Catch the Vision of
The Well-Educated Heart

Volume Three: Inspiration

MARLENE PETERSON

Libraries of Hope

Catch the Vision of
The Well-Educated Heart

Volume Three: Inspiration

Cover Image: The Day's Catch, by Daniel Ridgway Knight, (c. 1900). In public domain, source Wikimedia Commons.

Libraries of Hope, Inc.
Appomattox, Virginia 24522

Website www.librariesofhope.com
Email: librariesofhope@gmail.com

Printed in the United States of America

Table of Contents

Month 1 Podcasts

Podcast #17 Christopher Columbus

As we move into Month 1 of the rotation schedule, we open the year with an appropriate topic for Well-Educated Hearts: Discovery and Exploration. Young people love adventure and excitement and there's nothing that compares with these daring and courageous explorers who blazed new trails through danger and privations and all manner of suffering.

I want to start by highlighting Christopher Columbus and drawing out lessons from his life. His story was the very first one to go into the Forgotten Classics Family Library. It has been just ten years since then and little could I have imagined the hatred and contempt that would be stirred up against him in that time. I have heard of his statues being toppled, his holiday canceled and his name spoken only in derision. I am sad at the comments I read from moms in groups I am in as they struggle to share his story with their children. "How can I hold up such a man as this to them?" they say. "He is no hero in my book."

Well, first let me say that if only flawless, perfect men are allowed to be heroes, the list is pretty small. There is only one perfect man that I am aware of and we saw what the world did to Him and continues to do to Him. Far from the reverence and worship a true hero deserves, He is mocked and ridiculed in the vilest ways. The world at large isn't interested in making heroes. Rather our national pastime seems to be pulling heroes off their pedestals and trampling on them; relishing in magnifying their warts and imperfections. And then we wonder where all our heroes have gone?

We need heroes. Our children need heroes. And since we have no perfect people to draw from—only flawed ones—if we want any heroes left, we have to look at them through the eyes of an artist. When an artist paints a landscape, he doesn't paint everything exactly as he sees it. Rather, he selects those things that will convey beauty and truth in the eye of the beholder because his job is to lift and gladden the heart. There is plenty of time to get out in nature and see all the weeds and decaying rot the artist left off the masterpiece, but since the eye has been trained to see the beautiful, the weeds and the decay will not dominate the picture.

And so will it be with the great lives that are introduced in childhood. If you magnify the wart at first, the eye may never get past it. And the child may lose out on a lot of lessons he may not have otherwise.

No, we need a different criteria for a hero than perfection. I like Hamilton Wright Mabie's idea of a hero: "Men are not great or heroic because they are faultless; they are great and heroic because they dare, suffer, achieve and serve."

Using that criteria as we go along, I hope I can make my case for Christopher Columbus as one of my heroes.

Let me share some of the things I have discovered in my research. Only part of his story is being told out there.

The recent portrayal is that of a greedy, cruel, self-serving opportunist. Let's let him set the record straight in his own words, of what his motivation for the whole undertaking was, taken from his *Book of Prophecies*:[1]

> It was the Lord who put into my mind (I could feel His hand upon me) the fact that it would be possible to sail from here to the Indies. All who heard of my project rejected it with laughter, ridiculing me. There is no question that the inspiration was from the Holy Spirit, because he comforted me with rays of marvelous illumination, from the Holy Scriptures…encouraging me continually to press forward, and without ceasing for a moment they now encourage me to make haste.

> Our Lord Jesus desired to perform a very obvious miracle in the voyage to the Indies, to comfort me and the whole people of God. I spent seven years in the royal court, discussing the matter with many persons of great reputation and wisdom in all the arts; and in the end they concluded that it was all foolishness, so they gave it up. But since things generally came to pass that were predicted by our Savior Jesus Christ, we should also believe that this particular prophecy shall come to pass…

> I said that I would state my reasons: I hold alone to the sacred and Holy Scriptures, and to the interpretations of prophecy given by certain devout persons.

> It is possible that those who see this book will accuse me of being unlearned in literature, of being a layman and a sailor. I reply with the words of Matthew 11:25: "Lord, because thou hast hid these things from the wise and prudent, and hath revealed them unto babes…"

> I am a most unworthy sinner, but I have cried out to the Lord for grace and mercy, and they have covered me completely. I have found the sweetest consolations since I made it my whole purpose to enjoy His marvelous presence.

> For the execution of the journey to the Indies I did not make use of intelligence, mathematics or maps. It is simply the fulfillment of what Isaiah had prophesied. All this is what I desire to write down for you in this book.

> No one should fear to undertake any task in the name of our Savior, it if it just and if the intention is purely for His holy service. The working out of all things has been assigned to each person by our Lord, but it all happens according to His sovereign will even though He gives advice. He lacks nothing that it is in the power of men to give Him. Oh what a gracious Lord, who desires that people should perform for Him those things for which He holds himself responsible! Day and night moment by moment, everyone should express to Him their most devoted gratitude.

> I said that some of the prophesies remained yet to be fulfilled. There are great and wonderful things for the earth, and the signs are that the Lord is hastening the end. The fact that the gospel must still be preached to so many lands in such a short time— this is what convinces me.

But what about all that gold he was constantly searching for? First of all, you have to see the full picture to see what kind of pressure he was under to send gold back to Spain. The common man wasn't interested in spreading the light of the Gospel. Gold then, like it is now, is what speaks. If he produced no gold, the financing of his expeditions was over and he would be unable to fulfill the charge he was given. But beyond that, from the beginning he had an idea that the gold of the east could finance one last crusade with a 100,000 strong infantry and 10,000 horsemen to finally win back the Holy Sepulchre. For all the gold he sent back, where's the evidence of the wealth for his own comfort? Prior to his fourth and final voyage, he had "not enough with which to buy a cloak."

No, his desire was the religious advancement of mankind, not to make Christopher Columbus a wealthy and powerful ruler. The vision placed in his heart caused him to persist against great opposition for seventeen long years—seven of them in the royal courts of Spain. As Elbridge Brooks wrote: "Columbus tried to interest the rulers of different countries, but with no success. He tried to get help from his old home-town of Genoa and failed; he tried Portugal and failed; he tried the Republic of Venice and failed; he tried the king and queen of Spain and failed; he tried some of the richest and most powerful of the nobles of Spain and failed; he tried the king of England (whom he got this brother, Bartholomew Columbus, to go and see). People grew to know him as "the crazy explorer" as they met him in the streets or on the church steps of Seville or Cordova, and even ragged little boys of the town would run after this big man with the streaming white hair and the tattered cloak, calling him names or tapping their little foreheads with their dirty fingers to show that even they knew that he was "crazy as a loon."

Does not that singular act of determination for a worthy cause alone put him in the category of a hero?

But, you say, that doesn't excuse him from his cruelty to the natives nor the genocide he caused of an innocent people in a new world. And by the way, how can he be called a discoverer of a world if it's already inhabited?

To answer that question, you're going to need to weave many stories together, not the one that's being circulated that he spent his days enslaving and torturing natives. He had the heart of an explorer. "He was always ill at ease in administering and ruling…. He was happy and contented when he was discovering." Read the stories. But before I continue, you need to understand this, not only in the case of Columbus but for the study of all history. Just because something is written down doesn't make it true. Columbus had a lot of enemies in his day. A venture like this attracted the vilest of men who were interested in making a quick and easy buck. Furthermore, the ships were frequently filled with convicts who had been sentenced to banishment and were sent to a new world to work without pay. Columbus had insisted that families of respectable character be sent to colonize the new world. But that request was denied. He regretted that he was at times obliged to use force or ill-treatment, but says he would have done the same had his brother wished to kill him or wrest from him the government which the king and queen had given him to guard. He wrote: "For six months I was ready to leave to take to their Highnesses the good news of the gold and to stop governing a dissolute people who feared neither king nor queen, full of meanness and malice." Columbus begged that they would send someone at his expense to take command for he says bitterly that he has such a singular reputation that if he "were building churches and hospitals they would say they were cells for stolen goods."

Don't we see that today? People who are trying to do good whose intentions are maligned and twisted to fit someone's agenda?

But back to what I was saying that just because something is written down doesn't make it true. Even scholars are having a hard time sorting the truth from the fiction. There were many disgruntled speculators who were disappointed with their gains. Jealousy and vying for power and greed were rampant and many vicious letters were sent home to put Columbus in a bad light. We see public figures today maligned in the same way. I think of William Wallace who fought for Scotland's freedom. His enemies wrote all kinds of lies about him. Read cautiously— know that the account you may be reading may have been fabricated by someone with ill intent. Just because it's an original document doesn't mean it's true.

And consider this. When you read of his four voyages, he was constantly on the move. We have his diaries from three of the four voyages. And the second voyage has an account from someone who accompanied him. The second book in the *Stories of Christopher Columbus* from the Forgotten Classics library is the narrative taken from those diaries and journals by Edward Everett Hale, nephew to the great Nathan—I only regret I have but one life to give to my country—Hale. Columbus didn't stay long in the new world on his first voyage. When one ship abandoned him and the other was shipwrecked, the one small ship that was left couldn't bring all the men home again. And he was anxious to get back to Spain and bring back the good word. Sadly, while Columbus was away, the men who stayed behind evidently treated the natives who had been so kind to them in a horrible way and they were all killed. That wasn't Columbus' fault. The men of that first voyage were not exactly the upright men of the community. With the success of the first voyage, the second voyage attracted all kinds of dainty men who wouldn't lift a finger and expected to return home rich. They had little respect for Columbus or his rule. What could Columbus do? By the third voyage, you see a Columbus unjustly bound in chains and imprisoned by spiteful men, and he spent most of his fourth voyage shipwrecked on a desert island. Why aren't those stories being told? He was plagued by illness and nearly blind, fought against on every side, yet he never gave up.

Was there genocide? Yes. Were the Spaniards cruel? Yes. Columbus himself wished he could control them. Did Columbus engage in cruel acts? It's very possible. But let's share the responsibility. Let's place the blame where blame is due—on lawlessness, cruelty, selfishness, laziness, greed—none of which I have found evidence of in Columbus himself.

And one more part of the story that is left out. It is true Columbus took captives on his first voyage. The first time, it was so that they could be taught English so they could communicate with each other. As pressure mounted for payback from the expedition, he did resort to sending 500 slaves which Queen Isabella immediately rebuked and Columbus abandoned the enterprise. The man given charge over them treated them worse than animals and they died. It was terrible. But it wasn't Columbus.

Columbus later wished that he could use slave labor for just two more years in establishing colonies, but he said he would only use slaves that had been captured in war and insurrection. He was trying to build a settlement and he didn't exactly have any willing workers!

Which brings up another part of the story that is left out. It is true that the first natives they came in contact with were a delightsome and innocent people who welcomed them as messengers from heaven. They believed in a God and a life hereafter. In one interchange with one of their elders, Columbus described how the elder taught that they knew there were two paths—one leading to life and happiness and the other to darkness and misery. Columbus told him that was the message they had hoped to bring to them, but they already knew. I found it interesting that they found signs of the cross among the natives.

But there was another people there on nearby islands who were completely opposite. The Caribs, as they were called, were ferocious and would swoop down on these innocents and capture and eat their men and carry their women and children home, forcing them into slavery. I'm still learning about Columbus, but knowing what I know, I could see Columbus treating them with cruelty. Everything I have read indicates the innocents knew Columbus was their friend. I see acts of kindness and fairness with them. But he could get angry at injustice and wrongs.

All of these things and so much more you can read for yourself. My purpose is to put questions in your mind to challenge those things that are being fed to you today mainstream.

Most of all I take issue with the shortsightedness happening today that refuses to take in the full sweep of events and place them in context. They minimize the discovery by Columbus—and act as though they are privy to some grand secret that Leif Erickson discovered America before him and Chinese Buddhist priests came to America in the 5th century. In fact, Columbus never even saw the land that became the United States. Why should we honor him?

Well, thank goodness he didn't come to the United States first. He turned the attention of the gold-seeking Spaniards south, and you'll have to read the history of what happened there to appreciate that that wasn't our story.

But the timing of what he did could only have happened in the hand of a Providence who orders all things for our benefit. To appreciate that, you need to get a strong picture of what was happening in Europe—the hundreds of thousands of people who were massacred for their faith. At just the right time, when there were a people looking for a place of safety to worship according to the dictates of their own conscience, a new world had been mapped and explored and was ready to settle. The hundred years following Columbus' discovery was a time of preparation by an army of discoverers and explorers and adventurers. By the criteria of only perfect men as heroes, none of them would make the list. But collectively, their work and their daring and their suffering should never be forgotten by those of us who have reaped the blessing of freedom by their sacrifices. They are all heroes in my book.

Even in Columbus' day, haughty men who stayed in the comfort of their own homes while Columbus was pushing against overwhelming opposition, dismissed Columbus' accomplishment. Someone else would have found it, they said. No big deal. Columbus simply pulled out an egg and challenged them to stand it on end. None of them could do it. Then he broke off an end and placed it upright. See—he said—you just needed someone to show you how.

That's what Columbus did. He showed them it could be done. None of them had been brave enough or determined enough before he took the leap of faith. And look what followed. How was Columbus rewarded? He died alone. Broke. Obscure. And broken-hearted.

What annoys me most about the Columbus bashers today is that every comfort and every blessing of freedom of this beautiful country they enjoy was paid for dearly in suffering and hardship and privations. They remind me of spoiled children who have been bestowed with far too many unearned gifts and who bite the hand of the giver.

Christopher Columbus has my deepest gratitude for never giving up; for holding true to a mission and purpose God placed in his heart. And as God always does, we may mess things up in our weakness and imperfections, but he has a way of making beauty from our ashes. Those who mock Columbus are destroyers, not builders. America can never be great again if our children are made to hate and despise everyone who built it.

Do your own homework. And realize that you can read the story through whatever eyes you choose. In fact, I found this commentary interesting that I found in the preface of an 1892 book[2] written about Columbus.

The writer asked why it was that several well-educated, learned men can look at identical original source material and draw contradicting conclusions. Washington Irving greatly admired Columbus and Von Humboldt offered nothing but praise while Harrisse had nothing but cold criticism and Winsor gave a "sneering invective." I believe his response is worth considering:

> Where this amazing difference in judgment? Why does Mr. Winsor blame where others praise? Mr. Winsor thinks that it is due to his own superiority as a critical and scientific historian. Is Mr. Winsor right? Where does the province of the critical and scientific historian lie? In the gathering and sifting of historical evidence, in the full command of historical authorities, in the quick eye that sees historical contradictions and impossibilities, in the faculty sympathizing with the age and the feelings of the men he treats, in the power to see what under given environment is possible or impossible, is likely or unlikely. All this will aid the historian to form a just and a correct idea of a hero's character, and yet he may have all this, and err completely in his verdict.

> In every day life knowledge, human nature and knowledge of men is not the exclusive privilege of the man of many facts and varied lore. Often the plain man of common sense, the man who has studied men in the concrete, living among them with open eyes and keen quick wit, knows his fellow men more truly and do them justice more fairly, than the scholar who has conquered ten thousand volumes and swallowed the dust of libraries for a quarter of a century.

> What is there to hinder the man of action, who has seen again and again how men act in real life, amidst difficulties, and struggles and crises and triumphs and failures—what

is to hinder such a man when put in possession of the facts and placed face to face with the innermost thoughts of any great historical character to judge him and judge him correctly? Why may he not arrive at a fairer and truer verdict, than the scholar who has mastered dates and details, but fails to see flesh and blood, because the man of flesh and blood does not fit in with the imaginary world which the scholar has created in his mind?

All honor to the critical historian, when he collects, compares and sifts testimony, but if his judgment of the world's great men is to stand, he must prove himself to be more than a scientist and a critic, he must be a judge not only of books and facts, but of men—of their hearts, of their sympathies, of their feelings, of their passions, of their actions, of their judgments.

I would say your interpretation of Columbus will reveal more about you than him.

I have read a lot about Columbus, and the more I read, the more I love the man and am convinced our world has gotten him wrong, which isn't surprising for a world that has turned upside down; where good is seen as bad and bad as good; where every fault is magnified and every good is mocked. I love this summary given by one of Columbus' biographers, Charles Moores:[3]

A great vision came to Columbus and became the controlling influence of his life. Faith in the vision gave him courage to face hunger and pain and death. Disease beset him and blindness fell upon him. He believed that God had revealed a new world to him and had commissioned him to make the revelation known to men, and that God would take care of him until his divine errand was complete. The value of his life is measured by the vision that he saw as well as by the discovery that he made. Men would soon have found America. But the Italian dreamer whom the heavenly vision led into a new world remains one of the greatest of men because of the greatness of his faith.

That lesson alone makes Columbus a worthy subject to study.

And now a closing poem by Joaquin Miller

Behind him lay the gray Azores,
Behind the gates of Hercules;
Before him not the ghost of shores,
Before him only shoreless seas.
The good mate said: "now must we pray,
For lo, the very stars are gone.
Brave Adm'r'l, speak; what shall I say?"
"Why, say, 'Sail on, sail on! And on!'"

"My men grow mutinous day by day;
My men grow ghastly wan and weak."
The stout mate thought of home; a spray
Of salt washed his swarthy cheek.

"What shall I say, brave Adm'r'l, say,
If we sight not but seas at dawn?"
"Why, you shall say, at break of day:
'Sail on! Sail on! Sail on! And on!'"

They sailed and sailed as winds might blow
Until at last the blanched mate said:
"Why, now not even God would know
Should I and all my men fall dead.
These very winds forget the way,
For God from these dread seas is gone.
Now speak, brave Adm'r'l, speak and say—"
He said: "Sail on! Sail on! And on!"

They sailed. They sailed. Then spake the mate:
"This mad sea shows his teeth tonight:
He curls his lip, he lies in wait,
With lifted teeth, as if to bite:
Brave Adm'r'l, say but one good word;
What shall we do when hope is gone?"
The words leapt as a leaping sword:
"Sail on! Sail on! Sail on! And on!"

Then, pale and worn, he kept his deck
And peered through darkness. Ah, that night
Of all dark nights! And then a speck—
A light! A light! A light! A light!
It grew, a starlit flag unfurled!
It grew to be Time's burst of dawn.
He gained a world; he gave that world
Its greatest lesson: "On! Sail on!"

Podcast #19 Lessons from China

Before I share some lessons I've learned from a study of China, I thought it may be helpful to remind you of my objective in doing this. First of all, I'm not trying to tell you these are the things I think you should be studying. Rather, it's just done in the spirit of here's some interesting things I've learned and maybe something will spark an interest in you and maybe not. Maybe you're hearing this at the end of Month 1 and you're ready to move onto month 2. Just make a note to yourself that here's something you want to learn more about and when you come back next year, you have some studies to look forward to. Or, it's perfectly fine to extend studying Month 1 into Month 2. Like I keep saying, this rotation schedule is your servant, not your master. It adds enough structure to keep a little order about your learning but with lots of wiggle room.

But the bigger reason I am doing these "lessons learned" podcasts is because I have noticed it's really hard for some moms to get off the facts and information track. When I talk about gems and lessons learned, it's a completely foreign idea. They can't imagine what I'm talking about. And the thought of copying down a lot of facts in a notebook is daunting for sure. How do you begin to choose?

Face it—most of the modern books are filled with facts, and there's little to warm the heart and set it to pondering. I don't think it will take you long at all to catch on and you'll start finding gems all over the place, when you read these older books; little lessons and ideas and quotes that will grab hold of your heart and set you to thinking. And that's when learning gets really fun because you just naturally start talking about ideas and having conversations about things that matter. And the more you fill your heart, the more connections you'll start making and it all begins to feed itself.

Facts of themselves have no life. A name on a timeline, by itself, does little for us. But add the stories and imagination and the ideas start appearing. And ideas are very much living things.

So let's start with Marco Polo. For me, Marco Polo was a game you played in the swimming pool. One person was Marco and he'd close his eyes and call out "Marco" and other swimmers in the pool would reply "Polo." It was a kind of hide and seek game—he had to try and catch them just by the sound of their voice. Do you still play it?

I think I bumped into him a couple of times in a history class, but he was just a name and we moved on. As I've learned about him, I'm so sorry it's taken so long to make friends with him! He has an amazing story.

But let's take a detour before we dive into his story. While he was still a young boy at home in Venice, his father and uncle, who were merchants, made the long and treacherous trek to China, or Cathay as it was called, and were greeted by the great Kublai Khan who was delighted to have western visitors. He had never seen a European before, and the two brothers were very intelligent and had much to tell him. The great Khan was interested in civilizing his people and he asked about the emperors and how they administered justice and so forth and asked like questions about the kings and queens.

If you've seen the older black and white version of *The King and I* with Rex Harrison and Irene Dunne, it reminds me of the scenes between Anna and the King of Siam as he tries to learn to be civilized, etc., etc., etc. I love the musical, too, but this version is my favorite.

Anyway, he next inquired about religion. Here's what the record[4] says:

> When that Prince, whose name was Kublai Khan, Lord of the Tartars all over the earth, and of all the kingdoms and provinces and territories of that vast quarter of the world, had heard all that the Brothers had to tell him about the ways of the Latins, he was greatly pleased, and he took it into his head that he would send them on an Embassy to the Pope. So he urgently desired them to undertake this mission; and they replied that they would gladly execute all his commands.
>
> After this the Prince caused letters to the Pope to be written in the Tartar tongue, and gave them to the Two Brothers. Now the contents of the letter were as follows: He begged that the Pope would send as many as an hundred persons of our Christian faith; intelligent men, acquainted with the Seven Arts, well qualified to prove by force of argument to idolaters and other kinds of folk, that the Law of Christ was best, and that all other religions were false and naught; and if they would prove this, he and all under him would become Christians.
>
> And the Two Brothers promised they would return.
>
> When they got back to Venice, they found the Pope had died. These were very troublous times in the Church and no Pope was chosen for two years. Feeling anxious to return to the Khan, they decided to start the trip back right as a new Pope was appointed who ordered two priests to go with them. He could spare no more.
>
> And here's the thing! The priests went a short way, but soon turned back, because they were afraid of the perils of the journey! And so it happened that no missionaries reached China at that time. The Great Khan was determined to have some religion taught to his people, and so he sent to Tibet for Buddhist priests. It was in this way and at this time that Buddhism was introduced into northern China. If the Great Khan had received the hundred Christian missionaries that he asked for, it is likely that China would be today a Christian country!

Do you think the two priests, in the afterlife, did the ultimate face palm? Upon that seemingly small and insignificant decision, an entire nation was turned another way.

Lesson noted. Finish the task you set out to do.

Now back to Marco. He was only 17 years old when his father and uncle set out to China once more and they took him with them. It was a 5,000-mile trek in a straight line, but there was no straight-line road. Their actual trip was three times further—they traveled over 15,000 miles to get there. It took over three years and there was danger and peril every step of the way.

Pirates and robbers; snowy mountain peaks and deserts with little water or food.

When they finally arrived at the Imperial Palace, the Great Khan treated them with great honor and asked them many questions. And noticing Marco, he asked who he was. His father replied, "Sire, 'tis my son." "Welcome is he too," said the Emperor. Continuing now with the text: "Now it came to pass that Marco sped wondrously in learning the customs of the Tartars as well as their language, their manner of writing, and their practice of war; in fact, he came in brief space to know several languages. And he was discreet and prudent in every way, so that the Emperor held him in great esteem."

In fact, he made him an ambassador and even a governor while he was yet in his 20s. The Emperor trusted him implicitly and, because Marco was always giving his mind to get knowledge and to spy out and inquire into everything, he was sent out on many expeditions and came to visit more countries of the World than probably any other man.

Isn't that the kind of friend you'd like your teenage boy to have?

For 27 years Marco Polo lived in China. When he and his father and uncle returned to Venice, they found that all their property and possessions had been sold because everyone thought they were dead. Boy—I sure would have liked to see the faces when they came home after all those years. And the stories they had to tell!

Well, Marco wasn't interested at all in making himself the center of attention. He was ever polite and ever gracious. When he was asked questions, he answered with such kindly courtesy that every man felt himself in a manner his debtor.

He had no intention to write down any of his adventures. When you think about it, what would the point have been? There was no Simon and Schuster to publish it. There were no speaking tours. In fact, Gutenberg didn't even invent the printing press until after Marco Polo had been dead for a hundred years. It wasn't like you could pull out a pen and paper and write it down. Who was reading anyway? So he came home, married, had three children. But when Venice went to war, he was made commander of a ship that was captured and Marco Polo, with seven thousand others, were taken prisoner and put in chains.

What were the chances—Marco Polo ended up in a prison with a gentleman of Pisa name Puticiano. His cell mate was a man of letters—he could write! And during his extended imprisonment, with nothing else to do, he encouraged Marco Polo to tell his story while he wrote it down.

And history was changed because—what a coincidence—Marco was imprisoned in Genoa, the very city where 150 years later, Columbus was born. It was Marco Polo's writings that fueled the flame of desire in Columbus to travel to these wondrous lands Marco Polo described in such vivid detail. Scenes like the King's Great Palace: this is what he wrote. "You must know that it is the greatest Palace that ever was. The roof is very lofty and the walls of the Palace are all covered with gold and silver. They are also adorned with representations of dragons, sculptured and gilt, beasts and birds, knights and idols, and sundry other subjects. And on the ceiling, too, you see nothing but gold and silver and painting. On each of the four sides there is a great marble staircase.

"The Hall of the Palace is so large that it could easily dine six thousand people, and it is quite a marvel to see how many rooms there are besides. The building is altogether so vast, so rich, and so beautiful, that no man on earth could design anything superior to it."

No wonder Columbus kept looking to find this wondrous land of riches!

Have you ever thought about how many great things came out of prisons and captivity? Cervantes wrote *Don Quixote*, John Bunyan wrote *Pilgrim's Progress*, Thomas Malory wrote of the Legends of King Arthur while in prison. Do we remember that Daniel and Joseph were in captivity where they influenced the rulers of empires and kingdoms? John the Revelator wrote the book of Revelation and William Tyndale penned many of the words found in the King James version of the Bible while in exile. Sometimes what we think is a very horrible thing to happen turns into a blessing in disguise. Another lesson noted.

Marco Polo's story is full of adventure and excitement. And he proves himself a man of great character and integrity.

Which brings up one more lesson before we move on. There are scholars who doubt his story. There are always doubters, aren't there? But whether or not the stories were true, look at the effect they had on Christopher Columbus. Thank goodness the stories were allowed to do their work before some scholar somewhere got hold of it and threw it out because he couldn't positively verify the facts.

China has always been a mysterious country because they are very guarded and keep to themselves. There was just a small window in time that allowed Marco Polo to travel about and report back what he saw before that window was closed again. The world is indebted to that glimpse and happily that glimpse came to someone who was so observant. It has only been in recent years that we are learning as much about China as we are. And what a beautiful and fascinating civilization to discover and learn about! While the Western world was groveling through dark ages, the Chinese were a highly advanced civilization. I've enjoyed learning the wisdom of Confucius. Do you remember that I told you in the podcast on notebooking how frustrated I've been because I've lost stories along the way? One of the stories was about a city in China that actually did the very thing we're talking about—tending to the hearts of children. Remember, it was Confucius who taught:

> To put the world right in order
> we must first put the nation in order;
> To put the nation in order,
> we must first put the family in order.
> To put the family in order,
> we must first cultivate our personal life,
> we must first set our hearts right.

Well, this one town I read about actually put it into practice! And it became such a highly desirous city for people to live, rulers of nearby towns became jealous because all their subjects wanted to move there. The people were of such a high moral character that they were strong and it seemed impossible to bring them down. But they were finally conquered—and the thing that did it wasn't a force of arms. One of these jealous rulers sent over young girls to seduce the men. It so weakened them, they were finally able to conquer them.

Here's another lesson from China.

I keep noting times throughout history where rulers gain power over the people by destroying their books and history. This happened under Qin Shi Huang 200 years before Christ. In an effort to unify their thoughts and political opinions, and to keep scholars from comparing his reign with those who reigned in the past, he ordered their histories to be burned and those found with forbidden books were killed. In an old book, I read how the priests, at peril of their own lives, took the forbidden books and hid them in logs and caves and buried them in the ground so that when the madness was over, their history had been preserved.

As I watch our history being erased and books taken out of libraries and replaced with computers where access to thought can be easily controlled, maybe you will be like the priests of China and be a guardian of our heritage by the books you hold on to in your homes. That may sound like a crazy conspiracy theory, but history has shown me that freedom always has power grabbers lurking in the shadows and one of the age-old strategies is distancing a people from their heritage.

Did you see the story going around the internet recently? A proposal was made to drop millions of iPhones over North Korea. The strategy was that if the people could be exposed to the ideas that have been kept away from them, they would never allow themselves to be oppressed by a regime like that of Kim Jong-Un. The idea was under serious consideration.

During the Cultural Revolution of China under Chairman Mao, there was another book purge. If you haven't read Jung Chang's personal account of living in those times in her book *Wild Swans*,[5] it's very eye opening. And by the way, the book is banned in China. I copied a passage of her book in my notebook. I think it's difficult to comprehend the kind of mind control they were under. As it turned out, Jung was assigned to learn English and some librarians had saved some old books in their library attic because they were written in English and so didn't prove a threat.

As she read classics like *Little Women*, Jane Austen, the Brontes, and other European and American literature, she wrote, "My joy at the sensation of my mind opening up and expanding was beyond description." She continued: "Being alone in the library was heaven for me. My heart would leap as I approached it, usually at dusk, anticipating the pleasure of solitude with my books, the outside world ceasing to exist. As I hurried up the flight of stairs the smell of old books long stored in airless rooms would give me tremors of excitement.

"I became acquainted with Longfellow, Walt Whitman and American history. I memorized the whole of the Declaration of Independence, and my heart swelled at the words, 'We hold these truths self-evident, that all men are created equal' and those about men's 'unalienable rights' among them 'liberty and the pursuit of happiness.' These concepts were unheard of in China and opened up a marvelous new world for me. My notebooks, which I kept with me at all times, were full of passages like these passionately and tearfully copied out."

Sharing even that account with your children may help them appreciate something they may take for granted. While this isn't a book for young children, if you have mature high schoolers, I think it's a powerful book for teaching an appreciation for freedom by showing them clearly what it looks like to not be free.

As much as we condemn the loss of millions of lives under Chairman Mao, God has a way of turning the messes we make over for good and we are seeing a new China emerge after clinging tenaciously to so many traditions for thousands of years. The Cultural Revolution did provide a break with the past. The story isn't over.

Well, there are so many more things I could talk about, but I've gone on long enough for one day. China and their people fascinate me. We need to get to know them. One thing that made me smile was there was a part in *Wild Swans* where Jung said that as children, they were told by their parents to think about all the poor little capitalist children in America who were starving and eat all the food on their plates. I think we both have a lot of misconceptions about each other.

If you haven't read Gladys Aylward's story yet, if you want to be inspired with the power of love, it's a must read. And I noted that the way she opened hearts that were seeped in superstitions and traditions was through a story: long ago in a far-away land lived a carpenter who was gentle and kind. A simple story softened and changed the hearts of hardened generals and hardened criminals. It's a powerful book about courage and determination, but mostly love.

For today's poem, how about the classic poem written by Coleridge, the English poet. He had fallen asleep while reading Marco Polo's story and dreamed the poem beginning:

> In Xanadu did Kublai Khan
> A stately pleasure-dome decree,
> Where Alph, the sacred river, ran,
> Through caverns measureless to man,
> Down to a sunless sea.
> So twice five miles of fertile ground
> With walls and towers were girdled round;
> And there were gardens bright with sinuous rills,
> Where blossomed many an incense-bearing tree;
> And here were forests, ancient as the hills,
> Enfolding spots of sunny greenery.

Podcast #20 Lessons from India

Several years ago, one of my daughters took a leap of faith and moved cross country to Raleigh, North Carolina, where she hoped to get into a certain graduate program there. Well, the graduate program didn't work out, but she started dating a young man from India. After about a year, my husband got a phone call. "I'm on my way over to your daughter's home to propose marriage. Do I have your blessing?" Of course, we were thrilled because he's a very good man. And then my husband handed me the phone and my future son-in-law said, "I just need you to understand something. Sometimes these things happen very, very fast."

I'm thinking, OK, a month? Maybe two months? A little while later our daughter called, full of excitement. This was on a Thursday or a Friday. She said, "We're getting married—next Saturday!"

I panicked a little. Earlier, she had told me about her future sister-in-law's wedding. Her fiance's father had held an important government position, and in India, weddings are a really big deal. A family will save for years for the big event. And in this case, there had been over 1,500 guests over a 3-day celebration. Her dress was covered in jewels. What would they be expecting for their son?

Having raised eight daughters, in hindsight, I can definitely tell you the one-week wedding plan really is a good way to go. You don't have time to fuss over things that really don't matter and you take care of the essentials. My daughter has never cared about fancy things, so simple was just fine with her.

The reason for the rush was that his parents were flying home to India after an extended stay in the United States and there were certain cultural traditions that marriages needed to happen on certain days. It was either that day or it could be delayed for an unforeseen time.

Now, my son-in-law had been raised in the Hindu faith, but had converted to our LDS faith—or Mormonism—several years earlier. They wanted to be married in an LDS temple, but they also wanted to honor his parents' Hindu faith.

So we met early in the morning at the Raleigh LDS Temple. Knowing how important the marriage of their son was, I worried that his parents would be offended that they would not be allowed to go inside. But they were not. They were gracious and respectful. They asked questions of us. His father spoke English but his mother only spoke Hindi. But she has this bright, beautiful smile that speaks volumes of words. And then they waited patiently while we went inside for the wedding ceremony, which is a very simple ceremony in which a man and a woman are married for time and all eternity.

Afterwards, we took pictures on the temple grounds and then went to an Indian restaurant to eat. I had never eaten Indian food before and I have loved being introduced to all the new tastes and spices I've never even heard of before. My son-in-law has taught me to cook several

Indian dishes and buys spices for me. Yes—India has always been known for its spices! For a reason! My food world has expanded.

Then, that afternoon, his mother dressed me and my daughters in beautiful silk saris. I watched her take an incredibly long piece of fabric and skillfully pleat it around each of our waists and tie and wrap it and then we headed to a Hindu temple.

And then we were introduced to their culture as they now explained the meanings and significance of their traditions to us. Just as we took our shoes off as we entered the LDS temple, signifying a holy place, they asked that we remove our shoes as we entered the Hindu temple. We sat on the floor in the middle of a large intricately decorated hall where a much-simplified wedding ceremony over the normal one took place. Evidently, the full ceremony typically begins in the middle of the night and can go on for many, many hours. My husband and I were asked to repeat things in Sanskrit and there were candles and rice and so many things I can't remember.

And then we went home. Anshul had bought a big, beautiful home for them and his mother and sister had prepared the welcome to it. There were flower petals and more candles—the Indian culture celebrates Light, everything with a meaning and a significance. They dedicate their homes and everything is towards strong family ties and in being good, kind, decent human beings.

Here's the thing. Although the outward ceremonies were very different, the heart of them were the same. It was all about uniting families, about strong family bonds, of living lives of harmony and peace and love and joy; of welcoming children into families.

Our cultures are very different. But we are more alike than different.

There was a time when the Muslim could be found guarding Christian holy sites and Christian could be found honoring Muslim holy days. One of the surprises of the Crusaders was finding, upon arrival in the Holy Land, Muslim, Jew and Christian living side by side in harmony. An important part of the Muslim faith was cleanliness and there were beautiful water fountains everywhere. These Crusaders came from dark, damp, dirty castles where they gnawed on bones to a place where there were great delicacies, beautiful silks, colorful mosaics. They found an advanced civilization and many of them stayed.

I have learned so many things from my son-in-law over the years. It has been interesting to see America through his eyes. It's been hard for him to understand how Americans can live so disconnected from each other. In India, he said, you know all your neighbors very well. The mothers would all take their kids out to the playground in the afternoon and visit and they watched out for each other's kids. Here, he said, neighbors don't even talk to each other. We definitely don't see eye-to-eye on everything and we've had some lively discussions, but they always serve to expand my view and understanding. He challenges my thinking. I've learned so many things about India and the Hindu faith I didn't know. Which is a lot. He has a much different view of the English occupation of India and Gandhi than what I had read in the books. I haven't even scratched the surface, but my life has been enriched so much by being exposed to a new culture.

We all know the saying, "To know me is to love me." Isn't that why we want our children to study different cultures and different faiths? Do we not want to teach them to first seek to understand?

There are so many fears and prejudices out there. We have to begin to break them down as our world shrinks and we interact with people of all nations and cultures. It is possible to be different and still get along, isn't it?

How does the song go in *South Pacific?* "You've got to be taught, To hate and fear, You've got to be taught from year to year, It's got to be drummed in your dear little ear, You've got to be carefully taught. You've got to be taught to be afraid of people whose eyes are oddly made, And people whose skin is a different shade, You've got to be carefully taught. You've got to be taught before it's too late, Before you are six or seven or eight, To hate all the people your relatives hate, You've got to be carefully taught."

The song is right, but rather than teach our children to hate and fear, they've got to be carefully taught to love.

That is why cultural studies is an important part of the Well-Educated Heart. We want our children to learn about other people's faiths, about their holidays and traditions, their art and their music, their important buildings and monuments, their heroes and fanciful stories. Because through these things, we will begin to understand and thereby, to love.

I include crafts from holidays as well as foods from the various countries on Pinterest pages, but you can easily find many yourself to begin to introduce new cultures to your children. I wasn't very good at doing a lot when my children were growing up, but they remember our study of the Jewish faith. We cooked Jewish food and celebrated some Jewish holidays. And we went to a Jewish synagogue. They remember that. They don't look down on Jewish people. They respect their faith and understand who they are. Even though they believe differently than we do.

I cringe when so-called Christians get enraged when they hear their children being taught of the Muslim faith in schools or when they group all Muslims together into a group to be feared and hated. Do they not remember that God promised Abraham's son, Ishmael, that he would not forget his seed and would bless them? I accept that the Angel Gabriel visited Mohammed because the message was to remind these nomads who had become idol worshippers that there is one God. Do you know the five pillars of Islam? Faith, Prayer, Charity, Fasting, and a Pilgrimage to a Holy place.

They are taught there is one God and that one should pray to him many times a day, with a pure heart, signified by washing. They have a personal responsibility to care for the poor and the needy. They are taught to fast as a way to draw nearer to God. And at least one time in their life, they strive to make a pilgrimage to a holy place where they all dress alike in white, where there are no rich and no poor, all the same in the eyes of God.

Are these not all part of our Christian faith?

Have not Christians also perverted the simple teachings of Jesus; have kept the form and lost the meaning? Do we not also see among Christians an outward show while losing the true spirit of our faith? Did we not see Christian killing Christian in the slaughter of Protestant and Catholic? And the forcing by violence of the Christian religion during the Spanish Inquisition? Shall we shun all Christians because of what has been done in the name of their religion? Or shall we search for its roots and true understanding?

I'm not so quick to think that all Muslims are out to kill me. I know what it is to be part of a misunderstood religious group upon which a governor of our United States, stirred up by fear and misunderstanding, issued an extermination order driving men, women and children from their homes in the dead of winter, making refugees of them in our land of the free and the brave. And even now, we are mocked in a popular Broadway musical, shunned from Christian groups who will not let our families join their co-ops; who will boycott anything associated with a Mormon; who teach their children to fear and hate and avoid.

I was talking with Jim Weiss—and my understanding is he talked about this publicly so I believe I am at liberty to share this. He is a world-renowned storyteller who has spoken at homeschool conferences for years. He is a delightful and warm human being. But he was informed a couple of years ago that he was no longer welcome as a speaker at a major Christian homeschooling conference because he is a Jew.

Where, in all of Jesus' teachings is such a thing justified? For he taught us to love even our enemies; to do good to those who despitefully use us and hate us. To turn the other cheek. Because he knows there is a much greater power than hate. And that is the power of Love.

I don't remember who said it, but the comment was made that we rejoice in the discovery of electricity, but there is a much greater power that is real and tangible, and if we ever harness its power, it will transform the world.

That power is Love.

History is loaded with stories of cruel and barbarous people whose lives were turned around by Love. That love starts in the hearts of children who are carefully taught to love by their parents.

I have included a series in the Online Library called the Our Little Cousin series as well as the Twins Series. These wonderful books begin to introduce children of different cultures around the world to hearts of children. Sometimes you may bump into something in them that makes you cringe. For instance, in *Our Little Hindu Cousin*, in the preface it says something like, of course we know the Hindu race was a superior race to the dirty Muslims or something of the sort. Don't throw the book away—use it as a teaching moment with your children!! And yes, these stories don't represent life as it is today. Let your children know these are like reading the stories of little pioneer children in our country who lived a long time ago. You're trying to layer in a sense of cultural differences and these books weave in a lot of the traditions and histories of people around the world. Maybe one of you will one day write a new updated version. But for right now, this is what we have to work with.

Racism is a huge problem in our country today. It's overcome with stories and understanding. I love the story of Mary Bethune who was born into a slave family right after the Emancipation Proclamation. "Invest in the human soul," she said. "Who knows but that it may be a diamond in the rough." She rose against overwhelming challenges and founded a college. One day she met a little girl who had never seen a person with black skin and was afraid. But rather than be offended, Mary took a nearby bouquet of flowers and showed the little girl how pretty the bouquet was because there were so many different colors. "Likewise," she said, "God made a bouquet of people with many different skin colors. Isn't it beautiful?"

We have to be carefully taught.

The German Hessians were hired to fight the Americans because there weren't enough British who would fight their own people. They were fed all kinds of lies about the Americans—that we were a savage, uncivilized, brutal people. Their hatred was fed so they'd think they were doing the world a favor by killing us.

But then they came in contact with the kind farmer, the peace-loving Quaker, and some laid down their arms and became American as they found out the stories had been a lie.

This is an age of gathering. Every culture, every people, every nation in the world has treasures of knowledge and gifts to bring into the whole. Welcome these gifts! Bring the world to your children! We are all children of the same God. And, in the end, we'll find we really are more alike than we are different and that our Heavenly Father has gifted each of His children with a portion of His Light and Truth.

And now I'll close with the most famous poem written by Rudyard Kipling who was born in India and lived many years there. He is beloved by children the world over for his *Jungle Book* and Just So stories. Here's the poem:

> If you can keep your head when all about you
>   Are losing theirs and blaming it on you,
> If you can trust yourself when all men doubt you,
>   But make allowance for their doubting too;
> If you can wait and not be tired by waiting,
>   Or being lied about, don't deal in lies,
> Or being hated, don't give way to hating,
>   And yet don't look too good, nor talk too wise:
>
> If you can dream, and not make dreams your master;
>   If you can think, and not make thoughts your aim;
> If you can meet with Triumph and Disaster
>   And treat those two impostors just the same;
> If you can bear to hear the truth you've spoken
>   Twisted by knaves to make a trap for fools,
> Or watch the things you gave your life to, broken,
>   And stoop and build 'em up with worn-out tools:
>
> If you can make one heap of all your winnings
>   And risk it on one turn of pitch-and-toss,
> And lose, and start again at your beginnings

And never breathe a word about your loss;
If you can force your heart and nerve and sinew
 To serve your turn long after they are gone,
And so hold on when there is nothing in you
 Except the Will which says to them: "Hold on!"

If you can talk with crowds and keep your virtue,
 Or walk with Kings, nor lose the common touch,
If neither foes nor loving friends can hurt you,
 If all men count with you, but none too much;
If you can fill the unforgiving minute
 With sixty seconds' worth of distance run,
Yours is the Earth and everything that's in it,
 And, which is more, you'll be a Man, my son!

Podcast #21 Lessons from the South Seas

I'm going to turn to a story of a Presbyterian missionary today to draw today's lessons learned from the South Seas. If you want to teach your children to be selfless, to have courage through faith in the face of overwhelming odds, and to add a little perspective in their lives of what really matters, I can think of no better body of stories to draw from than the stories of missionaries and humanitarians. These are the unsung heroes of the world whose names have largely been forgotten, but who planted seeds that bore fruit for generations. These men and women found their lives by losing them. When they felt God place on their hearts a little corner in His garden to tend, they moved forward with no expectation, in many cases, of ever going home.

I found the story I'm going to share with you today on one of my used book store hunts. Some of my most treasured finds have been found "accidentally." If you are one to rely upon your book lists and the recommendations of others, I hope you will begin to let go and trust your own instinct. Pick up lots of books you've never heard of before, open them, read a few paragraphs here and there. Sometimes you'll just feel the warmth. That's when you know you've found a good one.

I picked up an old copy of *The Story of John G. Paton: or 30 Years Among the South Seas Cannibals told for Young Folks*[6] and was immediately drawn into the story. Living in the face of constant danger makes this a page turner for even your reluctant readers. I loved the book so much, I started sharing stories with my daughter who picked up her own copy and she loved it so much, she started telling the stories to the young man she was dating at the time in college, who also loved it so much, he'd call her almost every day, "Can I come have a little John G. Time?" And he'd come over and they'd go sit out on the grass and she'd read to him. She married someone else, but she gave her boyfriend a lifelong friend in John G.

So first a little background. New Hebrides, as it was called in John G.'s day, was a chain of eighty islands that stretch across 450 miles in the South Pacific. According to oral traditions and such, it's believed these islands had been inhabited for over 3,000 years when they were discovered first by a Spanish explorer, Fernandez de Quiroz, in 1606 and later by Captain James Cook in 1773 who gave them the name New Hebrides because they reminded him of the Hebrides Islands off the coast of Scotland. Today, these islands are known as the Republic of Vanatua.

The islands were inhabited by cannibals—a savage and uncivilized people that captured the hearts of a couple of missionaries from London who made the long trek, only to be eaten a couple of minutes after landing on shore. Another team was sent, and they were driven off within seven months. Missionary after missionary was killed. But that didn't deter a young Scotsman, John G. Paton who felt the call and arrived, at the age of 33, with his young pregnant wife on April 16, 1858. Within a year, both his wife and his newborn son died of the fever and he served alone on the island for the next four years under incredible circumstances of constant danger until he was driven off the island.

But that didn't deter him. He had been a popular preacher at home in Scotland and could have led a comfortable and prosperous life. He was constantly criticized for his foolish decision to go, and one respected elder chided him, "You will be eaten by cannibals!" to which Paton responded:

> Mr. Dickson, you are advanced in years now, and your own prospect is soon to be laid in the grave, there to be eaten by worms; I confess to you, that if I can but live and die serving and honoring the Lord Jesus, it will make no difference to me whether I am eaten by Cannibals or by worms.

He returned to another island which was eventually all converted to the Christian faith. But more importantly, the change that came into the lives of the natives was nothing short of miraculous. And that's what he wanted to show the skeptics and the doubters of the world—that the Christian faith has the power to take even the most uncivilized and savage of us, and change them for the good.

I won't even begin to attempt to share the stories of how that happened here. I'll leave you to read them for yourself. I have some excerpts in *Stories of Great Humanitarians and Missionaries*, but I'll link the whole book for you in the notes.

Here's what I do want to say today: What kind of home breeds that kind of faith, courage and compassion?

Let me share some glimpses from his writings.

First a description of his home as seen from a hill overlooking the village of his childhood.

> At your feet lay a thriving village, every cottage sitting in its own plot of garden, and sending up its blue cloud of "Peat reek," which never somehow seemed to pollute the blessed air; and after all has been said or sung, a beautifully situated village of healthy and happy homes for God's children is surely the finest feature in every landscape.

> There amid this wholesome and breezy village life, our dear parents found their home for the long period of forty years. There were born to them eight additional children, making in all a family of five sons and six daughters. Theirs was the first of the thatched cottages on the left.

> Our home consisted of a 'but' and a 'ben' and a 'mid room,' or chamber, called the closet. The one end was my mother's domain, and served all the purposes of dining room and kitchen and parlor, besides containing two large wooden erections, called by our Scotch peasantry 'box beds'; not holes in the wall, as in cities, but grand, big, airy beds, adorned with many-colored counterpanes, and hung with natty curtains, showing the skill of the mistress of the house. The other end was my father's workshop, filled with five or six 'stocking frames,' whirring with the constant action of five or six pairs of busy hands and feet, and producing right genuine hosiery for the merchants at

Hawick and Dumfries. The closet was a very small apartment betwixt the other two, having room only for a bed, a little table and a chair, with a diminutive window shedding diminutive light on the scene. This was the Sanctuary of that cottage home. Thither daily, and oftentimes a day, generally after each meal, we saw our father retire, and 'shut to the door,' and we children got to understand by a sort of spiritual instinct (for the thing was too sacred to be talked about) that prayers were being poured out there for us, as of old by the High Priest within the veil in the Most Holy Place. We occasionally heard the pathetic echoes of a trembling voice pleading as if for life, and we learned to slip out and in past that door on tiptoe, not to disturb the holy colloquy. The outside world might not know, but we knew, whence came that happy light as of a new-born smile that always was dawning on my father's face; it was a reflection from the Divine Presence, in the consciousness of which he lived. Never, in temple or cathedral, on mountain or in glen, can I hope to feel that the Lord God is more near, more visibly walking and talking with men, than under that humble cottage roof of thatch and oaken wattles. Though everything else in religion were by some unthinkable catastrophe to be swept out of memory, or blotted from my understanding, my soul would wander back to those early scenes, and shut itself up once again in that Sanctuary Closet, and, hearing still the echoes of those cries to God, would hurl back all doubt with the victorious appeal, "He walked with God, why may not I?"

And Jon's mother was no further behind as he described his mother, "a bright-hearted, high-spirited, patient-toiling, and altogether heroic little woman; who, for about forty-three years, made and kept such a wholesome, independent, God-fearing and self-reliant life for her family of five sons and six daughters, as constrains me, when I look back on it now, in the light of all I have seen and known of others far differently situated, almost to worship her memory."

As a young woman, she had noticed a young stocking-maker from the Brig End, was in the habit of stealing alone into the quiet wood, book in hand, day after day, at certain hours, as if for private study and meditation. It was a very excusable curiosity that led the young bright heart of the girl to watch him devoutly reading and hear him reverently reciting passages he could say by heart sixty years afterwards; and finally that curiosity awed itself into a holy respect, when she saw him lay aside his broad Scotch bonnet, kneel down under the sheltering wings of some tree, and pour out all his soul in daily prayers to God.

As to their home life, he wrote:

Family Worship had heretofore been held only on Sabbath Day in his father's house; but the young Christian managed to get the household persuaded that there ought to be daily morning and evening prayer and reading of the Bible and holy singing. And so began that blessed custom of Family Prayer, morning and evening, which my father practiced probably without one single avoidable omission till he lay on his deathbed, seventy-seven years of age.

Each of us, from very early days, considered it no penalty, but a great joy, to go with our father to the church; the four miles were a treat to our young spirits, the company by the way was a fresh incitement, and occasionally some of the wonders of city-life rewarded our eager eyes.

We had, too, special Bible readings on the Lord's day evening—mother and children and visitors reading in turns, with fresh and interesting question, answer and exposition, all tending to impress us with the infinite grace of a God of love and mercy in the great gift of His dear Son, Jesus, Our Saviour. Of course, if the parents were not devout, sincere, and affectionate—if the whole affair on both sides is taskwork, or worse, hypocritical and false, results must be very different indeed!

Oh, I can remember those happy Sabbath evenings; no blinds down, and shutters up, to keep out the sun from us, as some scandalously affirm; but a holy, happy, entirely human day, for a Christian father, mother and children to spend. Others must write and say what they will, and as they feel; but so must I. There were eleven of us brought up in a home like that; and never one of the eleven, boy or girl, man or woman, has been heard, or ever will be heard, saying that Sabbath was dull and wearisome for us, or suggesting that we have heard of or seen any way more likely than that for making the Day of the Lord bright and blessed alike for parents and for children. But God help the homes where these things are done by force and not by love!

As to the bond between father and son, well, I'll let him speak for himself. When an opportunity came to leave home, John wrote this:

Two days thereafter I started out from my quiet country home on the road to Glasgow. Literally on the road, about forty miles had to be done on foot, and thence to Glasgow by rail. My dear father walked with me the first six miles of the way. His counsels and tears and heavenly conversations on that parting journey are fresh in my heart as if it had been but yesterday; and tears are on my cheeks as freely now as then, whenever memory steals me away to the scene. For the last half mile or so we walked on together in almost unbroken silence—my father, as was often his custom, carrying hat in hand, while his long, flowing yellow hair (then yellow, but in later years white as snow) streamed like a girl's down his shoulders. His lips kept moving in silent prayers for me; and his tears fell fast when our eyes met each other in looks of which all speech was vain! We halted on reaching the appointed parting place; he grasped my hand firmly for a minute in silence, and then solemnly and affectionately said:

"God bless you, my son! Your father's God prosper you, and keep you from all evil."

Unable to say more, his lips kept moving in silent prayer; in tears we embraced, and parted. I ran off as fast as I could; and, when about to turn a corner in the road where he would lose sight of me, I looked back and saw him still standing with his head uncovered where I had left him—gazing after me. Waving my hat in adieu, I was round the corner and out of sight in an instant. But my heart was too full and sore to carry me farther, so I darted into the side of the road and wept for a time. Then, rising up cautiously, I climbed the dyke to see if he yet stood where I had left him; and just at that moment I caught a glimpse of him climbing the dyke and looking out for me! He did not see me, and after he had gazed eagerly in my direction for awhile he got down, set his face towards home, and began to return—his head still uncovered, and his heart, I felt sure, still rising in prayers for me. I watched through blinding tears, till his form faded from my gaze; and then, hastening on my way, vowed deeply and oft, by the help of God, to live and act so as never to grieve or dishonor such a father and mother as He had given me. The appearance of my father, when we parted—his advice prayers, and tears—the road, the dyke, the climbing up on it, and then walking away, head uncovered—have often, all through life, risen vividly before my mind, and do so now while I am writing, as if it had been but an hour ago. In my earlier years, particularly, when exposed to many temptation, his parting form rose before me as that of a guardian angel.

Do your children hear you pray for them? Do they see the light of God in your countenance? Is Sunday a day of delight, of windows thrown open and the sunshine pouring in? Do they love being with you? When you read scriptures, is it a forced item on a to-do list, or do they hear a reverence and a music in your voice? Do you love the scriptures? Do they feel a bond to you that is so strong that your children would never do anything to bring sorrow to your heart?

These were the gifts given to John G. Paton from his mother and father—a shining lesson of something for the rest of us to aspire to.

Such are just a few of my many, many South Seas lessons from the life of John G. Paton.

And now today's poem, which I think could have been written by John G., although we don't know the author.

A heart full of thankfulness,
A thimbleful of care,
A soul of simple hopefulness,
An early morning prayer.

A smile to greet the morning with,
A kind word is the key
To open the door and greet the day,
Whate'er it brings to thee.

A patient trust in Providence
To sweeten all the way,
All these, combined with thoughtfulness,
Will make a happy day.

Podcast #23 Lessons from Light and Sweden

The Month 1 topic for Nature Study is The Stars and we're also learning about Sweden. If you listened to my presentation on Nature Study, I laid out the rotation schedule for Nature and said that it generally follows the order of creation as laid out in the Bible. That doesn't hold true for Month 1 because the Creation of the sun and the moon and the stars didn't come until the 4th day when they were necessary for seasons to make things grow. Day One and the first step in all endeavors of creation, is: "Let there be Light."

To let means to allow or to permit.

I see us as educational re-formers who are trying to re-form education to let in the Light or, in other words, to allow or permit Light to be an integral part of the learning process. Letting in the light is the same work of educational re-formers like Pestalozzi who said he wished to rescue education from cheap, artificial teaching tricks and entrust it to the Light within; or Maria Montessori who hoped to bring Light into education. Or Charlotte Mason who taught that true education is between a child's soul and God, that there is no separation between the spiritual and intellectual lives of children.

This Light is the spark of life and a force that organizes raw materials into a usefulness for the purpose of increasing Light in the world. Love, Joy and Peace—the riches of eternity—are the fruits of education where Light is permitted and allowed. The alternative is darkness, decay and destruction.

The Pattern for Learning I keep talking about is all about increasing Light in learning's creative process. The application for this pattern can only be understood by the same Light. I cannot teach it directly. I wish I could. But we can see that our current educational methods are blocking the Light because we can see darkness overtaking the world. We are in need of educational re-forming.

Only by re-forming what we're doing can we turn the process around. And the first order of business is "Let there be Light."

Today I'd like to bring Helen Keller into the conversation who is an expert on this Light. I'm sure you all know Helen's story—that following an illness, possibly meningitis, as a 19-month old—she was left totally blind and deaf. Many of you have likely read the story of her life she wrote and have marvelled at all she was able to accomplish in her life without sight or sound. In the foreword to one of her books, it begins: "If a worldwide poll were to be taken to determine the most outstanding woman of our generation, no doubt the top selection would be Helen Keller. The good she has done throughout the world is enormous." A highly educated woman who knew several languages, she graduated from Radcliffe College. She worked up to 18 hours a day—carrying on extensive correspondence, preparing and delivering speeches—yes! She learned to talk despite never hearing language, and campaigning on behalf of the visually challenged. She traveled the globe six times over, visiting dignitaries in every land. If you have read any of her writings, her thoughts are deep and profound, expressed in elegant language.

How did she come to live such a magnificent and fruitful life in spite of her profound challenges?

Well, she wrote a lesser known book I happened to stumble across. This was actually the book about herself she wished everyone would read because it contained the secret behind her abilities and she wanted everyone to know. It was originally entitled *My Religion*. Those who were closest to her were indifferent to the project because of its religious nature, so Helen was left to herself to sit down at a typewriter and type out her thoughts for hours at a time. There was no one to help her pick up her thread of thought where she left off, so she feared the book was disjointed and fragmented. Her editor at Doubleday who had published her life story wasn't interested in a religious book, but she did find a publisher who saw the value and he introduced the book by saying, "My Religion is not a literary production prepared for publication; it is a public profession of faith, a spontaneous utterance of the heart." Decades later, someone took the time to help organize the thoughts and the book was renamed, *Light in My Darkness*.[7] Helen wrote, "My joy will know no bounds if what I have written turns out to be worthy of the light-bringer to the souls of men who are lost in the horror of the great darkness." And I'm going to use her words in this book generously throughout this podcast.

Helen tells of the friendship with a man and mentor who introduced her to the writings of a Swedish scientist who changed her life. She wrote:

> Those truths have been to my faculties what light, color and music are to the eye and ear. They have opened the gate of the Garden of Heaven for me and showed me fair flowering paths where I love to walk. What precious herbs of healing grow there! What sweet smells of celestial flowers greet me! What thresholds of quiet I pass over, leaving behind me all the harsh, loud futilities of earth-life. There the Lamb of God walks in beauty through the grass. In the Garden of the Lord sparkle countless rills and fountains. The trees, laden with golden fruit, murmur wisdom with their leaves, and the birds no longer sing wordless notes, but immortal truths. There, blessed figures arrayed in light pass me and smile companionship with me; their beautiful hands guide me in paths of peace.
>
> My soul is enabled to picture the beauty of the sky and listen to the songs of the birds. All about me may be silence and darkness, yet within me, in the spirit, is music and brightness, and color flashes through all my thoughts.
>
> Each day comes to me with both hands full of possibilities.

Wouldn't you love to greet each day with "both hands full of possibilities?"

Well, let me tell you more about this Swedish scientist. His name was Emanuel Swedenborg and he was born in Stockholm, Sweden, in 1688. Helen described his childhood, and it looks pretty well-educated heart-y to me:

"He and his father were constant companions. They climbed the hills around Stockholm and explored the fjords, collecting mosses, flowers and brightly colored stones. When they returned, the child wrote long reports of their outdoor experiences." Through these experiences, he developed, not only strong powers of observation, but the ability to interpret and record what he saw which prepared him for the work that followed.

And now notice the golden combination of heart and mind as she describes: "His was a rare blending of the practical and the beautiful, mathematics and poetry, invention and literary power." He spoke multiple languages.

He had a brilliant mind and quickly rose to positions of honor and prestige in the scientific community. He fell in love once, but evidently proposed marriage through a series of geometric proofs and a logical treatise of why it made sense that they join together. It didn't exactly woo her heart and he was rejected and never married.

Swedenborg lived in the great Age of Reason of the 17th and 18th centuries which some call the Age of Enlightenment, but others characterize it as the coldest, most depressing time in human history. The Christian religion was full of fear, hellfire and damnation with unbaptized babies and sinful people consigned to everlasting torment in purgatory and a monstrous hell. Swedenborg asked himself, "What is the use of all the knowledge I have gained when such a hideous shadow lies vast across the world?"

At the age of 56, his life changed. A friend of his recorded a conversation in which Swedenborg told him: "...in the night one had come to [me] and said that He was the Lord God, the Creator of the world, and the Redeemer, and that He had chosen me to explain to men the spiritual sense of the Scripture, and that He would explain to me what I should write on the subject. From that day I gave up the study of all worldly science, and labored in spiritual things, according as the Lord had commanded me to write. Afterward the Lord opened, daily very often, my eyes so that in the middle of the day I could see into the other world, and in a state of perfect wakefulness converse with angels and spirits."

Swedenborg wrote over 25 volumes of observations of this spiritual world that came to him over the next 25 years. The object wasn't to make money—he paid for the printing and distributed them freely to learned men and universities. The object wasn't fame. He already held positions of great renown. In fact, by embarking on this work, many thought he had lost his mind. He didn't even sign his name to many of the works, rather he used the pen name: "Servant of the Lord Jesus Christ." He sought no followers nor proselytes. He said the Lord told him He, the Lord, was about to establish a New Church in preparation for a New Jerusalem and Swedenborg didn't need to concern himself with that.

His object was to counter the coldness of an age that left out of Christianity its very heart of love. Helen said he was one of the noblest champions true Christianity has ever known, yet he has nearly been forgotten. He carved heavenly messages of love and help from God to his children.

To a Lutheran church official, he wrote:

> I can solemnly bear witness that the Lord Himself has appeared to me, and that He has sent me to do that which I am doing now, and that for this purpose He has opened the

interiors of my mind, which are those of my spirit, so that I may see things which are in the spiritual world and hear those who are there.

As Helen wrote, "Angels were his teachers, his guides. He lodged his soul in heaven; he sensed the magnitude of the Divine Providence, the tremendous circumstances of life eternal. He was permitted to walk the winding course of stars and to return to earth with wisdom in his hands. Swedenborg's humble, noble character and kind ways endeared him to all who knew him. He never hesitated to offer simple service to anyone in need."

On his deathbed—and he told his friends exactly what day he would be departing this life—he was asked if all he had written was strictly true or if he wished any parts to be retracted, and he replied with unfaltering warmth:

> I have written nothing but the truth, as you will have it more confirmed hereafter all the days of your life, provided you always keep close to the Lord, and faithfully serve Him alone, shun evils of all kinds as sins against Him, and diligently search His Word, which from beginning to end bears incontestable testimony to the truth of the doctrines I have delivered to the world.

Now, I'm not suggesting you all go out and study Swedenborg's writings in depth. But I have found much that has lifted me and inspired me and this little book written by Helen Keller, *Light in My Darkness*, contains much wisdom that pertains to the work we are doing here at The Well-Educated Heart; principles that I have gained from multiple sources. Test the truthfulness of it for yourself.

Let me share a few of these insights—some gems "brought back from heaven" as described in Helen Keller's words.

> True life is the heart's capacity for joy fulfilled.

> One is not happy unless one's heart is filled with the sun that never dissolves into gloom. God is that sun.

> Every pure delight we cherish, every lovely scene we dwell on, every harmony we listen to, every graceful or tender thing touched with reverent hands inspires a flock of sweet thoughts that neither care nor poverty nor pain can destroy.

> If those who seek happiness would only stop one little minute and think, they would see that the delights they really experience are as countless as the blades of grass at their feet or the drops of dew sparkling upon the morning flowers. Yet how few persons I meet realize this wealth of joy!

> It is not environment that alters a human being, but forces within the individual. The blind, the deaf, the prisoner for conscience's sake, even the poorest men and women with sound ideals have all proved that they can shape life nearer to their desires, no matter what the outward circumstances.

> It is a change that comes over us as we hope and aspire and persevere in the way of the Divine Commandments.

A simple, childlike faith in a Divine Friend solves all the problems that come to us upon the earth. The marvelous richness of human experience would lose something of rewarding joy if there were no limitations to overcome.

Swedenborg taught that God is a God of love; that He is incapable of being stern with His children. God created the universe because of his infinite need to give life and joy. Cooperation with God, confidence in his unwearying help, learning to understand more truths in the Word, living according to them, and doing good for its own sake—these are the only wholesome ways for mortals to rise out of their old selves and rebuild their world.... [As they do these things], they will forever find more to love, more to know, more to achieve.

God bestows existence upon each of us for the express purpose of imparting life to us. His infinite love impels him to be a creator, since love must have objects to which it can give its wealth of good-will and beneficence. In the love which is the life of God, we find the origin of creation. His infinite will cannot be satisfied with anything less than the existence of beings who can be...recipients of his own happiness. At the same time, such beings must have freedom and the rationality that accompanies true freedom. That is, his gift of life to us must be received voluntarily and thoughtfully if it is to become our own. That is why we pass through two distinct experiences—the birth into existence and the birth into life—to be born again.

[O]ur birth into life is a matter of choice: we have a very direct share in it, for no real spiritual life can be thrust upon us against our will. This is the meaning of God's constant, loving invitation to all of us—to come unto him and choose life, and be ever on our guard against the evils that would rob us of the life that we have chosen. Only by exercising our powers of thought and keeping our hearts always warm and pure do we become truly alive. But this beautiful work of re-creation comes not by observation; it is wrought in the quiet depth of the soul. We should think of conversion as a change of heart. It is the soul turning away from the ignoble instincts that tempt us to feel, think, speak and act for mere self-interest and the good opinion of the world, and finding joy in the unselfish love of God and a life of usefulness to others above all things. Our choice of life is this delight—this sweet expansion of mind and heart without which no worthwhile achievement is possible.

A wise teacher or friend or true reformer does not attempt to drag a wrongdoer into the right way by force. Anyone who, out of sheer goodness of heart, speaks a helpful word, gives a cheering smile, or smooths over a rough place in another's path knows that the delight felt in the giving is so returned as to make it an intimate part of one's own life— a rule to live by. The joy of surmounting obstacles that once seemed unremovable and pushing the frontier of accomplishment furtherBwhat other joy is there like it?

Let me interject a reminder here—I'm reading Helen's words as she interprets the words of Swedenborg. Now let me continue as she turns her thoughts to the education of children.

We can reorganize the whole educational system so that the bulk of humanity will grow up more happily prepared for creative service. The small group of believers who know must struggle on, bearing steadfast witness to their truth in schools, courts, workshops, offices and legislatures.

What induces children to learn but their delight in knowing? Why does the scientist often endure mental travail and repulsive tasks, if not for the delight felt in understanding new truths or rendering a new service to others?

The education of children he saw in heaven is a suggestion for our earthly schools: There they are taught largely by "representations"—pictures, instructive plays, and scenery—that is, by illustration and example. Isn't that what we're doing when we teach by story, poetry and pictures as well as our example?

Swedenborg uses a word reliquae as a powerful factor in molding life. The word signifies the lasting impressions of love and truth and beauty left in us from the days of our childhood. Only by having definite pictures of heavenly life stamped upon our memories can we learn to imagine more beautiful ones and make them living realities. Our reliquae are the holy places where we feel our kinship with the divine.

Children must advance step by step, accustoming their inner eyes to keener light before they can endure the dazzle of new truths, and they cannot be turned toward a good life except by their delights. For it is these delights that keep them free and at last give them the power to choose.

[A]lways God guards the right of everyone to act in freedom according to reason; for liberty and rationality are his primary means for the regeneration of mankind.

Sick or well, blind or seeing, bound or free, we are here for a purpose, and the purpose of education is to fit us to a usefulness.

We need a system of education that will teach us about all the varieties of use that surround us…and one that may impel us to choose the tasks to which our interest and fitness draw us most strongly. The old thought tells us we are given earth to prepare for heaven, but there is truth in seeing it the other way around. We are given a knowledge of heaven to fit us better for earth.

If people examine their personal delights, they will often realize they are self-centered because most of their energies are directed to shaping their own lives or acquiring knowledge for private ends; but it turns out that the more enduring joys are born of an unselfish purpose to serve others and create new life in the world.

Christianity is the science of love. Love teaches us the highest of all arts—the art of living. The essence of life is in the delight of those things we love. There is no interest when the heart is cold. As selfishness and complaint pervert and cloud the mind so love with its joy clears and sharpens the vision.

Think of all Helen's accomplishments. She took these truths to heart as she wrote:

Instinctively I found my greatest satisfaction in working with men and women everywhere who ask not, "Shall I labor among Christians or Jews or Buddhists?" but say rather, "God, in thy wisdom help me to decrease the sorrows of thy children and increase their advantages and joys."

It may be of interest to note: Evidently Johnny Appleseed was doing more than planting apple trees. He was spreading Swedenborg tracts. And if you study his life, you'll see in him the Light Within—a man who carried his kingdom in his heart and was beloved by all he came in contact with. He assisted in the work of tearing down old superstitions of fear and darkness and replacing them with seeds of hope and Light; of a God of Love and Joy; that in the Father's house were many mansions, many kingdoms of various degrees of Light and Glory. Some of you will find significance that Johnny planted these ideas in the hearts of settlers in Pennsylvania and the Ohio Valley in the early 1800s, opening their hearts to new truths. I've posted in the podcast notes a link to the little movie Disney made years ago about Johnny Appleseed—many of you will remember Johnny singing, The Lord is Good to Me—the message of those tracts.

Helen Keller sums it up with these words:

> The doctrines set forth by Swedenborg bring us by a wondrous path to God's City of Light. I have walked through its sunlit ways of truth; I have drunk of its sweet waters of knowledge; and the eyes of my spirit have been opened, so that I know the joy of vision that conquers darkness and circles heaven. His message has exalted my ideas of love, truth and usefulness. There is an exquisitely quieting and soothing power. I find in it a happy rest from the noisy insanity of the outer world with its many words of little meaning and actions of little worth.

Well, I could go on for hours. But I've gone on long enough for now so I'll close with a poem written by Helen Keller.

> O light-bringer of my blindness,
> O spirit never far removed!
> Ever when the hour of travail deepens,
> Thou art near;
> Set in my soul like jewels bright
> Thy words of holy meaning,
> Till death with gentle hand shall lead me
> to the Presence I have loved—
> My torch in darkness here,
> My joy eternal there.

May there be light in all your learning.

Podcast #78 Daily Sampler—Captain John Smith

As we start a new podcast season, I thought I would try something a little different. I know that when you go into the Libraries of Hope library, it can be overwhelming. A lot of the titles and authors are unfamiliar. So I thought what if I provide you a daily sample and talk about the writers or topics as we go along. I'll post all of these kinds of podcasts on the landing pages of the various topics so you can refer to them whenever you want.

If you are using the Well-Educated Heart planner, you can make a note of books you want to go back and revisit, either this time in the rotation or in the future.

I'll try and keep them short—under 15 minutes. It's a way to spend a few minutes together each day. And maybe it will spark an idea of something you can share with your kids.

So welcome to a brand new school year if you are following the rotation schedule. Exploration and discovery is one of our first topics—and what a perfect way to start the year.

Today's Daily sample comes from an 1879 book entitled *Stories of American History* written by Nathaniel Dodge. You'll find it in the Month 12 American Overview page or just enter it in the search field.

I've loved learning about Captain John Smith and this sample is Chapter 3, the Hero of Virginia.[8]

> In the settlement of America, there were many heroes. Columbus was a hero. Some of the navigators who followed Columbus were heroes. There was Hendrich Hudson, who discovered the North River and gave it his name; there were the Pilgrims. who settled Plymouth; there was William Penn, who founded the colony of Pennsylvania; they were all heroes. But in true heroism, not one was superior to Captain John Smith, who founded Virginia. Let us see:

> In the year 1606, when he sailed with one hundred and six others, in three ships, from England, to plant a colony in Virginia, he was only twenty-seven years old. And yet, from boyhood he had been engaged in adventures. He had built himself a hut in an English forest, and hunted and studied there four years; he had been to sea several voyages; he had been thrown overboard, and escaped to land by swimming; he had fought in many battles on the ocean and on land, and had several times been taken prisoner; he had travelled all over Europe, had killed three Turks in single combat, and was made a major for his gallantry; had been captured and reduced to slavery, and escaping at last, had wandered many days and nights in forests and deserts until he got back to England. There was never a braver man; such a thing as fear he did not know. In the very worst he was never disheartened; when a slave in Turkey he won the heart of his mistress, who set him at liberty; and when a Tartar prince, who had set him to threshing grain, insulted him, he beat out his master's brains with a flail, and fled to the

woods. All his life long he was in one trouble or another; but he was never discouraged, never faint-hearted, and never lost his self-reliance.

The three ships arrived safely in James river, and a town was founded called Jamestown. houses were built, trees were felled, fields were planted, roads were opened, forts were constructed, the Indians were dealt with fairly, every one of the colonists was set to work, and all the prospects were fair. Corn was sometimes scarce, and then Captain Smith, taking men with him, went among the Indians and traded for it. He explored the sea-coast and made charts, he sailed up the rivers and planned them on maps, he went far into the Indian country and bargained with the natives for land, and he was never weary in his efforts to make Jamestown a great and prosperous place.

To be sure he had trouble; all men who are in earnest do. The colonists were sometimes idle, and he made them work. The Indians were often ill-tempered and quarrelsome, but he quieted them with presents, or frightened them with guns. Many of the settlers wanted to go back to England, but he encouraged them with good words. Chief men in the colony revolted, but he brought them to obedience by good sense and firmness; and though for a time there was scant food, and much sickness, and many hardships, Captain Smith kept the people together by his brave heart.

He often made journeys up the rivers in a boat; along the coasts in one of the ships which brought the colonists over from England; and up the country on foot, attended by three or four of his men. Upon one of these expeditions, he sailed up the Chickahominy. When the boat could go no farther, he left her in charge of two of his men, telling them to keep watch, one to sleep while the other was awake, while he went farther. After he had gone, the men grew careless, and while both were asleep one night, the Indians killed them and captured the boat. Captain Smith knew nothing of this, but pressed onward by land, having with him an Indian guide. As he penetrated the forest, now ascending high mountains and then plunging through morasses and swamps, always observing where he went, and mapping the way on bits of paper; some Indians attacked him, shooting their arrows. He then tied his guide to his arm and made a shield of him, knowing that they would not willingly shoot a comrade. But though not wounded, Smith was at last taken prisoner, and the savages led him to their chief, Powhatan.

Powhatan was stretched out on a kind of throne of stones. Skins of wild beasts were spread around him; a blanket wrought with beads covered his legs; he had feathers in his hair, and paint on his face; one of his wives sat at his head and another at his feet; warriors stood near him, and altogether he seemed quite a king. Although he was greatly pleased with a pocket-compass which Captain Smith gave him, and put on a shirt which the Englishman had brought, and decked himself with the beads and buttons the colonists had sent, and accepted a jack-knife and brass ring and a string of bells and some red cloth and needles and thread from his prisoner, he determined to put him to death. So some of the savages seized the white man, bound him with green withs, threw him on the ground, and were ready to beat out his brains with their clubs.

Just at that moment a woman's scream was heard. Powhatan started up. The warriors were startled. In an instant a young Indian girl rushed from the crowd and threw herself on the prostrate victim. It was Pocahontas, the young daughter of Powhatan.

"Kill me," she cried, "kill me; you shall not kill him!" The warriors did not claro to strike. Their blows would have killed the girl. Powhatan's heart was softened. He forbade the execution. Smith was unbound, and after a time he was allowed to go back to Jamestown.

Here he found everything in confusion. Other ships with colonists had arrived. These new comers were young gallants who did not want to work. They had heard there was gold in Virginia, and it was that they were after. But Captain Smith knew better, It was with infinite trouble that he persuaded them to settle down to felling trees, and planting corn, and building huts, and making roads, and erecting saw-mills. Many were discontented. Some rebelled. A few went off into the woods and were taken by the Indians. But by energy and firmness he finally succeeded in making all contented. Jamestown grew up to be a prosperous colony. But for Captain Smith it would never have succeeded. He went back to England, returned with more colonists, and went back a third time. He was then created admiral of New England, a country not then settled. The charts he published, the maps he made, and the books he wrote, made the English people acquainted with America. He died in England at the age of fifty-four.

Pocahontas afterwards married a Mr. Rolfe. He took her to England. Everybody had heard of her heroism in saving Captain Smith's life. The people came in crowds to see her. When she rode through the streets they cheered her. The queen sent for her, and she went to court. Beautiful presents were made her; great entertainments were given her; she was shown the shops and public buildings, and churches, and bridges, and factories of England; artists painted her pictures; lords and ladies had her at their houses; so that the Indian girl became famous. She died just at the time she was about embarking for Virginia, and her little daughter grew up to be the mother of men and women, who were afterwards famous in Virginia.

Podcast #79 Daily Sampler—Marco Polo

Today's daily sample is from the writings of M.B. Synge—Margaret Bertha Synge. I can't tell you a lot about her, but I think you will really enjoy her series, *The Story of the World*, I posted in the Month 12 World Overview Section. Originally published in 1903.

I have linked these books to Yesterday's Classics and I want to say a word about that. Lisa Ripperton has provided a monumental service to us through the Baldwin Project. You will find hundreds of titles you can read for free on her site, but for those of you who prefer hard copies, she has brought many of these books back into print. *The Story of the World* is one of the series offered as a hard copy.

I wanted to give you a little background look at Marco Polo in today's sample. You'll actually find a number of great options to read about his adventures in China in the Month 1 China section. This is the chapter on Marco Polo found in *The Discovery of the World*,[9] one of the volumes in Synge's Story of the World.

> The Crusades had brought about a contact of East and West. But though they had raised the general standard of life, and made the riches of the East—gold, silks, spices, and jewels—familiar throughout Europe, yet the geography of the East was strangely misty and undefined. To the men of the Middle Ages, the world was still very limited. The great Atlantic, which was soon to open out a new world, was yet known as the Sea of Darkness, and many attempts to fathom its mysteries had ended in dismal failure. Still more alarming was the idea of a Sea of Pitchy Darkness, which was supposed to lie to the East of Asia.
>
> In the north the old Vikings, having discovered Iceland and sailed by the northern shores of America without knowing it, had become a settled people, and no longer terrified the world by their coasting raids. Africa, except for the strip of northern coast and Egypt, was still a closed book, and nothing was known of the south and west.
>
> This was somewhat the state of affairs when Marco Polo arose, travelled away to the far East, sailed on the Sea of Pitchy Darkness, and returned home, after many years, travel-stained and unrecognizable, to give the world an account of his wonderful doings.
>
> It seems somewhat natural to find that Venice was the birthplace of this early explorer, for Venice, as we have seen, had the enterprise of the whole world at this time.
>
> The very year that Marco Polo was born in Venice—1254—his father and uncle had started forth on a trading enterprise to Constantinople. They were away for some fifteen years, and when they came back, they had some wonderful stories to tell to the young Marco. They told him how they had reached China and been at the court of the Chinese ruler, the Great Khan, as he was called. The boy was fired with enthusiasm to go to this distant country, and to see for himself the wonders of the mysterious new

land.

Two years later, when the father and uncle started off again, they took young Marco with them. They sailed from Venice to Acre; but nothing is related of their journey except that they travelled towards the north-east and north, till, after three and a half years, they reached the city of the Great Khan, who was at his summer home among the hills to the north of Pékin. The great man, "Lord of all the Earth," as he was called, was very glad to see them, and asked at once who was the young man with them.

"Sire," answered his father, "'tis my son, and your liegeman."

"Welcome is he too," said the Great Khan.

Marco soon picked up the language and customs of the Chinese, and became a great favourite at this strange foreign court. Once the Great Khan sent him on a journey— "a good six months' journey distant." Marco returned safely; and so ably did he state all he had seen and heard that the Great Khan cried, "If this young man live, he will become a person of great worth and ability."

For seventeen years the three Polos stayed in China, and Marco explored countries which to this day are hardly understood. He was the first traveler to cross Asia, describing kingdom after kingdom that he had seen with his own eyes. He was the first to explore the deserts and the flowering plains of Persia, to tell the Western world of China, with its mighty rivers, its multitudes of people, its huge cities and great manufactures. He first told us of Thibet, Burmah, Japan, Siberia, and the frozen ocean beyond. So the years passed on, the Great Khan was growing old, and the Venetians yearned for home; but whenever they hinted at leaving China, the Khan growled refusal.

At last their chance came. A relation of the Great Khan was King of Persia. He had lately lost his wife, and now sent to China for a wife of his own nationality. The Polos were chosen to take her to Persia, because they were hardy and adventurous, and the lady must be sent by sea to Persia.

Fourteen ships were built by the Great Khan, each having four masts and able to carry nine sails, with some two hundred and fifty sailors in each. In these ships the Polos sailed away from China with the bride-elect on board. They took a sorrowful leave of the Great Khan, who gave them numbers of rubies and precious stones. After sailing for three months in the unknown China Sea they came to the island of Java, and after another eighteen months on the high seas they reached Persia, to find that the bridegroom was dead. But his son, the new king, married the lady without more ado, and the Venetians sailed on for home.

So one day, in the year 1295, three men appeared in the streets of Venice. They were dressed in Asiatic clothes and spoke with a foreign accent. It was therefore no great matter of surprise when they were refused admission to the family house of the Polos.

"We have been in the service of the Great Khan in China," they urged, but no one believed them.

So they invited a number of friends to a banquet prepared with great magnificence, and when the hour arrived for sitting down to table, all three came forth clothed in long crimson satin robes, after the fashion of the times. When the guests were seated, they took off these robes and put on others of crimson damask, whilst the first suits were cut up and divided among their servants. Soon after they again changed, this time to crimson velvet, while the damask robes were divided as before.

Dinner over, Marco rose, and fetched the three shabby garments in which they had arrived. With sharp knives they then slit up the seams, and from them took the most priceless jewels—rubies, diamonds, emeralds, and sapphires. So their astonished guests knew they spoke the truth, and all Venice came rushing to do them honour.

They stayed at home for a time, and then Marco Polo was made commander of a great and powerful galley to fight against Venice's rival seaport, Genoa. He was taken prisoner and shut up in Genoa. Here Marco Polo wrote his book of travels, which are interesting reading today; and we cannot do better than follow the good advice at the beginning of his book.

"Great Princes, Emperors, and Kings," he says, "and people of all degrees who desire to get knowledge of the various races of mankind and of sundry regions of the world, take this book and cause it to be read to you."

He was an old man when he had finished dictating his travels to his fellow captive, and he returned to Venice to die.

Podcast #80 Daily Sampler—The Stars

One of my earliest discoveries in this journey of learning how to educate hearts was the power of stories. And I learned about a revival in the art of storytelling among mothers in the early 1900s. I read every book I could find about storytelling from that era and what they stressed over and over was to put the book down and tell stories by heart; that that is the most powerful way of sharing life messages.

I still believe that with all my heart, but I've backed off of sharing that message because I have come to find out how truly story depleted our hearts are. We have a lot of heart work to do before we can become powerful storytellers again, but storytelling by heart has always been the aim of the Well-Educated Heart and will remain so.

I remember vividly my first attempt at telling a story to my little granddaughters several years ago. We were living with them at the time because their daddy had deployed for a year and my daughter was expecting another baby while he was away. It was a little cool that night and we all went out on the front porch. I was actually nervous to even attempt it and it felt awkward, but I have learned little children are easy to please and aren't hyper critical like we adults are.

We could easily see the big dipper from the porch and I pointed it out to them. And then I told them the story I'm going to share with you. It's found in *Restoring the Art of Storytelling in the Home*[10] and there's a free digital copy in the Storytelling section of the Mother's University. It's called the Legend of the Dipper.

You may think that when you teach your children about the Stars, you need to inform them of how far away the stars are and their relative sizes and the order of the planets in the Solar System. Those facts can come in time. My little story had nothing to do with those things. My granddaughters are older now and don't remember the details of the story. But when they look up at the Big Dipper in the sky, they remember the feelings of being together and how much their grandmother loves them. And that's the lesson I wanted them to take away.

So grab a blanket and go in the back yard and just snuggle up while you look up at the stars. And tell your children a story if you want. But even silence can be a wonderful teacher. I shared my most important childhood lesson about the Stars in another presentation. It was a Saturday night and I had just gotten out of the shower and still had a towel wrapped around my wet hair. As I walked by the front door, I saw my dad out on the front porch in the dark, so I went out and joined him. He smiled at me, but didn't say anything. He was just gazing up at the stars. I kept looking to see what he was looking at. Finally, he said, "Do you ever wonder what's out there?" And then the two of us gazed and wondered…in silence…together.

These are Star lessons for the heart.

Now the story.

The Legend of the Dipper

There had been no rain in the land for a very long time. It was so hot and dry that the flowers were withered, the grass was parched and brown, and even the big, strong trees were dying. The water dried up in the creeks and rivers, the wells were dry, the fountains stopped bubbling. The cows, the dogs, the horses, the birds, and all the people were so thirsty! Every one felt uncomfortable and sick.

There was one little girl whose mother grew very ill. "Oh," said the little girl, "if I can only find some water for my mother I'm sure she will be well again. I must find some water."

So she took a tin cup and started out in search of water. By and by she found a tiny little spring away up on a mountain side. It was almost dry. The water dropped, dropped, ever so slowly from under the rock. The little girl held her cup carefully and caught the drops. She waited and waited a long, long time until the cup was full of water. Then she started down the mountain holding the cup very carefully, for she didn't want to spill a single drop.

On the way she passed a poor little dog. He could hardly drag himself along. He was panting for breath and his tongue hung from his mouth because it was so dry and parched.

"Oh, you poor little dog," said the little girl, "you are so thirsty. I can't pass you without giving you a few drops of water. If I give you just a little there will still be enough for my mother."

So the little girl poured some water into her hand and held it down for the little dog. He lapped it up quickly and then he felt so much better that he frisked and barked and seemed almost to say, "Thank you, little girl." And the little girl didn't notice—but her tin dipper had changed into a silver dipper and was just as full of water as it had been before.

She thought about her mother and hurried along as fast as she could go. When she reached home it was late in the afternoon, almost dark. The little girl pushed the door open and hurried up to her mother's room. When she came into the room the old servant who helped the little girl and her mother, and had been working hard all day taking care of the sick woman, came to the door. She was so tired and so thirsty that she couldn't even speak to the little girl.

"Do give her some water," said the mother. "She has worked hard all day and she needs it much more than I do."

So the little girls held the cup to her lips and the old servant drank some of the water. She felt stronger and better right away and she went over to the mother and lifted her up. The little girl didn't notice that the cup had changed into a gold cup and was just as full of water as it was before!

Then she held the cup to her mother's lips and she drank and drank. Oh, she felt so much better! When she had finished there was still some water left in the cup. The little girl was just raising it to her own lips when there came a knock at the door. The servant opened it and there stood a stranger. He was very pale and all covered with dust from traveling. "I am thirsty," he said, "won't you give me a little water?"

The little girl said: "Why, certainly I will. I am sure that you need it far more than I do. Drink it all."

The stranger smiled and took the dipper in his hand, and as he took it, it changed into a diamond dipper. He turned it upside down and all the water spilled out and sank into the ground. And where it spilled a fountain bubbled up. The cool water flowed and splashed—enough for the people and all the animals in the whole land to have all the water they wanted to drink.

As they watched the water they forgot the stranger, but presently when they looked, he was gone. They thought they could see him just vanishing in the sky—and there in the sky, clear and high, shone the diamond dipper. It shines up there yet, and reminds people of the little girl who was kind and unselfish. It is called the Star Dipper.

Podcast #81 Daily sampler—How Pepper Helped to Discover America

One of the big objectives of studying history for the heart is to help children begin to appreciate the price others have paid that translate into blessings for our own lives and also to help us to see what we can do to improve the lives of those who follow after us. It's about fostering a sense of gratitude and linking generations together.

The sample I'm going to share today comes from a Month 1 book in the Middle School Exploration section called *Explorers and Settlers*, compiled by Charles Barstow.[11] I hope it will give you some ideas you can share with your kids around the dinner table. As you teach the heart, you always want to be looking for connections to familiar things, and most of us have a pepper shaker on the table. By unfolding this story about pepper, whenever they see that pepper shaker on their table, it will call up impressions and reminders of you have shared with them.

So here is today's sample—How Pepper Helped to Discover America. You'll also notice more lessons on what inspired Columbus to make his daring voyages to layer into your learning.

> How would you like a pie not only sweetened and spiced but made hot with a sprinkling of pepper? or a cake full of fruit and also strongly peppered? I rather think you would call these things spoiled, and beg to have them made in a different way. If, however, we had lived some four or five hundred years ago, we should have thought, like every one else in those days, that no dish, sweet or otherwise, was complete without the pungent taste of pepper. No doubt it is as well for our digestion that we in these times like our food prepared in simpler fashion.
>
> Perhaps it would surprise you to know that this taste for pepper, and the value which was once placed upon it, played an important part in the discovery of America. In case this last statement seems improbable, let me tell you something of the history of pepper, and its importance in the commerce of the world during the Middle Ages. There are a great many common things, you know, that have very interesting stories belonging to them, and they are generally worth hearing.
>
> The native country of the pepper-plant is southern India, and its culture there is very old. The berry, or peppercorn, which is ground for our use, is produced on vines which are trained against trees, very much as you may see the grape-vines in an Italian vineyard. The berries are dried in the sun and sent to market in bags. Black and white pepper are made from the same berries, but the black contains the ground husk, which the other does not. This addition of the husk gives the darker color and stronger flavor to black pepper.
>
> The old Eastern nations, the Egyptians, the Greeks, and the Romans all knew and used a great many spices, and among them was always pepper. How soon it came to be so highly esteemed as it was in the Middle Ages is not certain; but as early as 410, when the great Northern conqueror, Alaric the Visigoth, besieged Rome, and was induced to

retire by taking a ransom, three thousand pounds of pepper formed part of the treasure he carried away with him.

Later on, taxes began to be paid in pepper instead of money, and the Jews, especially, who dealt largely in this, among other spices, were obliged, in many cases, to give to the government so many pounds of it yearly. In the twelfth century, according to an old law, the Jews paid to the Pope a tribute of one pound of pepper and two pounds of cinnamon. From certain Provencal villages the archbishop received annually from one-half to two pounds of pepper, in payment for allowing the Jews to have a copy of the book of their law, a synagogue, lamp burning perpetually, and a cemetery. In 1385 the King of Provence imposed on the Jews in his dominions a tax of sixty pounds of pepper.

So much traffic in this spice came to the city of Alexandria that one of its streets and a gate were named for it; and as for Venice, an Italian proverb said, *"Il nero e il bianco hanno fatto ricca Venézia,"* which means, "The white and the black have made Venice rich." In other words, it was through the pepper and the cotton, brought from the East by the ships of Venice, and by her merchants sent all over Europe, that the city gained a large share of its vast wealth. In the fifteenth century pepper was the article, more than any other, that the Venetians sent to France, Flanders, England, and, above all, to Germany.

People used to make presents of pepper. Even kings and ambassadors gave and received it. When the republic of Venice wished to show special gratitude to the Emperor Henry V, they made him an annual gift of fifty pounds of it. After a victory gained by the people of Genoa in 1101, each soldier received as part of his pay two pounds of pepper.

In many countries there prevailed a curious system which obliged certain persons to furnish, at stated times, pepper in small quantities, in most cases about one pound. These payments were called "peppercorn rents," and the term has not entirely died out yet. In England the tax on pepper in 1623 was five shillings a pound, and even until the eighteenth century it amounted to two shillings and sixpence per pound.

You can easily imagine what a high price people had to pay for an article so much in demand, and what an enormous amount of it must have been used. I said that they put it even in sweet dishes, and, in fact, the rage for peppered food was so great that it was considered absolutely essential in every sauce. People would not have said then, "I haven't enough salt in my soup" or "on my meat," or "enough sugar in my pudding," but, "There isn't enough pepper."

You must imagine yourself in the Middle Ages, and think of all the difficulties then connected with carrying on business. When our merchants want anything, there are swift ships and fast trains everywhere; all countries are open, and we can telegraph from one end of the earth to the other. The products of India and Africa are at our very doors, and we have only to ask to obtain them. But it has not always been so, and ought to remember the long voyages taken, the weary searching made, the dangers from wild beasts and savage peoples encountered, before we, in our time, could obtain so comfortably and easily what seem to us only ordinary necessities.

Four and five hundred years ago there was, it is true, a great amount of luxury in France and Italy. People wore beautiful clothing, magnificent jewels, and ate choice food; art flourished, and science made great progress. But at what a cost were even the necessaries of living obtained! From the Far East to Europe, how long the journey was, and what months were consumed in bringing, over the deserts of Arabia, across the plains and mountains of Persia, under the burning sun of India, or in boats from Syrian and Turkish ports, the things which European civilization required. When we remember the difficulties of the medieval merchants, we can understand one of the principal motives which led so many persons to search for new and shorter routes to the countries where the spices grew, and where the land was rich in products which would bring them wealth. It was the love of adventure and the desire to see new and strange places which started large numbers of the early voyagers, but it was, more than all, for commercial reasons that most of the expeditions were undertaken.

In the year 1260 there passed through Constantinople two Venetians, named Maffeo and Niccolo Polo. They were on their way, as a matter of speculation, toward the East, and, by various chances and changes, went on until they reached Bokhara in Turkestan, where they felt a long way from home, and thought they had made a great journey. But here they fell in with certain envoys on a mission to Cathay, or China, and bound to the court of the great monarch Kublai Khan. The two brothers were induced to accompany them, and thus became, as far as we know, the first European travelers to reach China. There is no time to tell of how they found Kublai Khan at a place called Cambaluc (the old name of Peking), just rebuilt by him, or of his beautiful country-seat at Shangtu, north of the great wall.

But some day, when you read those lines which Coleridge left unfinished, and which begin—

> At Xanadu did Kubla Khan
> a Stately pleasure dome decree,

you might remember the visit the five Venetians paid the place.

The Chinese monarch was delighted to meet these intelligent men from the distant and civilized West, and when they went home he made them his messengers to the Pope, begging them to return with teachers and missionaries from Europe. After a long time they did reach China again, having visited home in the meanwhile, and although they had not succeeded in having the teachers sent, they brought with them Niccolo's son Marco, then fifteen years old, who became the famous traveler and the first European explorer to write a book about what he had seen.

When you read his book, you will notice how often he speaks of the spices of the Eastern countries, and how he mentions pepper as one of the most important articles of commerce in those lands. The Chinese, at that time, valued pepper so much that they willingly paid fifteen ducats for a bushel, and Marco Polo says that for one ship which left India with a cargo of pepper to be sent on to Alexandria, a hundred or more went to China.

Marco Polo's book made a great impression on his fellow-countrymen, and the interest already felt in the unexplored East was largely increased by reading his stories. One traveler after another sailed from the different ports Of Italy, and made voyages, more or less successful, in various directions. As at this time the principal traffic of Europe came through Venice, the Venetians were the first to interest themselves in expeditions to distant countries. Every year a Venetian squadron passed through the Straits of Gibraltar, and stopped at Lisbon on the way to England and Flanders. The sailors told stories of the Eastern countries with which their city carried on commerce, and the Portuguese and Spaniards were the next to catch the exploring fever, and began to make voyages of exploration for themselves. They went down the west coast of Africa, making their own one bit of territory after another, until, as you know, Vasco da Gama sailed quite around the Cape of Good Hope, and showed that path to India.

Prince Henry of Portugal, himself a navigator, was largely responsible for these African discoveries, and he was influenced by Marco Polo's book to attempt his own expeditions and encourage those of others.

Here in Portugal pepper was again of importance, for it is said that the desire to find it by an easy and cheap route, and thus to reduce its price, was one of the reasons why the Portuguese were so anxious to get to India by sea. Its price was certainly lowered after the merchants began to bring it directly from India and Ceylon in ships; and it became a monopoly of the Portuguese crown, continuing so until the eighteenth century. About this time the culture of pepper was extended to the Malay Archipelago, and part of the traffic was turned naturally from Italy to Portugal, as being in more direct communication.

Now let us go back a little, and this time to Florence, one of the greatest commercial cities of the past, particularly during the fourteenth and fifteenth centuries. Her merchants were of the richest in the world, and certain trades and arts flourished there as nowhere else.

Among these merchant families one called Toscanelli, and they carried on business in spices and in the other articles usually coming under that head in those days. They sent in every direction for their goods, and every year visited the old Italian town called Lanciano, where was held the great fair of spices, and where merchants carne to buy and sell from all countries of Europe, and even from Asia. Here one would be sure to find many travelers, and to hear many stories of strange lands and little known peoples, and here, no doubt, great impetus was given to research in new directions.

The Toscanelli family were rich, and owned a great deal of property in Florence, and a street in the city still bears their name. There is, too, a fine old villa, not far away, which belonged to them nearly five hundred years ago. But they are remembered especially for one famous representative of their name, and he was a man whom Americans should hold in great regard. Well known and esteemed in his own day, Paolo Dal Pozzo Toscanelli has almost been forgotten since by the world in general, until comparatively recent times. However, in 1871, at the meeting in Antwerp of the Geographical Congress, all the scholars, historians, and scientists present unanimously agreed in calling the inspirer of the discovery of America. He died in 1482, ten years before Columbus touched the shores of the New; but it was by the chart he drew, and according to his plans, that the great Genoese laid his course.

Toscanelli lived out the whole of his long life in Italy, a hard student, a skilful physician, and a remarkable scientist. He was the founder of modern astronomy, and was the first to mention some of the comets best known to later astronomers. His knowledge of mathematics was profound, and his interest in geographical researches intense. There is still, in the Cathedral of Florence, the gnomon, or sun-dial, he made, and it has been considered the Most perfect in existence.

On the death of his brother, he took the place almost of a father to his nephews, and, as they carried on the business, he interested himself largely in their success. It was for their sake that, aside from his scientific interest in the voyages of the day, he began to think and plan new routes and ways to the country of the spices. The Turks were interfering with the introduction into Venice, and thus into Italy, of the products of India, and Merchants of Florence were beginning to feel the effect of this obstacle to commerce, when Toscanelli declared it possible to reach the East by sailing west. On the chart which he made he traced a line from Lisbon, across the sea to Quin-sai (Han-chau), on the Chinese coast; and in a letter which he wrote on June 25, 1474, to his friend Christopher Columbus, he explained his ideas and theories regarding the voyage.

At the same time that Toscanelli sent this letter to Columbus (who was then at Lisbon), he also wrote to another person a letter to be given to the King of Portugal. In this letter, among other things, he said :

"Many other times I have reasoned concerning the very short route which there is by way of the sea from here to India,— the native land of the spices,— and which I hold to be shorter than that which you take by Guinea. For greater clearness of explanation, I have made a chart such as is used by navigators, on which is traced this route, and I send it to your Majesty. I have depicted everything from Ireland at the north as far south as Guinea, with the islands and countries, and I will show how you may reach the places most productive of all sorts of spices. Also I have shown in this chart many countries in the neighborhood of India, where, if no contrary winds or misadventures arise, you will find islands where all the inhabitants are merchants. Especially is there a most noble port, called Zaitou, where they load and unload every year a hundred great ships with pepper, and there are also other ships, laden with other spices. This place is thickly populated, and there are cities and provinces without number, under the rule of a prince, called the Great Khan, which name means 'King of Kings.' Here you will find not only very great gain and many rich things, but also gold and silver and precious stones, and all sorts of spices in great abundance. From the city of Lisbon you may sail directly to the great and noble city of Quin-sai, where are ten bridges of marble, and the name of the place signifies 'City of Heaven.' Of it are told most marvelous things of its buildings, of its manufactures, and of its revenues. This city lies near the province of Cathay, where the king spends the greater part of his time. You have heard of the island of Antillia, which you call the Seven Cities, and of the most noble island of Cipango, which is rich in gold, pearls, and precious stones, and the temples and royal palaces are covered with plates of gold. Many other things could be said, but I will not be too long. And so I remain always most ready to serve your Majesty in whatever you may command me."

With such ideas as these in his mind, you know why Columbus thought he was landing in the Orient when he stepped ashore on the island of San Salvador. He had even brought with him a letter and fitting gifts for the Great Khan, or Emperor of Cathay.

To-day pepper grows in many countries besides those of the East, though the best still comes from India, and a great deal of business is carried on in its cultivation, preparation, and exportation. It has become an ordinary thing to us, and we expect it on the table as a matter of course. Perhaps, however, when you remember its old importance, and that the trade in this spice really did help to lead voyagers toward America, you will regard it as something much more interesting than a mere every-day addition to your food.

> Then first Columbus, with the mighty hand
> Of grasping genius, weigh'd the sea and land;
> The floods o'erbalanced: — where the tide of light,
> Day after day, roll'd down the gulf of night,
> There seemed one waste of waters: — long in vain
> His spirit brooded o'er the Atlantic main:
> When sudden, as creation burst from nought,
> Sprang a new world through his stupendous thought,
> Light, order, beauty!

Podcast #82 Daily Sampler—Jenny Lind, The Swedish Nightingale

Many of you have enjoyed watching *The Greatest Showman* about PT Barnum. It was a feel-good movie with a strong theme of what matters most. I loved the movie for that, even though the portrayal of PT Barnum wasn't exactly accurate. And the portrayal of Jenny Lind was far from the truth.

So I thought it might be worthwhile to set the record straight.

PT Barnum said this of Jenny: "It is a mistake to say that the fame of Jenny Lind rests solely upon her ability to sing. She was a woman who would be adored if she had the voice of a crow."

I've read a number of books and accounts about Jenny, and her greatness was found in her heart through which her song flowed, which makes her story a vital one for heart-based learners. She had no desire for riches or fame. She gave most of her money away to charitable causes. She viewed her voice as a gift from God and recognized that this gift depended upon her purity of heart. She wrote, "If you knew what a sensation of the nearness of a higher power one instinctively feels when one is permitted to contribute to the good of mankind, as I have done, and still do! Believe me, it is a great gift of God's mercy."

Hans Christian Andersen fell in love with her, and although she loved him like a brother, she rejected his proposals of marriage. Poor Hans had a lifetime of such rejections and never married. Still, he wrote of her, "Through Jenny Lind I first became sensible of the holiness of Art. Through her I learned that one must forget one's self in the service of the Supreme. No books, no men, have had a more ennobling influence upon me as a poet than Jenny Lind." Several of his stories are attributed to her influence, including *The Nightingale*, which will be today's Daily Sampler.[12] Jenny was known as The Swedish Nightingale, and as you listen to the story, you will learn much about the secrets of her charm.

> In China, as you know, the Emperor is a Chinaman, and all the people around him are Chinamen too. It is many years since the story I am going to tell you happened, but that is all the more reason for telling it, lest it should be forgotten. The emperor's palace was the most beautiful thing in the world; it was made entirely of the finest porcelain, very costly, but at the same time so fragile that it could only be touched with the very greatest care. There were the most extraordinary flowers to be seen in the garden; the most beautiful ones had little silver bells tied to them, which tinkled perpetually, so that one should not pass the flowers without looking at them. Every little detail in the garden had been most carefully thought out, and it was so big, that even the gardener himself did not know where it ended. If one went on walking, one came to beautiful woods with lofty trees and deep lakes. The wood extended to the sea, which was deep and blue, deep enough for large ships to sail up right under the branches of the trees. Among these trees lived a nightingale, which sang so deliciously, that even the poor fisherman, who had plenty of other things to do, lay still to listen to it, when he was out at night

drawing in his nets. 'Heavens, how beautiful it is!' he said, but then he had to attend to his business and forgot it. The next night when he heard it again he would again exclaim, 'Heavens, how beautiful it is!'

Travellers came to the emperor's capital, from every country in the world; they admired everything very much, especially the palace and the gardens, but when they heard the nightingale they all said, 'This is better than anything!'

When they got home they described it, and the learned ones wrote many books about the town, the palace and the garden; but nobody forgot the nightingale, it was always put above everything else. Those among them who were poets wrote the most beautiful poems, all about the nightingale in the woods by the deep blue sea. These books went all over the world, and in course of time some of them reached the emperor. He sat in his golden chair reading and reading, and nodding his head, well pleased to hear such beautiful descriptions of the town, the palace and the garden. 'But the nightingale is the best of all,' he read.

'What is this?' said the emperor. 'The nightingale? Why, I know nothing about it. Is there such a bird in my kingdom, and in my own garden into the bargain, and I have never heard of it? Imagine my having to discover this from a book?'

Then he called his gentleman-in-waiting, who was so grand that when any one of a lower rank dared to speak to him, or to ask him a question, he would only answer 'P,' which means nothing at all.

'There is said to be a very wonderful bird called a nightingale here,' said the emperor. 'They say that it is better than anything else in all my great kingdom! Why have I never been told anything about it?'

'I have never heard it mentioned,' said the gentleman-in-waiting. 'It has never been presented at court.'

'I wish it to appear here this evening to sing to me,' said the emperor. 'The whole world knows what I am possessed of, and I know nothing about it!'

'I have never heard it mentioned before,' said the gentleman-in-waiting. 'I will seek it, and I will find it!' But where was it to be found? The gentleman-in-waiting ran upstairs and downstairs and in and out of all the rooms and corridors. No one of all those he met had ever heard anything about the nightingale; so the gentleman-in-waiting ran back to the emperor, and said that it must be a myth, invented by the writers of the books. 'Your imperial majesty must not believe everything that is written; books are often mere inventions, even if they do not belong to what we call the black art!'

'But the book in which I read it is sent to me by the powerful Emperor of Japan, so it can't be untrue. I will hear this nightingale; I insist upon its being here to-night. I extend my most gracious protection to it, and if it is not forthcoming, I will have the whole court trampled upon after supper!'

'Tsing-pe!' said the gentleman-in-waiting, and away he ran again, up and down all the stairs, in and out of all the rooms and corridors; half the court ran with him, for they none of them wished to be trampled on. There was much questioning about this nightingale, which was known to all the outside world, but to no one at court. At last they found a poor little maid in the kitchen. She said, 'Oh heavens, the nightingale? I know it very well. Yes, indeed it can sing. Every evening I am allowed to take broken meat to my poor sick mother: she lives down by the shore. On my way back, when I am tired, I rest awhile in the wood, and then I hear the nightingale. Its song brings the tears into my eyes; I feel as if my mother were kissing me!'

'Little kitchen-maid,' said the gentleman-in-waiting, 'I will procure you a permanent position in the kitchen, and permission to see the emperor dining, if you will take us to the nightingale. It is commanded to appear at court to-night.'

Then they all went out into the wood where the nightingale usually sang. Half the court was there. As they were going along at their best pace a cow began to bellow.

'Oh!' said a young courtier, 'there we have it. What wonderful power for such a little creature; I have certainly heard it before.'

'No, those are the cows bellowing; we are a long way yet from the place.' Then the frogs began to croak in the marsh.

'Beautiful!' said the Chinese chaplain, 'it is just like the tinkling of church bells.'

'No, those are the frogs!' said the little kitchen-maid. 'But I think we shall soon hear it now!'

Then the nightingale began to sing.

'There it is!' said the little girl. 'Listen, listen, there it sits!' and she pointed to a little grey bird up among the branches.

'Is it possible?' said the gentleman-in-waiting. 'I should never have thought it was like that. How common it looks! Seeing so many grand people must have frightened all its colours away.'

'Little nightingale!' called the kitchen-maid quite loud, 'our gracious emperor wishes you to sing to him!'

'With the greatest of pleasure!' said the nightingale, warbling away in the most delightful fashion.

'It is just like crystal bells,' said the gentleman-in-waiting. 'Look at its little throat, how active it is. It is extraordinary that we have never heard it before! I am sure it will be a great success at court!'

'Shall I sing again to the emperor?' said the nightingale, who thought he was present.

'My precious little nightingale,' said the gentleman-in-waiting, 'I have the honour to command your attendance at a court festival to-night, where you will charm his gracious majesty the emperor with your fascinating singing.'

'It sounds best among the trees,' said the nightingale, but it went with them willingly when it heard that the emperor wished it.

'Is it possible?' said the gentleman-in-waiting. 'I should never have thought it was like that. How common it looks. Seeing so many grand people must have frightened all its colours away.'

The palace had been brightened up for the occasion. The walls and the floors, which were all of china, shone by the light of many thousand golden lamps. The most beautiful flowers, all of the tinkling kind, were arranged in the corridors; there was hurrying to and fro, and a great draught, but this was just what made the bells ring; one's ears were full of the tinkling. In the middle of the large reception-room where the emperor sat a golden rod had been fixed, on which the nightingale was to perch. The whole court was assembled, and the little kitchen-maid had been permitted to stand behind the door, as she now had the actual title of cook. They were all dressed in their best; everybody's eyes were turned towards the little grey bird at which the emperor was nodding. The nightingale sang delightfully, and the tears came into the emperor's eyes, nay, they rolled down his cheeks; and then the nightingale sang more beautifully than ever, its notes touched all hearts. The emperor was charmed, and said the nightingale should have his gold slipper to wear round its neck. But the nightingale declined with thanks; it had already been sufficiently rewarded.

'I have seen tears in the eyes of the emperor; that is my richest reward. The tears of an emperor have a wonderful power! God knows I am sufficiently recompensed!' and then it again burst into its sweet heavenly song.

'That is the most delightful coquetting I have ever seen!' said the ladies, and they took some water into their mouths to try and make the same gurgling when any one spoke to them, thinking so to equal the nightingale. Even the lackeys and the chambermaids announced that they were satisfied, and that is saying a great deal; they are always the most difficult people to please. Yes, indeed, the nightingale had made a sensation. It was to stay at court now, and to have its own cage, as well as liberty to walk out twice a day, and once in the night. It always had twelve footmen, with each one holding a ribbon which was tied round its leg. There was not much pleasure in an outing of that sort.

The whole town talked about the marvellous bird, and if two people met, one said to the other 'Night,' and the other answered 'Gale,' and then they sighed, perfectly understanding each other. Eleven cheesemongers' children were called after it, but they had not got a voice among them.

One day a large parcel came for the emperor; outside was written the word 'Nightingale.'

'Here we have another new book about this celebrated bird,' said the emperor. But it was no book; it was a little work of art in a box, an artificial nightingale, exactly like the living one, but it was studded all over with diamonds, rubies and sapphires.

When the bird was wound up it could sing one of the songs the real one sang, and it wagged its tail, which glittered with silver and gold. A ribbon was tied round its neck on which was written, 'The Emperor of Japan's nightingale is very poor compared to the Emperor of China's.'

Everybody said, 'Oh, how beautiful!' And the person who brought the artificial bird immediately received the title of Imperial Nightingale-Carrier in Chief.

'Now, they must sing together; what a duet that will be.'

Then they had to sing together, but they did not get on very well, for the real nightingale sang in its own way, and the artificial one could only sing waltzes.

'There is no fault in that,' said the music-master; 'it is perfectly in time and correct in every way!'

Then the artificial bird had to sing alone. It was just as great a success as the real one, and then it was so much prettier to look at; it glittered like bracelets and breast-pins.

Then it again burst into its sweet heavenly song.

'That is the most delightful coquetting I have ever seen!' said the ladies, and they took some water into their mouths to try and make the same gurgling, thinking so to equal the nightingale.

It sang the same tune three and thirty times over, and yet it was not tired; people would willingly have heard it from the beginning again, but the emperor said that the real one must have a turn now—but where was it? No one had noticed that it had flown out of the open window, back to its own green woods.

'But what is the meaning of this?' said the emperor.

All the courtiers railed at it, and said it was a most ungrateful bird.

'We have got the best bird though,' said they, and then the artificial bird had to sing again, and this was the thirty-fourth time that they heard the same tune, but they did not know it thoroughly even yet, because it was so difficult.

The music-master praised the bird tremendously, and insisted that it was much better than the real nightingale, not only as regarded the outside with all the diamonds, but the inside too.

'Because you see, my ladies and gentlemen, and the emperor before all, in the real nightingale you never know what you will hear, but in the artificial one everything is decided beforehand! So it is, and so it must remain, it can't be otherwise. You can account for things, you can open it and show the human ingenuity in arranging the waltzes, how they go, and how one note follows upon another!'

'Those are exactly my opinions,' they all said, and the music-master got leave to show the bird to the public next Sunday. They were also to hear it sing, said the emperor. So they heard it, and all became as enthusiastic over it as if they had drunk themselves merry on tea, because that is a thoroughly Chinese habit.

Then they all said 'Oh,' and stuck their forefingers in the air and nodded their heads; but the poor fishermen who had heard the real nightingale said, 'It sounds very nice, and it is very like the real one, but there is something wanting, we don't know what.' The real nightingale was banished from the kingdom.

The artificial bird had its place on a silken cushion, close to the emperor's bed: all the presents it had received of gold and precious jewels were scattered round it. Its title had risen to be 'Chief Imperial Singer of the Bed-Chamber,' in rank number one, on the left side; for the emperor reckoned that side the important one, where the heart was seated. And even an emperor's heart is on the left side. The music-master wrote five-and-twenty volumes about the artificial bird; the treatise was very long and written in all the most difficult Chinese characters. Everybody said they had read and understood it, for otherwise they would have been reckoned stupid, and then their bodies would have been trampled upon.

The music-master wrote five-and-twenty volumes about the artificial bird; the treatise was very long and written in all the most difficult Chinese characters.

Things went on in this way for a whole year. The emperor, the court, and all the other Chinamen knew every little gurgle in the song of the artificial bird by heart; but they liked it all the better for this, and they could all join in the song themselves. Even the street boys sang 'zizizi' and 'cluck, cluck, cluck,' and the emperor sang it too.

But one evening when the bird was singing its best, and the emperor was lying in bed listening to it, something gave way inside the bird with a 'whizz.' Then a spring burst, 'whirr' went all the wheels, and the music stopped. The emperor jumped out of bed and sent for his private physicians, but what good could they do? Then they sent for the watchmaker, and after a good deal of talk and examination he got the works to go again somehow; but he said it would have to be saved as much as possible, because it was so worn out, and he could not renew the works so as to be sure of the tune. This was a great blow! They only dared to let the artificial bird sing once a year, and hardly that; but then the music-master made a little speech, using all the most difficult words. He said it was just as good as ever, and his saying it made it so.

Five years now passed, and then a great grief came upon the nation, for they were all very fond of their emperor, and he was ill and could not live, it was said. A new emperor was already chosen, and people stood about in the street, and asked the gentleman-in-waiting how their emperor was going on.

'P,' answered he, shaking his head.

The emperor lay pale and cold in his gorgeous bed, the courtiers thought he was dead, and they all went off to pay their respects to their new emperor. The lackeys ran off to talk matters over, and the chambermaids gave a great coffee-party. Cloth had been laid down in all the rooms and corridors so as to deaden the sound of footsteps, so it was very, very quiet. But the emperor was not dead yet. He lay stiff and pale in the gorgeous bed with its velvet hangings and heavy golden tassels. There was an open window high above him, and the moon streamed in upon the emperor, and the artificial bird beside him.

The poor emperor could hardly breathe, he seemed to have a weight on his chest, he opened his eyes, and then he saw that it was Death sitting upon his chest, wearing his golden crown. In one hand he held the emperor's golden sword, and in the other his imperial banner. Round about, from among the folds of the velvet hangings peered many curious faces: some were hideous, others gentle and pleasant. They were all the emperor's good and bad deeds, which now looked him in the face when Death was weighing him down.

'Do you remember that?' whispered one after the other; 'Do you remember this?' and they told him so many things that the perspiration poured down his face.

'I never knew that,' said the emperor. 'Music, music, sound the great Chinese drums!' he cried, 'that I may not hear what they are saying.' But they went on and on, and Death sat nodding his head, just like a Chinaman, at everything that was said.

'Music, music!' shrieked the emperor. 'You precious little golden bird, sing, sing! I have loaded you with precious stones, and even hung my own golden slipper round your neck; sing, I tell you, sing!'

But the bird stood silent; there was nobody to wind it up, so of course it could not go. Death continued to fix the great empty sockets of his eyes upon him, and all was silent, so terribly silent.

Suddenly, close to the window, there was a burst of lovely song; it was the living nightingale, perched on a branch outside. It had heard of the emperor's need, and had come to bring comfort and hope to him. As it sang the faces round became fainter and fainter, and the blood coursed with fresh vigour in the emperor's veins and through his feeble limbs. Even Death himself listened to the song and said, 'Go on, little nightingale, go on!'

'Yes, if you give me the gorgeous golden sword; yes, if you give me the imperial banner; yes, if you give me the emperor's crown.'

And Death gave back each of these treasures for a song, and the nightingale went on singing. It sang about the quiet churchyard, when the roses bloom, where the elder flower scents the air, and where the fresh grass is ever moistened anew by the tears of the mourner. This song brought to Death a longing for his own garden, and, like a cold grey mist, he passed out of the window.

'Thanks, thanks!' said the emperor; 'you heavenly little bird, I know you! I banished you from my kingdom, and yet you have charmed the evil visions away from my bed by your song, and even Death away from my heart! How can I ever repay you?'

'You have rewarded me,' said the nightingale. 'I brought the tears to your eyes, the very first time I ever sang to you, and I shall never forget it! Those are the jewels which gladden the heart of a singer;—but sleep now, and wake up fresh and strong! I will sing to you!'

Then it sang again, and the emperor fell into a sweet refreshing sleep. The sun shone in at his window, when he woke refreshed and well; none of his attendants had yet come back to him, for they thought he was dead, but the nightingale still sat there singing.

'You must always stay with me!' said the emperor. 'You shall only sing when you like, and I will break the artificial bird into a thousand pieces!'

Even Death himself listened to the song and said, 'Go on, little nightingale, go on!'

'Don't do that!' said the nightingale, 'it did all the good it could! keep it as you have always done! I can't build my nest and live in this palace, but let me come whenever I like, then I will sit on the branch in the evening, and sing to you. I will sing to cheer you and to make you thoughtful too; I will sing to you of the happy ones, and of those that suffer too. I will sing about the good and the evil, which are kept hidden from you. The little singing bird flies far and wide, to the poor fisherman, and the peasant's home, to numbers who are far from you and your court. I love your heart more than your crown, and yet there is an odour of sanctity round the crown too!—I will come, and I will sing to you!—But you must promise me one thing!—

'Everything!' said the emperor, who stood there in his imperial robes which he had just put on, and he held the sword heavy with gold upon his heart.

'One thing I ask you! Tell no one that you have a little bird who tells you everything; it will be better so!'

Then the nightingale flew away. The attendants came in to see after their dead emperor, and there he stood, bidding them 'Good morning!'

Podcast #83 Daily Sampler—Anna and the King of Siam

I have posted three movie versions of the story of Anna and the King of Siam on the Enrichment page for China and Asia. As you know, Siam is the modern-day Thailand. Your little ones will likely enjoy Rogers and Hammerstein's version of *The King and I*. Your older ones may enjoy the most recent version with Jodie Foster. This version is the most scenic, but keep in mind, you aren't seeing Thailand. When officials in Thailand read the script, they wouldn't allow them to film there and actually banned the movie after it was made. They claimed it was historically inaccurate and insulting to the royal family. My personal favorite is the black and white 1946 version with Irene Dunne and Rex Harrison.

Watch all three as a family and have a conversation about the differences. There are a lot of things to talk about! And here is a perfect example of the danger of the single story. There are a lot of layers to this story that I am still peeling back.

What I wanted to talk about today, though, is the real Anna Leonowens. The movies were all based on a fictionalized account of Anna's diaries written by Margaret Landon. But Anna's personal accounts are fascinating and will open up a world that, at least for me, was a place I had never visited in my imagination.

Anna is a perfect subject for this Month's Mother's University topic of A Mother's Influence. I came across this old 1915 book[13] written about Anna by someone who claimed to know her well. Let me share a little bit of what he shared.

He said that she was, "on the whole, the best, bravest and wisest among the many good and wise women he has known."

Her father died when she was young. Of her mother, he wrote:

> The mother, on whom devolved the entire charge of forming her character, was quite uncommonly fitted to undertake that sacred responsibility. She was evidently what her little girl afterwards came in eminent measure to be, a woman of force and stout heart. One incident in this mother's life sufficiently exhibits her quality....

> Mrs. Crawford—Anna's mother—had married a second time, and accompanied her husband, an English officer, to India. He had been appointed there, on one occasion, to survey a new road which was being built by the government in the dangerous neighborhood of the Province of Guzerat, much infested in those days by Bhil robbers; and was travelling with a considerable amount of public money in his charge to pay the workmen with. His wife went with him. She had—just as Anna would have done!—acquired a good working knowledge of the Guzerati language, which made her useful in many ways....

> The party had retired for the night. It so happened that her husband, wearied with his day's work in the sun, was sleeping heavily in an adjoining room, while she lay on a cot

close to the tumbril in which the treasure-box, with the government money in it, was wont to be conveyed from place to place. A small lamp stood in the midst between its two wheels, shedding a faint light. In the dead of the night she was roused by a shuffling noise, as of footsteps. Starting up she saw shadows moving along the screen made for them by the inner wall of the tent, which had two walls of canvas with a space between them; the solid darkness outside drawn close around it. She sat there staring, her heart nearly choking her. In a minute the shadows turned to squat shapes of dusky flesh entering one by one through the tent-door and only too plain in the glimmer of the lamp—six Bhils armed with bows and, as she well knew, poisoned arrows;... She was horribly afraid, but her head had never worked so clearly in her life. They had, of course, come to get the money, and they must not have it. She durst not cry for help. Her husband's appearance meant his instant death. She was the better watch-dog of the pair, because, as it flashed upon her, there was one thing the Bhils held inviolably sacred and would not profane unless in the very last extremity, and that was a woman's person. The blessed and noble superstition of these cut-throats was her one weapon. She had the heart to make full use of it, and defy them. To the assurance of the leader that they did not wish to hurt her but only to remove the contents of the cart, as they were much more in need of these than she was, she replied at once by throwing herself down in her long white night-dress, like a bar of white flame, in front of the treasure, exclaiming in Guzerati as good as their own: "You must trample on a woman's body to rob what has been entrusted to the care of her husband." She had shot her bolt. It nearly killed her. She lay there, more dead than alive, for half an hour, which seemed a year, not daring, even after all her senses had come back, to open her eyes. When at last she did open them, the robbers had gone, leaving the box untouched.

Like mother, like daughter! Many years after, that little daughter, then a young widow, was to have an astonishingly similar adventure. As she lay half-asleep in her room at Singapore, where she was living at that time, a well-oiled naked thug came sliding like a snake along the uncarpeted surface towards her bed. At first, she was frozen with terror. Then she remembered that in the small jewel-box under her bed there were some letters that she prized highly, her dead husband's. In an instant, hot rage took the place of fear. A thousand devils could not snatch those letters from her! She jumped up in the darkness, seized an extinguished glass lamp which stood on a table by her couch, smashed it to pieces upon the bare wooden floor, and in a voice with a tone one has heard from her, much more trying to the thief's nerves than the sudden clatter and ring of broken glass, cried out: "I will be the death of you!" He rolled out—much more speedily than he had glided in. Anna had come out true to type.

Her mother being of the mettle indicated, was likely to show the capacity, as valuable as it is scarce in these soft days of ours, of cultivating in her daughter some power of will and sense of what is meant by really doing a thing.

That phrase—these soft days of ours—really struck me. We fall apart if our 10-year-olds haven't memorized their multiplication tables and throw our hands up in the air and think we are failures! What will we do in the face of real danger?

It was this bravery of heart, when Anna was suddenly widowed at age 25 with two little children to care for and very little money, that led her to accept a teaching position in the court of the King of Siam where she became a true Mother of Influence to his army of wives and concubines and dozens of royal children. Following the death of the king, his son took his place. In this account I am sharing with you, is written this:

> Under the mild reign of his successor, the gentle intelligent prince, her own apt scholar, good days were in store for them. The spirit implanted in this receptive heart by his "English governess" bore fruit in all sorts of blessed changes for Siam. Her six years' labour had not been, like David's dear-bought draught from the well of Bethlehem, as water spilt upon the ground. She had, without knowing it, made a great and enduring contribution to the regeneration of that sick land, by permanently impressing something of her own character and ideals upon the nobly plastic mind of the creator of modern Siam. He never forgot her, or ceased to show with what reverence and gratitude he cherished her memory. A great part of Mrs. Leonowens still lives in the country where she "went forth in tears bearing precious seed," and loved and suffered much.

She wrote a book about her experiences called, *The English Governess at the Siamese Court; Recollections of Six Years in the Royal Palace at Bangkok.* There's a copy you can read in Internet Archive.

Here's a sampling from her preface, which, again, highlights her bravery.

> About a week before our departure for Bangkok, the captain and mate of the steamer Rainbow called upon me. One of these gentlemen had for several years served the government of Siam, and they came to warn me of the trials and dangers that must inevitably attend the enterprise in which I was embarking. Though it was now too late to deter me from the undertaking by any arguments addressing my fears, I can nevertheless never forget the generous impulse of the honest seamen, who said: "Madam, be advised even by strangers, who have proved what sufferings await you, and shake your hands of this mad undertaking."
>
> By the next steamer I sailed for the Court of Siam.

Anna Leonowens is a great soul worth spending time with. There's so much more I want to tell you about her, but I'll leave that to you to find for yourself.

But I just want to touch on one more thing. We live in an age of intolerance, and saddest of all to me is the intolerance I see going on in the Christian world among Christians themselves. How different our world would be if we could look at that which unites us rather than divides us.

Anna was a Christian, but when she was invited to teach, the king specifically told her she was not to try and convert his people to Christianity, reminding her, "as the followers of Buddha are mostly aware of the powerfulness of truth and virtue as well as the followers of Christ, and are desirous to have facility of English language and literature more than new religions."

Anna later wrote, "I was thankful to find, even in this citadel of Buddhism, men and above all women, who were 'lovely in their lives,' who, amid infinite difficulties, in the bosom of a most corrupt society, and enslaved to a capricious and often cruel will, yet devoted themselves to an earnest search after truth. On the other hand, I have to confess with sorrow and shame, how far we, with all our boasted enlightenment, fall short, in true nobility and piety, of some of our 'benighted' sisters of the East. With many of them, Love, Truth and Wisdom are not mere synonyms but 'living gods,' for whom they long with lively ardor, and, when found, embrace with joy."

And so in that spirit of sharing that which unites us, I want to share with you the Legend of the Maha Naghkon, found in the final chapter of Anna's book.[14] This was a story presented to her by the Supreme King of Siam.

> Many hundreds of thousands of years ago, when P'hra Atheitt, the Sun-god, was nearer to earth than he is now, and the city of the gods could be seen with mortal eyes,—when the celestial sovereigns, P'hra Indara and P'hra Insawara, came down from Meru, the sacred mountain, to hold high converse with mortal kings, sages, and heroes,—when the moon and the stars brought tidings of good-will to men, and wisdom flourished, love and happiness were spread abroad, and sorrow, suffering, disease, old age, and death were almost banished,—there lived in Thaisiampois a mighty monarch whose years could hardly be numbered, so many were they and so long. And yet he was not old; such were the warmth and strength and vigor imparted by the near glories of the P'hra Atheitt, that the span of human life was lengthened unto a thousand, and even fifteen hundred years. The days of the King Sudarsana had been prolonged beyond those of the oldest of his predecessors, for the sake of his exceeding wisdom and goodness. But yet this King was troubled; he had no son, and the thought of dying without leaving behind him one worthy to represent his name and race was grievous to him. So, by the advice of the wise men of his kingdom, he caused prayers and offerings to be made in all the temples, and took to wife the beautiful Princess Thawadee.

> At that very time P'hra Indara, ruler of the highest heaven, dreamed a dream; and behold! in his sleep a costly jewel fell from his mouth to the lower earth; whereat P'hra Indara was troubled. Assembling all the hosts of heaven, the angels, and the genii, he showed them his dream, but they could not interpret it. Last of all, he told it to his seven sons; but from them likewise its meaning was hidden. A second time P'hra Indara dreamed, and yet a third time, that a more and more costly jewel had fallen from his lips; and at last, when he awoke, the interpretation was revealed to his own thought,— that one of his sons should condescend to the form of humanity, and dwell on the earth, and be a great teacher of men.

> Then the King of Heaven imparted to the celestial princes the meaning of the threefold vision, and demanded which of them would consent to become man.

> The divine princes heard, and answered not a word; till the youngest and best-beloved

of Heaven opened his lips and spake, saying: "Hear, O my Lord and Father! I have yearned toward the race thou hast created out of the fire and flame of thy breast and the smoke of thy nostrils. Let me go unto them, that I may teach them the wisdom of truth."

Then P'hra Indara gave him leave to depart on his mission of love; and all the hosts of heaven, knowing that he should never more gladden their hearts with his presence, accompanied him, sorrowful, to the foot of Mount Meru; and immediately a blazing star shot from the mount, and burst over the palace of Thaisiampois.

That night the gracious Princess Thawadee conceived and became with child, and the P'hra Somannass was no longer a prince of the highest heaven.

The Princess Thawadee had been the only and darling daughter of a mighty king, and still mourned her separation from her beloved sire. Her only solace was to sit in the phrasat of the Grand Palace, and look with longing toward her early home. Here, day after day, she sat with her maidens, weaving flowers, and singing low the songs of her childhood. When this became known abroad among the multitude, they gathered from every side to behold one so famed for her goodness and beauty.

Thus by degrees her interest was aroused. She became thoughtful for her people, and presently found happiness in dispensing food, raiment, and comfort to the poor who flocked to see her.

One day, as she was reposing in the porch after her customary benefactions, a cloud of birds, flying eastward, fell dead as they passed over the phrasat. The sages and soothsayers of the court were terrified. What might the omen be? Long and anxious were their counsels, and grievous their perturbations one with another; until at last an aged warrior, who had conquered many armies and subjugated kingdoms, declaring that as faithful servants they should lay the weighty matter before their lord, bade all the court follow him, and approached his sovereign, saying:—

"Long live P'hra Chow P'hra Sudarsana, lord and king of our happy land, wherefrom sorrow and suffering and death are wellnigh banished! Let him investigate with a true spirit and a clear mind the matter we bring for judgment, even though it be to the tearing out of his own heart and casting it away from him."

"Speak," said the King, "and fear not! Has it ever been thought that evil is dearer unto me than good? Even to the tearing out of my heart and casting it to dogs shall justice be rendered in the land."

Then the sages, soothsayers, and warriors spake as with one voice: "It is well known unto the lord our King, that the Queen, our lovely lady Thawadee, is with child.

"But what manner of birth, is this that she has conceived, in that it has already brought grief and death into the land? For as the Queen sat in the porch of the temple, a great flight of birds that hastened, thirsty, toward the valleys of the east, when they would have passed over the phrasat were struck dead, as by an unseen spirit of mischief. Let the King search this matter, and put away the strange thing of evil out of our land, lest it make a greater sorrow."

When the King heard these words, he was sore smitten, and hung down his head, and knew not what to say; for the Queen, so gentle and beautiful, was very dear to him. But, remembering his royal word, he shook off his grief and took counsel with his astrologers, who had foretold that the unborn prince would prove either a glorious blessing or a dire curse to the land. And now, by the awful omen of the birds, they declared that the Queen had conceived the evil spirit Kala Mata, and that she must be put to death, she and the fiend with her.

Then the King in council commanded that the sweet young Thawadee should be set upon a floating raft, and given to the mercy of winds and waves.

But the brave chief who should have executed the sentence, overcome on beholding her beauty and innocence, interceded for her with the council; and it was finally decreed that, for pity's sake, and because the Queen was unconscious of any evil, she should not be slain, but "put away," after the dreadful birth. To this the stricken monarch thankfully agreed.

In due time the Queen was delivered of a male child, so beautiful that it filled all beholders with delight. His eyes were as sunshine, his forehead like the glow of the full moon, his lips like clustered roses, and his cry like the melody of many instruments; and the Queen loved him, and comforted herself with his beauty.

When the mother was strong again, the infant prince being then about a month old, the sentence of the council was carried into effect, and the poor princess and her child were banished forever from the beloved land of Thaisiampois.

Clasping her baby to her breast, she went forth, terrified and stunned. On and on, not knowing whither, she wandered, pressing her sleeping babe to her bosom, and moaning to the great gods above.

Then P'hra Indara, king of highest heaven, came down to earth, assumed the form and garb of a Bhramin, and followed her silently, shortening the miles and smoothing the rough places, until she reached the bank of a deep and rapid stream. Here, as she sat down, faint and foot-sore, to nurse her babe, there came to her a grave and venerable pilgrim, who gently questioned her sorrows and comforted her with thrilling words, saying her child was born to bring peace and happiness to earth, and not trouble and death.

Quickly Thawadee dried her tears, and consented to be led by the good old man, who had come to her as if from heaven. From under his garment he produced a shell filled with food from paradise, of which she partook with ecstasy; and gave her to drink water from everlasting springs, that overflowed her soul with perfect peace. Then he led her to a mountain, and prepared in the cleft of a rock a hiding-place for her and her child, and left her with a promise of quick return.

For fifty years she dwelt in the cave, knowing neither trouble nor weariness nor hunger, nor any of the ills of life. The young Somannass, as the good Bhramin had named him, grew to be a youth of wondrous beauty. The melody of his voice tamed the wild creatures of the forest, and charmed even the seven-headed dragons of the lake in which his mother bathed him every morning. Then again P'hra Indara appeared to them in the form and garb of the aged Bhramin; and he rejoiced in the strength and beauty of the young Somannass, and his heart yearned after his beloved son. But, hiding his emotion, he held pleasant converse with the Queen, and begged to be permitted to take the boy away with him for a season. She consented; and instantly, as in a flash of lightning, he transported the prince into the highest heaven, and Somannass found himself seated on a glorious throne by the side of P'hra Indara the Divine, before whom the hosts of heaven bowed in homage.

Here he was initiated in all the mysteries of life and death, with all wisdom and foresight. His celestial royal father showed him the stars coursing hither and thither on their errands of love and mercy; showed him comets with tails of fire flashing and whizzing through the centuries, spreading confusion and havoc in their path; showed him the spirits of rebellion and crime transfixed by the spears of the Omnipotent. He heard the music of the spheres, he tasted heavenly food, and drank of the river that flows from the footstool of the Most Highest.

And so he forgot the forlorn Queen, his mother, and desired to return to earth no more.

Then P'hra Indara laid his hand upon the brow of the lad, and showed him the generations yet to come, rejoicing in his prayers and precepts; and Somannass, beholding, stretched his arms to the earth again. And P'hra Indara promised to build him a palace hardly less grand and fair than the heavenly abode, a temple which should be the wonder of the world, a stupendous and everlasting monument of his love to men.

So Somannass returned to the Queen, his mother; and P'hra Indara sent down myriads of angels, with Phya Kralewana, chief of angels, to build a dwelling fit for the heavenly prince. In one night it was done, and the rising sun shone on domes like worlds and walls like armies. And because the seven-headed serpent, Phya Naghk, had shown the way to the mines of gold and silver and iron, and the quarries of marble and granite, the grateful builders laid the sign of the serpent on the foundations, terraces, and bridges; but on the walls they left the effigy of the Queen Thawadee, the beautiful and bountiful lady.

Then swift-winged angels flew to heaven, and, returning, brought fruits and flowers the most curious and exquisite; and immediately there bloomed a garden there, of such ravishing loveliness and perfume that the gods themselves delighted to visit it. Also they filled the great stables with white elephants and chargers. And then the angels transported Thawadee and Somannass to their new abode, the fame of which was so spread abroad that the great King Sudarsana, with all his court, and followers without number, and all his army, came to see it. And great was their astonishment to find again the fair and gentle Thawadee, who thus was reunited to her husband; and he took up his abode with her, and they lived together in love.

But the Prince Somannass built temples, and preached, and taught the people, and healed their infirmities, and led them in the paths of virtue and truth.

And the fame of his wisdom and goodness flew through all the lands, so that many kings became willing vassals unto him; but there came from a far-off country, where the heavens drop no rain, but where one great river suddenly floods the plains and then shrinks back into itself like a living thing, a king of lofty stature and exceeding craft. And the Prince Somannass was gracious toward him, and showed him many favors. But his heart was black and bad, and he would have turned the pure heart of the prince to worship the dragon and other beasts; wherefore Somannass changed him into a leper, and cast him out of his palace, and caused a stone statue to be made of him, which stands to this day, a warning to all tempters and evil-doers. And he caused the face of the great P'hra Indara to be carved on the north and on the south and on the east and on the west—so that all men might know the true God, who is God alone in heaven, Sevarg-Savan!

Podcast #84 Daily Sampler—Rudyard Kipling

And now let's take a look at India by paying a little visit to Rudyard Kipling. Don't you just love that name—Rudyard? Evidently he was named after the beautiful lake where his father fell in love with his mother—Lake Rudyard.

Let me start by giving you your daily sampler from a book called, *Famous Authors for Young People* by Ramon Coffman[15] found in the Elementary section of World Biographies. You'll find some interesting connecting stories in his life that will begin to interest even your youngest children in him. He is the author of the Just So Stories—so named because when he told the stories to his little children, they demanded that the words and sentences he used were identical to the way he had told the story before. They had to be told, "Just So." You will also recognize him as the author of *The Jungle Book* and maybe you are familiar with *Captain Courageous*, the story of a spoiled brat who falls overboard from a steamship and gets picked up by a fishing boat, where he's made to earn his keep by joining the crew in their work. There's a great old classic movie starring Spencer Tracy based on the book. And if you want to help give your older children a look at the people, culture and varied religions of India, you might interest them in reading the book *Kim*, which can be enjoyed by young adults. It is listed as one of the best-loved novels among the British. It's the adventures of an Irish orphan in India who becomes the disciple of a Tibetan monk while learning espionage from the British secret service.

But let me not get too far off track. Here's the sampler:

A small boy of English parentage took a walk alone one day in India. He was hardly four years of age, but he knew the way to the school in Bombay where his father taught art. Suddenly a large hen came from the edge of a small valley, and sprang at him. Running as fast as he could, he escaped; and when he reached the school he told his father of the event, sobbing as he spoke.

Many a child has kept an early fear through life, but John Kipling, the father of this child, did a wise thing. He wrote a little verse:

There was a small boy in Bombay
Who once from a hen ran away.
When they said, "You're a baby,"
He replied, "Well I may be:
But I don't like these hens of Bombay."

Before long little Rudyard Kipling was laughing about what had happened. Late in his life he said: "I have thought well of hens ever since."

India was Rudyard's birthplace and he lived there during his first five years. In that period he had native nurses who told him stories about jungle animals, and these stories he did not forget.

Another important thing about his early years is the fact that he learned to speak Hindustani. This is the most widely-used language in India. When he returned to the country years later, he was able to pick it up again.

There was to be a long period in his life in which he saw no more of India. He was to spend most of his childhood in England.

In company with his father and mother, Rudyard traveled toward England aboard a paddle-wheel steamboat. That was in the year 1871. The Suez canal was not in use at the time; so the Kipling family boarded a train to cross a desert at the edge of Egypt, to reach another seaport. Then another vessel took them the rest of the way. In England an old sea captain and his wife were given care of the boy, and he lived at Southsea for the next six years. His parents returned to India, where the father went on with his teaching.

For a time Rudyard was treated fairly well. The sea captain was kind to him and took him on long walks. One day he was shown a sailing vessel which had come back from a trip to the Arctic. The captain's wife was of a different nature; she was ill-tempered, and mistreated the lad from India.

While at Southsea, England, Rudyard Kipling was sent to "day school," and learned reading, writing and arithmetic. From time to time, letters came to him from his parents in India, and they also sent him interesting books.

Before long, unhappily, the sea captain died, and Rudyard's life outside school became miserable. The captain's wife showed her ill-temper more than before, and cuffed the lad around with little or no excuse.

If Rudyard had written to his parents about his bad treatment, he no doubt would have been placed in another household. As it was, he seems to have felt that this was the kind of life he was supposed to have.

He did not even complain to his aunt when he visited her during school vacations. He enjoyed himself to the limit during a month at her home each year, then went back to the Southsea house. Meanwhile, he had learned to love books, and many a spare hour he spent in reading.

At last his mother came from far India to visit him. He was at this time eleven years old. Mrs. Kipling found out about the bad treatment, and quickly took him away from the Southsea house. For months he enjoyed her company, and felt that "heaven on earth" had come to him.

Having to return to her husband in India, Mrs. Kipling was very careful to leave her son in a better household. Three kind-hearted women, who lived together, took care of the boy after she left. Soon Rudyard was a student at a new school. He was the only boy there who wore glasses. Although he was teased somewhat, he found good friends at this school. His poor eyesight kept him from taking much part in sports, but he wrote poems and essays which brought him some praise from his schoolmates.

The fun, the torments, and the school-boy pranks must have been remembered clearly years later when Kipling wrote "Stalky and Co." This is a story about English school life. Many boys read the book today and discover the wide difference between their own school days and young Rudyard Kipling's.

At sixteen young Kipling went back to India. There he worked on a small newspaper. When only twenty-one, he became assistant editor of the Allahabad Pioneer and soon afterward published several of his famous stories, including "Plain Tales from the Hills," "The Phantom Rickshaw" and "Wee Willie Winkie."

He also wrote poetry, some of it about India. A favorite poem with many people is "Gunga Din." It is a heroic story of a brave Indian water-boy who was shot while carrying water to wounded British soldiers in the thick of battle in India.

By the year 1892 Rudyard Kipling was a successful young author. He had written books which were widely read, and had a large sum of money in a bank. He had been married in London, England, to an American woman and was on his way around the world. The couple had crossed the Atlantic, and had enjoyed pleasant days in various parts of Canada, including Vancouver.

Leaving Vancouver, they had steamed over the Pacific to Japan. Life seemed most pleasant to them, until Kipling went to a bank in Yokohama, a branch of the British bank where he had placed his savings. He had visited the branch bank before, and had drawn money, but this time there was a sign on the door. It gave notice of the failure of the bank in England.

Now came the question of what to do.

"Why not make our home in the United States for a while?" suggested Mrs. Kipling. "I know a place where we could live cheaply."

Tickets clear around the world had been purchased, but a refund was obtained. There was enough money to buy passage to the United States, with several hundred dollars left over.

So it happened that Rudyard Kipling settled with his wife in a Vermont village, where two of his wife's grandparents had lived years before. They rented a house for ten dollars and called it Bliss Cottage. In that dwelling their first child, a daughter, was born.

Kipling was now twenty-seven years of age. Settling down to work, he soon began writing stories which grew into his famous "Jungle Books." The two "Jungle Books" contain stories of wild animals in India, where Kipling had spent about half of his life up to that time. In these books the animals talk together as if they were human beings.

After a short stay in America, Kipling returned, with his family, to England, where he lived until his death in 1936. He was known throughout the world as a poet and teller of tales.

There's another simple biography of Kipling you might enjoy sharing with your children, found in the online library, called *Kipling Storyteller of East and West* by Gloria Kamen.[16] It reads like a story. In this book, it tells how *Puck of Pook's Hill* came to be written, which you'll find in the online library under England Elementary Historical Fiction. When Kipling made England his home, the book says: "His thoughts turned to England's past, to the story his children had just begun to learn. Taking a pale blue paper and his pen he began to write a story about the early history of Britain with Puck, a fairy-like being, as the guide to the past.

"Puck of Pook's Hill made history come alive. The hill in his story was just beyond the garden and history was in its very soil." It's English history as a fairy tale. You may want to visit it when you get to Month 3. And yes, it was Rudyard Kipling who said, "If history was told in the form of stories, it would never be forgotten."

The Kiplings had three children. Josephine died in New York at the age of 7. Rudyard was himself hospitalized for whooping cough at the time and was not told of Josephine's death until he was recovered because his wife knew how deeply he would feel the loss. It was Josephine who repeated her father's bedtime stories to her doll, word for word. And it was for Josephine that he made up his first Just So Stories. After Kipling returned to England, he wrote, "I don't think it likely that I will ever come back to America. My little girl loved it dearly and it was in New York that we lost her."

He lost his son, Jack, in World War I. "He was made an officer in the Irish Guards and on his eighteenth birthday was shipped to France. Less than a week later, he was 'missing in action.' No trace of him was ever found. It is believed that he stepped on a land mind and was killed instantly." Rudyard worked through his grief in this sad poem, My Boy Jack:

> "Have you news of my boy Jack?"
> Not this tide.
> "When d'you think that he'll come back?"
> Not with this wind blowing, and this tide.
>
> "Has anyone else had word of him?"
> Not this tide.
> For what is sunk will hardly swim,
> Not with this wind blowing, and this tide.
>
> "Oh, dear, what comfort can I find?"
> None this tide,
> Nor any tide...

One of my favorite hymns is sung to *Rudyard's Recessional* written for Queen Victoria's Diamond Jubilee. It is hymn #80 in my hymnbook: God of Our Fathers, Known of Old

Verse 2 reads:

> The tumult and the shouting dies;
> The captains and the kings depart.
> Still stands thine ancient sacrifice,
> An humble and a contrite heart.

Lord God of Hosts, be with us yet,
Lest we forget, lest we forget.

You are also likely familiar with his famous poem, *If*, in which the last stanza reads:

If you can talk with crowds and keep your virtue,
Or walk with Kings, nor lose the common touch,
If neither foes nor loving friends can hurt you,
If all men count with you, but none too much;
If you can fill the unforgiving minute
With sixty seconds' worth of distance run,
Yours is the Earth and everything that's in it,
And, which is more, you'll be a Man, my son!

Kipling died in 1836 at the age of 71. His death was prematurely announced in a magazine, to which he wrote: "I've just read that I am dead. Don't forget to delete me from your list of subscribers."

Rudyard Kipling. Another great soul worth knowing.

Podcast #85 Daily Sampler—I Belong to Jesus Christ

If you have hung around me very much, you know that I don't separate spiritual from temporal learning. Inspiration is a vital part of the Pattern for Learning, or as is said in Charlotte Mason's writings, "True education is between a child's soul and God." While I respect people of all faiths, I, myself, am a Christian and believe that Jesus Christ is the source of all Truth and Light.

In our secularized world, I frequently field questions from moms who are worried about how to nurture faith in their children. And that is what I would like to address in this podcast. To open up the conversation, I'd like to turn to a hero of mine; a great soul who never fails to inspire my heart to do hard things and to trust in God. Her name is Gladys Aylward. She was a little woman—didn't even reach 5 feet tall. Growing up, she found church to be quite boring and didn't have much use for religion. In fact, she aspired to be an actress. Then one day, she tasted that love and connection to Jesus Christ that can't be explained in words. Around the same time, she learned that the people of China did not know Him and she couldn't bear the thought that there was a people who had never tasted of His love.

Her missionary society deemed she was too stupid to learn the language and would not offer their support in a Chinese mission. So, after saving every penny for a one-way train ticket to a remote village in China, she set off with nothing but $10 in her pocket and a firm faith and trust in God to supply the rest. And oh—what miracles they accomplished together!

I have listed a few books in the library about her. A personal favorite is the one she wrote with Christine Hunter called *Gladys Aylward: The Little Woman*.[17] You will never forget her.

I don't want to take away from what you'll read, but let me highlight a couple of experiences. At the time the Japanese invaded China, the people in her village were experiencing terrible hardships and sufferings. Let me let her tell you what happened:

> Two days after the Japanese retreated for the second time, a crowd of Chinese women trooped into my battered courtyard. They were bewildered, weary of war and unhappy, and I seized the opportunity of telling them that the great God I served care for them and could give them peace of heart even in these awful circumstances.
>
> I stood in the middle of the courtyard and held up a large Bible picture. I looked around on them all, my heart full of pity for them because they did not know God's love.

Unknown to her at the time was a hardened general who stood at the back of the crowd and listened. Over the next days, he came to taste of that love and went back to his troops, and said, "Up to this time we have been a bandit troop. I have led you into affrays largely for the sake of killing and looting, and we have always been successful. Now we will cease to be bandits and become honorable soldiers because last night I took Jesus Christ as my God. I find that this book [waving Glady's Bible] is against dishonesty and wickedness. Now will every man who is willing to join me come out and promise that we will cease to kill or loot for gain, but will serve this true God."

But he waited in vain for the men to come and promise their allegiance. Instead, he was arrested by his own men. They took away his clothes, tied him on a mule, and went off during the night.

For many months they continued as bandits, burning, looting and rioting. They dragged their general with them everywhere, afraid that he would expose them to the government if they let him go. In every possible way they tried to break his faith. He was tortured, starved, kicked and beaten, but still he held out. Fixed in his mind was the knowledge that because he belongs to Jesus Christ, he could no longer be a bandit.

After nine months of this terrible testing, a man came to where he was tied up one night and said, "We did far better when you were our leader. We want you back. Will you lead us again?"

"No, because I must still stand for Jesus Christ."

"Then if you are really sure, I will help you to get away."

After fifteen months of wandering, he made his way back to Gladys' village, where he entered her courtyard, instead of a bullying, cursing general, he came as a poor, battered, penniless beggar. She didn't even recognize him. "What is your name?" she asked gently.

"No name. I belong to Jesus."

He never really grew strong again and a year after his return, he died. The Christians in the village mourned him with great sorrow for he had become their Big Brother. The children of the village adored him and hung around him. He was truly loved.

Now let me touch upon one other experience.

Gladys' work took her to a city where hundreds of university students were converted. But then the Communist party took complete control of the university and demanded allegiance to the Communist party, which required an abandonment of their faith. Three hundred of five hundred students gave in. The Communist leaders then called the 300 and told them there was work for them to do. They could use what methods they liked—except that of actually taking life—to force those 200 into line.

For the next month, the most horrible forms of teasing, petty cruelty and unpleasant irritations went on. But at the end of that time, there were actually more converts, not less.

How had this happened? They began to make urgent inquiries and they learned that every morning the Christian students had held prayer meetings every morning before class at 7 A.M. to gain strength for the day of testing they knew lay before them.

When that study was broken up, the students gathered at 6 A.M. When their opponents discovered them, they rose earlier and met at 5 A.M. So it went on, until by the end of the month some of the Christians were getting hardly any sleep.

The authorities took immediate action. "We'll stop all this congregating together. We'll put an end to all this prayer and Bible reading," they announced.

Each Christian was isolated and put under the guard of ten red-hot Communists for three months. Their every movement was watched, and night and day they were talked at, jeered at, indoctrinated.

At the end of three months, they were all forced to appear in the market square. Under a huge squad of Communist police, 200 students marched into the square. A man stood with a long list of names. He called out the first.

A girl of seventeen stepped forward. She was refined and beautiful, and had been brought up in one of those lovely courtyards that belonged to the wealthy of Peking before the war.

"What position are you standing in now?" bellowed the man.

She walked to a little platform. She faltered a little, but then her voice rang out, suddenly clear and strong. "Sir, when I went for my three months' indoctrination I thought Jesus Christ was real. I thought the Bible was true. Now I know Jesus Christ is real, I know this book is true!"

One after the other of those two hundred names were called out, and not one faltered.

Every one of them was beheaded that very day in the marketplace. Before each execution the victim was given one last chance to recant; but even those at the end, who had been forced to watch the terrible butchery of all the others did not flinch.

Wow.

Is this the faith you want your children to have?

I believe faith is faltering in our young people because we are not following the Pattern for learning. We think to reach them by hammering them with doctrine and commandments to follow. But the first commandment is not to obey. The first commandment is to love.

The faith of all these examples was strong because they first knew and loved this Jesus Christ whom they chose to follow. They felt like they belonged to Him. Following His commandments become easy once you feel like you belong to Him. They become the expression of our love.

But they are not the way to love. Remember—the Pharisees strove for exactness in the keeping of all the laws and statutes of their religion. But their hearts were hard.

When doctrine and commandments become the foundation, the too-prone-to-err reasoning faculties begin to pick them apart in analysis. But when love is the foundation—when the heart is connected to Jesus Christ—all else follows in power and strength.

I have recommended it before, but I will recommend it again. There is an out of print book called *Christ and the Fine Arts* by Cynthia Maus.[18] There are usually used copies online. In her introduction is written:

> It is the conviction of the compiler of this anthology that if the youth of today, or for that matter of any day, are to get a clear vision and grasp of the contribution which Jesus Christ has made and is making through the centuries to the development and enrichment of human life, that vision and grasp will be better attained by looking at Christ through the eyes of the artist…than in any other way.

There is in every heart a love of the beautiful. We are made so that we respond to the ideal and the infinite even though we cannot and do not fully comprehend either. Through the ages men's intellects have been unable to agree about what and who Christ is; but human hearts in every generation have united in love for this matchless personality…

This anthology, therefore, is dedicated to youth and lovers of youth, who, through the fine arts, wish to see, to feel, and to discover with the eyes of the Spirit, the Christ of the centuries, the Friend, the Comrade, the Consoler of men through the ages.

More poems have been written, more stories told, more pictures painted, and more songs sung about Christ than any other person in human history, because through such avenues as these the deepest appreciation of the human heart can be more adequately expressed.

The purpose of the fine arts is to help us to see, to feel, and to appreciate the world in which we live…. In the landscape, the sea, the sky, the human soul and many another source, the fine arts discover and picture for those of us who would otherwise be inarticulate, the love, the light, the beauty of…Jesus Christ.

Art does not deal with things as they are in themselves. Science does that. Art, particularly religious art, deals exclusively with things as they affect the human soul.

And that's where we want to focus our attention.

So what is my recommendation for building faith in our children? It is to do exactly what we are learning here at the Well-Educated Heart—to become proficient in the languages of the heart and soul—Music, Art, Poetry and Story, so that we may connect to our Lord in the deepest places of our hearts. Inspired men and women have revealed Him in hymns; in masterful musical compositions, in fine art, in poetry, in beautiful literature. I would not only spend time with these creations, but with the great souls themselves who created them.

Furthermore, I would fill my children's hearts with stories of humanitarians and missionaries— like Gladys Aylward—who have changed lives for the better through Christ's love, in spite of personal suffering and sacrifice. I have provided you with an ample supply of such stories in the library.

And nowhere can we feel closer to our Creator than among His creations. This simple act of nature journaling we have been talking about gives us eyes to see the miracles and beauties all around us and fill our hearts with gratitude.

Yes—read from the scriptures. But let the music of those inspired words flow through the heart of someone who loves Him; not as a duty and a daily responsibility. Let hymns not be confined to Sunday worship service, but made a part of our everyday life. Never allow the beat of religious observance to drown out the melody of love.

I first heard the stories of Jesus as a toddler. And I loved Him instantly. I think little children have come so soon from His presence, they have not forgotten Him. As a 3-year-old, the story of this gentle carpenter on the cross bound my heart to His in a way that has never left me. Heaven, with its beautiful flowers, has lived in my imagination my whole life as a real place— my real Home. The lessons of church have often—as they did Gladys—irritated me because they are devoid of that love and beauty. Yet, I am still grateful for the fellowship that Church offers me.

The secret of my faith is that I belong to Jesus Christ.

So let me close with something I ran across last night. I was looking for some family games to play at our family reunion next week and the thought popped into my head to check out an old Family Recreation text I haven't looked at since my college years over 40 years ago. I didn't actually find a game idea, but I came across this little piece that apparently appeared in the Deseret News many years ago and fits in perfectly with this message that has been acting on my heart the last few days.

It's called *A Parable* by Jean Betzner.

> I took a little child's hand in mine. He and I were to walk together for awhile. I was to lead him to the Father. It was a task that overcame me, so awful was the responsibility. And so I talked to the child of the Father. I painted the sternness of his face, were the child to do something that would incur the Father's wrath. He walked under the tall trees and I said that the Father had power to send them crashing to the ground, struck by his thunderbolts. We walked in the sunshine, I told him of the greatness of the Father who made the burning blazing sun. And one twilight we met the Father. The child hid behind me; he was afraid. He would not take the Father's hand. I was between the child and the Father, and I wondered. I had been so conscientious, so serious.

> I took a little child's hand in mine. I was to lead him to the Father. I felt burdened with the many things I had to teach him. We did not ramble; we hastened from one spot to another spot. We compared the leaves of the different trees. While the child was questioning me about it, I hurried him away to chase a butterfly. Did he chance to fall asleep, I awakened him; lest he should miss something I wanted him to see. I poured into his ears all the stories he ought to know, but we were interrupted often by the wind blowing, of which we must study; by the gurgling brook, which we must trace to its source. And then, in the twilight, we met the Father. The child merely glanced at Him and then his gaze wandered in a dozen directions. The Father stretched out His hand. The child was not interested enough to take it. Feverish spots burned in his cheeks. He dropped exhausted to the ground and fell asleep. Again I was between the child and the Father. I wondered. I had taught him so many things.

> I took a little child's hand in mine, to lead him to the Father. My heart was full of gratitude for the glad privilege. We walked slowly, I united my steps with the short steps of the child. We spoke of the things the child noticed. Sometimes we picked the Father's flowers and stroked their soft petals and loved their bright colors. Sometimes it was one of the Father's birds. We saw the eggs that were laid. We wondered, elated at the care it gave its young. Often we told stories of the Father. I told them to the child

and the child told them again to me. We told them, the child and I, over and over again. Sometimes we stopped to rest, leaning against one of the Father's trees and letting his cool air soothe our brow, and never speaking. And then in the twilight, we met the Father. The child's eyes shone. He looked lovingly, trustingly, eagerly, up into the Father's face. He put his hand into the Father's hand. I was for the moment forgotten.

I was content.

Podcast #179 The Epic of India

Someone in our group this week posted a visual of the distribution of the world's population that was rather eye opening to me. I've included a picture on the podcast page. The two largest circles, by far, were China and India and the thought struck me, as the world shrinks, we have to be mindful of our neighbor's stories if we want to get along with and understand each other.

I don't remember studying anything about China and especially about India when I went through school. It has only been in recent years that China's story has even opened up to the Western world. I wasn't able to provide very many books on China or India's history in the Libraries of Hope site because I mostly offer pre-1923 public domain books and children's authors were not writing about these countries. So we need to piece together the story as best we can.

One author I have particularly come to love is Elizabeth Seeger who wrote a Newbery Award winning history of the Chinese people called *Pageant of Chinese History*. It was written in 1934 and covers China's history from mythological beginnings to the forming of their Republic in 1912. Unfortunately, copies of the book are hard to come by. I just did a quick search on Amazon and found five copies starting at $495! Thankfully, there are a handful of copies on AbeBooks for a lot less money. And last time I looked, there is no copy on Internet Archive. I own a copy and it is fascinating. I believe the copyright was not renewed—I'm still working on that—and would love to make it available to you if I can.

But she has other books as well and one is about India and that one is available on Internet Archive and can be printed out by you if you don't like reading online. This particular book is called *The Five Brothers*[19] and the best way to introduce you to it is to let her introduce you to why she wrote the book.

> The great epic stories of the world are few and their number will probably not increase— unless, for our sins, a new flood washes mankind from the face of the planet, leaving only another Noah or a Manu to start the long course of civilization over again.
>
> For the great epics came out of the dawn of the world, when everything was new: before man wrote or read, when intuition and experience were the only sources of his knowledge; when, amazed and stirred by the cosmic drama in the midst of which he found himself, he tried to find his part in it, his relation to the earth and its creatures, to the heavenly bodies and to his fellow men. He searched his memory to find a cause and a beginning and cast his vision far ahead to seek a purpose and an end. His findings were infinitely important to him and to all who have come after him. In order to record them he put them into stories that caught the rhythm of the turning earth. There is no better way to remember and to make others remember than to make a story and to put it into rhythmic speech.
>
> Because the epics were composed before writing was known or before it was widely used

in the country of their origin, they were not individual works but collective; for they were told by teacher to disciple, by parent to child, by storyteller to storyteller, each generation, each unusual person adding something until the story grew, like a Gothic cathedral, including many centuries in its final form. And, like a Gothic cathedral, it gathered in its growth the history, the beliefs and customs, the economy and the arts of the times it passed through, and preserved them for us. Only a great framework can hold all these things together and keep its own shape through so much handling; the epic, therefore, is always a magnificent story.

For these and other reasons it seems unlikely that further stories of this magnitude will be produced, and for these reasons the ones we have are particularly precious. There are none greater or more precious than the two epics of India, the Mahabharata and the Ramayana.

The Mahabharata in its entirety is the longest of all scriptures and of all poems; for it is three times as long as the Bible and eight times as long as the Iliad and the Odyssey put together. For two or three thousand years the story that forms its nucleus has been the vehicle for the moral philosophy and for the highest spiritual teaching of Hinduism; it has acquired not only enormous elaboration in the telling, but also enormous digressions amounting to whole volumes that are purely philosophical and only tenuously connected with the story. It has become the very encyclopedia of Hinduism: "The storehouse," as one scholar says, "of Indian genealogy, mythology and antiquity."

Since history, as understood in the West, has not been congenial to the Hindu mind, it seems impossible to find out, even approximately, the time when the events of this story may have taken place. Some Hindu scholars say 3000 B.C. and others about 1500 B.C.; Western scholars, after exhaustive research, say any time between 1700 b.c. and 700 B.C. There is no mention of the great battle in the vague historical records, although the Bharatas were known in very early times as powerful rulers of northwestern India who, indeed, gave it its early name—Bharata-varsha. There seems to be no doubt, however, that the story is based on actual events, though they were not of the colossal proportions claimed by the poem. For one of the quaint results of its long growth is the contrast between the claim of the Bharata kings to be "lords of the whole earth with its belt of seas" and a certain incident which proves them to be no more than tribal chieftains who raid each other's borders to steal cattle.

The poem, on the other hand, has its place in history. Professor Edward Washburn Hopkins in his book, The Great Epic of India, states that lays, or song cycles, about the Bharatas were current by 400 B.C., that this story, with its familiar characters, was known between 400 and 200 B.C., and that the poem had attained its present form and length at some time between 200 and 400 a.d. By that time it was written in Sanskrit and was available to priests and scholars.

During those many centuries and afterward, the story, its incidents and characters, became known to everyone in India and in those countries colonized or influenced by

India: Ceylon, Southeast Asia, and the Indies. It was and is now told in the homes, chanted in the temples, recited under the village tree; it was carved on the walls of Angkor and in the temples of Java; it was and is now shown in the shadow plays of Burma, Siam, and the Indies, played by living actors and danced in exquisite ceremonial dances. Indeed, it is so well known in the Indies that the Javanese began their history with these stories, believing them to be their own tradition.

The great arts of India, Indonesia, and Southeast Asia are as hard to understand, if one is ignorant of the two Hindu epics, as the arts of Western Europe would be if one were ignorant of the Greek myths and the Bible. Kunti and Draupadi are of the stature of Penelope, Antigone, and Alcestis; Yudishtira and Arjuna, Bishma and Vidura stand beside David and Solomon, Odysseus and Achilles, Arthur and Galahad and Roland. Is it not time for us to become as familiar with these great figures of Indian tradition as we are with those of our own? Is not the Aryan heritage ours also? And is it not well to know the sources of the culture of a great people whose newly won independence will make them increasingly important in the world?

The Indian epics do not belong so much to the past as ours do: they are alive and active in the life of India today. The grandmother or the mother tells them to the children; bands of actors and of minstrels travel about presenting them in town and village, where amateurs, too, love to enact them; priests recite the sonorous Sanskrit verses while interpreters translate them for the listeners; scholars and poets rhapsodize on solemn or festive occasions, taking one incident and improvising upon it, after the manner of the ancient Greek rhapsodes. The Pandavas, Kunti and Draupadi are the great examples of noble and virtuous behavior, held up to children and adults; their misfortunes still draw tears from the listener or spectator, and their victory brings an ever returning joy.

I seem to have forgotten that it is not the mighty Mahabharata that I am introducing, but my own humble version of its story. Yet even this volume has its place in the great tradition, for the noble tale has been in the hands of every sort of storyteller; many versions and condensations of it have been made in all the vernaculars of India and the many stories included in it— the stories of Sakuntala, Nala and Damayanti, Savitri, for example— have been told and retold in India and abroad. That great spiritual poem, the Bhagavad Gita, which is contained in the Mahabharata and yet is complete in itself, is known to all the world.

Month 2 Podcasts

Podcast #24 Lessons from Spain/Don Quixote

I thought I'd spend a little time today highlighting quite possibly the best-selling novel of all time, with an estimated 500 million plus readers. It's been translated into more languages than any other book, save the Bible, which speaks to its universal appeal to all people everywhere.

But especially I recommend it to you because it may be one of the most important books the well-educated child's heart can fall in love with because it speaks of the importance of dreams in fighting the battles of life and of joy in the journey, despite battle scars and wounds.

The book is *Don Quixote* by Cervantes, who lived in Spain, a Month 2 topic. Cervantes wrote the book over 400 years ago. He died in 1616—the same year as Shakespeare. He had an adventurous soul just like his Man from La Mancha. At age 24, he went off to fight in a war against the Turks, a venture that cost him the use of his left hand. Four years later, when he was sailing home, his ship was captured by Barbary pirates and he was taken to Algiers where he was forced into slavery for five years until his family and friends could raise enough money to ransom him and bring him home.

He had literary aspirations, but they didn't pay the bills. Like many of our modern vets, he sought compensation for the service rendered his nation, but there was none. He found a job for awhile as the purchasing agent for the Spanish Armada and later as a tax collector. Some irregularities in his bookkeeping were found that landed him in prison. He was also imprisoned for debts he couldn't pay. It was while he was in prison that *Don Quixote* was born—a fitting place to learn a truth he included in his book. He wrote: "Liberty is one of the most precious gifts that Heaven has bestowed upon mankind." The book that made him immortal was birthed while his family lived in wretched conditions.

Don Quixote was a dreamer—much like Cervantes himself. The realists around him thought he was insane. His modest home was filled with books about knights and chivalry which he read and read, until he fancied himself a knight-errant—called to right the wrongs of the world.

He reminds me of a little piece called *The Dreamers* by Herbert Kaufman:

> They are the architects of greatness. Their vision lies within their souls. They never see the mirages of Fact, but peer beyond the veils and mists of doubt and pierce the walls of unborn Time.

> The world has accoladed them with jeer and sneer and jibe, for worlds are made of little men who take but never give—who share but never spare—who cheer a grudge and grudge a cheer.

> Where, the paths of progress have been sobs of blood dropped from their broken hearts.

> Makers of empire, they have fought for bigger things than crowns and higher seats than thrones. Fanfare and pageant and the right to rule or will to love, are not the fires which

wrought their resolution into steel.

Grief only streaks their hair with silver, but has never grayed their hopes.

They are the Argonauts, the seekers of the priceless fleece—the Truth.

Through all the ages they have heard the voice of destiny call to them from the unknown vasts. They dare uncharted seas, for they are makers of the charts. With only cloth of courage at their masts and with no compass save their dreams, they sail away undaunted for the far, blind shores.

Their brains have wrought all human miracles. In lace of stone their spires stab the Old World's skies and with their golden crosses kiss the sun.

A flash out in the night leaps leagues of snarling seas and cries to shore for help, which, but for one man's dream, would never come.

Their tunnels plow the river-bed and chain the islands to the Motherland.

What would you have of fancy or of fact if hands were all with which men had to build?

Your homes are set upon the land a dreamer found. The pictures on its walls are visions from a dreamer's soul. A dreamer's pain wails from your violin.

They are the chosen few—the Blazers of the way—who never wear doubt's bandage on their eyes—who starve and chill and hurt, but hold to courage and to hope, because they know that there is always proof of truth for them who try—that only cowardice and lack of faith can keep the seeker from his chosen goal, but if his heart be strong and if he dream enough and dream it hard enough, he can attain, no matter where men failed before.

Walls crumble and the empires fall. The tidal wave sweeps from the sea and tears a fortress from its rock. The rotting nations drop from off Time's bough, and only things the dreamers make live on.

They are the Eternal Conquerors—their vassals are the years.

And I would add, the world and the realists often call them crazy.

Don Quixote teaches us that perception is everything. The way we choose to see the world is how it shall be. Aldonza is not a tavern prostitute: she is Dulcinea, a maiden of such exquisite beauty and purity that Quixote would rather die than deny her. He believes in her so much that she finally believes in herself. He sees giants in windmills and formidable armies of enemies in sheep. He blunders and fails and the realists mock and ridicule.

But because of his dream—because he has something worth fighting for—he relishes the struggles in the pursuit of his dreams.

Maybe I love this knight errant so much because I, too, have always been a dreamer. I don't remember the context of the conversation, but I remember one day my daughter said to me, "Mom, stop smooshing your dreams into my reality."

When our eight children were young, we made a daring and impractical move to Colorado from Utah. It was a feeling to go there. It made no sense. We didn't have the means. (A side note, yes, we have nine children—our 9th child falls between our last two daughters. She was born to another mother who raised her for her first 11 years. But now she's very much ours. Anyway, she's not part of the eight children I just mentioned because we didn't meet her until we got to Colorado. And you know, in retrospect, maybe our move there was to find her.)

Anyway, we were told we were fools to do what we did. Everything was an uphill battle. Everything went wrong. A few years later, we were destitute and heavily in debt—in fact, things got so bad, we were facing eviction from our rented home. We had exhausted every avenue. We had tried everything we knew to do. I had no idea where to turn—I started calling camp grounds to see if there was somewhere we could pitch a tent that we could afford. But we couldn't even afford that.

But I never stopped dreaming and I know that's what kept me moving forward. A few months earlier we had gone to some model homes and I found my dream home. It was 6,000 square feet and so spacious and open with lots of bedrooms for our large family. I could envision living there. I dreamed of living in a home like that.

Most of my kids will remember, I think, the little bank I brought home one day. It looked like a giant pencil but it had a place at the top to drop coins in. The name of the home I loved was the Crescendo and so I said this little bank was for our Crescendo dream. Because we all loved the house. So I said, let's drop our extra pennies in here and start saving up. Ridiculous, huh? An impossible dream. When someone had some loose change, it went in there. It never amounted to very much.

But it was always a visual reminder of the dream. And I never let the dream die no matter how bad things got.

Well, in the middle of the disaster when I was calling campgrounds, I remember I was vacuuming and an idea popped into my head of something we could do that was so clear and made so much sense, that I ran and told my husband, and he got excited, too. It was prom time and of course we couldn't afford to buy a prom dress, so I was trying to sew one up for my daughter. I had taken a part-time job during the day to bring in a little income so the only time I had to sew was at night. So I remember my husband and I worked straight through the night for the next 24 hours putting into action this plan that had come to my mind. He worked on laying out an advertising piece and I'd sew a few seams in the other room and then come back to where he was working and we'd talk through some ideas and he'd work on them and I'd sew some more.

Long story short, within two weeks, I paid the rent and within 6 months, not only were all our debts paid off, we were living in my dream home.

Realists would never have put a man on the moon. Realists would never have ventured across an unknown ocean or attempted to create devices by which I can instantly converse with someone on the other side of the globe as if they were sitting right by me.

Dreamers make the world move forward in spite of the naysayers and the scoffers and the doubters.

The well-educated heart is about raising a generation of dreamers who don't see the world as it is, but as it can be. And by that dream, set out to right the wrongs and find beauty where others only see ugliness.

As Cervantes wrote: "For neither good nor evil can last forever; and so it follows that as evil has lasted a long time, good must now be close at hand."

And: "When life seems lunatic, who knows where madness lies? Perhaps to be too practical is madness. To surrender dreams—this may be madness. Too much sanity may be madness—and maddest of all: to see life as it is and not as it should be."

To those who ridicule the dreamers and their seemingly failures and foibles, Cervantes would say:

> Obviously, you don't know much about adventures. The wounds received in battle bestow honor, they do not take it away.

> The greatest madness a man can be guilty of in this life, is to let himself die outright, without being slain by any person whatever, or destroyed by any other weapon than the hands of melancholy.

I love the Man of La Mancha. If you want to help your children love him, there's a version written by James Baldwin who wrote so many of the wonderful children's books of the Golden Age of Literature that I'll link in the program notes. Or there are other children's versions suggested in the additional reading lists.

There are numerous movies made of him. Of course, the famous version is the musical version of Man of La Mancha. The live productions strike me the deepest—keep your eyes out for a performance near you. Or there's the movie version starring Peter O'Toole. I will also link a Hallmark version starring John Lithgow.

Don Quixote is called a bible for humanity.

And now, there are no better words to close this podcast than with the lyrics to the popular song, The Impossible Dream.

> To dream the impossible dream
> To fight the unbeatable foe
> To bear with unbearable sorrow
> To run where the brave dare not go.

> To right the unrightable wrong
> To love pure and chaste from afar
> To try when your arms are too weary
> To reach the unreachable star.

> This is my quest: To follow that star

No matter how hopeless, no matter how far.
To fight for the right without question or pause
To be willing to march into hell for a heavenly cause.

And I know if I'll only be true to this glorious quest
That my heart will lie peaceful and calm
When I'm laid to my rest.

And the world will be better for this:
That one man scorned and covered with scars
Still strove with his last ounce of courage
To reach the unreachable stars.

Podcast #25 Lessons from William Bradford and the Pilgrims

While I've been so sad to watch what has happened to Christopher Columbus over the last few years, I thought to myself, at least no one can find fault with the Pilgrims. Not so fast. Coming to a town near you, the new twisted narrative: Pilgrims—America's first terrorist group.

We have to know our history, and, in this case, we have a critical piece of evidence: William Bradford's journal that recorded an eyewitness look at the events and the thought processes behind them. What we now call *Of Plimouth Plantation*[20] is a national treasure that actually went missing for about a hundred years. It had been left in the tower of the Old South Meeting House in Boston which was occupied by British soldiers and after the war was over, the journal had vanished. Some feared it had been destroyed when they ransacked the place. Others feared it had been carried off and carelessly thrown away.

Decades later, a man picked up a book in England that contained a history of the protestant Episcopal church and noticed that parts of Bradford's journal had been quoted. He reasoned—the only way that could have happened is if the journal had survived. A little detective work brought him to the Bishop of London's library at Fulham Palace. No one knows how it had gotten there and had it not been for that random connection, it may still be there, forgotten by the world at large. It would be another forty complicated years before it was brought home to America. Its arrival in 1897 was an occasion of great celebration. It was seen as "one of the most precious manuscripts on earth." Senator Hoar said, "If there were in existence in England a history of King Alfred's reign for thirty years, written by his own hand, it could not be more precious in the eyes of Englishmen than the manuscript is to us."

Another speaker said, "Wherever it shall go it will be an object of reverent care. I do not think many Americans will gaze upon it without a little trembling at the lips and a little gathering of mist in the eye, as they think of the story of suffering, of sorrow, of peril, of exile, of death and of lofty triumph which the book tells. There is nothing like it in human annals since the story of Bethlehem."

Well, 15 years ago when I heard about it, I was living in Salt Lake City. There was only one paperback version of this treasured manuscript in all the Salt Lake City, Salt Lake County, and Utah County library systems. I read it cover to cover and was moved beyond words at what I learned.

Later, when I started compiling the Forgotten Classics Library, I had intended to include a popular little story of the Pilgrims by Margaret Pumphrey. But after reading the journal, I thought how not true to the facts the little book is, although it is appealing to little children and therefore serves a purpose of awakening desire. So I looked for something else and came across a book written for children by one of the leading authorities on the Pilgrims history of the day, Roland Usher. In the preface, he noted that many legends had sprung up in the absence of Bradford's journal, but as it had recently resurfaced and had been brought back to

America, he used only those accounts that could be verified by the journal. That's the first book you'll find in *Stories of the Pilgrims* as well as the audio version that I'll post in the podcast notes. And you'll also find several excerpts from Bradford's journal in the back section of the Forgotten Classics book.

In the late 1800s, Woodrow Wilson was having a conversation with other thinkers of the day who were concerned with what was happening in our country. We were losing our national spirit. Our morals were declining. And Wilson remarked, "Our liberties are safe until the memories and experiences of the past are blotted out and the Mayflower with its band of pilgrims forgotten, until our public school system has fallen into decay and the nation into ignorance."

Those are sobering words for all liberty loving people!

These men concluded that refreshing our stories would wake the people up and renew their spirits. We need that today more than ever! William Bradford knew that, too, for he expressed in his journal, "We have noted these things, that you may see the worth of these things, and not negligently lose what your fathers have obtained with so much hardship…."

The story of the Pilgrims is one even young children can relate to because it's a story of families, unlike the Jamestown settlement 13 years earlier that was settled by dandies in their silks and their manservants out on their particular, dreaming of castles in the air. Over 80% of them died the first year because even with starvation staring them in the face, the thought of getting their hands dirty was repulsive to them.

No, the story of the Pilgrims is the story of young families, just like many of you—mothers and fathers in their 20s and their 30s. Of the 102 or so passengers on the Mayflower, 39 of them were children! William Bradford was just 30 years old. Those of you with a 4- or 5- or 6-year-old, take him, hold him and look him in the eyes, and imagine the feelings of William and Dorothy as they left their little 5-year-old son in the care of friends in Holland, not knowing if they would ever see him again. Dorothy didn't. While the Mayflower was anchored in the harbor and William was on shore trying to find a suitable place to settle, Dorothy somehow fell overboard and was drowned.

William remembered and recorded the scene of their departure from Holland:

> That night was spent with little sleep by the most, but with friendly entertainment and other real expressions of true Christian love. The next day (the wind being fair) they went aboard and their friends with them, where truly doleful was the sight of that sad and mournful parting, to see what sighs and sobs and prayers did sound amongst them, what tears did gush from every eye, and pithy speeches pierced each heart; that sundry of the Dutch strangers that stood on the quay as spectators could not refrain from tears …their reverend pastor falling down on his knees and they all with him and with watery cheeks commended them with most fervent prayers to the Lord and His blessing. And then with mutual embraces and many tears they took their leaves one of another, which proved to be the last leave to many of them.

> It was by many thought an adventure almost desperate; a case intolerable and a misery worse than death….

So what drove them to take such a drastic step?

Bradford noted they were "hunted and persecuted on every side…. Some were taken and clapped up in prison, others had their houses beset and watched night and day, and the most were fain to flee and leave their houses and habitations and the means of their livelihood."

And what was their crime? They had read the precious words of the Bible for themselves and longed to raise their children according to the simple and humble teachings of Jesus Christ.

For the simple act of reading the Bible, children were made to witness against their parents and watched their parents be burned at stakes with their Bibles around their necks. Believers were thrown in prisons and beheaded for going against their government.

Thank goodness we're more civilized and sensible, right? But do we not see homeschoolers, for example, living in fear of child protective services coming to their doors and taking their children away for not complying with government regulations? Or for being shunned by neighbors and friends for wanting to give their children a different kind of education? Can you not relate to the feelings of these Pilgrims as they longed for a place to be free and to raise their families without interference? How much would you sacrifice for the right to live according to the dictates of your own conscience? Or the right question appears to soon be, "How much will you sacrifice for the right to live according to the dictates of your own conscience? Will it be worth your home, your job, your standing in the community, your reputation?"

William reminds us: "All great and honourable actions are accompanied with great difficulties and must be overcome with answerable courages." And then he tells us again why he gave us the record that he did as he wrote: "I have been larger in these things…that their children may see with what difficulties their fathers wrestled in going through these things in their first beginnings; and how God brought them along, notwithstanding all their weaknesses and infirmities. As also that some use may be made hereof in after times by others in such like weighty employments."

He wrote to you and to me.

And his answer as to how they got through it was always the same: "These things did not dismay them, though they did sometimes trouble them; for their desires were set on the ways of God…. They rested on His providence, and knew Whom they had believed.

"They looked heavenward and quieted their fears. What could now sustain them but the Spirit of God and His grace?"

And while they did not escape sorrow and hardship, heaven did provide. The Mayflower was originally meant to take them to Virginia where they had been granted a charter. A fierce storm in the middle of the ocean crossing carried them off course and they found themselves in the Massachusetts Bay instead. Several attempts were made to go to Virginia, but the way was too dangerous and they had to settle on a new destination.

Was it coincidence that, in this accidental destination, there lived a native—Squanto—who had been kidnapped and carried to England where he lived and learned the language and had only recently returned to his home? His people had tragically been wiped out by an illness, he was alone, but he became friends and lived with the Pilgrims, teaching them how to survive in the New World. Which was a good thing because none of the seeds they had brought from England would grow. Bradford described him as "a special instrument sent of God for their good beyond their expectation."

After fighting off starvation for several seasons, the pilgrims planted and hoped for a good harvest. But William recorded:

> By a great drought which continued from the third week of May, till about the middle of July, without any rain and with great heart for the most part, insomuch as the corn began to wither away though it was set with fish. Yet at length it began to languish sore, and some of the drier grounds were perched like withered hay, part whereof was never recovered.
>
> Upon which they set apart a solemn day of humiliation, to seek the Lord by humble and fervent prayer, in this great distress. And He was pleased to give them a gracious and speedy answer, both to their own and the Indians' admiration that lived amongst them. For all the morning, and greatest part of the day, it was clear weather and very hot, and not a cloud or any sign of rain to be seen; yet toward evening it began to overcast, and shortly after to rain such sweet and gentle showers as gave them cause of rejoicing and blessing God. It came without either wind or thunder or any violence, and by degrees in that abundance as that the earth was thoroughly wet and soaked and therewith. Which did so apparently revive and quicken the decayed corn and other fruits, as was wonderful to see, and made the Indians astonished to behold. And afterwards the Lord sent them such seasonable showers, with interchange of fair warm weather as, through His blessing, caused a fruitful and liberal harvest, to their no small comfort and rejoicing. For which mercy, in time convenient, they also set apart a day of thanksgiving.
>
> …[F]amine hath not been amongst them since to this day.

It seems that William Bradford saw the naysayers of our day and addressed some of the very falsehoods I am seeing spread around. One of those stories is that for all their profession of Christian ideals, they weren't so pure. He wrote:

> [I]t may be demanded how came it to pass that so many wicked persons and profane people should so quickly come over into this land and mix themselves amongst them? Seeing it was religious men that began the work and then came for religion's sake? I confess this may be marveled at, at least in time to come, when the reasons thereof should not be known; and the more because here were so many hardships and wants met withal. I will therefore endeavour to give some answer hereunto.

And then he lists reasons.

1. According to that in the gospel, it is ever to be remembered that where the Lord begins to sow good seed, there the envious man will endeavor to sow tares.

2. Men being to come over into a wilderness, in which much labour and service was to be done about building and planting—many untoward servants sundry of them proved, that were thus brought over, both men and womenkind, became families of themselves which gave increase hereunto.

3. To make up their freight and advance their profit, cared not who the persons were, so they had money to pay them. And by this means the country became pestered with many unworthy persons, who, being come over, crept unto one place or other.

So, first, we need to understand that not everyone on board the Mayflower came for religious freedom. Only about half of them did. The other half consisted of workers hired to help, such as Miles Standish, a veteran of the Dutch wars, who came as a soldier for their protection, or John Alden who only planned on staying a short time. He was a cooper—his job was to make barrels. When Priscilla Mullins lost every member of her family, John fell in love with her and stayed. They married and had 11 children. But there were also loud, obnoxious, good-for-nothings like the Billingtons. The father had the distinction of being the first man to be hanged in America. His son nearly blew up the Mayflower playing in the gunpowder room. Keep in mind—those who financed the venture were interested in making money, not propagating freedom. The conditions of the agreement were harsh. But the Pilgrims had no other choice. They were nothing more than indentured servants to the financiers and they didn't care who came over. The Billingtons were evidently just warm bodies expected to produce some income. Who knows what they were fleeing from in England!

But ample examples are given of true Christianity in action as practiced by the true Pilgrims, starting with their conduct as they attempted to flee from England to the safety of Holland. They had already been betrayed once. Another attempt was made and due to precautionary measures, many of the husbands had boarded a ship when the authorities came to arrest and haul them back. In a panic, the captain hoisted anchor and sailed away to Holland, leaving the women and children behind, who happened to be carrying all the money and possessions. Bradford recorded: "…[P]itiful it was to see the heavy case of these poor women in this distress; what weeping and crying on every side, some for their husbands that were carried away in the ship; others not knowing what should become of them and their little ones; others again melted in tears, seeing their poor little ones hanging about them, crying for fear and quaking with cold."

They were arrested and paraded from town to town. No one knew what to do with them. But note this from Bradford: "Yet I may not omit the fruit that came hereby, for by these so public troubles in so many eminent places their cause became famous and occasioned many to look into the same, and their godly carriage and Christian behavior was such as left a deep impression in the minds of many."

Their godly carriage and Christian behavior—they let their light shine!

Another example is during that awful first winter when half of them died. When it was all over, only 4 of the 14 women were still alive. *But* most of the children had survived! I've heard it suggested maybe the reason the children lived is because the mothers were doing what mothers do—maybe they sacrificed their portion of the scanty measure of food for the sustenance of their children or maybe they lied their bodies over the children to keep them warm, but freezing themselves. We'll never know for sure. And isn't that something to think about—that most of who we call our Pilgrim fathers were children?

But this is the part I wanted to share as Bradford compared the way the Pilgrims treated each other in a spirit of Christian love and how the crew on board, that had stayed through the winter, treated each other.

Bradford wrote:

> So as there died some times two or three a day…that of 100 and odd persons, scarce fifty remained. And of these, in the time of most distress, there was but six or seven sound persons who to their great commendation spared no pains night nor day, but with abundance of toil and hazard of their own health, fetched them wood, made them fires, dressed them meet, made their beds, washed their loathsome clothes, clothed and unclothed them. In a word, did all the homely and necessary offices for them which dainty and queasy stomachs cannot endure to hear named; and all this willingly and cheerfully, without any grudging in the least, showing herein their true love unto their friends and brethren; a rare example and worthy to be remembered.

On the ship however:

> Half of the men on the ship died. For they that before had been boon companions in drinking and jollity in the time of their health and welfare, began now to desert one another in this calamity, saying they would not hazard their lives for them…would do little or nothing for them but, "if they died, let them die."

There had been a proud young man, one of the crew members, who had often cursed and scoffed at the passengers. Bradford continued: "But when he grew weak, they had compassion on him and helped him, then he confessed he did not deserve it at their hands, he had abused them in word and deed. 'Oh!' saith he, 'You, I now see, show your love like Christians indeed one to another, but we let one another lie and die like dogs.'"

Following that harsh winter, the captain of the Mayflower offered to carry anyone back to England who wanted to return. Isn't it incredible, given all the hardship and misery and suffering, not one took up the offer?

One more example—of doing good to those who despitefully use you; of honoring our commitments and being honest in our dealings.

After that first horrible winter, they laid up in store what they could to face another winter, which was barely sustainable as it was, a ship—the Fortune—sailed into the harbor. At first, they were excited—surely the ship brought badly needed supplies to them! Nope. It carried 35 more bodies, sent over by the financiers. They brought with them no food, no bedding, nor pot nor pan nor coat nor cloak. Just more mouths to feed. Yet, they were taken in and treated with care and kindness.

But even more painful was the letter sent over from Thomas Weston, who had been their agent between them and the money lenders. He was mad that they sent the Mayflower back with no products to sell. He wrote: "That you sent no lading in the ship is…worthily distasted. I know your weakness was the cause of it, and I believe more weakness of judgment than weakness of hands. A quarter of the time you spent in discoursing, arguing, and consulting would have done much more, but that is past."

And he signed the letter:

Your loving friend,
Thomas Weston

In part, Bradford's reply was:

You greatly blame us for keeping the ship so long in the country, and then to send her away empty. She lay five weeks at Cape Cod wilst with many a weary step (after a long journey) and the endurance of many a hard brunt, we sought out in the foul winter a place of habitation. Then, we went in so tedious a time to make provisions to shelter us and our goods; about which labour, many of our arms and legs can tell us to this day, we were not negligent. But it pleased God to visit us then with death daily, and with so general a disease that the living were scarce able to bury the dead, and the well not in any measure sufficient to tend the sick.

And now to be so greatly blamed for not freighting the ship doth indeed go near us and much discourage us. But you say you know we will pretend weakness. And do you think we had not cause? Yes, you tell us you believe it, but it was more weakness of judgment than of hands. Our weakness herein is great we confess, therefore we will bear this cheek patiently amongst the rest, till God send us wiser men. But they which told you we spent so much time in discoursing and consulting, their hearts can tell their tongues they lie. They cared not, so that they might salve their own sores, how they wounded others. Indeed, it is our calamity, beyond expectations, yoked with some ill-conditioned people who will never do good, but corrupt and abuse others…

Unfair as the accusations were, and as destitute their conditions, they loaded up the Fortune with good clapboard and two hogshead of beaver and otter skins and sent it back to England to begin to repay the debt.

But the cargo never made it. French pirates seized the ship and took everything on board. That didn't keep Bradford from honoring the agreement. He and a couple of the other leaders took on the burden of the debt and in time, completely discharged it.

What a lesson in honoring our obligations, no matter how unfair.

Another false impression is that of the Pilgrims being America's first terrorists. The fact is, they lived in friendship with the Native tribes around them and had decades of peace. There were other tribes who meant to do them harm, and their friends warned them and they had to deal with them with harsh measures, but their intention was to live in peace, which they did.

But always there was the problem of others who were coming to this New World, and Bradford wrote, "I fear these people will hardly deal so well with the savages as they should. I pray you therefore signify to Squanto that they are a distinct body from us, and we have nothing to do with them, neither must be blamed for their faults."

Oh my goodness. The riff-raff that came must have been so frustrating to deal with. Yet, time after time, Bradford and the Pilgrims treated them with kindness and compassion, even when betrayed and when harm was done to them. You'll have to read about all of those experiences yourself, including when Thomas Weston himself showed up begging in rags.

I love the story of the Pilgrims. I keep discovering new insights every time I come back to their story. And I feel sad every time I come to this entry in Bradford's journal. By the time he wrote this, the Puritans had settled in Boston. They weren't poor and with them came many opportunities for making money. It wasn't the suffering or the hardships that broke up their little Plymouth colony. In the end, it was prosperity. He wrote: "And thus was this poor church left, like an ancient mother grown old and forsaken of her children…thus, she that had made many rich became herself poor."

On a piece of paper, separate from his journal, he wrote:

> O sacred bond, whilst invioably preserved! How sweet and precious were the fruits that flowed from the same, but when this fidelity decayed, then their ruin approached. O that these ancient members had not died or been dissipated (if it had been the will of God) or else that this holy care and constant faithfulness had still lived, and remained with those that survived, and were in times afterwards added unto them. But (alas) that subtle serpent hath slyly wound in himself under fair pretences of necessity and the like, to untwist these sacred bonds and ties, and as it were insensibly by degrees to dissolve, or in great measure, to weaken the same. I have been happy, in my first times, to see, and with much comfort to enjoy, the blessed fruits of this sweet communion, but it is now a part of my misery in old age, to find and feel the decay and want thereof in great measure and with grief and sorrow of heart to lament and bewail the same. And for others' warning and admonition, and my own humiliation, do I here note the same.

The end of his journal simply has, at the top of the last two pages, Anno 1647, Anno 1648.

I sense sadness there.

Yet, as is the case with all of us, we cannot always see the ripple effect of our actions. They had undertaken the whole adventure with "a great hope and an inward zeal…of laying some good foundation or at least to make some way thereunto, for the propagating and advancing the gospel of the kingdom of Christ in those remote parts of the world; yea, though they should be but even as stepping stones unto others for the performing of so great a work."

Indeed—they were stepping stones! "Thus out of small beginnings greater things have been produced by His hand that made all things of nothing, and gives being to all things that are; and, as one small candle may light a thousand, so the light here kindled hath shone unto many, yea in some sort to our whole nation; let the glorious name of Jehovah have all the praise."

Today, more than 35 million Americans can trace their direct ancestry lines to the handful of passengers on the Mayflower, including my husband who is among William Bradford's descendants. If you'd like to find out if you are among them, I'm providing a link in the podcast notes.

The struggle for freedom continues. May we not negligently lose that which was bought by so dear a price by instilling the lessons of faith and trust and diligence in the hearts of our children, in part by never allowing the memory of the Mayflower and her Pilgrims from being blotted out.

I'll close with a poem by Felicia Hermans.

> The breaking waves dashed high
> On a stern and rock-bound coast,
> And the woods against stormy sky
> Their giant branches tossed;
> And the heavy night hung dark
> The hills and water o'er,
> When a band of exiles moored their bark
> On the wild New England shore.
>
> Not as the conqueror comes,
> They, the true-hearted, came;
> Not with the roll of the stirring drums,
> And the trumpet that sings of fame;
> Not as the flying come,
> In silence and in fear;
> They shook the depths of the desert's gloom
> With their hymns of lofty cheer.
>
> Amidst the storm they sang;
> And the stars heard, and the sea;
> And the sounding aisles of the dim woods rang
> To the Anthem of the Free.
> The ocean eagle soared
> From his nest by the white wave's foam;
> And the rocking pines of the forest roared,—
> This was their welcome home!
>
> There were men with hoary hair
> Amidst the pilgrim band;
> Why had they come to wither there,
> Away from their childhood's land?
> There was woman's fearless eye,
> Lit by her deep love's truth;

There was manhood's brow, serenely high,
And the fiery heart of youth.

What sought they thus afar?
Bright jewels of the mine?
The wealth of seas, the spoils of war?—
They sought a faith's pure shrine!
Ay, call it holy ground,
The soil where first they trod;—
They have left unstained what there they found—
Freedom to worship God.

It was almost as if he could see into the future and read the minds of these narrative twisters and address them.

And what better place to start than with the story of the Pilgrims.

"Our liberties are safe until the memories and experiences of the past are blocked out, and the Mayflower and its band of Pilgrims forgotten, until the public school system has fallen into decay, and the nation into ignorance." --Woodrow Wilson

Podcast #26 Lessons from Brave Little Holland

Brave Little Holland and What She Taught Us[21] is the title of a 1922 book I'm taking most of my information from to share with you today. William Griffis wrote it because he wanted to teach the boys and girls of America the lessons in liberty Holland left us. As John Adams wrote: "The origins of the two Republics are so much alike, that the History of one seems but a transcript from that of the other. The Dutch cast off the yoke of the Spaniards just as our fathers threw off the yoke of the British, because their rights were invaded and they were taxed without their consent. Like our fathers, also, they first formed a Union of states, and then made themselves free by a declaration of independence. Like us, they had a long war for freedom. Ours was 8 years; theirs was 80. Like us, they had trouble about threatened secession. They talked much about State Rights and the Union, but the Union was maintained. Only they were 200 years ahead of us. The Dutch even fly a flag of red, white and blue.

Let me start by painting a little picture for you of the Spirit of these Dutch people, taken from M.B. Synge's version in *The Awakening of Europe*.

> The fight for freedom had been going on for many years. City after city had been attacked and fallen. The Spanish Duke of Alva taunted them: "Like a hen calling her chickens, his Majesty still seeks to gather you all under the parental wing. But if you will not, every city in the Netherlands shall be burned to the ground."

> The siege of Leyden began in October of 1573. It was October 1574 when it ended, and all through this long dreary year the Dutchmen inside the town were fighting with famine and starvation; fighting for their religious liberty and freedom from the Spanish tyranny.

> In the very center of Leyden rose an old tower, standing high above the surrounding low country. From it could be seen the broad fertile fields which once had lain under the sea, and little villages with their bright gardens and fruitful orchards.

> As the long months wore on their condition became desperate. They were starving, but they would not yield; for if Leyden fell, Holland fell, too. Yet what could be done?

> The Prince of Orange, William the Silent knew what could be done. Better a drowned land than a lost land. If nothing else could save the city, the dykes could be opened, and the great stormy sea would once more ebb and flow over the country. Holland would be ruined, but it would not be in the hands of the Spaniards.

> "We have held out as long as we can," wrote the starving citizens. "Human strength can do no more."

> Then the Prince went himself and had the great dykes bored in sixteen places; the water-gates were opened, and the water began slowly to pour over the flat land.

The good news was carried into the despairing city. The citizens took fresh heart. Leyden, their city, would yet be saved. The besiegers, too, heard the news of the cutting of the dykes, but they did not believe in the possibility of the sea getting up so far as Leyden.

"Go up to the tower, ye beggars," they laughed; "go up to the tower and tell us if you can see the ocean coming over the dry land to your relief."

And day after day the citizens crept up the old ruined tower and strained their eyes out over the sea, watching, hoping, praying, fearing, and at last almost despairing of relief by God or man.

Meanwhile the Prince lay in a burning fever at Rotterdam. Under the strain of the last months, he had broken down. In his fever he seemed to hear the cries of the starving citizens. Would they give in before the ships could sail to their relief?

It was the 1st of September when the Sea Beggars embarked in their shallow boats on the water that was now slowly rising over the land. The little fleet made its way over fifteen miles of flooded country between the sea-coast and Leyden. So far a favourable wind had blown them onwards. Now the wind changed, the waters began to sink, and despair once more fell on the starving people within Leyden. They had eaten everything now. They had boiled the leaves of trees and eaten roots. Women and children dropped down dead in the streets, the burghers could hardly drag their weary legs up to the watch-tower. Yet they would not give up. Leyden was sublime in her despair. They must be true to their charge, true to their Prince, true to their country. The old burgomaster of the town spoke to the wavering from time to time.

"My life is at your disposal," he said one day. "Here is my sword. Plunge it into me and divide my flesh among you. But expect no surrender as long as I live."

"As well," shouted the angry Spaniards, "as well can the Prince of Orange pluck the stars from the sky as bring the ocean to the walls of Leyden."

On the 1st of October a violent gale swept over the waste of waters from the northwest. The waters rose rapidly, and the Sea Beggars sailed proudly forward in the darkness of the night.

Within the town all was mysterious. Would the Spaniards attack them or flee? Must they yet perish in sight of help?

But before morning had dawned the Spanish host had grown alarmed at the rapidly rising waters, and the crews of wild fierce sailors sailing ever nearer and nearer. And before the waters reached them they had crept away under cover of the darkness.

A long line of moving lights were seen to flit across the black face of the waters at dead of night, and when day dawned at last there was not a Spaniard left. So the Sea Beggars sailed to Leyden and the city was saved.

In honor of the bravery of Leyden's citizens, the story says the Prince of Orange offered to free them of their taxes for two years or to build them a University. Because of their love of learning, they chose the University and Leyden University became the foremost institution of learning in all of Europe for a season.

The Prince of Orange, or William the Silent as he is called for reasons you will learn of, is a life worth studying. Take note that William was taught by his mother, Juliana of Stolberg, a woman of rare abilities and a deeply religious character. He took the stand: "I cannot approve of monarchs who want to rule over the conscience of people, and take away their freedom of choice and religion."

In 1577 he wrote these words to the Dutch magistrates that became the cornerstone first of the Dutch and then the American Republic: "We declare to you that you have no right to interfere with the conscience of any one, so long as he has done nothing that works injury to another person, or a public scandal." A people who were seeking God, each after his own way, seemed to be good to him. He believed that they all, being Children of one Father, should live lovingly together as His children. He hated persecution and cruelty done in the name of religion. This was in the days of the terrible Inquisition and an era when hundreds of thousands were put to their deaths or tortured for their religious beliefs.

No wonder Holland became a place of temporary refuge to the Pilgrims until they could find a safe haven in the New World. In modern days, you find Corrie Ten Boom and her family hiding Jewish refugees, thereby endangering their own lives. And Holland was the place Anne Frank's Jewish German family fled to for safety.

Brave Little Holland is ridiculously small. And before we go on, no, Holland is not a country. It's one of 11 provinces of the Netherlands. It's like what Texas is to the United States. I am posting a little 3-minute video in the podcast notes to help clear up any confusion or possibly keep you confused. But Holland plays such an important role in their history, her name is frequently the one we hear. The whole kingdom of the Netherlands' 11 provinces is less than half the size of South Carolina, 1/3 the area of Ohio, and barely bigger than Maryland. You can drop 20 Netherlands into the state of Texas.

But don't let her size fool you as to her power or her influence. Good things do come in small packages. As Benjamin Franklin wrote, "In love of liberty and bravery in the defense of it, she has been our greatest example." Holland provided the training ground for such illustrious soldiers as Sir Walter Raleigh, Captain John Smith, and Miles Standish. When Alva's army arrived from Spain, tens of thousands of Dutch's best fled to England and not a few of these Dutch refugees emigrated to America. Some of the bluest blood of New England was Dutch before it was English. Four of our original 13 colonies were settled by the Dutch. In our Revolutionary War the Dutch sympathized with us, gave us aid, and lent us money. Her brave officers came to fight with us and for us. After the United States was formally recognized, the loan of Dutch merchants of fourteen millions of dollars came when our country needed it most. When in 1787 our fathers made the Constitution, the Dutch republic was the living example before their eyes. They borrowed many things directly from the Dutch system, though they also rejected many and improved most of its features. Alexander Hamilton, who married a Dutch woman, was a scholar of Dutch history and applied many of those lessons in laying the foundation of America.

For a thousand years, the Dutch fought the sea and dyked the land. Once a mudhole, by genius, energy, patience and faith of a noble people, the mud-hole has been changed into a garden. Neder-land means the land beneath as in a land beneath the ocean. The names of some of her famous cities like Amsterdam and Rotterdam, or Amsterdom as they would say it, and Rotter dam are so named for the dams placed on the rivers so that cities could be built.

Many of the arts, sciences, inventions and improvements which made Great Britain so rich and powerful came from Holland. The cookie is of Dutch origin and of course the Dutch oven. A taste for flowers was introduced at the time of the Crusades, and the Dutch became a nation of flower-lovers and skilled gardeners. As many as 24 editions of the New Testament and 15 editions of the Bible had been printed and published in the Netherlands before one copy had been printed in England.

A Dutch Golden Age followed their victory for freedom. Like a moth is drawn to the flame of a candle, the light of freedom drew some of Europe's greatest thinkers, scientists, writers, and artists to Holland where they were allowed freedom of thought and expression; where faith and reason, art and science, heart and mind could thrive. It was in this Golden age that the art of the Republic glorified the home. Instead of painting winged angels, mysteries, nuns and popes, they transfigured on the canvas the joys of pure wedded life, the mother, the baby in the cradle, their lovely meadows, and their glorious sunsets. In this Golden Age, over a million paintings were created in a span of just 20 years, although few have survived. Every home displayed works of art on their walls celebrating their love of life and joy in common things.

The central role of woman revolved around the home. She delighted in the arts of homemaking and creating a safe-haven from the lack of Christian virtue and immorality often found outside the home. They believed that so goes the home, so goes the Republic. Older women were looked up to and respected for their wisdom by the younger women.

Sadly, by the time our Republic was being born, the Republic of the Netherlands was dying. We would be wise to note some of the reasons for their decline. Do you recognize any of these among us, as described by Griffis?

There was too much concentration into the central government. The political machinery became clogged and at times almost suffered paralysis. Among the people, a spirit of luxury and extravagance took hold. They became weakened in old earnestness, integrity, devotion to high principles, sound ideas of honor, reverence for women, frugality and temperance. A money-loving spirit increased. Religion became formal. Manners declined. The love of strong liquors increased. Commerce, credit, the navy, and army declined. The virtues of republican faith in God, high motives, grand actions, and simplicity in dress, food and life had fallen to common levels.

So is there any hope for us? Can we turn things around? The more you study history, the more you see the cycles of history repeat themselves. As Lord Byron noted:

There is the moral of all human tales;
'Tis but the same rehearsed of the past,
First freedom, then Glory;
when that fails,
Wealth, vice, corruption, barbarism at last.
And History, with all her volumes vast,
Hath but one page…

Where will the spirit of freedom be born again that will give a generation the courage and stamina to stand up to tyranny in the face of starvation, sacrifice and death, as our friends at Leyden did that I shared at the beginning of this podcast?

Change always begins in the heart of one man or woman, such as Gerhard Groote who was born in 1340, who preached a religion independent of priests and church despotism and instead set people in search for inner peace. The priests weren't happy with him and revoked his license to preach. So he opened a private school and began the copying and multiplication of books. He revived many schools that had fallen in decay, where young men flocked, eager for knowledge. The people respected the fact that he earned his own living and worked with his own hands. He was a light to them and his sincere example ignited an educational movement that was rooted in the hearts of the common people who vied with each other to support it. Families gladly boarded poor students without cost. Although he died when he was only 45 years old, others picked up the work and raised up a generation of Christian patriots in the Netherlands. These men full of hope for the future, fond of books, with minds well trained, hungry for that food for the soul, furnished the intellectual stamina for the great struggle of the 16th century against giant Spain.

Pupils of Groote became some of the best teachers of Europe. And notice this: he brought back the old stories and re-introduced the reading of the old struggles for freedom in the ancient republics; thereby firing anew thoughts and desires for freedom.

Are you not doing the same thing as you fill the hearts of your children with the stories of the brave and the great and the noble preparing a generation for the fight ahead which history teaches us is looming?

The stories of brave little Holland will help fill that reservoir.

You can learn much about the Dutch people and their History from Mary Mapes Dodge's book, *Hans Brinker and the Silver Skates*, based on a true story. Younger children may not have the patience to sit through the history parts, but your middle schoolers and older will learn much about Dutch history and peoples, which was intentional on Mary Dodge's part. In her preface, Mapes wrote: "Should it cause even one heart to feel a deeper trust in God's goodness and love…the prayer with which it was begun and ended will have been answered." Also, I'll link another book of hers in the podcast notes called *The Land of Pluck*.

I was meeting with a group of young women and their leaders awhile back and we were trying to come up with some stories of courage and bravery and I suggested the story of the little boy of Haarlem, which is the capital of North Holland; the true story of a little boy who saved his village by holding his finger in the dyke. I was astonished to learn that not one girl or mother in that group had ever even heard of the story. So, in my effort to keep it out there, I'll close today's podcast with the story put to a poem.

The Leak in the Dike
by Phoebe Cary

The good dame looked from her cottage
At the close of the pleasant day,
And cheerily called to her little son
Outside the door at play;
Come, Peter, come! I want you to go,
While there is light to see,
To the hut of the blind old man who lives
Across the dikes, for me,
And take these cakes I made for him
They are hot and smoking yet;
You have time enough to go and come
Before the sun is set.

Then the good-wife turned to her labor,
Humming a simple song,
And thought of her husband, working hard
At the sluices all day long;
And set the turf a-blazing,
And brought the coarse black bread;
That he might find a fire at night,
And find the table spread.

And Peter left the brother
With whom all day he had played,
And the sister who had watched their sports
In the willow's tender shade;
And now, with his face all glowing,
And eyes as bright as the day
With the thoughts of his pleasant errand,
He trudged along the way;

And soon his joyous prattle
Made glad a lonesome place.
Alas! If only the blind old man
Could have seen that happy face!
Yet he somehow caught the brightness
Which his voice and presence lent;
And he felt the sunshine come and go

As Peter came and went.

And now, as the day was sinking,
And the winds began to rise,
The mother looked from her door again,
Shading her anxious eyes;

And saw the shadows deepen
And birds to their houses come back,
But never a sign of Peter
Along the level track.
But she said, He will come at morning,
So I need not fret or grieve
Though it isn't like my boy at all
To stay without my leave.

But where was the child delaying?
On the homeward way was he,
And across the dike while the sun was up
An hour above the sea.
He was stopping now to gather flowers,
Now listening to the sound,
As the angry waters dashed themselves
Against their narrow bound.

Ah! Well for us, said Peter,
That the gates are good and strong,
And my father tends them carefully,
Or they would not hold you long!
You're a wicked sea, said Peter;
I know why you fret and chafe;
You would like to spoil our lands and homes;
But our sluices keep you safe!

But hark! Through the noise of waters
Comes a low, clear, trickling sound;
And the child's face pales with terror,
And his blossoms drop to the ground.
He is up at the bank in a moment,
And, stealing through the sand,
He sees a stream not yet so large
As his slender, childish hand.
'Tis a leak in the dike! He is but a boy,
Unused to fearful scenes;
But, young as he is, he has learned to know,

The dreadful thing that means.

A leak in the dike! The stoutest heart
Grows faint that cry to hear,
And the bravest man in all the land
Turns white with mortal fear.
For he knows the smallest leak may grow
To a flood in a single night;
And he knows the strength of the cruel sea
When loosed in its angry might.

And the boy! He has seen the danger,
And shouting a wild alarm,
He forces back the weight of the sea
With the strength of his single arm!
He listens for the joyful sound
Of a footstep passing nigh;
And lays his ear to the ground, to catch
The answer to his cry.
And he hears the rough winds blowing,
And the waters rise and fall,
But never an answer comes to him,
Save the echo of his call.
He sees no hope, no succor,
His feeble voice is lost;
Yet what shall he do but watch and wait
Though he perish at his post!

So, faintly calling and crying
Till the sun is under the sea;
Crying and moaning till the stars
Come out for company;
He thinks of his brother and sister,
Asleep in their safe warm bed;
He thinks of his father and mother,
Of himself as dying and dead;
And of how, when the night is over,
They must come and find him at last;
But he never thinks he can leave the place
Where duty holds him fast.

The good dame in the cottage
Is up and astir with the light,
For the thought of her little Peter
Has been with her all night.

And now she watches the pathway,
As yester eve she had done;
But what does she see so strange and black
Against the rising sun?
Her neighbors are bearing between them
Something straight to her door;
Her child is coming home, but not
As he ever came before!

He is dead! she cries, my darling!
And the startled father hears,
And come and looks the way she looks,
And fears the thing she fears;
Till a glad shout from the bearers
Thrills the stricken man and wife:
Give thanks, for your son has saved our land,
And God has saved his life!
So, there in the morning sunshine
They knelt about the boy;
And every head was bared and bent
In tearful, reverent joy.

'Tis many a year since then; but still
When the sea roars like a flood,
Their boys are taught what a boy can do
Who is brave and true and good.
For every man in that country
Takes his son by the hand,
And tells him of little Peter,
Whose courage saved the land.

They have many a valiant hero,
Remembered through the years;
But never one whose name so oft
Is named with loving tears.
And his deed shall be sung by the cradle,
And told to the children on the knee,
So long as the dikes of Holland
Divide the land from the sea!

Podcast #97 Why the Colonists Came

As we move into Month 2 in the Rotation schedule, we won't really be leaving the Explorers behind. We'll revisit Spanish explorers this month and again in Month 9 when we talk about South America and we'll spend more time with the French explorers next month. They've been looking around for about a hundred years now, writing about what they are seeing and experiencing, and now the time is right to start colonizing the New World.

We'll spend a few months on this Colonial era of our history because it is a huge part of our story. From the time Jamestown was settled in 1607 until our nation was formed under our Constitution in 1787, 180 years went by. Add another 180 years to that, and it brings us to 1967 just before most of you were born. So the Colonial Era is almost half of our history.

To begin our study, I want to give you some daily samplers from the lives of some of the great souls who led and established these colonies. You will notice, as we spend time with Spain in a few days, that the motives the English had for settling North America were in sharp contrast to the motives the Spanish had in South America.

Of course, there is the danger of the single story. There were lots of reasons people came to America. Even the little band of Pilgrims that sailed on the Mayflower was a diverse group. But some of the greatest souls you will ever spend time with will be found establishing deep roots in America's soil.

Today's Daily Sampler comes from a book written in 1879: *Stories of American History* by N.S. Dodge.[22] I want to share the chapter called "Why the Colonists Came."

When I read the part about Roger Williams being a Baptist, that was new news to me. So I looked it up. He established the first Baptist congregation in North America, which I didn't know. It was a new faith, having originated in the Dutch Republic just a few years earlier in 1607. Just a little side note.

Now here's the chapter.

> Every one ought to love God. Those who do love Him have a right to worship Him in their own way. Quakers in their way, Catholics in theirs, Baptists in theirs. Everybody now in this country, and in many other countries, is allowed to worship God as he pleases; but a long time ago it was not so.
>
> In England the Puritans could not worship God as they wished to do. Their Sunday services were broken up, and the worshippers were thrown into prison. It was the same with the Catholics; it was the same with the Quakers. No matter how good citizens they were, they were opposed and persecuted and punished; they had not freedom to worship God.
>
> In France it was worse. There the Huguenots were not only opposed, but they were

driven from their country. A great many were killed, and a great many more were shut up in prison.

It was, then, for freedom to worship God, that the Puritans came to Massachusetts, and the Huguenots to South Carolina, and the Quakers to Pennsylvania, and the Catholics to Maryland.

The Puritans had now freedom to worship God in their new home; but they were not willing that Quakers should have that freedom, and whenever Quakers came among them, they were persecuted and banished. They sent away the Baptists, too, and the "New Lights," as they were called, and the Catholics. The Puritans wanted none to live with them who were not Puritans.

Nowhere in the whole world was it then understood what religious freedom meant. The Episcopalians in Virginia did not understand it, nor the Huguenots in South Carolina, nor the Quakers in Pennsylvania. They did not all persecute those who worshipped God differently from themselves, but they did not favor them.

"When Roger Williams, who was a good man, was banished from Massachusetts, he went to Rhode Island. There were no roads; no farms on the way; no people but savages. His only crime was that he was a Baptist. He found his path through the woods with a brave heart. There were people who went with him. The Indians were kind to him. The land was better than in Massachusetts. Other people shortly came to him, and in a little time there was a flourishing colony in Rhode Island. And in that colony every one— Congregationalists, Presbyterians, Catholics, Episcopalians, and Quakers—might worship God as they pleased. There was no persecution. The Baptists who settled Rhode Island had no more rights than the Quakers and others who came to live there. This was true religious freedom.

But Rhode Island was not the first colony which did this great and good thing. Two years before Roger Williams, with pack on back, trudged through the woods towards Providence, an English nobleman, named Lord Baltimore, sent two ships into the beautiful Chesapeake, with more than two hundred people on board, all of whom were Catholics. It was the richest body of colonists which had ever come to America. They were nearly all gentlefolk, well educated, refined, and good. They, too, had left England because they could not worship God as they desired.

It is a milder climate around the Chesapeake Bay, and the settlers did not suffer as the Puritans had in Massachusetts. Besides, it was a better time of the year, and the new comers had money, and furniture, and tools, and goods to sell to the Indians. Lord Baltimore selected choice land near St. Mary's, for which he paid the natives, and plantations were laid out, woods cut down, fences built, houses erected, and very shortly a charming settlement was growing up.

The new colony was called Maryland, in honor of the queen of Charles L, Henrietta Maria, and the new city was called Baltimore, from the founder. There was prosperity in Maryland from the first. The country is beautiful. A great sheet of water flows between two parts of it, and from both shores the land rolls back in hills and dales, green fields and rich meadows. People who live in Maryland think no other portion of the world is its equal.

Lord Baltimore made wise laws. Among them was one which gave entire freedom of conscience to every colonist. No matter what his religion, he might enjoy it undisturbed. Baptist or Methodist, Quaker or "New Light," he could worship God as he pleased.

Grave old men in other colonies shook their heads doubtfully, and said it would never do. Religion would get terribly mixed, and children would grow up not knowing what to believe. But it did do. Religion was not mixed, and no more religious children ever grew up.

As soon as it became known that Maryland law gave freedom of conscience, settlers began to come from all the world, and good, conscientious settlers, too. Episcopalians came from Virginia, and Puritans from New England, and Huguenots from Europe, and Swedes from Delaware, and Dutch from New York.

Roger Williams gave freedom of conscience to Rhode Islanders in 1636. Lord Baltimore gave freedom of conscience to the Marylanders in 1634. Maryland was the first community in the whole world in which entire freedom of conscience was ever given to every citizen.

Podcast #98 Daily Sampler—Sir Henry Vane

I'm sure you are as disheartened as I am at the level of corruption in leadership in high places, not only in America but around the world. It's hard to know who to trust anymore and it seems as though too many of our leaders are more interested in protecting their own interests than watching out for ours.

So let me counter that unsavory world and introduce you to three great souls over the next three podcasts who acted from a place of love and were willing to sacrifice their own personal comfort and even reputation in caring for the souls of others.

Today we visit one of those forgotten names in history, Sir Henry Vane, or Harry as he is called in the sampler I'm about to read to you. He was instrumental in the establishment of Harvard University, but his most valuable contribution was in moving forward our right to worship according to the dictates of our own conscience.

I first heard his name in the book I included in Volume 3 of the Freedom Series, *Stories of Early American History*. Technically, it's a Month 3 book because month three is where we see the push towards independence and this particular book reviews the events leading up to that time, including the settling of the 13 colonies. But I hope you can see by now there is a lot of overlap in our study and there is no need to be rigid as to what you read when.

The book I am referring to was written by Rebecca M'Conkey in 1874 and it's called *True Stories of the American Fathers, for the Girls and Boys all over the Land*.[23] She wrote it in the form of a beloved aunt gathering her nieces and nephews together each night for a story time where she unfolds the story of America to them.

At the place I will begin reading for today's daily sampler, she has already covered the explorers and has just told the story of the Pilgrims in Plymouth colony who have made it through that first tragic winter. We'll pick up the story here:

> They sent back words of cheer to their friends in England, who were still persecuted for conscience' sake, and advised them to follow them to the wilderness, for it was surely God's hand that had led them thither, and he would raise up a great nation to his honor and praise. The oppressed people heard and received it as a call from God, and they came. Ship after ship discharged on the shores of Massachusetts its precious freight of noble souls. Settlements sprang up as if by magic all through the wilderness. Far into the interior, and down the beautiful valley of the Connecticut River, the immigrant pushed their way, driving their flocks before them, their wives and little ones with them. The Indians were friendly to the early settlers, sold them lands, and made treaties of peace with them. They flourished and prospered. Comfortable dwelling-houses were built, then the churches, and soon the school-houses followed. In a few years thousands of English Dissenters had passed over the sea and made their homes in the Western

World. Many of them were people of noble birth, great intelligence, and ample wealth.

With this tide of population that poured into the flourishing New England settlements, many came who were not of their faith. This was a grief to the early Puritans, because they had forsaken all to possess this little corner of the earth where they could be safe from disputes and controversies; but they expected too much, for it is impossible for even good people to see eye to eye. The Puritans, we are sorry to record it, persecuted some who came among them; then they banished them from the colony, and it would have been better if they had remained away or gone to some other part of America, seeing there was abundance of room for all, but they would not. They came back and troubled them so much that at last the sturdy old Puritan magistrates had several of them hung as examples, declaring, however, that "we desired their lives absent rather than their deaths present."

It is grief to me to tell you this, children, but candor compels me. Perfection we cannot find in any thing human; it belongs not to man nor to any of his works. Our virtues and our religion are all tainted with human infirmity. The enemies of the Puritans are fond of charging them with intolerance and persecutions, but it ought to be remembered that the spirit of persecution was the spirit of that age. We must judge the past by its own light, not by ours in this better day. All sects and civil authorities persecuted those who differed from them, and the Puritans did less of it than any other people, except the Quakers. Besides, many of the Puritans themselves had risen above these narrow views, and were true followers of the great and good John Robinson, who led them out of England into Holland, but was too old and feeble to come with them to America. When they embarked on the 'Mayflower' he gave them a sublime charge: that they should not think they possessed the whole truth and had nothing more to learn. He told them the Lord had 'more truth yet to break forth out of his holy word,' and they must be willing to receive it with all humility. Among his followers were two young ministers of holy lives and 'precious gifts,' Roger Williams and Hooker, who went through the colonies preaching these sublime and glorious doctrines and winning many to their views. They declared it a sin to persecute any man for any religious opinion, and that truth would always be strong enough to overcome error without the aid of physical force.

Puritanism may lift its head without fear, graced with such names as Roger Williams, Winthrop, Hooker, and a host of others more than I have time to mention, though I must tell you of one, as noble a hero as ever sealed his truth with his blood. I mean the good Sir Harry Vane. He had been at one time governor of Massachusetts, but returned to England to plead the cause of the Puritans who were still persecuted there, and not alone their cause, but that of all who were wronged for religious opinions, whether it were Catholic, Puritan, Presbyterian, or Quaker. He was a man of great gifts and eloquence, and had such weight with the people that his enemies at last resolved to take his life. As you study history you will find, children, that those who are in error, when they find themselves out-argued and about to lose their cause, always resort to brute force. If they cannot kill the truth, they will try to kill the man who utters it. King Charles was persuaded that he ought to bring him to the block. But Sir Harry Vane went to the scaffold as calmly as he would have gone to his bed. The people followed him in throngs, weeping and blessing him who had been the friend of his race; not of his party, nor his sect, nor his class only, but of all mankind. He would have spoken to the poor weeping people, but his enemies would not let him, for they were afraid of the great and precious truths that fell from his lips, so they drowned his voice with the sound of their trumpets. But they could not take the glory and beauty out of his countenance, and the people "saw his face as it had been the face of an angel." He kissed and embraced his dear little children, and bade them not be troubled, for God would be a father to them. Thus he died with his soul full of peace, and in strong faith that though he died the truth would live. It does live; the liberties we enjoy in our dear country this day are the fruits of that truth. So we will bless and honor our Pilgrim Fathers for all they suffered and wrought for us.

When I read that, I thought this is someone I want to spend more time with. So I've read several accounts of his life. But nothing is as compelling as his own words. It was mentioned that he wrote a speech to be delivered at his execution, but his voice was drowned out by trumpets. Knowing that it was unlikely that he would be allowed to deliver it, he delivered copies of it to several trusted friends beforehand, thereby preserving the words for us.

Let me share with you parts of that speech, by which you can catch a glimpse of his heart and soul.

> The work which I am at this time called unto, in this place, is to Die, and receive a Discharge, once for all, out of Prison; to do that, which is but once to be done; the doing or not doing of which well, and as becomes a Christian, does much depend upon the life we have been taught of God to lead, before we come to this: They that live in the Faith, do also die in it: Faith is so far from leaving Christians in this hour, that the work of it breaks forth then into its greatest power; as if till then, it were not enough at freedom to do its office, that is, to look into the things that are unseen, with most steadfastness, certainty, and delight; which is the great Sweetener of Death, and Remover of its Sting.

Give me leave therefore in a very few words, to give you an account of my Life.

> I might tell you, I was born a Gentleman, had the education, temper and spirit of a Gentleman…being (in my youthful dayes) inclined to the vanities of the world…. But about the fourteenth or fifteenth year of my age, (which is about thirty four or five years since) God was pleased to lay the foundation or ground-work of Repentance in me, for the bringing me home to himeself, by his wonderful rich and free Grace, revealing his Son, in me, that by the knowledge of the only true God, and Jesus Christ whom he hath sent, I might (even whilst here in the body) be made partaker of Eternal Life, in the first-fruits of it.

When my Conscience was thus awakened, I found my former course to be disloyalty to

God, prophaneness, and a way of sin and death, which I did with tears and bitterness bewail, as I had cause to do. Since that foundation of Repentance laid in me, through Grace I have been kept steadfast, desiring to walk in all good Conscience towards God and towards men, according to the best light and understanding God gave me.

For this, I was willing to turn my back upon my Estate, expose myself to hazards in Foreign parts; yea, nothing seemed difficult to me, so I might preserve Faith and a good Conscience, which I prefer before all things; and do earnestly persuade all people rather to suffer the highest contradictions from me, than disobey God, by contradicting the light of their own Conscience.

In this, it is, I stand with so much comfort and boldness before you all this day, and upon this occasion; being assured, that I shall at last sit down in Glory with Christ, at his right hand. I stand here this day, to resign up my Spirit into the hands of that God that gave it to me. Death is but a little word, but 'tis a great work to die, it is to be but once done....

In all respects, wherein I have been concerned and engaged as to the Publick, my design hath been to accomplish Good things for these Nations. Then (lifting up his eyes, and spreading his hands) he said, I do here appeal to the great God of Heaven, and all this Assembly, or any other persons, to shew wherein I have defiled my hands with any mans Blood or Estate, or that I have sought myself in any public capacity or place I have been in.

For my Life, Estate and all, is not so dear to me as my Service to God, to his Cause, to the Kingdom of Christ, and the future welfare of my Country.... For if any man seek a proof of Christ in me, let him read it in his action of my Death, which will not cease to speak when I am gone...as my last words, leave this with you:

That as the present storm we now lie under, and the dark Clouds that yet hand over the Reformed Churches of Christ, (which are coming thicker and thicker for a season) were not unforeseen by me for many years passed: So the coming of Christ in these Clouds, in order to a speedy and sudden revival of his Cause, and spreading his Kingdom over the face of the whole Earth, is most clear to the eye of my Faith, even that Faith in which I die, whereby the Kingdoms of this world shall become the Kingdom of our Lord, and of his Christ, Amen. Even so, come, Lord Jesus.

Eyewitnesses to the event bore witness to his soul full of peace and in strong faith to the end. And it's to the likes of Henry Vane we owe our gratitude for our freedom to worship as we desire.

Podcast #99 William Penn

I am constantly amazed at all that was left out of my history lessons in school. While the name 'William Penn' is familiar, I knew him only as the colonizer of Pennsylvania. The part I didn't learn is that he is a wonderful example of a leader who governed by love and by faith.

As Kieran Doherty says in the introduction to his biography of Penn, "There are a few men and women throughout history who have led their lives based upon the strength of their convictions. William Penn is an extraordinary example of such a person. Early in his life William had a religious experience which convinced him of two things: first, that there was a God, and second, that God had plans for him."

With that firm knowledge in his heart, nothing could detract him from staying the course, whether it meant imprisonment, disinheritance, or ridicule. He fought for increased freedom of thought and many of the ideas he wrote about—innovative ideas—"became the foundation for the documents that preserve freedom and justice and tolerance of differences in the United States today."

Today's sample comes from the same book I shared part of Sir Henry Vane's story from—Rebecca M'Conkey's *True Stories of the American Fathers*.[24] I think you'll agree that you'll want William Penn to hang around your family for awhile, too.

"Penn was of noble birth, the son of a brave officer in the English navy, who had a great name at court for his gallant services to his country. William was his only son, and while he was yet at college, only seventeen years old, he heard one of these wandering Quaker preachers. His heart was stirred within him. He could never pray 'by the book' afterward. This was the rule at the college, so they fined him, and as he still refused, saying that God had taught him 'a more excellent way,' they expelled him. This was a heavy trial to the young ambitious student. But his trials were worse when he reached home, for his father was so enraged to think that his only son, the son of a noble house, would disgrace himself by going with such low people as the Quakers, that he whipped him and turned him from his door, thinking by this prompt treatment to bring him to his senses. His mother interceded for him, and his father gave him money, and sent him to travel in Europe, to divert his mind from his foolishness. Penn was a serious, observing traveler. While in France he studied the history of the people called Huguenots — I shall tell you more about them another time — and having gathered much wisdom by his travels, he returned to England. He is described, at this time; as most engaging and pleasing in manner and appearance, skillful in speech and debate, every way calculated to adorn the court of the king, and with every prospect of advancement, because of the high favor in which his father was held. But, alas! for this father's ambitious plans for his gifted son. Penn found his heart still drawn to that simple people called Quakers, and, while listening to one of them explaining 'the faith that overcometh the world' he embraced the doctrine, received the faith in his own heart, and, like Moses of old, refused the treasures of the king's court, choosing rather to suffer affliction with God's people. Thus beautifully he tells us of it: 'Into that path God in his everlasting kindness guided my feet in the flower of my youth, when about two and twenty years of age.'

"He was mocked and scorned by his family and friends, and it was told as a good joke that William Penn had turned Quaker, and his father had driven him without a penny from his door. You see, children, what Penn's principles cost him. His was no easy virtue. He could not possibly have borne all this except by that faith that overcomes the world and all that it contains. He was very brave. He went at once to court with his hat on to plead with the king and his ministers to allow the English people freedom of conscience, so that they might worship God as they saw best, and prayed him to let the Quakers out of the stocks and prisons where hundreds of them were now confined. They laughed at him, and handed him over to my Lord Bishop of London, and he sent him to the Tower, a prison where they put criminals of high rank. King Charles, however, did not like Penn to be shut up in the Tower, because of his brave father who had done such service to his country, and he sent another bishop to persuade Penn to give up his strange doctrines, and come out and behave like other young English noblemen. Penn sent word back to the king that the Tower was the worst argument in the world, and he continued from his prison to proclaim his principles, and send out light and truth from its dark recesses. After weary months the king granted his release.

"Just at this time his father died, and left him all his estate. He was of a brave, generous nature, regretted his treatment of his only son, and died in peace with him. Penn made good use of his fortune. He fed many poor children whose parents were in the prisons and dungeons all over England for being true to their own consciences. He devoted all his time, talents, and influence to obtain from parliament some laws to protect the English people in the enjoyment of their religious liberty; but it was in vain. Despairing of any better fate for his poor persecuted brethren in the land of their birth, he cast his eyes over the waters and longed to build a quiet habitation for them in the wilderness. The good tidings of the prosperity and happiness of the Pilgrim settlements in their forest homes had traveled back to England, and Penn resolved now to lead his people thither. You know I told you that Penn's father had been a great favorite at court with the king and the royal family. He was one of the bravest officers in the British navy, and for his services to his country during the Dutch war he received a claim upon his government of sixteen thousand pounds. How much is that in our currency, Albert?" "About eighty thousand dollars, aunty." "Well, this King Charles was one of the greatest spendthrifts that ever lived, and of course was always in debt. Penn offered to take the amount of this claim in lands in America. He had much opposition from many lords and bishops, who could not endure to think of a Quaker colony being left in peace even three thousand miles away from them. Yet Penn had a great many influential friends at court, and finally the king, rather than pay the money, granted him a large tract of land on the western bank of the Delaware River, and named it Pennsylvania, or Penn's

Woods. There were already some Dutch and Swedes living within the limits of this territory, and Penn immediately sent an agent over to tell them that he was coming out to live among them, to protect them and to do them good. He also wrote a letter to the sons of the forest, the Indians, telling them that they and he had the same Father, even the great God who made heaven and earth and all that it contains; that therefore they and he were brothers, and ought to love one another, and live in peace and good-will. His will was to be law throughout the colony, and he could have done much wrong to the people, and made himself rich by oppressing them, if he had been a selfish man; but fortunately he had but one wish, and that was that these people should be virtuous and happy. Then Penn made all his arrangements to lead out his colony to their new home. He left his beautiful and loving wife with his sweet children in England, that the children might be educated, admonishing her to 'live sparingly till my debts be paid; 'for he had spent so much money helping the poor people that his own family were poor, and were obliged to live very frugally. All being ready, the Quaker colony embarked for America, and on the 27th of October, 1682, William Penn landed at Newcastle, Delaware.

"The people crowded to the landing to welcome the 'Quaker king,' for thus he was called, and indeed his power was absolute over the territory he now owned. He spoke kindly to them, exhorted them to industry and sobriety, and promised them his friendly offices to do them all the good in his power. With a few friends he left Newcastle in an open boat, and journeyed up the Delaware, in the soft, mellow November days, to the beautiful banks fringed with trees, on which the city of Philadelphia was soon to be laid out. Here he met the chiefs of the various Indian tribes. They assembled beneath a great elm-tree, and Penn told them that the English and the Indians were to obey the same laws, both were to be equally protected in their pursuits and possessions, and if any difficulty arose it should be settled by an equal number of English and Indians. 'We meet/ said he, 'on the broad pathway of good faith and good will. No advantage shall be taken on either side, but all shall be openness and love. I will not call you children, for parents sometimes chide their children too severely. Nor brothers only; for brothers differ. The friendship between me and you I will not compare to a chain, for that the rains might rust or the falling tree might break. We are the same as if one man's body were to be divided into two parts; we are all one flesh and blood.' This treaty of peace and friendship was made under the open sky, by the side of the Delaware, with the sun and the river and the forest for witnesses. Penn came without arms; he declared his purpose to abstain from violence. He had no message but peace; and not a drop of Quaker blood was ever shed by an Indian. Here, on a neck of land between the Schuylkill and the Delaware, William Penn laid, at Philadelphia, the city of refuge, the mansion of freedom, the home of humanity. In after years 'Pennsylvania bound the northern and southern colonies in bonds stronger than chains; Philadelphia was the birthplace of American Independence, and the pledge of Union.'

"For several years Penn remained with his colony, directing and ruling for its best interests, and his heart was gladdened with the sight of its prosperity and happiness.

But he longed to sit once more at his own fireside, and look upon the dear home faces he had left. Besides, his colony was so well established, and governed by laws so mild and good, that the people had nothing to do but to be industrious, virtuous, and happy. Penn thought of the hundreds of English Quakers that still languished in dungeons and prisons. He felt that he must go back to England and do something for them. So he did; he labored day and night, and was instrumental in obtaining the release of not less than twelve hundred Friends. But he pleaded not only for the Quakers, for his sympathies were large enough to take in all mankind; and he, like Sir Harry Vane, claimed liberty of conscience for all men. He continued to watch over his American colony, sending out emigrants, and advancing its interests in every way. In extreme old age he writes to them as a father to his children, 'If the people want of me any thing that would make them happier, I should readily grant it.' He left the people of Pennsylvania free to alter their laws as they should think best, but the form of government devised by Penn's love and wisdom was so nearly perfect, that to this day its fundamental principles remain. These are some of the words of his farewell to his people: ' My love and my life are to you and with you, and no water can quench it nor distance bring it to an end. I have been with you, cared over you, and served you with unfeigned love; and you are beloved of me and dear to me beyond utterance. You are come to a quiet land; liberty and authority are in your hands. Rule for Him under whom the princes of this world will one day esteem it an honor to govern in their places. And thou, Philadelphia, the virgin settlement of this province, my soul prays to God for thee, that thou mayest stand in the day of trial, and that thy children may be blessed. Dear friends, my love salutes you all'

Podcast #100 James Oglethorpe and the Settling of Georgia

I hope you have been inspired by the leadership examples of Henry Vane and William Penn whose unselfishness, love and faith played such a vital role in the planting of religious freedom enjoyed by millions of people all over the world today; a freedom that we are, once again, at serious risk of losing if we are not vigilant.

Today we touch upon the work of James Oglethorpe, the last of the trio of leaders I chose to spotlight. The sample story is taken from a 1905 text called *Georgia History Stories* by Joseph Harris Chappell,[25] found in the High School section of the Colonies.

We'll pick up the story where it leads into how and why he colonized Georgia.

> When the Turkish war was over, [Oglethorpe] returned to England and settled down to ways of peace. His father and elder brothers died, and he inherited the family estates. He was now a very rich man, but he lived a simple and sober life. He was elected to Parliament and served as a member for many years. While he was in Parliament, an event occurred that turned his attention toward America and caused him to become the founder of Georgia. This is how it happened:

> There was a cruel law in England at that time by which a person in debt might be thrown into prison by his creditors and kept there until his debts were somehow paid. Many poor, unfortunate people, innocent of any crime, languished in these debtors' prisons. Oglethorpe had a dear friend, a Mr. Robert Castell, who was a scholar and an artist. He wrote a fine book on architecture, which he illustrated with splendid pictures drawn by his own hand. He was so much taken up with writing the book that he neglected his business affairs, and when the book was published instead of making money for him it brought him heavily in debt, and he was condemned to be cast into the debtors' prison.

> In the prison to which he was assigned, smallpox was at that time raging, and he had never had the disease. He begged the prison keeper, a heartless wretch by the name of Bambridge, to let him lie in the common jail until the prison should be freed of smallpox or until his friends could arrange to pay his debts for him, which he was sure would be done in the course of a few months. Bambridge agreed to do so if Castell would pay him down in cash a certain sum of money as a bribe, but poor Castell had not the money, so he was thrown into the smallpox-infested prison, where he soon contracted the disease; and after a few days' suffering he died an awful death, leaving his wife and little children poverty stricken and helpless.

> When Oglethorpe heard of this outrage his blood boiled with indignation. He at once introduced a bill in Parliament to have a committee appointed to examine the prisons of England and bring about a reform in their management. The bill was passed, Oglethorpe was made Chairman of the Committee, and, with the other members, he

spent several months visiting the prisons. He found in them practices of shocking cruelty, all of which were immediately abolished.

If Oglethorpe had done nothing more than bring about this reform, he would deserve the lasting gratitude of humanity, but he did not stop at this. While visiting the prisons his sympathies were deeply aroused for the poor debtors whom he found languishing behind iron bars, though innocent of any crime. He determined to try to do something to help them out of their sad condition.

By his earnest appeals he got Parliament to pass a law by which they might be set free, provided they would agree to go to America and establish there for England a new colony on a broad strip of unsettled country already claimed by her, south of the Savannah River. It lay next to Florida, which then belonged to Spain and had been colonized by her. The Spaniards were at that time one of the most powerful and warlike nations in the world, and in their hearts they were very hostile to the English, although not openly at war with them. The Spanish soldiers were bold, skillful, and heartless; so much so that some one said of them, "A Spanish soldier is a machine of steel with the devil inside of it!"

Fortunately for Oglethorpe's enterprise, King George II of England was anxious to plant colonies in his unoccupied possessions south of the Savannah River as a protection for South Carolina against the bold and unscrupulous Spaniards of Florida. So he gladly granted to Oglethorpe "for the use of debtors and other poor persons" all the country between Savanah and the Altamaha Rivers, and as far westward as they might choose to go.

This strip of country was named Georgia in honor of King George. A Board of Trustees, consisting of thirty-six members, among whom were some of the most distinguished men of England, was appointed by the King to have entire charge of planting, establishing, and governing the new colony.

They were to serve without pay or compensation of any sort. It must be purely a labor of love with them. The good and great Lord Perceval was president of the Board, and Oglethorpe was one of the members. The Trustees set about raising money to pay the cost of establishing the colony, for the poor people who were to go were not able to pay any part of their own expenses....

At one of the meetings of the Trustees it was suggested that some member of the Board, a man of education and ability, should go over to America with the first colonists as their Governor and live in Georgia with them until they were well and thoroughly established. Oglethorpe nobly volunteered to go, and the Trustees were delighted. In undertaking this trying service, Oglethorpe would have to give up his luxurious home, the pleasures of refined society, and the splendid public career that was fast opening to him in England and would have to endure untold hardships, privations, and dangers; and from it all he had nothing, in a worldly sense, to gain for himself. The Trustees had chosen as the official seal of the Board a group of silk worms spinning their cocoons and, written underneath, the noble motto, *"non sibi sed aliis!"* "Not for themselves but for others!" He was at this time forty-three years old and was yet unmarried....

When it was known that the great and good Oglethorpe himself would accompany the expedition, hundreds and hundreds of poor people, debtors and others, were anxious to go, but only a few could be taken. Out of the hundreds of applicants, the Trustees carefully selected forty strong, healthy men of good morals and with small families. All together, men, women and children, the party consisted of one hundred and twenty souls. Many poor wretches who begged to go had to be turned away with tears in their eyes and bitter disappointment in their hearts.

I'm sorry to tell you the story doesn't have a happy ending, but I'll let you discover the "rest of the story" for yourself after I paint this little scene and draw out a couple of lessons:

On the afternoon of February 12, 1733, they landed at the high bluff on the Savannah River. By sunset, they had spread under the tall pine trees four big, white tents; and in these the whole colony, one hundred and twenty souls men, women and children were stored away as snug as a bug in a rug. Thus they spent their first night on Georgia soil. Oglethorpe occupied by himself a little tent pitched under a group of three tall pine trees.

Early the next morning, the colonists were assembled in front of Oglethorpe's tent for prayers.... After prayers Oglethorpe gave them a kind, fatherly talk and some good advice; and then they went about their work....

For more than a year Oglethorpe continued to live in his little tent under the three great pine trees overlooking the river, while he directed the work of the colonists, all of whose hardships and privations he shared. He laid off in the great forest the plan of the town that was to be builded there. That plan is perfectly preserved in the city of Savannah today.

Of special interest to me was, again as we have seen with William Penn and William Bradford, the peaceful relationship they had with the Native Americans. The story being told today is that the White Man worked nothing but death and destruction among the Indians. It's the danger of the single story again; there were white men who were savage and Indians who were peaceful. But there were also white men who were peaceful and Indians who were savage.

But in several of these early stories, the white man and Native lived peacefully side by side. One of Oglethorpe's first order of business was to seek out 90-year-old chief, Tomo-chi-chi. Let me share that part of the story:

On reaching the village Oglethorpe called for Tomo-chi-chi and he stepped forth like a king. He was not surprised to see the white men. He had often seen white people before.... Oglethorpe told Tomo-chi-chi that he wished to settle with his colony in the woods near by, but that they would not interfere in any way with the Yamacraws; that they would do no harm but only good to the Indians.... He hoped they might always be good friends and live as peaceful neighbors. Oglethorpe's noble countenance, kind manner, and fine promises completely won old Tomo-chi-chi's heart, and he said: "There is plenty of room here for both red men and white men. Bring your people on to our woods. As soon as they get settled, we will call to welcome them."

But Tomo-chi-chi's tribe wasn't the only one occupying the area and you'll want to read about the coming together of all these tribes in establishing peace. Picture 56 tribal leaders dressed in full Native garb—not one of them is under 6 feet tall—gathered in one of Savannah's largest homes. It's an inspiring sight.

Over and over, I see that where there was mutual respect and tolerance, there was peace. Sadly, that wasn't always the case, but here is one example to hold up to the light.

Also of interest to me was that Tomo-chi-chi wanted to be taught about the Christian religion. When Oglethorpe returned to England for a short time, he brought back a young clergyman who served as his secretary for a time; a name you may recognize—John Wesley. Tomo-chi-chi was thrilled and said: "I am glad you have come to speak the great word to us. I will do my best to get my people to listen to you as well. But we don't want to be made Christians as the Spaniards make them. They put water on an Indian's head and say, You are a Christian, but we want you first to explain the great word to us so that we can understand it, then we will be baptized and will be real Christians."

But John Wesley, though a great and good man, was an utter failure as a missionary to these Native Americans. He lacked the power of winning their hearts and of teaching "the great word" in the simple way they needed. He explained the Christian religion to them in such a learned way that the poor Indians couldn't understand him.

Tomo-chi-chi had deep religious instincts, but after awhile lost all interest in the Christian religion. The reason came out one day when he was asked, "Tomo-chi-chi, why don't you become a Christian?" With flashing eye and scorn in his voice, the old man replied, "The people at Savannah are Christians, the people at Frederica are Christians, but they are no good; they get drunk, they tell lies, they fight, they beat weak people, they cheat poor Indians…. Me no Christian."

Whoa. There's a lot of lessons in there for instilling faith in our own children, isn't there?

Well, the story of the colony didn't end the way Oglethorpe had hoped, which you will find out. Two laws were instituted: no rum and no slavery, which made the people angry and disgruntled, even after all he had done for them in rescuing them from their prisons.

Here's the lesson I draw from that. We have become a people who are looking to our leaders to fix our problems. Here we have an example of exactly the kind of leader we would hope to have; one who is more interested in our welfare than our own; who labors out of love; who does all he can to make our lives better; who is honest and fair in all his dealings, actions and words.

But the fact was, he was dealing with a people who weren't used to taking care of themselves. And despite the best of his intentions, he couldn't overcome that fact.

While we ask which president is the best president our people can have, I say who are the best people a president can have? The children of Israel, like we in America, were given the great privilege of being self-governed, under God. It was when they demanded and expected a king to fight their battles that they were weakened and started down that slippery slope until they were divided, scattered and enslaved.

I wrote a little book while I was serving on the executive board of HomeMakers for America, now Moms for America, called *Restoring our Garden of Liberty*. I included a quote that has become a favorite of mine. It's from David Starr Jordan, the first president of Stanford University:

> If the experiment of government by the people is to be successful, it is you and such as you who must make it so. The future of the Republic must lie in the hands of the men and women of culture and intelligence, of self-control and of self-resource, capable of taking care of themselves and of helping others. If it falls NOT into such hands, the republic will have no future…. The problem of life is not to make life easier, but to make men stronger, so that no problem shall be beyond their solution…. The remedy for oppression is to bring in better men who cannot be oppressed.

So next time you want to throw your shoe through your computer or TV screen because of what you are seeing going on in the leadership of our country, remember the real corrective work is taking place in your homes and in your families as you raise that generation of "culture and intelligence, of self-control and self-resource, capable of taking care of themselves and of helping others…. The remedy for oppression is to bring in better men and women who cannot be oppressed."

And then if we, at the same time, raise leaders like Henry Vane, William Penn and James Oglethorpe, who labored for love, not personal gain, *Non sibi sed aliis*—Not for themselves but for others! What a beautiful world we will have!

That is the dream and the vision of The Well-Educated Heart and the stories like these that you plant in the hearts of your children will make that dream come true.

Podcast #101 Charles Morris and His Historical Tales

I plan on turning our attention to Spain for a few days, but before we do, I wanted to reaffirm why I spend so much time on history.

I don't view History as a subject to be studied and checked off the list. It is entirely possible to study it for years with little profit by looking only at the facts and the timeline. But when you study it "by heart," it reveals so much that is practical and inspirational.

For our sampler today, I want to read the introduction to a series of books I acquired and told you I would tell you more about them. They are called *Historical Tales* and were written by Charles Morris.

First, let me give you a little background on Charles Morris that I found on the Heritage History[26] site, which, by the way, I love. They wrote:

> Charles Morris was a prolific American writer of the late 19th century. After a brief career in academics, he began publishing a great number of books and articles under various pseudonyms, but his piece de resistance was his Historical Tales, a collection of romantic and entertaining stories from history, in fourteen volumes. [Although I've found sixteen; there may be more.]

> Although these tales are organized by civilization, and the stories occur in roughly chronological order, these books cannot be read as comprehensive histories, as he makes no particular attempt to tie them together, contenting himself to jump from one fascinating episode in history to another. For this reason, they are best read after one is already familiar with the basic outline of the history of a particular civilization.

> On the other hand, Morris is an outstanding writer, and he picks fascinating subjects for his stories. The stories are selected largely for their entertainment value, rather than purely for historical significance, so Morris treats his readers to a fascinating introduction to some compelling 'secondary' characters and events. He tells all of his stories in enough depth to make them truly entertaining, even when he is dealing with already well-known events. The Historical Tales are an entertaining treat, and though they are not recommended for introductory reading, they are a terrifically rewarding for intermediate or advanced readers of history.

I will add that Charles dedicated the series to "the memory of my father and mother, who, in my early childhood, instilled in me a taste for the study of great characters and events, which has done more to influence and mould my life than any other factor."

There it is the reason for the emphasis on the study of history as we do it here in the Well-Educated Heart. It has the potential to do "more to influence and mold" the lives of your children than any other factor.

Let me share now the beginning of the intro chapter to this series:[27]

John Wanamaker was once asked to finance an expedition to recover treasures which had lain for years in sunken frigates off the coast of the Bahamas. "Young man," he replied, "I know of a much better expedition than that right here. At your own feet lie treasures untold, and you can have them all by faithful study."

It is hardly necessary to emphasize the importance of education, for nowadays everyone agrees with Locke that "of all men we meet, nine out of ten are what they are, good or evil, useful or not, by their education."

But what is education? A few years at school and a little preparation for a chosen career? No! Man's education is never complete. Constant development is the first law of nature. Man is placed here to grow, and every cell of his mind must constantly absorb new power or he will be stunted. For, as Gladstone says, "The mind is but a barren soil—a soil which is soon exhausted, and will produce no crops unless it be continually fertilized and enriched."

It is the duty of every man to stand on the high plane for which he was created, and to do this he must take advantage of every opportunity to grow larger and broader. He must be ever filling his storehouse with useful knowledge to broaden his intellect and increase his ability. As Ex-President Harper of the University of Chicago said: "If there is one single necessity in life more vital than another it is the necessity for pressing forward intellectually from year to year. No greater sin can be committed than that of failing to obtain the highest degree of cultivation possible. The world divides itself into two classes—those who read at home, thus continuing to rise higher and higher; and those who do not read at home, and for this reason sink lower and lower in the grade of human life."

Yes, good literature constitutes the university in which everyone who wants a full-rounded education can and must get it. All distinguished men have been given to the habit of constant reading, and it utterly impossible to arrive at any degree of distinction without this habit. "The great instrument of mental culture," says Hugh Black, "is reading. A man who is ignorant of what others before him have thought and said and done, will turn down many a blind alley. In good literature we find the record of other people's experiences, thoughts and feelings, which widen our vision, extend our limited range of life, correct our own conclusions, and give us vast data for our thinking. We would indeed be poorly equipped for life if all we gained from good reading were taken away from us."

And of all reading, that along historical lines is the most important, for every person feels the need of being correctly informed regarding the past. History is being made so rapidly nowadays that it is impossible to keep pace with current events, or understand newspaper and magazine articles, or keep up one's end in ordinary conversations without a knowledge of the world's past history and the causes leading up to the present conditions.

No other kind of reading furnishes such positive benefit, for history is the basis of all knowledge. As Hamilton Wright Mabie says: "History is the background against the entire life of today, and nothing can be understood unless it is studied with this background in full view. The study of history is, therefore, a part of every other study— a kind of common ground on which philosophy, theology, politics, economy, art, literature and industry meet, and where alone they reveal their common origin in the needs, the capacities, and the conditions of the human soul."

And right along this same line Abraham Lincoln said: "History is the most valuable teacher of human nature, for it deals with the actual motives and actions of real men and women. All other forms of literature are of secondary importance. The fact is that nearly all the great masterpieces in other fields of literature are founded on the great events of history. And it is impossible to understand the principal works of literature and art unless one knows the true accounts of the historic events upon which such works are based."

Historical knowledge is indispensable to anyone who would hold a place in intellectual society. It is the corner-stone of culture, and without it a person can make no pretense to education. In every community there are persons who stand head and shoulders above their associates. If they read a masterpiece of literature they understand it better than others. If they listen to a lecture they get more good out of it than others who pay just as much for their seats. If they see a painting, or a piece of statuary, or some work of art, they enjoy and appreciate it, while others pass it by with a glance. What is the secret of their superiority? There is no magic about it. These persons simply have a good general knowledge of history, for the famous events and characters of history are what have inspired our literature and art, and there is hardly a lecture worth hearing, or an able sermon delivered, that is not full of historical allusions.

A person cannot get enjoyment from his travels unless he is "up" in history, because he knows nothing of the heroes of the past—the warriors, the scholars, the teachers, the reformers, the martyrs—of the victories they have achieved and the work they have accomplished in raising the world from savagery to civilization. He knows nothing of the various stages of the world's progress, the famous ruins, the historic buildings, the ancient landmarks, the renowned battlefields that make every country he visits an open book, every page of which is as interesting as a romance to the reader of history.

Historical knowledge is of no less importance in the practical affairs of life. It is a mere truism to say that no one may hope for success in any calling today without a knowledge of human nature. No one can expect to become a successful preacher, teacher, doctor, lawyer, editor or business man, who does not have a keen appreciation of the motives that govern men in the ordinary affairs of life. Knowledge in this domain is power and influence, while ignorance is weakness and inefficiency. For history is a study of humanity, not in an ideal condition, but as it has actually existed and must be dealt with, and familiarity with it gives one the power to be a leader of men rather than a mere follower.

Yes, and it is a patriotic duty which every man owes his country to be well versed in history. The state is but a collection of individuals, and the only way to better it is to better the individuals composing it. We must first know history before we can make history. A man cannot vote wisely and be a valuable citizen without a conception of what other men have stood and striven for, and what it has meant for them to win or lose.

And if this is necessary for the man of today, how much more necessary it is for him to bring up his children under the noblest influences. How important that those who are to wield the power and direct the affairs of the next generation shall be acquainted with the experiences of the generations that have gone before. The boys of today will fill the important places of tomorrow. Every year thousands of young men reach the age when they are allowed to share in the government of our nation, and they must be trained for the responsibilities that will come to them. They may be able to tell what year Columbus landed—they may be regular calendars so far as dates are concerned—but that amounts to little. What they need is the practical side of history—the part that will do them good through life. They need an insight into the lives of those heroes and patriots of other ages whose courage, strict devotion to duty, and heroic self-sacrifice represented the highest ideals and furnish lessons which will make more patriotic citizens, and consequently a better nation.

Yes, history is truly "the chiefest study among human studies, which enriches and illumines all the rest." It introduces us to the companionship of heroes who won the world's victories, statemen who made its laws, reformers who swept aside its evils, and martyrs who gave their blood to baptize its liberties. And to be associated with these great men and women through the pages of history is to be great ourselves.

But the mere reading along historical lines is not enough. To get the most out of what we read a definite plan must be followed. "You might read all the books in the British Museum, if you could live long enough" says Ruskin, "and still remain an entirely illiterate, uneducated person. But if you read ten pages of a good book in the right way you are forevermore, in some measure, and educated person."

It is not the amount of food we eat, but the amount we digest, that upbuilds our physical body; and, similarly, it is not the amount we read, but the amount we assimilate, that increases the capacity of our mental storehouse. "The most profitable reading," said Samuel Smiles, "is that which is conducted with a definite aim and object. By thoroughly mastering any given branch of knowledge we render it available for use at any moment…"

Food undigested weakens the organs of the body, and, in the same way, reading without thought or purpose is worse than wasting time—worse than the ignorance which comes from reading nothing—for it causes us to form desultory habits which are fatal to continuity of thought, and even have a detrimental effect upon our entire lives, making us unsystematic and careless.

Gladstone reminds us that the man with a method accomplishes more in a week than the hard-working sloven will accomplish in a month, and it is the duty of every person to adopt a definite course of reading that he may get the greatest benefit out of what he reads. For wisdom is not mere knowledge. It is the result of systematic reading by which the facts gained become a part of one's very being.

Stories like those found in *Historical Tales* serve to awaken interest in the hearts of your children to want to know more.

I know that many of you have very young children who are probably not old enough for many of the things I'm talking about in these podcasts, but I share these stories with you because I know there is a giant gap in most of us where the history of the world is concerned and I am trying to fill in that gap as fast as I can. You are to act as their guide through history, but how can you be a guide if you are unfamiliar with the territory? While there are many details to fill in on your own, I hope these podcasts are beginning to awaken interests in people and events that, at the right time, you can use to awaken an interest in your children.

You'll find Charles Morris' *Historical Tales* in the High School sections under History, sorted by country.

Podcast #102 The Alhambra

One of the big reasons I enjoy studying the stories of each nation individually rather than studying world history chronologically is because I pick up lessons I don't see otherwise. It's like our world is made up of many different families and each family, when studied individually, has a story to tell with something to teach us. Some families are well-governed and have beautiful lessons to share while other families are severely dysfunctional, but we learn from them as well.

I'm afraid I have to place Spain in the dysfunctional lot. Not that they didn't have their moment to shine or that they haven't made wonderful gifts and contributions to our world. Because they have! But they also became, for a time, one of the most hated nations in the world. Over the next few podcasts, I'm going to share some of the takeaways I am gleaning from their history lessons that can be applied even to what you are doing in the classrooms of your homes. We'll take a look again at what happens when you use force and compulsion, even with the best of intentions vs. allowing freedom of thought and tolerating individual differences. We also see what happens to a people when gold—the search for El Dorado and material comforts— becomes their god and the drive for their existence. How do we compare as a people who have made salary potential the highest aim of our education system and the measurement of our success? Where might that lead us? Is there another way? Their greed led them to commit atrocities and endure hardships that are nearly impossible for our modern minds to comprehend. But I see another lesson from it—God's ability to always raise beauty from the ashes of our human frailties.

Let's first stop by and visit the Alhambra. Alhambra, to me, was a city in Southern California not far from where I grew up. I certainly didn't learn about it in school. I vaguely remember hearing something about driving the Moors out of Spain, but I had no idea who they were. I assumed they were the bad guys and Queen Isabella and King Ferdinand were the good guys.

It was while I was searching for books about Christopher Columbus that I ran across Washington Irving's *Life and Voyages of Christopher Columbus* and learned that he went to Spain to do research for the book. And while he was in Spain, he was introduced to the Alhambra that captured his heart and his imagination. Alhambra was a beautiful palace in Granada built by the Moors, who were Muslim, and the last stronghold surrendered under the relentless pressures of Queen Isabella and King Ferdinand. It was their victory over the last of the Moors that allowed them to finally hear the cause of the Genoese sailor who had been following them from battle ground to battle ground for years. Columbus sailed the same year the Alhambra was surrendered. Because of Washington Irving's celebrity access, he was given the privilege of staying there for some time and he soon took up the cause of preserving the grandeur and enchantment of this beautiful palace through his writings which became *The Tales of Alhambra*.

Let me just read you a section from Charles Morris' *Historical Tales*[28] for a visual of this magnificent palace and refuge:

The rulers of France, England and Germany lived in rude buildings without chimneys or windows, with a hole in the roof for the smoke to escape, at a time when the royal halls of Arabian Spain were visions of grace and beauty. The residences of the Arabs had marble balconies overhanging orange-gardens; their floors and walls were frequently of rich and graceful mosaic; fountains gushed in their courts, quicksilver often taking the place of water, and falling in a glistening spray. In summer, cool air was drawn into the apartments through ventilating towers; in winter, warm and perfumed air was discharged through hidden passages. From the ceilings, corniced with fretted gold, great chandeliers hung. Here were clusters of frail marble columns…. The furniture was of sandal- or citron-wood, richly inlaid with gold, silver, or precious minerals. Tapestry hid the walls, Persian carpets covered the floors, pillows and couches of elegant forms were spread about the rooms. Great care was given to bathing and personal cleanliness at a time when such a thought had not dawned upon Christian Europe. Their pleasure-gardens were of unequalled beauty, and were rich with flowers and fruits. In short, in this brief space it is impossible to give more than a bare outline of the marvellous luxury which surrounded this people, recently come from the deserts of Arabia, at a time when the remainder of Europe was plunged into the rudest barbarism.

Much might be said of their libraries, their universities, their scholars and scientists, and the magnificence of their architecture, of which abundant examples still remain in the cities of Spain, the Alhambra of Granada, the palace which Boabdil so reluctantly left, being almost without an equal for lightness, grace and architectural beauty in the cities of the world.

Why did I not hear one word of this in all my years of school? That's a conversation for another day.

I have posted a school edition of *Tales of Alhambra* written by Josephine Brower in the Elementary Imaginative Section of Spain. For today's Sampler, I'd like to share the introduction to that book that will also serve as a brief introduction to the history of Spain. And then you might want to read some of the *Tales of Alhambra* found in this school edition. I particularly liked the Legend of Prince Ahmed al Kamel, a story of a Moorish prince, a Muslim—whose father locks him in a tower so he won't be exposed to anything contrary to what he wants him to see. The same happens to a beautiful Christian princess in a land far away. But look what happens when love leads the way.

And I think you'll know why I liked this little passage of the story:

[After years of careful academic tutelage, The Prince] completely abandoned his studies and took to strolling about the gardens, and musing about the side of the fountains. He had been taught a little music among his various accomplishments. It now endured a great part of his time, and a turn for poetry became apparent. The sage took the alarm, and endeavored to work these idle humours out of him by a severe course of algebra: but the prince turned from it from distaste.

"I cannot endure algebra," says he. "I want something that speaks more to the heart."

The sage shook his dry head at the words.

"Here is an end to philosophy," thought he. "The prince has discovered he has a heart."

I'll let you read for yourself what happens.

And by the way, as a side note, the daughter of the developer of the then new suburb of Los Angeles near where I grew up had just read Irving's book and suggested that her father name his development Alhambra. Which he did.

Now for the Introduction.[29]

> There is a promontory in the southwest corner of Europe which rises from the sea on one side and a once unknown ocean on the other, cliff above cliff, hill above hill, mountain above mountain. About its shores in Queen Dido's time prowled the high-beaked ships of Carthage hungry for trade. Curiously their wily captains scanned the mountain paths leading from inaccessible defiles down which, in order to traffic on the sea-beach, came tall, bold-featured Iberians. Having finished bargaining, the savages distrustfully turned away, remounted the stony trails, to melt into the mists that crowned their vast and gloomy tableland. What was it like up there, the Phoenician trader wondered?
>
> Years afterwards, when Carthaginian generals had crushed many a hardy and liberty-loving race, the Phoenicians wondered still more. For the taciturn Iberians silently withdrew from every attempt at conquest. Up within those melancholy mountains, nobody knew how, a race of men lived who could not be enslaved.
>
> One thing the old-world empires did know, however. Out of that unknown interior four great rivers wore their way westward into the Atlantic, and, as they fell toward the beach, they washed down gold. And it was the rumour of this gold that called those sailing kites of wealth, Carthage, Greece, Rome, the Goths, who make the first chapters of Spanish history. Each of these nations, in turn, conquered the green strip of Spanish shore. Not any one of them entered the guarded heart of Spain. Her invincible mountain-rampart rolled back the invaders as the cliffs rolled back the sea, while, from above, the ancient Iberians looked down in unconquerable manhood, silent, melancholy, honourable.
>
> By and by a fifth invasion came like lightning. Out of North Africa, across the straits, rushing up and over the mountain barriers that had kept out the great races before them, came the desert-born Moors! They came like wild-fire, scorching, blinding, and driving before them the old Iberian race until they hemmed it into the little northwest corner where afterwards Castile and North Portugal were outlined. There they passed it by for a time, while they poured through the defiles of the Pyrenees and streamed down into the green plains of France. The white barbs of the Moorish desert disdained to tread on Prankish soil, and, as they poised their dainty feet in air, the smooth steel caps of the riders with their quivering spikes and floating green veils caught the sunlight

and shimmered it away. Like a sea-tide the green and glancing Moslem host rolled into the history of Europe.

In its path waited a forlorn army. Fragments and remnants of the broken Roman empire had gathered together, dreary and desperate, for a last stand. Before them loomed one colossus, Charles the Sledge-Hammer, that day the saviour of a continent. It was on the plain of Tours in the year 732 that they fought one of the greatest battles of the world. Darkness and despair led by Charles the Sledge-Hammer broke and shattered the Moorish array. Abdurrahman was killed, and slowly and sullenly the Moors receded southward again.

And now begins the romance of Spain. The Moors had come back to stay. They built beautiful cities, graceful palaces, and barren old Spain began to blossom like a garden. Famous universities arose here and there. Music, poetry, literature, flourished under the kindly smile of the Khalifs. But behind this smile of peace the spirit of Iberia was gathering itself together up there among the mountains of Castile. The name Castile comes from the chain of castles which the hunted Spaniards had hung from cliff to cliff around their forbidding refuge. As soon as the Moors began to busy themselves in other ways than fighting, the gaunt Castilian knights began to let down their drawbridges. One day, when everything was ready, they rode forth followed by their men at arms, their priests blessing them as they went, their anxious ladies fluttering scarfs from the battlements and calling "God-speed, God-speed!" For they were going to fight against the infidels whose religion was a worse crime than their conquest. The old Castilian believed in the right of the strong to take what he could, but he never could be made to see that a man had the right to worship God according to his own conscience. Step by step the unconquerable Iberian stubbornness won back its country. At last, in the very same year when Columbus sailed for the discovery of the new world, the day came when Boabdil, with a handful of lamenting Moors, surrendered the last jewel of their kingdom, the most wonderful palace in the world. The Alhambra, and left forever the shores of Spain.

But the spirit of the Moor never has disappeared from Spain. Still he rules the Sierra Morena and haunts every watercourse of Andalusia. To this day, after nightfall, Spain is no Christian kingdom, but is ruled over by the Khalif. The Spanish peasant who lingers too late on the mountain roads, bringing down snow or wood to cool the water or build the fire of the Spanish city-dwellers, runs the risk of being overtaken and caught up by some phantom cavalcade, and swept away with them into their caverns deep under the mountains. There they sleep an enchanted slumber by day, and with the night come forth to resume their ancient realm. And all this is why Spain is the most romantic country of Europe; the genius of her Moorish conqueror enchanted her even while she drove him out.

The genius of the Moor enchanted her! She was ignorant. The Moor was skilled in every science known to that time. She could build just rude castles, and she loved the slender minarets and the swelling domes of Moorish mosque and palace. She could not help contrasting her dull grey stone walls with the glowing richness of Moorish stucco work, and her heart was wrung when she contrasted her rude war songs, her harsh trumpet notes, her massive religious chants, with the languorous and passionate music and poetry of her invader, his clashing cymbals, quiver of strings, the soft notes of the flageolet. The pride of the Castilian noble, accentuated by his honourable poverty, and his high-souled struggle for independence, was shamed by the oriental grace, the Epicurean serenity and courtliness of the benign Moslems. Lastly, his imagination took fire at some matchless stories that have held the world spellbound ever since the Spaniard retold them.

It is this union of the stern spirit of old Iberia with the rich imagination of the Moors which makes old Spanish stories about the finest ever told. They tell of the honour and the dignity and the pride of the Castilian fighting noble matched by an urbane and chivalrous foe. They display the glow and luxuriance of the most flexible of the tropic races side by side with the desolate sadness that broods over those barren and sun-scorched plains, whose solitudes to this day are dotted here and there only by a few taciturn herdsmen. Their plots are full of the mystery and fire of the Arabian Nights, full of castles with secret passages, mountains with subterranean caverns, beautiful ladies shut up in towers, music coming from no one knows where, mysterious physicians who practise magic, proud young cavaliers in velvet cloaks, their swords sticking briskly out beneath, incomparable señoritas throwing roses from moonlit balconies whose arabesques form tantalizing screens to their beauty, hard-hearted fathers becoming suddenly soft-hearted at the end of the story, and blessing runaway children. In other words these stories carry us where so many great conquerors of Spain could not fight their way, that is, into the dreaming heart of Spain.

A good many years ago, one of our countrymen travelled into this enchanted country on a sober errand of historical research. He was getting ready to write the life of the man who discovered America. It was this fortunate project which enabled him, four hundred years after Spain discovered America, to bring it about that America discovered Spain.

Washington Irving went to Spain in 1826. He was on a seventeen year visit to Europe. He had been in England, France, Germany, and Italy, and each country of them, especially England where he stayed the longest, made him think and write about his own country. But when he found himself across the Pyrenees, — for the first time, he lost himself in a country which has suffered less from change than has any other country of Europe. From the hour that he entered Spain until the end of his life Washington Irving was haunted by Moorish Iberia. It is to this that we owe a richness of style, a romantic feeling for the superb, which, but for Spain, the "Father of American Literature" would have lacked.

Some of the time Irving lived at court in Madrid, but best of all he loved the time he spent at Granada in the summer palace of the Moors. There he wandered by sunlight and by moonlight through the flower-scented courts, listening to the tinkle of water as it ran unceasingly through the deserted corridors into marble basin and tessellated reservoir. And there, on the very spot where it reached its glory, he recreated the strangest, most gifted, most unreal monarchy that ever reared its fabric for a time in Europe.

More pedantic critics than we may smile at Irving's gifts as a scholarly historian, but we who know that the highest and sweetest wisdom in every race finds expression in its legends will see to it that every generation of children in America shall be familiar with traditions as heroic and brilliant as any ever created.

The author of this arrangement of Irving's Alhambra stories loved these stories when she was a child, but was troubled by the necessity of hunting them out from their context. Therefore with rare and happy tact she has selected and simplified some of the narratives, enriching them with Mr. Charles E. Brock's fine drawings, for other children whose eyes turn eagerly to look through

"Magic casements opening on the foam
Of perilous seas in faery lands forlorn."

Frances Squire.

Podcast #104 El Cid

Today's sample comes from a book called *The Story of the Cid for Young People* by Calvin Dill Wilson.[30] Let's start with the Preface:

> All young people should know as much as they can of the great deeds that have been done and of the careers of the chief heroes of mankind. For, while most of our lives are placed amid ordinary surroundings, the knowledge of what others have been able to do, in the presence of difficulties than ours, makes us braver and stronger battle with our own circumstances. It is good also to read of great lives for information, that we may be familiar with famous characters as they are referred to in other books or in conversation.
>
> No hero ever won a larger place in song and story than he who is called The Cid, and no history is more entertaining or fuller of incident. This story has never heretofore been put into simple language and form suitable for young readers, and we are sure that this edition will carry the heroic tale into many young minds and hearts.

You will find within the stories of each nation, a great national hero that emerges that embodies the ideals of that nation. Spain was no different—as Richard Wyche taught, "This national hero towered above all other heroes. Upon him was heaped the ideals and aspirations of the race; he was glorious in form and person; great in prowess, but pure in heart and gentle in spirit; protected by the gods, but subject to pain and sorrow and death."

Knowing the stories of these epic and legendary heroes reveals much about the heart of a nation, which is why it is worth our time to study them.

El Cid is Spain's hero. Here is the beginning of his story:

> We are about to tell you the story of a very famous and wonderful man, whose real life was more remarkable than any which novel writers could invent. This man did such extraordinary deeds that almost from the day of his death the poets and chroniclers and minstrels began to write and sing about them, and his name was carried about the world until everybody had heard of the glory of "The Cid." Especially in his own country, Spain, he has always been looked upon as the greatest and the noblest of men; and the writers of that land speak of him as "The Perfect One," "The One Born in a Happy Hour," "My Cid," and in other like terms of praise and endearment.
>
> This most splendid of Spanish heroes, who is universally known as "The Cid," and whose real name was Rodrigo Diaz de Bivar, was born between the years 1030 and 1040, but the exact date is not certainly known. The poets and minstrels have mingled a good many legends with the facts of his life, but we shall relate the story with all its romance, and tell of the Cid as his countrymen have done. In spite of all the myths, it is beyond doubt that the real Rodrigo was one of the most wonderful men who has ever lived, and that he was the greatest warrior who fought in the long and fierce struggles between the

Christians and the Mahometans.

You will be anxious to know what the title, "The Cid," means, and why it was given to Rodrigo Diaz, and we shall not keep you in the dark, but explain this at the outset. This unique title was given to our hero by five Moorish kings whom he conquered in one battle, and who then acknowledged him as their lord, or, as that word is in the Arabic language, "El Seid." He was also called "Campeador" or Champion of his countrymen against the Moors. Thus he was often spoken of as "El Cid Campeador," or the Lord Champion.

In order to make clear the situation in Spain when the Cid lived and fought, we must go back for a moment into the history of that land previous to his time. Early in the eighth century the Moors, who were Arabs living in North Africa, made a raid into Spain, and having been entirely successful, they were encouraged to undertake the conquest of the country. This, under a succession of leaders, they partially accomplished, bringing a large part of Spain under their control, but they were unable to subdue all of that land. As the Moors were followers of the prophet Mahomet, Spain was now not only divided between two races, but two religions, the Mahometan and the Christian. Hence a series of struggles continued to take place between the two powers and the two religions, and lasted for many centuries.

In this period, when his country was occupied both by its natives and the Moorish invaders, and when constant warfare was going on between the two forces, Rodrigo Diaz, who was to become the greatest soldier of Spain, was born.

Let's continue when the baby has grown into a man.

At this time the king, Don Ferrando of Castile, was having a violent dispute with King Don Ramiro of Aragon, in regard to the city of Calahorra, which, being at the boundary between their kingdoms, each claimed as his own. In order to settle this question the king of Aragon proposed that it should be decided by single combat, as it was not unusual in those days for kings or generals to select a distinguished warrior for each side, and to agree to abide by the issue, instead of having whole armies fight. The king of Aragon chose as his champion Don Martin Gonzales, who was thought to be the greatest knight in all Spain.

King Don Ferrando agreed to this combat, and selected as his champion Rodrigo Diaz. As this warrior was not then present, the kings appointed a time when they would again meet, with their knights; and they promised each other that the knight who was victorious should win Calahorra for his master. When they had returned to their own countries, Ferrando told Rodrigo of the engagement he had made for him to fight on his behalf. Rodrigo rejoiced at this news, and said he would most willingly fight; but meanwhile, before the day for the contest arrived, he must go on a pilgrimage, as he had made a vow to do so.

To this end, Rodrigo set forth, in the company of twenty knights, and as he went he gave money to many beggars, and assisted the poor and needy whenever they crossed his path. Of this journey the following legend is told, and it serves to show the nature of the fanciful stories that are mixed up with the true tale of the Cid. This legend says that on the road they found a leper who was sinking in a bog, and who called to them to help him for the love of God; and that at this appeal Rodrigo got off his horse, and rescued the man from his peril, placed him before him on his horse, and carried him to an inn. The knights who were his companions found fault with this intimate treatment of one with so loathsome a disease.

But when supper was ready, Rodrigo went still farther in his kindness, and made the leper sit next to himself, and he ate with him out of the same dish. At this the knights rose up and left the room. But Rodrigo did not change his conduct toward the poor man, for he indeed slept with him in the same bed on that night. The legend tells that at midnight, when Rodrigo was fast asleep, the leper breathed against his back so strongly that the breath passed through his body. Then Rodrigo awoke, very much amazed at the strange feeling he had had, and he felt with his hands for the leper who had been with him in the bed, but he was not there; he called, but received no answer. Then he was afraid, and he rose up and asked for a light, and looked all through the room; but the man could not be found, so he returned to bed, and left the light burning.

After a while there appeared before him a figure dressed in white, and said, "Rodrigo, art thou asleep or awake?" Rodrigo answered, "I am not asleep; but who art thou, with light all about thee, and so pleasant an odor?" Then the other said: "I am St. Lazarus, and I was the leper to whom thou didst kindness for the love of God; and because thou didst this for His sake, God hath now granted thee a great gift. For whenever that breath which thou hast felt shall come upon thee, whatever thou desirest to do, and then begin, thou shalt accomplish, so that thy honor shall go on increasing from day to day. Thou shalt be feared both by Moors and Christians, and thy foes shall never prevail against thee; therefore go thou on, and always persevere in doing good." With that the figure disappeared, and Rodrigo arose and prayed until morning that his body and soul might be watched over in all his enterprises. In the morning he went on until he had finished his pilgrimage.

Who do you think could become America's hero if given a chance? Who do you think embodies our ideals and aspirations?

By the way, the book I am sharing isn't a book you'd likely want to share with your Elementary aged kids because there is a lot of brutality and such. In those younger years, just familiarizing them with the name of Spain's great hero should suffice and maybe even the story of his vision.

Podcast #105 Rembrandt

I'm going to leave Spain for a bit, but I'll come back to her before the month is over just to touch upon what happened when that lust for gold took over and her relentless search for El Dorado, which led to an age of piracy.

So let's turn to brave Little Holland. You may want to listen to Podcast #26 if you haven't yet. There are a lot of parallels between her story and the story of America as she fought to be free and to be independent from her Spanish oppressors. Which is why the study of Holland is linked to the study of Spain. And her story is linked to the study of the Pilgrims because they fled to Holland before they came to America. There were few places that would tolerate the freedom to worship according to the dictates of one's own conscience, and Holland was such a place of refuge.

Today's sampler is from a book called *Stories of Great Artists* by Olive Horne Brown.[31] You'll find this selection in *Stories of Paintings* in the Forgotten Classics series. It first creates a simple scene of life in Holland in the time of Rembrandt who was a young boy when the Pilgrims were living in Leyden. And then it unfolds the life of Rembrandt, told in a way that an elementary age child can understand.

Rembrandt's Native Land

Come with me far across the sea to Holland, and visit our good Dutch friends. Holland is a very small country. We shall see no mountains here, for the country is very low. Now you must know that low land is often wet land. Indeed, the word Holland means wet land. We shall find that this is a good name.

We can hardly believe it when we learn that Holland is lower than the ocean. "Why, then," we say at once, "does not the sea overflow the land? If that were true, the houses would be destroyed. The gardens and fields would be flooded, and the cattle would be drowned."

It is true that all these things would happen if the people did not have the dikes. Without them they could not live in Holland at all. These dikes are great walls of stone and earth. They are built along the beach. They keep back the sea. They are very high and are so wide that carts can be driven on their tops. In some places houses have been built on the dikes. How carefully the Dutch people watch for a leak in the dike! If one of these great banks should give way, many lives would be lost.

In Holland there are canals running in every direction. In some towns there are no streets at all. Canals are used instead. Many bridges span these canals.

Winter is the happiest season of the year for the Dutch children. Then all the canals are frozen. Every man, woman, and child has a pair of skates. What a crowd of happy people! Children race to school on their skates. The women skate to market. On their heads they carry baskets filled with cheeses and rolls of butter.

Almost anywhere in Holland one may see windmills. They are used for grinding com, sawing wood, and pumping water. The wind fills the sails of the windmills. The great arms whirl swiftly around. The machinery is set in motion. When the wind does not blow, no work can be done.

Let us visit one of the homes in this interesting country. How clean and orderly everything is! The copper pots and brass kettles hang above the broad fireplace. The dancing flames make them shine like polished gold. There are no carpets on most of the floors; they have been sprinkled with clean, white sand instead.

The furniture is waxed and polished. The chairs all stand back against the walls in straight rows. We are shown into the parlor, because we are visitors. The children are not allowed to enter this room except on Sundays and holidays. We must step very carefully, for patterns in the sand have been traced on the floor. We see good engravings hanging on the walls. In richer homes we should find oil paintings.

Now we must say good-by to the kind Dutch dame and her tidy house. As we pass through the yard we see the children scrubbing their wooden shoes with sand. When they are as white as snow, they will place them in a row outside the door.

The outside of the house is almost as spotless as the inside. Would it not seem strange to see some one washing the outside of a house? That is just what they do in Holland. Even that is not enough; they give the houses a fresh coat of paint each year.

Every home has a garden near it. The narrow paths are covered with fine, white gravel. They are as neat as everything else about a Dutch home. Here and there are bright beds of blossoming flowers. How beautiful the red and yellow tulips are in the bright sunshine! We are told that we may pick some of the gay blossoms. We are glad then that we came to Holland in the spring.

Nearly all of the houses are built on the banks of the canals. As we look down the canals, we see that the houses stand in straight rows. The trees have been planted in straight lines. Every house has a windmill. Even the windmills have been built in rows. The trees and windmills look like two rows of soldiers on each side of the canal.

One of the largest cities in Holland is Amsterdam. Much business is carried on there. Years ago it was even a busier place than it is now. Merchants from all over the world came to trade in Amsterdam. The people did well in their business. They had all the money they needed. Their homes were pleasant and happy. They liked to hang fine pictures on their walls. They also bought large oil paintings for halls and public buildings. For these reasons! many artists came to live in Amsterdam. They found it easy to sell their work there.

One of the smaller Dutch cities is called Leyden. It stands on the banks of the river Rhine. There are scores of bridges in this city. They are built across the canals and across the river also. The bridges reach from one island to another, for Leyden is built upon islands. This place is well known for its university.

Many, many years ago an army tried to capture Leyden. The Dutch people fought bravely. They were willing to give up anything to save their country. For many days they did not have enough to eat. At last the cruel war was over. The enemy had sailed away.

The prince of the country was called William of Orange, He wished to reward the brave people of Leyden. He said they might choose between a large gift of gold and a university. The people needed money to rebuild their homes. Yet they chose the university. Was not that a wise thing to do?

Boyhood of Rembrandt

About three hundred years ago a child called Rembrandt Van Ryn was born in Leyden. His father was a miller. His mill stood on the banks of the river Rhine. Van Ryn means of the Rhine. So the child was called Rembrandt Van Ryn to show where his home was. In Holland one can often tell from his name where a person lives.

Rembrandt's father was well-to-do. His mother was a good woman. She spent all of her time caring for her home and her children. Rembrandt had four brothers and sisters. They had a comfortable home near the mill. The children spent much of their time there. They liked to play in the dim, dusty, old place. They liked to watch the sails of the windmill turn swiftly about. They tried to help the dust-covered miller pile up the great sacks of grain.

The child Rembrandt was sent to school, as all other Dutch children were. He was a bright little fellow. He was so good-natured that all his play-mates liked him. By and by he grew to be a "tall, strong youth."

His parents asked him what trade he would like to follow. Rembrandt did not know which one to choose. He was sure, however, that he did not wish to be a miller. His parents hoped he would be a priest or a lawyer.

Do you remember that Prince William gave the people of Ley den a university? The lad was sent to this university at Leyden. It was surrounded by a park. Rembrandt spent much of his time there. Curious plants from many parts of the world grew in the hothouses. He was greatly interested in these odd plants.

Every Sunday he took a long walk into the country. He saw green meadows dotted with grazing cattle. There were fields shaded by great trees. He liked to watch the crimson and gold of the sunset light in the canals. Best of all, he liked the beautiful Rhine. All day ships were passing to and fro on the river. Rembrandt often sat for hours watching the procession of white and colored sails.

It is a great holiday. Years ago on this same day the enemy had been driven from the city. Banners of all colors are flying from the housetops.

Hark! Tramp, tramp, tramp come the soldiers down the street. In what straight lines they march! How well they keep step with the music! Rembrandt pushes his way to the very front of the crowd. He watches the glittering arms of the soldiers. How the sunlight gleams on their lances!

The younger soldiers are in the front ranks. See, the old soldiers are marching forward. The people cheer and cheer. The men and boys wave their hats in the air. The girls throw flowers in the path of the soldiers. Why do they greet the old soldiers in this way? Rembrandt never forgot the sights he saw in those days.

Rembrandt did not stay long at the university. He decided he did not wish to become a priest. He returned home. There were a number of artists in Leyden. Their pictures hung on the walls of the city hall. Rembrandt often visited that building. He looked at the engravings and the oil paintings. He liked the engravings better. He studied them for hours at a time.

"What trade shall our son learn?" said Rembrandt's father to his wife one day. "He will not be a miller, and does not care to be a priest." "The boy is very fond of fine pictures," said the mother. "Shall we not send him to an artist to study?"

Soon after, Rembrandt was sent to an artist in Leyden. Can you not fancy how pleased the boy must have been? He stayed with this master three years. His teacher was very kind to him. He learned rapidly. Everyone who saw his work said he would some day be a great artist. At the end of the three years, his teacher could help him no more. He went back to his home.

After awhile Rembrandt went to Amsterdam to study. He worked only three months with his second teacher. Once again he went to Leyden to live. He had made up his mind that Nature should be his only teacher.

Rembrandt fitted up a studio in his father's mill. It had only one small window. The boy often watched the rays of the sun come through this window. The light fell on only one part of the room. The objects in that part could be clearly seen. The rest of the room was in shadow. Rembrandt noticed this, and tried to show it in his pictures.

In this studio Rembrandt painted a picture of his father in the mill. The mill is lighted by a lantern. The miller is piling up the great sacks in the store- room. Most of the picture is in shadow. We can see the miller plainly, because the light of the lantern falls upon him.

Friends, who saw the picture, admired it very much. They told Rembrandt they thought he could sell it. So he took it to the city. A picture dealer gave him one hundred florins for it. That is about forty dollars in our money. This was the first money that the boy had ever earned. He carried it proudly to his mother.

Rembrandt kept at work in his little studio in the mill. He painted a great many portraits. His family posed for him. He painted portraits of his sister, his cousins, and his father. The best work he did at this time was of his mother. As long as she lived she posed for him. He never tired of painting his dear mother s face. In many of her pictures she holds a Bible in her hands. In others the Bible is close beside her.

Rembrandt in Amsterdam

Rembrandt was a young man now. He wished to live among artists. There were more artists in Amsterdam than in any other city in Holland, so he decided to make his home there. Once again he said good-by to his friends and to the old home. He journeyed to Amsterdam by canal. He lived there until he died.

People of this city had heard of Rembrandt's pictures. They were anxious to see the young artist. Some of the young men wished to become his pupils. He rented a large building for a studio. His pupils paid one hundred florins a year as tuition.

In many studios all the light comes from above. There are no windows in the walls. Rembrandt had such a studio. Sometimes he wished to have a strong light on only one object. Then he would darken all the windows but one. The light all fell in one place.

Perhaps Rembrandt is painting the portrait of a fine lady. He asks her to stand in the light. How beautiful is the rich silk and lace of her dress! Bands of pearls and rubies are about her throat and arms. Every jewel is a bit of light. Rembrandt showed all this in his picture—the shadow and the bright light, the silk, the lace, and the jewels.

When Rembrandt had been in Amsterdam only two years, his pictures were well known. He had more work than he could do. Many of the greatest people in the city wished him to paint their portraits. Priests, poets, rich merchants, and fashionable ladies came to him. He was very well paid.

Rembrandt removed to a better studio. Merchants from all over the world brought beautiful things to Amsterdam. Now the artist could afford to buy some of these things. He bought heavy silks and richly colored velvets. He decorated his studio with them. He saw in the shops strange swords and daggers from other countries. He bought these and many other curious things for his studio.

Sometimes Rembrandt painted things for a joke. Once he fitted a piece of canvas in the window of his room. Canvas is thick, and shuts out the light. Yet Rembrandt painted this canvas to look like a pane of glass. He also painted a picture of his maid servant standing before this window as if she were about to open it.

Rembrandt had much fun watching the people who came in. They did not realize that the window was covered with painted canvas. The work was so well done, that they were sure that they saw a real window with a maid servant standing before it. They wondered why she stood there so long.

Once an old gentleman spoke to her. She did not answer. He became impatient. He wished to see Rembrandt alone. He walked up to the girl. He meant to ask her to leave the room. He started to touch her shoulder, when he found himself in front of a picture instead of a living person. How surprised he was! He turned to Rembrandt. The artist was shaking with laughter.

It is said that Rembrandt made fifty pictures of himself. He would laugh as hard as he could. Then he would take up a mirror and look at himself laughing. He would try to paint just what he had seen in the hand glass. In this way he learned to put a laughing face into a picture.

Sometimes he looked sad or frowned. Again he looked frightened. Each time he studied his own face in the mirror. Afterwards he painted or engraved what he had seen. After such study as this, no wonder he could paint portraits well.

Often Rembrandt studied his own dress rather than his face. One day he put on a knight's armor. At another time he dressed himself as a nobleman in a rich velvet cloak. Taking a steel plate, he made an etching of himself in this dress.

Rembrandt was called the prince of etchers. His etchings are almost as well known as his paintings. He engraved very rapidly.

Once he was taking dinner with a friend. There was no mustard on the table. Hans, the servant, was sent for some. The artist said, "I'll wager I can engrave a picture before Hans returns." Rembrandt's friend replied, "I'll wager you cannot."

Rembrandt never went away from home without a copper plate. He took one from his pocket and began his picture. He worked with quick, firm strokes. In a little while Hans returned with the mustard. Just then, Rembrandt handed the finished plate to his friend. So the wager was won.

Rembrandt did not always choose beautiful things to paint. He often had beggars to pose for him. In some of Rembrandt's engravings we see these poor people. How ragged and uncared for they look! It became known in Amsterdam that the great artist was painting beggars. Many tramps gathered before his door every morning. Each one hoped Rembrandt would hire him to pose.

The great artist worked nearly every hour of the day. He let nothing keep him from his work. No one was allowed to disturb him. He would not have stopped his painting even for the king!

When Rembrandt was about twenty-seven years old, he married. His wife was a lovely young woman. Her name was Saskia. They had a very happy home. Rembrandt took great delight in giving Saskia beautiful presents. He bought her necklaces of beautiful jewels. He gave her heavy gold bracelets. Indeed, he thought nothing was too fine for his young wife.

Rembrandt did not care to paint his own picture now. Nothing gave him so much pleasure as to have his wife pose for him. In one picture her head rests upon her hand. Beneath the broad straw hat she wears, her face is sweet and smiling.

In another picture she is a princess. Her long gown is of softest silk. The jewels about her neck and in her hair are most costly and beautiful. One of the loveliest pictures Rembrandt made of Saskia is called The Jewish Bride.

Of all the artists in Amsterdam, the Dutch people liked Rembrandt the best. They were willing to pay large prices for his pictures. People from other cities also liked his work.

The Night Watch is Rembrandt's finest picture. It was painted in 1642. It represents a company of soldiers in the street. They have been called out suddenly.

In the center of the company is the captain. He is dressed in brown with a red sash about his waist. Near the captain stands another officer. His coat is yellow and his sash is white. He wears a plume in his big yellow hat.

Some children have heard the drum. They wonder what is the matter. They slip in among the soldiers. The men themselves do not know what the trouble is. They have rushed out quickly and are not in line. Neither the flag bearer nor the drummer is in his place. Some soldiers have snatched up lances. One has a gun and another a sword.

A great many men had asked Rembrandt to paint this picture. When it was finished, they would not pay for it. They did not like it. Each man wanted his own face to show most in the picture. Only two faces showed plainly. These two men were pleased. Those who were in the shadow were disappointed. The artist never received pay for his work. The Night Watch now hangs in a gallery in Amsterdam.

Rembrandt was the father of several children. All, except one, died when they were very small. The son who lived was called Titus. His father painted several pictures of Titus while he was a baby. One shows the little fellow asleep. In another picture, the happy baby lies on a rug before a blazing fire.

Rembrandt's happiest days were past. It made him sad that people did not like The Night Watch. He could not sell as many pictures as he had sold in former years. The death of his children filled his heart with sorrow. But a greater sorrow came to him. The gentle Saskia died.

The beautiful home seemed lonely without Saskia. Rembrandt was too sad to paint any more.

He had not paid for all the things in his home. The merchants wanted their money. Rembrandt's house was sold to pay his debts. All the furniture and pictures in the house were sold too. Even Saskia's jewels and beautiful gowns were taken by the merchants.

In these days Rembrandt read the Bible a great deal. Soon he began to paint again. His pictures all represented Bible stories. He was poor and unhappy. Yet he worked as hard as ever.

For many years Rembrandt lived in Amsterdam, almost without friends. People came no more to have their portraits painted. Merchants no longer paid high prices for his engravings.

A few years before his death, Rembrandt was given an order for a picture. This must have pleased the artist. The picture is called The Cloth Makers, The people in Amsterdam liked it. Rembrandt was no longer sad.

Of all Dutch artists, Rembrandt is the greatest. The people in Holland still love him. They are proud of The Cloth Makers and The Night Watch. Both of these pictures hang in Dutch galleries. Not only in Holland, but in many other countries is this artist admire

Podcast #107 Edward Bok

In *Stories of Great Writers*, on page 97 is a sweet story of a young boy's visit with the great poet, Longfellow. The boy's name was Edward Bok who was born in Holland. I thought you might enjoy hearing his story that I found in a book by Mary Parkman, called *High Adventurers*.[32] Bok was an Adventurer for Beauty.

Edward Box was not quite seven years old when the great adventure of his life began—the adventure of turning a little Dutch boy into an all-around American. He was born in the Netherlands, that land of thrift and courage, where strong dikes and untiring energy keep for men's uses the land hardly won from the sea. When he played as a tiny child by the great sea-walls or watched the turning windmills that pumped water from the low-stretching fields, he began to understand that the world was alive with many interesting things.

In his own home he listened to stories of high adventures of his own people. He was never tired of hearing about the rocky island where his grandfather had gone to drive away the pirates and make a place where people could live in safety and happiness. He could see the story in pictures as if one were turning the pages of a book while his grandmother told about the adventures of the strange long-ago times.

Five miles out from the Dutch shore in the North Sea was a bleak island where many ships were dashed up against the rocks in a time of storm. There pirates, like evil birds of prey, fell upon the shipwrecked voyagers, murdered those who were able to escape the fury of the waves, and seized their goods.

Edward could picture his grandfather at the time when he was a fearless young man, who had already proved himself to be a success as a lawyer, standing in the presence of his king.

"Your country is sending you to a dangerous island as mayor and judge," said King William. "You are not a man to run away from a hard task. We feel sure you will prove to be a leader who is not afraid of danger or hard work.

It was soon clear to every one that the king had chosen wisely. The young man brought hope and courage to the frightened people of the island. Soon all of the robbers and pirates had left a place where lawless people could no longer count on escaping punishment.

The mayor-judge looked about one day at the place that he now called home. What a bare ugly land it was—no trees, no parks, no gardens! The people thought that it was too cold for beautiful things to take root there. "We must make the best of it," they said.

"That is what I want you to do," replied the young mayor. "Make the best of it by making gardens and planting trees."

The people, however, were stubborn. "We are poor people with no time or money to spare, they said. "We will not waste the little we have on trees that cannot live through the winter storms." Their mayor answered by planting a hundred trees. These were hardy pioneers that seemed to have in their sturdy growth something of the courage of the man who planted them. Each year they stretched up new branches and each year the young leader planted more trees. The once bare island was now a place of greenness, famous for its song-birds. The "Island of Nightingales," people called it. Travelers from many lands came to see the beauties of the island and listen in the evenings to the song of the birds that had found a place of safety on that once forbidding shore.

There were not only nests of thriving birds, but also a large family of healthy, happy boys and girls growing up in the home nest that the mayor had built. The days for them were full of merry play and worth-while work. When any one of them was tempted to give up some hard thing as a bad job he was shamed out of it by just looking around at the proof of the way one person had persevered in the hard task of making his world a better place for all who lived there.

The story of the winning of the Island of Nightingales through the work of one man was told again and again.

"Don't forget that good work lives and grows just as trees do. Soon happy lives make their nests in places where once there was neither shelter nor safety," the grandmother would say; and then she would add, looking straight into the eager faces of the children, "Always remember that each of you must make the world better and more beautiful because you have lived in it."

Edward Bok could not remember when he had first heard those words. It must have been long before he was really able to understand their meaning. They were a part of his earliest memories of summer—a time of sunlight glancing through green branches, beneath which he and his brother used to play.

Then everything was suddenly changed. The family fortunes were at a low ebb and the father and mother told the boys that they must go to find a new home across the ocean, not on a little island, but in a country much larger even than Holland—the United States of America.

The big steamer called The Queen landed the family in New York, a strange place where everybody spoke a language new to the two boys of six and eight, who, the day after a place was found in Brooklyn for them to stay, were sent to a public school. The children could not answer back when a group of lively boys plied them at recess-time with questions. These boys thought it fun to see how far one could go in tormenting the newcomers.

It was evident, however, that even small boys from the Land of Pluck could take care of themselves. We know that bullies are always cowards and quick to give way before those who have the courage to stand up for their rights. These Dutch boys were not slow in proving that they had strong bodies and quick wits, as well as a plentiful supply of grit. Pluck is understood by every one, no matter what language happens to be spoken at the moment.

Edward and William Bok showed themselves quick to learn not only the ways but also the speech of their new country. It was not many weeks before the boys on the playground who called Edward "Dutchy" had forgotten that he was a new-comer in their midst.

Life was not easy for the boy. His father had hoped that America, which had proved for many a land of opportunity, would open the way to new wealth for one who had been so unfortunate as to lose a fortune in his native land. It is hard, however, to get a start anywhere, especially for those whose abilities and experience have been matched to conditions different from those they are forced suddenly to meet. Mr. Bok was no longer a young man, and though he had learned to speak English in the excellent schools of the Netherlands, he was unable to find the kind of work that he was able to do.

If Edward had not been the sort of boy who could find real fun in proving himself equal to hard work, he might have hated the first years of his American adventure. As it was, many times he was tired at the end of a day when, as often happened, he came home from school to help about the house. His mother was not strong enough to meet alone the many demands of the new life. She was used to Dutch cleanliness and order, but in the Dutch home there had been servants to share the drudgery. And as a good housewife who had been brought up in the ways of Dutch thrift, she often sighed and looked anxiously at her children when she saw everywhere signs of waste.

"We seem to have come to a strangely reckless land," she said. "I believe all the poor of the Netherlands could be fed on what American women throw out from their kitchens. Don't forget, Edward," she added, "that the person who wins in this life is the one who learns to turn things to good account, whether on a rocky island or in a wide country rich in many of Nature's gifts. People and nations gain when they use in the best way all that they have. When we waste we lose not only an opportunity but also something of real power in ourselves."

As she spoke there flashed before Edward's imagination the picture of an island of fair gardens and parks for rest and play. He, too, would try to make the world a better place because he lived in it.

First, there was the need of earning wherever possible, for the little family could not stop eating while a new-comer from Holland was trying to make the right sort of start for success in a new world. There were chilly mornings when there was neither wood nor coal for a fire, and the two boys went out to glean pieces of wood left on vacant lots and coal that was littering the streets near sidewalks where fuel had been delivered.

"It's all right for us to get what people have thrown away or wasted," argued Edward, when his mother shook her head as her two boys brought in before school a scuttleful of coal that had been collected along the neighboring streets. "This is America, where a person can do any sort of honest work.

One morning as Edward stood looking at the fresh buns in a baker's window and wondering how he could earn the money to add food to the family store, the chance came for his first real job. The baker too came to the shop door, to admire his display.

"No one could help seeing how good your things are if somebody would wash your window for you," suggested the boy. "Would you like to clean it?" asked the baker; and a bargain was made that Edward should come to the shop Tuesdays and Fridays after school to keep the show-window clear and shining for fifty cents a week. Since an opportunity well met generally opens the way to new adventure, Edward was soon finding that the precious after-school hours might be filled with different kinds of earning and learning. The baker gave him the chance to wait on customers and take home as wages another dollar, together with some of the bread and buns that could not be sold the next day as newly baked.

On Saturday afternoons as he went about delivering a weekly paper the idea came to him of a way to get a job as a news-gatherer. He wrote a paragraph about a party to which he had been invited, giving the names of all the boys and girls present, and took it to the office of the "Brooklyn Eagle."

"This is all right," he was told. "People will buy papers when they can see their own names and those of their neighbors in print. You can count on three dollars a column for this kind of copy." Soon Edward's schoolmates were enlisted as scouts to hand over timely items and the young reporter was often able to bring together enough to fill two or three columns.

The fortunes of the family were now beginning to look up. Mr. Bok succeeded in getting a position with a telegraph-company as translator. The man who was able to read several languages had at last found suitable employment.

Though there was no longer so great a need for help in the home, when he was thirteen Edward persuaded his parents to allow him to go to work as office-boy in the telegraph-office. "You will see that I shall not stop learning," he said.

As he worked, he watched the men in the office and tried to discover what it was in each that had helped him to win success. One day he decided that the prizes of life were won by those who could look far enough ahead to be ready to meet new opportunities and make the most of them.

At that time shorthand was a comparatively new art, but Edward was quick to see that if he S could be equipped with this means of saving time for busy men by taking down rapidly their directions and letters he would be able to advance in the office. He attended, therefore, a class in stenography at the Brooklyn Y.M.C.A., and because two lessons a week did not take him forward fast enough, joined a second class in a business school.

The instructor of each group was amazed at the lad 's talent for the quick pen-strokes and encouraged him to follow up his success.

The boy did not need urging to improve the opportunities that came his way. Indeed, he was always looking ahead for new possibilities just around the corner. He knew that it was his grandfather's steady hard work which had brought order and beauty to the Island of Nightingales. He had heard some one say that genius is at root a great "capacity for taking pains," and he believed that nothing could be won without persistent effort.

Some of his precious savings were spent for an encyclopedia, which he hoped might give him a clue to the different ways that great men had worked for success. Evening after evening he turned the pages, but somehow the living secret did not seem to be hiding between the covers of the volumes. Perhaps one of the men who had triumphed over difficulties would be willing to give a boy who had been forced to educate himself, a golden hint from the riches of his experience, which would help him to go ahead in the right way.

He had read in his encyclopedia that General Garfield (at that time a candidate for President of the United States) had taken the first steps of his career when as a boy he trudged along behind a mule on the tow-path of a canal. Edward decided to write a letter to the great man and ask if the book spoke the truth in so describing the first stage of his journey in life. He would ask also for a word that might help an ambitious young Hollander to win success in his adopted country.

General Garfield wrote a cordial answer, which increased the boy's interest in the biographies of great men and also gave him a new hobby. He would add to the information that books and newspapers might furnish by writing for first-hand reports on points of real interest. As the months went by he assembled a most interesting collection of letters, many of which (since the typewriter was not at that time in general use) were in the handwriting of the senders. Here was a collection of autographs of real importance, which proved not only the generosity of men in high places but also the genuine interest that the boy's letters aroused in different quarters.

General Grant not only answered his question concerning Lee's surrender, but enclosed a little sketch indicating the exact situation. Longfellow told the story of the writing of "Excelsior" and Whittier wrote something about "The Barefoot Boy."

Edward prized his collection of letters and autographs, which were not only interesting and valuable in themselves but led to a number of real adventures that had a great influence on his life. He watched the newspapers to learn when the writers of his friendly letters were staying in New York and ventured to call upon them. In one evening he was able to talk with General Grant, Jefferson Davis, and Mrs. Abraham Lincoln.

He spent a summer vacation in Boston, where he went to see the famous group of New England poets—Longfellow, Emerson, and Holmes. This was a time of high adventure for an ambitious boy, who was working now as a stenographer in a publishing house and hoping some day to command success 88 an author or editor.

The steps by which he advanced through seeing some opportunity unnoticed by others make an interesting story.

One evening at the theater his attention was caught by the restlessness between acts of the women in the audience. As his eye fell on the awkward, badly printed sheet that contained only the program and a few advertisements, an idea took shape in his mind.

"I believe an attractive booklet, easy to handle, and giving some lively items of interest, would be profitable because it could carry considerable space for advertising at a good rate," he said to himself.

Following this gleam of inspiration, he obtained from the theaters exclusive right to furnish without cost programs in the general form that is still in use. The little publication launched in this manner with a guaranteed circulation brought in from the start a dependable income through its advertisements.

Next there was a venture called "The Brooklyn Magazine," which was materially helped through a policy already tried out in the collecting of autograph letters from celebrities. Edward appealed directly to some of his generous correspondents for contributions to the columns of his paper and often secured without cost letters and articles of general interest. He thought of such topics for discussion as "Should America have a Westminster Abbey?" The next move was to write for the opinions of a group of prominent people and assemble their answers in a way to seize the eye and provoke debate. The paper for which he wrote was moved to New York with the new name of the "Cosmopolitan Magazine," but about this time Edward Bok decided to turn his efforts in another direction.

He thought that articles of general interest might be sold to a number of newspapers for publication in different cities, thus helping both publishers and writers. He soon learned, however, that he was not the first to take up the idea of "syndicate" news-material, and that he would have to furnish something novel, and better than that which two news-agencies were already putting out.

He looked over different papers and magazines to see if he could supply something of importance that was lacking. In a flash he made a discovery. There was nothing of especial interest for women. That was the reason, he felt sure, that women did not read newspapers as much as men did. If he could provide material to fill columns that would appeal especially to home-makers he was sure it would meet a real need.

For several years he divided his time between providing "Women's Page" features and advertising. Then came the offer from Cyrus H. K. Curtis, the publisher of "The Ladies Home Journal," to take the position as editor of that paper. This was in 1889, when the young man was twenty-six years old. At once he determined to take hold of the work as a new adventure and make of the magazine something that would be really worth while.

"I must discover what the readers of the 'Journal' want and then give them something in that line but just a little bit better. It is a good rule to find out the kind of room a person likes and make him comfortable there but also to see that the windows give him a view of something beyond," he said to himself.

He offered prizes for the best answers to three questions:

1.   What do you like best in this magazine and why?
2.   What do you like least, and why?
3.   What feature or department would you like to have added?

The thousands of answers that came into the editor's office were a great help to him in making plans for his magazine. Years after in telling his story, Edward Bok said:

"I learned that I was right in believing that the public expects its leaders to keep a notch above or a step ahead. People want something a little better than they ask for, and the successful man in catering to public demand is he who follows this golden rule."

Perhaps he remembered at this time his grandfather's adventure for beauty in his island home. When he planted the first trees there he was giving the islanders something a little better than the things that they knew they wanted. This policy, we know in advance, made the magazine a success and also opened the door to new opportunities for adventure.

"Why is it that builders of small houses give no thought to what is beautiful or homelike he said to himself, as he looked out of a train window one day. "Nature has given America a rich and beautiful land, but the people do not seem to care for beauty in their homes."

He decided to offer prizes for the best plans for houses that would not cost more than five thousand dollars. The winning plans were given a prominent place in the magazine, which also offered full descriptions and estimates so that any builder would be able to use the plans. In this way thousands of people who were unable to pay for the services of an architect could secure well-planned and attractive homes.

The magazine next went on a crusade for more beauty within the homes. Pictures were shown of well-planned rooms in contrast with furniture that was poorly chosen and arranged. The reader was told, "Look on this picture and then on that l" There could have been no better way of driving a point home.

Other campaigns in behalf of "Beautiful America" followed, to make people realize the extent to which signs and bill-boards had been permitted to spoil the charm of the country-side. Again pictures, of the before-and-after sort, told the story. Another series of pictures showed up "dirty cities," and while anger was aroused, together with threats to boycott the magazine, clean-up and paint-up drives became the order of the day in many places.

These are only a few of the ways in which Edward Bok was able to make his work as editor a real service to the cause of beauty and better living for many. It was, therefore, a great surprise to his friends, when, after thirty years of work with the magazine, the editor declared that it was time for him to retire.

"You're not an old man," they said, "and you 're not ill, are you? Why should you give up such successful work when you 're only fifty-six years young?"

"Because others are ready to carry on this work," was the reply, "and they should have a clear field. I, too, want the chance, while I am still young enough, to set out on a new trail. People spend many years in making a living, but often forget to take time to live," he added.

"What may I say you are planning to dot" asked a young newspaper reporter.

"If you must say something," replied Bok, with a smile, "you might inform your readers that I am planning nothing more than to be a citizen of Philadelphia."

It was soon evident that this citizen had only been waiting for the opportunity to do a number of interesting things. He wrote the story of his life, which he called "The Americanization of Edward Bok." He said that all of the events of the years since he came as a little boy to this country were adventures in the making of an American citizen. America had given him a chance to do worth-while work and he had been happy in the doing of it. He wished now to give to his adopted country some special service in return for the opportunities that he had enjoyed.

The idea came to him that most people were too much taken up with their special concerns to think about others who were doing different kinds of important work for their city. He decided that he would do something to make everybody wake up to the worth-while things that were going on around them. Prizes were provided each year for a policeman and a fireman who had done some outstanding service. This was, of course, a fine thing for the man, who was given an award of a thousand dollars, together with the recognition that he deserved from his fellow-citizens. It was an even better thing that all of the people stopped to think about those who were doing important work for the city.

The idea of a prize came to Bok as a means of leading many to take active part in work that would benefit all the people. He put the idea to the proof in several ways.

A prize was offered each year for the citizen of Philadelphia who was voted as the one who had done during the preceding twelve months something of outstanding worth for the whole community. One year the prize was given to the leader of the Philadelphia Orchestra, whose concerts were among the most important musical events in America; another time it went to the manager of the baseball league team who had helped his men win the championship for that year. These two instances will illustrate the way that the prizes encouraged many kinds of work for the city's welfare and happiness.

After the Versailles Treaty, which brought an end to the World War, had been signed, the people who had lived through the years of frightful destruction and suffering said there should be some way to stop the madness of wars between nations. Edward Bok hoped that his idea of an award might set thousands of people to working on plans for keeping the peace of the world.

"If the nations prepare for peace as thoroughly as they have prepared for war, the greatest menace to the safety and happiness of people everywhere will be conquered," he said.

Soon all of the papers and magazines in the country told the important news of the prize of $100,000 that Edward Bok was offering for the best plan by which America might "cooperate with other nations to achieve and preserve the peace of the world." Early in January, 1924, the winning plan was published, together with suggestions that other people had brought forward.

Many minds had been put to work, and millions of people were made to realize the need for making plans to prevent war.

It is clear that Edward Bok was using his time and his money to good purpose. As we have seen, he was trying in different ways to show his gratitude to America for the opportunities that had been given him in this land. During the last years of his life he was able to show his love for his adopted country by a wonderful gift to his fellow countrymen.

The story of that gift had its beginning long ago in the making of a bleak island into a place of beauty and in the message which he felt had been sent to him to carry on that work. The Dutch boy who came to the New World never forgot the splendid adventure of his grandfather across the sea. Always as he went on from one kind of work to another he knew that he was adventuring for beauty.

The great opportunity to make the thought of the Island of Nightingales take root and blossom in America came to Edward Bok while he was on a vacation in Florida. He chanced one day to see the bodies of some song-birds lying near the beach.

"Many birds that are migrating from the North to Cuba or South America lose their lives here every year," he was told. "Often when they are caught in a storm their strength does not hold out for the long journey that they make every spring and autumn."

In a flash then Edward Bok remembered the storm-driven birds that had found a refuge among the trees of the Island of Nightingales. Now he knew that he must make an island of rest and safety for tired birds and people in America. It should be a place of beauty and peace where many in need of renewal of strength and joy could come.

In the center of Florida, about midway between the Gulf of Mexico and the Atlantic Ocean, is a place three hundred and twenty-four feet above sea level—the highest ground in the State. This stretch of land, barren save for a growth of noble pine trees, Edward Bok selected for his island of beauty. A year was spent in providing the needed system for insuring a supply of water. Trenches were dug and pipes laid. Then a landscape architect began to transplant to the high ground trees and bushes, that grew in abundance in near-by swampy districts. Bushes with berries for the birds and underbrush for shelter were planted.

Among the trees that were introduced were the dogwood, magnolia, live-oak, wild plum, and mulberry. There were also masses of feathery golden acacia, hundreds of brilliant azalea plants, and everywhere the Florida blueberry bushes making a soft background with their dull gray-green foliage.

Two lakes were dug and surrounded with lilies and iris. Here wood-ducks, herons, and flamingoes were made welcome. A dozen nightingales were brought from England to found a colony in this bird paradise.

In the midst of Nature's gifts, rising more than two hundred feet from the hilltop, is a lovely Singing Tower. The base is made of the Florida coquina rock—the same mellow, light-tan stone that was used by the Spanish settlers in the building of the ancient fort at St. Augustine. Above this, built of pink Georgia marble, is the tower, which holds a wonderful carillon of sixty-one bells.

The name "Singing Tower" comes from Old World times when the people of Belgium and Holland built watch-towers from which sentinels could look out over the land and give warning of a break in the dikes or of danger from an enemy. A horn was blown in time of need as a signal from the watchers. Later on, bells placed in the tower sounded instead of the horn. In the seventeenth century famous carillons of bells pealed with the passing of the hours. The music of the bells that Edward Bok had heard as a child echoed in his memory with the quaint stories of long-ago times. That is the reason it came to pass that a Singing Tower was built in the heart of the bird sanctuary at Mountain Park, Florida. The bells from the tower are played at sunset each day and at noon on Sundays. There are, besides, special programs on Christmas Eve, New Year's and the birthdays of the three great Americans, Washington, Lincoln, and Lee.

At the entrance to this place of beauty, which was dedicated by President Coolidge at the time Edward Bok presented it to the American people, is placed this sign:

> The Sanctuary
> For the Humans and the Birds
> "I come here to find myself. It is so
> easy to get lost in the world."

In January, 1930, when Edward Bok came to the end of his earthly journey, his body was laid to rest in a crypt under the Singing Tower. The last of his adventures for beauty led to this sanctuary where we may hear echoed in the songs of birds and of pealing bells the message: "Make you the world a bit more beautiful and better because you have been in it."

Podcast #108 Mary Mapes Dodge

You may wonder why I am talking about a woman born in New York in 1831 in Month 2. The reason is simple. She is best known for her book, *Hans Brinker or the Silver Skates*. As one reader said, "On closing the book, one did not seem to have been reading about Holland, but to have been living *in* Holland." So let's start there.

Mary Mapes Dodge was filled with admiration for the heroic little nation after reading Motley's *Rise of the Dutch Republic and History of the United Netherlands*. If you haven't listened to Podcast #26, I hope you will where I talk about Brave Little Holland, a country whose story is reflected in our own American story. Mary started improvising a bedtime story about a brother and his little sister to her little boys and the book grew from there. She did her research and I quote: "She ransacked libraries, public and private, for books about Holland, made every traveler whom she knew tell her his tale of that unique country and submitted every chapter to the test of the criticism of two Hollanders living near her. It was the genius of patience and toil, the conscientious touching and retouching of the true artist, which wrought the seemingly spontaneous and simple task."

It was an instant success. And had that been her only achievement, she would remain a noteworthy woman. But let me give you a sampling of what was written about her, starting with a tribute paid to her[33] following her death, wherein she was described as "so triumphantly alive and joyous, so in love with life and raptured with the world; a woman of singular radiance and cheer."

She was the recognized leader in juvenile literature for nearly a third of a century. It was her mission to minister to the thoughts and interests and aspirations of childhood, and for this she was divinely fitted.

She married the love of her life at age 20, a young lawyer, but he suddenly and unexpectedly died just seven years later, leaving her with two little boys to raise. She determined that earning a living through writing was her best option and, after working for a time with Harriet Beecher Stowe on a magazine called *Hearth and Home*, she was offered a chief editor position over a new children's magazine wherein she was given complete rein. She wanted the name itself to appeal to children all over the world, and it was she who decided to call it St. Nicholas—the most successful children's magazine ever created, and she produced 12 monthly volumes a year for thirty years.

Her aim and her work was to make child-readers happy first, and through this happiness to lead them on to higher and nobler living. It was a golden treasury of stories, verses and pictures to raise a generation of children who were strong, warm, beautiful and true. She enlisted contributions from the great souls of her day: William Cullen Bryant, Longfellow, John Whittier, Lord Tennyson. Frances Burnett introduced her Little Lord Fauntlery in its pages. On meeting Rudyard Kipling, he asked Mary, "Aren't you going to ask me to write?" She replied, "Are you up to it?" After all, he had only written to adults up to that point. He replied, "I must and shall! For my sister and I used to scramble for St. Nicholas every month when I was a lad." A few weeks later, he sent her the first two of his famous Jungle Stories for the magazine.

To Whittier she wrote:

> I cannot help hoping that among your unwritten poems there may be some song or story for children; some Christmas thought or some personal reminiscence of a sleigh ride or boyish coasting. In short, a legend or something from school-life, home-life or thought-life that you may feel like giving to the children. If so thousands upon thousands of them will be glad and so will we editors be and so will you be, for I know you truly like making others happy.

Who could resist? She received his contribution shortly thereafter. By the way, you can read copies of this wonderful children's magazine on Internet Archive.

What she did was merely the expression of what she was. The inspiration of the magazine was a reflection of the power of her personality. It was but the "flowering of a noble nature of noble gifts, patiently and faithfully used for noble ends."

So you may be wondering, as I did, what kind of home did she grow up in that produced this woman, "so triumphantly alive and joyous, so in love with life and raptured with the world"?

We are given a few glimpses.

Her father, a much loved professor, never sent any of his daughters to school. They gained their education at home under carefully chosen tutors and governesses whose instruction included French, music, drawing and Latin. But her love and influence of great writers she owed to the influence of her father. There were no children's books in her youth, but their home was filled with books to which the children were given constant and ready access. The theory of her father was that children instinctively like good reading if they are fortunate enough to find it. So she was raised to love the Bible, the old English ballads, Shakespeare, Milton, Bunyan, Walter Scott. It was a home where the best people and the best influences found always an open door and an open heart.

When Mary became a mother, she patterned her own home after the home she was raised in. She filled it with rare and beautiful things, and there were books everywhere. The drawing room, library and music rooms were the center of her life; they were gathering places.

After her husband died, she went home. There had been some financial losses, and her father now lived in the countryside in more modest circumstances, but that didn't matter. There was an old abandoned cottage on the property and she took her little boys out there, knocked down a wall and cleaned it up. She didn't need money to make it cozy. She furnished it with used furniture pieces and hung mosses and leaves around the window where she could look out on the beautiful countryside and forests. Of course there were books and flowers—flowers everywhere. This became her work space where she could focus on her writing and still be close to her boys.

Her little boys were the joy of her life and she was ever their companion, helper and friend. She entered into all their daily interests, their work and play. She flew kites with them, skated with them, tramped miles beside them, collecting samples. Whatever subject interested them, she studied in secret.

When her elder boy, a born inventor, began to care for the things of his craft, it was she who was ready to explain to him the crystallization of iron, the effects of heat and cold and the laws of statics and dynamics.

When the younger, a born musician, began to think of harmonies, it was she who seemed to know more of the science and art of music than any teacher.

She kept before them the highest idea of character and left details of conduct to their instructed moral sense. There's a sentence worth pondering. Let me quote that again. She kept before them the highest idea of character and left details of conduct to their instructed moral sense. She remained their most intimate friend and advisor.

And she followed in her father's example. She was a brilliant conversationalist. She was known for her depth and tenderness of feeling, her intellectual poise, spiritual insight and simplicity of expression.

In the home where she grew up, vacant chairs always stood at the table for the chance a visitor may come and eat with them. And the world daily came to their door. She was raised on listening and engaging in conversations with men of science, poets, painters, statesmen, philosophers, journalists. The talk was of scientific achievements, of music, painting, and the drama; of great philanthropic and benevolent movements all over the world; of contemporary history, projected laws and reasons for those laws.

Her father was a gifted conversationalist as was his mother. His father patterned his home after the home he grew up in. His mother had been saluted by George Washington himself, had danced with Lafayette and she delighted her grandsons with stories of the historic past. Sunshine, music, flowers, the heartiest good-fellowship and with children as their companions filled the house. No atmosphere could be more delightful to live in.

It was said of Mary's home, much more than a housekeeper, she is a home-maker. The order and neatness, the economy and routine of her management, are simply the foundation on which the beauty and serenity of the home rest.

Is it any surprise that Mary's son established a home patterned after the home in which he was raised, which was patterned after the home in which his mother was raised which was patterned after the home in which his grandfather was raised? Sadly, her younger son didn't live to adulthood.

We may not be able to invite poets and painters and philosophers to our dinner table in person, but we can develop the art of conversation and share their stories, thoughts and ideas as though they are there and accomplish the wonderful things that brought such joy to Mary's life and which consequently influenced untold millions of children all over the world.

We can follow her example and be companions to our children, trusted confidants and advisors, more concerned with happiness than with things. We can fill our homes with sunshine, flowers, and books and create homes where:

> …gracious freedom, like the air
> of open fields; its silence hath a speech
> of royal welcome to the friends who
> reach its threshold.

An ideal worth reaching towards.

Month 3 Podcasts

Podcast #110 Robert Louis Stevenson

I had intended on devoting a podcast to Robert Louis Stevenson in Month 2 when we talk about pirates because he, of course, is the author of the most popular pirate book ever written—*Treasure Island*. He is the originator of *Fifteen men on a dead man's chest, Yo Ho Ho and a bottle of rum*. I could have also placed his story in Month 1 when we talk about the South Seas because of what he did there. Or we could talk about him in Month 5 when we talk about Poetry in the Mother's University because he wrote the much beloved *A Child's Garden of Verses*. Or I could talk about him in Month 6 where we talk about Storytelling—the native Samoans called him Tusitala—a Teller of Tales. His stories endeared himself to them.

But here we are in Month 3 and this is where I will start because Edinburgh, Scotland, is where he was born and raised—in a family of lighthouse builders.

One might say Stevenson, himself, is a lighthouse.

I think I will tell you his story by starting at the end. And when you hear, you will understand why I love this great author so much.

Stevenson was sickly his whole life. The cold, damp climate of Scotland was especially hard on him and it was for health reasons that he sailed to the warm, sunny islands of Samoa where he busied himself, not only with creating a home for his family, but in caring for the islanders he quickly came to love with all his heart.

And, oh, how they loved him. I'm going to share a couple of sections from Amy Cruses's biography of Robert Louis Stevenson to demonstrate that love.

The first scene follows an incident when several of the tribal chiefs who had been imprisoned were openly befriended by Stevenson, at his own personal risk.

> Almost as soon as they were released from prison, in September 1894, nine of them came up to Vailima for a consultation. (Vailima was Stevenson's home.) They sat in a solemn circle on the floor of the hall, and made known their intentions to Stevenson and his assembled family. He had, they said, done much to improve their position in prison and to hasten their release, and they had been considering what they could do in return. They had decided to make, with their own hands and the hands of their families, a road from the house at Vailima as far as the public way to Apia, to bear all charges and to supply their own food while the work was going on; ... Mrs. Strong describes how the "talking man" of the party began with the usual formal expressions and the usual Samoan composure of countenance, but when he began to speak of the love and gratitude they bore to Tusitala, of how they prayed for him and cherished the memory of his kindness, his calmness broke down, and he spoke with strong and real emotion. The whole incident touched Stevenson very deeply. Roadmaking was one of the most detested task of any in the whole island, and it was difficult to find men who,

either for the desire of high wages or the fear of punishment, would undertake it. But the chiefs entered on their task with the heartiest good-will and good-humour. In a few weeks the road was finished, and was known henceforward as "Ala Loto Alogfa," the Road of the Loving Heart.

When the road was finished, Stevenson invited all the workers and their families to a feast and made them a speech that embodies all his feeling for Samoa and his ideals and hopes for its future. "I love the land," he said. "I have chosen it to be my home while I live, and my grave after I am dead; and I love the people, and have chosen them to be my people, to live and die with them."

And now the final scene of his life—the end of his story, as found in a biography of Robert Louis Stevenson by Amy Cruse:[34]

Monday, the third day of the month, was mail day, and all the afternoon Stevenson was occupied in writing letters to his friends at home. When, at sunset, he joined the rest of the family on the verandah he was in the gayest spirits. He talked over plans for the future, and especially about a lecturing tour in America that he was eager to make; he joked with his wife, who had all day been oppressed by a presentiment of coming evil, and drew her to join with him in preparations for making of their evening meal a little festival. Suddenly he put both hands to his head, and cried out, "What's that?" and then, quickly, "Do I look strange?" and fell on his knees before his wife. Sosimo, his faithful attendant, came running in, and helped Mrs. Stevenson to carry him into the great hall and put him into the arm-chair, where he lay unconscious, but breathing heavily. Doctors were hurriedly sent for, and two soon arrived. Everything their knowledge and skill could suggest was done, but with no avail. The master of the house, the centre and mainspring of all its activities, was dying.

Loving hands lifted the unconscious form and laid it down gently upon a bed that had been brought in and placed in the middle of the hall. As the dire news spread over the estate, awe-stricken native servants stole silently in and seated themselves in a wide semi-circle on the floor, their dark, anxious faces all turned toward their chief, the well-loved Tusitala. His wife and the other members of his family gathered in anguish round his bed, and his missionary friend, Mr. Clarke, who had come hurrying to Vailima at the news of the attack, knelt and prayed aloud. The deep, painful breaths grew slower and fainter, then ceased. Robert Louis Stevenson was dead.

Silently his native servants went about the last sad duties they owed to their dead chief. The great Union Jack that his loyal heart had loved to see floating over the walls he had built in a strange land was hauled down and placed over his body; and under that symbol of home the Scotsman who was no more an exile lay at rest. His servants each knelt and reverently kissed the dead hand of their master. Not one could be induced to take any rest all through that long, sad night. There was no loud lamentation, but their mournful faces and dejected bearing showed how heavily this loss had fallen upon them. They sat silent, or chanted in a mixture of Latin and Samoan the long, solemn prayers that the Romish Church has ordained for use in the chamber of death, till the dawn came and brought in the day on which Tusitala must be laid in his grave.

Many feet trod that morning the Road of the Loving Heart, and chief after chief brought the customary offering of a fine mat to lay upon the body of the dead. Flowers, too, were brought, brilliant tropical flowers that filled the great hall with a blaze of colour.

An old Mataafa chief, one of those who had been in prison and who had afterward helped in building the road, came among the others; and as he crouched beside the dead body of Tusitala, he lamented over him in touching words. "I am only a poor Samoan, and ignorant," he said, "others are rich and can give Tusitala the parting presents of rich, fine mats; I am poor, and can give nothing this last day he receives his friends. Yet I am not afraid to come and look the last time in my friend's face, never to see him more till we meet with God…. We were in prison, and he cared for us. We were sick, and he made us well. We were hungry, and he fed us. The day was no longer than his kindness. You are great people, and full of love. Yet who among you is so great as Tusitala? What is your love to his love?"

Near at hand the grave was being prepared. Stevenson was to be buried in the place that he himself had chosen when he knew that he could not be laid with his fathers, "where the whaups and the plovers were crying," in the bleak Scotch graveyard at home. On the top of Vaea there is a small tableland no larger than a room; and here was to be his resting-place. No path led up to the steep side of the mountain, so forty of those who had gathered to offer their services were sent to hew one out with knives and axes, while a band of the Vailima servants, headed by Lloyd Osbourne, dug the grave on the summit.

The coffin, quickly made by the skilful hands of an old friend, was ready by noon, and Sosimo reverently placed the body of his master within it, posing the dead hands in the attitude of prayer. Then the tattered red ensign that had gone with him in his South Sea voyagings was laid upon the coffin, and it was borne on the shoulders of powerful Samoans up the steep path to the mountain top. The ascent was a work of almost incredible labour and difficulty, and each slow and painful step that brought them nearer to the summit tried most severely the strength of the devoted bearers. In all nineteen Europeans and about sixty Samoans assembled at the grave, where the Rev. W. E. Clarke read the Burial Service of the Church of England; and there, on the top of the mountain that had guarded his home, Robert Louis Stevenson was laid to rest.

His grave is marked by a tomb, built, in Samoan fashion, of great blocks of cement. On either side is a bronze plate. One bears in Samoan the words, "The Tomb of Tusitala." "Whither thou goest, I will go; and where thou lodgest, I will lodge; thy people shall be my people, and thy God my God; where thou diest, will I die, and there will I be buried." On the other plate is written in English two verses from his own "Requiem," with his name and the date of his birth and his death:

ROBERT LOUIS
1850 STEVENSON 1894

Under the wide and starry sky
Dig the grave and let me lie.
Glad did I live and gladly die.
    And I laid me down with a will.

This be the verse you grave for me:
Here he lies where he longed to be;
Home is the sailor, home from the sea,
    And the hunter home from the hill.

He was just 44 years old when he died. But what a lot of life he crammed into those short years. And so my question I wondered was, "What was the childhood that created such a loving heart?" For a glimpse of that, I'll turn to a story found in *Stories of Great Writers*.[35]

"What luck it is to have a lamp before our very own door," thought little Louis Stevenson as he stood by the nursery window to watch for the lamplighter.

One by one the lamps along Howard Place were touched into points of light, until the lamplighter reached No. 8, and then came the crowning joy of all, when Leerie stopped to light that special lamp. Would he look up and see the small face pressed against the window, and nod "good evening," or would he be too busy to think of little boys?

It was no wonder that the coming of the lamplighter was so eagerly looked for! The winter days were often long and wearisome to the little child shut up in the nursery there, and everything he could see from his window was interesting and exciting.

Louis, or "Smout" as his father called him, was so often ill, and caught cold so easily in the bitter cold Edinburgh winds, that he was often kept indoors the whole winter through, and all that he saw of the outside world was through his nursery window. They were happy days indeed when he was well enough to play about the nursery, to lie flat on the floor chalking and painting his pictures, and to watch for Leerie when the gloaming came. But there were many other days spent in bed, when Louis was obliged to make-believe a good deal to keep himself happy, as he sat up with a little shawl pinned round his shoulders and his toys arranged on the counterpane beside him.

It was all very well to make-believe in the daytime, when he could drill his soldiers and sail his ships and build his cities on "the pleasant land of counterpane," but when night came on it was weary work to lie long hours awake with a cough that hurt, dreaming half-waking dreams of wild terrors that were worst of all.

The wintry winds shrieked as they swept past, thumping at the window and howling away into the distance, and they sounded to the shivering child like a horseman galloping up into the town, thundering past with jingling spurs in fearful haste on some dreadful errand, only to turn and gallop back again with the same mysterious haste. Louis in his little bed, shaken with terrified sobs, said his prayers over and over again, and longed for the morning to come. It was so difficult to be brave when the night was so dark and he was so full of aches and pains.

But there was always someone at hand ready to comfort the child through those long dreadful hours. His nurse, Alison Cunningham, "Cummie" as he called her, never failed him. She was always there to drive away the terrors and soothe the pain, always patient and always gentle with the poor little weary boy. His nurseries changed first to Inverleith Row and then to No. 17 Heriot Row, but Cummie was always there. She was his sure refuge from terrors at night and the sharer of his joys by day; the feeling of "her most comfortable hand" he never forgot. Sometimes on those long watchful nights, when his wide-open eyes began to see fearful shapes, he would ask:

> *"Why is the room so gaunt and great?*
> *Why am I lying awake so late?"*

She would wrap a blanket round him and carry him over to the window, where he could look across the dark trees of the gardens beneath and see a few lights shining in the windows of the houses in Queen Street opposite. Safe in her arms, no shadows could touch him, and together they gravely discussed the question as to whether the lights meant that another wee laddie was awake watching with his nurse for the morn to come.

"When will the carts come in?" was the question always on his lips those weary nights. For the coming of the carts always meant that daybreak was at hand and the world was astir once more.

> *"Out in the city sounds begin,*
> *Thank the kind God, the carts come in!*
> *An hour or two more, and God is so kind,*
> *The day shall be blue in the window blind."*

But it was not only Cummie who watched over and cared for little Louis, there were his father and his mother too. Often during the night the nursery door would open gently, and his father would come in and sit by his bedside and tell him story after story, until the child forgot his pain and weariness and drifted away into the land of dreams. His father's tales always had a special charm for him and helped him through one terrible hour which he never forgot. He had been left alone in a room and by mistake had locked himself in, and then was unable to unlock the door. Evening was coming on, all his terrors of the dark began to gather round as the shadows crept nearer.

> *"All the wicked shadows coming tramp, tramp, tramp,*
> *With the black night overhead."*

But his father was close at hand, and his voice came through the keyhole talking about such delightful, interesting things that Louis held his breath to listen and quite forgot the shadows and the darkness until the locksmith arrived to open the door.

Then there was his young mother, "my jewels of mothers" as he called her, who was so ready to play with him and who always made even the dull nursery a sunshiny, happy place. She was not very strong, and Louis began early to try to take care of her. One day when he was only three years old, he was left alone with her after dinner and remembered that Cummie always wrapped a shawl about her; there was no shawl to be found, but he reached up and took a doyly off the table, carefully unfolded it, and spread it over as much of her as it would cover. "That's a wee bittie, mama," he said comfortingly. Cummie was very strict about Sunday, but his "jewelest of mothers" had a way of overcoming the difficulty, and if he promised to play nothing but the "Pilgrim Progress" game she sewed a patch on the back of one of his wooden figures, and lo! there was Christian, ready to flee from the City of Destruction, with all his exciting adventures ahead.

There was of course the Shorter Catechism to be learned, and there was no way of avoiding that, but afterwards came long chapters out of the Bible which Louis loved to listen to, and Cummie would read parts of the old writings of the Covenanters, and everything she read to him she managed to make most interesting. Louis himself learned to repeat long passages out of the Bible, besides Psalms and hymns, and he always recited them with a great deal of action, his small hands scarcely ever still, and his dark eyes shining with excitement.

With mother and Cummie to amuse him all day long, he was rather like a small prince in the nursery, and it was his will and pleasure that someone should constantly read to him. He never could listen quietly to any story, but must always try to act it, slaying dragons, attacking the enemy, galloping off on a fiery horse to carry news to the enemy, until he was tired out, and Cummie would smooth back the hair from his hot forehead, and try to persuade him to rest. "Sit down and bide quiet for a bittie," she said, and coaxed him to sew a piece of his kettle-holder, or knit the garter that was as black as only a child's grimy little hands could make it.

When spring came it brought new life to little Louis, and the long nights of pain and cold winter days were forgotten, as he played about the garden of his grandfather's manse at Colinton. Like the flowers, he began to lift up his head and grow strong in the sunshine. It was a different world to him when the sun shone and the sky was blue, and the splendid colours of the flowers made his days a rainbow riot of delight. There was no more lying in bed, no more coughs and wakeful nights, but instead, long warm summer days spent in the garden, or down by the river, where there was the joy of Louis's heart—a mill. There were cousins there too, in the sunny garden, ready to play all the games that Louis invented, to lie behind the bushes with toy guns watching for a drove of antelopes to go by, to be shipwrecked sailors on a desert island, where the only food to be had to keep them from starvation was buttercups, and even to eat those buttercups and suffer the after effects rather than spoil the pretending game.

There too was the kind aunt who brought out biscuits and calves'-foot jelly at eleven o'clock from her storeroom, which always had so delicious a smell of raisins and soap and spices. Never was there so kind an aunt, and never did anything taste so good as those biscuits and that calves'-foot jelly.

The children stood rather in awe of their grandfather, for he was very strict, and woe betide any small foot that left its mark on the flower-beds of the manse garden. It was whispered that their grandfather made a nightly round and examined each little muddy shoe put out to be cleaned at night, ready to fit it into the track which the evildoer had left on the flower-bed. It was enough to make them very careful where they stepped. It was awe-inspiring, too, to see their grandfather in the pulpit every Sunday, and though they admired his beautiful face and his white hair, there was something rather terrifying about him, and the cold dark room where he sat solemnly writing his sermons was seldom invaded by any of his grandchildren.

But there was something in that dark room which Louis longed with all his heart to possess. On the walls hung some very highly-coloured Indian pictures, just the sort of gorgeous colouring that Louis loved, and he wanted one more than anything else in all the world. At last there came a day when he was sent into the awesome room to repeat a Psalm to his grandfather, and his heart beat high with hope. Perhaps if he said his Psalm very nicely, his grandfather might reward him with a gift of one of those coloured pictures.

> *"Thy foot He'll not let slide, nor will*
> *He slumber that thee keeps"*

quavered the little voice, while Louis kept one eye on his grandfather's solemn face, and one on the Indian picture.

When the Psalm was finished, his grandfather lifted him on his knee, and kissing him gave him "a kindly little sermon" which so surprised Louis, who had a very loving little heart, that he quite forgot his disappointment about the gaily-coloured pictures he had longed for.

When those sunny summer days came to an end and Louis went back to Heriot Row, he had a companion with him now who made even the grey days cheerful. His cousin Robert Alan Stevenson spent a whole winter with him, and together they lived in a make-believe world of their own. Disagreeable things were turned into delightful plays, and even their meals were interesting. Instead of having to eat up a plateful of uninteresting porridge for breakfast, the magic of make-believe turned it into a foreign land, covered with snow (which was the sugar of course) or an island that was threatened by the encroaching sea (that was the cream), and the excitement of seeing the dry land disappearing or the snow mountains being cleared was so entrancing that the porridge was eaten up before the magic came to an end. Even cold mutton could be charmed into something quite delicious when Louis called it red venison, and described the mighty hunter who had gone forth and shot down the deer after many desperate adventures. Jelly was always a kind of golden globe of enchantment to him, and he was sure the spoon might at any moment reveal a secret hollow, filled with amber light. The boys possessed also very grand make-believe kingdoms which kept them very busy with the affairs of the nation. The kingdoms were called Encyclopædia and Nosingtonia, and were both islands, for Louis loved islands then as much as afterwards when "Treasure Island" took the place of Nosingtonia.

But perhaps the greatest joy of all was when Saturday afternoons came round and the boys went down to Leith to look at the ships, always the chief delight of their hearts. Passing down Leith Walk they came to a stationer's shop at the corner, where in the window there stood a tiny toy theatre, and piled about it a heap of playbooks, "A penny plain and twopence coloured."

Happy indeed was the child who had a penny to spend (for of course no self-respecting boy with paint-box at home ever thought of buying a "Twopence coloured"), who could walk into the shop with assurance and ask to see those books. Many a time did Louis stand outside, having no penny to spend, and try to see the outside pictures and to read as much of the printing as could be seen at such a disadvantage.

It was no use going in unless the penny was forthcoming, for Mr. Smith kept a stern eye on little boys, and seemed to know at a glance whether they were "intending purchasers" or not. Inside the dark little shop which "smelt of Bibles" he stood, and seemed to grudge them the pleasure of even turning over the pages of those thrilling plays.

"I do not believe, child, that you are an intending purchaser at all," he growled one day, sweeping the precious books away when Louis had "swithered" over his choice so long that no wonder dark suspicions were aroused.

It was those little books which opened to Louis the golden world of romance, the doors of which were never closed to him again.

It was not until Louis was eight years old that he began to read. His mother and Cummie had always been ready to read to him, and that, he thought, was the pleasanter way.

But quite suddenly he discovered that it was good to be able to read stories to himself, and it was a red-letter day when he first got possession of the *Arabian Nights*.

Long before he could write, he was fond of dictating stories to anyone who would write them for him, and poor patient Cummie would write sheet after sheet of nonsense, all of which she treasured and read to his mother afterwards. Sitting over the fire at night while Louis lay sleeping in his little bed, the mother and nurse whispered together over the cleverness of their boy, and anxiously tried to reassure each other that he was growing stronger, while they built their castles in the air always for Louis to dwell in as king.

Louis's school-days made but little impression upon him. He was so often kept away by ill-health, and the schools were so often changed, that he never won many laurels there. Whatever he liked to learn he learned with all his heart, and to the rest he gave very little attention whatever. He was not very fond of games, for he was not strong enough to play them well, and it was only when the make-believe magic began that he was in his element. He played football, but had to invent a tale of enchantment which changed the ball into a talisman, and the players into two Arabian nations, before he could enjoy it.

Far more exciting than any football was the business of being a lantern-bearer, that game of games, which he described with his magic pen long afterwards.

Picture Louis, stealing out of the house at North Berwick on a late September evening, his overcoat buttoned up tightly over something that bulged at the waist, his very walk betokening an errand of mystery. Presently, coming over the wind-swept shore, another dark figure is seen, also with a buttoned-up overcoat, and the same kind of bulge at the waist.

"Have you got your lantern?" breathed Louis. "Yes," comes the answer. All is well. Over the links and away to the shore the mysterious figures wend their way and are joined by others equally mysterious, and one by one they climb into an old boat and crouch together there at the bottom. The wind whistles and shrieks overhead, but down there they are sheltered, and the overcoats are slowly and carefully unbuttoned, and what seemed to be but a bulge is shown to be a tin lantern burning brightly, which quite accounts for the strong smell of toasting tin which has been hanging in the air about them.

In the dim light of these lanterns the lantern-bearers sit, and wild and exciting is the talk that mingles with the shriek of the wind, while the sky is black overhead, and the sound of the sea is in their ears.

No one can talk as Louis does, he lays a spell upon them all with his make-believe magic, but after all it is not the talk that is so fascinating, but rather the buttoning up of those overcoats over the lighted lanterns, the exquisite joy of knowing that unseen and unsuspected a hidden light is burning brightly there—that was the joy of being a lantern-bearer.

So it was that the make-believe magic kept Louis happy in his childhood's games, and when he grew up to be a man and left the games behind him, the make-believe magic was never left behind, but gave a great happiness to the world as well as to himself.

"Be good and make others happy" was his own particular rule, for he believed that everyone should be as happy as ever they could, and even children should remember that—

> *"The world is so full of a number of things,*
> *I'm sure we should all be as happy as kings."*

There are so many other things I'd love to tell you about Robert Louis Stevenson. I'll let you discover them on your own.

But did you notice—once again we see Stories, Songs, Rhymes, Imaginative Play and Nature, wrapped in love are the secret ingredients of well-educated and loving hearts?

Podcast #111 Moving Towards Independence

Before I dive into this podcast, let me plant a few seeds of thought:

Referring to the Greeks, Sir Edward Gibbon wrote: "In the end, more than they wanted freedom, they wanted security. They wanted a comfortable life, and they lost it all—security, comfort and freedom. When…the freedom they wished was freedom from responsibility, then Athen ceased to be free."

William Wallace chided his countrymen:

"You choose base slavery with safety rather than honest liberty with danger."

Somerset Maughan wrote: "If a nation values anything more than freedom, it will lose its freedom, and the irony of it is that if it is comfort or money that it values more, it will lose that, too."

One more: Woodrow Wilson. "I would rather belong to a poor nation that was free than to a rich nation that had ceased to be in love with liberty."

I'm going to spend the next several podcasts highlighting people who were in love with freedom. In month 3, we'll take a look at some of the early key players in America's fight for freedom. When I learned about the American Revolution in school, I pictured all the colonists on one side against England on the other. If you haven't picked up on it yet, you'll see how far from the truth that is. Only about a third of the colonists wanted to break away from England. A third were fence sitters and a third were staunch supporters of their mother country. Some of the greatest pressures and cruelties didn't come from the soldiers—it came from the neighbors. And there were a goodly number of England's leaders who were in favor of America's independence. These were family members to them—they didn't want to go fight family so German soldiers—the Hessians—had to be hired to do the fighting.

This month we'll look at some of the events leading up to the declaration of our independence and we'll study our mother country, England. She has given us so many wonderful gifts in spite of her sometimes unwise and arrogant kings. While we're in the British Isles, we'll look at the struggles of Ireland and Scotland to free themselves from England's strong arm. You will find so many heroes for your children to hang out with. The love of liberty that stirred within their souls was transplanted across the pond and many of our greatest freedom fighters were of Scottish and Irish heritage.

As you read the stories over the next few months, you can't help but feel a swell of gratitude for the sacrifices of those before us and a responsibility to not lose what was bought for us at such a high price. And perhaps the best way to help your children value freedom is to see clearly what life looks like without it.

Next month we'll devote a whole month to one man of virtue—George Washington—and the tremendous influence even one great soul can have. And in January we'll visit the Revolutionary War heroes, including the extraordinary Lafayette who sailed from France to help us win our freedom. He wanted nothing more than to bring the same gift back home to his own countrymen, but we'll see that it's not the Constitution that makes us free—it can only secure the freedom of a people who are already free in their hearts and know the personal requirements to remain so. France was not ready.

And then in Month 6—a New Nation is born as we devote a month to studying the Constitution and an experiment in government unlike anything the world had ever seen before. At the same time, we'll study the people of the Bible who also were free under God and take a look at the role the Bible has played in America's story.

Lots of great things ahead. So let me open this next chapter by sharing a story I included in *Stories of Great Americans*.[36] While we revere the names of Patrick Henry, Thomas Jefferson, Benjamin Franklin, George Washington and so many others, let us remember the unsung heroes; the wives and mothers who stayed behind and nurtured the rising generation while the husbands were out in the battle field.

Here is a mother's faith through the eyes of a child.

> My father was in the army during the whole eight years of the Revolutionary War, at first as a common soldier, afterwards as an officer. My mother had the sole charge of us four little ones.
>
> Our house was a poor one, and far from neighbors. I have a keen remembrance of the terrible cold of some of those winters. The snow lay so deep and long, that it was difficult to cut or draw fuel from the woods, or get our corn to the mill, when we had any.
>
> My mother was the possessor of a coffee mill. In that she ground wheat, and made coarse bread, which we ate, and were thankful. It was not always we could be allowed as much, even of this, as our keen appetites craved.
>
> Many is the time that we have gone to bed, with only a drink of water for our supper, in which a little molasses had been mingled. We patiently received it, for we knew our mother did as well for us as she could; and we hoped to have something better in the morning.
>
> She was never heard to repine; and young as we were, we tried to make her loving spirit and heavenly trust, our example.
>
> When my father was permitted to come home, his stay was short, and he had not much to leave us, for the pay of those who achieved our liberties was slight, and irregularly given. Yet when he went, my mother ever bade him farewell with a cheerful face, and told him not to be anxious about his children, for she would watch over them night and day, and God would take care of the families of those who went forth to defend the righteous cause of their country.
>
> Sometimes we wondered that she did not mention the cold weather, or our short meals,

or her hard work, that we little ones might be clothed, and fed, and taught. But she would not weaken his hands, or sadden his heart, for she said a soldier's life was harder than all.

We saw that she never complained, but always kept in her heart a sweet hope, like a well of water. Every night ere we slept, and every morning when we arose, we lifted our little hands for God's blessing on our absent father, and our endangered country.

How deeply the prayers from such solitary homes and faithful hearts were mingled with the infant liberties of our dear native land, we may not know until we enter where we see no more "through a glass darkly, but face to face."

Podcast #112 Patrick Henry

I don't know that we think much about what stirs our hearts. But as I learn more about America's fight for independence, I see the languages of the heart at work. One of the most powerful ways to reach the heart is a play—it's a story played out before our eyes and we are drawn into it in a way that we are almost living the events with the actors. I read somewhere that one of the most popular plays at the time of the Revolution was written by Addison and was based on one of Plutarch's lives, Cato, which we'll read more of in Month 4. The message of this play was that liberty was worth dying for. Some of our early founders watched it numerous times and it said that Washington commissioned the play to be performed at Valley Forge.

I have to wonder if Patrick Henry and Nathan Hale watched it as they gave us the two most quoted phrases of the time: Give me liberty or give me death and I only regret that I have but one life to give to my country.

In this podcast I want to turn to Patrick Henry—my neighbor. I've spent the last couple of 4th of Julys at his beautiful farm up the road and he always comes and shares the powerful speech that moved men's hearts forward at a time when their reluctance was paralyzing their action. The story I am sharing today is from a book called *Historic Americans* by Elbridge S. Brooks[37] and if you like his storytelling style, you might want to check it out for stories on other early patriots like Benjamin Franklin, James Otis, Samuel Adams and Thomas Jefferson.

"A king, by annulling or disallowing acts of so salutary a measure, from being the father of his people degenerates into a tyrant, and forfeits all right to his subjects' obedience."

The young lawyer paused for an instant; but in that instant men had sprung to their feet. Treason! Treason!" came the cry from different parts of the crowded court-room, and Mr. Lyons, the opposing counsel, appealed hotly to the bench where sat the young lawyer's own father as presiding justice. "Treason; the gentleman has spoken treason," he cried. your worships listen to that without showing your disapproval?"

Their worships said nothing. Instead, they sat mute and spellbound under the surprising flow of eloquence from the lips of one whom they had considered neither orator, pleader, nor lawyer, but who now, at one bound and by a sudden burst of eloquence, sprang into popularity, fame, and leadership.

The place was the stuffy little court-house in the county-seat of Hanover, in the Colony of Virginia; the time was the first day of December, 1763; the man was Patrick Henry.

He was arguing on the wrong side of an important case, in which both law and precedent were absolutely against him. It was a case of taxes, in which the council of the king of England had deliberately and contemptuously set aside a law made by the colony. In this case the king's council was right as to judgment, but wrong as to action.

The law it "disallowed" was an unjust one; but the high-handed manner in which king and council overruled and annulled it was not to be borne by the liberty and justice loving colonists who had enacted it.

That was the way in which the matter appeared to Patrick Henry, when, as a forlorn hope, he took up a case which other lawyers would not touch.

"The king of England has no right to meddle in the law-making of this colony. Virginia can look out for herself," he said, and in this spirit he defended a losing case and by his eloquence, earnestness, and argument overruled the judgment of the court, turned a defeat into victory, and won the case he had championed for his clients—the people.

This celebrated case known in American history as "the Parson's Cause"—made the name and established the fame of Patrick Henry as a resistless pleader and an impassioned orator. Up to that date he had not been a success. The son of a Virginia gentleman of small means, young Patrick Henry was left to himself for amusement and education, obtaining a good deal more of the first than of the second. He was a careless, happy-go-lucky country boy of the pleasant region of middle Virginia, loving hunting and fishing more than study and loafing more than books, never succeeding at anything, and sticking to nothing long. He failed as a farmer, failed in business, married a tavern-keeper's daughter when he had nothing on which to support her, and, failing at everything else, hastily concluded to try the law. He failed even in his examinations for that, and was only admitted to the bar through the good-nature of one of the examining lawyers and because of his own success at arguing the other out of a careless indifference. Such a man does not seem fitted to champion a great cause or teach new ideas to an energetic people. But something above the opportunity that lay beneath the Parson's Cause inspired and held young Henry; it gave him an earnestness that surprised and an eloquence that electrified his hearers; and those who hung their heads for shame when Patrick Henry began to speak, lifted him from the floor as he proceeded, and bore him out on their shoulders when he had concluded.

From that day success and fame were his. He sprang into instant popularity as "the people's champion." Practice as a lawyer flowed in upon him; he gained advancement in his own colony and power as a politician. He turned over a new leaf. He was no longer shiftless or unsteady. Popularity brought him business, and business brought him money; as a result he became an influential country gentleman with an estate of his own, with admirers and supporters throughout Virginia, and with the ability to gratify his leanings towards political preferment that speedily gave him position and importance. He was elected a member of the Virginia House of Burgesses, or Legislature; he became a political leader in Virginia, was sent as a delegate to the first and second Continental Congresses, was the first commander of Virginia's Revolutionary army, and was three times governor of Virginia. His fame spread throughout the land, and any office in the gift of the new nation might have been his had he cared to accept it. But he wished for no office. He declined to serve as member of the Constitutional Convention, as United States senator, as secretary of state, as governor of Virginia for the fourth time, as chief-justice of the United States, as ambassador to France, and as vice-president of the United States. He declined, you see, even more than he accepted office.

You know what gave him his greatest fame and led the people of the United States to know, to honor, and to respect him. It was his famous oration in old St. John's Church in Richmond, an oration that has not yet ceased ringing in the ears of Americans, and which, in certain of its impetuous utterances, has become a part of the proverbs and maxims of the Republic. Let me try to draw for you the picture of that remarkable speech in which he urged the arming of the Virginia militia in resistance to the British authorities; for, as Professor Tyler says, "it is chiefly the tradition of that one speech which to-day keeps alive, in millions of American homes, the name of Patrick Henry, and which lifts him, in the popular faith, almost to the rank of some mythical hero of romance."

It is a plain and unpretending little church today as it stands almost on the summit of one of beautiful Richmond's sightly hills—Church hill, it is called—at the corner of Broadway and Twenty-fourth street. Small as it is, the church is to-day much larger than it was on that day in 1775—Thursday, the twenty-third of March—when, rising to his feet, in the pew still shown to visitors and marked by a memorial tablet, Patrick Henry threw down the gauntlet to King George and declared war on the haughty prerogative of Great Britain.

The second Revolutionary convention of Virginia was assembled in that old church on the hill in Richmond. The first convention had met at Williamsburg the year before and had sent to the Continental Congress such representative Virginians as George Washington, Richard Henry Lee, Benjamin Harrison, and Patrick Henry, with others of equal ability, if of less prominence. There Patrick Henry, as pronounced an advocate of open resistance and organized protest as Samuel Adams, of Massachusetts, had advocated a union of all the colonies for mutual protection and defence against the aggressions of England, with equal representation and equal interests for all, saying grandly, as he pled for unity, "The distinctions between Virginians, Pennsylvanians, New Yorkers, and New Englanders are no more. I am not a Virginian, but an American!"

And now the second Revolutionary congress of Virginia had met to debate upon the question whether Virginia should declare for peace or war. Everywhere, throughout the colonies, the people were restless; everywhere there was talk of resistance, and from Massachusetts bay to Charleston harbor the local military companies were being organized for possible emergencies, and drilled to the use of arms. But prudence was keeping men back from act or speech that might be deemed aggressive; prudence was still holding men loyal to the king.

So, when the question of arming the militia of Virginia came up in the colonial convention, and Patrick Henry introduced a resolution that this colony be immediately put into a posture of defence and a committee be appointed to prepare a plan for embodying, arming, and disciplining such a number of men as may be sufficient for that purpose," prudence interfered to prevent so menacing a move.

"The resolution is premature," objected some of the more conservative members. "War with Great Britain may come," they said; "but it may be prevented."

"May come?" exclaimed Patrick Henry; "may come? It has come!" And then, rising in his place, in that narrow pew in old St. John's, he broke out into that famous speech which now, as Professor Tyler remarks, "fills so great a space in the traditions of Revolutionary eloquence."

Tall and thin in figure, with stooping shoulders and sallow face, carelessly dressed in his suit of "parson's gray," Patrick Henry faced the president of the convention, who sat in the chancel of the church, and began calmly, courteously, and with dignity.

"No man, Mr. President" he said, "thinks more highly than I do of the patriotism as well as the abilities of the very honorable gentlemen who have just addressed the house. But different men often see the same subject in different lights; and, therefore, I hope it will not be thought disrespectful to those gentlemen if, entertaining as I do opinions of a character very opposite to theirs, I should speak forth my sentiments freely and without reserve." Then he flung aside courtesy and calmness.

"This is no time for ceremony," he told them hotly. "The question before the house is one of awful moment to the country. For my own part, I consider it as nothing less than a question of freedom or slavery…

"Should I keep back my opinions at such a time, through fear of giving offence, I should consider myself," he declared impressively, "as guilty of treason toward my country, and of an act of disloyalty to the majesty of Heaven, which I revere above all earthly kings."

Then he begun his argument with that sentence which is still as a household word in the mouths of men: "Mr. President, it is natural for man to indulge in the illusions of hope; "and, showing how under existing circumstances hope was but a false beacon, and experience was the only safe guide, he called attention to the armament of England, and demanded: I ask gentlemen, sir, what means this martial array, if its purpose be not to force us to submission?"

Impressively he showed them that England's display of might was meant for America, "sent over to bind and rivet upon us those chains which the British ministry have been so long forging."

He demanded how his associates intended to oppose this British tyranny. Argument had failed, entreaty and supplication were of no avail, compromise was exhausted; petitions and remonstrances, supplications and prostrations, were alike disregarded— "we have been spurned with contempt from the foot of the throne," he said.

"There is no longer," he declared, any room for hope. If we wish to be free, if we wish not basely to abandon the noble struggle in which we have been so long engaged,"—he paused, and then, as one of his hearers said, "with all the calm dignity of Cato addressing the senate; like a voice from heaven uttering the doom of fate," he added solemnly but decisively, "we must fight! I repeat it, sir, we must fight! An appeal to arms and to the God of hosts is all that is left to us."

Then, his calmness all gone, his voice deepening and his slender form swayed with the passion of his own determination, he flung himself into that fervent appeal for union in resistance that we all know so well:

"Besides, sir, we shall not fight our battles alone. There is a just God who presides over the destinies of nations, who will raise up friends to fight our battles for us. The battle, sir, is not to the strong alone; it is to the vigilant, the active, the brave…. It is now too late to retire from the contest. There is no retreat now but in submission and slavery. Our chains are forged. Their clanking may be heard on the plains of Boston. The war is inevitable; and let it come. I repeat it, sir—let it come!"

Can you not almost hear that wonderful voice as it makes that terrible invitation with all the force of confident faith and repressed enthusiasm? Can you not almost see that swaying form, those forcible gestures, that face stern with purpose? Old men there were, years after its utterance, who could not forget that tremendous speech nor how, with their eyes riveted on the speaker, they sat, as one of them expressed it, "sick with excitement."

And then came that ending—one of those immortal bursts of eloquence, a fitting climax to what had gone before:

It is vain, sir, to extenuate the matter. Gentlemen may cry, Peace, peace, but there is no peace! The war is actually begun. The next gale that sweeps from the north will bring to our ears the clash of resounding arms. Our brethren are already in the field. Why stand we here idle? What is it that gentlemen wish? What would they have? Is life so dear, or peace so sweet, as to be purchased at the price of chains and slavery? Forbid it, Almighty God! I know not what course others may take, but as for me give me liberty or give me death!"

That wonderful speech has lived in men's memories and hearts for far over a hundred years. For other hundreds it will live as one of the trumpet calls leading men to fight for freedom or to die free men. To stand in that very pew in old St. John's, as I have done, and to recall that notable speech, thrills and inspires any true American. That speech has made Patrick Henry live forever as America's impassioned orator; but better still, it turned Virginia, as in a flash, for independence, and made her stand side by side with Massachusetts, leaders and coworkers in the fight for liberty.

How ready Patrick Henry was to live up to his grand principles of liberty or death we may discover in his story. From the convention he went speedily to the field. He was made commander-in-chief of Virginia's Revolutionary army, as George Washington was of the Continental forces, and almost the first overt act of the war in Virginia, so

Thomas Jefferson declared, was committed by Patrick Henry. With five thousand hurriedly gathered minute-men he marched upon the king's governor, Lord Dunmore, at Williamsburg and demanded the stolen powder of the province or reparation for its loss; and the king's governor wisely judged discretion to be the better part of valor and sent his receiver-general with three hundred and thirty pounds to pay for the stolen powder. Then he issued a proclamation declaring "a certain Patrick Henry" an outlaw and rebel; but the people of Virginia hailed the "outlaw" as their leader, and heaped him with honors, in the way of thanks and addresses.

There are many points of resemblance in the careers of Samuel Adams and Patrick Henry. Both were "architects of ruin," opponents of prerogative, foes to kingly authority. Both led the attack of the people upon British tyranny and by their matchless labors, with voice or pen, organized revolt, set on foot revolution, and showed the way to liberty and independence. Then, their higher mission accomplished, their work fell into other hands, and they, who had been leaders, became onlookers and critics. Each one was governor of his native State, and each felt alike the sun of popularity and the gloom of misrepresentation and defeat. Both enjoyed a well-merited old age, though Adams outlived his colleague alike in years and honors.

I have told you that Patrick Henry declined more honors than he accepted. One reason was, not that he could not march with the Republic, but because of continued ill-health, which so often dulls the edge of energy, makes a man critical, and keeps him dissatisfied. Alike the friend and critic of Washington, Patrick Henry was also friend and critic of the Republic he had helped to found, loving it for its liberty, but despairing, sometimes, of its future because things were not done as he would like to see them.

He retired from public life largely because of criticism; for, you see, there was a great deal of criticism in the air in those early days of the Republic, and criticism of his acts was one thing that Patrick Henry could not stand. Impetuous as James Otis, determined as Samuel Adams, like both those fervent patriots Patrick Henry chafed under restraint and hated to have his motives called in question. There are, after all, very few such superbly patient, gloriously self-governed men as George Washington and Abraham Lincoln.

But impetuosity is sometimes inspiration. This, at least, was one cause of Patrick Henry's eloquence. As an orator he had remarkable powers; but as a leader he was often uncertain and sometimes headstrong, to his own detriment and his country's peril.

But after all, it is as one who moves by the magic of his words that Patrick Henry's claims to remembrance as an historic American chiefly rest. Above everything else he was an orator; and it is as the orator of resistance, of liberty, and of patriotism that he has our loving and grateful reverence and will be remembered by America forever and ever.

His later years were spent in peaceful pursuits upon his beautiful farm at Red hill near historic Appomattox; and there he died on the sixth of June, 1799, surrounded by loving friends and mourned by America as its chief and most effective orator in the stormy days of protest and revolution.

Podcast #113 Nathan Hale

Continuing with my spotlights of our early heroes who were in love with liberty, I want to now turn to Nathan Hale. I so hope children today still know his story. This version of his story is taken from a 1915 book called *Pioneers and Patriots in Early American History* by Marguerite Dickson.[38]

Some day you will learn in your histories how it came about that the English settlements in America grew stronger than their French neighbors on the north or the Spaniards at the south. You will read about the struggle between French and English for: the Ohio Valley; and how New France was lost to the mother country, and was divided between England and Spain.

Thus it happened that England's possessions in the New World spread from the far north to Spanish territory in Florida. And every year the various colonies grew stronger.

To tell you how these English colonists quarrelled with the government of the mother country would be a long story. Some day you will learn that too in your histories. It is enough for us now to know that the quarrel arose, and that it led to war. No doubt you have already heard of the American Revolution, and the independence the colonists won by force of arms. The story I am now to tell you is the story of a hero of that war.

In a quiet room of a fine old mansion in the city of New York sat the commander-in-chief of the American army—the Continental army, as it was known. Before him stood a young officer, respectfully awaiting the final orders of his chief. For an hour General Washington explained the important mission to be undertaken.

We do not know what their last words were, as the general rose and took the young man by the hand; but the moment must have been a solemn one for both. Both knew the dangers to be encountered; both knew the fate awaiting a captured spy; both knew the scorn of the world for the spy's work; and yet that work must be done.

This important moment in the life of Captain Nathan Hale came when he was barely twenty-one years old. A fine young fellow he was, tall and well built, with handsome features and the glow of perfect health. He had graduated from Yale College only two years before, and had been a favorite with teachers, students, and the townspeople of New Haven. All expected for him a brilliant future, both because of his scholarship and his fine character.

"No young man of his years put forth a fairer promise of future usefulness and celebrity," says one who knew him in his college days.

The war called him from the schoolroom in which he was already making a success as teacher. When the news of the first fighting came, Nathan Hale cried, "Let us march immediately, and never lay down our arms until we have obtained our independence."

With the first company organized in the town he set forth.

That had been more than a year ago. He had already risen to the rank of captain, and was loved by his men as well as his superiors. The army was attempting the impossible task of holding. New York against double its own force of British soldiers and a British fleet. There had been a battle on Long Island which left the British in possession, and now Washington was waiting anxiously to discover the next move of the British commander, General Howe. Would he make an attack on the city itself? Or would he shut the Americans in by seizing some position north of them? Would he attack from the East River or the Hudson?

A constant lookout was kept from heights above the city with powerful field-glasses. But nothing was discovered. Washington called his officers to a council of war. There seemed only one thing to do. Some one must go into the British camp and find out the facts it was necessary to know.

Scarcely any harder task could have been proposed. It required military knowledge; bravery; coolness; caution; daring; judgment; faithfulness—in fact, it seemed as though no worthy quality of head or heart was not required. Who would undertake so delicate and dangerous a mission? Who would brave the scorn of the world, and perhaps suffer death and disgrace, to be a spy?

It was decided that a meeting of officers should be called, and the matter laid before them. The great need must be explained. Perhaps some one would volunteer to make the attempt.

The meeting took place. Colonel Knowlton, who commanded the "Connecticut Rangers," asked for a volunteer to serve the commander-in-chief. He explained the nature of the service. He reminded the officers that it was a case of desperate need. He appealed to their spirit of adventure, their ambition, their love of country. He paused and looked expectantly about the room.

A sudden silence had fallen. There was a look of astonishment on every face—on some a look of indignation. Colonel Knowlton was asking for a spy!

It would be impossible to describe the feelings aroused by Colonel Knowlton's words. Many, probably most, of the officers before him were young men. They had their dreams of the great things they were to do. Who among them wished the story of his life ended with "hanged as a spy"?

For a moment the silence continued. Then came a murmur of protest. And in spite of all that Colonel Knowlton could say, no one would consent to undertake the unwelcome task.

Just as the meeting was breaking up, a young captain in Colonel Knowlton's own regiment entered the room. A group of his friends immediately surrounded him, going over once more the question which had so agitated the meeting. The young captain asked few questions. He waited for no details. But, hearing merely that a volunteer was wanted for secret service for the chief, he turned calmly to Colonel Knowlton, saying, "I will undertake it." A perfect storm of remonstrance met him on every side. Surely he did not understand! It was a spy's work the chief wanted! Suppose he should be caught! Had he forgotten the fate of captured spies?

But no amount of protest changed the calm decision. "I will undertake it," he had said; and now, "I am fully sensible of the consequences of discovery and capture in such a situation.'

"I wish to be useful, and every kind of service necessary for the public good becomes honorable by being necessary." So he answered those who talked of dishonor or disgrace. There is something fine about the unhesitating way in which Nathan Hale made this decision. His country needed a certain service, and against his country's need nothing must count. So, resolutely and with his whole heart, he went the way leading to danger and death.

Almost immediately the young man went to General Washington for orders. Within a few hours he had taken leave of his fellow officers, and set out on his perilous mission.

The first step of his journey was taken that night. With two companions he travelled along the shore of Long Island Sound, looking for a safe place to cross. This was not easy to find, since the whole western end of Long Island was in the hands of the British, and their boats were guarding the Sound. They had reached Norwalk, fifty miles from New York, before they dared make the attempt. Here Hale laid aside his uniform, clothing himself once more in the plain garments of the schoolmaster. Then, bidding his companions await his return, he went on board the sloop which was to take him to the Long Island shore.

Once landed, he bade his boatmen return for him on a certain day. Then he assumed the character of a schoolmaster who was disgusted with the "rebellious Americans," and was himself a loyal supporter of King George. He was in search of employment as teacher. In this capacity he found little difficulty in making friends with loyalists and in gaining entrance to British camps. It is said he visited all the camps on Long Island, crossed to New York, which the British had now taken, and, returning to Long Island, made his way back to the place where his boatmen were to meet him.

So far his work had been done skilfully; in his shoes, beneath loose inner soles, were drawings of British fortifications and information written in Latin on the thinnest of paper. It was night, and before sunrise he would be on his way back across the Sound, to safety. Once on the safe side of the Sound, he might resume his uniform, and be himself once more—Captain Nathan Hale—on the way to rejoin his regiment, north of the city.

Only one night! but until he should be safe on board the sloop, he must still be the loyalist schoolmaster, with ear and eye quick to see danger, and with nerve strong and alert to meet it.

So it happened that a loyalist schoolmaster entered a tavern near the Long Island shore, to pass the night.

The tavern was a favorite meeting place for loyalists, and they were out in full force when the schoolmaster stepped in. Among them a red coat or two marked British soldiers. All were merry, and they called the schoolmaster to join them. He scarcely dared refuse. But it was the last night! Tomorrow, at dawn, he would find his friends awaiting him on the shore. Until then he must play his part.

It is said that a loyalist in the party looked keenly at the stranger—looked and looked again; then silently, still looking, passed out into the night and was seen no more.

We wonder at the nerve and coolness of this boy of twenty-one, seated among his bitter foes, and obliged to take his part in the gay and careless chatter of the hour. We wonder if he noticed the overcareful stare of the man who left his companions early, and if one thrill of fear disturbed his even heart-beat.

At last he was freed from the idle chatter. The house was quiet, and morning was not far off. He watched the slow change of the sky from black to gray. Masses of shadow showed at length as hills and trees. Faint streaks of light appeared in the eastern sky. A rosy flush told of coming day.

Silently the loyalist schoolmaster made his way from the tavern to the shore. His friends must be near. In a few minutes more, this strain would be over. Surely they would not fail him. No! he could see in the half light of the early morning, a boat cautiously approaching the shore.

Running swiftly down, he threw up his hand in signal, and in a moment was at the water's edge. The rest of the story is almost too sad and awful to tell. But we must hear it to value Nathan Hale at his true worth. Never was more courageous boy than he! Never was man with greater bravery than this man of twenty-one!

You will have guessed that the boat was manned by British soldiers. You will guess their errand on this lonely shore. Whether the watchful loyalist of the night before knew Hale and sent a message to the British we cannot tell. We know only that the brave boy stood on the shore with six British muskets levelled at his head. "Surrender or die was the curt order. A moment later the boat moved off, bearing among the redcoated soldiers a suspected spy.

Carried to a near-by British guard ship, Hale was searched, and the papers found in his shoes. Nothing more was needed to prove him the spy they had believed him to be. Taken now to the headquarters of General Howe, the British commander-in-chief, Hale made no effort to conceal his name and rank, or the work he had been doing, and why. We are told that General Howe was moved to pity by the fine, frank manner of the young officer, but he had no power to change the fate reserved for spies. He ordered Hale to be hanged before sunrise next morning. Hale was led away.

The last night of Nathan Hale's life was spent alone, under strong guard. Who can guess the thoughts that filled those wakeful hours? There is nothing to cause the belief that for a moment he felt regret for what he had done. He had been close to success—and life. An unhappy chance had sharply turned his steps toward failure—and death. He must face death as he had faced the task now to be forever unfinished—with calm decision and with a love of country so great as to blot out all else. Long before morning light, the prisoner was sent under guard to be delivered into the hands of the executioner.

The last test of the patriot spy was at hand.

A brutal man was the provost marshal into whose hands Hale fell. No last insult was too great for him to offer. Denied a minister, denied a Bible, denied even permission to write a farewell word to his mother, the hero Hale sat silent in a tent while the final preparations were being made.

A pitying officer brought a Bible and paper for letters. The boy wrote to his mother, his sisters, his sweetheart. But even that small comfort was of brief duration. The provost marshal read the letters and tore them to fragments before his victim's eyes. He said he had no idea of letting the rebels know they had a man who could die with such firmness.

Let us draw a veil over the rest of the sad story, lifting it only for a moment to catch the last words of Nathan Hale. In the last moment of Hale's life, the provost marshal tauntingly demanded a "confession."

Hale seemed not to hear him. With his fine head still lifted fearlessly. he looked out and through and beyond any taunts of men. And then he spoke—to himself, or perhaps to the world—to you, to me. These were his words:

"I only regret that I have but one life to live for my country."

And then he died; and by his death glorified the name of spy. For he loved his country, and he served her with his life, choosing not the shining road to fame and glory, but the darker one to lonely and embittered death. And the light of his devotion lights that path forever.

Podcast #116 Saint Patrick

C.S. Lewis wrote: "God can make use of all that happens." As I look at the story of the Pilgrims, while Holland was a difficult chapter in their lives, Bradford acknowledged that if they hadn't gone through the hardships there, they would have been too soft for life in the New World. None of them would have survived. I thought the same thing as I read the story of George Washington in the French and Indian War. No one loves war, but it served to prepare him to later lead his ragtag Continental troops to victory over the most powerful army in the world.

Today I'd like to share the story of Saint Patrick and you will, again, find God making use of all the hard things that happened in Patrick's life. Today's sampler is taken from Clayton Edward's 1920 book, *A Treasury of Heroes and Heroines*.[39] And then I'll be back at the end with some thoughts of what happened next.

> No saint's name is more familiar than holy Saint Patrick's. Legends have sprung up around it as thick as the grass of Ireland from which he is believed to have chased the serpents into the sea—but in all the calendar hardly a saint is known less about than this marvelous man, who carried the Christian religion to every corner of the emerald island.
>
> Saint Patrick was not a native of Ireland—he was born, perhaps in 373 a.d., in the little town of Banavem Taberniæ, a Roman town in ancient Scotland not far from the modern city of Glasgow. Rome had ruled the world for hundreds of years and the swords of her soldiers had been uplifted in every known land. Hence it was that Saint Patrick came into the world as a future citizen of Rome and the son of a wealthy and respected Roman colonist. His father was named Calpornius and was a deacon of the Christian church in the town where he lived, and the mother of the future saint was also a devout Christian, the niece of the renowned Bishop Martin of the city of Tours in France.
>
> Calpornius and his wife were so ardent in religion that they spent day and night in teaching their son the story of the gospel and the psalms. They desired first of all that he should be a good Christian and a bearer of the faith—but they wearied the growing boy with long hours of study and monotonous recitals of religious hymns and proverbs when he was eager to be ranging the hills or playing with his fellows. At that time he had no particular desire to be a priest, and, like most boys, was far more interested in the stories of heroes than the stories of saints, preferring to hear of the wild Scottish chiefs and the Roman Generals with whom they had engaged in bitter warfare.
>
> He thirsted for adventure, and adventure was to come to him. Those were wild days, and law only reached as far as it could be upheld by the sword and the arrow. Pirates harried the seas and from the north the galleys of the sea robbers were soon to range southward in search of lands where plunder was to be found and men and women to be carried into slavery.

One night, when a gale was blowing from the northeast, St. Patrick, we are told, sat with some friends in the glowing light of a great peat fire, where they warmed themselves at the same time that they told stories of adventure and sang Scottish songs as wild and melancholy as the wind that was scouring the hills. Saint Patrick was now a lad of sixteen, with well knit limbs and a powerful body that made him appear older than he really was, and at the same time gave promise of greater strength to come. He listened keenly to the singing, but at the same time gave ear to sounds that he heard without the hut, for the rough voices of men speaking an unknown tongue seemed to be mingling with the noise of the storm. At last he sprang up with a shout of warning, a shout that was answered by a battle cry from without. A pirate galley had made its way to the shore and the crew were engaged on a raid to capture slaves. Some of Saint Patrick's companions were clubbed or cut down where they sat, but he was thrown and strongly bound, dragged roughly to the shore and tossed on board the robber craft that quickly made its way to sea in spite of the tremendous surf that broke over the backs of the oarsmen.

For several days they fought the sea and at last came to the coast of northern Ireland, where Saint Patrick was sold as a slave to an Irish chief named Miliuc. It is probable that the pirates gained a rich reward for the clean-limbed boy, whose strength and ability were evident to all who saw him. When the bargain was finished they boarded their vessel and sailed away, leaving the luckless boy in the hands of his new master.

And straightway there commenced for Saint Patrick a bitterly hard life, for little kindness was wasted on those who were sold into bondage, and slaves were compelled to labor terribly with aching muscles and empty bellies, beaten and cuffed at the whim of their master—who had a perfect right to slay them if he so desired Hunger, blows and fatigue were Saint Patrick's portion and were added to the homesickness of a young man torn from affectionate parents.

And then Saint Patrick found consolation in the religious teachings that had been drummed into his unwilling ears, and in the midst of his suffering he turned to his faith for comfort. He remembered the psalms that had been taught by his father and mother and said them repeatedly, and he even forbore at times to eat his meagre rations, thinking that by fasting he might prove worthy in the eyes of the Lord.

And one night he had a dream in which he heard a voice, which said to him: "Fast no more, but fly, for a vessel now awaits you to carry you away from your bondage. Truly you shall behold your parents again and once more be free and happy."

Saint Patrick woke in amazement after this dream, but he was so certain that the voice which spoke to him was real that he did not hesitate to obey it. Watching his opportunity he slipped away from the chief who had held him for six years in bitter servitude, and walking and running by turns he made his way southward in search of the vessel that he knew must be awaiting him.

He did not concern himself about the path, for he felt that Heaven would guide him;

and indeed after he had marched for two hundred miles, he came to the coast, and just as he had dreamed a vessel lay at anchor near the shore and some of the sailors were standing on the beach.

Saint Patrick ran up to them and implored the captain to carry him away from Ireland back to his own country. His wild appearance startled the master of the vessel, but after considerable doubt the captain consented, and Saint Patrick boarded the ship where he was to work his passage across the channel.

They set sail at once and bent their backs to the oars, for in those days ships were moved over the water by rowers as well as by sails; and after three days they came not to Scotland, but the shore of France, landing in a wild and desolate region where no human habitation was to be seen. Their provision had run low and they were in danger of dying of hunger, when the captain, who had closely watched Saint Patrick during the voyage and observed his piety, asked him to pray to the Christian god to bring them food, for the captain himself was not a Christian and believed that his own prayers would be worthless on this account. And Saint Patrick knelt and prayed, and before he had risen to his feet again a wild boar ran from the thicket and then another and still a third, all of which were promptly slain and the meat roasted on sticks.

Then Saint Patrick bade farewell to his shipmates, and made his way to the city of Tours, where to his joy he met Bishop Martin, who was his own great uncle. And he stayed at the home of the Bishop for four years.

After this time he tried again to reach Scotland, to which he was drawn every hour by ties of blood and affection; and at last he embarked on a vessel bound to a port very near his own native town. He found his father and mother still living and they rejoiced mightily to see him, for to them he was as one who had returned from the dead. In place of the boy they had lost there appeared a tall and finely built man with a face hardened by toil but made noble by thought and suffering. And they had a feast to celebrate his return and wept for joy because they had their son again.

But the dreams that Saint Patrick had experienced in Ireland once more came to him, and in his sleep he heard the Heavenly voice telling him that he had been rescued from slavery for no mean or ordinary purpose, but must go again into Ireland as a priest, and teach the Christian religion to the savage Irish clans. So Saint Patrick knew that he must return to Ireland, and, bidding his parents farewell, he departed to become a priest in preparation for the labor that lay before him.

He studied to such purpose that he became a Bishop, celebrated for his learning and famous among the clergymen; and when this was accomplished he set sail once more for Ireland with a retinue of priests and clergymen accompanying him. But although he was going to a savage land where he had already experienced much bitterness and sorrow, he went unarmed, and among his entire company there was not so much as a single sword or lance.

He came to a place called Strangford Lough and there landed with his band of missionaries. The Irish fled at his approach, for they feared that the tall man who bore the cross was the leader of an invading army, and also that he possessed the arts of magic by which he would do injury to them.

Many of the Irish believed in the religion of the Druids—a strange faith that brought in the magic arts and endeavored to teach above all other things that a man's soul when he dies enters another human body. This belief was widely established throughout the world, and it is true that many persons beside the Druids believed in it; but the Druids had other beliefs that were cruel and dangerous. They were said to perform human sacrifices and their priests to practise black magic. These priests wore about their necks the "serpent's egg," a ball formed of the spittle of many poisonous snakes; they knew many strange things about animals and plants and held the oak tree to be sacred. For this reason they worshipped in oaken groves, and considered the mistletoe that grew around oak trees to have divine powers. It was cut by white-robed priests with golden knives in an impressive ceremony.

It can readily be seen that such people, who believed in such a faith, would not easily become Christians. Their priests were clever and knew how to place the stamp of fear and wonder on their minds. And—in company with all other people in those days—the Irish distrusted outsiders and were far more ready to believe them coming in treachery than in friendship.

When Saint Patrick and his followers set foot in Ireland it was the time of a great religious festival in which no lights were allowed to be lit or fires to be kindled for several days. Saint Patrick knew this, for he was well versed in the religious customs of the Irish, and he knew, too, that the penalty for disobeying the priestly order was a terrible death.

None the less, and in spite of being unarmed, he ordered his followers to build an enormous fire that could be seen for miles. When the great logs and the faggots were piled together Saint Patrick kindled the pile with his own hands and the flames shot high in the air, throwing strange shadows on the trees and causing the Irish to cry out in fear and astonishment. The Druid priests were greatly angered and perturbed at what Saint Patrick had done, and they went at once to the King, who was named Laoghaire MacNeill, telling him that the foreign band had desecrated the Druid faith and must be punished with death. Then the King told the priests to go and fetch Saint Patrick and bring him to judgment, but the priests feared the fire that had been kindled, thinking that it had magic powers. So they went as far as they dared and called out to Saint Patrick, summoning him to appear before the judges of the land.

Promptly and with fearless demeanor, Saint Patrick joined the priests and was taken before the King. And when the King demanded of him how he had dared to disobey the laws of the country and profane its religion, Saint Patrick answered that he did so because the light of the Christian faith was infinitely brighter than the light of any fire that he or any one else had power to kindle; and that the fire he had built was merely a sign to call the Irish to the worship of the true God. Then he preached, and his words were so wise and spoken with such weight of eloquence that many that heard him became Christians on the spot, and the work of converting Ireland was soon well under way.

There were many of the Irish that loved Saint Patrick, but he had many bitter enemies. On one occasion a powerful Irishman, who was enraged at the Saint for having taken a stone sacred to the Druids for a Christian altar, vowed that he must die. So he lay in wait in a patch of woods near a road over which he knew Saint Patrick would pass, with a sharp javelin to pierce his heart.

Saint Patrick had an Irish boy for his servant and this boy knew of the threat and the place and was greatly afraid for the life of his beloved master. But he knew, too, that it would be useless to ask Saint Patrick to go by another road, for fear was unknown to him. So the boy pretended to be weary and asked Saint Patrick to take the reins of the horse that they were driving; and the brave lad seated himself in his master's place. They came to the wood; there was a sudden stirring of the bushes and the hiss of a javelin which imbedded itself in the boy's heart, killing him instantly. The assassin had taken his master for the ordinary driver and Saint Patrick's life was saved.

Ardently the Saint set to work to bring about the conversion of the Irish, and he did his work so well that when he became an old man there were no heathen left in Ireland, and his name was loved and venerated from one end of the island to the other. And the legends grew up so quickly about him that it is hard to separate the true from the false.

He had written a famous hymn which was called "the breastplate," being as he said the best and strongest armor he or any other Christian could bear, since it was a confession of his faith in the Christian religion. On many occasions, when men sought his life, it is said he chanted this hymn and they let him pass.

Saint Patrick is said to have driven all the snakes out of Ireland into the sea—and it is notable that there are no snakes there to-day. And the other marvelous things he is believed to have accomplished are manifold. He died at a ripe old age and from the day of his death to the present one no man has been more revered in the land where he labored,—for the name of Saint Patrick is in every Irish heart and Saint Patrick's Day is celebrated by Irishmen in every part of the world.

One little observation: Did you notice how, even though in the moment, the stories and the hymns St. Patrick's very diligent parents planted in their son's heart, didn't appear to take, they surfaced in Patrick's moment of need and brought comfort and courage to him?

The story of St. Patrick is another example of the influence of one man of virtue. He is said to have converted over 100,000 souls to Jesus Christ—the entire island of Ireland. They had been a wild and barbaric people. I noted that their conversion wasn't to a religion of ritual; it was to Jesus Christ himself. They loved Him. The symbol of light was central to their lives as it symbolized the light of Christ burning in their hearts and the fervent love and devotion they felt in following and serving Him. And they understood that everything in creation was instilled with the divine spirit of Christ and therefore they had a heartfelt appreciation for nature, just like we're trying to do with our children.

And then came the miracle for which God had prepared. This Celtic Race was an exceptionally imaginative people and they expressed their faith through the creative arts. Their poets and storytellers were highly regarded and influential and God made use of that. This was at the time when the Roman Empire had fallen and the rest of Europe had fallen into a dark state of chaos and anarchy. Barbarians looted the artifacts, but seeing no value in the books, they burned them. So the Irish monks snatched up every piece of literature they could get their hands on and started copying it. Great libraries were established. The Emerald Isle became the center for learning for the rest of the world. And in due time, those monks went forth among the wasteland with books tied around their waists and a love of learning burning in their souls and they started planting seeds of light all over Europe.

Some scholars say the Irish saved civilization.

And Saint Patrick, who fearlessly followed where the Lord led, prepared the way.

Daniel Lattiere, who wrote an article for *Intellectual Takeout*, gives especially members of our Well-Educated Heart group good food for thought. He wrote:

> I've argued elsewhere we may be on the cusp of a new Dark Age, not due to the lack of books this time, but to a lack of knowledge of the contents of those books. As in the time of the Irish monks of the Middle Ages, what we desperately need are small communities of learners who dedicate themselves to the diligent study and passing on of those classical authors, ideas and languages that are no longer taught in schools today.

In other words, what we once again need are people who dedicate themselves to saving civilization.

Those monks who, day after day, copied words in their copy books may not have realized any more than your children do that what they are doing is saving civilization, but I have strong suspicion that one day, God is going to make use of that. Just like C.S. Lewis said.

Podcast #118 The Song of Caedmon

If we only realized the gift and power of song in our lives, we would give it its proper place of importance in the education of our children. Someone in the Facebook group posted a little blurb on what happens to the brain when singing. Neuroscientists have observed the whole brain lighting up. They said singing activates organizing and planning networks, language and listening networks, memory networks. It activates emotional networks, enhancing social bonding and empathy. And it releases dopamine—that feel-good chemical for the brain.

God knows these things and music has been used to move people and nations. In the introduction to my faith's hymnal, it reads: "Hymns can lift our spirits, give us courage, and move us to righteous actions. They can fill our souls with heavenly thoughts and bring us a spirit of peace."

In today's sampler, I want to share the story of the song of Caedmon, a story that ties together this month's British study as well as the Mother's University topic of Music. It's taken from a 1904 book called *Children's Stories in English Literature* by Henrietta Wright.[40]

Here is the chapter.

> The old British songs and the story of Beowulf belong to the time before England received the name it is now known by, and when the tribes which inhabited the land were often hostile, and always jealous of the power which each held. But as years passed the land grew more peaceful, and even the old warriors who had fought so fiercely at length came to imagine a future when there should be harmony between the different tribes, and when their children's children should no longer look upon one another as rivals, but all should be joined together by mutual interests, and the word English stand for all the people who called that country their home.
>
> And this time at last actually came, but in a way perhaps that the fierce sea-kings had never dreamed of, for the cause was so unlike anything that had ever influenced them, that it is no wonder they could know nothing of it. Differ as they might in many things, the Saxons and the Britons were all alike in their love for battle and the deep, undying hatred which they felt toward an invader of their homes. The British chieftain longed to die finally in battle, for his religion taught him it was the one glorious thing to do, and the Saxon chief was filled with the same desire, for the priests had taught him that only in this way could he win entrance to Valhalla, the Norseman's heaven.
>
> But there had come to Britain from across the sea, many years before the first Saxons landed on its shores, a little band of men who neither were dressed in glittering armor, nor held in their hands the cruel weapons of war, but who wore coarse garments such as the poorest might have worn, and bore a banner on which was wrought the figure of a dove, the emblem of peace.

They were Christian missionaries who had heard of the cruel religious practices of the Britons, and their love of revenge, and they had come to the island with the hope of winning them to a purer religion. Their simple ways of life, their honest service to their faith, their kindness to the poor, and the hope they gave of a better life beyond the grave, made a deep impression upon their listeners, who admired their courage in coming among a hostile people, sympathized with them in their indifference to hardship and deprivation, and found a strange pleasure in the thought that the new religion offered a strong field for battle, though the fighting was not to be with sword or spear, but against the strong powers of selfish courage and savage greed of power, and with the weapons of self-denial and a love that seemed all the greater because of its humility.

Many converts were won, and from this time Britain contained here and there little bands of native Christians who tried to lead their more savage brothers into gentler ways of living. Gradually churches and monasteries were established and the Christian religion was acknowledged by many, and Christian communities could be found in various places; and so extensive was the conversion that British bishops sat in the Council that was held in Arles, France, in 314, to discuss matters of importance to the Church. When the Saxon tribes came to Britain, bringing with them their religion of war and bloodshed, and finally succeeded in driving the Britons away from many places where they made Saxon settlements, the Christian religion suffered greatly from the change, and many of the British Christians went back to their ancient faith. Still, in the north of England, where the Church was too firmly established to perish before heathenism, the invaders gradually adopted the religion of the conquered, and the country became gradually rechristianized. Lona afterward Christian priests from Rome came to the Saxon settlements in the south and preached the new religion of love and mercy, and in time their doctrines won favor and the southern Saxons began again to accept Christianity and to dream of another life than one of continued fighting and feasting.

Perhaps the listening warriors remembered the story of Beowulf, and how his great battle was fought with other weapons than they knew any, thing of, and how he met death gloriously while trying unselfishly to serve the people he loved; perhaps they remembered that their great gods Odin and Thor, whose service was fear, were after all less loved by them than the gentle Baldur, whose service was peace, because all nature loved him. At any rate, from whatever reason, the new religion gradually spread from one part of the island to another, heathen temples were pulled down, heathen gods were forsaken, and there came at last a day when England could be called a Christian land from shore to shore. And then all over the country arose monasteries and churches, and the people were more firmly united than they had ever been before, for the new faith bound one and all, high and low, in the perfect brotherhood which the monks meant to establish when they told the story of how the new faith was first preached, not to great kings or mighty warriors, but to the humble shepherds who were watching their flocks on the hillsides around Bethlehem.

This great change could not take place without affecting the nation in many ways. War ceased to be glorified, and was looked upon as a fearful necessity and not the object of life. And the old war-songs and battle-chants gave place to Christian hymns, and it became more common to hear the sweet voices of nuns singing matins and vespers, than to start at the sound of the war-trumpet. And so it is not strange to find that about the same time that the story of Beowulf was written to please the warlike chieftains, another great poem should be sung by a Christian monk, to glorify the mission of the Church of peace, and should have for its subject the stories and incidents which are found in the Bible.

The author of this poem, known to us as Caedmon, from the name given to him by the monks when he was received into the monastery of Whitby, was born in 625, and had been perhaps, before his entrance into the community, a tenant-farmer on some of the abbey lands. In those days the lowliest born and the highest were alike in their love for song, and when we consider that their lives were for the most part spent in hard, monotonous labor, or warfare, and that what is called the beautiful had very little share in them, we do not wonder that they cherished the gift of song as the one bright thing in their existence. And so common was this gift among all classes, that it was looked upon as a reproach not to be able to sing.

According to a popular legend, Caedmon had not the gift of song at all, and felt his deficiency deeply, and this sorrow grew upon him so that he used to rise and leave the room when the harp was passed around, so that no one should see how deeply he was hurt. Thus his life was very lonely, and often sad, and as he wandered with the cattle over the meadows and heard the lark beginning the day with its sweet song, or listened to the music of the nightingale singing in the dark, when he sought to escape from the jeers of his companions, he felt that all nature had a voice and that he alone was dumb. But one night, when his friends were even merrier than usual at the feast, and the harp passed rapidly from one to another, Caedmon arose as was his custom and left the room. It was his turn to watch over the cattle during the night, and he lay down on his bed of straw and closed his eyes. But as he lay sleeping, a stranger with a face and form more beautiful than he had ever seen before, came to him in a dream, and touched him, and said, "Caedmon, sing." And Caedmon answered, "I cannot." But the stranger insisted and said, "Thou must sing." And as Caedmon looked on him he felt the birth of a new power in his soul, and his heart leaped with joy, for his visitor had brought to him the thing that he had desired above all others—the gift of song.

Then he was as eager to sing as a captive bird to use its wings, and he said to the stranger, "What shall I sing?" And he answered, "Sing me the origin of all things." Then in his dream Caedmon sang words and music that he had never heard before, in praise of the Creator of the world. And when the dream left him he still kept the music in his mind, and in the morning told the vision to an officer of the town, who led him to the Abbess Hilda, who had charge of the monastery, and who was so well beloved that everyone called her Mother. Hilda listened to Caedmon's song, and then called together all the learned men of the Order to determine the nature of his gift; for in those days it was often believed that anything uncommon might bring evil to its possessor. But as Caedmon sang, the holy men at once decided that his gift had come from heaven, for the music seemed to them divine. Then they read to Caedmon some portions of the Bible, and asked him if he could turn them into melody; and the next day he came again to the monastery and sang the words that had been given him, turning them into such sweet music that the abbess became convinced that he had been called by God to another way of life. So she persuaded him to become a monk and received him into the minster, and bade the wise among the company teach him the words of the Bible, so that he might sing the Scriptures and thus bring greater glory to their religion.

Caedmon listened to the accounts from the Bible and turned them all into song, so that a great part of the Scriptures became known to the people of that community through his singing, which was so unlike anything that had ever been heard before that he was looked upon as being especially endowed with the divine favor.

Caedmon lived in the monastery until he became an old man, loved by all the Order and the people of the neighborhood, and his fame spread abroad throughout all England, and many strangers came to Whitby, attracted only by the wonder of his voice. The monks wrote his songs down carefully, and they were learned by all the people, and became as familiar as the war-songs and love-ballads that were sung at their feasts. And though many other minstrels tried to sing of heavenly things and rival Caedmon, they could not, for his gift was the greater, and was considered by all to be divine from the manner of its coming to him. So his fame remained unrivalled, and after many years death came to him at last as the monks were singing nocturns, and so he had sweet music till the end.

Without accepting the miraculous part of this tradition we may easily see how the idea of paraphrasing the Scriptures may have come to Caedmon in a dream; and it has been conjectured that his never having sung before was due to religious scruple, fostered by the missionaries, against encouraging the warlike and unchristian feelings aroused by the minstrelsy of the time, and that he used his native gift as soon as he conceived the idea of singing the praises of religion with it. He was deeply religious, he lived where there had been the greatest mingling of the British and Saxon races, and though we cannot say positively that he was of Celtic blood, it is certain that he was inspired by the Celtic and missionary spirit, and was hostile to the traditions of the Saxon bards, who celebrated the victories of their chiefs and the deeds of Norse heroes.

Although the subjects of his verse were not original with him, yet in his Paraphrase Caedmon showed himself a true poet, at a time when the English race was considered almost as barbarian by the more enlightened nations. The literature of any other country was quite unknown to him, and it is from this fact that his poetry is peculiarly valuable, since we are sure that whatever beauty it possesses belongs to Caedmon alone.

I loved the lessons of good overcoming evil in this sample. But I especially loved the reminder of the divine influence on the hearts of true artists. Richard Wyche wrote—as did many of the heart educators—"No poet, painter, sculptor, builder, musician, writer or worker of any kind who has ever done abiding work did it apart from the spirit."

Are you having a gloomy day? A childhood song comes to mind:

> A song is a wonderful kind of thing
> So lift up your voice and sing.
> Just start a glad song, let it float let it ring
> And lift up your voice and sing.
>
> We shall make music to lighten the day
> We shall make music to brighten the way.
> Lift up your voice
> Lift up your voice
> Lift up your voice and sing.

Podcast #120 King Arthur and His Knights of the Round Table

This month has flown by and there are so many more things and people I wanted to share with you! But we'll be back by next year. But I can't leave England without talking about King Arthur and the spirit of Chivalry.

It is true that Chivalry, as it was practiced in the Middle Ages, is dead. But when we read these stories of King Arthur and his knights, we keep alive the spirit of chivalry in a new generation. The spirit of one high school was completely changed through the use of these stories. Richard Wyche wrote: "A teacher in a high school informs me that the study, dramatization, and an attempt on the part of the children to live again its spirit transformed the life of the school, bringing in a reign of kindness and courtesy that had never before been known in her classes."

I remember hearing of a Lady in England who would bring poor youth out of the crowded dirty London streets to her country estate for a sort of summer camp. She was appalled at their crude, coarse behavior and their profanity. Rather than tackling it directly, she immersed them in the stories of King Arthur and his knights and the change in their behavior was remarkable.

I've tried to provide you a variety of books to choose from so that you can find something that is appropriate for the ages of your children. For my daily sampler, I am going to read you the first chapter in a 1905 version written by Maude Radford[41] for 5th and 6th graders so you can get a sense of it. This is probably the simplest of the King Arthur versions and I especially liked it because of the picture images she creates in telling the story. You'll see what I mean.

But before I do that, let me share a few excerpts from the introduction of another book, *Stories of King Arthur*,[42] to give you a little background on where the Arthurian legends came from and also to give you a brief look at the beginnings of chivalry and what happened to it. The oath of the Knight was really one of service to his God and to society to protect the oppressed and to uphold the right. A knight took a solemn vow "to speak the truth, to succor the helpless and oppressed and never turn back from an enemy."

We could use a little more of that in our world today, don't you think?

Here's the intro first.

> Among the best liked stories of five or six hundred years ago were those which told of chivalrous deeds—of joust and journey and knightly adventure. To be sure, these stories were not set forth in printed books, for there were no printed books as early as the times of the first three King Edwards, and few people could have read them if there had been any. But children and grown people alike were eager to hear these old-time tales read or recited by the minstrels, and the interest in them has continued in some measure through all the changing years of taste…
>
> In these early romances of chivalry, Arthur and his knights of the Round Table are by far the most popular heroes, and the finding of the Holy Grail is the highest

achievement of knightly valor. The material for the Arthur stories came from many countries and from many different periods of history. Much of it is wholly fanciful, but the writers connected all the incidents directly or indirectly with the old Britain king of the fifth century, who was the model of knighthood, "without fear and without reproach."

Perhaps there was a real King Arthur, who led the Britains against the Saxon invaders of their land, who was killed by his traitor nephew, and who was buried at Glastonbury—the valley of Avilion of the legends; perhaps there was a slight historical nucleus around which all the romantic material was crystallizing through the centuries, but the Arthur of romance came largely from the imagination of the early writers.

And yet, though our "own ideal knight" may never have trod the soil of Britain or Roman or Saxon England, his chivalrous character and the knightly deeds of his followers are real to us, if we read them rightly, for "the poet's ideal was the truest truth." Though the sacred vessel—the Holy Grail—of the Christ's last supper with his disciples has not been borne about the earth in material form, to be seen only by those of stainless life and character, it is eternally true that the "pure in heart" are "blessed," "for they shall see God." This is what the Quest of the Holy Grail means, and there is still many a true Sir Galahad, who can say, as he did,

> "My strength is as the strength of ten,
> Because my heart is pure,"

and who attains the highest glory of knighthood, as before his clear vision

> "down dark tides the glory glides,
> And starlike mingles with the stars."

We call these beautiful stories of long ago Stories of Chivalry, for, in the Middle Ages, chivalry influenced all that people did and said and thought. It began back in the times of Charlemagne, a hundred years before our own King Alfred, and only very gradually it made its ways through all the social order. Emperor Charlemagne was really a very great man, and because he was so, he left all Western Europe a far better place to live in than he found it. Into the social life of his time he brought something like order and justice and peace, and so he greatly helped the Christian Church to do it work of teaching the rough and warlike Franks and Saxons and Normans the gentle ways of thrift and helpfulness.

Charlemagne's "heerban" or call to arms, required that certain of his men should attend him on horseback, and this mounted service was really the beginning of what is known as chivalry. The lesser nobles of each feudal chief served their overlords on horseback, a cheval, in time of war; they were called knights, which originally meant servants— German *knechte*; and the system of knighthood, its rules, customs, and duties, was called chivalry—French *chevalerie*.

When rightly exercised chivalry was a great blessing to the people of its time. It offered high ideals of pure-minded, warm-hearted, courtly, courageous Christian manhood. It did much to arouse thought, to quicken sympathy, to purify morals, to make men truly brave and loyal. Of course this ideal of character was not in the days of chivalry—ideals are not often now—very fully realized. The Mediaeval, like the Modern, abused his power of muscle, of sword, of rank. His liberty as a knight-errant sometimes descended into the license of a highwayman; his pride in the opportunity for helpfulness grew to be the braggadocio of a bully; his freedom of personal choice became the insolence of lawlessness; his pretended purity and justice proved wanton selfishness.

Because of these abuses that crept into the system, it is well for the world that gunpowder at last came, to break through the knight's coat of mail, to teach the nobility respect for common men, roughly to end this age of so much superficial politeness and savage bravery, and to bring in a more democratic social order.

The books of any age are for us a record of how the people of that age thought, how they lived, and what kind of men and women they tried to be. The old romances of chivalry give us clear pictures of the knights and ladies of the Middle ages, and we shall lose the delight and the profit they may give us, if we think only of the defects of chivalry, and close our eyes to the really worthy motives of those far-off times, and so miss seeing what chivalry was able to do, while it lasted, to make men and women better and happier.

After giving ideas to generation after generation of romance writers of many countries and in many languages, these same romantic stories were, in the fifteenth century, skillfully brought together into one connected prose narrative—one of the choicest of the older English classics, "Le Morte Darthur," by Sir Thomas Malory. Those were troublous times when Sir Thomas, perhaps after having himself fought and suffered in the Wars of the Roses then in progress, found some quiet spot in Warwickshire in which to put together in lasting form the fine old stories that already in his day were classics.

[Fifteen years later, when Caxton set up the first printing press in England, the nobility of the age requested he print the "noble history of the Holy Grail and of the most renowned Christian king—Arthur."]

Generation after generation of readers and of writers have drawn life from its chapters, and the new delight in Tennyson's "Idylls of the King," shows that the fountain has not yet been drained dry.

Chivalry of just King Arthur's kind was given up long ago, but that for which it stood—human fellowship in noble purpose—is far older than the institution of knighthood or than even the traditions of the energetic, brave, true, helpful King Arthur himself. It links us with all the past and all the future. The knights of the twentieth century do not set out in chain-armor to right the wrongs of the oppressed by force of arms, but the best influences of chivalry have been preserved for the quickening of a broader and a nobler world than was ever in the dreams of knight-errant of old. Modern heroes of the genuine type owe more than they know to those of Arthur's court who swore

198

"To reverence the King, as if he were
Their conscience, and their conscience as their King,
To break the heathen and uphold the Christ,
To ride abroad redressing human wrongs,
To speak no slander, no, nor listen to it,
To honor his own word as if his God's,
To lead sweet lives in purest chastity,
To love one maiden only, cleave to her,
And worship her by years of noble deeds,
Until they won her."

"Antiquity produced heroes, but not gentlemen," someone has said. In the days of Charlemagne and Alfred began the training which, continued in the days of Chaucer and Sir Thomas Malory and many, many more, has given to this our age that highest type of manhood, the Christian gentleman.

And now Chapter 1: How Arthur Became King.[43]

Once upon a time, a thousand years before Columbus discovered America, and when Rome was still the greatest city in the world, there lived a brave and beautiful youth whose name was Arthur. His home was in England, near London; and he lived with the good knight Sir Hector, whom he always called father.

They dwelt in a great square castle of gray stone, with a round tower at each corner. It was built about a courtyard, and was surrounded by a moat, across which was a drawbridge that could be raised or lowered. When it was raised the castle was practically a little island and very hard for enemies to attack.

On one side of the moat was a large wood, and here Arthur spent a great deal of his time. He liked to lie under the trees and gaze up at the blue of the sky. All about him old oaks stood like giant guardians watching sturdily over the soil where they had grown for centuries. Arthur could look between the trunks and see rabbits and squirrels whisking about. Sometimes a herd of brown deer with shy dark eyes would pass, holding their graceful heads high in the air; sometimes a flock of pheasants with brilliant plumage rose from the bushes. Again there was no sound except the tapping of a bright-crested woodpecker, and no motion but the fluttering of leaves and the trembling of violets half buried in green moss.

At times, when it was dim and silent in the wood, Arthur would hear bursts of merry laughter, the tinkling of bells, and the jingling of spurs. Then he would know that knights and ladies were riding down the road which ran beside the trees. Soon the knights would appear on horses, brown, black, and white, with gaily ornamented saddles, and bridles from which hung silver bells. Often the saddles were made of ivory or ebony, set with rubies or emeralds. The knights wore helmets laced with slender gold chains, and coats of mail made of tiny links of steel, so fine and light that all together hardly weighed more than a coat of cloth. Usually the legs of the knights were sheathed in steel armor; and their spurs were steel, or even gold. The ladies sat on horses with long trappings of silk, purple, white, or scarlet, with ornamented saddles and swinging bells. The robes of the ladies were very beautiful, being made of velvet or silk trimmed with ermine. Arthur liked to watch them, flashing by; crimson, and gold, and blue, and rose-colored. Better still, he liked to see the pretty happy faces of the ladies, and hear their gay voices. In those troublous times, however, the roads were so insecure that such companies did not often pass.

Sometimes the knights and ladies came to visit Sir Hector. Then Arthur would hurry from the forest to the castle. Sir Hector would stand on the lowered drawbridge to greet his guests, and would lead them, with many expressions of pleasure, into the courtyard. Then he would take a huge hammer hanging from a post, and beat with it on a table which stood in a corner of the courtyard. Immediately from all parts of the castle the squires and servants would come running to take the horses of the knights and ladies. Sir Hector's wife and daughters would then appear, and with their own hands remove the armor of the knights. They would offer them golden basins of water, and towels for washing, and after that put velvet mantles upon their shoulders. Then the guests would be brought to the supper table.

But Arthur did not spend all his time dreaming in the woods or gazing at knights and ladies. For many hours of the day he practiced feats of arms in the courtyard. It was the custom in England to train boys of noble birth to be knights. As soon as they were old enough they were taught to ride. Later on, they lived much among the ladies and maidens, learning gentle manners. Under the care of the knights, they learned to hunt, to carry a lance properly, and to use the sword; and having gained this skill, they were made squires if they had shown themselves to be of good character.

Then, day by day, the squires practiced at the quintain. This was an upright post, on the top of which turned a crosspiece, having on one end a broad board, and on the other a bag of sand. The object was to ride up at full gallop, strike the board with a long lance, and get away without being hit by the sand bag.

Besides this, the squires had services to do for the knights, in order that they might learn to be useful in as many ways as possible, and to be always humble. For instance, they took care of the armor of the knights, carried letters and messages for them, accompanied them at joustings and tournaments, being ready with extra weapons or assistance; and in the castle they helped to serve the guests at table. After months of such service, they went through a beautiful ceremony and were made knights. In the country round about, Arthur, of all the squires, was the most famous for his skill in the use of the lance and the sword, for his keenness in the hunt, and for his courtesy to all people.

Now, at this time there was no ruler in England. The powerful Uther of Wales, who had governed England, was dead, and all the strong lords of the country were struggling to be king in his place. This gave rise to a great deal of quarreling and bloodshed.

There was in the land a wise magician named Merlin. He was so old that his beard was as white as snow, but his eyes were as clear as a little child's. He was very sorry to see all the fighting that was going on, because he feared that it would do serious harm to the kingdom.

In those days the great and good men who ruled in the church had power almost equal to that of the monarch. The kings and the great lords listened to their advice, and gave them much land, and money for themselves and for the poor. So Merlin went to the Archbishop of Canterbury, the churchman who in all England was the most beloved, and said:

"Sir, it is my advice that you send to all the great lords of the realm and bid them come to London by Christmas to choose a king."

The archbishop did as Merlin advised, and at Christmas all the great lords came to London. The largest church in the city stood not far from the north bank of the Thames. A churchyard surrounded it, filled with yew trees, the trunks of which were knotted with age. The powerful lords rode up in their clanking armor to the gate, where they dismounted, and giving their horses into the care of their squires, reverently entered the church.

There were so many of them that they quite filled the nave and side-aisles of the building. The good archbishop, from where he stood in the chancel, looked down on them all. Just behind him was the altar covered with a cloth of crimson and gold, and surmounted by a golden crucifix and ten burning candles. In front of him, kneeling under the gray arches which spanned the church, were the greatest men in the kingdom. He looked at their stern bronzed faces, their heavy beards, their broad shoulders, and their glittering armor, and prayed God to make the best man in the land king.

Then began the service. At the close of the first prayer some of the knights looked out of the window, and there in the churchyard they saw a great square stone. In the middle of it was an anvil of steel a foot high, and fixed therein was a beautiful sword. On the sword was some writing set in with gold which said:

"Whosoever pulls this sword out of this stone and anvil is the real king of all England."

The knights who read this told the archbishop, but he said:

"I command you all to keep within the church and still pray to God. No man is to touch the sword until all the prayers are said."

After the service was over, the lords went into the churchyard. They each pulled at the sword, but none could stir it.

"The king is not here," said the archbishop, "but God will make him known. Meantime, let ten good knights keep watch over this sword."

The knights were soon chosen, and then the archbishop said that on a fixed day every man in the kingdom should try to pull the sword out of the anvil. He ordered that on New Year's day all the people should be brought together for a great tournament to be held on the south bank of the Thames, near London bridge. After a few days spent in jousting among the knights, each man should make the trial to find out whether or not he was to be king.

The brave youth Arthur did not know of the contest that was to be made for the sword. Sir Hector told him that he was to go to a tournament, but he did not tell him the reason for holding the tournament. So Arthur rode to London with Sir Hector; and Sir Kay, who was Sir Hector's oldest son, was with them.

Sir Hector and Sir Kay rode soberly in front. They were tall, stalwart men and rode black horses, their dark figures making shadows on the light snow that had fallen. Arthur, riding behind them, felt exhilarated by the crisp winter air which caused the blood to dance in his veins. Sometimes he stood up in his saddle and flicked with his sword the dead leaves on the oaks. Again he made his horse crush the thin crust of ice that had formed in tiny pools on the road. He was so happy in the thought of the tournament he was to see, that he could have sung for joy.

The road was not very wide, for few carts passed upon it, but it had been well worn by riders. Sometimes it wound through a bit of thick woods; again it rose up over a gently rolling hill. From the hilltops the riders could see London far in the distance. It looked at first like a gray haze; then, as the three came nearer, the buildings, large and small, grew plain to the sight. The castles and huts, barns and sheds, smithies, shops and mills, stood out in the keen sunlight. A high wall surrounded them, while on one side flowed the river Thames.

After they had entered the city, and had passed the churchyard, and had almost reached London bridge, Sir Kay discovered that he had left his sword at home.

"Will you go back for it?" he asked Arthur.

"That I will," said Arthur, glad of the chance to ride longer in the delightful air.

But when he reached their dwelling, he could not get in. The drawbridge was raised, and he could not make the warden hear his calling. Then Arthur was disturbed and said to himself:

"I will hasten to the churchyard we passed, and take the beautiful sword which I saw in the stone. It does not seem to belong to anyone, and my brother Kay must have a weapon."

So he rode on till he reached the churchyard, dismounted, and tied his horse to a sapling. The ten knights who guarded the sword had gone away to see the combats in the tournament. Arthur ran up and pulled lightly but eagerly at the sword. It came at once from the anvil. He hurried to Sir Kay, who was waiting for him on London bridge. Sir Kay knew that the weapon was the one that had been fixed fast in the stone, but he said nothing to Arthur, and the two soon overtook Sir Hector, who had ridden slowly to the field where the tournament was taking place. Sir Kay immediately told his father what had happened.

The good knight at once spoke with great respect to Arthur.

"Sir," he said, "you must be the king of this land."

"What mean you, sir?" asked Arthur.

Sir Hector told the wondering youth the reason why he was destined to be king. Then he said:

"Can you put this sword back in its place and pull it out again?"

"Easily," replied Arthur.

The three returned to the great stone, and Arthur put back the sword. Sir Hector tried to take it out, but failed.

"Now, you try," he said to Sir Kay.

But Sir Kay, in spite of great efforts, also failed. Then Arthur, at Sir Hector's bidding, tried, and at once pulled forth the sword. At that Sir Hector and Sir Kay knelt before Arthur.

"Alas," said Arthur, raising them from the ground, "my own dear father and my brother, why do you kneel to me?"

"Nay, my lord Arthur," said Sir Hector, "I am not your father. You are of higher blood than I am. Long ago, when you were a little baby, Merlin brought you to me to take care of, telling me that you were to be the king."

"Then whose son am I?" cried Arthur.

"There are two stories: the one that Merlin tells, and the one that old Bleys, the master of Merlin, tells. Merlin brought you to me, saying that you were the son of King Uther and Yguerne his wife. But because the king was dead and the lords powerful and jealous, he told me to guard you in secrecy lest your life be taken. I did not know whether the story was true or false then, but you were a helpless child, and Merlin was a wise sage, and so I took you and brought you up as my own."

Arthur was so astonished that he did not ask to hear the tale that Bleys told. He stood gazing at Sir Hector, who said:

"And now, my gracious lord, will you be good to me and mine when you are king?"

"I will, indeed," replied Arthur, "for I am more beholden to you than to any one else in the world, and also to my good lady and foster mother, your wife, who has reared me as if I were her own child. If it be God's will that I shall sometime become king, ask of me then what you will."

"Sir," said Sir Hector, "I ask that you make my son Sir Kay, your foster brother, the steward of all your lands."

"That shall be done," said Arthur, "and more. He shall have that office as long as I live."

Then the three went to the Archbishop of Canterbury and related to him the story of Merlin and all that had occurred. At his request they told no one else.

At the command of the archbishop on Twelfth day, which is the sixth of January, all the great lords assembled in the churchyard. Each tried to draw forth the sword, and each failed. Then the untitled people came and tried. Everyone failed until at last Arthur stepped forward. He hardly more than touched the sword when it came away in his hand.

At this many of the great lords were angry.

"He hardly more than touched the sword"

"He is but a boy," they said, "and not of high blood."

They refused to believe the story of his birth told by Merlin and Sir Hector. And because of all the quarreling, it was decided to have another trial at Candlemas, which fell in the month of February. Again Arthur was victorious. Then the great lords decreed that there should be another trial at Easter, and again Arthur succeeded. Next they decided to have a final trial at the feast of the Pentecost, which fell in May.

Meanwhile, Merlin advised the archbishop to see that Arthur had a bodyguard. So the archbishop selected several knights whom the former king, Uther, had trusted. These were Sir Ulfius and Sir Brastias and Sir Bedivere; Sir Geraint and Sir Hector and Sir Kay were also chosen. These brave men formed a bodyguard for Arthur until the feast of the Pentecost.

At this time Arthur again drew out the sword from the anvil. Then the common people, who had so far let the lords have their will, cried out:

"We will have Arthur for our king, and we will have no more delay, for we see that it is God's will that he shall be our ruler."

Then all the people knelt down, high and low, rich and poor, and begged Arthur's pardon for the delay he had undergone. Arthur forgave them, and taking his sword, reverently placed it on the great altar beside which the archbishop stood. This was a sign that he meant to dedicate himself and his sword to God.

Afterward the crowning was held, and all the brave men and fair ladies in the land were present. The lords wore beautiful robes of velvet and ermine, with gold and jewels on their breast-plates. The ladies' robes were of purple and white and scarlet and gold and blue, and they wore many pearls and rubies and diamonds, so that all the place where they were assembled was glowing with light and color.

But Arthur, who wore a plain white robe, did not think of the beauty and richness. He was very grave, knowing that he was about to take a solemn oath. He bowed his head, while the archbishop set upon it the golden crown, which gleamed with jewels. Then he stood up before his people, and vowed that he would be a good king and always do justice. All the people uncovered their heads and vowed to serve and obey him; and when he smiled kindly on them as he rode slowly through the throng, they threw up their caps and shouted joyfully: "Long live King Arthur! Long live the King!"

King Arthur chose worthy men for his officers, making Sir Kay steward as he had promised; Sir Ulfius he made chamberlain, and Sir Brastias warden. Arthur gave offices also to Sir Hector and Sir Bedivere and Sir Geraint.

After his crowning the king set about righting all the wrongs that had been done since the death of King Uther. He gave back the lands and money that had been taken from widows and orphans, and would permit no unkindness to any of his subjects. Thus, at the very beginning of his reign, his people began to call him "Good King Arthur."

Podcast #121 Robert Bruce

We started out the month with some podcasts about people who loved freedom so much, they were willing to die for it. So as we leave Month 3 for now, I'd like to share a story about Robert Bruce of Scotland, another lover of freedom. It's found in a book called *Heroes of the Middle Ages* by Eva March Tappan.[44]

In the days of King John the English had their hands full with only one king to manage, but a time came in Scotland when there were thirteen persons who claimed the throne. Finally it was clear that two of them had stronger claims than the other eleven. They were John Baliol and Robert Bruce. Baliol was the grandson of the eldest daughter of a certain royal David, and Bruce was a son of the second daughter of this same king. People in Scotland took sides, some in favour of Baliol and some in favour of Bruce, and feeling was so strong that there was danger of civil war. 'King Edward of England is a wise king. Let us leave the question to him," said the Scottish nobles, and it was done. This was a fine chance for King Edward. He declared at once that neither Baliol nor Bruce, but he himself had the best claim to the Scottish throne. Baliol, however, might rule under him, he said. But Baliol did not prove obedient enough to please him, so Edward carried him and the famous Stone of Scone off to London together. The Scots prized the stone highly. They had a tradition that Jacob's head had rested upon it the night that he had his dream of angels ascending and descending between heaven and earth; and whenever a Scottish king was to be crowned, he always took his seat upon this stone. Edward had it put underneath the seat of the chair in Westminster Abbey, in which English sovereigns sit at their coronation; and perhaps he thought that Scotland had yielded, and there would be no more trouble. On the contrary, in a very little while William Wallace led the Scots against the English and defeated them in a great battle. Soon after this, however, he fell into the hands of Edward and was put to death.

After a few years the Scots found a new leader. This was the grandson of Robert Bruce, and his name, too, was Robert Bruce. He was crowned King of Scotland, and the Scots flocked to his standard. Then came Edward with a large force, and soon the king of Scotland was hiding first in the Grampian Hills, then on a little island off the north coast of Ireland. He was almost in despair, for he had tried six times to get the better of the English and had failed. One day, it is said, he lay in a lonely hut on a heap of straw, wondering if it would not be better to give it up and leave Scotland to herself. Just then he caught sight of a spider trying to swing itself from one rafter to another. Six times it tried, and six times it failed. "Just as many times as I have failed," thought Bruce, and he said to himself, "If it tries again and succeeds, I, too, will try again." The spider tried again and it succeeded. Bruce tried again, and he, too, succeeded. Edward died, and before his son Edward II was ready to attend to matters in Scotland, Bruce had captured most of the castles that Edward I had taken, and had brought an army together.

When Edward II was at last ready to march into Scotland, some two or three years later, he came with a large force as far as Stirling. Bruce met him with one only one-third as large, but every man in it was bent upon doing his best to drive away the English. Bruce dug deep pits in front of his lines. Many of the English cavalry plunged into these and were slain, and the rest were thrown into confusion. Then as the English troops looked at the hill lying to the right of the Scottish army, they saw a new army coming over the crest. It was really only the servants and wagons and camp followers; but Bruce had given them plenty of banners, and the English supposed they were fresh troops. Then King Edward and his men ran away as fast as they could; but the Scots pursued, and the king barely escaped being taken prisoner. This was the Battle of Bannockburn, the most bloody defeat that the English ever met with in Scotland. The victory of the Scots freed Scotland from all English claims; and a few years later England acknowledged her independence.

It was of this battle that Robert Burns wrote:

> Scots, wha hae wi' Wallace bled,
> Scots, wham Bruce has aften led;
> Welcome to your gory bed,
> Or to victory!
> Now's the day, and now's the hour;
> See the front of battle lour;
> See approach proud Edward's power –
> Chains and slavery!
>
> Wha will be a traitor knave?
> Wha can fill a coward's grave?
> Wha sae base as be a slave?
> Let him turn and flee!
> Wha for Scotland's king and law
> Freedom's sword will strongly draw,
> Freeman stand, or Freeman fa',
> Let him follow me!
>
> By oppression's woes and pains!
> By your sons in servile chains!
> We will drain our dearest veins,
> But they shall be free!
> Lay the proud usurpers low!
> Tyrants fall in every foe!
> Liberty's in every blow! –
> Let us do, or die!

In 1603 James VI of Scotland became James I of England, but although for the next hundred years the two kingdoms were ruled by the same sovereign, the parliaments were not united. This followed, however, in 1707, and England and Scotland were henceforth one country under the name of Great Britain.

Month 4 Podcasts

Podcast #28 Lessons from Plutarch

There was a man named Cincinnatus who lived on a little farm not far from the city of Rome. He had once been rich, and had held the highest office in the land; but in one way or another he had lost all his wealth. He was now so poor that he had to do all the work on his farm with his own hands. But in those days it was thought to be a noble thing to till the soil.

Cincinnatus was so wise and just that every-body trusted him, and asked his advice; and when any one was in trouble, and did not know what to do, his neighbors would say—

"Go and tell Cincinnatus. He will help you."

Now there lived among the mountains, not far away, a tribe of fierce, half-wild men, who were at war with the Roman people. They persuaded another tribe of bold warriors to help them, and then marched toward the city, plundering and robbing as they came. They boasted that they would tear down the walls of Rome, and burn the houses, and kill all the men, and make slaves of the women and children.

At first the Romans, who were very proud and brave, did not think there was much danger. Every man in Rome was a soldier, and the army which went out to fight the robbers was the finest in the world. No one staid at home with the women and children and boys but the white-haired "Fathers," as they were called, who made the laws for the city, and a small company of men who guarded the walls. Everybody thought that it would be an easy thing to drive the men of the mountains back to the place where they belonged.

But one morning five horsemen came riding down the road from the mountains. They rode with great speed; and both men and horses were covered with dust and blood. The watchman at the gate knew them, and shouted to them as they galloped in. Why did they ride thus? and what had happened to the Roman army?

They did not answer him, but rode into the city and along the quiet streets; and everybody ran after them, eager to find out what was the matter. Rome was not a large city at that time; and soon they reached the market place where the white-haired Fathers were sitting. Then they leaped from their horses, and told their story.

"Only yesterday," they said, "our army was marching through a narrow valley between two steep mountains. All at once a thousand sav-age men sprang out from among the rocks before us and above us. They had blocked up the way; and the pass was so narrow that we could not fight. We tried to come back; but they had blocked up the way on this side of us too. The fierce men of the mountains were before us and behind us, and they were throwing rocks down upon us from above. We had been caught in a trap.

Then ten of us set spurs to our horses; and five of us forced our way through, but the other five fell before the spears of the mountain men. And now, O Roman Fathers! send help to our army at once, or every man will be slain, and our city will be taken."

"What shall we do?" said the white-haired Fathers. "Whom can we send but the guards and the boys? and who is wise enough to lead them, and thus save Rome?"

All shook their heads and were very grave; for it seemed as if there was no hope. Then one said, "Send for Cincinnatus. He will help us."

Cincinnatus was in the field plowing when the men who had been sent to him came in great haste. He stopped and greeted them kindly, and waited for them to speak.

"Put on your cloak, Cincinnatus," they said, "and hear the words of the Roman people."

Then Cincinnatus wondered what they could mean. "Is all well with Rome?" he asked; and he called to his wife to bring him his cloak.

She brought the cloak; and Cincinnatus wiped the dust from his hands and arms, and threw it over his shoulders. Then the men told their errand.

They told him how the army with all the noblest men of Rome had been entrapped in the mountain pass. They told him about the great danger the city was in. Then they said, "The people of Rome make you their ruler and the ruler of their city, to do with everything as you choose; and the Fathers bid you come at once and go out against our enemies, the fierce men of the mountains."

So Cincinnatus left his plow standing where it was, and hurried to the city. When he passed through the streets, and gave orders as to what should be done, some of the people were afraid, for they knew that he had all power in Rome to do what he pleased. But he armed the guards and the boys, and went out at their head to fight the fierce mountain men, and free the Roman army from the trap into which it had fallen.

A few days afterward there was great joy in Rome. There was good news from Cincinnatus. The men of the mountains had been beaten with great loss. They had been driven back into their own place.

And now the Roman army, with the boys and the guards, was coming home with banners flying, and shouts of victory; and at their head rode Cincinnatus. He had saved Rome.

Cincinnatus might then have made himself king; for his word was law, and no man dared lift a finger against him. But, before the people could thank him enough for what he had done, he gave back the power to the white-haired Roman Fathers, and went again to his little farm and his plow.

He had been the ruler of Rome for sixteen days.

This story[45] is one of James Baldwin's retellings and is found in the Great Lives book in the Story Hour Series. Do you see why George Washington has been called a modern-day

Cincinnatus? He was the first modern day leader to turn over power freely and retire from public life. At least he tried to. This connection between George Washington and an ancient Roman, Cincinnatus, one of Plutarch's Lives—provides the connecting link for Month 4's topics.

But that's not the only connection. I read that in that frigid winter in Valley Forge, where the men literally walked around practically naked, in rags, starving and miserable, Washington commissioned the performance of a play written by Addison based on another one of *Plutarch's Lives*—Cato—wherein were the words: "A day, an hour of virtuous liberty is worth a whole eternity in bondage." The message was that liberty was worth dying for. It was a play that was frequented by many of those early patriots and you hear the message reflected in Patrick Henry's "Give me liberty or give me death" and Nathan Hale's "I only regret that I have but one life to give to my country."

The influence of *Plutarch's Lives* cannot begin to be measured. Ralph Waldo Emerson called it a "bible for heroes." He said, "We cannot read Plutarch without a tingling of the blood." After the Bible, Plutarch was the most quoted source among the Founders. Alexander Hamilton said, "Students of politics could do no better than to have Plutarch in one hand and Holy Writ in the other." It provided them a survey of all manners of government and in particular the role of individual character in those forms of government.

Plutarch's Lives was the first Book of Virtues. Montaigne wrote, "He is a philosopher that teaches us virtue…he sought to bring back to the Romans a reminder of the qualities which in their forefathers conquered the world and also gave a warning that the loss of morals must sooner or later entail political disintegration and national decay."

Aren't we seeing that for ourselves today?

Plutarch's Lives inspired Shakespeare to write some of his most powerful plays and gave him the materials to write them from.

In a preface to one of the Plutarch for young people books I've posted in the online library, I read: "King Henry IV of France, upon being told that his wife was pleased with the perusal of Plutarch's Lives, wrote to her: 'You could not have sent me tidings more agreeable. To love Plutarch is to love me, for he was the instructor of my early years; and my good mother, to whom I owe so much, who watched over the formation of my character…put this book into my hands when I was little more than an infant at the breast. It has been my conscience, and has whispered in my ear many good suggestions and maxims for my conduct and the government of my affairs.'"

Jean Jacques Rousseau affirmed that he never read Plutarch without profit; that he knew the Lives by heart by the age of eight; Madame Roland referred to it as the pasture of great souls' and the learned Theodorus Gaza of the 15th century, uttered what is perhaps the most striking tribute ever rendered to the genius of Plutarch. Being asked if learning were doomed to suffer general shipwreck, and it was given him to choose the one author that should survive, he replied, "Give me Plutarch."

I don't know about you, but I never even heard Plutarch's name once through all my school years. Emerson made the prophecy that Plutarch will be perpetually re-discovered from time to time, as long as books last.

Given his neglect in our generation, and the profound influence for good he has had throughout the ages, maybe it's time to help him get re-discovered.

So who was Plutarch? I think you'll find in him someone you would care to know; someone you can relate to. He was born just a few years after the time of Christ in a small village in Greece. His parents made sure he had the best education available and he traveled widely. In time, he was given increasingly responsible and influential positions in Rome and was widely respected for his wisdom and scholarship. Although he was promised a brilliant career in Rome, he turned his back on it and went home to his humble place of birth and opened a small private school. He wrote, "I prefer to live in a small city that it may not become still smaller." No job was beneath him. He was criticized for carrying home some pickled fish from the market in his own hands. But he relished such small tasks.

He loved his family and his dear wife, Timoxena. They had four sons and evidently had to wait some time before a daughter came along whom they adored. Tragically, she died while Plutarch was away from home. The letter he wrote to his wife has survived. He wrote: "The messengers you sent to announce our child's death apparently missed the road to Athens. I was told about my daughter on reaching Tanagra. Everything relating to the funeral I suppose to have been already performed." Can we imagine the grief? And in fact, the rest of the letter addresses that grief to not allow it to overcome them. "But should I find your grief excessive, my trouble on your account will be greater than on that of our loss. I am not a 'stock or stone' as you, my partner in the care of our numerous children, every one of whom we have ourselves brought up at home, can testify. And this child, a daughter, born to your wishes after four sons, and affording me the opportunity of recording your name, I am well aware was a special object of affection."

After referring to the sweet temper and loving ways of the child, the father says, "Yet why should we forget the reasonings we have often addressed to others, and regard our present pain as obliterating and effacing our former joys?" The letter closes with expressions of his belief in the immortality of every human soul.

Plutarch lived in an age we can also relate to. His beloved homeland was a shell of what it once was. The people had forgotten their heritage; of who they had been. And that was one of the main objectives of writing his Lives—to remind them of the great lives that had gone before in the hopes of having it awaken and stir something in their own hearts.

Bear in mind, he wrote, "My purpose is to write lives, not history. The most glorious exploits do not always give the clearest views of virtues and vices in men; sometimes a mere trifling happening, a mere jest, informs us better about a man's character than the report of the bloodiest battle he ever won. Portrait painters are more exact in showing the lines and features of the face, in which the character is seen. And in the same way I give more attention to the personal words and acts that reveal the souls of men…. My original purpose in writing lives of the great was to teach others, but I found more and more that I am the one who gets the most profit from lodging these men one after the other in my house. The virtues of these great men serve me as a sort of looking glass; in it I may see how to adjust and adorn my own life. Through daily living and associating with them I perceive all their qualities and select all that are noblest and worthiest."

He was criticized for his use of anecdotes and the lack of facts. But already the facts had become obscured, so he simply used the device, "The story goes…" He wrote, "It is so hard to find out the truth of anything by looking at the record of the past. The process of time obscures the truth of former times, and even contemporaneous writers disguise and twist the truth out of malice or flattery." As George Grant wrote in an essay on Plutarch, "Whether an event actually occurred was of little consequence to him. What mattered was how the lessons of that event passed into cultural consciousness."

I see the same dilemma for the study of history today with our children. Are you more focused on trying to get at facts, which are difficult to come by at all in history, or are you trying to use the stories to draw out the lessons for life and pass into their "cultural consciousness"? The influence for good Plutarch has had throughout the ages should help us answer the question as to what will be the most valuable.

Plutarch gave life and personality to Demosthenes, Pericles, Cicero, Lycurgus, so many others who may have vanished in the dust bins of history otherwise.

His Lives consists of 25 parallel lives. He paired an ancient Greek with an ancient Roman. And I just about fell out of my chair when I read why. He could see clearly that it was the hearts of the Greeks that gave power to the glory of Rome with her focus on Law and Order. He knew the Greeks were the foundation to Rome's greatness, they were the roots that gave the Romans nourishment and they needed to be reminded of that, just as we are trying to remind our children of our heritage. It was the arts of Greece that gave life and meaning to Rome. It's the pattern for learning—heart and art first. Plutarch knew that.

Studying the lives of the Ancient Greeks and Romans which Plutarch has made possible may become some of the most interesting lives your children will study because human nature doesn't change. And they have so much to teach them.

I'll link James Baldwin's *Fifty Famous Stories Retold* that includes some wonderful first stories like my opening story of Cincinnatus that can be read to children as young as seven or eight. Developmentally, waiting to around age 10 or 11 makes more sense before diving into the study of these moral heroes, but you know your children best. The book I chose to include in *Great Greeks and Romans* in the Great Lives Series includes a reprint of Plutarch's Lives aimed at the youngest audience I could find. It's a good place to start. Familiarity is the key to the beginning of learning. So let the names themselves become familiar. I think even little children enjoy the music of hearing names like Diogenes and Aristides. I've linked some other versions of Plutarch's Lives for young people in the G3 online library and if I find more, that's where I will place them. I also included Dryden's translation. Ambleside Online has a good discussion on why study Plutarch and some of the different versions out there that I will link as well. You'll also find some simpler stories of ancient Greeks in the S9 history book in the Story Hour series.

I hope you'll give Plutarch a chance and that one of these resources will be just the right thing to get you started. And now I'll close with a few verses from Longfellow's Psalm of Life.

> Lives of great men all remind us
> We can make our lives sublime,
> And, departing, leave behind us
> Footprints on the sands of time;
>
> Footprints, that perhaps another,
> Sailing o'er life's solemn main,
> A forlorn and shipwrecked brother,
> Seeing, shall take heart again.
>
> Let us, then, be up and doing,
> With a heart for any fate;
> Still achieving, still pursuing,
> Learn to labor and to wait.

Podcast #29 Lessons from Rome and Ben-Hur

We're in Month 4 and you may think that studying the Holy Land at Christmastime would make more sense than a study of Rome. We're going to get to the Holy Land in 2 months, but to truly appreciate what the arrival of Jesus Christ meant, we need to have a clear view of the world into which he was born.

The people of His day were looking for a Savior who would save them from their oppressive government. Fix the government, they thought, and they would be happy. His message for them is the same message for us today—tend first to the inner kingdom and the outer will take care of itself. Few accepted the message then and few accept it today, but for those who do, they find a peace and joy in their lives the world can never give and which stands independent of all outward circumstances.

And as God always does, He turns all things for good. Rome was necessary for the advancement of His kingdom. I thought Olivia Coolidge sums it up pretty good in her *Roman People*:[46]

> The Roman world of Augustus is the world that Jesus Christ was born into, which gives it an extra interest for us. Indeed, the spread of early Christianity is mainly due to the Romans. They persecuted it from the first, but they helped it far more. They helped it by having a world at peace through which missionaries could travel. They helped it by spreading common languages throughout their empire. Most of all they helped it by mixing together all sorts of people with different backgrounds and religions who talked to each other, got over their own prejudices, and became interested in new ideas. All this was happening in the days of Augustus before Jesus had started to preach. The world was ready.

The influence Rome had on the nations that followed and in our world is immeasurable. As you continue studying the individual nations, including America, you'll find the influence of Rome in many of their beginning stories. One of my book recommendations to help you take a look at the political and religious conditions of the world at the time of Jesus' coming is Lew Wallace's *Ben-Hur*.

Ben-Hur is considered to be the most influential Christian book of the 19th century. In fact, only the Bible exceeded it in sales. It's been translated into over 20 languages. It has never been out of print since 1880. One of the things that boosted its sales was the school book companies published the chariot race chapter in its readers and piqued the interest of children who then wanted to read the rest of the book. That's a good way for you to pique interest, too. It continued to be the #1 bestseller here in America until *Gone With the Wind* came along and it slipped until Charlton Heston starred in the movie and it edged out the lead again. I'm surprised at how many in the younger generation have never heard of it before. They remade the movie recently, but personally, I wouldn't waste my time with it. I'm kind of sorry I did.

The more I learn about Lew Wallace, the more I like him. His father was a successful lawyer and so sent him to the best schools money could buy, but I'm afraid Lew played hookie more than he attended classes. He said:

> I did not desert the schools entirely, but my attendance was so provokingly irregular and my indifference so supreme, I wonder now that I was tolerated at all. But I had one mainstay: I loved to read. I was a most inordinate reader. In some lines of literature, especially history and some kinds of fiction, my appetite was insatiate, and many a day, while my companions were clustered together in the old red brick schoolhouse, struggling with their problems in fractions or percentage, I was carefully hidden in the woods near by, lying upon my elbows, munching an apple, and reveling in the beauties of Plutarch, Byron or Goldsmith.

When he finally found something he wanted to write, he realized his deficiency in grammar and math and was then ready for its exacting study.

I've heard it said that we all have a book in us, but for those of you waiting for life to clear out a block of time, Lew Wallace frequently had to write in the evenings after he finished his day job, one of which was serving as the governor of New Mexico, or squeeze it into the moments of the day. It took him seven years to finish the book. He dedicated the first edition to his wife. It read: "To the wife of my youth," but so many people sent letters of condolences thinking she had died, he later had to add, "who still abides with me."

And many of you will relate to his fondest desire of building himself a study out among his roses which he called his "pleasure-house for my soul"; a detached room away from the world and its worries. He wanted a place where he could make speeches to himself and play his violin at midnight if he wanted to. Evidently you can still visit it in Indiana.

I think the most interesting thing I learned about *Ben-Hur* is that Lew Wallace was not a religious man at all when he started the book. But let me take a little time and let him tell you[47] all about how the book came to be written and the personal effect it had on him.

General Wallace has given this detailed account of the writing of Ben-Hur:

"'How came I to write Ben-Hur?'

"The question has been put to me so often, and in the same form, that the world shall have an answer; although I confess it not a little difficult, seeing the different aims the interrogation may take.

"The very beginning of the book lies in a quotation from St. Matthew:

"'Now when Jesus was born in Bethlehem of Judea, in the days of Herod the king, behold, there came wise men from the east to Jerusalem, saying, Where is He that is born King of the Jews? For we have seen His star in the east, and are come to worship Him.'

"Far back as my memory goes of things read by or to me, those lines took a hold on my imagination beyond every other passage of Scripture. How simple they are! But analyze them, and behold the points of wonder!

"The saying that they came from the east is altogether unsatisfactory. How many were they? And oh, the star! the star!

"It was a speaking star, for we are left to infer it told them a king was born to the Jews, and that they must go find and worship Him; and when, doubtless, they asked where He was, they were bid follow it, for it was the King's star. So, too, it could not have been set in the heavens, else it could not have led them; for one may go round the globe, and up and down from pole to pole, without ever getting under the far pin-point of light called the north star.

"Then when, after months and possibly years of journey to and fro, on ship or horse or camel, bearing presents of value—they could not have walked—how did they know their journey at last finished?

"And when they entered a cave near an obscure hamlet, Bethlehem by name, and beheld a speechless baby in swaddling-clothes, and nowise different in appearance from other babies, who told them it was He they were seeking? What, a king in a stable-manger!

"But they did not laugh; they stopped there and worshipped the little boy, and gave Him their gifts. Was the mother astonished, or was she looking for them?

"In 1875—the date is given from best recollection— when I was getting over the restlessness due to years of service in the War of the Rebellion, it occurred to me to write the conceptions which I had long carried in my mind of the Wise Men. A serial upon the subject would admit of any number of illustrations, and might be acceptable to one of the magazines.

"So I wrote, commencing with the meeting in the desert, numbering and naming the three upon the authority of the dear old tradition-monger, Father Bede, and ending with the birth of the Child in the cave by Bethlehem.

"At that time, speaking candidly, I was not in the least influenced by religious sentiment. I had no convictions about God or Christ. I neither believed nor disbelieved in them.

"The preachers had made no impression upon me. My reading covered nearly every other subject. Indifference is the word most perfectly descriptive of my feelings respecting the To-morrow of Death, as a French scientist has happily termed the succession of life. Yet when the work was fairly begun, I found myself writing reverentially, and frequently with awe.

"This was purely natural; for it is with me, presumably, as with every writer who creates as he goes. My characters are essentially living persons. They arise and sit, look, talk, and behave like themselves.

"In dealing with them I see them; when they speak I hear them. I know them by their features. They answer my call. Some of them I detest. Such as I most affect become my familiars. In turn they call me, and I recognize their voices. Such being the case, think of the society to which the serial directly admitted me!

"Think of riding with Balthasar on his great white camel to the meeting appointed beyond Moab; of association with the mysterious Three; of breaking fast with them in the shade of the little tent pitched on the rippled sand; of hearing the 'grace' with which they began their repast; of listening as they introduced themselves to one another, telling how and when and where they were severally summoned by the Spirit; of the further guestship in the final journey to Jerusalem, the star our guide!

"Think of attending a session of the Sanhedrim; of hearing Herod the Builder ask Hillel, more than a hundred years a scholar, where the new King of the Jews was most likely to be discovered!

"Think of lying with the shepherds in their sheepfold that clear, crisp, first Christmas night; of seeing the ladder of light drop out of the window of heaven; of hearing the Annunciator make proclamation of his glad tidings!

"Think of walking with Joseph from the Joppa gate across the plain of Rephaim, past the tomb of Rachel, up to the old khan by Bethlehem; of stealing glances at the face of the girl-wife on the donkey, she who was so shortly to be, in good old Catholic phrase, the Blessed Mother of God!

"Think of seeing that face so often and with such distinctness as to be able to pronounce that there are but portraits of her in the world, Raphael's and Murillo's, all the others being either too old, too vulgar, or too human! Then tell me, was it strange if I wrote reverentially, and sometimes with awe? Or that I was unconsciously making ready to cast my indifference as a locust casts its shell?

"Well, I finished the proposed serial and deposited it in my desk, waiting for a season of courage in which to open communication with the Harpers.

"In the time of writing, down to the hour I laid the manuscript by, as said, never once did the possibility of a formal book occur to me.

"If any reader before whom this confession may chance to fall will return to the volume now known as Ben-Hur: A Tale of the Christ, and examine critically the commencement of the part designated Book Second, he cannot fail to be struck with its similitudes to the opening of a novel. Such, in fact, it was.

"It is possible to fix the hour and place of the first thought of a book precisely enough; that was a night in 1876. I had been listening to discussion which involved such elemental points as God, heaven, life hereafter, Jesus Christ, and His divinity. Trudging on in the dark, alone except as one's thoughts may be company good or bad, a sense of the importance of the theme struck me for the first time with a force both singular and persistent.

"My ignorance of it was painfully a spot of deeper darkness in the darkness. I was ashamed of myself, and make haste now to declare that the mortification of pride I then endured, or, if it be preferred, the punishment of spirit, ended in a resolution to study the whole matter, if only for the gratification there might be in having convictions of one kind or another.

"Forthwith a number of practical suggestions assailed me: How should I conduct the study? Delve into theology? I shuddered. The theology of the professors had always seemed to me an indefinitely deep pit filled with the bones of unprofitable speculations.

"There were the sermons and commentaries. The very thought of them overwhelmed me with an idea of the shortness of life. No; I would read the Bible and the four gospels, and rely on myself. A lawyer of fifteen or twenty years of practice attains a confidence peculiar in its mental muscularity, so to speak.

"Next the subject was considered dry. Was there no way of making it the least bit light and savory? No incidental employment or task which would give it a color of pastime, and, while compelling thorough investigation, keep me interested? Then it came!

"The manuscript in my desk ended with the birth of Christ; why not make it the first book of a volume, and go on to His death? I halted—there was a light in my mind! And it brought the difficulties—a host of them —to the surface.

"One ought never to speak except he sees his opening and conclusion; the intermediate will take care of itself —so a successful after-dinner orator is reported to have said. The remark applies well to addresses; but I doubt its wisdom in the matter of book-making. Here in the very outset the intermediate presented itself a Giant Despair.

"I had my opening; it was the birth of Christ. Could anything be more beautiful? As a mere story, the imagination of man has conceived nothing more crowded with poetry, mystery, and incidents pathetic and sublime, nothing sweeter with human interest, nothing so nearly a revelation of God in person. So, too, I saw a fitting conclusion.

"Viewed purely and professionally as a climax or catastrophe to be written up to, the final scene of the last act of a tragedy or a tale, what could be more stupendous than the Crucifixion?

"But the unities are inexorable. Because they run through every life they must be observed. And here in this story there was a lapse of eighteen or twenty years—being the interval between the remarkable appearance of the Holy Child in the Temple, what time He came up to the Passover, and His reappearance a man with a mission.

"The Days of Ignorance of the Arabs, when there was no history, were not denser with a want of knowledge than that interval. What was I to do with it? Now it seemed a gulf in my way; now an Illimani high as the sky.

"I scarcely dare tell of my travail; but after weeks of reflection, at last I decided to use the blank to show the religious and political condition of the world at the time of the coming. Perhaps those conditions would demonstrate a necessity for a Saviour.

"Having weathered this point, I passed on to the constituents of the tale. There was no lack of incident, none of persons; only, I was hampered in the selection by the requirement to discard all which did not serve the conditions mentioned.

"Rome furnished the politics, and made the evolution of Messala easy. Save the few pearls of faith glistening on the marble steps of the Gate Beautiful in the Herodian Temple at Jerusalem, there was nowhere a suggestion of religion; out of that circumstance I wrought Ben-Hur, his mother and sister, Simonides and Esther—naming the latter after my own dear mother, departed long ago in the fairness of her youth.

"The commitment to the galley, the sea - fight, the chariot-race and its preceding orgies were Roman phases; just as the love marking the Hur family, the steady pursuit of vengeance by the son, and his easy conversion by Simonides to the alluring idea of the Messiah a ruler like Cæsar, were Jewish.

"The derivation of what may be termed the Christian incidents is apparent. Wanting to convey a commensurate conception of the awful power underlying a miracle, I struck the mother and sister of my hero with leprosy. It was cruel, but essential. Finally, wanting a connecting thread for the whole story, but more particularly for the two periods so wide apart—that given to Christ the Child, and that given to Christ the Saviour—I kept Balthasar alive to the end.

"In the next place, I had never been to the Holy Land. In making it the location of my story, it was needful not merely to be familiar with its history and geography, I must be able to paint it, water, land, and sky, in actual colors. Nor would the critics excuse me for mistakes in the costumes or customs of any of the peoples representatively introduced, Greek, Roman, Egyptian, especially the children of Israel.

"Ponder the task! There was but one method open to me. I examined catalogues of books and maps, and sent for everything likely to be useful. I wrote with a chart always before my eyes—a German publication, showing the towns and villages, all sacred places, the heights, the depressions, the passes, trails, and distances.

"Travellers told me of the birds, animals, vegetation, and seasons. Indeed, I think the necessity for constant reference to authorities saved me mistakes which certainly would have occurred had I trusted to a tourist's memory.

"But the greatest of the difficulties! Veterans in the fine art of story-telling are likely to say off-hand it was either the invention of incidents or the choice of characters. No, no!

"The Christian world would not tolerate a novel with Jesus Christ its hero, and I knew it. Nevertheless, writing of Him was imperative, and Ile must appear, speak, and act. Further, and worse as a tribulation, I was required to keep Him before the reader, the object of superior interest throughout.

"And there was to be no sermonizing. How could this be done without giving mortal offence? How, and leave the book a shred of popularity? It does not become me to intimate any measure of success in the accomplishment; yet I may be pardoned for an outright confession of the rules I. prescribed for my government in the dilemma.

"First, I determined to withhold the reappearance of the Saviour until the very last hours. Meantime, He should be always coming—to-day I would have Him, as it were, just over the hill yonder; to-morrow He will be here, and then—to-morrow. To bring Balthasar up from Egypt, and have him preaching the Spiritual Kingdom, protesting the Master alive because His mission, which was founding the kingdom, was as yet unfulfilled, and looking for Him tearfully, and with an infinite yearning, might be an effective expedient.

"Next, He should not be present as an actor in any scene of my creation. The giving a cup of water to BenHur at the well near Nazareth is the only violation of this rule.

"Finally, when He was come, I would be religiously careful that every word He uttered should be a literal quotation from one of His sainted biographers.

"Of the more than seven years given the book, the least part was occupied in actual composition. Research and investigation consumed most of the appropriated time.

"I had to be so painstaking! The subject was the one known thoroughly by more scholars and thinkers than any other in the wide range of literature.

"After comparing authorities, I had frequently to reconcile them; failing in that, it remained to choose between them. There is nothing, not even a will-o'-thewisp, so elusive as a disputed date. Once I went to Washington, thence to Boston, for no purpose but to exhaust their libraries in an effort to satisfy myself of the mechanical arrangement of the oars in the interior of a trireme.

"Nor must it be supposed I wrote day after day continuously. I wanted to; but through the whole period I was a bread-winner. Consequently my book-making hours were such as I could snatch from professional employment.

"Sometimes Ben-Hur or Simonides or Balthasar or Sheik Ilderim the Generous would call me imperiously; and there being no other means of pacifying them, I would play truant from court and clients. There are numberless paragraphs in the volume recognizable as having been blocked out on the cars 'between cities' or in the waits at lonesome stations.

"Thus Tirzah's little song, 'Wake Not, but Hear Me, Love,' is the resultant of a delayed passage from Indianapolis home. A man can carry his mind with him as he carries his watch; but like the watch, to keep it going he must keep it wound up.

"Of course most of the writing was done at Crawfordsville, with night as the favoring time. Of summer days, business permitting, the preferred spot was beneath a beech-tree, one of many kings of its kind airing their majesties around our homestead. Its spreading branches droop to the ground, weighed down by their wealth of foliage, and under them I am shut in as by the walls of a towering green tent.

"How often, while lending me its protection and fragrant coolness, it has been the sole witness of my struggle to whip an obstinate thought into comeliness of expression; and how often, out of respect for me, it has maintained a dignified silence when it might have laughed at my discomfiture.

"I am under the great gray arms of the same tree at this present writing. The hum of singing things imparts life to the silence; the sunlight freckles the sward, the birds hunt their prey almost to my feet, all as when I wandered with Ben-Hur through the Grove of Daphne."

[He went on to describe the old adobe governor's house he lived in in New Mexico. The final book was written in one of its dark, cavernous chambers. He continued:]

"My custom when night came was to lock the doors and bolt the windows of the office proper, and with a student's lamp, bury myself in the four soundless walls of the forbidding annex.

"The ghosts, if they were ever about, did not disturb me; yet in the hush of that gloomy harborage I beheld the Crucifixion, and strove to write what I beheld.

"As this article is in the nature of confessions, here is one which the reader may excuse, and at the same time accept as a fitting conclusion: Long before I was through with my book, I became a believer in God and Christ."

After Wallace died, a close friend was asked what keepsake he would like, and he replied that he would like the spectacles General Wallace looked through at the world.

He could not write what he wrote without seeing what he saw. I just read that the difference between an idea and an ideal is that an idea is vague and hazy while an ideal is a perfect image in the mind. As Wallace pieced together the perfect image of this humble carpenter of 2,000 years ago, it changed him. He said, "I was in quest of knowledge, but I had no faith to sustain, no creed to bolster up. The result was that the whole field of religious and biblical history opened up before me, and, my vision not being clouded by previously formed opinions, I was enabled to survey it without the aid of lenses. I believe I was thorough and persistent. I know I was conscientious in my search for the truth. I weighed, I analyzed, I counted and compared. The evolution from conjecture into knowledge, through opinion and belief, was gradual but irresistable; and at length I stood firmly and defiantly on the solid rock.

Upward of seven hundred thousand copies of *Ben-Hur* have been published [I will add, it's in the millions now], and it has been translated into all languages from French to Arabic; but, whether it has ever influenced the mind of a single reader or not, I am sure its conception and preparation, if it has done nothing more, has convinced its author of the divinity of the lowly Nazarene who walked and talked with God.

Podcast #30 Lessons from George Washington

The American History topic for Month 4 is George Washington: One man of virtue. In today's world, the word "virtue" has primarily been connected with sexual purity. But if you go back to Webster's 1828 dictionary, the word is so much richer in meaning. Virtue, Webster says, is nothing but voluntary obedience to truth. It means strength and moral goodness, but doesn't stop there. It is that strength by which a person acts and produces effects on other bodies. A virtuous person lifts all around him.

Virtue is the perfect word for George Washington. Who else could have held together a starving, ragtag army of merchants and farmers against the greatest military force in the world? Washington was a man of few words, but when he spoke, everyone listened. Insurmountable odds could not crush him, and power could not corrupt him.

Do you remember what Dr. Gordon Neufeld said about the young attaching to someone and growing to be like that to which it has attached? It's fitting that Washington, who had no children of his own, should come to be known as the Father of our country. When he is held up as an ideal to our children, by virtue of his goodness, they will want to grow up to be like him. And if the ideals of Washington became America's ideals, what a nation we would have for we would be a people of faith, compassion, humility, mercy, duty, selfless determination, honesty, love of home and family.

Each of us must reconstruct him in our hearts before we can truly see the man he was. If you listened to the podcast about Plutarch, I talked about how Plutarch understood it wasn't in the battle field or the big events that the heart of a great man is revealed, but in the small, seemingly insignificant acts.

I would like to add some brush strokes to this canvas you are painting in your heart of this great general, first president and loving husband, so that you can see him clearly and by his virtue, be lifted and strengthened where you stand.

I've chosen some lesser known events that illustrate his character—little scenes from his life— taken from a 1911 book compiled by Wayne Whipple called *The Story-Life of Washington: A Life History in 500 True Stories, Selected from Original sources and Fitted Together in Order.*[48] Don't you love those old long titles? I'll link it in the podcast notes and you can also find it in the F4 online library.

Scene 1:

> Once the General was engaged in earnest consultation with Colonel Pickering until after night had fairly set in. Washington prepared to stay with the Colonel over night, provided he had a spare blanket and straw. "Oh, yes," said Primus, who was appealed to, "plenty of straw and blankets, plenty."
>
> In the middle of the night Washington awoke. He looked about him and descried the

negro. He gazed at him a while and then spoke.

"Primus," said he, "Primus!" Primus started up and rubbed his eyes.

"What, General?" said he.

Washington rose up in his bed. "Primus," said he, "what do you mean by saying you had blankets and straw enough? Here you have given up your blankets and straw to me, that I may sleep comfortably, while you are obliged to sit through the night."

"It's nothing, General," said Primus. "It's nothing! I'm well enough! Don't trouble yourself about me, General, but go to sleep again. No matter about me, I sleep very good!"

"But it is matter, it is matter," said Washington. "I cannot do it, Primus. If either is to sit up, I will. But I think there is no need of either sitting up. The blanket is wide enough for two. Come and lie down with me."

"Oh, no, General!" said Primus, starting and protesting against the proposition. "No, let me sit here."

"I say come and lie down here," said Washington. "There is room for both; I insist upon it."

He threw open the blanket as he spoke, and moved to one side of the straw. Primus professed to have been exceedingly shocked at the idea of lying under the same covering with the commander-of-chief, but his tone was so resolute and determined that he could not hesitate. He prepared himself therefore and laid himself down by Washington; on the same straw under the same blanket, and the General and the negro slept until morning.

Scene 2.

Two days before the battle of Brandywine, Washington called to Morris's office in Philadelphia and said that they were so far in arrears with the soldiers' pay, and then men were in such hardships that they had little heart for battle…

"Can you help us?" pleaded the commander-in-chief, in a voice husky with emotion.

Morris shook his head sadly, saying:

"I have used up my own means and credit. I am deeply grieved to admit that I can do nothing now—nothing!"

General Washington, covering his face with his large hands, so that the fingers touched his forehead, burst into an abandon of weeping, and as he sat there sobbing, the tears trickled through his fingers and dropped down his wrists.

The General soon gained his normal composure, arose and went out without a word. The financier also got up and silently followed him, looking sadly after Washington as he passed slowly down the street.

Two days later, September 11, 1777, Washington met Lord Howe at Brandywine and was defeated.

Scene 3

One day a Tory, who was well known in the neighborhood, was captured and brought into camp. His name was Michael Wittman, and he was accused of having carried aid and information to the British in Philadelphia. He was taken to West Chester and there tried by court-martial. It was proved that he was a very dangerous man and that he had more than once attempted to do great harm to the American army. He was pronounced guilty of being a spy and sentenced to be hanged.

On the evening of the day before that set for the execution, a strange old man appeared in Valley Forge. He was a small man with long, snow-white hair falling over his shoulders. His face, although full of kindliness, was sad looking and thoughtful; his eyes, which were bright and sharp, were upon the ground and lifted only when he was speaking.

His name was announced.

"Peter Miller?" said Washington. "Certainly. Show him in at once."

The old man went in.

"General Washington, I have come to ask a great favor of you," he said in his usual kindly tones.

"I shall be glad to grant you almost anything," said Washington, "for we surely are indebted to you for many favors. Tell me what it is."

"I hear," said Peter, "that Michael Wittman has been found guilty of treason and that he is to be hanged at Turk's Head tomorrow. I have come to ask you to pardon him."

Washington started back, and a cloud came over his face. "That is impossible," he said. "Wittman is a bad man. He has done all in his power to betray us. He has even offered to join the British and aid in destroying us. In these times we dare not be lenient with traitors; and for that reason, I cannot pardon your friend."

"Friend!" cried Peter. "Why, he is no friend of mine. He is my bitterest enemy. He has persecuted me for years. He has even beaten me and spit in my face, knowing full well that I would not strike back. Michael Wittman is no friend of mine."

Washington was puzzled. "And still you wish me to pardon him?" he asked.

"I do," answered Peter. "I ask it of you as a great personal favor."

"Tell me," said Washington, with hesitating voice, "why is it that you thus ask the pardon of your worst enemy?"

"I ask it because Jesus did as much for me," was the old man's brief answer.

Washington turned away and went into another room. Soon he returned with a paper on which was written the pardon of Michael Wittman.

"My dear friend," he said, as he placed it in the old man's hands, "I thank you for this example of Christian charity."

It was a matter of fifteen miles, by the shortest road from Valley Forge to West Chester, which was then known as Turk's Head, and the road at that time was almost impassable. The evening was already far gone, and Michael Wittman was to be hanged at sunrise in the morning. How was the pardon to reach him in time to save his life?

Old and feeble though he was, he began to run. From the top of the hill a welcome sight appeared. The straggling village of Turk's Head was just before him, and the sun had not yet risen. He saw a commotion in the street; men were hurrying toward the village green; a body of soldiers was already there, drawn up in order beneath a tree.

Summoning all his strength, Peter ran on and soon entered the village. Close to the tree stood Michael Wittman with his hands tied behind him. A strong rope was dangling from one of the branches. In another minute the sun would begin to peep over the snow-clad hills. An officer had already given orders to place the rope around the traitor's neck. Peter Miller, still running, shouted with all his might. The officer heard and paused. The crowd looked around and wondered. Panting and out of breath, Peter came up, waving a paper in his hand.

"A pardon! A pardon!" he gasped. "A pardon from General Washington."

The officer took the paper and read it aloud.

"Unbind the prisoner and let him go," he commanded of his only enemy. Michael Wittman, with his head bowed upon his breast, went forth a free man and a changed man. The power of Christian charity had rescued him from a shameful death, and the cause of patriotism need have no further fears of being harmed by him.

Scene 4

Although Washington had no children of his own, he adopted the widow Custis' two children and loved them as their father. While the shouts of triumph were heard at the surrender of Yorktown, word came to Washington that his stepson, who he loved dearly and who had been serving as an aid to the Commander-of-Chief, had fallen ill of camp fever in the trenches before Yorktown. When the doctor announced there was no longer hope, Washington, attended by a single office and a groom, left his headquarters at midnight and rode with all speed 30 miles to where his stepson lay.

The anxious watchers of the dying were, in the gray of the twilight, aroused by a trampling of a horse, and looking out, discovered the commander-in-chief alighting from his horse in the courtyard. He immediately summoned Dr. Craik. "Is there any hope?" Craik mournfully shook his head. The General retired to a room to indulge his grief, requesting to be left alone. In a little while the poor sufferer expired. Washington, tenderly embracing the bereaved wife and mother, observed to the weeping group around the remains of him he so dearly loved, "From this moment I adopt his two youngest children as my own." Absorbed in grief, he then waved with his hand a melancholy adieu, and, fresh horse being ready, without rest or refreshment, he remounted and returned to camp.

Scene 5

In his retirement, Mt. Vernon was frequented by guests and visitors. A Mr. Elkanah Watson visited in the winter of 1785. He says, "I trembled with awe, as I came into the presence of this great man. I found him at table with Mrs. Washington and his private family…who put me at my ease, in a free and affable conversation."

In the evening Mr. Watson sat conversing for a full hour with Washington after all the family had retired. Mr. Watson had taken a severe cold in the course of a harsh winter journey, and coughed excessively. Washington pressed him to take some remedies, but he declined. After retiring for the night, his coughing increased. "When some time had elapsed," writes he, "the door of my room was gently opened, and, on drawing my bed curtains, I beheld Washington himself, standing at my bedside with a bowl of hot tea in his hand. I was mortified and distressed beyond expression. This little incident occur-ing in common life with an ordinary man, would not have been noticed; but as a trait of the benevolence and private virtue of Washington, deserves to be recorded.

How about a couple more.

Scene 6

Immediately after the organization of the present government, the chief magistrate repaired to Fredericksburg, to pay humble duty to his mother, preparatory to his departure for New York. Seeing how disease had ravaged her body, he said that as soon as he could tend to necessary business of the new government, he would hasten back to Virginia to see her. She interrupted him with: "…you will see me no more; my great age, and the disease which is fast approaching my vitals, warn me that I shall not be long in this world; I trust in God that I may be somewhat prepared for a better. But go, George, fulfil the high destinies which Heaven appears to have intended for you; go, my son, and may Heaven's and a mother's blessing be with you always."

The President was deeply affected. His head rested upon the shoulder of his parent, whose aged arm feebly yet fondly encircled his neck. That brow on which fame had wreathed the purest laurel virtue ever gave to created man, relaxed from its awful bearing. That look which could have awed a Roman senate, was bent in filial tenderness upon the time-worn features of the aged matron.

He wept.

Scene 7

Washington's last days, like those that preceded them in the course of a long and well-spent life, were devoted to constant and careful employment. His correspondence both at home and abroad was immense. Yet no letter was unanswered. One of the best-bred men of his time, Washington deemed it a grave offence against the rules of good manners and propriety to leave letters unanswered. He wrote with great facility and it would be a difficult matter to find another who had written so much, who had written so well. General Harry Lee once observed of him:

"We are amazed, sir, at the vast amount of work you get through." Washington answered, "Sir I rise at four o'clock, and a great deal of my work is done while others sleep."

And the final scene I'll share for now took place exactly 218 years ago today, on December 14, 1799. Washington was just 67 years old and had taken a ride around his beautiful Mt. Vernon property that he loved so much on December 12th. An eyewitness wrote, "Soon after he went out, the weather became very bad, rain, hail, and snow falling alternately with a cold wind. I observed to him that I was afraid he had got wet; he said no, his great coat had kept him dry. He came to dinner without changing his dress. In the evening he appeared as well as usual.

"A heavy fall of snow took place on Friday which prevented the General from riding out as usual. He had taken cold and complained of a sore throat. He however went out in the afternoon to mark some trees that were to be cut down. He had a hoarseness which increased in the evening, but he made light of it. He sat in the parlor with Mrs. Washington and myself reading until about nine o'clock. He was very cheerful and when he met with anything interesting or entertaining, he would read it aloud as well as his hoarseness would permit him. On his retiring I observed to him that he had better take something to remove his cold. He answered, no. "You know I never take anything for a cold. Let it go as it came."

Between 2 and 3 o'clock on Saturday morning, he awoke Mrs. Washington and told her he was very unwell. She observed that he could scarcely speak and breathed with difficulty; and would have got up to call a Servant; but he would not permit her lest she should take cold.

The doctor was summoned in the morning, and despite applying remedies, his condition worsened rapidly. By the afternoon, Washington said, "I find I am going, my breath cannot last long. I believed from the first that the disorder would prove fatal." He gave instructions to his assistant to arrange his papers, accounts and books and asked if there was anything which it was essential for him to do, as he had but a very short time to continue among us. His assistant said, "I told him I could recollect nothing; but that I hoped he was not so near his end; he observed smiling, that he certainly was, and that as it was the debt that all must pay, he looked to the event with perfect resignation."

"As the evening came on, he said to his Physicians: "I feel myself going, I thank you for your attentions; but I pray you to take no more trouble about me, let me go off quietly, I cannot last long."

"About ten minutes before he expired, between ten and eleven o'clock at night, his breathing became easier; he lay quietly; he withdrew his hand from mine, and felt his own pulse. I saw his countenance change. I spoke to Dr. Craik who sat by the fire; he came to the bed side. The General's hand fell from his wrist—I took it in my mine and put it into my bosom. Dr. Craik put his hands over his eyes and he expired without a struggle or a sigh.

"While we were fixed in silent grief, Mrs. Washington (who was sitting at the foot of the bed) asked with a firm and collected voice,

"'Is he gone?'

"I could not speak, but held up my hand as a signal that he was no more.

"''Tis well,' said she in the same voice. 'All is now over. I shall soon follow him! I have no more trials to pass through!'"

She joined him just two and a half years later.

"The sublimest figure in American history is Washington on his knees at Valley Forge. He was in that hour and place the American people personified, not depending on their own courage or goodness, but asking aid from God, their Father and Preserver. Washington knew that morals are priceless, but he knew that morals are from within. And he knew that in that dread day when all, save courage, had forsaken the American arms, appeal must be to that Power beyond ourselves, eternal in the heavens, which after all, in every crisis of the lives of men and nations, has been their surest source of strength.

"That is why the snows of Valley Forge are his altar, and on his knees asked aid from Him whom the enemy had forgotten. The enemy trusted in numbers and munitions— in infantry, cavalry, artillery. Washington trusted in those things, too; but he also trusted in the God of men and nations. And Washington won."

> With his lean, ragged levies, undismayed,
> He crouched among the vigilant hills; a show
> To the disdainful, heaven-blinded foe.
> Unlauded, unsupported, disobeyed,
> Thwarted, maligned, conspired against, betrayedB
> Yet nothing could unheart him. Wouldst thou know
> His secret? There, in that thicket of snow,
> Washington knelt before his God and prayed.

> Washington at Valley Forge Canon R.G. Sutherland

Podcast #122 George Washington: One Man of Virtue

Over time, words tend to take on different meanings. One word that was used frequently in the vintage children's books was "gay." Obviously, it meant something much differently then than it does now. When I was compiling the Forgotten Classics library, while I left the word in for the most part, occasionally I replaced the word because I knew it could be very confusing to a child in today's world. For example, "the prince was gay"

When we use the word virtue today, it is usually attached to sexual purity. But I have come to love the meaning of the word as defined in Webster's 1828 dictionary. By the way, if you haven't discovered this dictionary yet, you can search online and find a free, easy-to-use version there. I love to gather deeper meanings in words by going there first. But back to virtue. Although the definition includes moral goodness and moral excellence and Webster says, "Virtue is nothing but voluntary obedience to truth," I love the very first definition:

> Strength. That substance or quality of physical bodies, by which they act and produce effects on other bodies.

And I thought what a perfect descriptive word for George Washington. His very presence—even without saying a word—inspired confidence and courage in people. In fact, he was often silent in meetings. But when he spoke, everyone listened.

What a bright shining example of what one person of virtue can accomplish.

Let me share one example taken from a favorite book of mine about George Washington, *The Real George Washington* by Jay Parry and Andrew Allison.[49] You can buy copies through the National Center for Constitutional Studies.

Here's the sample:

> On March 10, 1783, Washington learned that an unauthorized meeting of general and field officers had been called by an anonymous circular. At the same time, he was handed a fiery message to all officers, encouraging them to forcibly seek redress from a long-delinquent Congress…. [The] words were not designed to soothe, but were incendiary, deliberately designed to inflame and incite. The men in the army, already at the end of their emotional rope, were ripe for such a message….
>
> Washington was stunned by the inflammatory appeal. Members of his army were advocating use of arms to force their way upon Congress and the states. It was a dangerous and horrifying prospect! He immediately issued strict orders condemning the meeting and calling for another meeting to be held on the fifteenth of March. At that time the officers could openly discuss their many grievances and come to a more intelligent solution to their problems.

Even though Washington had taken this preliminary step, he instinctively knew that the situation could still explode out of control. Only through vigorous action would he be able "to arrest on the spot the foot that stood wavering on a tremendous precipice, to prevent the officers from being taken by surprise while the passions were all inflamed, and to rescue them from plunging themselves into a gulf of civil horror from which there might be no receding."

Initially, he had hoped to let the officers work out their grievances on their own, but on careful reflection he decided to address the meeting himself.

After a fitful, sleepless night, Washington arose on the fifteenth with the fears of the day looming ominously before him. At the appointed time, he strode to the large wooden dance hall his soldiers had erected a few weeks before and without formal introduction took over the crude lectern at the front. He began by apologizing for attending personally; such had not been his original intention, but he finally realized he must. He disparaged the paper that had circulated, characterizing it as "addressed more to the feelings and passions than to the reason and judgment of the army."

Washington agreed that Congress was shackled. But he insisted it was peopled by honorable men who eventually would be certain to do the army 'complete justice.' He had respect for these men and said the labor of Congress "to discover and establish funds for this purpose has been unwearied and will not cease till they have succeeded…. Why, then, should we distrust them and…adopt measures which may case a shade over that glory which has been so justly acquired, and tarnish the reputation of an army celebrated throughout Europe for its fortitude and patriotism?"

Washington solemnly pledged to continue to promote the army's cause 'to the utmost extent of my abilities.' But he added that both officers and soldiers must continue to be patient while Congress was addressing these problems…

Washington concluded his carefully prepared remarks. Some of the men had been swayed, but others continued to stare with hardened faces that were determined not to bend. Then, almost as an afterthought, the General pulled from his pocket a letter he had received from Joseph Jones, a Congressman from Virginia who expressed deep sympathy toward the army and pledged his help. Perhaps if he read aloud selected parts of that letter, Washington thought, it would underscore the things he had been saying.

He opened the letter and tried to read it, but stumbled badly. He paused, then pulled from his pocket a pair of new spectacles, which only his closest aides had ever seen him wear. He fumbled to put them on, but seemed to have difficulty. Finally, he said simply, "Gentlemen, you must pardon me. I have grown gray in your service and now find myself growing blind."

That humble, honest statement suddenly made a difference. Stern faces softened and strong soldiers wept.

Major Samuel Shaw recalled the commanding power of the moment:

"On other occasions, [Washington] had been supported by the exertions of an army and the countenance of his friends; but in this he stood single and alone. There was no saying where the passions of an army, which were not a little inflamed, might lead. Under these circumstances he appeared, not at the head of the troops, but as it were in opposition to them; and for a dreadful moment the interests of the army and its General seemed to be in competition! He spoke—every doubt was dispelled, and the tide of patriotism rolled again in its wonted course. Illustrious man!"

After Washington left the room, the officers voted to sustain their beloved commander in chief and to wait patiently on Congress. No one voted nay, and there was only one abstention.

Washington was relieved and gratified by the officers response…. But he could not let Congress close its eyes to the deadly peril he had momentarily averted. He wrote that they must act speedily to fulfill all their promises.

In retrospect, historians recognize how critical these decisive actions by Washington truly were. As one writer observed, "Americans can never be adequately grateful that George Washington possessed the power and the will to intervene effectively in what may well have been the most dangerous hour the United States has ever known." If Washington had not intervened—or had his efforts been ineffective—the army might very well have made good on their angry threat to use armed force. Had they done so, a new military dictatorship could have been born.

A year later, in 1784, Jefferson acclaimed Washington's decisive actions in the Newburgh crisis: "The moderation and virtue of a single character have probably prevented this revolution from being closed, as most others have been, by a subversion of that liberty it was intended to establish."

I hope that is an idea you can plant deeply in your children's hearts—the influence of the virtue of a single character—that who they are speaks louder than what they say and that one person of virtue really can make a difference in our world. Over the next few days, I'll highlight a few other persons of virtue—particularly virtuous mothers and the effect they have had on our world's history.

But before I go today, let me share one more example from Washington's life and tie it into our study of Rome this month. George Washington has been likened to Cincinnatus, a leader in the early Roman republic. Like Cincinnatus, Washington might have seized and held on to power for himself. He was in position to do so. Few people in the history of the world have been able to resist such power. But when the suggestion was given to Washington to make him king, he wasted no time in letting his opinion of the matter be known:

"You could not have found a person to whom your schemes are more disagreeable. If you have any regard for your country, concern for yourself or posterity, or respect for me, …banish these thoughts from your mind, and never communicate, as from yourself or anyone else, a sentiment of the like nature." His desire was to quietly return to his home and tend to his farm. Just like Cincinnatus. A man of virtue.

Podcast #123 Mary Washington, Mother of George

Several years ago when I was at the very beginning of this Well-Educated Heart journey, as I was learning about the power of stories, I went to my local Barnes and Noble in search of some books that would inspire my grandchildren. I went back to the children's section and asked the sales person for some help. I told her I was looking for some books that would be ennobling and would teach moral truths.

She took me to the back wall where we scanned book titles together. She shifted from one foot to another, scratched her chin, and finally reached over and pulled out *If You Give a Mouse a Cookie* and said, "I'm pretty sure this has a moral."

Now, I love *If You Give a Mouse a Cookie*, but it wasn't quite the depth I was going for. I thanked her and asked her to show me the biography section—that maybe I could find something there.

I was disappointed to see it occupied only a couple of small lower shelves and most of the books were about current celebrities. But I did find a little section of George Washington books and thought I couldn't go wrong there.

So I pulled out the first book—opened a page— and read this:

> What, finally, can we say about George Washington? The first thing is that he was no man of marble. He sometimes lost his temper, he was quick to jump into battle, he liked nothing better than a day spent on horseback followed by a jolly dinner with friends and family.
>
> But George Washington had a passion for what was in those days called fame. Today people become famous for being good athletes, well-known musicians, popular actors. In Washington's time, fame meant something like lasting honor. A person could not become famous simply because he could hit a baseball far or sing in a popular style. He or she had to do something that was really important to a nation or the world.
>
> Washington believed that if he helped to found a great nation he would earn undying fame.

Seriously? Fame was his motive?

How about what he said? "I was summoned by my country, whose voice I can never hear but with veneration and love."

OK. Maybe not that book. I picked up the next one, opened it up and read, "George Washington never liked his mother." I turned a few more pages—"He wanted to go to sea probably to get away from his mother." A few more pages—"We know he didn't like his mother because he addressed all his letters to Honored Madam."

Really?

I don't think I've been back to Barnes and Noble since. But what a treasure trove of inspiring stories I have found online in the old children's books written so long ago.

So for today's sampler, let's take a look at a story about George Washington's mother, Mary, and see what you think. I see a woman of virtue—a virtue that was instilled into the soul of her son.

The story was originally found in an 1892 book, *The Mothers of Great Men and Women* by Laura Holloway,[50] but I included an adapted version of the story in *Stories of Great Wives and Mothers*[51] in the Forgotten Classics library.

Here is the story.

> Had the mother of Washington been associated with the daily life of her distinguished son after he reached man's estate, hers would have been a familiar historical character. As she was not, the world knows but the barest incidents of her life as compared with its knowledge of Washington's wife.
>
> Like the mothers of all great and earnest men, she was a praying woman. Her Bible was her constant companion, and its precepts were ever on her lips. A silent, serious woman she was, self-contained, self-respecting, and reserved. During the forty-six years of her widowhood she managed her household and farm without the assistance of any adviser, and reared her children to usefulness and honor, and saw them go forth into the world equipped for its work and pain. That they each and all revered her, and sought her counsel in every emergency, is sufficient testimony of her worth and ability.
>
> Mrs. Washington's lack of personal ambition and her constitutional reserve were qualities which prevented her from becoming popularly known to the public, even at a time when the people were eager for any opportunity to show her honor. But no demonstration was ever made in her behalf, and there is but one instance recorded when she appeared in public with her son. This was after the surrender of Lord Cornwallis, when Washington, accompanied by his suite and many distinguished military men, went to Fredericksburg. A grand ball was given in his honor, and the proud old mother was the belle of the evening, the observed of all observers as she passed from group to group, leaning on the arm of her happy son. The beautiful devotion of Washington to his mother endeared him to her neighbors and to the people of Virginia, and the honors that were paid him on that occasion were doubly sincere because they were a recognition of his worth, not alone as a patriot, but as a son.
>
> Mother and son were much alike in character, personal appearance, and conduct. Washington, in the most trying emergency of his career as commander-in-chief, did not display more self-control and courage than did his mother in hiding from her children for months and years the distressing face that she was a sufferer of cancer. This circumstance it was that strengthened her resolve to live alone, which she did up to the last few months of her life, and her mode of life probably had much to do with prolonging her existence to the great age she attained.

The last duty that Washington performed previous to leaving Virginia for the seat of war at the breaking out of the rebellion, was to go to Fredericksburg and remove his mother from the country into the city, where her married daughter was residing. He was unwilling to go away leaving her on the farm, and to overcome her opposition he knew that a personal appeal must be made. The prospects of a long war and the uncertainty of his return were shown her in their conversation, and when convinced that it was to add to his peace of mind when away, she consented, and removed at once, leaving a competent man in charge of the farm, subject to her daily supervision. And supervise it she did every day of her life, riding about the fields, directing the planting and the gathering of crops, ordering repairs, and buying supplies. She had what would not be termed an old-fashioned buggy and a gentle horse, and every morning both were before her door awaiting her. She lived out of doors the greater part of the later years of her life.

Her children were grown and gone from her, and her eldest son was engaged in duties that exposed him more or less to constant danger and separated him almost entirely from her. It was wisdom in her so to live, and the disease that had very gradually come upon her was kept at bay for many years by her uniform, quiet, and peaceful life. Where another mother of less fortunate temperament would have found occasion for constant worry and anxiety, in her son's prolonged absence and trying if high position, Mrs. Washington fretted not at all, and troubled no one with her heart experiences. She had great native sense, and she was strong of will and firm of faith, and her outlook on life was in consequence extended.

As a child on her father's Virginia plantation, Mary Ball was trained religiously, and as she grew to womanhood she became a church member, and all her associations were of a religious nature. The children of the early settlers of this country and their immediate descendants were strenuous advocates of church worship, and they gave of their means and their time to build meeting-houses. The Sabbath was the day of all others most filled with important duties. All the week the colonists worked hard, and at the meetings on Lord's day they met together and were companions in devotion. They learned the Bible, and could repeat large portions of it.

Mary Ball was, by reason of her careful rearing and her natural disposition, altogether fitted for the position of stepmother, which position she assumed when she became the wife of Augustine Washington, her father's friend and neighbor. She was twenty-four years old when she married—an age not considered very young in that day.

The Washingtons were planters of considerable means in Westmoreland County, and the home to which Augustine conducted his wife was one of the most comfortable in that section of the country. In this pretty country home was born on the 22nd of February, 1732, George, the first child of Mary and Augustine Washington. Six children were born to Mr. and Mrs. Washington, five of whom lived to maturity.

It was a very religious household: both father and mother were members of the

Episcopal Church. Family prayers were said morning and evening. The Bible was read, and the servants of the household were always present. The mother instructed her children constantly on religious subjects, and as often as not her reproofs were made in scriptural language. In this way she inspired their hearts with respect, and impressed upon their unfolding minds the dignity and responsibility of a mother.

Mr. Washington died at the age of forty-nine years, leaving to his wife the responsibility of rearing her young children, the eldest of whom was but a small lad. Mrs. Washington found little difficulty in bringing up her children. They were disciplined in obedience, and a simple word was her command. She was not given to any display of rage, but was steady, well-balanced, and unvarying in her mood.

A relative and playmate of George in boyhood, who was often a guest in her house, says: "I was often there with George—his playmate, schoolmate and young man's companion. Of the mother I was ten times more afraid than I ever was of my own parents. She awed me in the midst of her kindness, for she was indeed truly kind. I have often been present with her sons, proper tall fellows too, and we were all as mute as mice; and even now, when time has whitened my locks, and I am the grandparent of a second generation, I could not behold that remarkable woman without feelings it is impossible to describe. Whoever has seen that awe-inspiring air and manner, so characteristic in the Father of his Country, will remember the matron as she appeared when the presiding genius of her well-ordered household, commanding and being obeyed."

Mr. Sparks, than whom there is no better authority, says:

"It has been said that there never was a great man, the elements of whose greatness might not be traced to the original characteristics or early influences of his mother. If this be true, how much do mankind owe to the mother of Washington?"

Mrs. Washington permitted her son to spend his holidays at Mount Vernon, with his brother Lawrence, and there he was brought into contact with military men and naval officers. The martial spirit was always strong in the lad, and he was a careful listener to the conversations held in that home on the Potomac. Lawrence encouraged George in his desire to become a military man. An opportunity offered to secure for him a midshipman's position on a British man-of-war, and Lawrence urged Mrs. Washington to let him accept it. George also petitioned her, and the trial was a severe one to her. She refused finally, on the ground that there was no reason why her son (he was then fourteen years of age) should be thrown out into the world, and separated so far from his kindred. The professions she objected to also as one that would take her boy from her permanently. She could not bring herself to see that it was to his advantage to go to sea, and we may feel assured she made it the burden of many prayers.

There was a neighbor of hers who was a friend of her stepson's and this man, Mr. Jackson, at the request of Lawrence, went to see her regarding the matter. After visiting Mrs. Washington, he wrote to Lawrence as follows:

"She seems to dislike George's going to sea, and says several persons have told her it was a bad scheme. She offers trifling objections, such as fond, unthinking mothers habitually suggest."

Mr. Jackson, who rated his worldly judgment against a mother's intuition! His obtuseness in styling her an "unthinking" mother was sufficient to have made a woman of her strong sense distrust advice from such a quarter. Had she been persuaded against her will, her son's great future would have been marred, and the probabilities are that his career would have been a comparatively obscure one.

In the archives of Mount Vernon may be seen a manual compiled by Mrs. Washington from Sir Matthew Hale's "Contemplations, Moral and Divine," which she wrote out for her son, and which he preserved until the day of his death. It stands to reason that a son who heeded every other instruction would yield implicit obedience in a matter of so much importance, and it is an historical fact that he in after years alluded to it with expressions of gratitude to his mother for preventing him from taking a step that would have been unfortunate if not fatal to his future.

It was a not a great while after the circumstance narrated above that the French and Indian War broke out, and George Washington received his mother's consent and blessing when he made known his desire to go. From that time henceforth he was with her only on occasional visits.

When the war broke out he paid her, as has been said, a visit before starting north to assume command. In the long years that passed before she saw him again, he wrote her repeatedly, and lost no opportunity to relieve her mind of anxiety concerning him. The lavish praises bestowed upon him by all who saw her hardly ever received any other recognition than a quiet reminder that Providence was ordering all things. For herself, she found her self-control in prayer, and much of her time was spent alone.

The surrender of Cornwallis at Yorktown was the auspicious event that hastened their reunion. A messenger was sent to apprise her of the fact, and as soon as possible public duties were laid aside, and Washington visited her, attended by his staff. His presence in Fredericksburg aroused the enthusiasm of all classes. For the first time in six years mother and son met, and it may be imagined that her heart rejoiced over the meeting. She was then over seventy-years of age. On this occasion the people of Fredericksburg gave a ball in his honor, and it was attended by a brilliant throng of military officers and foreigners. Washington presented the American and European officers to his mother, who regarded her with undisguised pleasure and astonishment. Tradition says she was the picture of beautiful simplicity, moving among the dazzling throng dressed in the appropriate costume of a Virginia matron of the olden time.

At the close of the Revolution Washington endeavored, as he had done before, to have his mother reside with him at Mount Vernon. She was now past seventy, and he was unwilling that she should live alone at her time of life. Her children all shared this feeling. Nothing could shake her determination. Her reply was, "I thank you for your dutiful and affectionate offers, but my wants are few in this life, and I feel perfectly competent to take care of myself."

Very often Washington visited her, and always with increasing anxiety. During the latter portion of her life, when the pitiless disease from which she had suffered for years was making rapid headway, it was her habit to repair daily to a secluded spot near her dwelling, and their commune with her Maker. She sought by this means to gain strength to live out her days without harrowing the feelings of others with the sight of her sufferings. But for this disease, cancer in the breast, which had exhibited itself years before, she would in all probability have lived with her son, or at least her daughter. But as long as she could hide the cruel secret from her children, she did, and it was not until the last years of her life that her son knew of it. His alarm and anxiety she quieted by her resolute course, and her own courage and calmness helped the others.

When Washington was elected President of the United States, he paid her a farewell visit. He was soon to start for the seat of government, and he felt that he would not see her again. This was the year of her death, and she knew when she gave him her last blessing that the end was not far off. The separation was intensely painful to him. He rested his head on her shoulder while she folded her feeble arms about his neck. Both wept, the mother silently, while Washington, unable to control his feelings, sobbed as she gently released herself from his embrace. She bade him do the duty Providence had assigned him, and live his life through with her blessing on his head.

The trial was bitter to her, because she was fast hastening away, and would have gladly had his loving support to the end. But it was not to be, and controlling herself with great effort, she met the parting with more composure than he could summon.

After intense sufferings, she died on the evening of the 25th of August, 1789, in her eighty-third year, and the forty-sixth of her widowhood. Mrs. Lewis, after the last sad rites were paid her, wrote to Washington informing him of the end. He had been extremely ill, and the intelligence deeply affected him. His letter included the following:

> *My Dear Sister:*
>
> *Under these considerations, and a hope that she is translated to a happier place, it is the duty of her relatives to yield due submission to the decrees of the Creator. When I was last in Fredericksburg, I took a final leave of my mother, never expecting to see her more.*

Mrs. Washington's business integrity throughout her life was one of her finest characteristics, and in her last worldly transaction she recorded the fact that her estate was encumbered by no debts.

She died as she had lived, a grand character, one of the noblest this country ever has produced or ever will produce.

Her grave was unmarked, even by a headstone, until the year 1833, when the cornerstone of a monument to her memory was laid by President Jackson, in the presence of a great concourse of people. The day, the seventh of May, was beautiful, the soft spring air and cloudless sky making it seem the perfection of weather. The grave was made near the spot where she was accustomed to retire and pray, and it recalled the memories of her last years to very many who stood on ground consecrated by her presence. The simple but eloquent inscription it contains is:

MARY,
the Mother of
WASHINGTON.

Mrs. L.N. Sigourney's poem and tribute read on the occasion contains the following touching lines:

A nation's liberty and earth's applause,
Making Mount Vernon's tomb a Mecca haunt
For patriot and for sage, while time shall last,
What part was thine, what thanks to thee are due,
Who 'mid his elements of being wrought
With no uncertain aim—nursing the germ
Of Godlike virtue in his infant mind,
We know not—Heaven can tell!
Rise, noble pile!

And show a race unborn who rests below,
And say to mothers, what a holy charge
Is theirs—with what a kingly power their love
Might rule the fountains of the new-born mind;
Warn them to wake at early dawn, and sow
Good seed before the world doth sow its tares,
Nor in their toil decline—that angel bands
May put the sickle in, and reap for God,
And gather to His garner.

Podcast #124 Monica, the Mother of St. Augustine

As I continue highlighting persons of virtue, I now turn to a mother of great virtue whose influence on the history of the world is incalculable. The story takes place in some of the final years of the Roman Empire. For any of you who have had children grow up and depart from the ways you so carefully taught them, this story is one of hope.

The story is found in the 1892 book, *Mothers of Great Men and Women* by Laura Holloway and an abridged version is found in *Stories of Great Wives and Mothers*.[52]

> Those not familiar with ecclesiastical biography may need to be reminded that there were two St. Augustines who have left illustrious records in the annals of Christianity. One of them was a monk, who with forty of his comrades was sent by Pope Gregory the Great to Christianize Britain, and who, landing on the coast of Kent, became the first Archbishop of Canterbury. But the other and greater St. Augustine, who became after his conversion first a priest and then Bishop of Hippo in Africa, is he whose mother has left an example of encouragement and benediction to the Christian mothers of all time. It is of her that we would now speak.
>
> St. Augustine was born under very different auspices from those of the Christians in the nineteenth century. Although Christianity had a large domain in the fourth century, and the Roman emperors were nominally
>
> Christians, yet the dissensions of Christians as to doctrine were so great and their morals were so largely influenced by heathenism, that when the third century closed it seemed as if the salt of Christ's followers had lost its savor and the light and sweetness of Jesus had deserted his professed disciples. A wholesale relapse into paganism seemed imminent until St. Augustine lifted up the cross anew, and "the plague was stayed."
>
> It is from his own "Confessions," a work that has been translated again and again into all the languages of Europe, that we must gather the chief characteristics both of his mother and himself. His father, Patricius, was a heathen until within a few years of his death, which occurred when St. Augustine was a lad of seventeen.
>
> Monica's birth took place in 332, and she was raised in the Catholic faith, to which her parents steadily adhered. They were persons of genteel poverty who kept a small retinue of servants. One of these servants had nursed the father of Monica in his infancy, and had obtained great authority in the household. She also cared for the future mother of St. Augustine, and it was through her restraining influence that Monica, after her marriage with Patricius, was enabled to live peaceably with her mother-in-law, who, at first, did all she could to prejudice the pagan husband against his unoffending Christian wife. Monica returned good for evil, and when her mother-in-law and the servants whispered against her, "she so overcame by observance, and persevering endurance and meekness, that in the end these whispering tongues were silenced," and the wife and

mother of Patricius lived together "with a remarkable sweetness of mutual kindness." It is her illustrious son who tells us this, and who exclaims, "Such was she, Thyself, O God, her most inward instructor, teaching her in the school of the heart…"

We hear much in our time of the dangers and temptations of college life. Carthage, which was now a part of the Roman Empire, was the seat of the best learning of the time, and thither St. Augustine was sent, in the year 371. Here he studied rhetoric, heathen literature, and philosophy. The Scriptures appeared to him trivial when compared with the heathen classics, and especially with Cicero. Augustine remained at Carthage until his nineteenth year, at Monica's expense, his father having died two years before.

It was a great consolation to Monica that her husband had become a Christian before his death, and that the last few years of their union had been peaceful and affectionate. It had not always been so. Patricius was a man of violent temper, who had abused, though he did not beat her, had impeded her religious doctrines, mocked at her high standard of virtue, and when Monica learned that her son Augustine, long given to immorality, had become the father of an illegitimate child, Patricius only laughed as though his sowing of wild oats were a matter of course. For the mother of this boy Augustine entertained a sincere affection, although their relations, which continued for fifteen years, were unlawful.

Among those whom Monica interested in the mental and moral struggles of her son was a bishop who bade her leave Augustine alone and trust to prayers and time for the longed-for change, and who cheered her with the words, "It cannot be that the son of such tears should perish." There followed a hard period of sorrow and probation both for the mother and the son. Monica believed in dreams. On one occasion, while she slept, there appeared to her a youth of shining aspect, who had, as it were, the face of an angel, and who whispered words of hope and consolation to her regarding the future conversion of her son. She herself seemed to be standing safely upon a bridge, which no storm could shake or waters of destruction reach. The radiant messenger assured her that "where she was there should her son be also." She awoke, and beheld Augustine standing at her side. Through the long years of waiting that were yet to come she drew comfort from the recollection of this vision, and pondered it in her heart.

Slowly and silently the change was wrought. Augustine had a dear friend, Nebridius. "I had made one friend, only too dear for…and, like myself, in the fresh opening flower of youth." Nebridius was taken sick of a fever, and lay unconscious and nigh unto death. He seemed to be getting better, but one day was attacked again with fever, and so departed. Augustine sorrowed long and bitterly for the loss of his "one friend." Augustine at this time was occupied with the study of the beautiful, and, like Edmund Burke, wrote a book upon the subject. He dedicated it to a famous orator in Rome, and to Rome he himself set out from Carthage. He caught a sickness on his arrival, and while sick studied the Scriptures with more attention. From Rome he set out for Milan, where he had received an appointment as a teacher of rhetoric.

Augustine was now thirty years old: it was the year 385. Monica had for some time been kept anxious by the despondent tone of Augustine's letters, and at last resolved, at all hazards, to rejoin him at Rome. In those days the journey was a difficult one, especially for a woman. She was at this time residing at her native place, Tagaste. To meet the expenses of the journey she had to sell her valuables. But she made her way to Carthage, from which her son had sailed two years before while she was waiting on the shore, and embarked. Hardly had the vessel sailed when a violent storm set in. The hearts of all on board sank with apprehension, and even the captain and sailors gave up all hope. But the faith which had enabled St. Paul to tranquillize a ship's company when he too was traveling Romeward, inspired poor Monica with courage. She cheered the sailors and restored their courage. She told them that though the waves of the sea were mighty and raged horribly, the Lord who ruled them was mighty and could still their raging. And so it was.

They reached Civita Vecchia, and Monica hastened on to Rome, only to find that her son had left for Milan. The latter city is two hundred leagues from Rome, and to reach it one must cross the Apennines. This did not scare her. The mountain passes had no more terrors for her than the stormy sea. So, after one day's rest, she set out for Milan, where the long desire of her soul was to be accomplished, and her son, after all his wanderings in the far country of sin and unbelief, was to be converted by the preaching of St. Ambrose, "whom," said Monica, "I shall ever think of as an angel of God," and receiving baptism in the spirit of a little child was to learn the eternal strain, "Thou art the King of Glory, O Christ."

Except for St. Paul, Christianity had never gained a greater convert than St. Augustine, so far as intellect was concerned. Augustine stayed the sceptic process that was fast destroying the life of the Western Church. His marvellous gifts were transferred at once from the school of heathenism to the school of Christ; from the vain babbling of false philosophy to the service of absolute truth. His natural characteristics became sanctified and consecrated to higher uses. The eye that was so keen to note things beautiful in books and nature now saw the beauty of the City of God.

Deep were his thoughts while yet a youth, and they grew deeper still when he discovered that God has created the soul and reason of man for His own abode, and that happiness and contentment can be found in Him alone.

The angel who wrestled in prayer for him and shed such tears of anguish was his mother, Monica. His "Confessions" are full of the most grateful acknowledgments to God for what she had wrought for him. "Thy faithful one," he says, "weeping to Thee for me, more than mothers weep the bodily death of their children; for discovered the death wherein I lay, and Thou didst not despise her tears when, streaming down, they watered the ground in every place where she prayed." It was not until after seventeen years of anxious wandering and doubt that the voice of enfranchisement was heard.

The immediate circumstances are worth narrating.

An old friend from Africa named Pontitianus, one of "them that were of Caesar's household," being a military officer of the imperial court, but a fervent Christian, paid Augustine and his mother and his friend Alypius a visit at Milan. The old soldier of Christ and of Caesar had travelled much in Gaul, in Spain, in Italy, and in Egypt, and his talk was much upon religious houses which had taken rise from St. Antony, in Alexandria, and had spread to Africa. Augustine listened eagerly as the old man narrated that, while the Emperor was at the circus, he had gone with three or four friends to walk in some gardens near the town. On their road two of them went into a hermit's cell and found a manuscript life of St. Antony, which they began to read. "Tell me," said one to the other, "to what, after all, does our life tend? What do we seek or hope for? The favor of the Emperor? But that is here today and gone tomorrow! Instead of that, if we will seek the favor of God, it is ours at once, now, and forever!"

When Pontitianus and the others joined them, the two men declared their purpose of devoting themselves henceforth to the service of God. Augustine, who with his friend Alypius was moved at the story, went into the garden, whither Alypius soon followed him. "What are we doing?" said Augustine. "Do you not hear? The ignorant, the unlearned, carry the kingdom of heaven by storm, while we, with our boasted science, grovel on the earth. Is it not a shame that we have not the courage to imitate them?" Abruptly quitting Alpius, he threw himself under a fig-tree and began to weep in misery.

Suddenly a child's voice seemed to reach him, singing and repeating the words, "Take and read!" These words appeared to him as a revelation from heaven. Seizing a copy of the New Testament, he opened the passage, "Let us walk honestly, as in the day; not in rioting and drunkenness; not in chambering and wantonness; not in strife and envyings. But put ye on the Lord Jesus Christ, and make not provision for the flesh to fulfill the lusts thereof." "Instantly," he says himself, at the end of the sentence, "by a light, as it were, of serenity infused into my heart, all the darkness of doubt vanished away." Henceforth, until her death, a spiritual union was added to the natural affection subsisting between the now happy mother and her transformed son. Many were the conversations about high and heavenly things which they enjoyed together.

"Son, for my part," said Monica, "I have no further delight in anything in this life. What do I here any longer, or to what end I am here, I know not, now that my hopes in this world are accomplished. One thing there was for which I desired to linger for a while in this life—that I might see thee a true Christian before I died. My God hath now done this for me more abundantly, that I now see thee, despising earthly happiness, become His servant. What do I here?"

The shadows of life's evening were indeed closing around the mother of Augustine. About five days after this, she was taken with a fever, and said to him, "Here shall you bury your mother." And when some lamented that she was about to die so far from her old home in Africa, she meekly answered, "Nothing is far to God; and I do not fear that He should not know where to find me at the resurrection morning."

"I closed her eyes," said her son, "and there flowed a mighty sorrow into my heart. O my God, what comparison is there between the honor that I paid to her and her slavery for me? Being then forsaken of so great comfort in her, my soul was wounded.... And behold the corpse was carried to the burial. We went and returned without tears. And then by little and little I recovered my former thoughts of Thy handmaid; her holy conversation toward Thee; her holy tenderness and observance toward us; whereof I was suddenly deprived."

Such was the mother of whom Augustine, to the close of his own life, declared, "It is to my mother that I owe everything. If I am Thy child, O my God, it is because Thou gavest me such a mother. If I prefer the truth to all other things, it is the point of my mother's teachings. If I did not long ago perish in sin and misery, it is because of the long and faithful tears with which she pleaded for me." By prayer and patience she won her great son Augustine from unbelief and sensuality to that faith and self-consecration which made him a burning and shining light to all ages of the Church and of the world. His influence upon Christian civilization can hardly be overestimated.

Podcast #125 Roman Mothers of Virtue

Continuing on with taking a look at mothers of virtue—virtue meaning the effect they have on the lives of their children because of their personal strength—let's visit a few more Roman mothers. You can read about them in *Stories of Great Wives and Mothers*.[53] The final story is another sample from James Baldwin's *Fifty Famous People*.[54]

Mothers of Antiquity

The theory that mothers were the ruling influence on the characteristics of their children is not a new one, having been held by the ancients as an indisputable truth. To the mothers they looked as the source of the improvement or degeneracy of the race.

Jerome speaks in his writings of his mother and his maternal grandmother as the teachers of his infancy, and gives testimony to the fact that to his mother he owed his religious training.

Chrysostom owed to his mother, Anthusa, the widow of an imperial general, the tenderest care, and he gave in return the sincerest affection. When her son had made up his mind to retire to a convent and spend his life apart from the world, as his nearest friend had done, his mother prevented such a step, believing that his usefulness to the world would be more marked outside than within the convent walls. He tells us how she influenced his decision. Taking him by the hand, she led him into her chamber, where she broke into tears and "into words more moving than any tears." She told him of her grief over the death of his father soon after birth, and spoke of the efforts she had made to provide for his education and preserve to him her husband's property. Her request to him was that he would not leave her in a second widowhood, or renew a sorrow that had been partly assuaged. "Wait, at least," she said, "until I am dead; and that will not be long."

Obeying his mother, Chrysostom attained to a dignity and usefulness that would not have been reached by him perhaps within the cloister.

So potent and beneficent had been his mother's influence over him that he honored all women, and entertained an exalted idea of the power, of a Christian mother. The position he accorded a Christian woman in the fourth century is more advanced than that granted her in many denominations in this nineteenth century. In a letter to a noble Roman lady, he thus expressed his views on the subject:

"In the order of affairs of this world, as in that of nature, each sex has its particular sphere of action: to the woman, household affairs; to the man, public business, the government of the city, discussions in the agora. But in the work which has the service of God for its object, these distinctions are effaced, and it often happens that the woman excels the man in the courage with which she supports her opinions, and in her holy zeal…. Do not consider as unbecoming to your sex that earnest work which in any way promotes the welfare of the faithful. On the contrary, I urge you to use every effort to calm, either by your own influence or by that of others whom you can convince, the fearful storm which has burst upon the Eastern churches. This is the great work which I beg you to undertake with the utmost diligence; the more frightful the tempest, the more precious the recompense for your share in calming it."

A Story of Old Rome

There was a great famine in Rome. The summer had been very dry and the corn crop had failed. There was no bread in the city. The people were starving.

One day, to the great joy of all, some ships arrived from another country. These ships were loaded with corn. Here was food enough for all.

The rulers of the city met to decide what should be done with the corn.

"Divide it among the poor people who need it so badly," said some. "Let it be a free gift to them from the city."

But one of the rulers was not willing to do this. His name was Coriolanus, and he was very rich.

"These people are poor because they have been too lazy to work," he said. "They do not deserve any gifts from the city. Let those who wish any corn bring money and buy it."

When the people heard about this speech of the rich man, Coriolanus, they were very angry.

"He is no true Roman," said some.

"He is selfish and unjust," said others.

"He is an enemy to the poor. Kill him! kill him!" cried the mob. They did not kill him, but they drove him out of the city and bade him never return.

Coriolanus made his way to the city of Antium, which was not far from Rome. The people of Antium were enemies of the Romans and had often been at war with them. So they welcomed Coriolanus very kindly and made him the general of their army.

Coriolanus began at once to make ready for war against Rome. He persuaded other towns near Antium to send their soldiers to help him.

Soon, at the head of a very great army, he marched toward the city which had once been his home. The rude soldiers of Antium overran all the country around Rome. They burned the villages and farmhouses. They filled the land with terror.

Coriolanus pitched his camp quite near to the city. His army was the greatest that the Romans had ever seen. They knew that they were helpless before so strong an enemy.

"Surrender your city to me," said Coriolanus. "Agree to obey the laws that I shall make for you. Do this, or I will burn Rome and destroy all its people."

The Romans answered, "We must have time to think of this matter. Give us a few days to learn what sort of laws you will make for us, and then we will say whether we can submit to them or not."

"I will give you thirty days to consider the matter," said Coriolanus.

Then he told them what laws he would require them to obey. These laws were so severe that all said, "It will be better to die at once."

At the end of the thirty days, four of the city s rulers went out to beg him to show mercy to the people of Rome. These rulers were old men, with wise faces and long white beards. They went out bareheaded and very humble.

Coriolanus would not listen to them. He drove them back with threats, and told them that they should expect no mercy from him; but he agreed to give them three more days to consider the matter.

The next day, all the priests and learned men went out to beg for mercy. These were dressed in their long flowing robes, and all knelt humbly before him. But he drove them back with scornful words.

On the last day, the great army which Coriolanus had led from Antium was drawn up in battle array. It was ready to march upon the city and destroy it.

All Rome was in terror. There seemed to be no way to escape the anger of this furious man.

Then the rulers, in their despair, said, "Let us go up to the house where Coriolanus used to live when he was one of us. His mother and his wife are still there. They are noble women, and they love Rome. Let us ask them to go out and beg our enemy to have mercy upon us. His heart will be hard indeed if he can refuse his mother and his wife."

The two noble women were willing to do all that they could to save their city. So, leading his little children by the hand, they went out to meet Coriolanus. Behind them followed a long procession of the women of Rome.

Coriolanus was in his tent. When he saw his mother and his wife and his children, he was filled with joy. But when they made known their errand, his face darkened, and he shook his head.

For a long time his mother pleaded with him. For a long time his wife begged him to be merciful. His little children clung to his knees and spoke loving words to him.

At last, he could hold out no longer. "O mother," he said, "you have saved your country, but have lost your son!" Then he commanded his army to march back to the city of Antium.

Rome was saved; but Coriolanus could never return to his home, his mother, his wife and children. He was lost to them.

Podcast #126 Socrates

Now let's travel over to Greece in search of more men and women of virtue where we will spend a little time with Socrates. He left no writings of his own, no great masterpieces of art, and yet his influence has been felt through hundreds and even thousands of years and continues to be felt.

Today's sample is a chapter from *Aunt Charlotte's Stories of Greek History for the Little Ones* by Charlotte Yonge.[55] With a title like that, you may be expecting a watered down, simple retelling of the story. But here is another example of how far we have fallen in our expectations of what children are capable of taking in.

After reading the story, you may want to visit the Mother's University Art section where you will find a YouTube describing a painting called The Death of Socrates by Jacques Louis David painted in 1787.

And now, today's sampler, which begins about 400 years before Christ.

> Of the men who sought after God in the darkness, "if haply they might feel after Him," none had come so near the truth as Socrates, a sculptor by trade, and yet a great philosopher, and, so far as we can see, the wisest and best man who ever grew up without any guide but nature and conscience. Even the oracle at Delphi declared that he was the wisest of men, because he did not fancy he knew what he did not know, and did not profess to have any wisdom of his own. It was quite true—all his thinking had only made him quite sure that he knew nothing; but he was also sure that he had an inward voice within him, telling him which was the way in which he should walk. He did not think much about the wild tales of the Greek gods and goddesses; he seems to have considered them as fancies that had grown up on some forgotten truth, and he said a healthy mind would not dwell upon them; but he was quite sure that above all these there was one really true Most High God, who governed the world, rewarded the good, punished the bad, and sent him the inward voice, which he tried to obey to the utmost of his power, and by so doing, no doubt, his inward sight grew clearer and clearer. Even in his home his gentleness and patience were noted, so that when his scolding wife Xantippe, after railing at him sharply, threw some water at his head, he only smiled, and said, "After thunder follows rain." He did not open a school under a portico, but, as he did his work, all the choicest spirits of Greece resorted to him to argue out these questions in search of truth; and many accounts of these conversations have been preserved to us by his two best pupils, Plato and Xenophon.
>
> But in the latter days of the Peloponnesian war, when the Athenians were full of bitterness, and had no great deeds to undertake outside their city, a foolish set of arguing pretenders to philosophy arose, who were called the Sophists, and who spent their time in mere empty talk, often against the gods; and the great Socrates was mixed

up in people's fancy with them. A comic writer arose, named Aristophanes, who, seeing the Athenians fallen from the greatness of their fathers, tried to laugh them into shame at themselves. He particularly disliked Euripides, because his tragedies seemed, like the Sophists, not to respect the gods; and he also more justly hated Alkibiades for his overbearing ways, and his want of all real respect for gods or men. It was very hard on Socrates that the faults of his pupils should be charged against him; but Aristophanes had set all Athens laughing by a comedy called "The Clouds," in which a good-for-nothing young man, evidently meant for Alkibiades, gets his father into debt by buying horses, and, under the teaching of Socrates, learns both to cheat his creditors and to treat respect for his father as a worn-out notion. The beauty and the lisp of Alkibiades were imitated so as to make it quite plain who was meant by the youth; and Socrates himself was evidently represented by an actor in a hideous comic mask, caricaturing the philosopher's snub nose and ugly features. The play ended by the young man's father threatening to burn down the house of Socrates, with him in it. This had been written twenty years before, but it had been acted and admired again and again, together with the other comedies of Aristophanes—one about a colony of birds who try to build a city in the air, and of whom the chorus was composed; and another, called "The Frogs," still more droll, and all full of attacks on the Sophists.

Thus the Athenians had a general notion that Socrates was a corrupter of youth and a despiser of the gods, for in truth some forms of worship, like the orgies of Bacchus, and other still worse rites which had been brought in from the East, were such that no good man could approve them. One of the thirty tyrants had at one time been a pupil of his, and this added to the ill-feeling against him; and while Xenophon was still away in Asia, in the year 399, the philosopher was brought to trial on three points, namely, that he did not believe in the gods of Athens, that he brought in new gods, and that he misled young men; and for this his accusers demanded that he should be put to death.

Socrates pleaded his own cause before the council of the Areopagus. He flatly denied unbelief in the gods of his fathers, but he defended his belief in his genius or in-dwelling voice, and said that in this he was only like those who drew auguries from the notes of birds, thunder, and the like; and as for his guidance of young men, he called on his accusers to show whether he had ever led any man from virtue to vice. One of them answered that he knew those who obeyed and followed Socrates more than their own parents; to which he replied that such things sometimes happened in other matters—men consulted physicians about their health rather than their fathers, and obeyed their generals in war, not their fathers; and so in learning, they might follow him rather than their fathers. "Because I am thought to have some power of teaching youth, O my judges!" he ended, "is that a reason why I should suffer death? My accusers may procure that judgment, but hurt me they cannot. To fear death is to seem wise without being so, for it is pretending to understand what we know not. No man knows what death is, or whether it be not our greatest happiness; yet all fear and shun it."

His pupil Plato stood up on the platform to defend him, and began, "O ye Athenians, I am the youngest man who ever went up in this place—"

"No, no," they cried, with one voice; "the youngest who ever went down!" They would not hear a word from him; and 280 voices sentenced the great philosopher Plato to die, after the Athenian fashion, by being poisoned with hemlock. He disdained to plead for a lessening of the penalty; but it could not be carried out at once, because a ship had just been sent to Delos with offerings, and for the thirty days while this was gone no one could be put to death. Socrates therefore was kept in prison, with chains upon his ankles; but all his friends were able to come and visit him, and one of them, named Krito, hoped to have contrived his escape by bribing the jailer, but he refused to make anyone guilty of a breach of the laws for the sake of a life which must be near its close, for he was not far from seventy years old; and when one of his friends began to weep at the thought of his dying innocent, "What!" he said, "would you think it better for me to die guilty?"

When the ship had come back, and the time was come, he called all his friends together for a cheerful feast, during which he discoursed to them as usual. All the words that fell from him were carefully stored up, and recorded by Plato in a dialogue, which is one of the most valuable things that have come down to us from Greek times. It was not Socrates, said the philosopher, whom they would lay in the grave. Socrates' better part, and true self, would be elsewhere; and all of them felt sure that in that unknown world, as they told him, it must fare well with one like him. He begged them, for their own sakes, never to forget the lessons he had taught them; and when the time had come, he drank the hemlock as if it had been a cup of wine: he then walked up and down the room for a little while, bade his pupils remember that this was the real deliverance from all disease and impurity, and then, as the fatal sleep benumbed him, he lay down, bidding Krito not forget a vow he had made to one of the gods; and so he slept into death. "Thus," said Plato, "died the man who, of all with whom we were acquainted, was in death the noblest, in life the wisest and the best."

Plato himself carried on much of the teaching of his master, and became the founder of a sect of philosophy which taught that, come what may, virtue is that which should, above all, be sought for as making man noblest, and that no pain, loss, or grief should be shunned for virtue's sake. His followers were called Stoics, from their fashion of teaching in the porticos or porches, which in Greek were named stoai. Their great opponents were the Epicureans, or followers of a philosopher by name Epicurus, who held that as man's life is short, and as he knew not whence he came, nor whither he went, he had better make himself as happy as possible, and care for nothing else. Epicurus, indeed, declared that only virtue did make men happy; but there was nothing in his teaching to make them do anything but what pleased themselves, so his philosophy did harm, while that of the Stoics did good. A few Pythagoreans, who believed in the harmony of the universe, still remained; but as long as the world remained in darkness, thinking men were generally either Stoics or Epicureans.

Podcast #127 Greek Mythology

I frequently see threads among homeschool groups—particularly Christian homeschoolers—where they refuse to share Greek mythology with their children. They say it is corrupting and goes against their faith in Jesus Christ.

I do not agree with them. Although there is much in many of the re-tellings that is not appropriate for children, they are like everything else—we must be discerning and seek the jewels.

My heart-educator friends were gifted in this ability and if you will turn to their writings and retelling of the Greek myths, you will find much treasure for the hearts of your children.

I thought it may be helpful to share some of their insights with you, so I've compiled a sampling of their thoughts for this podcast. Let me start with Kate Douglas Wiggin, who you may recall as the author of *Rebecca of Sunnybrook Farm*. She also wrote *The Birds' Christmas Carol* which I have included in my *Stories for Christmas* volume in the Forgotten Classics. She originally wrote the story to raise money for the first kindergartens that were being established among poor families in California, little dreaming of its success. It's a simple story—some may even call it cheesy—but when I finished it, I sat at my desk and wept at the deep feelings it stirred inside of me.

Anyway, here is what she says in the introduction to her *Tales of Wonder*[56] about the power of stories, generally.

> There is a Chinese tale, known as "The Singing Prisoner," in which a friendless man is bound hand and foot and thrown into a dungeon, where he lies on the cold stones unfed and untended.
>
> He has no hope of freedom and as complaint will avail him nothing, he begins to while away the hours by reciting poems and stories that he had learned in youth. So happily does he vary the tones of the speakers, feigning in turn the voices of kings and courtiers, lovers and princesses, birds and beasts, that he speedily draws all his fellow-prisoners around him, beguiling them by the spell of his genius.
>
> Those who have food, eagerly press it upon him that his strength may be replenished; the jailer, who has been drawn into the charmed circle, loosens his bonds that he may move more freely, and finally grants him better quarters that the stories may be heard to greater advantage. Next the petty officers hear of the prisoner's marvellous gifts and report them everywhere with such effect that the higher authorities at last become interested and grant him a pardon.
>
> Tales like these, that draw children from play and old men from the chimney corner; that gain the freedom of a Singing Prisoner, and enable a Scheherazade to postpone from night to night her hour of death, are one and all pervaded by the same eternal

magic. Pain, grief, terror, care and bondage are all forgotten for a time when lakes of gems and enchanted waterfalls shimmer in the sunlight.

"Childish wonder is the first step in human wisdom."

And then she reminds us the value of the older tales with this story:

There was once a little brown nightingale that sang melodious strains in the river-thickets of the Emperor's garden, but when she was transported to the Porcelain Palace the courtiers soon tired of her wild-wood notes and supplanted her with a wonderful bird-automaton, fashioned of gold and jewels.

Time went on, but the Emperor, wisest of the court, began at last to languish, and to long unceasingly for the fresh, free notes of the little brown nightingale. It was sweeter by far than the machine made trills and roulades of the artificial songster, and he felt instinctively that only by its return could death be charmed away.

The old, yet ever new, tales are like the wild notes of the nightingale in the river thicket, and many are the emperors to whom they have sung.

Whenever we tire of what is trivial and paltry in the machine-made fairy tale of today, let us open one of these [old tales] and hear again the note of the little brown bird in the thicket.

Edward St. John has this to say:

So great is the charm of the Greek myths, …and so strongly do they appeal to the interests of children and youth, that it is with real regret that many teachers have put them aside because of the moral imperfections of the gods and the polytheistic conceptions with which they are filled. They are right in putting the moral and religious results above all others that are involved, and, from the days of Plato on, many educators have felt the same necessity and have reached the same conclusion. But the rejection of all these stories is not as essential as it seems at first thought. The elimination of such of the stories as cannot be so edited as to remove accounts of the grosser forms of immorality and to emphasize the fact that vice and virtue meet their certain rewards meets the ethical requirement. The gods of the Greeks were only men of superhuman powers, and the stories of their lives have the same educational values as others of the ideal type.

The polytheistic element still remains as an objection on the side of religious education, but it may be readily overcome. One may introduce the myth by saying, "You know, children, that our Father in heaven made the earth and everything about us, and that he takes care of us all. Many years ago there were people who had never heard of this; but when they looked out upon the beautiful world and saw the sun rising every morning, and the stars shining at night, and the flower blooming, and the fruits opening in the trees, they knew that someone must care for all of these. Since they did not know of the one great God who can do all things, they thought there must be one god for the sun and one for the stars, another for the flowers and still another for the fruits. I am going to tell you of some of the things that they thought these gods did." When one has finished the story he may add, "That is the way they told it long ago, but we know that it is really our Father in heaven who cares for all the creatures that he has made." So the thought of these old days may stir the simple religious feelings of the child—the wonder and love and trust that he shares with the men of that early age—and that without giving him wrong conceptions of God.

Julia Darrow Cowles reminds us: "The child who is made familiar with the old mythology by means of stories and verse, holds the key of understanding to the countless allusions of the world's best literature. He may not comprehend the deeper meaning, nor understand that they were the religion of an ancient people, but when in his later reading of some masterpiece of poetry or prose he finds an allusion to Phaeton, to Apollo, or to Neptune, he will experience the same delight that comes to one who meets an old playfellow in a foreign land…. Those which contain an objectionable element may readily be withheld; there are plenty which are beautiful in their form and true in their teaching."

James Wood agrees: "…there is much in them calculated at once to purify and elevate both the intellect and the heart of the very best among us…. The thoughts of men true to the divine are the key to the thoughts of God…. Man's power of fancying, or fantasying, in harmony with the 'truth,' is the divinely-appointed means withal whereby the fact itself is brought home to our affections."

Emma Firth says: "Aside from their use as a means of strengthening the imagination, the myths embody ethical truths…

> There is an instinct in the human heart
> Which makes all fables it has coined—
> To justify the reign of its belief,
> And strengthen it by beauty's right divine—
> Veil in their inner cells a mystic gift,
> Which, like the hazel twig in faithful hands,
> Points surely to the hidden springs of truth.

If by means of a story, well told, [a child] can grasp the simple truth contained in it, he is making progress in the right direction. He is getting a foundation for the future study of literature, and gaining an appreciation for the beautiful in art. All modern tendencies are to make children too realistic, and to stifle, rather than to cultivate, the fine imagination necessary to the creation or enjoyment of art and literature. By presenting these myths…because of their beauty and simplicity, we are giving him good material for the growth of a healthful imagination.

And I love the thoughts of Charles Kingsley contained in a letter written to children in the introduction of his book, *The Heroes*:[57]

My dear Children:

Some of you have heard already of the old Greeks; and all of you, as you grow up, will hear more and more of them. …You will hardly find a well-written book which has not in it Greek names, and words, and proverbs; you cannot walk through a great town without passing Greek buildings; you cannot go into a well-furnished room without seeing Greek statues and ornaments, even Greek patterns of furniture and paper; so strangely have these old Greeks left their marks behind them upon this modern world in which we live....

Now I love these old Greeks heartily; and I should be very ungrateful to them if I did not, considering all that they have taught me; and they seem to me like brothers, though they have all been dead and gone many hundred years ago. So as you must learn about them, whether you choose or not, I wish to be the first to introduce you to them, and to say, "Come hither, children, at this blessed Christmas time, when all God's creatures should rejoice together, and bless Him who redeems them all. Come and see old friends of mine, whom I knew long ere you were born. They are come to visit us at Christmas, out of the world where all live to God; and to tell you some of their old fairy tales, which they loved when they were young like you."

For nations begin at first by being children like you, though they are made up of grown men. They were children at first like you—men and women with children's hearts; frank, and affectionate, and full of trust, and teachable, and loving to see and learn all the wonders round them; and greedy also, too often, and passionate and silly, as children are.

Thus these old Greeks were teachable, and learnt from all the nations round…. Therefore God rewarded these Greeks and made them wiser than the people who taught them in everything they learnt; for He loves to see men and children openhearted, and willing to be taught; and to him who uses what he has got, He gives more and more day by day. So these Greeks grew wise and powerful, and wrote poems which will live till the world's end, which you must read for yourselves some day. And they learnt to carve statues, and build temples, which are still among the wonders of the world; and many another wondrous thing God taught them, for which we are the wise this day.

For you must not fancy, children, that because these old Greeks were heathens, therefore God did not care for them, and taught them nothing.

The Bible tells us that it was not so, but that God's mercy is over all His works, and that He understands the hearts of all people, and fashions all their works. And St. Paul told these old Greeks in after times, when they had grown wicked and fallen low, that they ought to have known better, because they were God's offspring, as their own poets had said; and that the good God had put them where they were, to seek the Lord, and feel after Him and find Him, though He was not far away from any of them. And Clement of Alexandria…who was as wise as he was good, said that God had sent down Philosophy to the Greeks from heaven, as He sent down the gospel to the Jews.

For Jesus Christ, remember, is the Light who lights every man who comes into the world. And no one can think a right thought, or feel a right feeling, or understand the real truth of anything in earth and heaven, unless the good Lord Jesus teaches him by His Spirit, which gives man understanding.

But these Greeks, as St. Paul told them, forgot what God had taught them, and, though they were God's offspring, worshipped idols of wood and stone, and fell at last into sin and shame, and then, of course, into cowardice and slavery, till they perished out of that beautiful land which God had given them for so many years.

For, like all nations who have left anything behind them, beside mere mounds of earth, they believed at first in the One True God who made all heaven and earth. But after a while, like all other nations, they began to worship other gods…. Zeus, the Father of gods and men—who was some dim remembrance of the blessed true God—and Hera his wife, and Apollo the Sun-God and Athena who taught men wisdom and useful arts, and Aprhodite the Queen of Beauty…and many other dreams they had, which parted the One God into many;… and when their philosophers arose, and told them that God was One, they would not listen, but loved their idols, and their wicked idol feasts, till they all came to ruin. But we will talk of such sad things no more.

But, at the time of which this little book speaks, they had not fallen as low as that. They worshipped no idols, as far as I can find…and knew well what was right and what was wrong. And they believed—and that was what gave them courage—that the gods loved men, and taught them, and that without the gods men were sure to come to ruin. And in that they were right enough, as we know—more right even than they thought; for without God, we can do nothing, and all wisdom comes from him.

Now, while they were young and simple they loved fairy tales, as you do now. All nations do so when they are young…. But…there are no fairy tales like these old Greek ones, for beauty, and wisdom, and truth, and for making children love noble deeds, and truth in God to help them through…. The stories are not all true, of course, nor half of them; you are not simple enough to fancy that; but the meaning of them is true, and true for ever, and that is—"Do right, and God will help you."

And finally a few thoughts from James Baldwin:[58]

Perhaps no other stories have ever been told so often or listened to with so much pleasure as the classic tales of ancient Greece. For many ages they have been a source of delight to young people and old, to the ignorant and the learned, to all who love to hear about and contemplate things mysterious, beautiful and grand. They have become so incorporated into our language and thought, and interwoven with our literature, that we could not do away with them now if we would. They are a portion of our heritage from the distant past, and they form perhaps as important a part of our intellectual life as they did of that of the people among whom they originated.

That many of these tales should be read by children at an early age no intelligent person will deny….

Will you deny your children this treasure trove of stories?

As Mary MacGregor said: "Poets and philosophers lived in Athens and so literature and art spread the glory of Greece far and wide, moulding the thoughts and quickening the deeds of many people. Before the glory of Greece faded, Europe had learned from her to follow truth, to love beauty."

You will find many choices of collections of these wonderful Greek fairy tales and stories of heroes in the website that have been filtered through the hearts of these heart educators who see the beautiful and the true.

So let us begin: "Far, far away from our own country, across wide seas and many strange lands, is a beautiful country called Greece. There the sky is bluer than our own; the winters are short and mild, and the summers long and pleasant. In whatever direction you look, in that land, you may see the top of some tall mountain reaching up toward the sky. Between the mountains lie beautiful deep valleys, and small sunny plains, while almost all around the land stretches a bright blue sea.

The people who live in that country are called Greeks, and are not very different now from ourselves....

Enjoy your journey.

Podcast #128 The Legend of the Christmas Rose

Combining this month's study of Italy with the Nature topic of Plants, and given that Christmas is almost here, I thought for today's sampler I would share a story from Amy Steedman's 1909 book, *Legends and Stories of Italy for Children*,[59] called The Legend of the Christmas Rose. You will love the beautiful, colorful illustrations as well.

But before we get to the story, sharing her Preface is well worth a minute or two.

Preface

'I want a hidden pearl story to-day,' said the child.

'What kind of a story is that?' asked the saint. She was a real saint, although every one could not see the golden halo that shone round her dear head.

'One of the old stories which you say are like the common shells that have a pearl hidden inside,' answered the child.

'Ah, then you must listen with your heart as well as your ears,' said the saint, 'or you will not find the pearl. Mother Earth takes care to hide away her gold and precious stones deep down in the earth. The diver, too, must seek in the depths of the sea before he gathers the rough shells in which the shining pearls lie hid. So it is with the hidden treasure which lies wrapped up in these old legends and stories. Those who would find it must seek carefully and patiently, for only thus can it be found. For just as the sweet green grass and common flowers cover the earth where treasure lies hid, just as the rough shell holds in its heart the soft, shining pearl, so these stories may seem at first but simple, common tales, but those who look beneath will find at the heart of them a living truth more precious than gold or shining pearls.'

'I will listen carefully,' said the child, 'but I love even the rough shells of your pearl stories.'

The Story

It was the night on which our Blessed Lord was born, and the angels had brought their message of peace and goodwill to the shepherds upon the lonely hillside.

The glory of that heavenly vision had left the men awed and silent as they gathered round their fire. The news of the birth of the long looked for Infant King filled their hearts so full of wonder and of joy that for a while they could not speak. But ere long they roused themselves and in low tones began to talk of what they had seen and of all that the message of the angels meant. There was surely but one thing to be done—they must set out at once to seek the new-born King. So they began to plan how they might safely leave their sheep, and to pile the fire high with dry branches that the blaze might keep away all evil beasts.

So intent were they on their preparations, and so filled with the wonder of that night, that none of them gave a thought to the little child who lay in the warm shelter of a rock close to the fire. She had been helping her father tend the sheep all day, and had crept into the bed of dry leaves to rest, for she was very tired. The shepherds never noticed her as she lay in the shadow of the rock, and even if they had, they would have deemed her far too young to understand the glorious vision of that starry night.

But the little maid had seen the opening of heaven's gates and heard the angels' message. With wondering eyes she had gazed upon those white-robed messengers of peace and listened to their words. There was much that she did not understand, but this at least she knew, that a little Baby had been born that night in the village close by, that He was the King of Heaven and had brought God's love and forgiveness to all the poor people upon earth.

Now as she lay in her warm corner watching the bright flames as they rose and fell, a little lamb nestling close at her feet for warmth, she had but one thought in her heart, How could she see this Bambino, this new-born King. Very anxiously she watched the shepherds and tried to hear what they were saying. She saw one lift a lamb in his arms, another take a home-made cheese from their little store, another a loaf of barley-bread. Then there was a movement away from the fire, and she saw they were preparing to set out down the hill. They were going to seek the King, and if she followed she would see Him too.

In an instant she had left her warm corner and was speeding after the men. Quickly and silently she crept along behind them, trying always to keep out of sight lest one of them should turn his head and bid her go home. But the shepherds were all too eager to think of aught but the wonderful quest which lay before them, and they never thought of looking back, nor did they hear the patter of small bare feet upon the frozen ground.

It was a bitterly cold night. The moon shone down on ice-bound streams and fields white with hoar-frost. Not a sound was to be heard but the soft sighing of the wind passing gently through the bare branches of the trees. Not a light was to be seen in any of the huts they passed, for every one was fast asleep. But overhead there shone a wonderful star like a silver globe of light going before them as they went. So the little company passed on, and the child kept bravely up behind, although the ground was rough and hard and sorely hurt her bare feet. It was not easy to keep pace with the men's swift stride, but she never stopped to rest until she had entered the village street of Bethlehem, and the shepherds paused before a little shed over which the silver star was shining down.

Here they halted and talked together in low tones, while the child drew aside into the shadow of the house to watch what they would do.

She saw them take out from their wallets the things which they had brought, and realised for the first time that they were presents for the Infant King. There was the loaf of barley-bread, the home-made cheese, a handful of dried fruit and the fleece of a lamb, white and soft, fit to wrap around a baby's limbs this cold wintry night. There were other things besides, but all were poor simple gifts, and the shepherds looked at the array half sadly.

'They make but a poor show,' said one with shame.

'They are indeed but simple offerings,' said another; but He will understand that it is our best we give with the true love of our hearts.'

'Ay, surely,' said a third, 'and poor though they be, they are better than nothing. It would be a sin indeed to come empty-handed to greet our King this night.'

Those words fell on the listening ears of the child, and when she heard them, all hope and joy died out of her heart. She had no gift to offer. She looked down at her little empty sun-browned hands and a great sob rose in her throat. If it were a sin to go in without a gift, then she must stay outside. She had come so far and longed so greatly to see the Infant King, and now it was all no use, the sight was not for her. Perhaps if she crept near the door she might peep in when it was opened and catch if it were only a glimpse, while she herself remained unseen.

The shepherds knocked at the door and reverently bared their heads. A low sweet voice bade them enter, and the door was opened. Pressing forward, the child tried to look in. There in the soft light she saw a fair young mother with head bent low, and behind her an ox and an ass feeding from a low manger. She tried to see the Bambino, but the forms of the kneeling shepherds came between, and even as she looked, the door was shut and she was left outside.

Then it seemed as if her heart would break. She was so weary and so footsore, and all her trouble had been for nought. The King was so near, only a wall between Him and her, and yet she was not to see Him. She threw herself down on the hard gravel and buried her head in her arms, while the sobs came thick and fast and her tears made the very ground wet.

Presently the door opened and the shepherds came out with slow and reverent steps, They did not see her, for she had crept close to the wall, and when they started on their homeward way she did not move to follow them. She was too tired and sorrowful to care what became of her now.

But presently as she lay there, with the tears still dropping one by one, she started and looked closely at the ground. What were those pale-green shoots that were bursting up between the cracks of the stones? Now they were growing into glossy leaves. She held her breath with wonder, but true it was that wherever a tear had fallen and thawed the frozen earth, a bud had begun to swell. The pale-green shoots grew taller and taller, the glossy leaves unfolded and showed pink-tipped buds hanging between, which, as she gazed, opened into blossoms with petals as silver white as moonbeams upon the glistening snow.

A glad thought came into the child's sorrowful heart. Why, here was the very gift she was seeking, and she 8 yet might see the King. Eagerly she stretched out her hands and gathered the open blossoms and pink flushed buds, with one or two glossy leaves to place around them. Then she went close to the door and timidly ventured on a very little knock. She waited, scarcely daring to breathe, but no one answered, and so putting both hands against the door she pushed it a little way open.

The Madonna was sitting in the poor stable by the little bed of hay on which the Gesu Bambino slept. She was bending over Him and softly singing a lullaby, her eyes still shining with quiet joy over the thought of the wondrous tale told her by the simple shepherds. Suddenly a draught of cold air came sweeping in, and she turned her head to see who had opened the door. A little child stood there with flushed cheeks on which the tears were scarcely dry. Wistful eyes were raised to hers, and two small hands held out a bunch of snowblossoms.

The Madonna needed no words to tell her what it meant. Her mother-heart understood at once what the little one wanted. Very gently she drew her in and led her to the little manger-bed and bade her lay her flowers there in the little, helpless hands of the new-born King. The child knelt and gazed at the sleeping Bambino. She forgot her tiredness and weary feet, she forgot her tears and disappointment, and she dimly felt that the happiness that filled her heart would live on and on forever.

And now when winter-time comes and the days are dark and the nights are long, when the snow covers up all the sleeping flowers and the Christmas bells ring out, the white blossoms of the child's flowers appear above the cold, dark earth. We call them the Christmas roses now, in memory of the little one who had no other gift to offer that first Christmas morning, but the gift of her sorrowful tears.

Podcast #129 The Knights of Art

With our Mother's University topic of Art this month, our study of Italy and the Christmas season, I thought it would be appropriate to give you a sampler from Amy Steedman's 1907 book, *Knights of Art, Stories of Italian Painters*.[60] I'll begin with her wonderful introduction, and then share the story of Raphael who painted the most famous and beloved of all the Madonnas, the Sistine Madonna, that I highlighted in a podcast earlier.

Introduction

What would we do without our picture-books, I wonder? Before we knew how to read, before even we could speak, we had learned to love them. We shouted with pleasure when we turned the pages and saw the spotted cow standing in the daisy-sprinkled meadow, the foolish-looking old sheep with her gambolling lambs, the wise dog with his friendly eyes. They were all real friends to us.

Then a little later on, when we began to ask for stories about the pictures, how we loved them more and more. There was the little girl in the red cloak talking to the great grey wolf with the wicked eyes; the cottage with the bright pink roses climbing round the lattice-window, out of which jumped a little maid with golden hair, followed by the great big bear, the middle-sized bear, and the tiny bear. Truly those stories were a great joy to us, but we would never have loved them quite so much if we had not known their pictured faces as well.

Do you ever wonder how all these pictures came to be made? They had a beginning, just as everything else had, but the beginning goes so far back that we can scarcely trace it.

Children have not always had picture-books to look at. In the long-ago days such things were not known. Thousands of years ago, far away in Assyria, the Assyrian people learned to make pictures and to carve them out in stone. In Egypt, too, the Egyptians traced pictures upon the walls of their temples and upon the painted mummy-cases of the dead. Then the Greeks made still more beautiful statues and pictures in marble, and called them gods and goddesses, for all this was at a time when the true God was forgotten.

Afterwards, when Christ had come and the people had learned that the pictured gods were not real, they began to think it wicked to make beautiful pictures or carve marble statues. The few pictures that were made were stiff and ugly, the figures were not like real men and women, the animals and trees were very strange-looking things. And instead of making the sky blue as it really was, they made it a chequered pattern of gold. After a time it seemed as if the art of making pictures was going to die out altogether.

Then came the time which is called 'The Renaissance,' a word which means being born again, or a new awakening, when men began to draw real pictures of real things and fill the world with images of beauty.

Now it is the stories of the men of that time, who put new life into Art, that I am going to tell you—men who learned, step by step, to paint the most beautiful pictures that the world possesses.

In telling these stories I have been helped by an old book called The Lives of the Painters, by Giorgio Vasari, who was himself a painter. He took great delight in gathering together all the stories about these artists and writing them down with loving care, so that he shows us real living men, and not merely great names by which the famous pictures are known.

It did not make much difference to us when we were little children whether our pictures were good or bad, as long as the colours were bright and we knew what they meant. But as we grow older and wiser our eyes grow wiser too, and we learn to know what is good and what is poor. Only, just as our tongues must be trained to speak, our hands to work, and our ears to love good music, so our eyes must be taught to see what is beautiful, or we may perhaps pass it carelessly by, and lose a great joy which might be ours.

So now if you learn something about these great artists and their wonderful pictures, it will help your eyes to grow wise. And some day should you visit sunny Italy, where these men lived and worked, you will feel that they are quite old friends. Their pictures will not only be a delight to your eyes, but will teach your heart something deeper and more wonderful than any words can explain.

Raphael

Among the marvellous tales of the Arabian Nights, there is a story told of a band of robbers who, by whispering certain magic words, were able to open the door of a secret cave where treasures of gold and silver and precious jewels lay hid. Now, although the day of such delightful marvels is past and gone, yet there still remains a certain magic in some names which is able to open the secret doors of the hidden haunts of beauty and delight.

For most people the very name of 'Raphael' is like the 'Open Sesame' of the robber chief in the old story. In a moment a door seems to open out of the commonplace everyday world, and through it they see a stretch of fair sweet country. There their eyes rest upon gentle, dark-eyed Madonnas, who smile down lovingly upon the heavenly Child, playing at her side or resting in her arms. The little St. John is also there, companion of the Infant Christ; rosy, round-limbed children both, half human and half divine. And standing in the background are a crowd of grave, quiet figures, each one alive with interest, while over all there is a glow of intense vivid colour.

We know but little of the everyday life of this great artist. When we hear his name, it is of his different pictures that we think at once, for they are world-famous. We almost forget the man as we gaze at his work.

It was in the little village of Urbino, in Umbria, that Raphael was born. His father was a painter called Giovanni Santi, and from him Raphael inherited his love of Art. His mother, Magia, was a sweet, gracious woman, and the little Raphael was like her in character and beauty. It seemed as if the boy had received every good gift that Nature could bestow. He had a lovely oval face, and soft dark eyes that shone with a beauty that was more of heaven than earth, and told of a soul which was as pure and lovely as his face. Above all, he had the gift of making every one love him, so that his should have been a happy sunshiny life.

But no one can ever escape trouble, and when Raphael was only eight years old, the first cloud overspread his sky. His mother died, and soon after his father married again.

The new mother was very young, and did not care much for children, but Raphael did not mind that as long as he could be with his father. But three years later a blacker cloud arose and blotted out the sunshine from his life, for his father too died, and left him all alone.

The boy had loved his father dearly, and it had been his great delight to be with him in the studio, to learn to grind and mix the colours and watch those wonderful pictures grow from day to day.

But now all was changed. The quiet studio rang with angry voices, and the peaceful home was the scene of continual quarrelling. Who was to have the money, and how were the Santi estates to be divided? Stepmother and uncle wrangled from morning until night, and no one gave a thought to the child Raphael. It was only the money that mattered.

Then when it seemed that the boy's training was going to be totally neglected, kindly help arrived. Simone di Ciarla, brother of Raphael's own mother, came to look after his little nephew, and ere long carried him off from the noisy, quarrelsome household, and took him to Perugia.

'Thou shalt have the best teaching in all Italy,' said Simone as they walked through the streets of the town. 'The great master to whose studio we go, can hold his own even among the artists of Florence. See that thou art diligent to learn all that he can teach thee, so that thou mayest become as great a painter as thy father.'

'Am I to be the pupil of the great Perugino?' asked Raphael, his eyes shining with pleasure. 'I have often heard my father speak of his marvellous pictures.'

'We will see if he can take thee,' answered his uncle.

The boy's heart sunk. What if the master refused to take him as a pupil? Must he return to idleness and the place which was no longer home?

But soon his fears were set at rest. Perugino, like every one else, felt the charm of that beautiful face and gentle manner, and when he had seen some drawings which the boy had done, he agreed readily that Raphael should enter the studio and become his pupil.

Perugia had been passing through evil times just before this. The two great parties of the Oddi and Baglioni families were always at war together. Whichever of them happened to be the stronger held the city and drove out the other party, so that the fighting never ceased either inside or outside the gates. The peaceful country round about had been laid waste and desolate. The peasants did not dare go out to till their fields or prune their olive-trees. Mothers were afraid to let their little ones out of their sight, for hungry wolves and other wild beasts prowled about the deserted countryside.

Then came a day when the outside party managed to creep silently into the city, and the most terrible fight of all began. So long and fiercely did the battle rage that almost all the Oddi were killed. Then for a time there was peace in Perugia and all the country round.

So it happened that as soon as the people of Perugia had time to think of other things besides fighting, they began to wish that their town might be put in order, and that the buildings which had been injured during the struggles might be restored.

This was a good opportunity for peaceful men like Perugino, for there was much work to be done, and both he and his pupils were kept busy from morning till night.

Of all his pupils, Perugino loved the young Raphael best. He saw at once that this was no ordinary boy.

'He is my pupil now, but soon he will be my master,' he used to say as he watched the boy at work.

So he taught him with all possible carefulness, and was never tired of giving him good advice.

'Learn first of all to draw,' he would say, when Raphael looked with longing eyes at the colours and brushes of the master. 'Draw everything you see, no matter what it is, but always draw and draw again. The rest will follow; but if the knowledge of drawing be lacking, nothing will afterwards succeed. Keep always at hand a sketch-book, and draw therein carefully every manner of thing that meets thy eye.'

Raphael never forgot the good advice of his master. He was never without a sketch-book, and his drawings now are almost as interesting as his great pictures, for they show the first thought that came into his mind, before the picture was composed.

So the years passed on, and Raphael learned all that the master could teach him. At first his pictures were so like Perugino's, that it was difficult to know whether they were the work of the master or the pupil.

But the quiet days at Perugia soon came to an end, and Perugino went back to Florence. For some time Raphael worked at different places near Perugia, and then followed his master to the City of Flowers, where every artist longed to go. Though he was still but a young man, the world had already begun to notice his work, and Florence gladly welcomed a new artist.

It was just at that time that Leonardo da Vinci's fame was at its height, and when Raphael was shown some of the great man's work, he was filled with awe and wonder. The genius of Leonardo held him spellbound.

'It is what I have dreamed of in my dreams,' he said. 'Oh that I might learn his secret!'

Little by little the new ideas sunk into his heart, and the pictures he began to paint were no longer like those of his old master Perugino, but seemed to breathe some new spirit.

It was always so with Raphael. He seemed to be able to gather the best from every one, just as the bee goes from flower to flower and gathers its sweetness into one golden honeycomb. Only the genius of Raphael made all that he touched his very own, and the spirit of his pictures is unlike that of any other master.

For many years after this he lived in Rome, where now his greatest frescoes may be seen—frescoes so varied and wonderful that many books have been written about them.

There he first met Margarita, the young maiden whom he loved all his life. It is her face which looks down upon us from the picture of the Sistine Madonna, perhaps the most famous Madonna that ever was painted. The little room in the Dresden Gallery where this picture now hangs seems almost like a holy place, for surely there is something divine in that fair face. There she stands, the Queen of Heaven, holding in her arms the Infant Christ, with such a strange look of majesty and sadness in her eyes as makes us realise that she was indeed fit to be the Mother of our Lord.

But the picture which all children love best is one in Florence called 'The Madonna of the Goldfinch.'

It is a picture of the Holy Family, the Infant Jesus, His mother, and the little St. John. The Christ Child is a dear little curly-headed baby, and He stands at His mother's knee with one little bare foot resting on hers. His hand is stretched out protectingly over a yellow goldfinch which St. John, a sturdy little figure clad in goatskins, has just brought to Him. The baby face is full of tender love and care for the little fluttering prisoner, and His curved hand is held over its head to protect it.

'Do not hurt My bird,' He seems to say to the eager St. John, 'for it belongs to Me and to My Father.'

These are only two of the many pictures which Raphael painted. It is wonderful to think how much work he did in his short life, for he died when he was only thirty-seven. He had been at work at St. Peter's, giving directions about some alterations, and there he was seized by a severe chill, and in a few days the news spread like wildfire through the country that Raphael was dead.

It seemed almost as if it could not be true. He had been so full of life and health, so eager for work, such a living power among men.

But there he lay, beautiful in death as he had been in life, and over his head was hung the picture of the 'Transfiguration,' on which he had been at work, its colours yet wet, never to be finished by that still hand.

All Rome flocked to his funeral, and high and low mourned his loss. But he left behind him a fame which can never die, a name which through all these four hundred years has never lost the magic of its greatness.

Month 5 Podcasts

Podcast #35 Lessons from the American Revolution

At the end of last summer, my husband and I and a couple of our children visited Valley Forge. It's beautiful in the summertime—one of the most beautiful places I've ever visited. There were only a few people there…so it's the kind of place where you can ponder and feel. In such a peaceful, lush green setting, it was difficult to picture in my mind's eye that frigid, bitter winter of 1777 and the starving, ragged soldiers huddled in their huts.

This month as we take a look at the American Revolution, I've suggested that you compare it to another revolution taking place in France. They, too, were fighting for their liberty, but what a different outcome it had. Lafayette, who fought so gallantly and bravely here, wanted to do the same for his countrymen as he had done in America. It's in the heart of the people that the differences between the two Revolutions can be so clearly seen. The mobs behind the Reign of Terror are in sharp contrast to the scenes I am about to paint to you. We are reminded by the fox in *The Little Prince*—by the way, a good read for our France topic—"Only the heart sees rightly; what is essential is invisible to the eye." The difference between the American and the French Revolution lies in the hearts of the countrymen. Not all of our hearts were the same.

As a child, I pictured the Americans united in a cause, all self-sacrificing patriots. It's been eye-opening to discover that only about a third supported the cause of independence. A third remained loyal to the British crown and a third were fence sitters. Far from being united to a cause, the colonies were jealous, petty, bickered with each other. While merchants, farmers and simple folk left their homes and gave their lives for freedom, their neighbors weren't opposed to making themselves rich by supplying the British with food, shelter and supplies. The unprotected wives back home were often more fearful of the robbers among them taking advantage of the situation than of the British. It was dangerous times.

Many of our generals had fought in the British army not many years before. They were fighting friends. Back home in Britain, the king couldn't raise enough troops because they refused to fight their family and friends in the colonies, so he had to hire the Hessian soldiers from Germany to do the deed. And the odds of an untrained, woefully undersupplied ragtag army of common folk defeating the most powerful army in the world are staggering.

The key players are so young: at the time of the signing of the Declaration of Independence, Lafayette was just 18 years old. Alexander Hamilton, 21, James Madison, 25. Henry Knox, 25. John Paul Jones, 28. Nathaneal Greene, 33. Thomas Jefferson, 33. Betsy Ross was 24.

All these thoughts went through my mind as I walked around Valley Forge. And I realize more every day, the victory wasn't won out on the battlefields any more than our fight for freedom today can be won in war or even in the halls of Congress. It was truly won in the hearts of the few. And that part of the story is rarely told. As a witness to the Revolution observed:

> "You see, these history writers go about hunting up every incident relating to the war, now, and after a while they'll know more about it—or say they do—than the men who

were actors in it… These historians may not know as much of the real spirit of the people at that period, but that they should be better acquainted with the mass of facts relating to battles and to political affairs is perfectly natural." The old man…mumbled …that nobody could know the real state of things who was not living among them at the time.

So, come take a walk around Valley Forge with me[61] and listen to the players who took part so we can hear the untold story. Let's first walk to the huts.

It was a terrible season. It's hard to give a faint idea of it in words; but you may imagine a party of men, with ragged clothes and no shoes, huddled around a fire in a log hut— the snow about two feet deep on the ground, and the wind driving fierce and bitter through the chinks of the rude hovel. Many of the men had their feet frost-bitten, and there were no remedies to be had…. The sentinels suffered terrible, and looked more like ghosts than men, as they paced up and down the lines of huts.

General Washington…saw how the men were situated, and, I really believe, his heart bled for them. … Washington's head-quarters was near the camp, and he often came over to see the poor fellows, and to try to soothe and comfort them; and I tell you, the men loved that man as if he had been their father, and would rather have died with him than have lived in luxury with the red-coat general.

I recollect a scene I beheld in the next hut to the one in which I messed. An old friend, named Josiah Jones, was dying. He was lying on a scant straw bed, with nothing but rags to cover him. He had been sick for several days, but wouldn't go under the doctor's hands, as he always said it was like going into battle, certain of being killed. One day, when we had no notion of anything of the kind, Josiah called out to us, as we sat talking near his bed, that he was dying, and wanted us to pray for him. We were all anxious to do anything for the man, for we loved him as a brother; but as for praying, we didn't exactly know how to go about it. To get clear of the service, I ran to obtain the poor fellow a drink of water to moisten his parched lips.

While the rest were standing about, not knowing what to do, someone heard the voice of General Washington in the next hut, where he was comforting some poor wretches who had their feet almost frozen off. Directly, he came to our door, and one of the men went and told him the state of things. Now, you see, a commander-in-chief might have been justified as being angry that the regulations for the sick had been disobeyed, and have turned away; but he was a nobler sort of man than could to that. He entered the hut, and went up to poor Josiah, and asked him how he was. Josiah told him that he felt as if he was dying, and wanted someone to pray for him.

Washington saw that a doctor could do the man no good, and he knelt on the ground by him and prayed. We all knelt down, too; we couldn't help it. An old comrade was dying, away from his home and friends, and there was our general kneeling by him, with his face turned towards heaven, looking, I thought, like an angel's. Well, he prayed for Heaven to have mercy on the dying man's soul; to pardon his sins; and to take him to

Himself; and then he prayed for us all. Before the prayer was concluded, Josiah's spirit had fled, and his body was cold and stiff. Washington felt the brow of the poor fellow, and, seeing that his life was out, gave the men directions…and then left to visit the other parts of the camp.

He continued:

General Washington was the main pillar of the Revolution. As a general, he was vigilant and skillful; but if he not been anything more, we might have been defeated and crushed by the enemy. He had the love and confidence of the men, on account of his character as a man, and that enabled him to remain firm and full of hope when his countrymen saw nothing but a gloomy prospect.

Now let's go into General Washington's headquarters, on loan to him by a Quaker, Isaac Potts. It's not very big and is unique as a historical site because, rather than a recreation, the actual home still stands. When you go inside and hold the stair railing going upstairs, it's the same wood Washington held. The stones are the very stones that made up the walls. I stood in his quarters where I pictured this scene as described by a soldier:

Meantime General Washington was doing everything in his power to alleviate our distresses. The light in that man's quarters was often seen burning all night long. I've seen it. We've all seen it. He was writing letters, hundreds of them, to governors, to Congress, to men of influence everywhere, begging and imploring their assistance. Precious little he got of it. And the time, too, was coming right along when the army (if such a lot of ragamuffins can be called one) ought to take the field again. And we were expected to win battles! I've no patience when I think of it. No man alive, but Washington, could have held that hungry, ragged, and dispirited crowd together. God bless him!

In a woods nearby, we now turn to a scene entered in the Pennsylvania Historical Record, told by Isaac Potts himself:

I was a Tory once for I never believed that America could proceed against Great Britain whose fleets and armies covered the land and ocean. But something very extraordinary converted me to the good faith.

"Do you see that woods, and that plain?" I was about a quarter of a mile from the place we were riding. "There," said he, "laid the army of Washington. It was a most distressing time of the war, and all were giving up the ship but that one good man. In that woods," pointing to a close in view, "I heard a plaintive sound, as of a man at prayer. I tied my horse to a sapling and went quietly into the woods and to my astonishment I saw the great George Washington on his knees alone, with his sword on one side and his cocked hat on the other. He was at Prayer to the God of the Armies, beseeching to interpose with his Divine aid, as it was ye Crisis and the cause of the country, of humanity, and of the world.

Such a prayer I never heard from the lips of man. I left him alone praying. I went home and told my wife, "I saw a sight and heard today what I never saw or heard before," and just related to her what I had seen and heard and observed. We never thought a man could be a soldier and a Christian, but if there is one in the world, it is Washington. We thought it was the cause of God, and America could prevail.

In the God of battles trust!

Although I was not standing on the battlefield described in the next scene, I could picture what it looked like, standing on the meadows and fields of Valley Forge:

Just before the battle of Germantown, "All day long, on the tenth of September, 1777, both armies were in the vicinity of each other…. At length, as the day closed, both armies encamped within sight of each other, anxiously awaiting the morrow, to decide the fate of the devoted city…

The sun was just sinking behind the dark hills of the west, gilding the fading heavens with an autumnal brightness, and shedding a lurid glare upon the already drooping and discolored foliage of the surrounding forests. It was an hour of solemn calm. The cool evening breeze stole softly through the air…and the national standard flapped lazily from the tall flag-staff on its banks.

In the American camp, interspersed between groups of tens and stacks of arms, might be seen little knots of weary soldiers seated on the ground, resting from the fatigues of the day, and talking in a low but animated tone of the coming contest.

The bugle sounded… Obedient to the signal, the greater part of the soldiers assembled in front of the marquee of the commander, near the center of the encampment.

All was hushed in expectation: soon the tall form of Washington, wrapped in his military cloak and attended by a large body of officers, was seen advancing in their midst. All present respectfully saluted them, to which they bowed courteously, and then took their seats upon camp-stools set for them by a servant. The venerable Joab Prout, chaplain of the Pennsylvania line, then stood upon the stump of a tree, and commanded silence—for it was the hour of prayer.

Here was a scene of moral grandeur unsurpassed by anything in the annals of war. There, on that still, cool evening, when the sky was darkening into night, were assembled some eight thousand men; very many of whom would never look upon the glorious sunset again. From the humble cottages in the quiet valley of Connecticut— from the statelier mansions of the sunny South—at the call of liberty, they had rushed to the tented field; and now, on the eve of battle, as brethren in heart and deed, had met together to implore the God of battles to smile upon their noble cause.

Oh! It was a thrilling and an august sight! The mild and dignified Washington looked around him with proud emotion, and turned enquiringly to the fair young stranger, Lafayette, beside him, as if to ask, "Can such men as these be vanquished?'

The bold and fearless Wayne was there; the undaunted Pulaski, and the whole-hearted

Kosciusko; and they bowed their heads in reverence to Him in whose presence they were worshipping.

Never beneath the vaulted dome of the stately temple—never from the lips of the eloquent divine—was seen such a congregation, or was heard such a discourse, as on that September evening, from that humble old man, with his grey locks streaming in the wind…

"They may conquer us on the morrow! Might and wrong may prevail, and we may be driven from this field—but the hour of God's own vengeance will surely come!…in the hour of battle, when all around is darkness, lit by the lurid cannon glare and the piercing musket flash—when the wounded strew the ground, and the dead litter your path—then remember, soldiers, that God is with you. The eternal God fights for you—

"…You have taken the sword, but not in the spirit of wrong and ravage. You have taken the sword for your homes, your wives, for your little ones. You have taken the sword for truth, for justice and right, and to you the promise is, Be of good cheer, for your foes have taken the sword in defiance of all that man holds dear.…"

The last ray of lingering light had departed, and they were left in darkness. A parting prayer was proposed, and immediately every head was uncovered and bowed in reverence, while, with outstretched hands, that sincere old man in the homespun garb thus addressed the throne of grace.

Those who survived the battle of the next day never forgot the spirit they felt that still, autumn night. After a hard fight, the battle was lost. But one of the old soldiers reminisced, "It was all for the best. We shouldn't have known our enemies nor ourselves without losing that battle. The harder the struggle for liberty, the more we enjoy it when won… The freedom dearest bought is highest prized, and Americans have learned the value of that inestimable gem.

Let's make one more stop, to a simple, humble home.

My father was in the army during the whole eight years of the Revolutionary War, at first as a common soldier, afterwards as an officer. My mother had the sole charge of us four little ones.

Our house was a poor one, and far from neighbors. I have a keen remembrance of the terrible cold of some of those winters. The snow lay so deep and long, that it was difficult to cut or draw fuel from the woods, or get our corn to the mill, when we had any.

My mother was the possessor of a coffee mill. In that she ground wheat, and made coarse bread, which we ate, and were thankful. It was not always we could be allowed as much, even of this, as our keen appetites craved.

Many is the time that we have gone to bed, with only a drink of water for our supper, in which a little molasses had been mingled. We patiently received it, for we knew our mother did as well for us as she could; and we hoped to have something better in the morning.

She was never heard to repine; and young as we were, we tried to make her loving spirit and heavenly trust, our example.

When my father was permitted to come home, his stay was short, and he had not much to leave us, for the pay of those who achieved our liberties was slight, and irregularly given. Yet when he went, my mother ever bade him farewell with a cheerful face, and told him not to be anxious about his children, for she would watch over them night and day, and God would take care of the families of those who went forth to defend the righteous cause of their country.

Sometimes we wondered that she did not mention the cold weather, or our short meals, or her hard work, that we little ones might be clothed, and fed, and taught. But she would not weaken his hands, or sadden his heart, for she said a soldier's life was harder than all.

We saw that she never complained, but always kept in her heart a sweet hope, like a well of water. Every night ere we slept, and every morning when we arose, we lifted our little hands for God's blessing on our absent father, and our endangered country.

How deeply the prayers from such solitary homes and faithful hearts were mingled with the infant liberties of our dear native land, we may not know until we enter where we see no more "through a glass darkly, but face to face."

I don't know about you, but what I take away from these scenes is the reassurance that a few people, relying upon God in faith, can change the course of a nation; and that while modern society may say the private virtue of our leaders is of no consequence or matter to us, I can see how one leader of virtue can move a cause forward against unspeakable odds. These words of General Washington apply to us today as much as they did when he spoke them over 200 years ago:

> [T]he time is near at hand, which will determine whether Americans are to be freemen. The fate of unknown millions will depend, under God, on the courage and conduct of this army. [Which I will add you and I are part of.] Let us rely on the goodness of our cause, and the aid of the Supreme Being, in whose hands victory is, to animate and encourage us to great and noble actions.

And now I'll close with the final stanza of a poem written by John Pierpont, called Warren's Address. Joseph Warren fought as a volunteer at Bunker Hill. He was the last to leave the field and as a British officer called to him to surrender, a ball struck him in the forehead, killing him instantly.

In the God of battles trust!
Die we may,—and die we must;—
But, O, where can dust to dust
Be consigned so well,
As where Heaven its dews shall shed

On the martyred patriot's bed,
And the rocks shall raise their head,
Of his deeds to tell!

Podcast #142 New Year's Eve in Canada

As we continue with our study of the American Revolution in Month 5, I want to share a story that bridges into our study of Canada, which is one of our topics for this month, as well. The event happened to fall on New Year's Eve, 1775. Our hero of the story, Richard Montgomery, is just 37 years old. After serving in the British military, he acquired some land just north of New York City, married the love of his life, and settled down to the quiet life of a farmer. He and his wife were living in a small cottage while he was building them a larger home; a time when he said to his wife he was never so happy in all his life, when the call to serve his country, his new country, came to him. His self-sacrifice and bravery is the hallmark of these early patriots to whom we owe so much and whose stories we should never forget.

This telling of his story is taken from a book I included in the Forgotten Classics Family Library in Volume 3 of the Freedom Series. A favorite aunt is telling the story of America to her eager nieces and nephews each night. Let's join them for tonight's story "The Canadian Expedition—Richard Montgomery."[62]

> "All aboard for Canada!" was Harry's salutation this evening. Albert had wheeled up the lounge toward Aunt Edith, so that Stevey might lie comfortably and listen. Little Grace was curled up at the other end of the lounge with her kitten in her lap, for she had learned to sit quite still while the talk flowed over her young head.
>
> "All aboard for Canada!" repeated Aunt Edith. "We can easily say that, Harry, beside this bright winter fire, with our comfortable surroundings; wait until I draw the picture of our brave Revolutionary soldiers marching barefoot and half-clothed through Canadian snowdrifts, and we shall be able to measure the long distance between reading or talking about heroes and being heroes ourselves. Generals Schuyler and Montgomery were ordered to assemble their forces at a point on Lake Champlain. Here General Schuyler fell ill and was obliged to return home, leaving the expedition, its dangers and glories, to the youthful Montgomery. He was a man of great military experience for his years; full of gifts, graces, and accomplishments; one of the most admired and beloved of the Revolutionary heroes. The order to take charge of the Canadian expedition reached him in his beautiful home on the banks of the Hudson, where with his young wife, whom he tenderly loved, he had settled, hoping for quiet years of domestic happiness in a home adorned with every refinement. But Montgomery loved honor more than life, and liberty more than happiness. He obeyed the call of his country. Albert, take your map and show the children the Sorel River, which joins Lake Champlain and the River St. Lawrence. Do you see any forts named there?"
>
> "Yes, aunty," said Nannie, "Fort St. John and Fort Chambly."
>
> "Since the Americans had taken Forts Ticonderoga and Crown Point the English had much strengthened these forts, especially St. John, as they were the only remaining

defenses of Canada on that line. It was necessary to take it by siege. As soon as Montgomery's little band, not more than one thousand in number, were armed and equipped, their gallant commander led them on until they came near Fort St. John, when they proceeded to invest it."

"What does that mean, aunty?" asked little Alice.

"Albert, will you tell us how it is done?"

"Sometimes by taking positions on hills or eminences outside the fort and mounting cannon to bear on it, sometimes by digging trenches until approaches are made near enough to make a final assault."

"Yes, that's it. This fort was well armed and garrisoned, and its capture was a work of time. Hearing that Fort St. John was thus closely besieged, the British General Carleton came with a large force, intending to engage Montgomery in battle outside and thus relieve the fort, or, as military men call it, raise the siege. But Montgomery was ready to receive him. Carleton suffered a defeat and retreated with great loss. Montgomery proceeded with the siege. Fort Chambly being feebly garrisoned, he had dispatched a small number who surprised and captured it; this afforded him a further supply of cannon and ammunition. The provisions of the garrison of St. John were now nearly exhausted. Montgomery's trenches were near enough for the assault; he therefore sent a summons to the commander to surrender and thus save further bloodshed, informing him also of Carleton's defeat. Seeing no hope of succor from any quarter, he accepted Montgomery's terms and surrendered the post. The colors taken from the English were presented to Congress. Leaving a garrison to hold the fort, Montgomery hastened on toward Montreal. So rapid were his movements and so well-planned his attack, that General Carleton, after a slight resistance, fled in disguise to Quebec. The city capitulated, and many vessels and naval stores fell to the victors. Montgomery's object was to make friends of the Canadians and induce them to join the cause of the Colonies. Though they did not do this, yet they received the Americans kindly, and supplied them and their army with all that they needed. The news of this brilliant train of victories spread over the land. Montgomery's praises were on every tongue, and Congress voted him the thanks of the nation. But the young soldier's heart was sad. After leaving garrisons at Chambly, St. John, and Montreal, he found himself with only three hundred effective men left him to attempt the capture of Quebec, which was, by natural position and military art, the most strongly fortified city in America. A Canadian winter was upon them, and their perils and hardships had but just commenced. Sad presentiments chilled Montgomery's heart. He often thought of his peaceful home in the bosom of the hills, the loving wife sitting in her loneliness there. He would have bartered all the glory he had won for one hour at that hearthstone. Should he ever see it again?

"Washington had forseen the situation in which Montgomery would find himself, and, knowing that without the capture of Quebec the expedition (the object of which was the conquest of Canada) would be a failure, had dispatched a column from his own camp near Boston to penetrate the State of Maine and come out into Canada at Quebec. He even hoped that they would reach it in time to surprise and take it while Montgomery was operating against Montreal. If not, they were to await his coming and operate with him. This force consisted of ten companies of New England infantry, one of Virginia riflemen under the brave Morgan, and two companies of Pennsylvanians. In all the records of ancient or modern valor I have read nothing equal to this wrestle of heroism and endurance with toil and suffering. Let us follow these noble soldiers on the map. They were to sail up the Kennebec River as far as navigable, then they were to take flat-boats, which Washington had ordered to be constructed for their use; thence up the Dead River, a branch of the Kennebec. After that their path lay through an uninhabited wilderness until they came to the sources of the Canadian River, called the Chaudiere, which empties itself into the St. Lawrence River quite near Quebec."

"It looks tolerably easy by the map," said Albert.

"Yes, by the map; but as they advanced up the Kennebec the stream became rapid and violent over its rocky bed; often they could not row, but had to drag their heavily-laden boats up the swift current, waist deep. It was winter, remember; the mountains were covered with snow and the waters at a deadly chill. Beds of rock, falls and rapids, often forbade the passage of their boats at all. They had to be unloaded, arms, ammunition, baggage and provisions, and the boats themselves carried by the men through tiresome pathless forests until the stream would bear their boats again. Leaving the Kennebec, they dragged every thing over a rough mountain-ridge and through swamps and bogs, sinking knee-deep, to the Dead River. Their course now lay up this river for eighty-three miles, and no less than seventeen times, because of falls and rapids, they were forced to unload their boats and carry them, as I have before described. Winter winds howled around them; their shoes were gone; briers and rocks had torn their clothes from their backs; storms drenched them; they had no shelter at night, except what they made with the boughs of trees; their provisions were nearly gone; famine and death marched with them, until they were forced to kill their faithful dogs that had followed their masters' steps into the wilderness. But the love of liberty and their country kept its flame alive on the altar of their hearts and they toiled on. They had dragged their boats one hundred and eighty miles of the journey; they had carried them on their shoulders with all their contents, forty miles, through frightful thickets, ragged mountains, and knee-deep bogs, till at last they reached the Chaudiere, which goes foaming down its rocky bed at too rapid a speed; for it whirled over three of their boats, and they lost much of the stores and ammunition which they had brought so far with so much labor. They were nearing their journey's end, and the first French Canadians who saw them wondered if they had fallen from the clouds, Arnold had sent forward several letters to Montgomery by the hands of friendly Indians to apprise him of his coming. Unfortunately, these letters were intercepted."

"O don't tell us that," said Harry, with a world of vexation in his face.

"Yes, but for this it was very possible that Arnold's brave heroes, worn and tattered as they were, coming suddenly upon the garrison, might have surprised and carried the defenses of the city; but the British strengthened their works and stood well upon their guard. Arnold bravely offered them battle outside the fort, but they did not accept it, and he was forced to march away some miles and wait for Montgomery's arrival. It was a glad day when their eyes caught the first sight of the American colors borne by Montgomery's men. There was a joyful meeting of friends in that far-off winter-land. Montgomery had brought them woolen clothing and boots; he also gave them words of cheer and encouragement for their almost superhuman achievements. Counting their little band, those who remained to Montgomery after battle, siege, and assault, and those who remained to Arnold from the perils of the wilderness, they amounted to a few less than one thousand, including two companies of Canadians. This handful of men appeared in mid-winter before Quebec, defended by two hundred pieces of cannon and a garrison of twice their number, well provisioned. Montgomery spoke hopefully to his men, but in his heart he carried a weight of despair. To return without taking Quebec was to throw away all the brave work he had done. Congress expected it; the nation waited for it. A soldier's fame is dear to him as life; to a patriot the cause of his country is above all else. No time was to be lost; the rigors of winter were becoming intolerable, and the sufferings of the men were beyond endurance. Two diseases attacked the camp, small-pox and homesickness."

"Poor fellows!" said Nannie, the tears standing in her eyes. "Dear aunty, what did put it into their heads to go in the winter?"

"Sure enough," added Albert. "You said Washington never made mistakes, but that seemed very much like one."

"They did not choose the winter, but they accepted it as a necessity. England had no army in Canada at this time, in the spring she would have. It was now or never for the capture of Canada; moreover, Congress ordered the Canadian expedition; being ordered, Washington contributed to the best of his ability to its success. Montgomery and Arnold used every honorable provocation to induce General Carleton to come out of his defenses and fight; they would then have had a fair chance of success. But the British general thought 'prudence the better part of valor.' Finding all his efforts unavailing, Montgomery said, 'To the storming we must come at last.'

"The year was growing old, but a few days remaining of 1775. The term of enlistment of most of the men expired with it. The generals planned for a night assault. 'The night of the 26th of December was clear, and so cold that no man could handle his arms or scale a wall. The 27th was hazy, and the troops were put in motion; but the sky cleared, and Montgomery, tender of their lives, called them back and waited for a night of clouds and darkness, with a storm of wind and snow.'

"On the thirtieth, the New Year's eve, a north-east snow-storm set in. The troops were divided for attack at different points, Montgomery reserving the post of danger for himself. Two of the attacks were to be mere pretenses, to draw attention from the real points, which were to be assaulted by Arnold on one side and Montgomery on the other. The snow had changed to driving hail that cut the men's eyes and faces; they advanced with heads down and their guns under their coats to keep them dry. A braver man than Arnold never led men to battle. They assailed their point of attack with the greatest fury. A musketball in his leg disabled Arnold early in the action, and he was borne to the rear. Morgan took command, and cheering on his men with words of victory, they carried the battery and took its defenders prisoners, though with great loss of life. He held for a time the lower part of the town, and there they waited and watched for the promised signals from Montgomery's side.

"He with three hundred men and his two aids, MacPherson and Cheeseman, two gallant young soldiers, took their course along a steep and rocky path, made so slippery and dangerous by the frozen snow and hail that it was a constant effort to keep their feet. On they went, Montgomery opening the path though the snow with his own hands. A battery intercepted their path—it must be taken. Montgomery ordered them to 'double-quick,' himself leading, with the words, 'Come on, brave boys, you will not fear to follow where your general leads.' A flash, a 'well-served cannon discharge,' Montgomery, MacPherson, and Cheeseman fall dead. The drifted snow was the winding-sheet of the beautiful and brave on the morning of the New Year 1776, before the gates of Quebec. Seeing their leaders fall, the men had no courage to advance over their dead bodies. They retreated. Morgan and his men waited on the other side of the town for the signals, which, alas! they should never see. They waited too long. The enemy, released from defending other points, surrounded and took them prisoners. To General Carleton's praise be it spoken, the bodies of the noble fallen received burial with all the honors of war. Montgomery had fought under England's banner in his youth, and had even then won a name for honor and valor. When the news of his death reached England, the 'great defenders of liberty in the British Parliament vied with each other in his praise,' and wept as they pronounced his eulogy. Washington bewailed his loss, for he loved him as a brother. All over the land men wept as for a 'heart friend.' Congress, 'desiring to transmit to future acres an example of patriotism, boldness of enterprise, and contempt of danger and death, reared a monument of marble to the glory of Richard Montgomery.'

"But the bitterest tears were shed in that pleasant home amid the hills of Hudson; a grief was there for which earth had no balm, for Montgomery's wife took no other love in his stead. Years after the toils of war had passed, Washington kept state in the city of New York as first President of the Republic for which Montgomery had died, and for which Washington had lived. It is related that on reception-days ' it was the custom for the secretaries and gentlemen of the household to hand ladies to and from their carriages; but when the honored widow of Montgomery came, the President himself performed these complimentary duties.'"

The little group sat silent for a moment, and Albert said, "I can't help thinking, aunty, that it was a great mistake for them to undertake this expedition."

"If we consider it as a piece of offensive warfare, perhaps it was, though the cause of failure seemed to be the accident of Montgomery's death at the critical moment; for it was afterward found that the battery was served only by a handful of men, and if Montgomery had not fallen its capture would have been an easy matter. He without whom the sparrow does not fall gave the final orders. We 'rough hew' our destinies, but He 'shapes' them as he wills. It would doubtless have been better if they had stood upon their defense, instead of entering a neutral province, and had contented themselves with putting strong garrisons into the forts on the Lakes, on our own territory, thus keeping the doors into Canada well locked on this side. No success attended them afterward, though Congress, against Washington's advice, continued their efforts to accomplish their designs there. War is a horrible wickedness, and includes every form of suffering and wrong. It is unmitigated barbarism from beginning to end, except in defense of a just cause. In that case we are commanded to 'resist unto blood,' and every man who lays down his life fairly earns the name of martyr.

"Montgomery gave his life to win for us those civil and religious liberties which have made our country 'the glory of all lands.' The hero keeps his quiet, unbroken slumber in the grave-yard of St. Paul's Church, New York, just a step aside from Broadway. Of all the busy, toiling, hurrying millions that yearly pass and repass above the sacred dust, how many pause to lay upon his grave the chaplet of a grateful memory?"

Podcast #143 Liberty or Loyalty in the American Revolution

When I learned about the American Revolution in school, I got the impression all the colonists were united against the British. But that simply isn't true. I read that only about a third truly supported the cause, a third were fence sitters and a third had no desire to sever ties with the King.

Today's sampler talks about this very thing and is taken from a 1915 book called *Pioneers and Patriots* by Marguerite Dickson.[63]

Liberty or Loyalty

We must not make the mistake of supposing that every American in Revolutionary days fought for independence, or, if not fighting, gave what help he could in other ways. There were many people of America who looked upon the war as a "most wicked rebellion against his Gracious Majesty, King George." They could not understand how their neighbors and friends could take part in such wicked business. Most of them at the beginning of the struggle had no doubt that England would make short work of subduing the rebellious colonists, and they looked forward to long lives as subjects of the king.

Naturally enough, many of these "loyalists," as they were called from their loyalty to the English government, wanted to help the English soldiers to put an end to the war, and so they joined the British army. There were whole regiments fighting for England which were made up of American loyalists.

Others had no heart to fight against their neighbors and one-time friends. Some of these left their homes, going to Halifax or to England. Some tried to live quietly at home. Some gave secret aid to the king's soldiers, and, if they were found out, received rough treatment. Some received rough treatment anyway, simply because they were loyalists, or Tories, as the other party called them.

The name Tory in itself meant nothing bad or disgraceful. Whig and Tory were the names of English political parties, as Republican and Democrat are in our own country to-day. Of course there were Whigs and Tories in the English colonies too. The Whigs in both the colonies and the mother country took the part of the resisting Americans, and the Tories believed the English government was right. So when an American called another American a Tory, he meant merely a man loyal to the English government. Of course as war went on the feeling between Whigs and Tories grew bitter, and the very word Tory came to imply scorn.

All sorts of cruel deeds were done as the war spirit grew. Quiet and harmless Tories were tormented because they could not believe as their neighbors did. Others were imprisoned or driven away from their homes. Tories, on the other hand, did their share of tormenting. They spied upon their Whig neighbors, and many a patriot soldier at home for a glimpse of wife and children was captured by bands of Tories or by British soldiers warned by Tory spies.

Perhaps the most hated of all were those who would take neither side, or who changed sides during the war. Nobody trusted them—nobody dared trust them. It would perhaps be too much to expect that every man should be true to his best self at such a time. There were selfish men, who would be sure to follow the stronger side for their own advantage. There were the timid ones, who dared not choose the weak side even though they believed it right. And there were others that seemed to change with every wind that blew. When a British army encamped near them, they were all for "England and the Crown." When a turn of battle brought an American army, they were just as devoted to the cause of liberty and independence. Thus they hoped to make sure of their own safety.

Michael Doherty, of Delaware, was an unfortunate example of this changeable nature. He was a sergeant in the Continental army, but was taken prisoner by the British. While in prison he was approached by a British officer who offered him his freedom if he would take the king's side. Michael, won by what he calls the offcer's "perpetual blarney" and "the king's money" slipped into his hand, became a duly enlisted soldier in the British regiment which had captured him. Alas, for Michael! His regiment was ordered to garrison Stony Point, and there "Mad Anthony's men gave him an ugly wound and took him prisoner again. No doubt he had time to think over the matter seriously while his wound was healing; at any rate he changed his sympathies and was forgiven and received back with kindness by his comrades in his old Delaware regiment. But at the battle of Camden in South Carolina the British won the day, and poor Michael soon found himself marched to the coast and shut up on a British prison ship. By that time changing sides had probably become a habit, so we are not surprised to hear that, in the battle at the Cowpens, Michael was again a valiant British soldier, and, when the battle was over, again a prisoner to his friends, the enemy. What became of him after that I cannot say, but he lived to tell the tale, which he concluded with these words: "1 feel some qualms at the thought of battle since, take whatever side I will, I am always sure to find it the wrong one."

I must tell you the story of Doctor Byles and his two daughters, of Boston. For more than forty years the learned doctor was pastor of a church in his native town, but when trouble came between the colonies and the English government, his people were not satisfied with the good doctor's stand.

He was careful not to say a word about politics or the questions that everybody else was talking excitedly about. Other preachers wrote sermons about "the duty of the colonies to the king," or "the wrongs of the American colonies," but never a word from Doctor Byles. At last some one asked him why he expressed no opinion. His reply was: "In the first place, I don't understand politics; in the second place, you all do, every man and mother's son of you; in the third place, you have politics all the week, pray let one day in seven be devoted to religion."

This, however, did not satisfy his Whig congregation. The people believed he was a Tory at heart. And so he was, but of the sort that was disposed to keep out of the quarrel and allow those who felt more strongly than he to settle it.

It was not long before his Tory sympathies cost him his church; but he lived on in his old house in Boston. His daughters were far more interested than he. They welcomed to their father's house the British officers then stationed in Boston; they watched anxiously for news of British victories; they prayed for the success of England and the welfare of the British king.

The old doctor was closely watched, you may be sure, and, at one time during the war, he was tried and sentenced to be shut up in his own house under guard. It might have been worse, of course, and the old man, always cheerful, made the best of it, although the daughters more than offset his mildness by their indignant exclamations.

One day it happened that the doctor was alone in the house, before which the sentinel marched back and forth on his usual guard duty. It also happened that the doctor found himself much in need of a servant or a messenger boy to do an errand for him. Unfortunately he could not go himself, and there was no one else. Quite annoying, surely! Suddenly, with a twinkle in his shrewd old eyes, the doctor threw open the front door and hailed the guard.

Now, I haven't a doubt that the militiaman pacing up and down before the doctor's door was very tired of his task. And I should be very little surprised to know that it seemed to him rather a foolish precaution to guard this white-haired old man who had done nothing worse than to wish success to England in the war. Even so, he stood in open-mouthed astonishment when the doctor coolly proposed that he — the guard — go on an errand for his prisoner!

"But, sir," he stammered, "who—who—who would stand guard over you, sir?"

"I am quite capable of shouldering a musket myself," replied the old doctor. "Go on. I'll do sentry duty." The strangest part of the story is that the sentinel agreed, leaving the prisoner to march gravely back and forth for an hour or more, till his return.

Once the doctor and his daughters were ordered to be sent to England, but the sentence was not carried out. Instead they remained in their old home, while the war went on and finally ended in the independence of the American colonies.

The hopes and prayers of the doctor's daughters had gained them nothing. still, however, they were loyal to King George. The father died, but the daughters lived in Boston for fifty years after the war, unchanging loyalists to the days of their death. The people around them might yield to the rulers of "the states." They were as they had always been, subjects of the king. Their old-fashioned house was kept as in their father's day. Their treasures were "from England" and as old or older than themselves. They talked of the old days when they were taken to walk on the Common by General Howe and Lord Percy of the King's Army, and of the band which played beneath their windows by the order of these officers. As death approached, they found great comfort in the knowledge that "not a creature in the states will be any better for what we shall leave behind us."

To them the war was always "a rebellion," and they never forgot nor forgave the deeds of their "misguided countrymen." We cannot help feeling sorry for the poor old ladies, although we rejoice in America's freedom and in the deeds of our patriot forefathers, which won it.

There is a story of another old minister in Massachusetts, which shows him, like his fellow-Tory, Doctor Byles, a gentle and peace-loving man. For many years before the Revolution he had been wont to pray as other ministers did for "our excellent King George" and one Sunday after the war began, he, in an absent-minded way, offered the same prayer. He had scarcely spoken the words "King George," however, when he realized what he had said and that his people would surely object; so he immediately went on, "O Lord, I mean George Washington."

There were not many Tories as harmless to the patriot cause as Doctor Byles, nor many who could have been trusted to stand guard over themselves. On every hand we hear of Tory deeds. In the Mohawk Valley, in New York State, they gathered together bands of Indians and, with their aid, carried on the most cruel and awful warfare. There were raids and massacres, murder and scalping—warfare not only against men, but against women and children.

Everywhere through the middle colonies and the south there were more Tories than in New England; and the patriots of these sections had to fight not only British soldiers, but neighborhood Tories. Stories are still told in Pennsylvania of the five Doane brothers, who left their home, and carried on their warfare from the woods. They were the terror of the neighborhood, spying, robbing, dashing out from their hiding places, and doing all manner of harm to the patriot cause.

Scarcely a town, north or south, but has its stories of Tory misdeeds. There is a story of a southern patriot, whose plantation was left for months at a time in charge of his faithful slaves, while the master fought for liberty. One night the master suddenly appeared, and the slaves were rejoiced to see him, although they feared for his safety, for there were many Tories in the neighborhood.

After a long talk about plantation matters, the weary soldier sought his bed, and was soon sleeping soundly. The slaves kept watch, lest he should be surprised and captured. Suddenly in the dark hours of the night, the slaves came running to rouse their master.

"The Tories are coming, massa. They are coming, sure," they cried, even shaking the sleeping man to rouse him to his danger. He had scarcely wakened when he knew the slaves were right. Voices and hoof beats told the story. There was little time in which to flee.

Reassuring the frightened negroes, the soldier ran down the stairs, and, still in his night-clothes, hastily concealed himself in a thickly growing shrub close to the house. There was no time to seek a more distant refuge. Scarcely had the crackling of twigs and the rustling of leaves ceased before the Tory band was upon him. He hardly dared breathe.

In a moment the leader of the company was roughly demanding that the slaves lead him to their master. They protested loudly that they did not know where he was. And indeed they did not. They knew only that he was hidden somewhere. The voices grew louder and angrier. The slaves grew more and more frightened, but they were loyal in spite of fright. The Tories threatened them with whipping and with torture, but were at last convinced that they really did not know.

Close beside the hiding place of the soldier, the Tories gathered, and soon decided that they would burn the house. "He's probably in it somewhere, so we'll get him dead if not alive," said one. In a short time there was smoke and the crackling of flames. The fire burned rapidly, and the man in the bushes began to suffer from the heat. He had torn his scanty garments in getting to his hiding place, and now the heat was blistering his back and arms. It seemed as though he must cry out. But crying out meant, capture and perhaps death. He bit his lips, and endured the torment.

At last the Tories, seeing that the house was doomed, turned about, and, with a last threat flung toward the weeping negroes clustered at a little distance, rode off. Then the master crept forth, scratched and bleeding, scorched and blistered. But he lived to fight again for liberty.

One of the saddest things about the war for independence was the turning against each other of one-time friends and neighbors. But in most cases, people favored the side which they thought right, and we must allow to each the liberty of his own belief. Whigs and Tories called each other hard names; and when the Whigs were victorious and won independence, they treated the defeated Tories harshly. It is only in these later years that we can see that, if they were honest, they could only defend the right as they saw it.

Podcast #144 Another Story from the American Revolution

I'd like to introduce you to an author who has written a number of books to bring the American Revolution to life for young people. His name is Everett T. Tomlinson. I happened across a lecture he gave to the American Library Association in 1909 entitled *The Historical Story for Boys* in which he says, "It is better to put the yeast in the bread before the bread is put into the boy. And that yeast is the story. The normal boy demands a story…this is the law of life. It is more, it is as vital as breathing."

So today, I'll share one of his stories of the American Revolution called *How the Red Doe Changed Owners*.[64] It is only through story that your children will sense the sacrifices made by others for them.

How the Red Doe Changed Owners

"I'm afraid it's the last day I'll ever see."

So David Hunter said to himself as he rode on in the midst of the band of twenty men. Strange, determined-looking men were all of them, and as David glanced again at the leader, in spite of his own danger, he could but admire the strength and zeal of his captor. For David Hunter was a prisoner of David Fanning and his band of "outliers."

Just an hour before this time they had swept suddenly down upon his home, having learned in some way that the zealous Whig had returned, and before he could give the alarm, or make an attempt to escape, the house had been surrounded and he had been carried away. Even now he could not shut out the sight of his weeping wife and children as they watched his departure, and the great fear in David's heart was not of what might befall him, but of what would become of those whom he had left behind.

Did it pay? In spite of himself, the question forced its way into his mind. He had been laboring day and night for the good of the colonies ever since the summer of 1776, and now it was the spring of 1781. And what had been accomplished? Cornwallis had raised the royal standard at Hillsboro on February 22d, 1781, and apparently the feelings of both Whigs and Tones had become more intense than ever before. The end seemed to be far away.

David Hunter smiled grimly at the thought of the part he himself had taken. Early and late he had been zealous in the defence of his friends and neighbors, and up to the present day had escaped all the plottings of his enemies.

Now, however, he was a prisoner of David Fanning, one of the most desperate of all the "outliers" in South Carolina in 1781—1782. He recalled many of the stories he had heard of his daring, and that he had been a carpenter until Major Craig had occupied Wilmington. Then a new field presented itself to Fanning's ambition. Clad in a long, white hunting shirt, Indian leggings and cavalry boots, and mounted on a common draught horse, he had first appeared as the leader of a band of eight or ten marauders. He had no home, seldom entered a house, and generally passed his nights alone in some solitary place. But Major Craig appreciated his energy and fearlessness, and had secured for him an appointment as colonel in the militia. Then the white hunting shirt gave place to a gorgeous British uniform, and the sword and holster of pistols which the major also gave him were ever near him.

Proud as he was of these things, however, his chief pride was in the beautiful horse he rode—the Red Doe—a gift from a royalist named Lindsey. She had become famous for her speed and intelligence before the "outlier" owned her, and in his desperate ventures she also became one of his main reliances. Through her aid and that of his followers he had captured Colonel Philip Alston at his own house, and not long after swept suddenly down upon Pittsborough and carried away with him all the Continental officers stationed there.

David Hunter also thought of how his own near neighbors, Charles Spearing and Captains Dreck and Dye, had been shot by this man. Fanning had gone to Spearing's home one night, and, after calling for him to come forth, had shot him as he stood in the doorway. And hangings and plunderings and murders had increased until all the people in the region between the Cape Fear and Peedee rivers were living in a constant state of terror, for no one knew when his turn to suffer might come.

And David Hunter's turn had indeed arrived. He thought of all these things as once more he glanced ahead at the leader. Fanning was mounted on the Red Doe, and his sword and holster of silver-mounted pistols could be seen as clearly as his brilliant-hued uniform.

"There's no sympathy to be found there," thought David, as he looked away from Fanning at his other companions. "No, nor there, either," he added, as he noticed the grim expressions and forbidding looks of the men. "Well, I'm sorry for Mary and the babies. I should have liked too to live for my country; but if I have to die, I'll do it as a man and a Christian ought. I hope those who will be born a hundred years after I'm gone will appreciate the price we had to pay to give them a home and a country."

Still the men rode silently forward. Not a word had been spoken since they had left David Hunter's house and had swiftly followed the Red Doe and her rider mile after mile. Whither were they going? At times a faint-hope arose in Hunter's mind that they were keeping him as a prisoner, and that they would deliver him up to some of the British officers. But that was not Fanning's method, as a rule, and he braced himself to meet the worst when it should come; for when he recalled the neighbors whose bodies had been left hanging from some tree by the roadside, he knew that he had little right to expect a better fate for himself.

Still on and on sped the men. The Red Doe apparently was as fresh as when they started, but many of the other horses were already showing signs of distress. The pace was a swift one, and apparently the leader had no thought of resting. The horses' hoofs struck the earth together, and the appearance they presented was that of one large body moving swiftly and steadily up the road.

"Perhaps I've a chance yet," thought Hunter, when at last the men halted by the roadside and a consultation took place between the leaders. Apparently no one was heeding him; but he well knew that the first suspicious movement on his part would call forth a shot. No, his only hope lay in being quiet and waiting; but no one will ever know the breathless interest with which he watched the men as they stood and talked together.

Soon a band composed of half the men remounted their horses and retraced their way. David Hunter watched them until they were out of sight, and then turned just as the consultation ended. His heart. sank and his lips became pale when he saw one of the men take a rope from his pack, and throwing one end over the limb of a tree arrange a noose in the other.

He knew just what those signs of preparation meant for him. If he had had any doubts, they would have been dispelled when Fanning approached him and said, "Well, Hunter, you'll have to follow the other Whigs we've sent on their way before you."

"And you can't send me on to Charleston as a prisoner?" David Hunter spoke calmly; but he felt as if he never could draw breath again. It seemed to him as if his heart were held as in a vice and never would beat again; but none of his fear was betrayed in his manner or in his words.

"Can't be done," replied the "outlier." "I did think at first we'd keep you, for you're quite a fellow, if you are a traitor; but our plans have changed. You'll have to swing."

"Think of my wife and babies," pleaded Hunter. He saw no mercy in the man before him, but in his anguish the cry broke out almost without his knowledge.

"Other men had wives and babies, and they had a king too. You should have thought of the king, and your wife and babies would have been all right. No; you'll have to swing. Come!"

Well knowing that further pleadings would be useless, David controlled his emotion, and quietly followed the brutal leader until he stood beneath the swinging rope. Then for a moment he glanced about him. The men and horses were standing in a semicircle, but the sight of a struggling, desperate man had become so common to them all that no one displayed any special interest.

At the extreme right, and only about a yard from him, stood the Red Doe, and David thought that from her eyes there shone a gleam of pity. She had been well trained, and Fanning had no need to tie her on an occasion like this. The other horses followed her as their leader, as the men did her rider. But no help, no hope, could the unfortunate man see on any side of him.

"Come; we'll give you two minutes to say your prayers in. Be quick, for we've other business to attend to," said Fanning roughly, stepping back behind the prisoner as he spoke.

And David Hunter folded his hands and knelt beneath that terrible rope hanging just over him. He had always been a God-fearing man, and every morning, in his home, with his wife and children kneeling about him, had prayed to Almighty God for help through the coming day. But how different it all was now. The sight of the rope had been almost like that of a twisting, crawling serpent.

And he could not shut out the vision of that rude little house that had been home to him for five long years. And what would become of his wife and babies now, without a protector in these terrible times when every man's hand seemed to be against his neighbor? He could not have told just what he was asking for; but he was thinking of One who had declared that not even a sparrow fell to the ground without the notice of the Great Father of all. "Fear ye not, therefore, ye are of more value than many sparrows."

David opened his eyes. He did not realize how long he had been praying. It might have been for hours, so far as he knew. There stood the Red Doe still looking at him with curious, pitying eyes. There stood the men just as they had been, not one having changed his position. And David still knelt, though his eyes were open now, and a new and sudden, perhaps wild, impulse was in his heart.

"Finished your prayers? If you have, we'll go on with the hanging." It was Fanning who was speaking, and his voice, though rough, was not altogether unkind.

"Yes, I've finished my prayers," replied David Hunter, as with one quick bound he leaped to his feet and threw himself upon the back of the Red Doe.

A quick pull at the bridle, a sharp word of command, and the beautiful beast was off up the road like a flash of light. It all happened so quickly, that for a moment the band of "outliers" were speechless with surprise; but it was only for a moment. David, bending low on the Red Doe's beautiful neck, glanced backward as he heard the shout of astonishment and anger which came a moment later.

He saw the guns quickly raised to the shoulders of the men; he heard the sharp command of Fanning to "aim high," and even then was dimly conscious that the leader was thinking of his fleet little steed; he closed his eyes and waited for the report.

In a moment the sound of the volley rang out, and he felt a sharp pain in his left shoulder, and knew at once that the arm was useless, but also that only one bullet had hit him. Releasing his grasp on the bridle, he took a firm hold of the Red Doe's mane with his right hand, and leaning low on her neck began his race for life. From behind came the shouts and calls of the angry men; but their muskets were empty now, and David knew that if the Red Doe could gain in the first of the pursuit, the end would take care of itself.

So on and on he urged the beautiful mare, which seemed to realize that life and death were hanging on her efforts. Her hoofs seemed hardly to touch the ground. In long, steady leaps she rushed forward, and David Hunter was clinging desperately to her neck. He could feel the red drops trickling from his left hand, and knew that by them the pursuers would have little difficulty in tracing his course.

Under him he could feel the holster of silver-mounted pistols, which, next to the Red Doe herself, had been the pride of David Fanning's heart. Not an effort would be spared by him to regain the double prize. But the prize before David Hunter was far greater than either or both, for it was life itself.

On and on he urged the Red Doe. Soon she was flinging the foam from her lips, and her heaving sides were wet. Her nostrils were like burning coals, and above her head appeared the white and agonized face of David Hunter, who seemed to know no mercy for the beautiful beast beneath him. From time to time the shouts of his pursuers could be heard, now loud and now dim and distant; but David well knew they would follow him to the end.

The minutes passed, the hot sun mercilessly poured its heat upon beast and rider, but still the Red Doe sped on. The click of her hoofs grew monotonous; but whenever David thought of halting, he would hear that far-away call, and again would urge his noble steed forward. Suddenly she stopped and snorted with fear, and her rider lifted his head in surprise.

Before him lay Little River, and the road ended on the high bluff on the bank. The waters were high, and he knew at once there was no ford. Just then he again heard the call of the "outliers," and it was nearer than before. Something must be done, but what could he do? For a moment David hesitated, but only for a moment, for with his jaws set and an agonized expression on his face, he drew the Red Doe several steps back from the bank.

He waited a moment, but again that terrible cry of the "outliers" rang out, and then, with one quick word of command, David urged her forward, and with one strong leap she shot out over the bank and disappeared in the waters of Little River.

In a moment she rose to the surface, and after one snort of fear, arched her beautiful neck and struck out for the farther shore with David still clinging to her back. In a brief time she gained the bank, and her rider led her within the shadows of the forest, and then turned to see what his pursuers would do.

Soon they made their appearance; but the pursuit was ended, for not one of them dared or cared to follow the course of the fleet Red Doe. When David saw them turn backward in the road, he once more dropped on his knees; but this time, there was no fear of the dangling noose before his eyes. It was a prayer of gratitude and not one for release, and it was not long before David Hunter, with the beautiful Red Doe, and the no less beautiful holster of silver mounted pistols, was safe from all pursuit.

David Fanning remained in the field until the spring of 1782, when he made his way to

Charleston and afterward to Digby, Nova Scotia, where he died in 1825, after having been a member of the assembly from Queen's County, New Brunswick, and serving as a colonel in the militia. Doubtless there the passions of the Revolution were forgotten, and his energy found a proper field in which to display itself.

As for the Red Doe, there are many of her descendants to-day whose owners are as proud of her story as they are of her beautiful offspring.

As for us, we cannot forget the question that arose in David Hunter's mind, and I am wondering whether to-day we are as brave, and are doing as much for our country as David, and many men like unto him, did in the time of her troubles. They labored, and we have entered into their labors. They paid the price, and we have received the value.

Podcast #145 Israel Israel's Experience with the Tories

Let's end the week with one more American Revolution story from *Pioneers and Patriots*.[65] This time we'll see the bravery of a young wife.

In the early twilight of a winter afternoon in 1777, a young man walked rapidly along the road from Wilmington to Philadelphia. He was closely wrapped in a large cloak, inside which he carried various bundles and packages, including a small bag of money. He was clearly anxious to reach his journey's end, yet as he approached the ferry, he lingered along the road until darkness fell and the lights of the city began to appear in the distance. Then under the friendly cover of the darkness, he walked boldly toward the British sentinel who guarded the ferry entrance.

Philadelphia was at this time in the hands of the British General Howe, and his soldiers were quartered in the city. The Tories of Philadelphia were joyful indeed because of the presence of the British, but Whigs unfortunate enough to remain suffered inconvenience and sometimes real hardship. Among the Whig families thus suffering were the mother and sisters of the young man at the ferry; and his present journey was to carry them relief.

Hailed by the British sentinel with the customary question, "Who goes there?" the young man promptly answered, "A friend," and when further questioned, gave quite as promptly the British countersign for the night.

"Pass, friend!" said the sentinel. The young man hurried on, glad to escape his searching eyes.

This man, Israel Israel, was the elder of two sons of a widowed mother. When war broke out, both of the brothers desired to fight for liberty, but the aged mother, two sisters and Israel's young wife seemed to need the protection and support of one of the young men, and it was decided that one must remain at home. It was hard to choose between them. It was finally settled that they should draw lots, and this ended in the lot's falling upon Joseph, the younger brother, who therefore went to fight.

Israel continued to live upon his little farm in Wilmington, making frequent visits to the old mother and sisters in Philadelphia. Since the British had seized the city, only "king's men," or loyalists, were permitted to pass in and out. Israel heard strange stories of the rough treatment Whigs within the city were receiving, and he grew daily more fearful. He tried to devise some way to get inside the British lines.

At length help came from an unexpected source. A Tory neighbor, knowing of Israel's longing to learn how his mother was faring, obtained for him the British countersign; and thankfully accepting his neighbor's kindness, Israel had passed the sentinel, as we have seen, and was soon walking rapidly in the direction of his mother's house.

Once within, the young man was relieved to find his mother and sisters well, though sorely in need of the supplies he had brought. Soldiers were quartered in the house, they told him, and the timid women were very weary of their rough, noisy ways. Then cautiously they led Israel to an inner room, where he was surprised to find a soldier in Continental uniform.

"Why, 'tis Joe," he cried, and the brothers clasped hands joyfully. "How did you get here, man?" asked Israel. "Did some Tory friend help you as mine helped me?"

"'Tis too long a tale to tell," answered Joseph. "'Tis enough that I am here. Indeed I must soon be gone. I must be far from the city before light."

It was fully eleven o'clock when the happily united family sat down to supper, still talking busily of their experiences in these trying times. Suddenly the tramp of horses in the street without was followed by loud knocking at the door. In a moment Joseph had left his untasted supper, for to be caught here in Continental uniform meant imprisonment and perhaps worse.

The rest rushed after him up the stairs, helped him out of the telltale uniform, and saw him safely out of sight on the roof before they descended to open to the pounding, shouting soldiers below.

It was Israel himself who unbarred the door. Upon him the soldiers rushed, shouting, "Now we have him, the rebel rascal!"

"Who calls me a rebel?" calmly asked the young man, shaking off the rough hand of the Hessian sergeant who commanded the group.

"Your own slave admits it," answered the sergeant, pointing to an old negro who stood with hanging head in the doorway.

The master fixed his keen eye upon the trembling slave, as he said carelessly, "There's a mistake here, gentlemen. It's my brother, Joe, you're looking for, no doubt. He fights in the rebel army. But he isn't here." And as he spoke, Israel could only hope his words were true, and that Joe was indeed some distance away by this time.

"Stay," he added, as if a new thought had just come to him, "I believe an old uniform of Joe's has been left in the house. I'll get it, and you may see for yourselves whether I'm its rebel owner."

So, still calmly, he went upstairs, and returned with the garments so lately thrown aside by the escaping soldier. Now it chanced that Joe was a small man, while Israel was tall and broad, quite a giant in fact. Even the soldiers could only laugh when Israel struggled, but all in vain, to get into the uniform.

The sergeant made all due apologies, and dismissing his men, proposed that, since supper was on the table, he stay and share it. Little as the family desired his presence, they dared not object, and they made a place for the self-invited guest.

When the officer had taken his departure, Israel bade his mother and sisters good-by, and set out upon his homeward journey. Passing the sentinel safely, he tramped the thirty miles between the ferry and his home, arriving weary, but relieved that his dangerous errand was safely accomplished.

At home, however, he met fresh difficulties. The friendly Tory who had given him the countersign proved far from friendly at heart, for he had betrayed the secret of the journey to the British, and now Israel found himself arrested and accused of entering the British lines as a spy.

Together with his wife's brother, the young man was carried off to a British warship in the Delaware, to be tried for his life. While it was not true that he was a spy, his activity in the patriot cause could not be denied, and his Tory neighbors were more than ready to testify against him.

The Roebuck, on which the prisoners were confined, lay not far from the town, directly opposite, it happened, to Israel's little farm. As he lay on the deck, on the coil of rope which was his only bed, he could see the lights in his windows, telling of the lonely young wife within the house, trembling for his safety.

Only nineteen years old, she was now left quite unprotected.

In the morning, Israel saw his cattle driven out upon the meadow by the riverside and knew the brave wife was caring as she could for the home in his absence. His enemies were on hand early with their tales of his evil deeds. He had been a rebel from the first, they said. He had given no provisions for the use of his Majesty's soldiers and fleet. Indeed he had been heard to say he would sooner drive his cattle as a present to General Washington than to sell them for a cartload of British gold.

"Indeed," said the commander of the Roebuck." And where are these precious cattle?"

"There, on the meadow, sir, in plain sight," responded the Tory informers. Then the commander sternly ordered men ashore to drive the cattle down to the river, where they should be slaughtered before their rebel owner's eyes.

The young wife, having risen at dawn, was watching eagerly from an upper window of the farm-house for some sign of her husband's fate. She saw the soldiers rowed ashore from the ship, saw them land and march toward the meadow. Guessing their errand, she ran down with a sudden determination to resist.

No one was in sight to help her but the small boy who had driven the cows to the pasture, and he was only eight years old. Calling him to follow, she started for the pasture, and, pulling down the bars, ran to drive the cattle out. With the small boy who helped valiantly, she soon started the herd in the right direction. The soldiers were coming nearer now and were shouting angrily that they would fire—and fire they did. By this time Mrs. Israel was thoroughly aroused, and she only called back, "Fire away!" while she ran hither and thither with the boy, guiding the frightened cattle.

With the balls falling around them, the young woman and the little boy braved death in defence of those rebel cattle. "This way, Joe! Head them this way! Don't let a single one escape." With the last one through the bars, Mrs. Israel caught up the little boy, stumbling in his terror, and fastened the cattle securely in the barnyard.

The soldiers, perhaps a little ashamed of making war upon a woman and a child, turned back to the ship. On the deck of the Roebuck officers and prisoners had watched the scene, and the prisoners at least must have gloried in the courage shown by the young wife. The trial went on, but strange to say, the officers for some reason changed their harsh attitude toward the prisoners and sent them home free men. They even rebuked the Tories who had accused a man bound on a peaceful errand of duty to his old mother. Israel went home in honor on a splendid barge, with presents for his brave wife from the officers of the Roebuck, British man-of-war.

Podcast #149 Marie Curie

Today I want to share a story about Marie Curie from a book called *Heroines of Service*, written in 1917 by Mary Parkman.[66] Although Marie was born in Poland and you can certainly study about her in Month 10 when we get to Poland—I included her in our French studies because she married a Frenchman, Pierre, and lived in France most of her life. Her discovery of radium took place in France.

I wish the story included how long and hard that process of discovery was and the sacrifices involved, but I will leave you to read about that on your own. I chose this telling of her story because you will recognize several Well-Educated heart principles woven into the story. How many can you find?

> You would hardly think that a big, bare room, with rows of battered benches and shelves and tables littered with all sorts of queer-looking jars and bottles, could be a hiding-place for fairies. Yet Marie's father, who was one of the wise men of Warsaw, said they were always to be found there.
>
> "Yes, little daughter," he said, "the fairies you may chance to meet with in the woods, peeping from behind trees and sleeping in flowers, are a tricksy, uncertain sort. The real fairies, who do things, are to be found in my dusty laboratory. They are the true wonder-workers, and there you may really catch them at work and learn some of their secrets."
>
> "But, Father, wouldn't the fairies like it better if it wasn't quite so dusty there?" asked the child.
>
> "No doubt of it," replied the professor.
>
> "We need one fairy more to put us to rights."
>
> At a time when most little girls are playing with dolls, Marie was playing "fairy" in the big classroom, dusting the tables and shelves, and washing the glass tubes and other things that her father used as he talked to his students. "I think we might see the fairies better if I make all these glasses clear and shiny," said Marie.
>
> "Can I trust your little fingers not to let things fall?" asked her father. "Remember, my funny glasses are precious. It might cost us a dinner if you should let one slip."
>
> The professor soon found that his little daughter never let anything slip—either the things he used or the things he said. "Such a wise little fairy and such a busy one!" he would say. "I don't know how we could do our work without her."
>
> If Professor Ladislaus Sklodowski had not loved his laboratory teaching above all else, he would have known that he was overworked. As it was, he counted himself fortunate in being able to serve Truth and to enlist others in her service. For the professor's zeal was of the kind that kindles enthusiasm. If you had seen the faces of those Polish

students as they hung on his words and watched breathlessly the result of an experiment, you would have known that they, too, believed in the wonder-working fairies.

It seems as if the Polish people have a greater love and understanding of the unseen powers of the world than is given to many other nations. If you read the story of Poland's tragic struggles against foes within and without until, finally, the stronger surrounding countries—Germany, Austria, and Russia—divided her territory as spoil among themselves and she ceased to exist as a distinct nation, you will understand why her children have sought refuge in the things of the spirit. They have in a wonderful degree the courage that rises above the most unfriendly circumstances and says:

> One day with life and heart
> Is more than time enough to find a world.

Some of them, like Chopin and Paderewski, have found a new world in music; others have found it in poetry and romance; and still others in science. The child who dreamed of fairies in her father's classroom was to discover the greatest marvel of modern science—a discovery that opened up a new world to the masters of physics and chemistry of our day.

Marie's mother, who had herself been a teacher, died when the child was very small; and so it happened that the busy father had to take sole care of her and make the laboratory do duty as nursery and playroom. It was not strange that the bright, thoughtful little girl learned to love the things that were so dear to her father's heart. Would he not rather buy things for his work than have meat for dinner? Did he not wear the same shabby kaftan (the full Russian top-coat that looks like a dressing-gown) year after year in order that he might have material for important experiments? Truth was, indeed, more than meat and the love of learning more than raiment in that home, and the little daughter drank in his enthusiasm with the queer laboratory smells which were her native air and the breath of life to her.

The time came when the child had to leave this nursery to enter school, but always, when the day's session was over, she went directly to that other school where she listened fascinated to all her father taught about the wonders of the inner world of atoms and the mysterious forces that make the visible world in which we live. She still believed in fairies—oh, yes!—but now she knew their names. There were the rainbow fairies—light-waves, that make all the colors we see—and many more our eyes are not able to discover, but which we can capture by interesting experiments. There were sound-waves, too, and the marvelous forces we call electricity, magnetism, and gravitation. When she was nine years old, it was second nature to care for her father's batteries, beakers, and retorts, and to help prepare the apparatus that was to be used in the demonstrations of the coming day. The students marveled at the child's skill and knowledge, and called her with admiring affection "professorowna," (daughter-professor).

There was a world besides the wonderland of the laboratory, of which Marie was soon aware. This was the world of fear, where the powers of Russia ruled. In 1861 the Poles had made a vain attempt to win their independence, and when Marie was a little girl (she was born in 1867), the authorities tried to stamp out any further sparks of possible rebellion by adopting unusually harsh measures. It was a crime to speak the Polish language in the schools and to talk of the old, happy days when Poland was a nation. If any one was even suspected of looking forward to a better time when the people would not be persecuted by the police or forced to bribe unprincipled officials for a chance to conduct their business without interference, he was carried off to the cruel, yellow-walled prison near the citadel, and perhaps sent to a life of exile in Siberia. Since knowledge means independent thought and capacity for leadership, the high schools and universities were particularly under suspicion. Years afterward, when Marie spoke of this reign of terror, her eyes flashed and her lips were set in a thin white line. Time did not make the memory less vivid.

"Every corridor of my father's school had finger-posts pointing to Siberia!" she declared dramatically.

When Marie was sixteen, she graduated from the "gymnasium" for girls, receiving a gold medal for excellence in mathematics and sciences. In Russia, as in Germany, the gymnasium corresponds to our high school, but also covers some of the work of the first two years of college. The name gymnasium signifies a place where the mind is exercised and made strong in preparation for the work of the universities.

The position as governess to the daughters of a Russian nobleman was offered to the brilliant girl with the sweet, serious eyes and gentle voice. As it meant independence and a chance to travel and learn the ways of the world, Marie agreed to undertake the work.

Now, for the first time in her life, the young Polish girl knew work that was not a labor of love. Her pupils cared nothing for the things that meant everything to her. How they loved luxury and show and gay chatter! How indifferent they were to truth that would make the world wiser and happier.

"How strangely you look, Mademoiselle Marie," said the little Countess Olga one day, in the midst of her French lesson. "Your eyes seem to see things far away."

Marie was truly looking past her pupils, past the rich apartment, beyond Russia, into the great world of opportunity for all earnest workers. She had overheard something about another plot among the students of Warsaw, and knew that some of her father's pupils had been put under arrest.

"Suppose they should try to make me testify against my friends," said the girl to herself. "I must leave Russia at once. My savings will surely take me to Paris, and there I may get a place as helper in one of the big laboratories, where I can learn as I work."

The eyes that had been dark with fear an instant before became bright with hope.

Eagerly she planned a disguise and a way to slip off the very next night while the household was in the midst of the excitement of a masquerade ball.

Everything went well, and in due time she found her trembling self and her slender possessions safely stowed away on a train that was moving rapidly toward the frontier and freedom. No one gave a second thought to the little elderly woman with gray hair and spectacles who sat staring out of the window of her compartment at the fields and trees rushing by in the darkness and the starry heavens that the train seemed to carry with it. Her plain, black dress and veil seemed those of a self-respecting, upper-class servant, who was perhaps going to the bedside of a dying son.

"I feel almost as old as I look," Marie was saying to herself. "But how can a girl who is all alone in the world, with no one to know what happens to her, help feeling old? Down in my heart, though, I know that life is just beginning. There is something waiting for me beyond the blackness—something that needs just little me."

It was a wonderful relief when the solitary journey was over and the elderly disguise laid aside. "Shall I ever feel really young again?" said the girl, who was not quite twenty-four. But not for a moment did she doubt that there was work waiting for her in the big, unexplored world.

During those early days in Paris, Marie often had reason to be grateful for the plain living of her childhood that had made her independent of creature comforts. Now she knew actual want in her cold garret, furnished only with a cot and chair, like a hermit's cell. She lived, too, on hermit's fare—black bread and milk. But even when it was so cold that the milk was frozen—cold comfort, indeed!—the fire of her enthusiasm knew no chill. Day after day she walked from laboratory to laboratory begging to be given a chance as assistant, but always with the same result. It was man's work; why did she not look for a place in a milliner's shop?

One day she renewed her appeal to Professor Lippman in the Sorbonne research laboratories. Something in the still, pale face and deep-set, earnest eyes caught the attention of the busy man. Perhaps this strange, determined girl was starving! And besides, the crucibles and test-tubes were truly in sad need of attention. Grudgingly he bade her clean the various accessories and care for the furnace. Her deftness and skill in handling the materials, and a practical suggestion that proved of value in an important experiment, attracted the favorable notice of the professor. He realized that the slight girl with the foreign look and accent, whom he had taken in out of an impulse of pity, was likely to become one of his most valuable helpers.

A new day dawned for the ambitious young woman. While supporting herself by her laboratory work, she completed in two years the university course for a degree in mathematics, and, two years later, she won a second degree in physics and chemistry. In the meantime her enthusiasm for science and her undaunted courage in the face of difficulties and discouragements attracted the admiration of a fellow-worker, Pierre Curie, one of the most promising of the younger professors.

"I love you, and we both love the same things," he said one day. "Would it not be happier to live and work together than alone?"

And so began that wonderful partnership of two great scientists, whose hard work and heroic struggle, crowned at last by brilliant success, has been an inspiration to earnest workers the world over.

Madame Curie set up a little laboratory in their apartment, and toiled over her experiments at all hours. Her baby daughter was often bathed and dressed in this workroom among the test-tubes and the interesting fumes of advanced research.

"Irene is as happy in the atmosphere of science as her mother was," said Madame Curie to one of her husband's brother-professors who seemed surprised to find a crowing infant in a laboratory. "And if I could afford the best possible nurse, she could not take my place! For my baby and I know the joy of living and growing together with those we love."

What was the problem that the mother was working over even while she sewed for her little girl, or rocked her to sleep to the gentle crooning of an old Polish folk-song whose melody Chopin has wrought into one of his tenderest nocturnes?

The child who used to delight in experiments with light-waves in her father's laboratory, was interested in the strange glow which Prof. Becquerel had found that the substance known as uranium gave off spontaneously. Like the X-rays, this light passes through wood and other bodies opaque to sunlight. Madame Curie became deeply interested in the problem of the nature of the Becquerel rays and their wonderful properties, such as that of making the air a conductor for electricity. One day she discovered that pitchblende, the black mineral from which uranium is extracted, was more radioactive (that is, it gave off more powerful rays) than the isolated substance itself, and she came to the conclusion that there was some other element in the ore which, could it be extracted, would prove more valuable than uranium.

With infinite patience and the skill of highly trained specialists in both physics and chemistry, Madame Curie and her husband worked to obtain this unknown substance. At times Pierre Curie all but lost heart at the seemingly insurmountable obstacles in the way. "It cannot be done!" he exclaimed one day, with a groan. "Truly, 'Nature has buried Truth deep in the bottom of the sea.'"

"But man can dive, cher ami," said his wife, with a heartening smile. "Think of the joy when one comes up at last with the pearl—the pearl of truth!"

At last their toil was rewarded, and two new elements were separated from pitchblende—polonium, so named by Madame Curie in honor of her native Poland, and radium, the most marvelous of all radioactive substances. A tiny pinch of radium, which is a grayish white powder not unlike coarse salt in appearance, gives out a strange glow something like that of fireflies, but bright enough to read by. Moreover, light and heat are radiated by this magic element with no apparent waste of its own amount or energy. Radium can also make some other substances, diamonds for instance, shine with a light like its own, and it makes the air a conductor of electricity. Its weird glow passes through bone almost as readily as through tissue-paper or through flesh, and it even penetrates an inch-thick iron plate.

The Curies now woke to find not only Paris but the world ringing with the fame of their discovery. The modest workers wanted nothing, however, but the chance to go on with their research. You know how Tennyson makes the aged Ulysses look forward even at the end of his life to one more last voyage. The type of the unconquerable human soul that ever presses on to fresh achievement, he says:

> All experience is an arch where-thro'
> Gleams that untravel'd world, whose margin fades
> Forever and forever when I move.

So it was with Pierre Curie and his wife. Their famous accomplishment opened a new world of interesting possibilities, a world which they longed above all things to explore.

Their one trouble was the difficulty of procuring enough of the precious element they had discovered to go on with their experiments. Because radium is not only rare, but also exceedingly hard to extract from the ore, it is a hundred times more precious than pure gold. It is said that five tons of pitchblende were treated before a trifling pinch of the magic powder was secured. It would take over two thousand tons of the mineral to produce a pound of radium. Moreover, it was not easy to secure the ore, as practically all the known mines were in Austria, and those in control wanted to profit as much as possible by this chance.

"It does seem as if people might not stand in the way of our obtaining the necessary material to go on with our work," lamented Pierre Curie. "What we discover belongs to the world—to any one who can use it."

"We have passed other lions in the way. This, too, we shall pass," said Madame Curie, quietly.

They lived in a tiny house in an obscure suburb of Paris, giving all that they possessed— the modest income gained from teaching and lecturing, their share of the Nobel prize of $40,000, which, in 1903, was divided between them and Professor Becquerel, together with all their time and all their skill and knowledge, to their work.

For recreation they went for walks in the country with little Irene, often stopping for dinner at quaint inns among the trees. On one such evening, when Dr. Curie had just declined the decoration of the Legion of Honor, because it had "no bearing on his work," his small daughter climbed on his knee and slipped a red geranium into his buttonhole, saying, with comical solemnity: "You are now decorated with the Legion of Honor. Pray, Monsieur, what do you intend to do about it?"

"I like this emblem much better than a glittering star on a bit of red ribbon, and I love the hand that put it there," replied the father, his face lighting up with one of his rare smiles. "In this case I make no objection."

Other honors, which meant increased opportunity for work, were quietly accepted. Pierre Curie was elected to the French Academy—the greatest honor his country can bestow on her men of genius and achievement. Madame Curie received the degree of Doctor of Physical Science, and—a distinction shared with no other woman—the position of special lecturer at the Sorbonne, in Paris.

One day in 1906, when Dr. Curie, his mind intent on an absorbing problem, was absent-mindedly hurrying across a wet street, he slipped and fell under a passing truck and was instantly killed. When they attempted to break the news to Madame Curie by telling her that her husband had been hurt in an accident, she looked past them with a white, set face, and repeated over and over to herself, as if trying to get her bearings in the new existence that stretched blackly before her, "Pierre is dead; Pierre is dead."

Now, as on that night when she was leaving Russia for an unknown world, she saw a gleam in the blackness—there was work to be done! There was something waiting in the shadowy future for her, something that she alone could do. As on that other night, she found her lips shaping the words: "The big world has need of little me. But oh, it will be hard now to work alone!" Then her eyes fell on her two little girls (Irene was now eight years old and baby Eve was three), who were standing quietly near with big, wondering eyes fixed on their mother's strange face.

"Forgive me, darlings!" she cried, gathering her children into her arms. "We must try hard to go on with the work Father loved. Together is a magic word for us still, little daughters!"

Everybody wondered at the courage and quiet power with which Madame Curie went out to meet her new life. She succeeded to her husband's professorship, and carried on his special lines of investigation as well as her own. The value of her work to science and to humanity may be indicated by the fact that in 1911 the Nobel prize was again awarded to her—the only time it has ever been given more than once to the same person.

At home, she tried to be father as well as mother. She took the children for walks in the evening, and while she sewed on their dresses and knitted them mittens and mufflers, she told them stories of the wonderland of science.

"Why do you take time to write down everything you do?" asked Eve one day, as she looked over her mother's shoulder at the neat note-book in which the world-famous scientist was summing up the work of the day.

"Why does a seaman keep a log, dearie?" the mother questioned with a smile. "A laboratory is just like a ship, and I want things shipshape. Every day with me is like a voyage—a voyage of discovery."

"But why do you put question marks everywhere, Mother!" persisted the child.

It was true that the pages fairly bristled with interrogation points. Madame Curie laughed as if she had never noticed this before. "It is good to have an inquiring mind, child," she said. "I am like my children; I love to ask questions. And when one gets an answer—when you really discover something—it only leads to more questions; and so we go on from one thing to another."

When Madame Curie was asked on one occasion to what she attributed her success, she replied, without hesitation: "To my excellent training: first, under my father, who taught me to wonder and to test; second, under my husband, who understood and encouraged me; and third, under my children, who question me!"

It is the day of one of Madame Curie's lectures. The dignified halls of the university are a-flutter with many visitors from the world of wealth and fashion. There, too, are distinguished scientists from abroad, among whom are Lord Kelvin, Sir Oliver Lodge, and Sir William Ramsay. The President of France and his wife enter with royal guests, Don Carlos and Queen Amélie of Portugal, and the Shah of Persia. The plodding students and the sober men of learning, ranged about the hall, blink at the brilliant company like owls suddenly brought into the sunlight.

At a given moment the hum of conversation dies away and the assemblage rises to its feet as a little black-robed figure steps in and stands before them on the platform. There is an instant's stillness—a hush of indrawn breath you can almost hear—and then the audience gives expression to its enthusiasm in a sudden roar of applause. The little woman lifts up her hand pleadingly. All is still again and she begins to speak.

She is slight, almost pathetically frail, this queen of science. You feel as if all her life had gone into her work. Her face is pale, and her hair is only a shadow above her serious brow. But the deep-set eyes glow, and the quiet voice somehow holds the attention of those least concerned with the problems of advanced physics.

Bank and wealth mean nothing to this little black-robed professor. It is said that when she was requested by the president to give a special demonstration of radium and its marvels before the Shah of Persia, she amazed his Serene Highness by showing much more concern for her tiny tube of white powder than for his distinguished favor. When the royal guest, who had never felt any particular need of exercising self-control, saw the uncanny light that was able to pass through plates of iron, he gave a startled exclamation and made a sudden movement that tipped over the scientist's material. Now it was the Lady Professor's turn to be alarmed. To pacify her, the Shah held out a costly ring from his royal finger, but this extraordinary woman with the pale face paid not the slightest attention; she could not be bribed to forget the peril of her precious radium. It is to be doubted if the eastern potentate had ever before been treated with such scant ceremony.

In 1911, Madame Curie's name was proposed for election to the Academy of Sciences. While it was admitted that her rivals for the vacancy were below her in merit, she failed of being elected by two votes. There was a general protest, since it was felt that service of the first order had gone unrecognized merely because the candidate happened to be a woman. It was stated, however, that Madame Curie was not rejected for this reason, but because it was thought wise to appoint to that vacancy Professor Branly, who had given Marconi valuable aid in his invention of wireless telegraphy, and who, since he was then an old man, would probably not have another chance for the honor. As Madame Curie, on the other hand, was only forty-three, she could well wait for another vacancy.

Since the outbreak of the present war the world has heard nothing new of the work of the Heroine of Radium. We do not doubt, however, that like all the women of France and all her men of science, she is giving her strength and knowledge to the utmost in the service of her adopted country. But we know, also, that just as surely she is seeing the pure light of truth shining through the blackness, and that she is "following the gleam." When the clouds of war shall have cleared away, we may see that her labors now, as in the past, have not only been of service to her country, but also to humanity. For Truth knows no boundaries of nation or race, and he who serves Truth serves all men.

Podcast #150 Joan of Arc

I never tire of hearing the story of Joan of Arc. It's a reminder to me of how God can use the least of us to accomplish mighty works. Who else would choose a young peasant girl to free a nation? And had there been no France, there may not have been an America.

I want to share a story that can be used to introduce her to your younger children. It leaves out the whole being burned at the stake thing, but will likely spark an interest to want to know more. The focus is on Joan as a child. It's from a book called *Boys and Girls Who Became Famous* by Amy Cruse. But before I share that, I thought you might like a little background on my favorite Joan of Arc book written by Mark Twain called *Personal Recollections of Joan of Arc*.

Let me read from some glimpses I included in *Stories of Great Writers*[67] in the Forgotten Classics series.

The Inspiration for Joan of Arc

> …an incident occurred which may be looked back upon now as a turning-point in Samuel Clemens's life. Coming home from the office on afternoon, he noticed a square of paper being swept along by the wind. He saw that it was printed—was interested professionally in seeing what it was like. He chased the flying scrap and overtook it. It was a leaf from some old history of Joan of Arc, and pictured the hard lot of the "maid' in the tower at Rousen, reviled and mistreated by her ruffian captors. There were some paragraphs of description, but the rest was pitiful dialogue.

> Sam had never heard of Joan before—he knew nothing of history. He was no reader. Orion was fond of books, and Pamela; even little Henry had read more than Sam. But now, as he read, there awoke in him a deep feeling of pity and indignation, and with it a longing to know more of the tragic story. It was an interest that would last his life through, and in the course of time find expression in one of the rarest books ever written.

> The first result was that Sam began to read. He hunted up everything he could find on the subject of Joan, and from that went into French history in general—indeed, into history of every kind. Samuel Clemens had suddenly become a reader—almost a student. He even began the study of languages, German and Latin, but was not able to go on for lack of time and teachers….

We'll pick up the story in another book:[68]

> At Villa Viviani, an old, old mansion outside of Florence, on the hill toward Settignano, Mark Twain finished Tom Sawyer Abroad, also Pudd'nhead Wilson, and wrote the first half of a book that really had its beginning on the day when, an apprentice-boy in Hannibal, he had found a stray leaf from the pathetic story of Joan of Ar. All his life she had been his idol, and he had meant some day to write of her. Now, in this weather-

stained old palace, looking down on Florence, medieval and hazy, and across to the villa-dotted hills, he began one of the most beautiful stories ever written, *The Personal Recollections of Joan of Arc*. He wrote in the first person, assuming the character of Joan's secretary, Sieur Louis de Conte, who in his old age is telling the great tale of the Maid of Orleans. It was Mark Twain's purpose, this time, to publish anonymously. Walking the floor one day at Viviani, and smoking vigorously, he said to Mrs. Clemens and Susy:

"I shall never be accepted seriously over my own signature. People always want to laugh over what I write, and are disappointed if they don't find a joke in it. This is to be a serious book. It means more to me than anything else I have ever undertaken. I shall write it anonymously."

So it was that the gentle Sieur de Conte took up the pen, and the tale of Joan was begun in the ancient garden of Viviani, a setting appropriate to its lovely form.

He wrote rapidly when once his plan was perfected and his material arranged. The reading of his youth and manhood was now recalled, not merely as reading, but as remembered reality. It was if he were truly the old Sieur de Conte, saturated with memories, pouring out the tender, tragic tale. In six weeks he had written one hundred thousand words—remarkable progress at any time, the more so when we consider that some of the authorities he consulted were in a foreign tongue. He had always more or less kept up his study of French, begun so long ago on the river, and it stood him now in good stead. Still, it was never easy for him, and the multitude of notes that still exist along the margin of his French authorities show the magnitude of his work. Others of the family went down into the city almost daily, but he stayed in the still garden with Joan. Florence and his suburbs were full of delightful people, some of them old friends. There were luncheons, dinners, teas, dances, and the like always in progress, but he resisted most of these things, preferring to remain the quaint old Sieur de Conte, following again the banner of the Maid of Orleans marshaling her twilight armies across his illumined page.

The Story of Joan of Arc[69]

It was a fair, bright day of early summer in the year 1424, and the pleasant land of Lorraine lay green and fresh under blue skies and golden sunlight. In a meadow near the little village of Domremy a group of country girls were minding their fathers' sheep. In that quiet place the sheep needed very little watching except when the cruel war that was rending France brought bands of rough soldiers to plunder the country-side. Then the church bell rang with quick, loud strokes, and the terrified children drove the sheep and pigs into the courtyard of the old disused castle that stood in a bend of the river, while the housewives gathered up their few treasures and followed. But on this day all was peaceful; the bells were silent except when they rang softly to mark the hour of prayer.

The girls wandered over the meadow picking handfuls of lovely summer flowers; then they sat down on a bank where the meadow-sweet grew tall behind them, and the one who had the most skilful fingers wove the flowers into a garland.

"We will take it to the Fairies' Tree," said a brownhaired, sturdy maiden, whose name was Guillemette, "and hang it on a branch, and we will dance round the tree and drink some of the water from the fountain."

"Which of us shall hang it there?" asked another, and then there were cries of "Let me! Let me!" For the children of Domremy loved to hang garlands on the great beech which was called "The Fairies' Tree." They thought that perhaps the "little people" might show themselves to the child who paid them this honour.

"Let us run a race, and the one who wins shall take the garland," suggested Hauviette, who was long-legged and swift in running, and the others agreed. So when the garland was finished the girls ran laughing to the end of the field and prepared for their race. There was a dark, happyfaced maid among them, tall and straight and full of health and vigour, and when the word was given to start this girl sped along like a young greyhound, so that her laughing companions were soon left behind.

"Jeanne, I saw you flying close to the earth," cried Hauviette as, breathless, they threw themselves down to rest, while the sheep who had moved uneasily as the racing figures passed them bent their heads once more to the sweet grass.

"Jeanne," cried a voice from the side of the field, "you are to go home at once; your mother needs you."

Jeanne looked up quickly. A boy stood by the gate, who was calling to her and waving his hand. She could not see his face very clearly. It was a village boy, perhaps one of her brothers. She got up at once and ran off.

"Come back as soon as you can, Jeanne," called the others, and she answered merrily from the other end of the meadow where her swift feet had already carried her. Then she ran on to the comfortable cottage where lived Jacques d'Arc and his wife Isabella.

"I am come, Mother," she cried, putting her face in at the door, but her mother, who was busy with household work, only looked up for a moment.

"And why have you come?" she asked, a little sharply; "leaving the sheep to stray as they will. Get you back, my maid. I want you not."

So Jeanne went out again into the garden where the birds were singing and the scent of flowers made the air sweet. She was very happy, for she loved her home and all the country pleasures of the bright summer days, the sewing and spinning that her mother taught her, the sheep-minding that was more play than work, the scouring and washing and baking. The thought of change had never come into her head; she was content, and more than content, with things as they were.

She danced gaily down the garden path singing a little song; then stopped. A light so bright that it made the afternoon sunshine look pale filled the space before her, and in it moved shadowy forms. A voice, sweeter and kinder than any she had ever heard before, said:

"Jeanne, my child, the King of Heaven speaks to you. He has great pity on His fair realm of France and He bids you go forth and save her from her enemies. He bids you put on armour like a man and ride at the head of His army. But the time is not yet. Only be ready. Be a good girl and go often to church, and God will show you how to do His Will."

The voice ceased, the light faded. Jeanne stood by the garden gate her face pale, her breath coming quickly. It had not been a dream, she was certain of that. She had seen and heard as plainly as she had ever seen and heard in her life. What did it mean? A girl of thirteen, poor, untaught, who could not even read—how could she save France? Jeanne loved her country and grieved sorely over the stories that came to Domremy of battles and slaughter, of towns destroyed, and the country-side laid waste; but, as was natural, she thought more of her own village; of the hills and the fields and the river she knew so well, than of the unknown lands that lay beyond. She to save France! It seemed to her, as it would have seemed to any girl of her age and her circumstance, a wild, even a monstrous thing. Yet she was not frightened. The voice had been kind and mild, with something in it that had roused her courage and her loyalty. She felt the stirring of a new spirit within her, and she went thoughtfully back to the meadow not quite the same childish, untroubled Jeanne who had left it so blithely only a little while before.

From that day a new life began for her. She still played merrily with the other children of the village, she still sang as she scoured the pots or sat knitting in the doorway; but the feeling that a great charge had been laid upon her made her serious and less childlike. The voices came again and again, two or three times a week, and always they told her to be good, and to prepare herself for the great work that God had willed she should do.

The shadowy forms she had seen on that first afternoon grew clearer. One was a noble, mail-clad warrior whom she knew from the pictures she had seen to be St. Michael; and there were two gracious and beautiful ladies who wore crowns upon their heads and flowing silken garments. These, because she heard them speak to each other, she had learned were St. Catherine and St. Margaret. Jeanne loved them with all her heart, and longed to serve them. They told her to be good, and in her simple way she tried to obey them. She went often to church, she worked hard, she nursed the sick in the village and gave a helping hand wherever she could. Once when some people from another village came fleeing to Domremy because they had been driven from their homes by a band of raiding soldiers Jeanne gave up her bed to one of the poor fugitives. She had always been a favourite in the village because of her sweet temper and her happy face, but in these years when she was growing from a child into a maiden every one loved her and spoke well of her. She was quick and active and strong, and the voices she listened to did not make her dreamy or idle. She seemed to gain grace and dignity of bearing from her saintly guides, but she was still a peasant maid, downright in her speech and manners, ignorant of book-learning, but with much sound common sense and native wit.

The years went on and gradually Jeanne became used to the thought of herself as the saviour of France, though always she shrank in pain and horror from the thought of leaving her quiet home and taking so heavy a charge upon herself. But she was ready to do God's will, and when she thought of the plight of her unhappy country she longed for the day when she might begin her work, even though she knew it would lead her swiftly to her death. She grew restless, looking for a way and finding none. The curé, to whom she told her secret in confession, had no encouragement to give her; and, later, when she confided in some village friends they laughed and mocked at her. Her father, who perhaps had heard some rumours of the voices that spoke to her, dreamed that he saw her leave the village in company with some men-at-arms. "In that case," he said to his sons, "you must drown her, or I will." There was no one to whom she could look for help or sympathy; if she entered on this great mission she must enter on it alone and unaided.

By the beginning of 1428 Jeanne believed that the voices were urging her to action. "Go to the Dauphin," they said, "and tell him you are sent by God to deliver him from his enemies and lead him to be crowned at Rheims."

Yet what could she do, a girl of sixteen, poor and without friends? Charles the Dauphin was at Chinon, four hundred and fifty miles away, and much of the land that must be travelled to reach him was in the hands of the Duke of Burgundy, who was in league with the English. Jeanne did not expect a miracle by means of which she would be in some wonderful manner carried to Chinon. She was a plain, practical peasant girl, and her common sense told her that if she wished to make the journey she must find herself a horse and a guide. So she set her wits to work.

The nearest town held for the Dauphin was Vaucouleurs, twelve miles from Domremy. Its governor was Robert de Baudricourt, who was well known throughout the district. Jeanne had heard of him as a rough, blunt soldier, the last person to sympathize with a tale such as she had to tell him. Yet Baudricourt was, she saw clearly, the person to whom she must go. He could, if he would, send her on her way.

The first thing to do then was to get to Vaucouleurs. Jeanne remembered that she had a cousin living at Little Burey, close by the town. This cousin had married a wheelwright named Lassois who had always been friendly and kind to Jeanne. She begged him now to ask her to his house for a time, and he agreed, giving as a reason that his wife was ill and needed help. In May, Jeanne went to Little Burey, and from there she persuaded Lassois to go with her to Baudricourt at Vaucouleurs.

Jeanne, in the plain red dress that the peasant girls of that district wore, and Lassois in his working-man's garb gained little attention from the men-at-arms who were gathered in the courtyard of the castle. When they asked to see the Governor they were met with laughter and rough jests. Jeanne bore herself calmly and steadfastly; she was not easily put out, and she was so intent on her purpose that she took little notice of gibes. Her good temper and her frank country ways won over the men, and at last she was brought before Baudricourt.

She had come, she told him, with a message. Voices had told her that she was to save France, and she must go to the Dauphin at Chinon. Would Baudricourt help her and would he send to Charles and say, "Guard yourself well, and do not offer battle to your foes, for the Lord will send you succour by next mid-Lent"?

Baudricourt listened, almost as much astonished as he was amused, and when the maid had finished he and the men around him laughed long and loudly. Here was a fine thing they had heard! This slip of a girl was proposing to take a hand in a war between two great kingdoms that had striven together for years, and neither, for all its power and all its valiant fighting-men, had been able to tread the other down. And she was going to "save France"! Little wonder that they laughed!

"Go home," said the jovial Baudricourt, not unkindly; "get back to your sewing and such-like maid's work. Put all this nonsense out of your head and come not to me with such tales. Box her ears," he said, turning to Lassois, "and send her back to her father." And they all laughed again.

Jeanne seemed scarcely to hear the laughter and the ridicule.

"Will you not send my message to the Dauphin?" she said. "It is a message from God, of whom the Dauphin holds his kingdom, though it is given by a poor girl, and God wills that he should have it."

Baudricourt laughed louder than ever. "There would be scant reward for the bringer of that message, I trow," he said, "save to be soused in the moat as a saucy jester. Get you home, my girl."

Jeanne and her companion were led out of the castle by the men-at-arms, while gibes and laughter and mocking cries followed them. But the girl held herself fearlessly and looked not the least cast down. She was doing the will of those who had sent her. They knew she had done her best, and they would help her when the right time came.

She went home and took up her old life, working in the cottage and in the fields. She spoke openly now of her mission and of the voices that were guiding her, and the people of Domremy for the most part believed that in Jeanne would be seen the fulfilment of the old prophecy they all had heard that a maid should save France. Even her father no longer opposed her, and, little by little, it came to be understood in the village that when the right time came she would go forth on her mission.

There was indeed great need that some help should come to the unhappy country, for the English were pushing their way farther and farther southward. In July a small force was sent against the district round about Vaucouleurs and the people of Domremy left their homes and took refuge at Neufchateau, six miles away. The force did little except lay waste tracts of the country, and after about a fortnight the villagers returned to their roofless cottages and blackened fields. The war became more real and terrible to them after that, and they listened to Jeanne's message more eagerly.

By October the English had taken some of the smaller towns on the Loire and were besieging Orleans, and in January Jeanne once more set out to Vaucouleurs. She went in sorrow, shrinking from the fate that was before her, hating the work she had to do. "I would sooner be torn by wild horses than do this thing did not my Lord command it," she said. She knew that she would never see her home again. She said many times that little more than a year of life was to be given her to do her work. But her faith in her mission never wavered and she kept a brave heart and a cheerful face through all her trouble. Only on the last morning she wept as she looked on the old familiar places and the faces of her friends. She dared not say good-bye to Hauviette, who had been her closest friend since they were tiny children together, and she stole away in the grey morning while the other girl was sleeping.

She stayed with her cousin at Little Burey and for three weeks she tried to persuade Baudricourt to send her to Chinon, but he still treated her message with derision.

"I must be with the Dauphin by mid-Lent," she said, "though I wear my legs down to the knees. No one in the world can recover the kingdom of France, nor hath the Dauphin any succour save from myself; though I would liefer be sewing beside my poor mother. For this deed is not convenient to my station. Yet go I must, and this deed I must do because my Lord wills it."

At last her perseverance and her determination won her friends. The first was a young man-at-arms who knew her father and mother. He swore to go with her and help her in every way he could. Then the Duke of Lorraine heard of her and sent to her to come to him. He believed her story and gave her money to help her on her way; and at length Baudricourt, too, came over to her side. Perhaps he thought that things were so bad it was well to try any remedy, even so wild a one as this project of the maid's; perhaps the faith the people had in Jeanne moved him in her favour. He wrote to the Dauphin telling him of the peasant girl and her mission, and he provided her with an escort of two men-at-arms and two servants. The people of Vaucouleurs subscribed to buy her a horse and Baudricourt gave her a sword. She took the dress of a page because it was more convenient than her peasant girl's garb, and on February the twenty-third, in the dusk of the evening the party rode out toward Chinon.

The rest of Jeanne's story belongs to the history of England and of France. It is not a story of which either nation can be proud, but for Jeanne it is full of glory. She followed faithfully where her voices led her, through danger and cruel suffering, until the sad day when she died bravely in her country's cause.

Podcast #151 Marie Antoinette

Until recent years, the only thing I knew about Marie Antoinette is that she lost her head after telling starving peasants, "Let them eat cake." I viewed her as frivolous, extravagant and clueless.

But, like everything else, the more I dig, the more I find how much I don't know and how distorted and incomplete my views are. Today I am going to share a story from an 1892 book called *Mothers of Great Men and Women* by Laura Holloway[70] that focuses on Marie Antoinette as a wife and a mother where you may see her, as I did, through fresh eyes which has caused me to look at her with new respect and compassion.

I was going to say more about the spirit of the mobs of that time, how cruel they became, wondering if we are seeing a trend toward that here in America today....but I'll save that conversation for another time.

But I do want to call attention to just one more interesting little point since we are also studying the American Revolution this month I just hadn't made the connection myself before. When we sent over our statesmen to appeal to the king and queen of France for help, we were appealing to this very young and newly crowned couple.... Marie Antoinette and her husband, Louis XVI. Their story is intertwined with ours.

Now the story.

> The world has never seen and never can see a sadder and more pathetic biography than that of Marie Antoinette. Here is a woman supported through such experiences as make the least emotional of us shudder even now to think of, and we wonder how she retained her reason and her trust in God. In other tragedies there is an interlude of light and hope; in this one there is none. From the discovery and arrest of the fugitive royal family at Varennes to the scaffold that faced the gardens of the Tuileries, there is no respite, no relief, no ray of hope, no parenthesis of pity. From palace to prison, from prison to dungeon, from the Tuileries to the Temple, from the Temple to the Conciergerie, from the Conciergerie to the common felons' prison and the guillotine—this is the cumulative story of the royal victim, these the steps of the ladder that bore her heroic footsteps from earth to heaven. Marie Antoinette Josephe Jeanne was the youngest daughter of Francis, eventually the Emperor of Germany and of Maria Theresa more generally known as the Empress-Queen who bore sixteen children. She was born on the 2nd of November, 1755. Her parents preferred greatly to their gorgeous palace at Vienna a smaller one which they possessed in the neighborhood where they could cultivate rural and domestic tastes and bring up their children healthily.
>
> In this quiet home Marie Antoinette passed a happy childhood. Her beauty, intelligence, and affectionate disposition made her the favorite of her father, and the first sorrow she ever knew was at his death, which occurred in 1765, before she was ten

years old. He was going to Innspruck on some business, and his carriage was drawn up in the courtyard of his palace. Before starting he asked for his little daughter, that he might kiss her goodby. "Adieu, my darling child. Papa wished to press you once more to his heart," are the words ascribed to him. If so, they were prophetic, for he was seized with illness at Innspruck, where he died, and they never saw each other again.

The superintendence of her vast empire occupied a far larger share of his widow Maria Theresa's attention than the education of her children. But as Marie Antoinette grew in beauty and attractiveness, the empress-queen, her mother, saw a prospect of cementing more closely her recent alliance with France by a marriage between Marie Antoinette and the Dauphin of France, grandson of the reigning King, Louis XV. For this purpose she made proficiency in French the chief aim in the young girl's education. Metastasis taught her Italian; and Gluck gave her lessons on the harpsichord.

Marie Antoinette was perhaps too fond of play to apply steadily to her studies. At any rate, she herself regretted sincerely in after life her own want of literary information and culture, and endeavored to make up her deficiencies by taking lessons in more than one accomplishment during the first years of her residence at Versailles. She felt, when afterward Queen, her inferiority in culture to the ladies of the old French noblesse, and once exclaimed sadly, "What a resource amid the casualties of life is a well-cultivated mind! One can then be one's own companion, and find society in one's own thoughts."

Such, then, was Marie Antoinette, when, at the age of fifteen, she went to Paris and became the bride of the Dauphin, afterward Louis XVI. On the day on which she set out from Vienna, her mother had written the following letter to her future son-in-law:

"Your bride, my dear Dauphin, has just left me. I do hope that she will cause you happiness. I have brought her up with the design that she should do so, because I have for some time foreseen that she would share your destiny.

"I have inspired her with an eager desire to do her duty to you, with a tender attachment to your person, with a resolution to be attentive to think and do everything which may please you. I have also been most careful to enjoin upon her a tender devotion toward the Master of all Sovereigns, being thoroughly persuaded that we are but badly providing for the welfare of the nations which are intrusted to us when we fail in our duty to Him who breaks sceptres and overthrows thrones according to His pleasure.

"I say, then, to you, my dear Dauphin, as I say to my daughter: 'Cultivate your duties toward God. Seek to cause the happiness of the people over whom you will reign (it will be too soon, come when it may). Love the king, your grandfather; be humane to him; be always accessible to the unfortunate. If you behave in this manner, it is impossible that happiness can fail to be your lot.' My daughter will love you, I am certain, because I know her. But the more that I answer to you for her affection and for her anxiety to please you, the more earnestly do I entreat you to vow to her the most sincere attachment.

"Farewell, my dear Dauphin. May you be happy. I am bathed in tears."

The earlier years of the married life of Marie Antoinette were frivolous rather than happy. Her husband treated her with respectful coldness, for his nature was not demonstrative of attention. He had no idea of wounding her feelings, but he did not see her society in private, and had no perception that marriage was to her, as a warmhearted woman, anything more than the matter of convenience and acquiescence that it was to himself.

Married at the early age of fourteen years and a half to a youth only a few years older than herself, the pair was childless for eight and a half years after their union. Louis XV died on the 10th of May, 1774 and the Dauphin and Dauphiness became King and Queen of France. There seemed little prospect of a family, and this disappointment was keenly felt by the queen. Her natural desire for children of her own was greatly increased when her sister-in-law, the Countess d'Artois, presented her husband with a son. She treated the young mother with sisterly affection, but she could not restrain her feelings on the subject when writing to her mother, and she expressed candidly the extreme pain she suffered "at thus seeing an heir to the throne who was not her own child." At a pavilion her husband had given her at her own request, about a mile from the palace of Versailles, she sought to quench her grief in a constant whirl of pleasurable excitement.

Little did the yearning but giddy young queen imagine that she was helping by her extravagance to bring on that revolution of which hatred to rank and wealth was the spark that was to consume herself and her husband and all her dearest friends.

Her joy at the prospect of having a child was fully shared by her husband. All his coldness and apathy seemed to vanish, and he wrote himself both to her mother and her brother Joseph, the Emperor. The news created equal joy at Paris and Vienna, and the poor young queen showed her grateful sense of happiness by liberal gifts to the poor, and by founding a hospital for women in a similar condition as her own.

On the 19th of December, 1778, she gave birth to a princess, who was named Maria Theresa, in honor of her imperial grandmother. She alone of the four children of Marie Antoinette lived to maturity and a good old age.

"Boys will come after girls," wrote Maria Theresa to her daughter. The birth of the princess came near being the death of the queen. By the barbarous custom of that time in France, every one, even the rabble, who could gain an entrance into the chamber, was admitted to be witness of the royal birth. The heat was so intense that the queen became insensible and had to be bled in the foot. The king rushed to the windows and with all his strength, got them open. His was the voice that whispered tenderly to her that she had been delivered of a daughter. She herself was not disappointed. When the nurse brought her the babe, she whispered, "Poor little thing; you are not what was desired, but you shall not be the less dear to me. A son would have belonged to the state; you will be my own: you shall have all my care, you shall share my happiness and sweeten my vexations."

Besides the gifts to the poor and the hospital which were made before the birth, the happy mother now sent large sums of money to the prisons to release poor debtors, gave dowries to one hundred poor maidens, applied to the chief officers of the army and navy to send her a list of veterans worthy of reward, and to the clergy of Paris for the names of worthy objects for her bounty. She also settled pensions on a number of poor children who were born on the same day as the princess, one of whom, who owed her education to this pension, became known to fame as Madame Mars, the greatest of comic actresses in Paris.

In the spring of 1780 Marie Antoinette was shocked by the news of her mother's death. They had been much attached to each other since Marie became a queen, and had corresponded regularly upon important subjects. Maria Theresa gave far more prudent advice to her daughter than did the haughty Catharine of Russia, who once wrote to her that kings and queens should do as they pleased and pursue their own plans, regardless of the interest of their dogs of subjects.

On the morning of October 2nd, 1782, a son and heir to the throne blessed the love of Louis XVI and Marie Antoinette. The king, whose affection for her had steadily grown in intensity since she began to have children, would not allow her life to be endangered this time by a crowd of strangers in her apartments. He forbade any one but himself to announce to her the sex of the child, and it was with a heart full of joy and pride that he told her that their hopes of an heir were fulfilled.

The child was not destined to live. The Dauphin, whose sad lot and early death from neglect and illtreatment form one of the tragedies of that awful series, was Marie Antoinette's third child, not yet born. The elder son and second child was sickly, and had spinal complaint from his birth. He had no stamina to support him through the ordinary ailments of children, and he died on June 4th, 1789, when not yet seven years old. On the 27th of March, 1785, the future desolate and slowly murdered Dauphin came into the world, which was for him a prison and a slaughterhouse, a habitation of cruelty, and the grave of all his young affections. The reader of history thanks the justice of a crime-permitting Providence, that his keeper, Simon the shoemaker, who starved him and beat him and kept him in filth and darkness for the last three years of his young life, was carried to the guillotine before the child-victim's death.

The Princess Sophie Helene Beatrix was the fourth and last child of Louis XVI and Marie Antoinette. She was born on the 9th of July, 1786, was a sickly child and died on the 9th of June, 1787, aged eleven months.

We have Marie Antoinette before us at the beginning of the Revolution as the mother of two children only, the Princess Royal, now nine, and the Dauphin, seven years old, the two others having died. She made it her happiness and her duty to study the dispositions of the young prince and princess. Her mind was bent on training her son not as a common child, but as one who was heir to the throne of a great and illustrious nation.

In a letter to Madame de Tourzel dated July 25th, 1789, the mother writes:

"I have always accustomed my children to have great confidence in me, and when they have done wrong, to tell me themselves; and then, when I scold them, this enables me to appear pained and afflicted at what they have done rather than angry. My son cannot read, and he is very slow at learning; but he is too giddy to apply. He has no pride in his heart, and I am very anxious that he should continue to feel so. Our children always learn soon enough what they are. He is very fond of his sister, and has a good heart. Whenever anything gives him pleasure, whether it be going anywhere or that any one gives him anything, his first movement always is to ask that his sister may have the same. He is lighthearted by nature. It is necessary for his health that he should be a great deal in the open air; and I think it is better to let him play and work in the garden on the terrace, than to take him longer walks. The exercise which children take in running about and playing in the open air is much more healthy than forcing them to walk, which often makes their backs ache."

The letter proves her to have been a good, a prudent, and a watchful mother. Poor little Louis! A far different fate awaited him from what she fondly hoped for. The Committee of Public Safety decreed that the young Capet, as they called him, should be placed in solitary confinement, under the charge of the brutal shoemaker Simon, who had private orders to get ride of him by degrees. It was night when the officers of the Committee came to carry him away. His mother flung her arms around him, and resisted all efforts to tear him from her, exclaiming, *"Tuez moi donc d'abord"*—"Then kill me first." They only prevailed by threatening to kill the child, when she relaxed her hold and sank exhausted with the struggle. The unhappy Dauphin was shut up for nearly two years before his merciful release by death, in solitude, without employment, without human sympathy or kindness, denied even the light and air. When the door was opened it was to place a flagon of dirty water and a crust of bread for him. He was never washed and his clothes and linen were never changed. It was a slow death in a living tomb. His limbs became rigid, his mind vacant and insensible. After his keeper was executed for his other crimes, his persecutors relented, but it was too late. The celebrated physician, Dersault, was sent to his lowly bedside. His mother's image—that mother from whom he had been so cruelly separated two years before, when she was doomed to the guillotine, but whom he was not perhaps to rejoin in everlasting reunion—was the last that filled his dying vision. The physician asked him if he suffered much. "Oh, yes, I suffer still," he answered, "but much less than I did, the music is so beautiful." "On what side do you hear this music?" "There, on high; listen! listen!" Then, after a brief silence, his eyes kindled with the heavenly light, and he exclaimed, with the rapture of an enfranchised and departing soul, "Amidst all the voices, I have recognized that of my mother." He waved his hand, wafted a kiss to her, and sank back dead.

The opening of the year 1789 was the beginning of troubles for Marie Antoinette. Hitherto she had been alternately lauded and insulted by the artisans of Paris. Now the very refuse of humanity were to fling their dirt at her. Hers is one of those characters that are washed and made white by passing through great tribulation. All that was frivolous and extravagant in her conduct disappeared forever, and the heroic queen was only less admirable than the devoted wife and mother. The vilest slanders were circulated against the queen, one of them being that she had a mine ready to blow up the Parliament of Paris, or National Assembly.

On the 14th of July the cry "To the Bastile!" was echoed from mouth to mouth by a drunken mob along the banks of the Seine. This was the third day of the insurrection and they stormed the iron and stone forms of the Bastile, and murdered the governor and military that defended it, who had been taken by surprise and could make little resistance. At midnight couriers arrived at Versailles to apprise the king and queen of the terrible aspect of affairs.

On the 6th of October, 1789, when the mob insisted that she should make her appearance, she came forth on the balcony, holding the Dauphin with one hand and the Princess with the other. "No children!" was the angry cry. She led them away, and reappeared alone. Even the insensate crowd was astonished at her calmness and courage, and with true French fickleness burst into rounds of applause.

On the night of the 13th of April, 1790, the king, after vainly looking for her in her own apartments, found her in the Dauphin's nursery, holding him in her arms. "Madame," said Louis, "I have been looking for you everywhere, and you have caused me much uneasiness." "Sire," replied Marie Antoinette, "I am at my post."

When Versailles was attacked, Louis tried to induce his wife to fly with the children, but she refused to leave her husband, declaring that her place was by his side, and that, as a daughter of Maria Theresa of Austria, she had no fear of death. It was a sorrowful journey which the king, now accompanied by the queen and his children, took back to Paris. The procession was painfully slow, and as no food had been provided for the journey the little Dauphin cried from hunger. The good mother, who never shed a selfish tear, wept at the sufferings of her child. She begged him to be patient, and the little fellow ceased complaining. "Mamma," he said, when they reached the Tuileries, which had been neglected, and whose chambers were dismantled, "how bad everything looks here!" "My boy," she replied, "Louis XIV lived her comfortably enough."

It would be beside our purpose to stain our pages with the nameless and inhuman crimes of the Reign of Terror. Let us cling to the queen-woman, true and noble to the last, who is so soon to leave us. A little plot of ground was railed off in the garden of the Tuileries for the Dauphin's amusement, and one of her favorite recreations was to watch him working at the flower-beds with his little rake and hoe, although neither she nor he were left for a moment without the grenadiers of the city guard, who watched her as though she were a criminal already condemned. Privacy and rest were never to be hers again in this world. "The king," said Mirabeau, "has but one man about him, and that is his wife." More than one attempt was made to murder her. "If my death only secures the throne to my son, I shall willingly die." Even in their imprisonment in the

Temple they had at least for a time the consolation of each other's society, and that of their children. But they were soon separated, and worse than the bitterness of death was the separation of the wife and mother, first from her husband, then from each of the children.

On the 11th of December, 1792, the mock trial of the king took place. On the 21st of January, 1793, he met death like a man.

Marie Antoinette, now a widow still young, but with locks white as snow through sorrow, was removed to solitary imprisonment and the last inhuman cruelty that can be inflicted on a mother fell upon her in the seizure of her darling son. Dearly did she love him, and when, while they were yet together, her friends proposed a plan of escape, she refused the offer, and wrote: "The interest of my son is my sole guide; and whatever happiness I might find in being out of this place, I cannot consent to separate myself from him…I could enjoy nothing if I were to leave my children."

And when, on the night of the 3rd of July, the little king was sleeping, and, as we have already told, was snatched from her embrace, the last words which the unhappy child of misfortune was ever to hear on earth from his poor mother's lips were these: "My child, they are taking you from me; never forget the mother who loves you tenderly, and never forget God! Be good, gentle and honest, and your father will look down on you from heaven and bless you!"

To the Princess Elizabeth, her true sister in affliction, and who was soon to share the same fate, she wrote from the common prison in which she was herded with the lowest felons, her last letter, dated October 16th, 4:30 a.m, in which she said:

"It is to you, my sister, that I write for the last time. I have just been condemned, not to a shameful death, for such is only for criminals, but to go and rejoin your brother. Innocent like him, I hope to show the same firmness in my last moments. I am calm, as one is when one's conscience reproaches one with nothing. I feel profound sorrow in leaving my poor children: you know that I only lived for them and for you, my good and tender sister. You who out of love have sacrificed everything to be with us, in what a position do I leave you!

"I have learned from the proceedings at my trial that my daughter was separated from you. Alas! Poor child; I do not venture to write to her; she would not receive my letter. I do not even know whether this will reach you. Do you receive my blessing for both of them. I hope that one day, when they are older, they may be able to rejoin you, and to enjoy to the full your tender care. Let them both think of the lesson which I have never ceased to impress upon them, that the principles and the exact performance of their duties are the chief foundation of life; and then mutual affection and confidence in one another will constitute its happiness.

"Let my daughter feel that at her age she ought always to aid her brother by the advice which her greater experience and her affection may inspire her to give him. And let my son in his turn render to his sister all the care and all the services which affection can inspire. Let them, in short, both feel that, in whatever positions they may be placed, they will never be truly happy but through their union. Let them follow our example. In our own misfortunes, how much comfort has our affection for one another afforded us! And in times of happiness, we have enjoyed that doubly from being able to share it with a friend; and where can one find friends more tender and more united than in one's own family?

"Let my son never forget the last words of his father, which I repeat emphatically: let him never seek to avenge our deaths. I have to speak of one thing" [referring to the depositions which the captive little son had been compelled by his persecutors to sign, containing accusations against his aunt and his mother] "which is very painful to my heart; I know how much pain the child must have caused you. Forgive him, dear sister; think of his age, and how easy it is to make a child say whatever one wishes, especially when he does not understand it. It will come to pass one day, I hope, that he will better feel the value of your kindness and of your tender affection for both of them…I beg pardon of all the vexations which, without intending it, I may have caused you. I pardon all my enemies the evils they have done me. I bid farewell to my aunts, and to all my brothers and sisters. I had friends. The idea of being forever separated from them and from all their troubles is one of the greatest sorrows that I suffer in dying. Let them at least know that to my latest moment I thought of them.

"Farewell, my good and tender sister. May this letter reach you. Think always of me; I embrace you with all my heart, as I do my poor, dear children. My God, how heartrending it is to leave them forever! Farewell! Farewell!" Her apprehensions proved well founded. The letter never reached her sister-in-law, but fell into the hands of Fouguier, who preserved it among his special papers. Had one spark of humanity survived in the monsters of the Reign of Terror, they would have respected the doomed prisoner's last wishes and last words.

Those almost dying thoughts and anxieties, let it be remembered to her immortal honor, were not for herself, but for her children and her friends. It was dark when she began the letter, but now the faint beams of sunrise stole through the narrow window of her cell. She lay down on her straw bed and tried to sleep. At seven the executioner came in. The streets were thronged by that Parisian mob, whose faces, lurid with cruelty, were like a vision of pandemonium. She was used to their looks and their revilings, and minded them no more. Other women, and strong men also, have gone stark, raving mad at one tenth part of the sufferings this sublime woman endured. Yet the wounds were deep, and had left their scars in the white hair, and the wan, furrowed face, upon which still those lines of beauty lingered which had evoked the praises of Europe.

A few weeks before her death she struck her head against a door in following her jailer. Being asked if she was hurt, she answered, "No, nothing can hurt me now." An English lady saw her in her dungeon for any one who asked was allowed to look at her, on the one condition of expressing no sympathy, and said in a letter: "She was sitting on an old worn-out chair made of straw, which scarcely supported her weight. Dressed in a gown which had once been white, her attitude bespoke the immensity of her grief."

In a common cart, seated on a bare plank, the executioner by her side holding the cords with which her hands were already bound, she was borne to the place of execution. Her last words showed the true lady and the queen. In descending from the cart she had stepped on the executioner's food. "Excuse me, sir," she said, "I did not do it on purpose," and she added, "Please make haste." In a few moments all was over.

So perished, by a death which as she nobly said was to her not ignominious because she was no criminal, one of the very noblest wives and mothers. She had never injured or borne malice against a single human being.

Benevolence was native to her soul, and her charities were only bounded by her means. She had those virtues of purity, fidelity, courage, and affection which exalt humanity and redeem our fallen race. She was an angel whom accident had put under the power of devils. If families are reunited in a brighter world than this, there is no reunion that heavenly spirits would more gladly gaze upon than that of these poor Capets, King and Queen of France.

One more victim from that family was still to follow her—the saintly, meek and self-sacrificing aunt. Madame Elizabeth, as the king's sister was called since titles had been done away, committed the orphan children to God's holy keeping, and went calmly from those who, in the words of Socrates, falsely call themselves judges upon earth, to the presence of eternal justice. Her life and character are a study worthy of a volume by itself. How little does the world appreciate the quiet life-service of such an aunt and sister as the Princess Elizabeth had proved herself to her brother Louis and his wife and children.

Young and beautiful, she had chosen to share their sorrows when she might have wedded nobly or passed a brilliant life in the court of other brothers, two of whom were in turn Emperors. At Vienna the Reign of Terror could not have made her a victim and a martyr, but she was one of those sweet women of whom, let us thank God, there are still many in a selfish world, who have no thought of self, who forego all thoughts of marrying and giving in marriage to tend a brother's or a sister's little ones, and who resemble in this our blessed Saviour, who came "not to be ministered to, but to minister and to give His life a ransom for many."

Podcast #152 Henry Wadsworth Longfellow

Henry Wadsworth Longfellow is rightly known as the children's poet. I'm sure most of you are familiar with his Midnight Ride of Paul Revere or that you sang his I Heard the Bells on Christmas Day during the Christmas season.

In the little sample I'll share with you today, he says that his favorite poem was Evangeline. In tomorrow's podcast I'll tell you the true story of Evangeline as told by her adopted mother, which includes a story of Canada for this month's topic and is so fitting with today's headlines where we hear of exiles and immigrants and families torn apart.

I can't help but wonder if he loved Evangeline because it was reflective of the sorrows of his own life. It's a story of two young people in love who are suddenly and cruelly separated. Longfellow's first wife, after they had been married for only a short time, died while they were on a trip abroad in Europe. He remarried and had several children and one day his wife was sealing packets of their children's hair as keepsakes and a drop of the sealing wax fell on her dress and ignited it on fire. Longfellow was in the other room and heard her screaming. He rushed in to help her, extinguishing the flames with his own body, burning himself badly in the process. But the injuries were too severe and she died.

Adding to that sorrow, his son was wounded in a Civil War battle. It was when he rushed off to his side that he felt the gloom of the world around him and penned the words I Heard the Bells on Christmas Day and resolved, in spite of all his sorrows and anguish, "God is not dead, nor doth He sleep."

I'm going to link a book in Internet Archive called *The Children's Longfellow*[71] that has a section of Evangeline as well as some of his other most popular works. One of my favorites is the Village Blacksmith that reminds us of the way our lives our forged daily by our deeds and thoughts. You can almost hear the pounding of the anvil in the rhythm. Let me share it:

> Under a spreading chestnut-tree
> The village smithy stands,
> The smith, a mighty man is he,
> With large and sinewy hands;
> And the muscles of his brawny arms
> Are strong as iron bands.
> His hair is crisp, and black, and long,
> His face is like the tan;
> His brow is wet with honest sweat,
> He earns whate'er he can,
> And looks the whole world in the face,
> For he owes not any man.
>
> Week in, week out, from morn till night,

You can hear his bellows blow;
You can hear him swing his heavy sledge,
With measured beat and slow,
Like a sexton ringing the village bell,
When the evening sun is low.

And children coming home from school
Look in at the open door;
They love to see the flaming forge,
And hear the bellows roar,
And catch the burning sparks that fly
Like chaff from a threshing-floor.

He goes on Sunday to the church,
And sits among his boys;
He hears the parson pray and preach,
He hears his daughter's voice,
Singing in the village choir,
And it makes his heart rejoice.

It sounds to him like her mother's voice,
Singing in Paradise!
He needs must think of her once more,
How in the grave she lies;
And with his hard, rough hand he wipes
A tear out of his eyes.

Toiling,—rejoicing,—sorrowing,
Onward through life he goes;
Each morning sees some task begin,
Each evening sees it close
Something attempted, something done,
Has earned a night's repose.

Thanks, thanks to thee, my worthy friend,
For the lesson thou hast taught!
Thus at the flaming forge of life
Our fortunes must be wrought;
Thus on its sounding anvil shaped
Each burning deed and thought.

There is also a poem called The Building of the Ship. I don't know about you, but I am so sad at what I see happening in our country today; the divisions, the ignorance, the lack of understanding of our story and the sacrifices others made to gift us what we have. In a few days as we begin Month 6 we'll be talking about our New Nation and especially the gift of freedom. This final stanza of Longfellow's poems stirs my heart as I think about these things.

Thou, too, sail on, O Ship of State!
Sail on, O Union, strong and great!
Humanity with all its fears,
With all the hopes of future years,
Is hanging breathless on thy fate!
We know what Master laid thy keel,
What Workmen wrought thy ribs of steel,
Who made each mast, and sail, and rope,
What anvils rang, what hammers beat,
In what a forge and what a heat
Were shaped the anchors of thy hope!
Fear not each sudden sound and shock,
'Tis of the wave and not the rock;
'Tis but the flapping of the sail,
And not a rent made by the gale!
In spite of rock and tempest's roar,
In spite of false lights on the shore,
Sail on, nor fear to breast the sea!
Our hearts, our hopes, are all with thee,
Our hearts, our hopes, our prayers, our tears,
Our faith triumphant o'er our fears,
Are all with thee, — are all with thee!

And now I want to share today's sampler. In month 2, I shared the story of Edward Bok from Holland who, as a young man, visited the great and noble men of his time and shared his experiences with them. One of those men was Longfellow and this is his account[72] of the day spent with him that gives you a wonderful glimpse into the kind and warm heart of the poet.

When Edward Bok stood before the home of Longfellow, he realized that he was to see the man around whose head the boy's youthful reading had cast a sort of halo. And when he saw the head itself he had a feeling that he could see the halo. No kindlier pair of eyes ever looked at a boy, as, with a smile, "the white Mr. Longfellow," as Mr. Howells had called him, held out his hand.

"I am very glad to see you, my boy," were his first words, and with them he won the boy. Edward smiled back at the poet, and immediately the two were friends.

"I have been taking a walk this beautiful morning," he said next, "and am a little late getting at my mail. Suppose you come in and sit at my desk with me, and we will see what the postman has brought. He brings me so many good things, you know."

"Now, here is a little girl," he said, as he sat down at the desk with the boy beside him, "who wants my autograph and a 'sentiment.' What sentiment, I wonder, shall I send her?"

"Why not send her 'Let us, then, be up and doing'?" suggested the boy. "That's what I should like if I were she."

"Should you, indeed?" said Longfellow. "That is a good suggestion. Now, suppose you recite it off to me, so that I shall not have to look it up in my books, and I will write as you recite. But slowly; you know I am an old man, and write slowly."

Edward thought it strange that Longfellow himself should not know his own great words without looking them up. But he recited the four lines, so familiar to every schoolboy, and when the poet had finished writing them, he said:

"Good! I see you have a memory. Now, suppose I copy these lines once more for the little girl, and give you this copy? Then you can say, you know, that you dictated my own poetry to me."

Of course Edward was delighted, and Longfellow gave him the sheet as it is here:

> Let us, then, be up and doing,
> with a heart for any fate,
> Still achieving, still pursuing,
> Learn to labor and to wait.
>
> Henry W. Longfellow

Then, as the fine head bent down to copy the lines once more, Edward ventured to say to him:

"I should think it would keep you busy if you did this for every one who asked you."

"Well," said the poet, "you see, I am not so busy a man as I was some years ago, and I shouldn't like to disappoint a little girl; should you?"

As he took up his letters again, he discovered five more requests for his autograph. At each one he reached into a drawer in his desk, took a card, and wrote his name on it.

"There are a good many of these every day," said Longfellow, "but I always like to do this little favor. It is so little to do, to write your name on a card; and if I didn't do it some boy or girl might be looking, day by day, for the postman and be disappointed. I only wish I could write my name better for them. You see how I break my letters? That's because I never took pains with my writing when I was a boy. I don't think I should get a high mark for penmanship if I were at school, do you?"

"I see you get letters from Europe," said the boy, as Longfellow opened an envelope with a foreign stamp on it.

"Yes, from all over the world," said the poet. Then, looking at the boy quickly, he said: "Do you collect postage-stamps?"

Edward said he did.

"Well, I have some right here, then," and going to a drawer in a desk he took out a bundle of letters, and cut out the postage-stamps and gave them to the boy.

"There's one from the Netherlands. There's where I was born," Edward ventured to say.

"In the Netherlands? Then you are a real Dutchman. Well! Well!" he said, laying down his pen. "Can you read Dutch?"

The boy said he could.

"Then," said the poet, "you are just the boy I am looking for." And going to a bookcase behind him he brought out a book, and handing it to the boy, he said, his eyes laughing: "Can you read that?"

It was an edition of Longfellow's poems in Dutch.

"Yes, indeed," said Edward. "These are your poems in Dutch."

"That's right," he said. "Now, this is delightful. I am so glad you came. I received this book last week, and although I have been in the Netherlands, I cannot speak or read Dutch. I wonder whether you would read a poem to me and let me hear how it sounds."

So Edward took "The Old Clock on the Stairs," and read it to him.

The poet's face beamed with delight. "That's beautiful," he said, and then quickly added: "I mean the language, not the poem."

"Now," he went on, "I'll tell you what we'll do: we'll strike a bargain. We Yankees are great for bargains, you know. If you will read me 'The Village Blacksmith' you can sit in that chair there made out of the wood of the old spreading chestnut-tree, and I'll take you out and show you where the old shop stood. Is that a bargain?"

Edward assured him it was. He sat in the chair of wood and leather, and read to the poet several of his own poems in a language in which, when he wrote them, he never dreamed they would ever be printed. He was very quiet. Finally he said: "It seems so odd, so very odd, to hear something you know so well sound so strange."

"It's a great compliment, though, isn't it, sir?" asked the boy.

"Ye-es," said the poet slowly. "Yes, yes," he added quickly. "It is, my boy, a very great compliment."

"Ah," he said, rousing himself, as a maid appeared, "that means luncheon, or rather," he added, "it means dinner, for we have dinner in the old New England fashion, in the middle of the day. I am all alone to-day, and you must keep me company; will you? Then afterward we'll go and take a walk, and I'll show you Cambridge. It is such a beautiful old town, even more beautiful, I sometimes think, when the leaves are off the trees.

"Come," he said, "I'll take you up-stairs, and you can wash your hands in the room where George Washington slept. And comb your hair, too, if you want to," he added; "only it isn't the same comb that he used."

To the boyish mind it was an historic breaking of bread, that midday meal with

328

Longfellow.

"Can you say grace in Dutch?" he asked, as they sat down; and the boy did.

"Well," the poet declared, "I never expected to hear that at my table. I like the sound of it."

Then while the boy told all that he knew about the Netherlands, the poet told the boy all about his poems. Edward said he liked "Hiawatha."

"So do I," he said. "But I think I like 'Evangeline' better. Still," he added, "neither one is as good as it should be. But those are the things you see afterward so much better than you do at the time."

It was a great event for Edward when, with the poet nodding and smiling to every boy and man he met, and lifting his hat to every woman and little girl, he walked through the fine old streets of Cambridge with Longfellow. At one point of the walk they came to a theatrical bill-board announcing an attraction that evening at the Boston Theatre. Skilfully the old poet drew out from Edward that sometimes he went to the theatre with his parents. As they returned to the gate of "Craigie House" Edward said he thought he would go back to Boston.

"And what have you on hand for this evening?" asked Longfellow.

Edward told him he was going to his hotel to think over the day's events.

The poet laughed and said:

"Now, listen to my plan. Boston is strange to you. Now we're going to the theatre this evening, and my plan is that you come in now, have a little supper with us, and then go with us to see the play. It is a funny play, and a good laugh will do you more good than to sit in a hotel all by yourself. Now, what do you think?"

Of course the boy thought as Longfellow did, and it was a very happy boy that evening who, in full view of the large audience in the immense theatre, sat in that box. It was, as Longfellow had said, a play of laughter, and just who laughed louder, the poet or the boy, neither ever knew.

Between the acts there came into the box a man of courtly presence, dignified and yet gently courteous.

"Ah! Phillips," said the poet, "how are you? You must know my young friend here. This is Wendell Phillips, my boy. Here is a young man who told me to-day that he was going to call on you and on Phillips Brooks to-morrow. Now you know him before he comes to you."

"I shall be glad to see you, my boy," said Mr. Phillips. "And so you are going to see Phillips Brooks? Let me tell you something about Brooks. He has a great many books in his library which are full of his marks and comments. Now, when you go to see him you ask him to let you see some of those books, and then, when he isn't looking, you put a couple of them in your pocket. They would make splendid souvenirs, and he has so many he would never miss them. You do it, and then when you come to see me tell me all about it."

And he and Longfellow smiled broadly.

An hour later, when Longfellow dropped Edward at his hotel, he had not only a wonderful day to think over but another wonderful day to look forward to as well!

He had breakfasted with Oliver Wendell Holmes; dined, supped, and been to the theatre with Longfellow; and to-morrow he was to spend with Phillips Brooks.

Boston was a great place, Edward Bok thought, as he fell asleep.

Podcast #153 The True Story of Evangeline

In the last podcast, I mentioned that Longfellow once said that Evangeline was his favorite poem that he wrote. Today I want to share the true story of Evangeline as told by her adopted mother: *Acadian Reminiscences, The True Story of Evangeline* by Felix Voorhies.[73] In the telling of the story, you are going to learn about the Acadians, a group of French families who settled in Acadia which is present-day Nova Scotia and nearby areas in Canada as well as parts of Maine. When the British scattered them, many of them relocated to Louisiana where the Acadians became known as the Cajuns—if you happen to like Cajun cooking, that's where the name came from—those French Acadians.

There are many lessons woven into this story… Here we go.

Acadian Reminiscences, depicting the True Life of Evangeline, is a story centered about the life of the Acadians whose descendants are not resident of the Teche Country.

These people lived a pure and simple life with an unbounded devotion to their religion and with an unshakable faith in their God. Their love for one another is unparalleled in the annals of human history.

The author, Judge Felix Voorhies, relates the story as it was told to him by his grandmother.

> "My native land is called Acadia. It is a cold and desolate region during winter, and snow covers the ground during several months of the year. IT is rocky, and huge and rugged stones lie strewn over the surface of the ground in many places, and one must struggle hard for a livelihood there, especially with the poor and meagre tools possessed by my people. Yet I grieve for my native land, with its rocks and snows, because I have left there a part of my heart in the graves of those I loved so well and who sleep under its sod."

And as she spoke thus, her eyes streamed with tears and emotion choked her utterance.

> "You must know, petiots, that less than a hundred years ago Acadia was a French Province, whose people lived contented and happy. The king of France sent brave officers to govern the province, and these officers treated us with the greatest kindness.

> "Our manner of living in Acadia was peculiar, the people forming, as it were, one single family. Although poor, they were honest and industrious, and they lived contented with what little they had, without envying their neighbors, and how could it be otherwise? If any one was unable to do his field work because of illness, or of some other misfortune, his neighbors flew to his assistance, and it required but a few days work, with their combined efforts to weed his field and save his crop.

> "Thus it was that, incited by noble and generous feeling, the inhabitants of the province seemed to form one single family, and not a community composed of separate families.

We lacked none of the comforts of life, and although not wealthy, we were not in want, as our wishes were few and easily satisfied.

"Plainness and simplicity of manners are the mainsprings of happiness, and he that wishes for what he may never have or acquire, must be miserable, indeed, and worthy of pity. Alas! that this simplicity of our Acadian manners should have already degenerated into extravagance and folly! Ah! The Acadians are losing, by degrees, the remembrance of the traditions and customs of the mother country, the love of gold has implanted itself in their hearts, and this will bring no happiness to them.

"In Acadia, early marriages were highly favored. No obstacle was thrown in the way of a loving couple who desired to marry. The lover accepted by the maiden obtained the ready consent of the parents, and no one dreamed of inquiring whether the lover was a man of means, or whether the destined bride brought a handsome dowry, as we are wont to do nowadays. Their mutual choice proved satisfactory to all, and, indeed, who better than they could mate their hearts, when they alone were staking their happiness on the venture? And, besides, it is not often that marriages founded on mutual love turn out badly.

"As soon as the marriage of a young couple was determined, the men of the village, after having built a cozy little home for them, cleared and planted the land parceled out to them; and while they so generously extended their aid and assistance, the women were not laggards in their kindness to the bride. To her they made presents of what they deemed most necessary for the comfort and utility of her household, and all this was done and given with honest and willing hearts.

"Everything was orderly and neat in the home of the happy couple, and after the marriage ceremony in the church and the wedding feast at the home of the bride's father, the happy couple were escorted to their new home b the young men and young maidens of the village. How genial was the joy that warmed our hearts and brightened our souls on these occasions; how noisy and light the gaiety of the young people; how unalloyed their merriment and happiness!

"I will now relate to you what befell them.

"It was on a Sunday, I remember this as if it were but yesterday, we were attending mass, and when our old curate ascended his pulpit, as he was wont to do every Sunday, he announced to us that war was being waged between France and England. 'My children,' said he in sad and solemn tones, 'you may expect to witness awful scenes and to undergo sore trials, but God will not forsake you if you put your trust in his infinite mercy'; and then kneeling don, he prayed aloud for France, and we all responded to his fervent voice, and said amen! From the depths of our hearts. A painful silence prevailed in the little church until mass was over. As we left the church, the people grouped themselves on all sides to discuss the sad news, and we retired mournfully and quietly to our homes.

"This intelligence troubled us, and we tried, in vain, to shake off the gloom that darkened our souls. England had enlisted hundreds of Indians in her armies, and we knew that the bloodthirsty savages spared no one, and inflicted the most exquisite tortures on their prisoners.

"Then we argued ourselves into a different mood by thinking that this news might, after all, be exaggerated, and that our apprehensions were unfounded. Why should England wage war upon us? Acadia, so poor, so desolate, so sparsely peopled, was surely not worth the shedding of a single drop of blood in its conquest. The storm would pass by without even ruffling our peace and tranquility. We argued thus to rid ourselves of the gloomy forebodings that troubled us, but despite our endeavors, our fears haunted us and made us despondent and miserable.

"The news that reached us, now and then, were far from being encouraging. France, whelmed in defeat, seemed to have abandoned us, the English were gaining ground, and our Canadian brothers were calling for assistance.

"Six months passed away without our receiving the least intelligence. We knew, however, that the war was still progressing, and that the French were losing ground every day. The English directed all their efforts against Canada, and seemed to have los sight of Acadia in the turmoil and fury of battle. In spite of our anxiety and apprehensions, the peace and quiet of the colony remained unruffled. Alas! we had been lulled to security by deceitful hopes, and the storm that had swept along Canada, was about to burst upon us with unchecked fury. Our day of trial had dawned, and, doomed victims of a cruel fate, we were about to undergo sufferings beyond human endurance, and to experience unparalleled outrages and cruelties."

Our own grandmother, at this point, was overcome by her emotion and hung her head down. Having mastered her emotions, she brushed away her tears and resumed her narrative as follows:

"One morning, at dawn of day, a young man was lying unconscious on the green near the church. His arm was shattered, and he had bled profusely; it was with the greatest difficulty that we restored him to life. When he opened his eyes his looks were wild and terrified, and, despite his weakness, he made a desperate effort to rise and flee.

"We quieted him with friendly words, and when he had recovered from the exhaustion occasioned by the loss of blood, he related to us what had happened to him, and we listened to his words with breathless suspense and anxiety.

"'The English', said he, 'have landed troops on the eastern coast of Acadia, and are committing the most atrocious cruelties. Their inhumanity surpasses belief. They pillage and burn our villages, and even lay sacrilegious hands on the sacred vessels in our churches. They tear the wives from their husbands, the children from their parents, and they drive their ill-fated victims to the seashore, and stow them on ships which sail immediately for unknown lands. They spare only such as become traitors to their Faith and to their King. They raided our village at dusk yesterday. They reduced it to ashes. They have driven its inhabitants to the seashore like cattle, and when through sheer exhaustion, one of their victims fell by the road side, I have seen the fiends compel him with the butts of their muskets, to rise and walk. I have escaped, in the darkness of night, with an arm shattered by a random shot, and I have run exhausted by the loss of blood, I fell where you have found me. They will overrun Acadia, and they will not spare you, my friends, if you show any hostility to them. Your town will be raided shortly, and you cannot resist them, my friends. Abandon your homes, and seek safety elsewhere, while you have the time and chance to do so.

"You may well imagine, petiots, that our trouble was great when we heard this terrible news. We stood there, not knowing what to do. In our predicament and in so critical an emergency, our only alternative was to apply to our old curate for advice.

"He gave us words of encouragement, and withdrew with our elders to his room. At last our elders, accompanied by our old curate, sallied out of that house with sorrowful countenances, but with steady step and firm resolve written on their brows. Their countenance bespoke the gravity of the situation, far more serious, indeed, then we then realized, and as they approached us, in the deathlike silence that prevailed, we could distinctly hear the throbbings of our hearts.

"One of our elders spoke as follows: 'My good friends, said he, 'our hopes were illusory and the future is big with ominous threats for us. A cruel and relentless enemy is at our doors. The story of the wounded man is true, the English are applying the torch to our villages, and are spreading the scattering ruin as they advance. They spare neither old age nor infirmity, neither women nor children, and are tender hearted only to renegades and apostates. Are you ready to accept these humiliating conditions, and to be branded as traitors and cowards?'

"'Never,' we answered; 'never!'

"'Then let exile be our lot. Let us prepare for the worst, for today, we bid adieu forever, perhaps to Acadia, to our homes, to the graves of those we loved so well. We leave friendless and penniless for distant lands; we leave for Louisiana, where we shall be free to honor and reverence France, and to serve our God according to our belief.'

"These words chilled our hearts, and yet, without a tear, without a complaint, we resigned ourselves to our fate.

"Ah! It was a cruel day to us. We were leaving Acadia, we were abandoning our homes where our children were born and raised. Everything that we saw, every object that we touched, recalled to our hearts some sweet remembrance of days gone by. We were leaving them forever. The terrible ordeal we were undergoing did not shake our resolve, and submitting to the will of God, we preferred exile and poverty before dishonoring ourselves by becoming traitors and renegades.

"Our people, so meek, so peaceable, became frenzied with despair. The women and children wandered from house to house, wailing and uttering piercing cries. Every object of spoil was destroyed, and the torch was applied to the houses. Oh, the ruin, the ruin, petiots; it was horrible.

"We left St. Gabriel numbering about three hundred, whilst the ashes of our burning houses, carried by the wind, whirled past us like a pillar of light to guide our faltering steps through the wilderness that stretched before us.

"As darkness came, we cast a sad look toward the spot where our peaceful and happy St. Gabriel once stood. Alas, we could see nothing but the crimson sky reflecting the lurid glare of the flames that devoured our Acadian villages.

"Not a word fell from our lips as we journeyed slowly on, and as night came its darkness increased our misery, and such was our dejection, that we would have faced death without a shudder.

"At last we halted in a deep ravine shadowed by projecting rocks, and we sat down to rest our weary limbs. We built no fires and spoke only in whispers, fearing that the blazing fire, that the least sound might betray us in our place of concealment; with hearts failing, oppressed with gloomy forebodings, the events of the day seemed to us a frightful dream.

"Oh! That it only had been a dream!

"Our elders had withdrawn a few paces away from us to decide on the best course to pursue, for, in the hurry of our departure, no plan of action had been decided upon, our main object being to escape the outrages and ill-treatment of a merciless and cruel soldiery. It was decided to reach Canada the best way we could, after which, after crossing the great northern lakes, our journey was to be overland to the Mississippi river, on whose waters we would float down to Louisiana, a French colony inhabited by people of our own race, and professing the same religious creed as ours.

"But to carry out this plan, we had to travel thousands of miles through a country barren of civilization, through endless forests, and across lakes as wide and deep as the sea; we were to overcome obstacles without number and to encounter dangers and hardships at every step, and yet we remained firm in our resolve. It was exile with its train of woes and of misery; it was, perhaps, death for many of us, but we submitted to our fate, sacrificing our all in this world for our religion, and for the love of France.

"We knelt down to implore the aid and protection of God in the many dangers that beset us, and, trusting in His kind Providence, we lay down on the bare ground to sleep.

"When the moon rose, dispelling by degrees the darkness of night, we again pursued our journey. We made the least noise possible as we advanced cautiously, our fears and apprehensions increasing at every step. All at once our column halted; a deathlike silence prevailed.

"We had not advanced two hundred yards when we were halted by a company of English soldiers. Ah! Petiots, our doom was sealed. We were in a narrow path surrounded by the enemy, without the possibility of escape. How shall I escribe what followed. The women wrung their hands and sobbed piteously in their despair. The children, terrified, uttered shrill and piercing cries, while the men, goaded to madness, vented their rage in hurried exclamations.

"The officer in command approached us: 'Acadians,' said he, 'you have fled from your homes after having reduced them to ashes; you have used seditious language against England, and we find you here, in the depth of night, congregated and conspiring against the king, our liege lord and sovereign. You are traitors and you should be treated as such, but in his clemency, the king offers his pardon to all who will swear fealty and allegiance to him.'

"'Sir,' answer Rene Leblanc, under whose guidance we had left St. Gabriel, 'our king is the king of France, and we are not traitors to the king of England whose subjects we are not. If by the force of arms you have conquered this country, we are willing to recognize your supremacy, but we are not willing to submit to English rule, and for that reason, we have abandoned our homes to emigrate to Louisiana, to seek there, under the protection of the French flag, the quiet and peace and happiness we have enjoyed here.'

"The officer who had listened with folded arms to the noble words of Rene Leblanc, replied with a scowl of hatred: 'To Louisiana you wish to go? To Louisiana you shall go, and seek in vain, under the French flag, that protection you have failed to receive from it in Canada. Soldiers,' he added, with a smile that made us shudder, 'escort these worthy patriots to the seashore, where transportation will be given them free in his majesty's ships.'

"These words sounded like a death knell to us; we saw plainly that our doom was sealed. They treated us most brutally, and had no regard either for age or for sex. They drove us back through the forest to the seashore, where their ships were anchored, and stowing the greater number of our party in one of their ships, they weighed anchor, and she set sail. The balance of our people had been embarked on another vessel which had departed in advance of ours.

"Is it necessary, petiots, that I should speak to you of our despair when thus torn from our relatives and friends, cooped up in the hull of that ship as malefactors?

"We were huddled in a space scarcely large enough to contain us. We could not lie down to rest our weary limbs. With but scant food, with the water given grudgingly to us, barely enough to wet our parched lips; with no one to care for us, you can well imagine that our sufferings became unbearable.

"At last our ship was anchored, and we were told that we had reached the place of our destination. Was it Louisiana? we inquired. Rude scoffs and sharp invectives were their only answer. We were disembarked with the same ruthless brutality with which we had been dragged to their ship. They landed us on a precipitous and rocky shore, and leaving us a few rations, saluted us in derision with their caps and bidding farewell to the noble patriots, as they called us. Our anguish, at that moment, can hardly be conceived We were outcasts in a strange land; we were friendless and penniless, with a few rations thrown to us as to dogs. The sun had no set, and we were in an agony of despair.

"Our only hope rested in the mercy of a kind Providence, and with hearts too full for utterance, we knelt down with one accord and silently besought the Lord of Hosts to vouchsafe to us that pity and protection which he gives to the most abject of his creatures. Never was a more heartfelt prayer wafted to God's throne. When we arose, hope, once more smiling to us, irradiated our souls and dispelled, as if by magic, the gloom that had settled in our hearts. With a clear conscience, we lay down to sleep under the blue canopy of the heavens.

"The dawn of day found us scattered in groups, discussing the course we were to pursue, and our hearts grew faint anew at the thought of the unknown trials that awaited us.

"At that moment, we spied two horsemen approaching our camp. Our hearts fluttered with emotion. We felt as if Providence had not forsaken us. When the cavaliers alighted, they addressed us in English, but in words so soft and kind, that the sound of the hated language did not grate on our ears, and seemed as sweet as that of our tongue. They bowed gracefully to us, and introduced themselves as Charles Smith and Henry Brent. 'We are informed,' said they, 'that you are exiles, and that you have been cast penniless on our shores. We have come to greet you, and to welcome you to the hospitality of our roofs.' These kind words sank deep in our hearts. 'Good sirs,' answered Rene Leblanc, 'you behold a wretched people bereft of their homes and whose only crime is their love for France and their devotion to the Catholic faith,' and saying this, he raised his hat, and every man of our party did the same. 'We thank you heartily for your greeting and for your hospitality so generously tendered. See, we number over two hundred persons, and it would be taxing your generosity too heavily, no one but a king could accomplish your noble design.'

"'Sir,' they answered, 'we are citizens of Maryland, and we own large estates. We have everything in abundance at our homes, and this abundance we are willing to share with you. Accept our offer, and the Brent and Smith families will ever be grateful to God, who has given them the means to minister to your wants, assuage your afflictions and soothe your sorrows.'

"How could we decline an offer so generously made? It was impossible for us to find words expressive our gratitude. Unable to utter a single word, we shook hands with them, but our silence was far more eloquent than any language we could have used.

"The same day, we moved to their farms, which lay near by, and I shall never forget the kind welcome we received from these two families. They vied with each other in their kind offices toward us, and ministered to our wants with so much grace and affability, that it gave additional charm and value to their already boundless hospitality.

"Petiots, let the names of Brent and of Smith remain enchased forever like precious jewels in your hearts, let their remembrance never fade from your memory, for more generous and worthier beings never breathed the pure air of heaven.

"Thus it was that we settled in Maryland after leaving Acadia.

"Three years passed away peacefully and happily, and during the whole of that time, the Smith and Brent families remained our steadfast friends. Our party prospered, and plenty smiled once more in our homes. We lived as happy as exiles could live away from the fatherland, ignorant of the fate of those who had been torn from us so ruthlessly. In vain we had endeavored to ascertain the lot of our friends and relatives, and what had become of them; we could learn nothing. Many parents wept for their lost children; many a disconsolate wife pined away in sorrow and hopeless grief for a lost husband; but the saddest of all was the fate of poor Emmeline Labiche.

"Emmeline Labiche was an orphan whose parents had died when she was quite a child. I had taken her to my home, and had raised her as my own daughter. How sweet-tempered, how loving she was! She had grown to womanhood with all the attractions of her sex, and, although not a beauty in the sense usually given to that word, she was looked upon as the handsomest girl of St. Gabriel. Her soft, transparent hazel eyes mirrored her pure thoughts; her dark brown hair waved in graceful undulations on her intelligent forehead, and fell in ringlets on her shoulders, her bewitching smile, her slender, symmetrical shape, all contributed to make her a most attractive picture of maiden loveliness.

"Emmeline, who had just completed her sixteenth year, was on the eve of marrying a most deserving, laborious and well-to-do young man of St. Gabriel, Louis Arceneaux. Their mutual love dated from their earliest years, and all agreed that Providence willed their union as man and wife, she the fairest young maiden, he the most deserving youth of St. Gabriel.

"Their nuptial day was fixed, and their long love-dream was about to be realized, when the barbarous scattering of our colony took place.

"Our oppressors had driven us to the seashore, where their ships rode at anchor, when Louis, resisting, was brutally wounded by them. Emmeline had witnessed the whole scene. Her lover was carried on board of on e of the ships, the anchor was weighed, and a stiff breeze soon drove the vessel out of sight. Emmeline, tearless and speechless, stood fixed to the spot, motionless as a statue, and when the white sail vanished in the distance, she uttered a wild, piercing shriek, and fell fainting to the ground.

"When she came to, she clasped me in her arms, and in an agony of grief, she sobbed piteously. 'Mother, mother,' she said, in broken words, 'he is gone; they have killed him; what will become of me?'

"I soothed her grief with endearing words until she wept freely. Gradually its violence subsided, but the sadness of her countenance betokened the sorrow that preyed on her heart.

"Thus she lived in our midst, always sweet tempered, but with such sadness depicted in her countenance, and with smiles so sorrowful, that we had come to look upon her as not of this earth, but rather as our guardian angel, and this is why we called her no longer Emmeline, but Evangeline, or God's little angel.

"Emmeline had been exiled to Maryland with me. She was my adopted child, and she followed me in my long pilgrimage from Maryland to Louisiana. I shall not relate to you now the many dangers that beset us on our journey, and the many obstacles we had to overcome to reach Louisiana. When we reached the Teche country, we found there the whole population congregated to welcome us. As we went ashore, Emmeline walked by my side, but seemed not to admire the beautiful landscape that unfolded itself to our gaze. She lived in the past, and her soul was absorbed in the mournful regret of that past.

"She walked beside me with a measured step. All at once, she grasped my hand, and, as if fascinated by some vision, she stood rooted to the spot, and with silvery tones of a voice vibrating with joy: 'Mother! Mother!' she cried out, 'it is he! It is Louis! pointing to the tall figure of a man reclining under a large oak tree.

"That man was louis Arceneaux.

"With the rapidity of lightning, she flew to his side, and in an ecstasy of joy: "Louis, Louis,' said she, "I am your Emmeline, your long lost Emmeline! Have you forgotten me?'

"Louis turned ashy pale and hung down his head, without uttering a word.

"'Louis,' said she, painfully impressed by her lover's silence and coldness, 'why do you turn away from me? I am still your Emmeline, your betrothed, and I have kept pure and unsullied my plighted faith to you. Not a word of welcome, Louis?' she said, as the tears started to her eyes. 'Tell me, do tell me that you love me still, and that the joy of meeting me has overcome you, and stifled your utterance.'

"Louis Arceneaux, with quivering lips and tremulous voice, answered: 'Emmeline, speak not so kindly to me, for I am unworthy of you. I can love you no longer; I have pledged my faith to another. Tear from your heart the remembrance of the past, and forgive me,' and with quick step, he walked away, and was soon lost to view in the forest.

"Poor Emmeline stood trembling like an aspen leaf. I took her hand; it was icy cold. Her eye had a vacant stare.

"'Emmeline, my dear girl, come,' said I, and she followed me like a child. I clasper her in my arms. 'Emmeline, my dear child, be comforted; there may yet be happiness in store for you.'

"'Emmeline, Emmeline,' she muttered in an undertone, as if to recall that name, 'who is Emmeline?' Then looking in my face, she said in a strange, unnatural voice: 'Who are you?' and turned away from me. Her mind was unhinged; this last shock had been too much for her broken heart; she was hopelessly insane.

"How strange it is that beings, pure and celestial like Emmeline, should be the sport of fate, and be thus exposed to the shafts of adversity. Is it true, then that the beloved of

God are always visited by sore trials? Was it that Emmeline was too ethereal a being for this world, and that God would have her in his sweet paradise? It does not belong to us to solve this mystery and to scrutinize the decrees of Providence; we have only to bow submissive to his will.

"Emmeline never recovered her reason, and a deep melancholy settled upon her. When poor, crazed Emmeline strolled upon the banks of the Teche, plucking the wild flowers that strewed her pathway, and singing in soft tones some Acadian song, those that met her wondered why so fair a gentle a being should have been visited with God's wrath.

"She spoke of Acadia and of Louis in such loving words, that no one could listen to her without shedding tears. She fancied herself still the girl of sixteen years, on the eve of marrying the chosen one of her heart, whom she loved with such constancy and devotion.

"Sinking at last under the ravages of her mental disease, she expired in y arms without a struggle, and with an angelic smile on her lips.

"She now sleeps in her quiet grave, shadowed by the tall oak tree near the little church at the Poste Des Attakapas, and her grave has been kept green and flower-strewn as long as your grandmother has been able to visit it. Ah! petiots, how sad was the fate of poor Emmeline, Evangeline, God's little angel.

And burying her face in her hands, grandmother wept and sobbed bitterly.

"As I have already told you, during three years, we had lived contented and happy in Maryland, when we received tidings that a number of Acadians, exiles like us, had settled in Louisiana, where they were prospering and retrieving their lost fortunes under the fostering care of the French government.

"The desire to seek our brother exiles grew keener every day, and became so deeply rooted in our minds, that we concluded to leave for Louisiana, where the banner of France waved over true French hearts.

"We announced our determination to our benefactors, the Brent and Smith families, and, undismayed by the perils that awaited us, and the obstacles we had to overcome, we prepared for our pilgrimage from Maryland to Louisiana.

"We set out on our journey with sorrow. We were parting with friends kind and generous; friends who had relieved us in our needs, and who had proved true as steel, and loving as brothers. When we grasped their hands in a last farewell, words failed us, and our tears and sobs told them of our gratitude for the benefits they had, so generously, showered upon us. They, too, wept, touched to the heart by the eloquent, though mute, expression of our gratitude. Their last words, were words of love, glowing with a fervent wish that our cherished hopes might be realized.

"Our journey was slow and tedious, for a thousand obstacles impeded our progress. We encountered deep and rapid streams that we could not cross for want of boats; we traveled through mountain defiles, where the pathway was narrow and dangerous, winding over hill and dale and over craggy steeps, where one false step might hurl us down into the yawning chasm below. We suffered from storms and pelting rains, and at night when we halted to rest our weary limbs, we had only the light canvass of our tents to shelter us from the inclemency of the weather.

"Ah! We were undergoing sore trials! But we were lulled by the hope that far, far away in Louisiana, our dreamland, we would find our kith and kin. That radiant hope illumined our pathway; it shone as a beacon light on which we kept our eyes riveted, and it steeled our hearts against sufferings and privations almost too great to be borne otherwise.

"Thus we advanced fearlessly, aye, almost cheerfully, and at night, when we pitched our tents in some solitary spot, our Acadian songs broke the silence and loneliness of the solitude.

"During days and weeks, we had to march slowly and tediously through endless forests. Thus we toiled on day after day, and night after night, during two long weary months on our seemingly endless journey, until, dispirited and disheartened, our courage failed us.

"It was a dark hour, full of alarming forebodings, and we witnessed the depression of our brother exiles with sorrow and apprehension.

"But a kind Providence watched over us. The hope of finding our lost kindred stimulated our drooping spirits. We had been told that Louisiana was a land of enchantment, where a perpetual spring reigned. A land where the soil was extremely fertile; where the climate was so genial and temperate, and the sky so serene and azure, as to justly deserve the name of Eden of America. It smiled to us in the distance like the promised land, and toward that land we bent our weary steps.

"At last we launched on the turbulent waters of the Mississippi and floated down that noble stream as far as Bayou Plaquemines, in Louisiana, where we landed. As the tidings of our arrival spread abroad, a great number of Acadian exiles flocked to our camp to greet and welcome us. How can I describe our joy and rapture, when we recognized countenances familiar to us. Grasping their hands, with hearts too full for utterance, we wept like children. Many a sorrowing heart revived to love and happiness on that day. Many a wife pressed to her bosom a long lost husband. Many a fond parent clasped in rapturous embrace a loving child. Ah! such a moment repaid us a thousand-fold for all our sufferings and privations, and we spent the day in rejoicing, conviviality and merriment.

"You must not imagine that the Teche region was, at that time, dotted all over like nowadays with thriving farms, elegant houses and handsome villages. No, it required the nerve and perseverance of your Acadian fathers to settle there. Although beautiful and picturesque, it was a wild region inhabited, mostly, by Indians and by a few white men, trappers and hunters by occupation. Such was the region your ancestors settled, and which, by their energy, they have transformed into a garden teeming with wealth.

"The Acadians enriched themselves in a country where no one will starve if he is industrious, and where one may easily become rich if he fears God, and if he is economical and orderly in his affairs.

"And my tale is told. Your Acadian fathers were martyrs in a noble cause, and you should always be proud to be the sons of martyrs and of men of principle."

"Grandmother," we said, as we kissed her fondly, "your words have fallen in willing and loving hearts, and they will bear fruit. We are proud not of being called Acadians, for there never was any people more noble, more devoted to duty and more patriotic than the Acadians who became exiles, and who braved death itself, rather than renounce their faith, their king and their country."

Podcast #154 William Tell

As we get ready to leave Month 5 countries for another year, I want to take a quick stopover in Switzerland and share the story of William Tell. I found this telling in a wonderful set of Music Appreciation books written by Hazel Gertrude Kinscella that I plan on sharing with you over the next while. They mostly haven't been digitized yet and actual copies out there are rare, so I am trying to find other ways to share them with you.

William Tell is the perfect segway into Month 6 where we celebrate our New Nation and where we take a closer look at freedom. Tell was another one of those great souls who refused to be oppressed by tyrants. Tomorrow I'll share the second part of the story from the Music Appreciation Reader—where Hazel talks about the William Tell Overture written by Rossini for a quick music appreciation lesson.

And now, the story.

The Brave Mountaineer

> There is an old story which is often told by the people who live in the Hasle Valley of Switzerland. This is the story of how the beautiful country of Switzerland came to be settled.

> The story tells us that the Swiss you live in this district were originally descendants of a band of Swedes, who, many centuries ago, were driven from their native land in the north of Europe.

> There was at that time a terrible famine in Sweden. So many people were without food that something had to be done at once. The men, therefore, drew lots, and every tenth man was forced to take his family and leave his old home.

> In this way, a great army of men and women and their children moved southward and crossed the Baltic Sea into Germany. They wandered across Germany until they came to the forest-covered mountains of Switzerland. Here they stopped, settling in the valley where the Riiver Muotta flows between wide green meadows. They built themselves homes and founded the old village of Schwyz. After a time, some of the families moved to and settled in other parts of Switzerland. Century after century passed, and the brave mountaineers lived on in their villages and homes, happy and undisturbed.

> High up among the Alps, in the very heart of Switzerland, are three districts, or Cantons, which came to be known as the Forest Cantons. These forest cantons are famous in history, for here lived a race of mountaineers and free men who were proud of their independence.

> In a canton over in the valley of the River Rhine lived the Hapsburg family, whose leaders were very rich and very powerful. Some of the men in this family became dukes

of Austria, and one of them became Emperor Albert the First.

As soon as he became Emperor, Albert declared that all the Swiss highlands belonged to him by right. Then he sent a band of soldiers to Switzerland to govern the people there.

One of the men sent by Albert to be governor was Hermann Gessler, and as a tyrant he had no equal. He was cruel and oppressed the people in many ways, especially by making them pay very heavy taxes. Even the lesser offences of the Swiss people were severely punished.

In one of the forest cantons, there lived at this time a mountaineer named William Tell. There was no man in all Switzerland who knew its lakes and its mountains so well, and there was no one in the whole nation so skilled in the use of the bow and arrow. This was in the days before the general use of guns and firearms, and hunting was always done with bow and arrow.

All the time that Gessler was taxing the people and punishing them severely for each little offence, the Swiss leaders were planning how they might rebel and free their land.

One dark night, a number of them met in a lonely meadow and took a solemn vow to work together for freedom. For more than a year they held their secret meetings. They made many plans and gathered provisions and arms which they hid away safely for future use.

Just at this time, Gessler decided that he must show his authority over the swiss in some new manner. So he had a tall pole set up in the market place of the village of Altdorf. On the top of the pole he hung his hat, then had bands of soldiers announce that every Swiss man, woman, or child who passed by, must bow to his hat on the pole as they would to the Emperor.

On the day when the pole was set up in the market place, William Tell chanced to come down from his home higher up in the mountains to do some trading. His young son, Walter, came with him, and when they neared the Square, the boy said to his father, "Oh, look at the tall pole, Father! See the man's hat on it!"

William Tell did not know then why the pole had been set up, and he walked on across the square without giving it any more notice. When one of the soldiers on guard stopped him, he refused to bow, and was at once arrested.

Gessler had heard of William Tell. He hated him already because of his independence. Now he offered to release Tell if he would do just one thing, and that was to shoot an apple off the head of his own son.

You can imagine how William Tell felt when the tyrant asked him to do this. He loved his son dearly. If he should shoot, and his arrow should fail to strike the apple, he would kill the boy. Because of this, William Tell, who had never been frightened before, was afraid to try the shot. The little boy, though, was as brave as his father.

"You won't miss it, Father!" he said. "I shall stand so still."

"Do you think I fear an arrow from my father's hand? Not I! I'll wait firmly, nor so much as wink! Quick, Father, show them that thou art an archer! He doubts thy skill—he thinks to ruin us."

The soldiers placed the apple on Walter's head, and William Tel aimed so well that he shot the apple into two pieces.

When he saw that his son was safe, Tell dropped his bow beside him. Gessler, who had been watching all the time, noticed that another arrow lay by the bow on the ground.

"For whom is the second arrow?" he asked.

"For you, tyrant, had I killed my son!" answered the fearless William Tell.

Of course Gessler would not think of letting William Tell go free after that answer. That night, he put Tell into a boat which was to carry him to a famous prison across the lake.

After the group of soldiers and their prisoner set out across the lake in the small open boat, a terrible mountain storm arose. The soldiers were afraid that they would never reach the shore again. They took the chains off William Tell and asked him to help row the boat. This he did until they came near the shore, when he sprang to an overhanging rock and escaped into the woods.

That night there were signal fires on every mountain and by dawn of the following day, the village of Altdorf was filled with Swiss soldiers all ready for battle. Gessler, the cruel governor, was glad to escape with his life, and the Swiss won a great victory.

Some years later, Gessler returned to the forest cantons with a large army. As he and his soldiers marched through a narrow pass in the high mountains, the Swiss soldiers hurled large trees and rocks, and avalanches of dirt down upon them. Many of the soldiers were buried under the heavy rocks, and the others were glad to turn back home. Gessler, their leader, was killed by a flying arrow. Thus were the Austrians defeated. The men of the forest cantons united in the Republic of Switzerland. Five other cantons soon joined them.

Should you ever go to Switzerland and to Lake Lucerne, you will see there the very rock upon which William Tell is said to have sprung when he escaped from the boat full of soldiers. Here, a beautiful "William Tell Chapel" has stood for many years. Inside it, on each of the four walls, is a wonderful painting. Each one of these four paintings tells some part of the old story of the tyrant Gessler and the brave mountaineer, William Tell.

—Retold from Schiller's "William Tell"

Podcast #155 William Tell Overture

In the last podcast, I shared the story of William Tell as told in the Hazel Gertrude Kinscella Music Appreciation Readers. Today I want to include the part where she talks about the story behind the William Tell Opera by Rossini and then, I'll include the music of the popular and recognizable William Tell Overture for you to enjoy. True, the Lone Ranger hijacked the fourth part, but it was really intended for our hero, William Tell.

Enjoy.

The Opera "William Tell"

As long ago as 1470, the shepherds of Switzerland sang a ballad which told of William Tell. This was long before the poet Schiller became so charmed by the old historic tale. Still later, a great Italian composer named Rossini set the story to music and made of it a famous opera.

Rossini was born in the Italian seaport town of Pesaro in 1792. His father was the town trumpeter, and his mother was a fine singer. The young boy heard much music both at home and in the streets of this home town, for all the people who lived there, as in many other towns and cities of Italy, were very fond of music and sang most of the time.

As the boy grew up, he too learned to play a horn and was never so proud as when he first played a duet with his father in the town hall. He was also taught to play the harpsichord and the cello and, when still older, to write music.

After he had been studying music for a time, Rossini decided that he would like, best of all, to know how to write operas. As he sang quite well, he begged for a chance to sing small parts and to sing in the chorus of the operas that were given in the town.

So well did Rossini learn how operas should be written that he himself wrote more than fifty operas before he died. Not all of these were perfect, but many of them were effective, and are still favorites not only with the people of Italy, but of all the world. He not only learned to write music well but he also wrote it very quickly, and it is certain that he wrote the opera "Barber of Seville" in exactly thirteen days.

After Schiller had written the drama, "William Tell," Rossini chanced to read it. He so admired the brave hero that he at once decided to use the story for the next opera he should write. So it was that the opera, "William Tell," came to be written and was first sun when the composer was thirty-seven years old. Everyone liked the opera, and from that day to this, it has been considered Rossini's finest work.

Horns were still favorite instruments with Rossini, and so he used them in many parts of the "William Tell" music. They were used in such a way as to suggest to the audience the alpine horns of the Swiss herdsmen. In several other parts of the opera, Rossini wrote directions that tiny bells should be played by the orchestra which furnished the accompaniments for the singers. These bells were added to suggest the bell-music of the Alpine herds, which always sounds so dainty and beautiful when heard from a Swiss mountain side.

Woven into some of the Rossini "William Tell" music is also the melody of the "Ranz des Vaches," or Swiss herdsman's song, so dear to the herdsmen whom William Tell, the brave Swiss patriot, helped to free.

One of the finest parts of the entire opera is the overture which was written to be played before the stage curtain rose. So beautiful is this music that it is now often played by great orchestras as a separate concert piece. This overture is really written in four parts. Each part was given a name by the composer.

The first part, called "At Dawn," suggests the sunrise in the Alpine mountains. The first part of the Overture is played by the cello in the string section of the orchestra. Toward the end of this part of the Overture there is heard a rumble of thunder, suggested by the kettle-drum.

The second part, called "The Storm," is a musical description of the great storm which overtook William Tell and the boat-load of Austrian soldiers while they were rowing on Lake Lucerne. In this music, we hear the cattle call of Swiss shepherds played on the flute. Then the lightning is suggested by the quick short notes played on piccolo and flute; thunder by "rolls" from the kettle-drums; rain and wind by the quickly descending and ascending scales.

The third part of the Overture, "The Calm," describes the joy of the mountain shepherds after the storm is passed. It is in this part of the Overture that the "Ranz des Vaches" is heard. This "Herdsman's Song" is played by the English Horn and the Flute in the woodwind section of the orchestra, after which the singing of birds is suggested by the flute.

The fourth part, called the "Finale"—an Italian word meaning "the end"—is very gay music, and describes the march of the Swiss soldiers as they assemble for battle.

So it is that the fame of the brave William Tell, and his equally brave son, live on in music.

Month 6 Podcasts

Podcast #31 The Madonna in Art

Our Mother's University topic for Month 4 is Art and since we are celebrating Christmas this month and we are a group of mothers, I thought I would focus this podcast on the Madonna in Art. I'm going to share sections from a book called *The Madonna in Art* by Estelle Hurll written in 1897[74] which I'll link in the podcast notes. But before we dive in, I think it bears repeating a couple of quotes from the audio I did in connection with Art. Our learning objective in studying art is captured in this little experience, shared by one of our heart-educator friends:

> The first time I saw Raphael's Disputa, which decorates one of the walls in one of the rooms of the Vatican in Rome, I had set out with my guidebook, intending to study all the paintings by Raphael that decorate these rooms. I entered the first room, and I suppose looked around the other walls, seeing the other paintings, but all I recall during this visit was the Disputa. I sat down before it and remained seated! I do not know how long, but the morning slipped away. What I thought about as I looked at the picture I cannot tell you. My impression is that I did not think at all; I only felt. My spirit was lifted up and purified and strengthened with happiness. Returning to my hotel, I read about the picture in my guidebook. It appeared that one of the figures represented Dante. I had not noticed it; and as I read on, I noticed other things that I had missed; that indeed, the whole subject as far as it could be put into words escaped me. I had no knowledge what the painting was about; only I had felt its beauty.

> Since then I have studied more about the picture and discovered some of the means Raphael employed to arouse this depth of feeling, and the knowledge has helped me to find beauty in other things.

John Van Dyke wrote: "You must look at pictures studiously, earnestly, honestly. It will take years before you come to a full appreciation of art; but when at last you have it, you will be possessed of one of the purest, loftiest and most ennobling pleasures that the civilized world can offer you."

Let me start today's discussion by sharing part of Estelle Hurll's introduction:

> This little book *The Madonna in Art*—is intended as…a study of Madonna art as a revelation of motherhood. With the historical and legendary incidents in the life of the Virgin it has nothing to do…. Out of the great mass of Madonna subjects are selected, here, only the idealized and devotional pictures of the Mother and Babe.

> It is now about fifteen centuries since the Madonna with her Babe was first introduced into art, and it is safe to say that, throughout all this time, the subject has been unrivalled in popularity. It requires no profound philosophy to discover the reason for this. The Madonna is the universal type of motherhood, a subject which, in its very nature, appeals to all classes and conditions of people. No one is too ignorant to understand it, and none too wise to be superior to its charm. The little child appreciates

it as readily as the old man, and both, alike, are drawn to it by an irresistible attraction. Thus, century after century, the artist has poured out his soul in this all-prevailing theme of mother love until we have an accumulation of Madonna pictures so great that no one would dare to estimate their number. It would seem that every conceivable type was long since exhausted; but the end is not yet. So long as we have mothers, art will continue to produce Madonnas.

Then she goes on to talk about how overwhelming it is to approach the subject without some kind of system for studying the art. While an historical student may group the paintings according to the era in which they were painted, and an art critic may group them by the technical schools they represent or there may be other scholarly groupings, Estelle first groups them according to the setting of the composition and then with their inner significance, which will hopefully make more sense as we go along.

I've created a little video from the paintings she talks about in her book that you can watch and gain a quick overview of these paintings as she has grouped them. I hope the brief descriptions I'll share here will help you appreciate what you're looking at. Then, if you'd like to go back and study each painting in greater detail, you can do that from the book I've linked in the podcast notes.

So let's take a look at the first five groups the settings of the paintings. I'll let Estelle teach you herself.

First, there is the Portrait Madonna in which the figures are half-length against an indefinite background. We turn with relief to a simple portrait mother like this. It is another case where the simplest is best.

Next, the Madonna Enthroned where the setting is some sort of throne or dais. In every true home the mother is queen, enthroned in the hearts of her loving children. There is, therefore, a beautiful double significance, which we should always have in mind, in looking at the Madonna enthroned. The picture stands for the Virgin Mother as Queen of Heaven. Understood typically, it represents the exaltation of motherhood.

The story of Cimabue's Madonna an example of the Madonna Enthroned—is one of the oft-told tales we like to hear repeated. How on a certain day, about 1270, Charles of Anjou was passing through Florence; how he honored the studio of Cimabue by a visit; how the Madonna was then first uncovered; how the people shouted so joyously that the street was thereafter named the Borgo dei Allegri; and how the great picture was finally borne in triumphal procession to the church of Santa Maria Novella. Sir Frederick Leighton has preserved for future centuries this story, already six hundred years old, in a charming pageant picture: Cimabue's Madonna carried through the streets of Florence.

Third, the Madonna in the Sky or the Madonna in Gloria where the figures are set in the heavens, as represented by a glory of light, by clouds, by a company of cherubs, or by simple elevation above the earth's surface. It is of pictures like this that our poet Longfellow is speaking, when he wrote:

> Thou peerless queen of air,
>> As sandals to thy feet the silver moon dost wear.

The fourth grouping is the Pastoral Madonna, with a landscape background. It was many centuries before art, at first devoted exclusively to figure painting, turned to the study of natural scenery. Thus it was that Madonna pictures, of various kinds, had long been established before the idea of landscape setting was introduced. In the ideal pastoral, the landscape entirely fills the picture, and the figures are an integral part of it. Such paintings are so rare that we write in golden letters the names of the few who have give us these treasures. The pastoral Madonna is the sort of picture which can never be outgrown. The charm of nature is as perennial as is the beauty of motherhood, and the two are always in harmony.

Finally, we have The Madonna in a Home environment, where the setting is an interior. A subject so sacred as the Madonna was long held in too great reverence to permit of any common or realistic treatment. The pastoral setting brought the mother and her babe into somewhat closer and more human relations than had before been deemed possible; The Madonna as a domestic subject, represented in the interior of her home, was hesitatingly adopted, and has been rarely treated. The Northern painters the Dutch and the Flemish—led the way. Peculiarly home-loving in their tastes, their ideal woman is the hausfrau, and it was with them no lowering of the Madonna's dignity to represent her in this capacity.

As you watch the slideshow, you'll notice Estelle arranges the paintings in the order of historical development so far as possible.

The second grouping addresses the question, Which aspects of motherhood are displayed in the Madonna pictures or in other words, in what relation to her child has the Madonna been represented? The answer includes the following three subjects:

1. The Madonna of Love in which the relation is purely maternal. The emphasis is upon a mother's natural affection as displayed towards the child. Undoubtedly the most popular of all Madonna subjects certainly the most easily understood is the Madonna of Love. The mother's mood may be read at a glance; she is showing in one of a thousand tender ways her motherly affection for her child. She clasps him in her arms, holding him to her breast, pressing her face to his, kissing him, caressing him, or playing with him. Love is written in every line of her face; love is the key-note of the picture. Pictures like these constantly reiterate the story of a mother's love an old, old story, which begins again with every new birth.

2. The Madonna in Adoration in which the mother's attitude is one of humility; contemplating her child in awe. The first tender joys of a mother's love are strangely mingled with awe. Her babe is a precious gift of God, which she receives into trembling hands. A new sense of responsibility presses upon her with almost overwhelming force. Hers is the highest honor given unto woman; she accepts it with solemn joy, deeming herself all too unworthy.

This spirit of humility has been idealized in art in the form of Madonna in Adoration. It represents the Virgin Mary adoring her son. Sometimes she kneels before him, sometimes she sits with clasped hands, holding him in her lap. Whatever the variation in attitude, the thought is the same: it is an expression of that higher, finer aspect of motherhood which regards infancy as an object not only of love, but of reverent humility. It is a recognition of the great mystery of life which invests even the helpless babe with a dignity commanding respect.

A picture with so serious an intention can never be widely understood. The meaning is too subtle for the casual observer. But though the sacred mystery of Mary's experience sets her forever apart as blessed among women, she is the type of true motherhood in all generations.

Before such pictures as these, gleaming in the dim light of quiet chapels, many a heart, before unbelieving, may learn a new reverence for the mysterious sanctity of motherhood.

Finally, The Madonna as Witness, in which the Mother is preeminently the Christ-bearer, wearing the honors of her proud position as witness to her son's great destiny. In proportion to a mother's ideals and ambitions for her child does her love take on a higher and purer aspect. The noblest mother is the most unselfish; she regards her child as a sacred charge, only temporarily committed to her keeping. Her care is to nurture and train him for his part in life; this is the object of her constant endeavor. Thus she comes to look upon him as hers and yet not hers. What is true of all motherhood finds a supreme illustration in the character of the Virgin Mary. She understood from the first that her son had a great mission to fulfil, that his work had something to do with a mighty kingdom. Never for a moment did she lose sight of these things as she pondered them in her heart. Her highest joy was to present him to the world for the fulfillment of his calling.

As a subject of art, this phase of the Madonna's character requires a mode of treatment quite unlike that of the Mother as Love or the Mother as Adoration. The attitude and expression of the Virgin are appropriate to her office as the Christ bearer. Both mother and child, no longer absorbed in each other, direct their glance towards the people to whom he is given for a witness. The mother's lap is the throne for the child, from which, standing or sitting, he gives his royal blessing.

It will be readily understood that so lofty a theme cannot be common in art. The progress of painting, and the growing love of beauty, at length wrought a change. The time came when art saw the possibility of uniting, with the religious conception of previous centuries, a more natural ideal of motherhood. Thus, while the Madonna continues to be preeminently a witness of her son's greatness, it is not at the sacrifice of motherly tenderness.

Raphael's Sistine Madonna is the greatest ever produced, from every point of view. Its theme is the transfiguration of loving and consecrated motherhood. Mother and child, united in love, move towards the glorious consummation of the heavenly kingdom.

It has been said that Raphael made no preparatory studies for this Madonna, but, in a larger sense, he spent his life in preparation for it. The Sistine Madonna is above all words of praise; all extravagance of expression is silenced before her simplicity. Hers is the beauty of symmetrically developed womanhood; the perfect poise of her figure is not more marked than the perfect poise of her character. Not one false note, not one exaggerated emphasis, jars upon the harmony of body, soul and spirit. Confident, but entirely unassuming, serious, but without sadness; joyous, but not to mirthfulness; eager, but without haste; she moves steadily forward with steps timed to the rhythmic music of the spheres. The child is no burden, but a part of her very being. The two are one in love, thought and purpose. Sharing the secret of his sacred calling, the mother bears her son forth to meet his glorious destiny.

Art can pay no higher tribute to Mary, the Mother of Jesus, than to show her in this phase of her motherhood. We sympathize with her maternal tenderness, lavishing fond caresses upon her child. We go still deeper into her experience when we see her bowed in sweet humility before the cares and duties she is called upon to assume. But we are admitted to the most cherished aspirations of her soul, when we see her oblivious of self, carrying her child forth to the service of humanity. It is thus that she becomes of his "witnesses unto the people" it is thus that all generations shall call her blessed.

I'll divert a bit from Estelle Hurll's writings to add a little more about this final painting which I will link as a PDF so you can print it out and study it in greater detail. In fact, you'll find a link to the PDFs of all these paintings in the podcast notes if you'd like to study them more in depth, using Estelle's writings to guide you through an appreciation of each of them.

The Sistine Madonna was Raphael's final Madonna painting and said to be his crowning achievement. I thought it was interesting that Lew Wallace mentioned, as he researched the characters to write *Ben-Hur* and they came alive to him in his imagination, there were only two Madonna's that did justice to the Mary created on his heart. One of them was Raphael's Sistine Madonna.

The curtains are suggestive to me of a stage as though there was a role to be played; an act to be performed in this stage of life. In the clouds, you see the faces of unborn babies. So many lives are dependent upon the successful completion of this act. It is said that when the painting was first placed, it was set opposite a crucifix that would have been the object of sight and that the expressions on the faces of mother and child reflect the dread and yet the resolution of that supreme offering that lie ahead.

The two other figures in the painting are Saints. The figure on the left is Pope Sixtus II, a 3rd century martyr who some say is pointing to the scene of the Crucifixion or others say he is calling attention to the myriads of souls who are watching in anticipation of the events to unfold. The figure on the right is Saint Barbara who is always connected with her tower, which you see faded in the background, largely hidden behind the curtain. Saint Barbara's pagan father locked her in a tower to keep her away from the world's influences, yet despite his efforts, she became converted to Christianity and endured torture and her eventual beheading at the hands of her father rather than deny her faith. I noted the perfect peace on her face that gift of the Prince of Peace that stands independent from outward circumstances. Peace I leave with you, My peace I give unto you not as the world giveth, give I unto you. Let not your heart be troubled, neither let it be afraid.

I hope I have given you enough of a background to enjoy the slideshow of Madonna paintings I've prepared for you. Estelle Hurl said to notice that as we go from Madonna as Love to Madonna as Adoration and from Madonna as Adoration to Madonna as Witness, we advance farther and farther into the experience of motherhood. At the same time there is an increase in the dignity of the Madonna and to her importance as an individual. In the Mother as Love paintings, she is subordinate to her child, absorbed in him, so to speak; his infantine charms often overmatch her own beauty.

When she rises to the responsibility of her high calling, she is, for the time being, of equal interest and importance.

In conclusion, Estelle said through studying both the settings and the internal meanings of the paintings, we are admitted to some new secret of a mother's love.

The music I chose as a background to the Madonna slide show is a movement from Vivaldi's Gloria in d Major which is frequently performed at Christmastime. Based on an ancient text that can be traced back to the 2nd century, the words, in part, read:

> Glory, glory to God in the highest and on earth peace and goodwill to men.
> We praise you, we bless you, we adore you, we glorify you,
> We give you thanks because of your great glory

A fitting accompaniment, don't you think?

And now I'll close with a single stanza from a poem written by Bertha Andersen Kleinman:

> Oh, let me enfold thee, my baby, tonight;
> While legions are singing in joyous delight.
> A new star has risen to hail thee divine,
> For you are a king, but tonight you are mine.

Podcast #33 There Is a Balm in Gilead

I talk a lot about a Pattern for Learning in the Well-Educated Heart. The pattern, again, is simply this: all learning begins in the heart and is connected to our desires. We want to raise children who love and desire the good, the beautiful and the true. Then comes obedience and living in harmony with universal principles, rules and laws. The combination of loving and obeying increases our capacity for Light; a spiritual grace and power that quickens our understanding and inspires us to use that learning in a way that bears good fruit, or in other words, increases Love, Goodness and Truth in the world, and thereby Joy.

Out of reverence, I rarely use the name of Jesus Christ as the source of that Light, but I believe He is the Source because He said He is: I am the Light of the World. That light shines upon the believers and the unbelievers. An unbeliever who desires that which is good and lives in harmony with universal laws will feel a measure of that Light in their lives. But I believe our capacity increases as we acknowledge the true source and come to know Him.

I believe in this Pattern for Learning, not because I read about it somewhere in a book, but because I have experimented upon the word. And the fruits have come into my life as promised. It is given to each person to know the truthfulness by the same process of proving it by applying it.

Today is Christmas Eve and we prepare to celebrate the birth of the One who has brought the glad tidings of great joy to the world. Some of you may question sharing the message I'm about to share in this podcast setting because of its religious nature. But to me, there is no separation between what we are trying to do in the Well-Educated Heart and in the message I am about to deliver. Everything I share with you is for the purpose of softening, refining and purifying hearts and learning to identify true principles so that there is a greater capacity to receive the spiritual gifts of learning.

But I also want to share it for another reason. I am a member of the Church of Jesus Christ of Latter-day Saints commonly known as Mormons. I know not all of you share my faith and that is perfectly fine with me. All are welcome. But it always puzzles me when the question is asked if Mormons are Christians. There are even some Christian congregations who are hostile towards the Mormons; who reject the very idea of associating with them. My intention is not to convert, but I hope I can build some bridges. First of all, the name of our Church should answer the question to if we are Christians. We are The Church of Jesus Christ. If a Christian is defined as someone who loves the Lord Jesus Christ with all his or her heart and desires to walk the path He has marked and in which He has led the way; who looks to Him as Savior and Redeemer because we cannot perfect ourselves and acknowledges that without His spiritual grace we can never be saved; who seeks to build His Kingdom here upon the earth, by that definition I am a Christian. And I am not ashamed to own it.

So the message I am sharing today is a talk I gave in my church a few weeks ago. It unfolded to my heart a couple of years ago in the early morning hours and I have shared pieces of it here and there. The message is that no life is so messed up; no heart is so broken that it is beyond the healing grace and power of our Lord. And you will recognize that the way of that healing is the same as the Pattern for Learning. "Come unto Me" He says, "all ye that are heavy laden and I will give you rest." This is the message of Christmas. This is the true aim of learning. This is the glad tidings of great joy the angels declared to the shepherds. Each soul is precious to Him and He is the great Healer of our lives and our world, if we will invite Him into our hearts.

Here is the talk I gave:

Balm of Gilead

I'm a bit hesitant to say what I'm going to say. I feel to share a personal struggle I've been going through and frankly it's embarrassing. It's not the kind of thing you want others to know about you. But the truth is, I happen to know there's a good chance that many of you are secretly dealing with the same thing or will in the future or have a loved one going through it. I've never heard it directly addressed over the pulpit so given the commonality of this experience, I decided it's time to bring it out into the light and talk about it openly.

Naturally, what I'm talking about is, of course, toenail fungus. I worry about a lot of things but toenail fungus never even made my list. I suspect I picked it up when some friends took me to get a professional pedicure. At first, it just appeared as a little white line at the base of my right big toenail. I didn't give it any thought until one day my little granddaughter said to me, "Ew, Grandma, what's wrong with your toenail?" That's when I knew I had a problem.

I still wasn't too worried about it, though. I'd just go online and see what I needed to pick up at the store to take care of it. That's when I stumbled upon millions of sufferers fighting a battle in secret that I soon learned for myself is not won easily. Some of these people had been dealing with it for 10, 20, 30 years. I read of longings to run barefoot on sandy beaches again without shame; of throwing on a pair of flip flips and running into the grocery store without embarrassment.

Yes, there was a prescription, but even doctors were reluctant to give it out because of its price and the potential liver damage and there was no guarantee of its effectiveness. I read account after account of people who had spent thousands of dollars on their doctors, whose livers had been damaged, and still the fungus persisted.

I saw images of thick, gnarled, yellowed toenails with green goo oozing from beneath the nail and read descriptions of the accompanying putrefying stench. I was horrified! This was not something to be trifled with!

This was serious business. So I started applying every remedy I could find. I soaked it in hot, salty water, applied cotton balls drenched with apple cider vinegar with 'the mother,' wrapped it in really raw honey, dabbed it with melaleuca oil, buried it in corn meal. And still the fungus continued to eat its way up my toenail. I can tell you that if you're going to try Listerine, be sure and use the amber color because the blue Listerine will turn your toe blue.

For months, I kept it away from my husband and when I finally told him, he reacted exactly the way I feared: "Ewww. That's gross. Keep it away from me."

I knew this was going to have to be my battle.

Sometimes I'd sit on my bed and look down at my two big toes side by side and wonder—would my right toenail ever be healthy and pink and whole again? How could a simple toenail cause so much grief?

But as I continued my search for solutions, I kept reading about a balm—b-a-l-m, not b-o-m-b—a little $2 jar of ointment I'd had all along. Apply it daily, they said. It may take weeks or months before you actually see a change, but trust the process. Never miss a single day—apply it diligently and you will heal your toenail.

I had tried everything else. What else could I do? So I started faithfully applying the balm morning and night. At first, nothing happened. In my discouragement, I was tempted to give up. In those times of doubt, it was the testimony of others and drawing hope from their success that kept me going. And then, one day, I noticed the tiniest little pink moon at the base of my toenail. I was cautiously optimistic—it had happened once before, but the fungus had overcome it. It would take days or weeks before I could know for sure. There was no way to rush the process.

Ever so gradually, it continued to grow—pink and healthy and whole. By then the fungus had enveloped my entire toenail and had lifted it from the bed so I now started to cut away the corrupted part, exposing more of the soft fleshy part underneath where I could directly apply the balm. The new nail continued to grow. And then, one glorious day—there it was! My toenail had been restored! It had taken months of daily, diligent effort, and I relished the victory.

Oh, that I was as abhorred by and as diligent in ridding myself of my sins—especially the little white ones that lie at the base of my…soul, for, as the Lord has spoken, "I the Lord cannot look upon sin with the least degree of allowance" for all sin contains seeds of corruption that are as damaging to our souls as the fungus was to my toenail.

And yet, my efforts against sin sometimes seem as futile as my initial attempts to rid myself of toenail fungus. While I am tending to one sin, another one creeps in. I cannot stay ahead of them. It's like an eternal game of wack-a-mole—when I bop one sin on the head, another pops up. King Benjamin reminds us: "…I cannot tell you all the things whereby ye may commit sin; for there are divers ways and means, even so many that I cannot number them."

What hope do I have?

My hot, salty tears of themselves do not have the power to rid me of those corrupting seeds of sin. Where is the Balm for my soul?

And deep within, I feel the answer. I've had it all along:

> There is a Balm in Gilead to heal the sin-sick soul;
> There is a Balm in Gilead to make the wounded whole.

Every Sunday, the Sacrament prayer reminds us of how to apply the balm.

The first step is to always remember Jesus Christ. But how do we remember someone we have not seen with our eyes or talked with face to face? How do we remember someone where a veil of forgetfulness has been drawn over our minds? I was thinking about that one day and the thought occurred to me that every single one of us has to recreate Him on a blank canvas on our heart. Every word He spoke, every scene from His life, every image we see of Him are the brush strokes on that canvas. The more brush strokes there are, the more clearly we can see and remember. If we find our faith faltering or we're feeling a spiritual deadness, maybe it's because the canvas has faded and needs to be refreshed. Or maybe there were never enough brush strokes applied to clearly see this Jesus who is the object of our faith, our adoration and our profound reverence. How have you painted His eyes? Are they stern and disapproving? Are they disinterested and looking away? Or are they tender, full of compassion and mercy? I have come to believe our eternal destiny may well be determined by how His eyes have been painted in our hearts. And how frequently we look into them.

When I paint scenes in my heart so I can remember, I try and paint myself in them. Do you do that too? I am sitting on the Mount as He teaches me how to be happy. I am filled by the loaves and fishes. I am the woman of Samaria—flawed and imperfect, who sits at his feet—I long to drink of the living waters and never thirst again. I am in the midst of the storm and I watch the winds and waves obey His voice; I cast my nets over the side of the boat and they are filled. I am the woman who has touched the hem of his garment and been healed; I am blind and He has given me my sight, I am deaf and He has made me to hear again. I am lame, and now I walk. I am the leper, the outcast of society, and He has made me whole. I hear His voice call to me, though I am dead, "Daughter, arise." I am the woman caught in adultery; He has taken my hand and lifted me up—"Neither do I condemn thee; go thy way and sin no more." I hear His invitation: "Come unto me, all ye that are heavy laden, and I will give you rest."

For I am "the Way, the Truth and the Life."

I follow Him into the Garden. I witness his anguish…those drops of blood…they are shed for me. He is mocked and scourged…I follow Him to Calvary and see the nails driven into His hands and His feet—I hear His groans of pain and agony, I fall to the ground and weep. "I tremble to know that for me, He was crucified; that for me, a sinner, He suffered and bled and died."

As I remember all these scenes and more, my heart swells with love and gratitude. Oh, dear Lord, Thou hast given me so much, what can I possibly give thee in return?

And I hear His voice: "If ye love me, keep my commandments." Here is the second part of the application process—to keep his commandments which He has given me. Both parts are essential. The first commandment is not to obey; the first commandment is to love and out of that love, to obey. To keep the law without the love is to be as the Pharisees who prided themselves in living the law with exactness to perfection. But to love without keeping the law is to be as the hypocrites to whom the Lord gave the chastening words: "Why call me Lord, Lord and do not the things I say?"

"But, Lord, it seems there are so many things. Where do I start? I am so weak." And He patiently replies, "Be thou humble and I will lead thee by the hand." "By the power of the Holy Ghost thou shalt know all things that thou must do."

So I take hold of His hand, and although still deeply flawed, I trust that, if I don't let go, He will lead me on a path to perfection; to wholeness. To know what He would have me do becomes my daily quest and desire. I gladly take His name upon me. I want to be His. I listen for His voice and I obey because I love Him and want to show Him that love. And somehow, in ways that are inexplicable, through that process of loving and obeying; of always remembering Him and keeping His commandments; of my faith and my works; something begins to happen deep within me as His healing and sanctifying spirit—His grace—begins to pour into my soul. At first, sometimes imperceptibly. But over time, I begin to notice the peace, the love, the joy—the fruits of the Spirit that begin to adorn my life.

He somehow takes my stony heart and gives me a new soft and fleshy one, a purified heart. Blessed are the pure in heart for they shall see God, not only in the life to come; but in the stars and the flowers, the pages of history, in inspired works of literature, music and art; they see God everywhere. It is as though I am born again. He restoreth my soul. He leadeth me beside still waters; He maketh me lie down in green pastures. I no longer worry about keeping track of all the ways I may be tempted to sin, for I lose my disposition to do evil. I am encircled in the warm arms of His love and I never want to leave. My heart is bound to His eternally.

And my past sins? He remembereth them no more.

Though they were as scarlet, He has made me as pure and white as the fresh fallen snow.

These are the scenes I try and paint on my heart and always remember.

If, in a year from now, you take me aside after the block of meetings and put your arm around my shoulder and say, "Sister Peterson, I've been applying the balm, and my toenail is healthy, pink and whole, I will clap my hands in joy and rejoice with you for I will have felt your shame and your sorrow, but more importantly, I will understand the daily diligence required of you to come to this place. If I can feel so much joy in the restoration of a toenail, what joy must be felt in the heavens over each precious soul that doth repent, which is simply a word meaning to turn back to the Lord.

There is a balm in Gilead to make the wounded whole.

There is a balm in Gilead to heal the sin-sick soul.
It is Jesus Christ, Our Savior, our Healer, our Friend.

Of this I bear my testimony and my personal witness—I have experimented upon His words and have proven these promises to be true for myself.

May you and your family feel wrapped in the warm arms of His love, not only this Christmas season, but in all the days ahead.

Podcast #156 Birth of a New Nation

Today, as I record this podcast, marks the 230th anniversary of the voting in of George Washington as the first president in the birth of our new nation. It has been a risky, long and difficult labor. America didn't suddenly come into being July 4, 1776. That just marked the impending and hopeful birth announcement. It would be another 11 years—and lots of blood shed—before these immortal words were presented to the world:

> We, the People of the United States, in order to form a more perfect union, establish justice, insure domestic tranquility, provide for the common defense, promote the general welfare, and secure the blessing of liberty to ourselves and our posterity, do ordain and establish this Constitution to the United States of America.

In a day when we see single laws 2,500 pages long, it is a miracle that this document that secured our liberty and has held us together for over 200 years was written on just four pages of parchment. I went and saw it in person last year and I teased that they had moved it—I saw it hanging by threads from the ceiling. Sometimes it appears to be hanging by a thread as ignorance is tearing us apart and dividing us as a people; where its provisions are seen as mere suggestions and the call is that it's time for something new.

How little such voices seem to know of the price paid and the miracle that this government of, by and for the people is.

So today I want to share a few of the resources you can draw from to teach your children about the Constitution and the gift of freedom they enjoy.

Last year I recorded an 1879 book called *The Story of Liberty* by Charles Coffin that was included in the Podcasts. You can still access it there, starting with Podcast #37 in the February 2018 archives. It is also found in Month 6 of BelMonde. One of the best ways to help your children appreciate freedom is to see what life looks like without it. And this book offers a vivid impression, although I don't recommend it for younger children. There are lots of sad things—martyrs being burned at the stake, for instance. For you, it will give you quite an education of the events leading up to the settling of America pertaining to the story of liberty. I highly recommend it.

In Volume 6 in the Freedom Series, *Stories of the Government*, I included a book that explains the workings of our government and some of the landmarks in Washington, D.C., through the eyes of four young children on tour with their knowledgeable uncle. True, things have changed since then and I tried to make note of them, but it will help them see things as they were first intended. For instance, it was a rule that any new bill introduced to Congress had to be read aloud 3 times before a vote was taken. I'll leave you to consider how adhering to that one rule could affect what is happening in Congress today.

Also in that volume is a look at our Constitution written for young people where the

Constitution is explained line by line. The middle book in that volume gives a brief overview of events leading up to the formation of a new nation.

I also want to call attention to another book by Eva March Tappan called *The Story of Our Constitution* written in 1922. You'll find a link to the book in the Middle School section a New Nation.

When you look at the strong opinions and the divisions and the difficulty of getting anything accomplished in our government today, it was no different when they came together to write a new Constitution. Human nature never changes and there was hard headedness and hard heartedness, tempers, jealousies, stubbornness, divisions and necessary compromises. Those involved saw that it was a miracle that it came together…and it almost didn't. This book gives you a glimpse into the problems facing them, including the issue of slavery and the 3/5 clause. Let me share some selections from that book, starting with the Preface:[75]

Preface

It is a thrilling story, the tale of four million people deliberately choosing a form of government for themselves and promising to live in obedience to its laws. It is a story of dreaming of union, but dreading to be bound; of dreaming of separation, but fearing to be free; a story of peering into the future like the seers of old, and of balancing sordid advantages and disadvantages like the most penurious of misers. And what of that noble group of men, unconsciously great, who without a thought of their own gain moved quietly about the task of saving a nation from lawlessness and anarchy? Why is it that histories which are elsewhere interesting become so often dry and dull when the wonder-story is touched upon?

It is from such thoughts as these that this book has grown.

And part of Chapter 1: The Days of Weakness and Confusion.

There was once a family of boys who were somewhat inclined to quarrel. One day the father called them together and handed the youngest a bundle of short sticks. "See if you can break that," he said. The boy tried, but he could not even crack them. Then the next boy tried, and the next, and finally the oldest of the four, but the bundle was tied closely together and remained as firm as ever. While the boys stood wondering what their father was trying to do, he untied the string and gave each boy a stick. Even the youngest could break one, and the father said, "You boys are like the sticks. If you quarrel and each one stands alone, you are weak; but if you are good friends and stand together, no one can ever harm you."

It is a pity that the Americans could not have read this old fable every morning of the first years following the Revolutionary War. They had had a severe struggle, and they had won the victory. Naturally, they were somewhat puffed up and just a bit proud of themselves. No one should step on their toes, whether he were George III or a man from a neighboring State.

They had opinions of their own, and every man was prodigiously sure that his were correct. Some of these opinions, whether correct or not, were certainly remarkable. One sturdy Vermonter fled to the newspapers with a wrathful declaration that nothing but luxuries ought to be taxed, that lawsuits were luxuries and served chiefly for the entertainment of idle, quarrelsome people, and therefore lawsuits ought to be taxed. Another went even farther, for he was much aggrieved that any of the tax money should go to the support of the courts. "I never had a case in court," he declared virtuously, "and why should I be taxed to help pay the costs of settling other people's quarrels?"

About the Society of the Cincinnati there was a real tempest in a teapot. This society was formed of the surviving officers of the Revolution. It was merely an association of friends who agreed to help one another if any need for help should arise. At the death of each member, his oldest male descendant was to have the right to take his place. There does not seem to be anything especially alarming in this, but in the eyes of many worthy Americans of the day, it was fraught with awful danger to the democracy of the country. Hereditary honors and a "hereditary nobility "were bad enough, but much worse was the fact that foreign officers who had fought in the war were actually allowed to become members; and from this there was no knowing what evils might arise. Even the fact that Washington was president of the Cincinnati did not soothe the fears of the apprehensive people.

Another alarm arose at the demand of Congress for a standing army, although it does not seem as if its proposed size need have startled any one. According to the treaty of peace with England, the confiscated property of the Tories, or those who had been on the English side during the war, was to be returned to them and all private debts were to be paid. Congress asked the different States to do this, 'but they paid no heed to the request. England refused to give up the western forts till it was done, and a motion was introduced in Congress to requisition some nine hundred men as a defense in case of necessity. The people were angry and alarmed. What right had Congress, they demanded, to require an army to be furnished by the States in time of peace? There was no knowing where this might end. If Congress once had armed troops at its command, who could foresee what it might do? This storm was at length quieted by the change of a single word; Congress no longer "requisitioned," it "recommended," and quiet was restored.

So it was that everything that Congress did or proposed to do was watched, not only by the people as individuals, but as States. Every State was jealous of every other State. New York on the one side and New Jersey and Connecticut on the other, almost came to blows. New Jersey served New York as a great truck farm. Whenever market day came around, fleets of boats weighed down with fruit, vegetables, fowls, cheese, and butter, sailed from New Jersey to the wharves of New York; and from Connecticut came almost as many piled up with great loads of fire-wood.

New York began to take heed of the amount of money that was going from the pockets of her citizens into those of her thrifty neighbors. It was highly improper, she thought, for so many good pounds and shillings to be carried off to rival States. That she was getting a fair return for her money did not affect the matter; and her assembly passed a decree that all boats over twelve tons must be entered and cleared at the custom house; that is, they must pay their neighboring State as large dues for selling to her citizens as if the vessels had been foreign craft.

The Jersey folk meditated on how to strike back. They could raise the price of wood and vegetables, of course, but the probabilities were that the New Yorkers would then refuse to purchase. There was one way, however, in which New Jersey could get her revenge. New York, it seemed, needed a lighthouse on Sandy Hook, and some time before this had bought of its New Jersey owner four acres of ground and had put up a light-house. Nothing was simpler than for the New Jersey assembly to increase the taxes on that four acres; and New York was promptly notified that her annual tax would be $1,800, a sum worth far more than it is now. As for Connecticut, a league of business men agreed not to sell one article to New York for a year.

Each State was looking out for itself. Kentucky and Tennessee, for instance, wished to trade with New Orleans; but Spain held the land about the lower Mississippi, and she refused to allow American vessels to use that part of the river. New England wished to have a commercial treaty with Spain, and Spain replied, "Very well, I will agree to such a treaty, provided all American vessels are forbidden to enter the lower Mississippi." Kentucky and Tennessee and the Southern States were indignant at being shut off from the mouth of the river; New England was indignant at the "obstinacy and selfishness" of the South. Both groups of States threatened to leave the Union. "What I buy and sell and how I buy and sell it is my own business," was the claim of each and every State.

At the end of the war, we were hardly a United anything!

And poor Washington who had already given so much for his country, was called back into service. Let me a read a little from that chapter:

Washington had hesitated about accepting his appointment as delegate. The Cincinnati were to meet at the same time and in the same city and wished him to accept a second term as their president. He had refused on the ground of private business, and now felt that he could not properly accept this later appointment. Moreover, as he said, he did not wish to be swept back into the tide of public affairs. His life since the close of the war had been as fully occupied as it was during the struggle. He had taken leave of his officers with great affection, and with tears in their eyes they had silently watched him while he entered the barge that was to carry him to Paulus Hook, New Jersey, on his way to Mount Vernon. For his services as commander-in-chief of the army he had refused any compensation, but had agreed to keep an account of his expenses. This account he now presented to the comptroller of the treasury, in Philadelphia. In Annapolis, where Congress was then in session, he formally laid down his sword. "I here offer my commission," he said, "and take my leave of all the employments of public life."

So it was that he returned to beautiful Mount Vernon, which he had not seen for eight years; but the peace and quiet for which he had longed he could not find even there.

Guests came in a constant stream. Everybody wrote to him. Some sent him inquiries which, as he said, "would require the pen of a historian to satisfy." People applied for favors of all sorts. One requested the loan of his private papers to assist in writing a history of the events of the war. One asked him to write to Europe for a wolf-hound. Another wished permission to dedicate an arithmetic to him. The Empress of Russia begged him to collect for her the vocabularies of some of the Indian tribes—and he did. Little Mademoiselle Lafayette, eight years old, wrote him a letter, which received a prompt reply. Those who could think of nothing else to write about, sent him pages of compliments. Everybody who had ever wielded a paint-brush wanted him to sit for his portrait.

And all this while he was longing to give his time to his family and his estate. That his place should have some attention was very necessary. During his long absence he had received weekly reports from his overseer; but for eight years Mount Vernon had missed its master's hand, and it was sadly in need of care. This was the "private business" which demanded his presence.

His finances were troubling him. For two years his crops had failed. He could not collect debts that were long overdue. His living expenses were much increased by the numerous visitors. He wrote his mother that he had no idea where he could get a shilling toward the taxes that were due; he would not be in debt, and he feared lest he should have to sell part of his estate. His country was not ungrateful; but when he learned that through Congress the whole nation was to be invited to unite in a gift to him, he gratefully declined it in advance; he would take no rewards for serving his own land. Even when the companies formed to connect the Virginia rivers with the Ohio wished to present him with shares worth many thousands of dollars, he refused to accept the gift, because he believed that he could arouse the interest of the people in the undertaking more surely if they knew that he had no selfish concern in it.

Surely, no one could have blamed Washington if he had left public business to others and had spent a little time in attending to his own affairs. When he left the army, he said that he hoped to pass the remainder of his life "in a state of undisturbed repose," and he felt sure that becoming a delegate would be the beginning of a return to public life. But duty to his country came first with him, and when Shay's Rebellion showed so plainly the lawlessness of the land, he laid aside all thoughts of his own advantage and accepted the appointment.

We are indebted to Washington for all his sacrifices.

Finally, when I was serving on the Executive Board from HomeMakers for America, now called Moms for America, I wrote a little booklet that contained the vision I had of what we need to do, as mothers, to correct the course going forward. I had recently completed the Freedom Series and as I pondered all that I had learned, a simple formula emerged; a sort of 3-legged stool that is required for a people to remain free. The three pillars of liberty are Faith, Virtue and Patriotism. Remove any one of them, and it topples. We are in danger of knocking out all three. In later years, I could see in this formula the same Pattern for Learning that I share in the Well-Educated Heart. In our Faith is our love of God who gives us a vision and a desire for liberty. "Where the spirit of the Lord is, there is liberty." It requires faith to see the hand of God in the stories of the nations and especially in the story of America. Virtue is abiding the laws of God; universal laws upon which happiness is based; laws such as temperance, frugality, industry, chastity, honesty, courage, loyalty, gratitude, patience, reverence. And Patriotism is not intended as merely the waving of flags and decorating with red, white and blue, but patriotism in its active sense of doing the work required of a free people of serving, and voting, and being involved not out of mere duty but out of a love for our country and its ideals. When Patriotism dies, the soul of our nation dies.

These three pillars are best taught in the home and mothers, as you know I believe, have the most influence over the hearts of their children. I linked a free copy of this little book on the Landing page for A New Nation.

If you are concerned about the direction we are heading, you the mothers in your homes are the ones who can change it. Your children can become tomorrow's leaders. Everything we do here at the Well-Educated Heart is all part of this work. As Calvin Coolidge wrote:

> We do not need more material development,
>   we need more spiritual development.
> We do not need more intellectual power,
>   we need more moral power.
> We do not need more knowledge,
>   we need more character.
> We do not need more government,
>   we need more culture.
> We do not need more law,
>   we need more religion.
> We do not need more of the things that are seen,
>   we need more of the things that are unseen.

> It is on that side of life that it is desirable to
> put the emphasis at this time.

> If that side is strengthened,
> the other side will take care of itself.

> It is that side which is the foundation of all else.
> If the foundation be firm, the superstructure will stand.

Podcast #159 The Price Paid for Freedom

I have talked about how some of the best ways to help our children appreciate freedom are to show them what life without freedom looks like and to share stories of the price that was paid to secure that freedom.

Today I want to share the story of a father and a son and the price they paid for us. The stories are taken from N.S. Dodge's American History stories.[76]

Henry Laurens

The tower of London is a great state prison, more than a thousand years old. Here kings have been confined, and princesses beheaded, and statesmen shut away from their families and the world, ever since England was a kingdom. Perhaps one distinguished American only was ever imprisoned here, and his crime was love of his country. For two long years, sometimes not permitted for weeks to go out on the walls to see the sun or breathe the air, supplied with bad food, furnished with a damp bed, and forbidden his accustomed comforts, did this great and good man suffer here. He might have been free any day, if he would have acknowledged George Third as his king. He might have had honors and command, as well. But he would do no such thing. He spurned the bribes that were offered. Imprisonment and death to him were better than treachery. And so, heart-sick and ill and lame, while his property was being destroyed at home and his family were broken up, did this noble Christian gentleman suffer without a murmur, for devotion to his country.

Henry Laurens was a South Carolina planter. When the war commenced he was in England, known as a great and good man; he had tried to prevent his friends in Parliament from acting against the colonies. He opposed the stamp act. He called the tax on tea a "crazy crusade." Together with thirty-eight other South Carolinians who were in London, he signed a remonstrance against the Boston Port Bill. But all was in vain. England was obstinate. And in 1776, Mr. Laurens took his son John, whom he had been educating in Europe, and came back to South Carolina. John entered the army. His father was sent to Congress. The two, who dearly loved each other, never met again.

In the Continental Congress Mr. Laurens had great weight. He was a handsome man, with gray hair and pleasant face. His voice was musical, his manners were gentle, and his presence was commanding. When he spoke in public every one listened. His opinions had the respect even of those who differed from him. He was also a methodical man. He had a place for everything, and everything was in its place. At an early part of his life he had been a merchant, and in his business all was done like clock-work. In Congress it was the same. He was always present, always attentive, never in a hurry, but always at work.

When John Hancock left, Mr. Laurens was elected president of the Congress. He presided with great dignity. Rarely was he ever severe, and never was he angry. All the members respected him. Benjamin Franklin was his friend. John Adams said he was the wisest man in America. Thomas Jefferson loved him like a brother.

By-and-by a time came for the United States to send an ambassador to Holland. An ambassador should be a gentleman, a man of wisdom, and acquainted with other languages than his own. Unfortunately, all ambassadors are not so; but Mr. Laurens was. He was therefore made ambassador or minister from the United States to Holland, and soon set sail for that country.

Passing through the English channel, the ship in which he sailed was overhauled and searched by a British man-of-war. When Mr. Laurens heard the demand of the British officer, "Heave-to your ship, and I will send a boat aboard you!" and saw a pinnace launched to bring search officers, he was alarmed. Going hastily to his state-room, he tied all his papers in a parcel, in the inside placing an inkstand for a weight, and came back on deck to sink them. He was too late.

The pinnace was close by. As he threw the package into the water a British sailor reached out and caught it while sinking. When opened, the papers showed Mr. Laurens to be a minister from the United States to Holland, and he was sent to the tower.

It was not till General Cornwallis had surrendered, and Great Britain had given up her colonies, that Laurens was released, Ile was then employed as commissioner, together with Benjamin Franklin, John Jay, and John Adams, to negotiate peace with England.

Mr. Laurens returned home at the conclusion of the war. He found his houses burned, his stock destroyed, his plantations ravaged, and all his improvements overturned. He had left America rich; he returned poor. But he did not complain. He set to work with his usual energy and method to put things to rights, and would no doubt have succeeded in time. But his long sufferings in the tower had weakened his constitution, and he did not long survive.

John Laurens

Four young undergraduates were chatting together on a seat under the great oak of Christ's college-yard, Oxford. A fifth came up, and nodding to the others, asked, "Have you heard the news from America?"

They all answered, "No. Tell us what it is." "Our troops," he replied, "have whipped at Bunker Hill those cowardly Americans."

"Those what?" said one of the four, springing suddenly to his feet. "Those what, sir? Say it again at your peril."

He was a fine, tall fellow, with black, curling hair, and dark, flashing eyes, who thus suddenly challenged the other to repeat his remark. The offender hesitated, looked for a moment into the face of his opponent, and then slowly repeated the offensive words.

"I said, sir, that British soldiers had whipped the cowardly Americans."

"Then take that, sir," replied the first, "from an American who tells you that you lie!" and with a blow of his fist, planted squarely in the speaker's face, he felled him to the ground.

The whole affair was of an instant. The others had no time to interfere. It was a word and a blow. With blackened eye and bleeding nose the Englishman picked himself up, saying:

"You will be sorry for this, Laurens."

"Perhaps so," replied the young southerner; "but any man who dares in my presence to call my countrymen cowards will fare as you have."

John Laurens was then twenty years old. He had been educated in France and Germany, and spoke their languages like his own. He was now graduating from Oxford University. His father had spared no expense to make him accomplished. He was a good scholar; on the violin he could discourse sweet music; at ball, or on the slack rope, or in running a race, he had no equal; and as a truthful, brave, outspoken young gentleman, there was not his superior in his college. His father loved him dearly, and wanted to make him a great lawyer.

In 1776 he left England with his father and sailed for America. On shipboard everybody liked him. He climbed the ropes, became intimate with officers and sailors, and in the sports which passengers have at sea, would lift the heaviest weight and perform the adroitest rope feats. Before the ship reached land, a pilot came on board and told of the British being driven out of Boston, and of Washington's success at the head of the American army.

There was no more thought of law. "I must go into the army, father," said the young man; and before many weeks, after the ship had come to port, John Laurens had buckled on his sword, said good-by to his friends, and was an aide-de-camp of General Washington.

And now it was just the same. He would write despatches all night, that they might be ready in the morning. He would sleep on the ground, if his tent were wanted. A dry crust of bread in his saddle-bags was all he needed for food. To ride sixty miles a day right through the enemy's pickets was easy to him. He feared nothing. What fatigue was, he did not know. His gray mare—Fanny Grey he called her—would gallop all day, and then lay down by his side all night. Washington had no one he loved so well, or trusted so much.

Young Laurens was commander often, as well as aide-de-camp. He was wounded at Brandywine, but would not dismount till the battle was over. He fought at Germantown with such bravery, that old soldiers said, "He will surely be killed." He was in the thickest of the fight at Monmouth and Charleston. And to brave old Moultrie, when he was battling stoutly against the British, Laurens was most useful of all his captains.

Ready upon all occasions, quick, intelligent, goodnatured, without vices and without fear, faithful to friends and generous to foes, no wonder Washington called him after a famous soldier of old time in France, "the Chevalier Bayard of the army."

It was not his courage only, nor his handsome person, nor his agreeable manners, that served his turn. Elis French and German were of great service. He was secretary and interpreter and foreign correspondent to the commander-in-chief. When French officers, who could not speak English, came to headquarters, it was Colonel Laurens who welcomed them. When orders had to be sent to the French troops, it was Colonel Laurens who carried them. When despatches in French had to be prepared, it was Colonel Laurens who wrote them.

At one time Congress wanted money to pay the army. LaFayette advised to borrow it in France. "Whom shall we send?" the speaker asked. Some said, "Send General LaFayette." Others said, "Send Colonel Hamilton." But when Washington was asked, he replied, "Send John Laurens."

Colonel Laurens went and got the money; but, as Benjamin Franklin said, "it was by the skin of his teeth." Count Vergennes, the minister, would not listen to him. He could not get the ear of any of the princes. Our ambassador could not help him. He concluded, therefore, to appeal directly to the king, did so, and succeeded.

Poor fellow, he was killed in the little battle of Chehaw, when only twenty-five years old. The whole country mourned for him. Washington wept when he heard the news. And to this day old people in South Carolina tell the tales they heard from their grandmothers, about brave and handsome John Laurens.

Podcast #160 There is Hope

I just finished recording the third book in the Young Folks' Bible Library I've been telling you about that was published in 1911, primarily written by mothers. I'll start recording the 4th one today entitled *The Wonderful Story of Jesus*. My heart is filled to overflowing as I have been immersed in these stories.

Which is ironic because the stories themselves are really disturbing. One of my daughters is doing a final review after the editing before she posts them and she said, "Why were these people so messed up? They were all awful!" And these were the Chosen People! Even the ones who were supposed to be the great ones like King David. Committing adultery and then killing a spouse to cover his tracks isn't exactly on our list of heroic traits. And what about his sons? They were beyond disastrous. They were horrible! And what about this chosen people who are wiping out cities killing all the inhabitants and taking possession of them and a prophet calling out the bears to kill the children who made fun of his baldness. And even Jehovah seems like a God full of wrath and anger and vengeance.

Are these really the stories we want to be telling our children?

Actually, yes.

Because as I have immersed myself in these stories, my heart is seeing things far more clearly; understanding that is being found in the white spaces between the lines, like Mr. Rogers talks about.

Here are some of the lessons that are emerging which are so relevant to the problems America is facing today as well as the world.

We, too, were a 'chosen' people brought to a promised land where no king would rule over us. God was to be our ruler, and for a time, He was. When the children of Israel demanded a king shifting from personal responsibility to having someone to fight their battles for them, Samuel warned them of the dangers. And everything he warned them about came true. As I watch the role of government in our everyday lives grow bigger, and as I see corrupt leaders and a people who reject God, I see the same weakening of us as a nation as happened in Israel.

I almost hate to check the news every day because I am appalled at what is going on and it feels impossible to fight against. The prophets of the Old Testament felt the same way. The messages they delivered in their day which were dismissed, mocked, and scoffed at, and over which the prophets were even killed—were messages like these: Turn back to God. Live a moral life. Strengthen your family. Quit taking advantage of your neighbor. Quit making idols of your riches. Quit living the outward forms of your religion, God requires the heart. The prophets promised their people—If we turn back to God, He will fight our battles for us. That is the message of the Old Testament. And when we look at the problems we are facing, it is our solution as well. I'm afraid it's being met in the same way: dismissed, mocked and even reviled.

Furthermore, what came through these stories loud and clear was no matter how horrible you are—and these people in the Old Testament were some of the worst—God is ever full of loving kindness and He never gives up on us. If He can love such a degenerate people, He can love me in my petty weaknesses. We are not beyond help or hope.

For today's sampler, I want to share the final chapter from the book I just finished recording, *Lessons from the Great Teachers.* Here are the books we typically avoid; at least I did because I didn't understand—the books of Haggai, Obadiah, Habakkuk, Joel, Zechariah. These prophets were poets and their messages are buried in poetic expression. But these wonderful mother storytellers who wrote this particular series have given them personalities and placed them in their proper setting to help us make sense of their messages. And the messages are for us.

The children of Israel of that day looked for a King—a deliverer to save them from their oppression and difficulties. Just as many people today look for a new president or new elected officials to solve our problems. But the solution Jesus brought to the world then is the same one in place today Love God. Love your neighbor. Purify your hearts. It is not the Constitution that will make us free; it can only keep us free if we are a people living under the rule of God; if we love God.

Will we ever get it right? That's where there is hope because the answer is yes!! That day of universal peace is assured. And you and I are right in the middle of the task of making it such. We have a role to play and I believe the mothers of this generation are key. God has planned and prepared for this day all along. He knows exactly what He is doing even though it looks pretty messy from our point of view, just as it looked pretty hopeless in the eyes of the Old Testament prophets. Yet they never lost hope. In the chapter called Malachi's Promise, it reads:

> Another element in the teaching of the prophets was that there would always be a pure remnant of the people…. Isaiah had always believed that there would be a remnant that would be true. So Malachi was sure of a certain few that were followers of Jehovah and he was sure that those few were never forgotten by their God…. And God would use that remnant to keep a light shining in the world; a light that would grow brighter and brighter until the perfect day.

I believe you are of the remnant. If your heart is turned to God and you are striving to do His will, you most assuredly are.

As you share these stories with your children, may they stir their hearts to where they say enough! We will stop the madness and we will be true to our loving Father and share His message of love to the world. For that is the meaning of the elect—they are elected to be a light and bring others to the love and joy only found in the one true God.

As Moses declared: "would…that all the LORD'S people were prophets."

Here, now, is that concluding chapter from *Lessons from the Great Teachers.*[77]

> As we look back over the stories of the prophets we find that they were preaching to Israel for about four hundred years. They were men of marked difference of condition and training. Elijah came from the desert, Amos was a herdsman, Micah was a man of

the countryside, Isaiah and Zephaniah were noblemen, Jeremiah, Ezekiel and Zechariah were priests. Some of these men had the best learning that their day afforded. Some were men of the people.

There are differences also in their conduct and in their sermons. Elijah with fiery zeal destroys the prophets of Baal and the king's soldiers. Nahum and Obadiah rejoice in the vengeance that overtakes their foes. The prophecy of the exile breathes a universal compassion. The story of Judah exhibits Jehovah as caring for the children and even for the cattle of the heathen. There was a growth in the recognition of the goodness and the mercy of God.

Yet in their great essentials the prophets may be regarded as belonging to one order and as exhibiting the same characteristics. They were all patriots. Never among any people has there been a succession of public men, extending through four centuries of national life, who have exhibited a nobler and more sacrificial patriotism than these preachers of Israel. They were not always regarded as patriots, for they had not that cheap and stupid love of country, which cares only for national advantage and prosperity. Their patriotism was in their longing for their country to be so good that it therefore must be great. And for this hope of national righteousness the prophets were willing to die.

We must include as a general characteristic of all the prophets that they were men of remarkable eloquence. They are not all on an equality in this respect. Isaiah's lofty oratory is perhaps the most superb. The Exile Prophecy of Redemption is the most sublime. Jeremiah exhibits the deepest feeling. But in most of the prophets there is a grandeur, a dramatic power, a poetic sweetness, a gracious appeal, that puts this succession of men, taken as a whole in the front of the world's orators.

The prophets were men of intense religious faith. They knew God. He was not to them an abstraction but a reality. Jehovah was their friend, with whom they spoke as a man speaks to his friend. The people had a very narrow view of Jehovah, thinking of Him as a national deity side by side with other national deities. But the prophets believed that the God of their little land was Jehovah of hosts, the God of the whole earth. They believed that all of the great events of the world were conducted by His power. This made them men of intense religious conviction.

Growing out of this religious conviction was that passion for righteousness which burned in the would of every prophet. Religion never meant to them mere formalities, it always meant conduct. The sermons of the prophets are simply a succession of stern and stirring demands that the people shall be righteous. The one great need, as all the prophets saw it, was that "justice should roll down as waters, and righteousness as a mighty stream."

And righteousness in the minds of the prophets was always a social matter. They never thought of mere personal goodness which a man might have alone with God. They always believed that religion and national prosperity alike were founded on the right relations of common life. The purity of the family, the love of husband and wife, or parents and children; justice between the rulers and judges and the people; fair dealing in business; kindness between the rich and the poor, the employer and the servant, the lender and the borrower; these were the great duties. Micah summed it all up when he said, "what doth Jehovah require of thee, but to do justly, and to love kindness, and to walk humbly with thy God?" And so spoke all the prophets.

They were true optimists. While they pointed out the evils of their time in the most unsparing fashion they always believed in the coming good. In different ways and under different forms they ever looked to a glorious future. The righteousness which they preached so passionately they were sure would at last prevail: the peace that they so ardently hoped for they were certain would become universal. Sometimes they thought a great king, full of the spirit of Jehovah would bring this blessed future. Sometimes they thought that the religion of Jehovah, full of righteousness and peace, would win the allegiance of the world. Sometimes they saw the deep truth that the salvation of men comes through the vicarious suffering of the righteous. But always they expected the world to become a place of blessing, and they expected Israel would be the servant of Good to bring it to pass.

Israel's great gift to the world was the preaching of her prophets. Assyrian, Babylonian, Egyptian empires passed away. The splendid palaces of that ancient world are in ruins. But the burning words of the great Hebrew orators never die.

Many years after the last prophets had spoken there lived a Jewish boy on the borders of that same fertile plain of northern Israel which the poet-prophets had so often celebrated in song. He read with keen interest the stories of the great preachers. They were his people. They spoke to his heart. His soul kindled as he read their words. He too was a patriot longing for his nation's good. He lived with God in a fellowship so beautiful and simple that God was to him a Father. He saw that righteousness was the only glory of life and the only ground of happiness. He believed in the good time that was coming. He read and re-read the words of the prophets. And when at last there came to his heart the same call to go forth and preach that head come to the young prophets before him, he spoke their words. He lifted those words into a greater beauty and a finer truth, but he always spoke from the preparation that the prophets had given him.

So our own faith is joined with that of the prophets of old Israel, for Jesus of Nazareth, our Lord, was the greatest of the prophets.

Month 7 Podcasts

Podcast #70 Lessons from The Soul of an Indian

If you are looking for some authentic writing to help you see the life and traditions of a Native-American, I suggest taking a look at the writings of Charles Eastman. He was the first Native-American to write an autobiography and to talk of their way of life from a first-person point of view.

When he was born in 1858, he was named Hakadah, meaning pitiful last. His beautiful mother died not long after giving birth to him, her fifth baby. As a young boy, there was a massacre of his village and his 60-year-old grandmother and uncle whisked him away to safety where they took care of him for the next ten years. Later in life, he wrote of his boyhood experiences to share with young people in a book called *Indian Boyhood* which became a huge bestseller and was translated into many languages. I highly recommend it to you, but be warned—there is a chapter on his First offering in which he is to make a sacrifice of his most beloved possession. He has a little dog he loves dearly—I had a hard time making it through that one.

His grandmother's name was 'Stands Sacred' and she was strong and brave. At one point she had to swim across a river with Hakadah on her back. As we are always on the lookout for lessons on being better mothers, let me share some of his thoughts of the role of mother and grandmother in his culture.[78]

> It has been said that the position of woman is the test of civilization, and that of our women was secure. In them was vested our standard of morals and the purity of our blood…. She was to us a tower of moral and spiritual strength, until the coming of the border white man, the soldier and trader, who with strong drink overthrew the honor of the man, and through his power over a worthless husband purchased the virtue of his wife or his daughter. When she fell, the whole race fell with her.

> Before this calamity came upon us, you could not find anywhere a happier home than that created by the Indian woman. … Her early and consistent training, the definiteness of her vocation, and, above all, her profoundly religious attitude gave her a strength and poise that could not be overcome by ordinary misfortune.

> A woman's name usually suggested something about the home, often with the adjective 'pretty' or 'good' and a feminine termination.

> The American Indian was an individualist…he had neither a national army nor an organized church. There was no priest to assume responsibility for another's soul. That is, we believed, the supreme duty of the parent…since it is his creative and protecting power which alone approaches the solemn function of Deity.

> The Indian was a religious man from his mother's womb. From the moment of her recognition of the fact of conception to the end of the second year of life, it was supposed by us that the mother's spiritual influence counted for most. Her attitude and

secret meditations must be such as to instill into the receptive soul of the unborn child the love of the "Great Mystery" and a sense of brotherhood with all creatures. Silence and isolation are the rule of life for the expectant mother. She wanders prayerful in the stillness of the great woods…and to her poetic mind the imminent birth of her child prefigures the advent of a master-man—a hero, or the mother of heroes—

And when the day of days in her life dawns—the day in which there is to be a new life, the miracle of whose making has been entrusted to her, she seeks no human aid. She has been trained and prepared in body and mind for this her holiest duty, ever since she can remember. The ordeal is best met alone…where all nature says to her spirit: "'Tis love! 'Tis love! The fulfilling of life!" When a sacred voice comes to her out of the silence, and a pair of eyes open upon her in the wilderness, she knows with joy that she has borne well her part in the great song of creation!

Presently she returns to the camp, carrying the mysterious, the holy, the dearest bundle! She feels the endearing warmth of it and hears its soft breathing. It is still a part of herself, since both are nourished by the same mouthful, and no look of a lover could be sweeter than its deep, trusting gaze.

She continues her spiritual teaching, at first silently—a mere pointing of the index finger to nature; then in whispered songs, bird-like, at morning and evening. To her and to the child, the birds are real people, who live very close to the 'Great Mystery;' the murmuring trees breathe His presence; the falling waters chant His praise.

If the child should chance to be fretful, the mother raises her hand. "Hush! Hush!" she cautions it tenderly. She bids it be still and listen—listen to the silver voice of the aspen, or the clashing cymbals of the birch; and at night she points to the heavenly, blazed trail, through nature's galaxy of splendor to nature's God. Silence, love, reverence—this is the trinity of first lessons; and to these she later adds generosity, courage and chastity.

In the old days, our mothers were single-eyed to the trust imposed upon them; and as a noted chief of our people was wont to say: "Men may slay one another, but they can never overcome the woman, for in the quietude of her lap lies the child! … [A] gift of the Great Good to the race, in which man is only an accomplice."

This wild mother has not only the experience of her mother and grandmother, and the accepted rules of her people for a guide, but she humbly seeks to learn a lesson from ants, bees, spiders, beavers, and badgers. She studies the family life of the birds, so exquisite in its emotional intensity and its patient devotion, until she seems to feel the universal mother-heart beating in her own breast. In due time the child takes of his own accord the attitude of prayer, and speaks reverently of the Powers.

At the age of about eight years, if he is a boy, she turns him over to his father for more training. If a girl, she is from this time much under the guardianship of her grandmother, who is considered the most dignified protector of the maiden. Indeed, the distinctive work of both grandparents is that of acquainting the youth with the national traditions and beliefs. It is reserved for them to repeat the time-hallowed tales with dignity and authority, so as to lead him into his inheritance in the stored-up wisdom and experience of the race. The old are dedicated to the service of the young, as their teachers and advisers, and the young in turn regard them with love and reverence.

The expectant parents conjointly bent all their efforts to the task of giving the new-comer the best they could gather from a long line of ancestors. A pregnant woman would often choose one of the greatest characters of her family and tribe as a model for her child. This hero was daily called to mind. She would gather from tradition all of his noted deeds and daring exploits, rehearsing them to herself when alone. In order that the impression might be more distinct, she avoided company. She isolated herself as much as possible, and wandered in solitude, not thoughtlessly, but with an eye to the impress given by grand and beautiful scenery.

Those ideas which so fully occupied his mother's mind before his birth are not put into words.... He is called the future defender of his people, whose lives may depend upon his courage and skill. If the child is a girl, she is at once addressed as the future mother of a noble race.

Very early, the Indian boy assumed the task of preserving and transmitting the legends of his ancestors and his race. Almost every evening a myth, or a true story of some deed done in the past, was narrated by one of the parents or grandparents, while the boy listened with parted lips and glistening eyes. On the following evening, he was usually required to repeat it.... The household became his audience, by which he was alternately criticized and applauded.

This sort of teaching at once enlightens the boy's mind and stimulates his ambition. His conception of his own future career becomes a vivid and irresistible force. Whatever there is for him to learn must be learned; whatever qualifications are necessary to a truly great man he must seek at any expense of danger and hardship.

...our manners and morals were not neglected. I was made to respect the adults and especially the aged.... We were taught generosity to the poor and reverence for the "Great Mystery." Religion was the basis of all Indian training. ... "Be strong of heart..." my grandmother used to say.

It was supposed that Hakadah's father and siblings had been killed in the massacre, but imagine the joy when some ten years later, his father and brother reappeared. His father had been imprisoned and sentenced to be executed for his role in the uprising, but Abraham Lincoln pardoned him. In his confinement, he had become a Christian. In time, Hakadah also converted and adopted a Christian name, Charles Eastman.

One of the last books Eastman wrote was *The Soul of the Indian* where he describes in great detail the religion of his people, which he said was the same as the Christian. Only when the Christian priests came to convert them, the manner of their lives was a huge obstacle. Charles recalled an old battle-scarred warrior who sat among the young preachers and exclaimed, "Why, we have followed this law you speak of for untold ages! We owned nothing, because everything is from Him. Food was free, land free as sunshine and rain. Who has changed all this? The white man, and yet he is the believer in God! He does not seem to inherit any of the traits of his Father, nor does he follow the example set by his brother Christ."

They were puzzled that the white man showed neither respect for nature nor reverence toward God. They would take His name in vain. Everything was about money and material possessions. They gave them fire water that ruined their lives. They didn't honor their promises.

In the Foreword to Eastman's book, he opened with a quote by the great Seneca orator, Red Jacket: "We also have a religion which was given to our forefathers, and has been handed down to us their children. It teaches us to be thankful, to be united, and to love one another! We never quarrel about religion."

He then said this book was an attempt to paint the religious life of the typical American Indian as it was before he knew the white man.

> The original attitude of the American Indian toward the Eternal, the 'Great Mystery' that surrounds and embraces us, was as simple as it was exalted. To him it was the supreme conception, bringing with it the fullest measure of joy and satisfaction possible in this life.

> The worship of the "Great Mystery" was silent, solitary, free from all self-seeking. It was silent, because all speech is of necessity feeble and imperfect… It was solitary, because they believed that He is nearer to us in solitude, and there were no priests authorized to come between a man and his Maker… Among us all men were created sons of God and stood erect, as conscious of their divinity…

> There were no temples or shrines among us save those of nature…. He needs no lesser cathedral!

> That solitary communion with the Unseen which was the highest expression of our religious life is partly described by the word babeday, literally 'mysterious feeling.' It may better be interpreted as 'consciousness of the divine.'

Isn't that beautiful? The Native American is far from the savage, superstitious barbarian image created in later days.

Eastman went on to graduate from Dartmouth and received his training as a doctor at Boston University. He was the only physician on site to treat the survivors at the massacre at Wounded Knee. How I would have loved to see his methods of healing as he combined the traditions of his people with modern medicine. Let me take a minute to share what he wrote about that:

> I always regarded my good grandmother as the wisest of guides and the best of protectors…. I distinctly recall one occasion when she took me with her into the woods in search of certain medicinal roots.

> "Why do you not use all kinds of roots for medicines?" said I.

> "Because," she replied, in her quick, characteristic manner, "the Great Mystery does not will us to find things too easily. In that case everybody would be a medicine-giver,

and Ohiyesa must learn that there are many secrets which the Great Mystery will disclose only to the most worthy. Only those who seek him fasting and in solitude will receive his signs."

With this and many similar explanations she wrought in my soul wonderful and lively conceptions of the 'Great Mystery' and of the effects of prayer and solitude. I continued my childish questioning.

"But why did you not dig those plants that we saw in the woods, of the same kind that you are digging now?"

"For the same reason that we do not like the berries we find in the shadow of deep woods as well as the ones which grow in sunny places. The latter have more sweetness and flavor. Those herbs which have medicinal virtues should be sought in a place that is neither too wet nor too dry, and where they have a generous amount of sunshine to maintain their vigor.

"Some day Ohiyesa will be old enough to know the secrets of medicine; then I will tell him all. But if you should grow up to be a bad man, I must withhold these treasure from you and give them to your brother, for a medicine man must be a good and wise man. I hope Ohiyesa will be a great medicine man when he grows up. To be a great warrior is a noble ambition; but to be a mighty medicine man is a nobler!"

She said these things so thoughtfully and impressively that I cannot but feel and remember them even to this day.

Elsewhere he wrote:

> There is no doubt that the Indian held medicine close to spiritual things, but in this also he has been much misunderstood; in fact, everything that he held sacred is indiscriminately called 'medicine.' As a doctor, he was originally often successful. He employed only healing bark, roots, and leaves with whose properties he was familiar. He could set a broken bone with fair success, but never practiced surgery in any form. In addition to all this, the medicine-man possessed much personal magnetism and authority, and in his treatment often sought to re-establish the equilibrium of the patient through mental or spiritual influences.

> The Sioux word for the healing art is "wah-pee-yah," which literally means readjusting or making anew. "Pay-jee-hoo-tah," literally root, means medicine, and "wakan" signifies spirit or mystery. Thus the three ideas, while sometimes associated, were carefully distinguished.

> It is important to remember that in the old days the 'medicine man' received no payment for his services, which were of the nature of an honorable function or office. When the idea of payment and barter was introduced among us, and valuable presents or fees began to be demanded for treating the sick, the ensuing greed and rivalry led to many demoralizing practices, and in time to the rise of the modern 'conjurer,' who is generally a fraud and trickster of the grossest kind.

Charles Eastman, in addition to being a writer, humanitarian and doctor, was instrumental in setting up 32 chapters of the YMCA for Native-Americans. He was a key player in the establishment of the Boys Scouts of America as well as the Campfire Girls and many of the original camp and nature experiences came from his upbringing.

I can well imagine why he resisted assimilation into the white man's world. In his declining years, he built a simple log cabin by a lake and spent his last days there.

I believe the Native American has yet a significant future role to play in our story. He has been sorely treated and dismissed, but among their people is a powerhouse of faith and lessons we desperately need. The final paragraph of Soul of the Indian reads:

> Such are the beliefs in which I was reared—the secret ideals which have nourished in the American Indian a unique character among the peoples of the earth. Its simplicity, its reverence, its bravery and uprightness must be left to make their own appeal to the American of today—who is the inheritor of our homes, our names, and our traditions. Since there is nothing left us but remembrance, at least let that remembrance be just!

May we teach our children to learn and remember a forgotten heritage.

And now I'll close with a poem by Coleridge that Eastman included in the front of Soul of the Indian:

> God! Sing ye meadow streams with gladsome voice!
> Ye pine-groves, with your soft and soul-like sounds!
> Ye eagles, playmates of the mountain storm!
> Ye lightnings, the dread arrows of the clouds;
> Ye signs and wonders of the elements,
> Utter forth God, and fill the hills with praise! …
> Earth, with her thousand voices, praises GOD!

Podcast #71 Lessons from the Saracens

My husband and I watched *The Hiding Place*—again—the other night. We've watched other movies about the Holocaust as well and every time I ask myself: "How could people treat the Jews the way they did? How could neighbors turn and look the other way or even join in the persecution?

And I've asked myself—are the Muslims to be the Jews of today because there are many voices out there that would make us afraid of them; make us afraid to associate with them. I've heard of parents who are appalled when their children are taught of Muslim holy days or of their religion, traditions, or their prophet, Mohammed.

This is definitely a case where we can see the danger of the single story. There is no single story of the Muslim any more than there can be a single story of the Christian. On the one hand, you read that the intent of the Muslim religion is to wipe the infidel off the planet and we have seen horrific acts of terrorism committed in the name of Islam. But then you read of interactions with faithful Muslim families who are not so different than we are; who have a faith in God, live lives of compassion and goodness. If you listened to *The Story of Liberty*, you saw horrific acts committed in the name of Christianity.

And even if the Muslim was truly our enemy, for those of us who profess to be Christian, can we allow one shred of hatred to enter our hearts? Didn't Jesus teach us to love our enemies and do good to them that persecute us? I have in my reservoir of stories miracles worked through the power of love even among hardened and ferocious people, which, by the way, I don't believe describes the majority of the Muslim population.

So what is my point here. My point is that we need to teach our children about the Muslims and their faith that they may understand who they are because the Muslims are playing a huge role in our world today. Will you teach your children to fear them or to love them?

Last month we studied the stories of the Holy Land and we learned that Abraham had a son named Ishmael who, although outcast, was given promises through Abraham. It was Ishmael's descendants living in the Arabian desert that Mohammed was called to be a prophet to. They were worshippers of many gods and idols, a scattered, nomadic people.

When Mohammed said that the Angel Gabriel visited him, I believe him for so have angels appeared to prophets throughout the ages. I recognize the same truths I have been raised with in my Christian faith in the five Pillars—the foundation of Islam beliefs. Here are the five Pillars:

1. Faith—There is only one God.
2. Prayer—We should pray to God many times a day.
3. Charity—All things belong to God. We each have a personal responsibility to ease the economic hardships of others and strive towards eliminating inequality.

4. Fasting—We fast to seek nearness and to look for forgiveness from God; to express our gratitude and dependence on Him and to remind us of the needy. We refrain from violence, anger, envy, greed, lust, profane language or gossip.

5. Pilgrimage to Mecca—a holy place. At least once in a lifetime, when they are prepared, they make such a pilgrimage and when they arrive, all dress in white—signifying all are alike before God. There is no rich or poor.

True, over the years, just as has happened in Christianity, the simple rules are often embellished and changed. But for those Muslims—and Christians—who find the heart and spirit of their religions, we find our common ground.

So I'd like to share a few things I've learned that I was completely unaware of until a few years ago and that give us hope that we can live together in peace even in our diversity. Not once in all of my schooling—elementary through college years—did I even once hear the name Saracen. The first time I came across it was in a book I found written by Rose Wilder Lane called *The Discovery of Freedom*.[79] If you're a *Little House on the Prairie* fan, Rose was Laura Ingalls Wilder's daughter. I'll link the book in the notes—it's so thought provoking. Here are a few excerpts:

> During the stagnation of Europe that is called the Dark Ages, the world was actually bright with an energetic, brilliant civilization, more akin to American civilization and more fruitful today for everyone alive, than any other in the past.

> Millions upon millions of human beings, thirty generations, believing that all men are equal and free, created that civilization and kept creating it for eight hundred years.

> To them the world owes modern science—mathematics, astronomy, navigation, modern medicine and surgery, scientific agriculture…

> These men were of all races and colors and classes, cultures and many religions; by no means all of them were Moslems. They were former subjects or descendants of subjects of all former empires. There is no one name that applies to them all. Europeans called them Saracens.

> Their own records of the eight hundred years, of their civilization, its institutions, and the causes of its collapse, are largely locked in the Arabic language. Since American scholars and intellectuals in general are European-minded, an American can get only glimpses of the Saracens' world, seen through European indifference or hatred.

The draw to this civilization was that it was a place where people were safe to think for themselves. And look what happened in education!

> The refugee scientists in Persia…opened their schools, from Baghdad to Granada, their schools were crowded with students. In two centuries, there were great universities, the world's first universities.

> For hundreds of years, these universities grew. The University in Cairo was more than a thousand years old and still had forty thousand students, when I was there.

These universities had no organization whatever. (Mohammed said that organization corrupts knowledge.) A Saracen university had no program, no curriculum, no departments, no rules, no examinations; it gave no degrees nor diplomas. It was simply an institution of learning. Not of teaching, but of learning. A man, young or old, went to a university to learn what he wanted to know, just as an American goes to a grocery to get the food he wants.

Men who knew (or thought they knew) something, and wanted to teach it, opened a school to sell their knowledge. Success depended upon the demand for the knowledge they had. If they prospered, other teachers joined them.

The teachers lectured in open classrooms. Anyone was welcome to listen. An incoming student wandered about, listening. When he decided upon the teacher he wanted, they discussed privately whatever he wanted to learn and needed to study, and agreed upon fees. Then he joined the class regularly. If he was not satisfied, he could quit at any time and find another teacher. When he had learned what he wanted to know, he left the university to use his knowledge.

A thousand years after the Saracens built these universities, far away in time and on a continent that they never knew existed, a revolutionary leader, Thomas Jefferson—who knew little or nothing about the Saracens—realized the dream of his life when he created the University of Virginia. His dream was a new kind of education.

Proudly, almost bragging a little, he wrote to a friend in the medieval-university system of Harvard, 'We shall allow them [the students] uncontrolled choice in the lectures they shall choose to attend. Our institution will proceed on the principle…of letting everyone come and listen to whatever he thinks may improve the condition of his mind.'

For more than nine hundred years the University of Cairo proceeded on precisely that principle. Until the end of the 19th century, Europeans were not able to impose upon that university any tinge of the European belief that minds acquire knowledge, not be actively seeking to know, but by passively being taught whatever Authority decides they should know.

Whoa! I wish that idea could catch on today!

Here was another startling discovery. I had heard stories of the Crusaders, but what a surprise they found when they got there! They found a people far from barbaric or uncivilized. Let me continue reading from Rose's writing:

Moslems had held the Holy Land for five hundred years and Christians had been worshiping at its Christian shrines, which Moslems reverently guarded. Christian shrines and Moslem shrines and Jerusalem has always been a Holy City to Moslems, who revere Abraham, Moses, Gideon, Samuel and Christ as prophets of God.

Saracens had set the guard that still stands—or did, when I was in Jerusalem—at the Church of the Holy Sepulchre. Night and day for more than a thousand years an armed

Moslem has stood there, to keep Christians from killing Christians of rival sects at the tomb of Christ.

Of the 426,000 Crusaders who invaded the country, 30,000 reached Palestine. They found palm groves, the vineyards, the orchards of figs, the villages and towns and the white-walled city of Ramlah.

A hundred Crusaders rode into Bethlehem and found it a Christian town built around the Cathedral of the Virgin Mary. The people, priests and monks entertained them royally. They rode back toward Jerusalem, and came to the peaceful church of the Blessed Mother of Christ, in the garden of Gethsemane on the Mount of Olives.

How does it happen that the Crusaders found so many Christians living among the infidels? Why, Christians lived there all the time. They were part of the Saracens' world. Moslems did not exterminate people whose religious belief was different; …it was Europeans who massacred heretics.

The Crusaders whose castles were rude stone walls and floors of earth or damp stone covered thick with rotting reeds, came into rooms like jewels, the floors tiled, the walls and ceilings of mosaic. …the most amazing thing to the Crusaders must have been its cleanliness. Moslems bathed five times a day. Mohammed taught that a clean body is essential to a clear mind and a pure spirit. He tied cleanliness to his plan for keeping the truth in men's minds without a church organization. … So the Crusaders came into a country where…fountains were everywhere.

No European had ever seen so many cereals, vegetables, and fruits that the Saracens ate: rice and spinach and asparagus, lemons, melons, peaches…. And these Saracen goods are still renowned from their world: damask linens, mohair fabrics, muslin, Morocco leather, Syrian silks, oriental rugs, mosaics, inlaid woods, glassware and porcelains, enamels, filigree and inlaid work in metals."

I can't begin to touch the advancements that happened in the Moslem world of these centuries. It didn't last, of course, but there's much for us to learn and benefit from. I hope you'll take time to learn more. I've included other writings in the *Stories from Arabia* book in the Forgotten Classics. I certainly discovered a huge gap in my understanding of their history. I'm still piecing things together.

Let me call your attention to one more book. There's a book written by Marcus Bach called *Had You Been Born in Another Faith*.[80] I included it in *The Stories of Spiritual Leaders*. His intention in writing the book was to help us begin to understand the faith of others. And so he talks of the faith of the Hindu, the Moslem, the Protestant, the Confucionist, the Jew, the Catholic, the Mormon. To understand does not mean we have to embrace, but understanding is the beginning of love.

He wrote: "Most of all, I was impressed by my own realization that we understand others best when we understand what they believe, and that we can never truly enter into their belief until we stand for a little while where these people stand.

"Of course, this requires a bit of doing… But since we must learn to live together or none of us will live, what else is there to do? And since we have tried every other known avenue for understanding, why not try this?"

The question he sought to answer was: "Had I been born in another faith, what would my faith—and I—be like?"

As he traveled the world in search of understanding the faith of others by standing in their places of worship and conversing with them, he concluded that the spirit inherent in religions is found to be one spirit when we truly put ourselves in the other person's place. "If a man reachest the heart of his own religion, he has reached the heart of others, too."

Dr. Albert Schweitzer was a true lover of all mankind and his philosophy was:

"Impart as much of your faith as you can to those who walk the road of life with you, and accept as something precious that which comes back to you from them."

Bach concluded: "All too long, each group has lived in its own restricted sphere, unaware of its close kinship with other groups. With hatred and suspicion increasing in the world, the warning has become all too real: we must learn to live together or none of us will live.

"…whenever we investigate the other person's way of life, we reinvestigate our own. And whoever approaches religion in this way is not going to condemn anything, but is going to discover that religion's likenesses are greater than its differences."

I love that thought.

I hate to close on a negative note, but the words in Rodgers' and Hammerstein's song in *South Pacific* ring true, even though they took a lot of criticism for the song. The fact is, children must be taught to hate. They aren't born with that hate.

> You've got to be taught to hate and fear
> You've got to be taught from year to year
> It's got to be drummed in your dear little ear
> You've got to be carefully taught.
>
> You've got to be taught to be afraid
> Of people whose eyes are oddly made
> And people whose skin is a diff'rent shade
> You've got to be carefully taught.
>
> You've got to be taught before it's too late
> Before you are six or seven or eight
> To hate all the people your relatives hate
> You've got to be carefully taught.

Will you carefully teach your children to love or hate those people who are different from them? Tomorrow's world will reflect your answer.

Podcast #106 Opal Stanley Whiteley

If you haven't already met her, today I'd like to introduce you to Opal Stanley Whiteley and her diary. She was another one of those accidental finds on the way to looking for something else, but two things drew me into her book: The first thing was that her name was Whiteley and some of my most favorite people on the planet go by that name. But secondly, it was 'the diary of an understanding heart.' I'm sure you know why that intrigued me.

I posted links to her book in the Mother's University Imagination month, but I could just as well have placed it in this month's topic of Nature Study.

It look me about one page to fall in love with this little girl. Her *Fairyland Around Us*[81] book dedication page reads:

> To you little children over the world who are dreaming of a fairyland far distant and who are longing to know the fairies, this book of the fairyland around us in God's outdoors is dedicated, and also to you grown-ups who have kept your faith in childhood and who are seeking inspiration for your work in the everyday things around you, this book is dedicated by one who loves this fairyland around us and who has found therein a bigger vision of life and of life's supreme joy, Service.

Opal was thought to have been born a French princess but was raised in poverty as her adopted family moved from lumber camp to lumber camp in Oregon. Let me start by letting her tell her own story.[82] Notice the methods her mother used to teach her and the long-lasting influence and impression they made on her even though she was so young.

> Of the days before I was taken to the lumber camps there is little I remember. As piece by piece the journal comes together, some things come back. There are references here and there in the journal to things I saw or heard or learned in those days before I came to the lumber camps.

> There were walks in the fields and woods. When on these walks, Mother would tell me to listen to what the flowers and trees and birds were saying. We listened together. And on the way she told me poems and other lovely things, some of which she wrote in the two books and also in others which I had not with me in the lumber camps. On the walks, and after we came back, she had me to print what I had seen and what I had heard. After that she told me of different people and their wonderful work on earth. Then she would have me tell again to her what she had told me. After I came to the lumber camp, I told these things to the trees and the brooks and the flowers.

> There were five words my mother said to me over and over again, as she had me to print what I had seen and what I had heard. These words were: What, Where, When, How, Why. They had a very great influence over all my observations and the recording of those observations during all the days of my childhood. And my Mother having put

such strong emphasis on these five words accounts for much of the detailed descriptions that are throughout my diary.

No children I knew. There were only Mother and the kind woman who taught me and looked after me and dressed me, and the young girl who fed me. And there was Father in those few days when he was home from the far lands. Those were wonderful days—his home-coming days. Then he would take me on his knee and ride me on his shoulder and tell me of the animals and birds of the far lands. And we went for many walks, and he would talk to me about the things along the way. It was then he taught me comparer.

There was one day when I went with Mother in a boat. It was a little way on the sea. It was a happy day. Then something happened and we were all in the water. Afterward, when I called for Mother, they said the sea waves had taken her and she was gone to heaven. I remember the day because I never saw my Mother again.

The time was not long after that day with Mother in the boat, when one day the kind woman who taught me and took care of me did tell me gently that Father too had gone to heaven while he was away in the far lands. She said she was going to take me to my grandmother and grandfather, the mother and father of my Father.

We started. But I never got to see my dear grandmother and grandfather, whom I had never seen. Something happened on the way and I was all alone. And I didn't feel happy. There were strange people that I had never seen before, and I was afraid of them. They made me to keep very still, and we went for no walks in the field. But we traveled a long, long way.

Then it was they put me with Mrs. Whiteley. The day they put me with her was a rainy day, and I thought she was a little afraid of them too. She took me on the train and in a stage-coach to the lumber camp. She called me Opal Whiteley, the same name as that of another little girl who was the same size as I was when her mother lost her. She took me into the camp as her own child, and so called me as we lived in the different lumber camps and in the mill town.

With me I took into camp a small box. In a slide drawer in the bottom of this box were two books which my own Mother and Father, the Angel Father and Mother I always speak of in my diary, had written in. I do not think the people who put me with Mrs. Whiteley knew about the books in the lower part of the box, for they took everything out of the top part of the box and tossed it aside. I picked it up and kept it with me, and, being as I was more quiet with it in my arms, they allowed me to keep it, thinking it was empty. These books I kept always with me, until one day I shall always remember, when I was about twelve years old, they were taken from the box I kept then hid in the woods. Day by day I spelled over and over the many words that were written in them. From them I selected names for my pets. And it was the many little things recorded there that helped me to remember what my Mother and Father had already told me of different great lives and their work; and these books with these records made me very eager to be learning more and more of what was recorded in them. These two books I studied much more than I did my books at school. Their influence upon my life has been great.

Listen to some of the names of her pets! Her shepherd dog was Brave Horatius. A baby chicken was Edmund Spencer. Elizabeth Barrett Browning was a pet cow with poetry in her tracks. A little squirrel was Geoffroi Chaucer. Even the trees had names—the tallest tree in the forest was Charlemagne. A grand fir tree with an understanding soul was named Michael Angelo Sanzio Raphael. And her most dear lamb that had needs to be mothered was Menander Euripides Theocritus Thucydides—a mouthful for a 7-year-old, don't you think?

Now let me continue this sampler as the publisher of her book picks up the story.

> Opal Whiteley—so her story runs—was born about twenty-two years ago—where, we have no knowledge. Of her parents, whom she lost before her fifth year, she is sure of nothing except that they loved her, and that she loved them with a tenacity of affection as strong now as at the time of parting. To recall what manner of people they were, no physical proof remains except, perhaps, two precious little copybooks, which held their photographs and wherein her mother and father had set down things which they wished their little daughter to learn, both of the world about her and of that older world of legend and history, with which the diarist shows such capricious and entertaining familiarity. These books, for reasons beyond her knowledge, were taken away from Opal when she was about twelve years of age, and have never been returned, although there is ground for believing they are still in existence.
>
> Other curious clues to the identity of her father and mother come from the child's frequent use of French expressions, and sometimes of longer passages in French, and from her ready use of scientific terms. It is, perhaps, a fair inference that her father was a naturalist by profession or native taste, and that either he or her mother was French by birth or by education.
>
> After her parents' death, there is an interlude in Opal's recollection which she does not understand, remembering only that for a brief season the sweet tradition of her mother's care was carried on by an older woman, possibly a governess, from whom, within a year, was taken and, after recovering from a serious illness, given to the wife of an Oregon lumberman, lately parted from their first child—Opal Whiteley—whose place and name, for reasons quite unknown, were given to the present Opal.
>
> From some time in her sixth year to the present, her diary has continued without serious interruption; and from the successive chapters we shall see that her life, apart from the gay tranquility of her spirit, was not a happy one. Her friends were the animals and everything that flies or swims; her single confidant was her diary, to which she confided every trouble and satisfaction.
>
> When Opal was over twelve years old, a foster-sister, in a tragic fit of childish temper, unearthed the hiding-place of the diary and tore it into a myriad of fragments. The work of years seemed destroyed, but Opal, who had treasured its understanding pages, picked up the pitiful scraps and stored them in a secret box. There they lay undisturbed for

many years.

[Let me interject here—there were those who said she was a fraud. Mystery still surrounds her life. The world certainly does 'veil the spirit,' but understanding hearts will feel the beauty and sincerity of her writings and above all, her childlike faith in God which never left her.

Back to the story told by the editor in the Preface of her diary:]

Last September, late one afternoon, Opal Whiteley came into the Atlantic's office, with a book which she had had printed in Los Angeles. It was not a promising errand, though it had brought her all the way from the Western coast, hoping to have published in regular fashion this volume, half fact, half fancy, of *The Fairyland Around Us*, the fairyland of beasts and blossoms, butterflies and birds. The book was quaintly embellished with colored pictures, pasted in by hand, and bore a hundred marks of special loving-care. Yet about it there seemed little at first sight to tempt a publisher. Indeed, she had offered her wares in vain to more than one publishing house; and as her dollars were growing very few, the disappointment was severe. But about Opal Whiteley herself there was something to attract the attention even of a man of business—something very young and eager and fluttering, like a bird in a thicket,

The talk went as follows:—

"I am afraid we can't do anything with the book. But you must have had an interesting life. You have lived much in the woods?"

"Yes, in lots of lumber-camps."

"How many?"

"Nineteen. At least, we moved nineteen times."

It was hard not to be interested now. One close question followed another regarding the surroundings of her girlhood. The answers were so detailed, so sharply remembered, that the next question was natural.

"If you remember like that, you must have kept a diary."

Her eyes opened wide. "Yes, always I do still."

"Then it is not the book I want, but the diary."

She caught her breath. "It's destroyed. It's all torn up." Tears were in her eyes.

"You loved it?"

"Yes; I told it everything."

"Then you kept the pieces."

The guess was easy (what child whose doll is rent asunder throws away the sawdust?), but she looked amazed.

"Yes, I have kept everything. The pieces are all stored in Los Angeles."

We telegraphed for them, and they came, hundreds, thousands, one might almost say millions of them. Some few were large as a half-sheet of notepaper; more, scarce big enough to hold a letter of the alphabet. The paper was of all shades, sorts, and sizes: butchers' bags pressed and sliced in two, wrapping-paper, the backs of envelopes—anything and everything that could hold writing. The early years of the diary are printed in letters so close that, when the sheets are fitted, not another letter can be squeezed in. In later passages the characters are written with childish clumsiness, and later still one sees the gradually forming adult hand.

The labor of piecing the diary together may fairly be described as enormous. For nine months almost continuously the diarist has labored, piecing it together sheet by sheet, each page a kind of picture-puzzle, lettered, for frugality (the store was precious), on both sides of the paper.

The entire diary, of which this volume covers but the two opening years, must comprise a total of a quarter of a million words. Upwards of seventy thousand—all that is contained in this volume—can be ascribed with more than reasonable definiteness to the end of Opal's sixth and to her seventh year. During all these months Opal Whiteley has been a frequent visitor in the Atlantic's office. With friendliness came confidence, and little by little, very gradually, an incident here, another there, her story came to be told. She was at first eager only for the future and for the opportunity to write and teach children of the world which she loved best. But as the thread of the diary was unraveled, she felt a growing interest in what her past had been, and in what lay behind her earliest recollections and the opening chapters of her printed record.

If the story of Opal were written by another hand than her own, the central theme of it would be faith. No matter how doubtful the enterprise, the issue she always holds as certain, simply because the world is good and God loves his children. Loving herself all created things, from her barrel-full of caterpillars, whose evolution she would note and chronicle from day to day, to the dogs and horses, squirrels, raccoons, and bats which peopled the world she lived in, she would thank God daily for them, and very early in her life determined to devote the rest of it spreading knowledge of them and of their kind far and wide among little children.

To accomplish this, needed education, and an education she would have. Those about her showed no interest; but by picking berries, washing, and work of all rough sorts, Opal paid for the books which the high school required. But she must do more than this. She must go to college. To the State University she went, counting it nothing that she should live in a room without furniture other than a two-dollar cot, and two coats for blankets. Family conditions, however, made college impossible for her. After the illness and death of Mrs. Whiteley, Opal borrowed a little money from friends in Cottage Grove, Oregon, and started alone for Los Angeles, determined to see her livelihood by giving nature lessons to classes of children.

The privations and disappointments of the next two years would make an heroic tale;

but she persevered, and her classes became successful. The next step was her nature book, for which, by personal canvass for subscriptions, she raised not less than the prodigious sum of $9,400. But the printers with a girl for a client, demanded more and still more money, and when the final $600 necessary to make the booty mount to $10,000 was not forthcoming, with a brutality that would do credit to Thenardier, first threatened, and then destroyed the plates.

A struggle for mere existence followed, but gradually Opal triumphed, when she was overtaken by a serious illness and taken to the hospital. New and merciful friends, such as are always conjured up by such a life as Opal's, came to her assistance, and after her recovery she soon started eastward, to find a publisher for her ill-fated volume. The rest we know.

Yet, after all, our theme should not be Opal, but Opal's book. She is the child of curious and interesting circumstance, but of circumstance her journal is altogether independent. The authorship does not matter, nor the life from which it came. There the book is. Nothing else is like it, nor apt to be. If there is alchemy in Nature, it is in children's hearts the unspoiled treasure lies, and for that room of the treasure-house, the Story of Opal offers a tiny golden key.

Her Fairyland book was eventually published. She loved teaching children about nature and became known as The Sunshine Fairy. David Starr Jordan, the first President of Stanford University and a great soul we'll talk about more in a few months, wrote this introduction to that book which is a lesson to us as we study the importance of Nature Study in the lives of our children:

> It was a French story-teller who said: "We must lay up a stock of enthusiasms in our youth, or else we shall reach the end of our journey with an empty heart, for we lose a great many of them by the way."

> It is the finest part of education to fill the mind of youth with these enthusiasms, to teach him to know the world about him because he loves it—to love the world about him because he knows it—to make friends with all the things of nature, great and small, he meets when he goes forth every day—to know and love the little world about him which is after all the fairer part of the great world we call the Universe of God.

> And the joys of seeing and knowing and doing are the real joys of life. We may know a real joy from a spurious pleasure by this—it leaves no sting, it brings no weakness, it clears the way for more joys and more strength. Moreover, as Agassiz used to say: "This is the charm of Nature herself: She brings us back to absolute Truth—every time we wander."

> This is a word of greeting to a unique Nature book, the work of a young woman who is a real lover of Nature. It is an effort to give our boys and girls a right start in the joys of life. It opens their eyes to the charms and glories shown all around them. It draws them toward a sympathy with the problems of life which beset every man and beast and bird among us and which one way or another we are called on to solve. It swells the stock

of these youthful enthusiasms which so long as they last keep the heart young and make life the better worth living.

His words were followed by the publisher of the book:

God's Wonder-world is very largely wasted on us, nowadays, because we pay no attention to it. We don't see the beauty in the blade of grass, nor in the drop of rain, nor in the love-making of the flower, nor in the industry of the bee, nor in the reason why some birds have beautiful songs and others beautiful coats. We could not turn around even a city lot without finding something to fascinate us, if we had either the knowledge or the imagination of what is there.

As every mother knows, the way to keep youngsters out of "mischief" is to employ their minds and hands. Any youngster who becomes interested in the birds and flowers and beasties will have a lot of mental occupation and no real excuse for getting into "mischief."

I hope I have piqued your interest. And by the way, Barbara Cooney illustrated a beautiful little picture book called *Only Opal* that you may be able to find in your public library, but would be a worthwhile addition to own a copy that will introduce your very youngest children to her story and love of nature.

Sadly, Opal spent the last 50 years of her life in a psychiatric hospital in England where she was known as The Princess. She committed herself—perhaps the stresses of life were too great for her and at least she was safe there. She was buried at Highgate Cemetery. Her tombstone bears her name and the simple inscription: I spake as a child.

It's fitting to close this podcast with her words:

"Now Brave Horatius and me and Thomas Chatterton Jupiter Zeus are going to prayers in the cathedral. The great pine tree is saying a poem, and there is a song in the tree-tops."

Podcast #161 James Baldwin

Today I want to tell you about a book called *In My Youth* by Robert Dudley[83] and was published in 1914. It goes along with our topic of the westward expansion. But Robert Dudley was only a pen name. It is considered to be the autobiography of James Baldwin and offers one of the best glimpses into the everyday lives of those rural settlers who pushed our boundaries west that I have ever read. I absolutely love this book which is why I wanted to add it to the listening library, although I have to admit my attempt to read the backwoods dialogue made my daughter, who is helping to edit these audios, laugh out loud.

So who is this James Baldwin and why would you care to know about him?

If you have read William Bennett's *Book of Virtues*, you have read many of James Baldwin's writings. And if you are familiar with Lisa Ripperton's incredible Baldwin Project in connection to Yesterday's Classics, she named the project after him. And for good reason! He not only wrote more than 50 books for children, including biographies, histories and the retelling of classic stories, at one time, of all the school books used in the United States, over half of them had been written or edited by him. He also compiled the Baldwin, Harper and Expressive Readers. Over 26 million copies of his books were distributed worldwide, including China and Indonesia.

A pretty big accomplishment for someone who grew up in a humble cabin in the New Settlement of rural Indiana, with little opportunity for formal education. He was largely self-educated. Which is why I think you'll love his story because through this story, you will see the simple life events that shaped this great man who went on to accomplish such great things. You will see a lot of Well-Educated Heart principles in action. It's another testament of the power of books to shape lives and of the small and simple means that grow great men and women. His influence cannot begin to be measured. And yet, today, few people recognize his name or know of his work. I have searched in vain for more details on his life but this one volume, I think, tells all the essentials.

He never had children of his own, although the book was written for his unseen posterity which is actually all of us. I have to admit when I finished the book, there may have been tears and it was one of those books I hugged and didn't want to end.

I suspect by the time you finish the book, you will feel like James Baldwin is a real friend; someone you'll want to hang out with for the rest of your life. As much as I love progress, I'm glad I can ride in air conditioned cars and drive to the store to pick up food, I couldn't help but feel that something has gone missing in our lives and I found myself longing for simpler times.

The editor for the original publisher for this book wrote:

> It is difficult to describe just what there is so remarkable about this book, but it is undeniably wonderful. It is literature. It is a strange combination of autobiography and

fiction, and records only the simplest happenings the life of people in the Indiana backwoods, the primitive life, the commonplace experiences, the visits between neighbors. To tell about it in this way does not make it sound remarkable, yet it is. The style is simple and clear; there's a quiet humor running through it, and in other places, the reading brings tears to the eyes.

This is a book for the whole family. I hope you enjoy it.

Podcast #162 Orison Swett Marden

I have had the loveliest and most inspiring guest stay at my home the last couple of weeks. It's a minor detail that his body was laid in the ground nearly a hundred years ago. He has been filling me with his words of wisdom—if you were paying attention, you'll see that I have been sharing a few of those words the last few days in my Facebook posts. He saw you mothers a hundred years ago—he knows: "The very foundation of our national life is laid in the home, and the wife and mother is the center, the mainspring of all true home life...."

He confided in me that "[o]ur wives and mothers have as yet hardly entered the outer chamber of the beautiful edifice of the ideal home of the future. It is the holy of holies of evolution, and in it lies the very secret of human progress....

"The highest civilizations have scarcely as yet glimpsed the possibilities of home."

He told me he believes, "The time will come when our children will be taught...to consider beauty as a most precious gift...and regarded as a divine instrument of education." For, he said, "[b]eauty is a quality of divinity, and to live much with the beautiful is to live close to the divine. Every beauty in any form...refines and elevates character...."

I told him that is happening right now through you in your homes. And he smiled.

Sadly, I told him I have a lot of things piling up on my to do list and other guests who I have kept waiting and I have to make room for them. He understood and said I have an open invitation to invite him back any time I want. Still, I didn't want him to go. I told him it is such a shame that he, who influenced so many millions of lives for good all over the world, should be practically unknown in our world today.

But I told him I'd like to remedy that and that I wanted to tell you moms his story. So we stayed up together last night, way into the late night hours, while he shared his story with me so that I can tell you.

I almost forgot to tell you his name! His name is Orison Swett Marden.

His sweet mother died at the age of 22 when he was only 3 years old. While he didn't get to keep any pictures, his entire life he had a vivid recollection of her beautiful face and her auburn hair as she tucked him in his bed. His grief-stricken father—a tall, rugged 6-foot-2 man—took on the role of father and mother in their backwoods home in the hills of New Hampshire. He not only carried on his duties of farming, hunting and trapping, he took care of all the household tasks of cooking and cleaning and sewing and caring for the three little children left behind. Orison cherished the memory of the little Christmas outfit his father stayed up late to sew for him.

He loved his father. But one day, when he was out checking on a bear trap in the forest, there was an accident with the trap that brought down a large tree upon him. He managed to drag himself home, but he died just a short time later.

Orison now had no home. He was separated from his sisters, this little boy of seven, and sent to homes who took him in as the 'hired boy.' He would pass through five such homes before striking out on his own. He was cuffed and whipped, starved, worked to the limits of human endurance, abused and insulted. There was no one to give him comfort or love or answer his questions. Yet, it was out of the bitterness of his own experiences—his joyless childhood and the utter starvation of body and soul—that he was able to learn the glorious secrets of real happiness.

And one of those secrets was the gifts of Nature.

He told me:

> Everything in Nature seemed to speak to me to try to make up to me for my homelessness and loneliness. I loved every bit of it. Often in an ecstasy of emotion I would throw my arms around the trees and hug them…. They filled me with a sense of the very presence of God, and I felt that I could read His thoughts in the flowers, in the grass, in the trees, in the birds—in all the beauty He created.

> Something spoke through all these things to me; gave me assurance and hope, and in a measure satisfied my hunger for love. When out in the sunshine, under the blue sky, I could not believe that I was left quite alone in this great universe, just because my father and mother had left me. It did not seem right to me that I should be cut off from communication with all who had any interest in me. Indeed, I fancied that I could feel the pulse of the unseen life, and that I could communicate with the spirit, the reality of my father and mother through the things I loved so much.

> This love of Nature was a special refuge. I only knew that I was happy when out in the fields or in the woods, listening to the birds and watching the butterflies and the bees gathering honey from the wild flowers whose fragrance and beautiful colors delight my heart….

He added this story from his adulthood:

> I was going through the Yosemite region. After riding one hundred miles in a stage coach, over rough mountain roads, I felt so utterly exhausted that it did not seem possible for me to hold on to my seat while we covered the ten more miles that lay between us and our destination. But we toiled on and at length reached the summit of the mountain.

> Never shall I forget the sight that greeted my eyes on looking down. The sun, just breaking through the clouds, which until then had hung over the landscape, shone out in all its noonday splendor on the wonderful Yosemite Falls and the surrounding scenery. Spread out below us, above us, around us, there was revealed a picture painted by the Almighty Himself—a picture of such rare beauty, of such marvelous form and coloring, such an infinite variety of texture and tinting that my soul was ravished. Every particle of fatigue, mental exhaustion, and muscle weariness, which had threatened

physical collapse, vanished. My whole being thrilled with a winged sense of sublimity, grandeur, and beauty which I had never before experienced. I felt a spiritual uplift which brought tears of joy to my eyes. I seemed to stand in the visible presence of God, in the very Holy of Holies.

In that moment's spiritual vision a new life had entered into me. I had been recreated. All my hurts were healed. A new ambition surged through me, filled me with a desire to attempt great things—to do something bigger than I had before thought possible to me....

Like the mythological giant, Antaeus, whose strength was renewed every time he touched his Mother Earth, I felt a new and wonderful strength throbbing through my veins—I was a new man!

Said the Psalmist: "I will lift mine eyes unto the hills, from whence cometh my help."

There was a silence—a break in our conversation—as I tried to take in all he was saying. And then he quietly added, "Remind your mothers, when you are jaded and worn from the strenuous life of motherhood; when exhausted after a year's run, struggling with the daily problems that face you—it is to the 'everlasting hills' you must turn for help—for health, for physical and spiritual renewal. You must go into God's laboratory, the great outdoors, where Mother Nature will 'take her own way with you.'"

If you give yourselves to her unreservedly, she will lay her healing hand upon you, overhaul and repair your exhausted bodies, restore your flagging spirits—renew you physically and spiritually—and, in due time, send you back to your tasks, new women.

Now back to the story. When he was in his early- to mid-teens, he happened upon a dilapidated copy of a book stored away in an attic that was the turning point in his life. It was written by a Scottish man named Samuel Smiles—the book was called *Self Help*. He wrote it to give hope to the young boys and girls of England who were living in such dire poverty and circumstances. Orison said, "I felt like a poor man who had just by accident discovered a gold mine. The book was a perpetual delight to me, and I treasured it as if it were worth its weight in diamonds, reading and re-reading the precious pages until I had almost committed them to memory."

It was a book of stories; stories of great men and women who had overcome hard challenges in their lives. It lit a fire of hope in his own heart, and by sheer perseverance and push, he went on to graduate from the Harvard School of Medicine and the Boston University School of Law within a year of each other as well as earning degrees in science and art. He put himself through school by working in hotels—which he later owned.

Then came the depression of the late 1800s and he experienced great financial loss, including the loss of his hotels. Yet, it wasn't growing a hotel empire that held his heart. For fifteen years, he had used every spare moment to gather stories of great men and women because he wanted to do for the youth of America what Samuel Smiles had done for the youth of England—and for him. It was his way of paying it forward.

He was preparing the manuscript from his thousands of pages of notes he had gathered when a fire broke out in the hotel where he was staying. He escaped the fire with nothing but his nightshirt on. His labor of years went up in smoke.

He immediately walked down the street to buy some necessary clothes. As soon as this was attended to, he bought a twenty-five cent notebook, and while the ruins of the hotel were still smoking, began to write from memory the manuscript of his dream book.

Of course, he was overwhelmed and heartbroken. He had little money, but with what he had, he bought a train ticket to Massachusetts, rented a small, plain room and diligently set to work. After a short time, he made 3 manuscripts of the book, sent it to three local publishers, and all three of them offered to publish it.

Pushing to the Front became a runaway bestseller. Within 25 years, there had been 250 editions in the United States alone. Letters poured in from presidents like William McKinley, Theodore Roosevelt, the British Prime Minister William Gladstone, kings and rulers from around the world, telling him of how it had influenced their lives. A noted educator of the Italian Parliament strongly recommended the book be made obligatory reading in the schools of Italy, because he regarded it as 'a civilization builder.' The government schools of Japan and Peru and other countries adopted it into their studies. The book inspired Henry Ford, Thomas Edison, Harvey Firestone and JP Morgan. Orison received thousands of letters from people in nearly all parts of the world, telling how the book had aroused their ambition, changed their ideals and aims, increased their confidence, and how it had spurred them to the successful undertaking of what they before had thought impossible.

Many of these letters came from youths telling how it had encouraged them to return to school or college after having given up in despair; to go back to vocations which they had left in a moment of discouragement; enheartened to take up other dropped or neglected tasks with new hope and new ambition; and how the book had proved a turning point in their careers; the cause of their success.

He went on to write 50 more books—publishing nearly two books a year. He started a magazine to inspire hearts: it was called *Success*. And it failed in 1912. But that didn't phase him. In 1918, a new version appeared that stayed in print until after his death.

Yet, for all the fame and fortune, he knew the true secrets of happiness and that's what he taught and lived. They were the treasures of the heart—that there is something greater than wealth, grander than fame; that character is success, and there is no other.

As much as he wanted a home and a family, it didn't happen until he was in his 50s. He married a young woman and together they had three children. He wanted to leave them a legacy that they would prize more than they would a money legacy—he wanted them to have a precious recollection, a sweet, beautiful memory of a happy childhood, a happy home, a kind, loving father.

He bought a farm on Long Island and there he lived a blissful life at home with his wife and children. In after years one of the children said, "Father looks at Mother as if she were an angel just come down from heaven, and might at any moment unfold her wings and take flight again."

This perfectly expressed his attitude toward his wife from the beginning to the end of their married life. He never seemed to have gotten over the joy and wonder of having won her.

After he closed his story for the night, I told my guest that after I told you about him, you were likely going to want him to come visit your homes, too. And he said that would be his delight.

I told him that I have been recording his book he wrote especially for the youth in school— *Stories from Life*. I am posting the stories at mybelmonde.com. I told him I put it in the Westward Expansion section under great lives because he is certainly expanding our minds!

He was happy that I included links to some of his books in the Joy section of the Mother's University. "You know," he said with a twinkle in his eye, "the whole world is full of unworked joy mines. Everywhere we go we find all sorts of happiness-producing material, if we only know how to extract it."

How can we ever thank you, I asked him.

He hugged me, and said that if something he has written opens wider the door of some narrow life and awakens powers before unknown, he will feel amply repaid for his labor.

My dear friend, Orison Swett Marden—bye bye, until we meet again.

Podcast #163 Albert Payson Terhune's Mother

I don't get to the Nature side of the rotation schedule as much as I'd like in these podcasts, but today I'd like to share a bit about Albert Payson Terhune. Before there was Lassie, there was Lad, a Dog, a much beloved classic about the love of a collie written largely from Albert's own experiences. He went on to write over 30 books, mostly about dogs. You'll find a link to the book in the Animals section. Just fair warning, evidently there are parts of the book that are racist, but don't let that keep you away. Use it as a teaching moment of how people viewed different races in another time. Learn from it. I haven't had a chance to read the book yet, but I am recommending it on the basis of how many generations have loved this book.

I'll tell you something about Albert that made me appreciate him more. His first wife died when she was only 23 years old, four days after she gave birth to their daughter. They had only been married none months. He eventually remarried, but never had more children. I always make note of such things, even though very sad, as a reminder that people get through hard things; that there is life after tragedy. And I can't think of many sorrows harder than this one.

But neither Albert nor his book are really the focus of this podcast. I want to tell you about his mother. Or rather, I am going to have Albert tell you about his mother. I found an old magazine article written in October of 1926 entitled *Why I Think My Father and Mother Were Great* by Albert Payson Terhune.[84] I'll let it speak for itself.

> May I introduce my mother to you. She is worth your meeting; for she was almost as great in her own way as my father.
>
> My mother was a dire disappointment to my grandmother. From the time she was ten years old, she used to occupy her leisure time in scribbling stories in her copybook. This was an unheard-of form of mental perversion. Her mother hoped the child might outgrow it.
>
> When she was fourteen, my mother wrote a story, called "Marrying Through Prudential Motives" and she sent it to a fifty-dollar prize contest that was waging in "Godey's Lady's Book." This was in 1845; an era when respectable young girls were no more supposed to write for publication than they were supposed to go into the prize-ring.
>
> She did not wish to disgrace her family by writing the tale under her own name, on the off chance that it might be printed and her shame blazoned to the world. So she hit on the pen name that thereafter was hers. Her name was Mary Hawes—Mary Virginia Hawes. She kept the initials of her first and last names and used them for a nom de plume which would sound as much as possible like the original without betraying her identity. This, so she would be able to tell to her girl friends, in secret, that she was the author of the story; with some chance of being believed.
>
> Hence, she evolved from "Mary Hawes" the pseudonym "Marion Harland."

My mother did not send her address with the story, nor stamps for its return. Six months later, she saw in "Godey's Lady's Book" an announcement that "Marion Harland" had won the contest's first prize of fifty dollars; and a request that she send her address.

"What did you do with the fifty dollars?" I asked, when she told me about it.

"I spent half of it on a black silk dress for my mother," she answered, "and gave the other half, anonymously, to our church's building fund. You see, I had a feeling I had done something wicked; and that it would be wrong to profit by it."

My grandmother's pleasure (if any) in the silk dress did not balance her horror at her fourteen-year-old daughter's sin. She lectured her severely and weepingly on the unwomanliness of writing stories; and besought her never again to yield to such an unworthy temptation.

For two solid years my mother was so oppressed with a sense of guilt that she did not write another word. She told me those were the two unhappiest years of her life. Story plots kept bubbling into her brain, and her fingers itched to set them down in words. The strain told on her health. In a moment of confidence, she confessed to her father the sinful yearning of her heart to go in writing; and she asked him how best to overcome it.

He demanded that she hunt up any of her stories she might still have kept, and show them to him. He spent a whole evening reading them, in his study. Late that night, he finished the heap of scribbled manuscripts and went up to her room with them. She woke to see him standing at the foot of her bed.

"Daughter," said the grim old Presbyterian, "you can serve God and mankind as worthily with a gift like yours, as you could by going as a missionary to the heathen. God gave you the rare power to write. You would be ungrateful to Him if you neglected it. Go on with your work."

From then to his death he read and reread every word she wrote; and looked upon her with a queer awe. She, alone of his army of children, did not fear him, and had no need to.

When she was eighteen, she finished her first novel, "Alone." In Presbyterian Richmond, in the late 1840s, novel reading was done in secret, for the most part. Such books usually were kept from The Young. Trembling, my mother took "Alone" to a local publisher. He rejected it. She sent it to a Northern publisher, who sent it back almost by return mail.

Then she told her father what she had done. He read the book's manuscript all of one business day and late into the night. Next morning he took it to the Richmond publisher who had refused it, and bade him issue a goodly edition of it and to send him the bill. My mother told me she lay awake all that night, wondering if her father would get back a penny of his wild investment.

The novel passed the hundred thousand mark, in an age when large book sales were pitiably few. Longfellow and young Aldrich and Whittier and N.P. Willis wrote glowingly congratulatory letters about it to the unknown girl; letters she treasured all her long life.

She had arrived.

Thenceforward the road was clear. Book followed book. All of them successful.

She and my father met at a dinner, in Richmond. Each was twenty-four. Each disliked the other at sight. My father had said he "had a contempt for women who wrote books." My mother heard of this. She had said she would sooner die than marry a clergyman; and that my father had the ugliest jaw she had seen on a man. (That was nearly twenty years before I was born with a jaw that matched it, line for line.) Kind friends carried this absurd speech to him.

A year later, he and she were married. They came to New Jersey to live—to Newark, which in that day was well-nigh as strait-laced as Richmond…

His religious faith was as simple as a child's. So was my mother's. This simple and utter faith—a faith past mere argument—is the richest of their many heritages to me.

It was when I was still a small child that my mother's lungs broke down; and we went to Europe to stay for several years. It was during this time, too, that I drove my mother almost to desperation.

It happened in Rome. We had a furnished apartment there, on the Piazza de Spagna. My mother was a splendid disciplinarian and she was rigidly careful, besides, as to my diet and sleep hours. I rebelled often and fruitlessly at this restraint. I used to cite the happy children who were allowed to sit up till ten o'clock at night, and to eat pastry and candy and the like; and who were not forced to eat hideous oatmeal porridge at breakfast or be in bed by seven. In irritation, once, my mother answered:

"When I am gone, you'll have a pretty stepmother with golden hair and blue eyes, and she'll let you sit up as late as you want to and eat everything you like; and she will give you pounds of candy a day!"

She spoke in vexed joke and, I think, more for the benefit of my father than for myself. But the mischief was done. My boyish imagination took hold. Instead of bursting into tears at chance of losing her, I was thrilled to the very soul at the prospect she had painted for me.

Of course, I loved my mother, and of course I didn't want her to die. But she had to die—well, golden hair and blue eyes were a grand combination. And the pretty stepmother would let me sit up all night if I wanted to, and she would feed me heaps of candy and let me have Italian pastry for breakfast and all manner of other heavenly food.

That began it. I knew my mother was truthful. She never broke her word. She had promised me this fascinating and generous stepmother. Therefore, the stepmother must soon appear, her white arms laden with rich gifts for me—mostly things to eat. Of course this couldn't happen while my mother lived. But—

Morning after morning I ran to my mother's room as soon as I was awake, to peer keenly at her over the foot of the bed, and to ask how she was feeling.

Sometimes—very tactfully, for I began to see it was not a popular theme of discourse with her—I would seek to lure her into more detailed descriptions of the stepmother, who by this time had been clothed by my flaming imagination with all the most desirable aspects of Santa Claus.

"Could I have a saddle horse and a collie dog of my very own, did she suppose? Of course, not right now, but when—when—?"

She told me years afterward that my ghoulishly speculative glares at her and my incessant hints about the beautiful stepmotherly times ahead did more to rouse in her an angry resolution to live than did all the climate and medicines.

She had gone to Europe to die. Every doctor said so; and on that ground they had advised my father against taking her thither. Stubbornly he had insisted, declaring he was going to bring her back alive and well. His forecast came true. She returned to America at last in splendid health and she remained so for another forty years.

It was before that first European sojourn and before her health broke down that she won another battle in regard to her writing—a battle almost as arduous as the one my grandfather had helped her through. She was the best housekeeper—except my own wife—that I have known. This in a day when cookbooks were few and semi-useless and when housewives perforce turned to their elders for culinary lore.

She decided to write a cookbook which could be understood and followed by the newest bride. She wrote it. She called it "Common Sense in the Household." I believe that something close to a half-million copies of it have been sold first and last.

Then came the struggle to get it published. Long since, her many novels had found a ready and growing market. But this was a different matter. Her own publishers would not touch the new venture. They and other experts said there was no possible sale for a cookbook, and that the volume must be a lamentable failure.

At length she took the unwanted cookbook to Charles Scribner, senior. He accepted it—not, as he confessed to her later on, that he had any idea it could sell a dozen copies, but in the hopes that his publishing it would induce her to let him bring out her next novel.

At once, "Common Sense in the Household" justified her belief in it. It did more. It condemned its author to be known henceforth as a writer on domestic topics instead of a novelist; and to build her future fame on what had been a mere experiment.

"It isn't literature, this household stuff I write," she told me once, with a whimsical resignation. "I know that. But it is influence. And it helps people. Perhaps that is even more worthwhile than to feel that my next novel is looked forward to by those same people."

Yet I knew it galled her, unspeakably, that a younger generation should look upon her as a kind of super-cook and not a popular novelist. She bore it pluckily, even gayly; as was her way. And she made the most of it. But always it hurt.

She kept on with her novels too; and even won for herself a merited fame as a biographer. But primarily, from that time on, she was known to the public at large only as an authority on household themes. To me, there is a glint of tragedy in that. She won her campaign for the betterment of American homes; but in winning it she threw away her high vogue as a fiction writer.

Two more successful battles, on a smaller scale, marked her after-life. At seventy-three she broke her right wrist. Never did it mend enough for her to write again by hand, except for a very few scrawling words at a stretch. At that age, for the first time, she bought and mastered a typewriting machine; presently using it as fast and as well as many a professional typist, and learning to compose on it as readily as one she had written by pen. That by itself was something of a victory, for a woman her age, I think.

At ninety, she went blind. We told her it was double cataract, and that soon she could be operated on and would see as well as ever. But it was not cataract. It was an incurable form of blindness.

Unwilling to wait with her hands folded in her lap for the supposed operation, she hired a secretary and taught herself to dictate. She dictated an entire novel ("the Carringtons of High Hill"), and numberless household articles, in the remaining eighteen months of her life. To me that seems her supreme triumph. For the work was vigorous and excellent, showing no sign of its author's great age nor of her unaccustomed new medium of expression.

She was the hardest and most conscientious worker imaginable. I do not believe there was a week-day a month, year after year, on which she did not average at least seven busy hours at her desk, besides superintending every detail of the household.

Neither the quality of the work nor that of the home suffered in any way by this dual achievement. When I say she spent seven hours at her desk, I don't mean she sat there mooning or fidgeting or chatting; but that she was writing every minute, and with every ounce of energy and concentration she possessed.

She endured, from us children or from the servants or from visitors, an incessant bombardment of interruptions which would send me insane, or which, at the very least, would shatter for the whole day my ability to do acceptable or even coherent work. Never have I seen her lose her none-too-placid temper at such interruptions. Always, if they were justified—and often if they were not—she would attend to whatever detail of business was brought up by them; and then would go back to her work, joining its frayed threads where they had been broken off.

I dropped in to see her at dusk, just after her eighty-ninth birthday. She was resting.

"I'm a little tired," she told me. "I was at my desk nine solid hours today. There was an article the editors wanted in a hurry. Yes, I'm really tired," she added worriedly. "Do you suppose it is a sign I'm getting old?"

There were six of us children, to begin with. Three of us lived past childhood. I was the youngest, being born on my mother's forty-second birthday. She used to say she and I were twins.

Apart from her manifold other labors, she taught all of us to read and write; and prepared us for school so thoroughly, along every branch of study, that we entered classes with children two or three years older than we. I should like to brag that we continued to hold the gratifying scholastic start she gave us; but, in my own case, it would not be true. I slipped back with startling promptitude.

As to our home life during my childhood—looking back on it over the lapse of so many years, the only real flaw I can recall is my mother's insistence that we bet at the breakfast table at a most ungodly early hour. She herself was up and about by daybreak. She had no love at all for sleep, and she had only puzzled scorn for those who enjoyed it. Said my father to me, half-mournfully, when I had incurred disgrace, a usual, through over sleeping:

"Your dear mother is ready to believe that God's mercy is wide enough to embrace all ordinary sinners; but she is quite certain there is no forgiveness either in heaven or on earth for anyone who lies in bed after seven in the morning."

She outlived my father by fifteen years; though she had always declared most positively that he would outlive her. Less than a year before his death, he and she celebrated their golden wedding, at Sunnybank; the home they had bought and built and loved in the early days of their married life, the home that now is mine.

Podcast #164 James Russell Miller

I made a new friend this morning. A member of our group introduced me to him. He wrote a piece about Pictures in the Heart and by the time I got through reading it, I thought this is someone I have to get to know better.

I believe his name is familiar among Presbyterians, but I had never heard his name before. His name is James Russell Miller and he was born in 1840 and died in 1912 and Pennsylvania was home. Let me introduce him by way of the foreword in a biography of him written by John Faris:[85]

> Dr. Miller was too much occupied with things deemed by him more important to give any attention to the selection and putting aside of material concerning his life. He was so busy writing and speaking and living and loving, with the shaping of the lives of others in view, that he took no time to think of the world's interest in his life. It never occurred to him that there would be any demand for the story of his life, and he discouraged the efforts of friends who sought to gather material for a biography.

> Yet Dr. Miller was the author of the truest possible description of himself. He did not think of it as a description—in giving it he was only telling the reality of his faith in his Master. But all who knew him agree that the description was true and accurate. He said, "Jesus and I are friends."

I love that. When he died, he didn't want any flowers on his grave or eulogies offered, although people gathered far and wide to share memories of him and lessons learned from this gentle soul. He said, "Let us seek to make our lives immortal, not in shafts and monuments, not in riches and earthly honors, but by making the world better, by putting touches of beauty into our lives, by teaching and blessing little children, by encouraging the weary and disheartened, and by comforting human sorrow. Then we shall need no grave with its marble memorial, to keep our name alive. We shall live in the things we have done."

Aren't those exactly the words you would expect to come from a Friend of Jesus?

So, of course, my mind always wonders about the childhood of such a person. And here are a few glimpses from Faris' biography. I think you will recognize some of the same methods you are incorporating into your homes.

> The poets were his great delight, and his mind and soul were enriched by many of their treasures.

> It was his habit to try to reproduce from memory sentences and paragraphs which impressed him, thus making them his own. Then he would write original sentences and paragraphs modeled on those of the masters.

> He was fond of illustrations that would be like windows through which the visions of

the soul might become real to others.

He took equal delight in studying the book of Nature which was spread out so entrancingly before him. Long walks in the country increased his love for God and God's world and all mankind.

His associates knew that his life was renewed by daily contact with Him, whom, even then, he was fond of calling His Friend. When he gifted his brother a Bible, he inscribed: Read this Book as a letter from the dearest of all friends.

There was no holier-than-thou spirit about him. The home in which religion was given such prominent and constant place was not the abode of gloom. The children were glad to spend the evening in the company of their parents. Music was their solace during many of these evenings. They would sing together or James would play on his violin.

Frequently there would be a guest in the family circle. And the conversation of these visitors did much to shape James's purpose in life.

So let me share the piece I read this morning called *Pictures in the Heart*[86]—what a beautiful vision of a Well-Educated Heart.

Niebuhr, the distinguished traveler, became blind in his old age. But, having traversed many lands, amid the fairest and loveliest scenes of the world, he had stored away in his memory, countless pictures of landscapes, mountain-scenery, valleys of rare beauty, and great and splendid cities. Then, as he lay upon his bed or reposed on his easy-chair, his face would often brighten into a rich glow, as if some inner light was shining through. He was pondering once more, some *splendid scene* he had looked upon in the sunny Orient. The chamber-walls of his memory were hung all over with pictures which filled his darkened years with joy and beauty. It mattered not to him—that the light had gone out, leaving thick gloom all about him. His *heart* was his world, and there was no darkness there. No putting out of sun—could obscure the *pictures that hung in that sacred house of his soul.*

In a far truer sense than many of us are aware—do our *hearts* make our *world* for us. The things we behold—are but the shadows of the things that are *in* us. If we have bright pictures in our heart—the whole world, wherever we go, will be a lovely picture-gallery! Every scene—will be a *panorama of beauty*. The most repulsive objects—will wear a tinge of loveliness. On the other hand, a somber, cheerless heart—clothes the whole world in shadow and gloom.

A writer says: "A *cold firebrand* and a *burning lamp* started out one day to see what they could find. The *firebrand* came back and wrote in its journal, that the whole world was very dark. It did not find a place wherever it went, in which there was light. Everywhere was darkness. The *lamp* when it came back wrote in its journal: 'Wherever I went—it was light. I did not find any darkness in all my journey. The whole world was light. The lamp carried light with it, and when it went abroad it illuminated everything. The dead firebrand carried no light, and it found none where it went.'"

Just so, men and women go through the world, and, returning, write records of observation just as diverse as these. Some find only gloom—in the fairest paths; and amid the lovely scenes—nothing beautiful. Others find nothing but beauty and brightness, even in the deepest valleys of earth. Each one finds—just what he takes out in himself. The colors he sees—are the tints of his own inner life.

Many people move amid unbroken music, hearing not one note; so, in a spiritual world full of heavenly presences, men remain unconscious of the love and companionship that linger about them. Having eyes—they see not; and having ears—they hear not. Their sorrows go uncomforted, while the Comforter stands close beside them. The world seems dreary and cold, while tender warmth and rich beauty lie close around them!

This is true in our commonest life. How many of us find all the good there is in our lot? Do we extract the *honey* from every flower that blooms in our path? Do we find all the *gold* that lies in the hard rocks over which our feet stumble? Do we behold all the *beauty* that glows along the ways of our sore toil? Do not many good things pass through our hands and slip away from us forever, before we even recognize their loveliness or their worth? Do not *angels* come to us unaware in homely disguise, walk with us, talk with us, minister to us, and then only become known to us—when their place is empty and they have spread their radiant wings in flight which we have no power ever to recall?

The *baby* seemed very troublesome as it broke your night's rest with its cries, and you were compelled to rise and care for it. But when it lay bashed and still, forever among the flowers—what would you not have given to have heard it cry again? We never see the beauty of our friends—until they are vanishing out of our sight. While they were with us—we were impatient with their faults. Their habits fretted us. But when death touched them—it clothed them in a garb of brilliant beauty. They appeared *transfigured*. Out of the dull, faulty character, sprang a radiant angel-form, and hovered just beyond our reach forever. What joy and blessing it had brought to our lives, to have seen the beauty and the worth—*before* the vanishing!

So it is in all life. It really takes but very little, to make anyone happy—yet there are many who cannot extract even a reasonable happiness from *a world of luxuries and blessings*. There are some who see nothing to admire—in the most magnificent collections of rare works of art, while others stand enraptured before the crudest picture.

There are those who will go through a forest on a June morning when a thousand birds are warbling—and hear not one note of song; while others are thrilled and charmed by the coarsest bird-note that falls out of the air. One man sees no beauty in the most picturesque landscape; another finds some tender bit of loveliness in the barest and most ragged scenery. One cannot find pleasure or contentment amid the most lavish abundance; another finds enough in the sheerest poverty, to give deep happiness and evoke hearty praise.

In nothing does this distinction come out more clearly than in the way *the ills of life* appear. One class of people see nothing but ills. Everything wears to them a somber aspect. Smallest trials are magnified into crushing disasters! All troubles look *exaggerated* to their vision. These see nothing but *adversity* in all their days. They find some cause for *discontent* in the serenest circumstances.

Then others find only blessing wherever they go. Their sorrows are struck through—with the glory of God's love. In the chapel at Pisa the dome is so constructed that sounds uttered below come back in a delightful response of melodious music, and even a discord is converted into a harmony as it floats up into the resonant vault and returns to the ear. Such a dome hangs over these souls. Even the *painful* and *discordant* things—are changed into rich harmonies!

Life seems different to different people—because their *hearts* differ! One man listens to thrilling music—and is not moved; under the same strains—another feels his soul kindled into rapture. The first has no music in his own bosom to interpret the melody that strikes his ear from without; the other has a singing angel in his heart, that responds to every sweet note that breathes through the air about him. "You must have the bird in your heart," says someone, "before you can find it in the bush."

It is not, then, half so much the *outward* in life that we need to have changed—as the spirit of the *inner* life. The cause of discontent is not in men's circumstances—but in their own spirit and temper. Get the song into your heart—and you will hear songs all about you. Even the wailing storm will but make music for you. Get the beauty and the good into your own soul—and you will see only beauty and good in all things. Get the peace deep into your own life—and you will find peace in every lot.

Our *hearts* make our *world* for us. The things we *see* around us—are but the shadows of our inner experiences, which are cast outside. The things we *hear* are but the echoes of our own inner thoughts and feelings. Pictures in the heart, fill all the world with ugliness—or loveliness!

And let me close this podcast with a few words of encouragement from Miller to you mothers.

The work you do may be unheralded to the world, but you are the living force that will decide the future of our world.

The battle was over. Two mighty armies had met in terrible conflict, and the earth had quivered beneath the shock. Great destinies had been decided.

After the battle, gentle women came upon the field, and went quietly and quickly among the wounded and dying with water and wine and food, and words of cheer and kindness.

There was diviner power in the ministry of these angels of comfort who came after the battle, when all was still, than in the awful force of the battle itself.

We are strong only as we are gentle. Gentleness is the power of God working in the world.

We may learn the finest arts of life music, painting, sculpture, poetry, or may master the noblest sciences, or by means of reading, study, travel and converse with refined people, may attain the best culture; but if in all this we do not learn love, and become more gentle in spirit and act, we have missed the prize of living.

It matters not how much Bible reading and prayer and godly teaching there may be in a home, if gentleness if lacking. A child must have love. Love is to life what sunshine is to plants and flowers. No young life can ever grow to its best in a home without gentleness.

> The lonely heart that knows not love's
> Soft power, or friendship's ties,
> Is like you withering flowering that bows
> Its gentle head touched to the quick
> For that the genial sun hath hid its light,
> And, sighing, dies.

There may be fine furniture, rich carpets, costly pictures, a large library of excellent volumes, instruments of music, and all luxuries and adornments; and there may be religious forms, good instruction; but if gentleness is wanting in the family, the lack is one which leave an irreparable hurt in the lives of the children.

There is a legend of a great artist. One day he had wrought long on his picture, but was discouraged, for he could not produce on his canvas the beauty of his soul's vision. He was weary, too; and sinking down on a stool by his easel, he fell asleep. While he slept an angel came; and taking the brushes which had dropped from the tired hands, he finished the picture in marvellous way.

> If only we strive to be pure and true,
> To each of us all there will come an hour
> When the tree of life shall burst into flower,
> And rain at our feet the glorious dower
> Of something grander than we ever knew.

I believe that…with all my heart.

Podcast #186 Helen Hunt Jackson

I frequently use a quote from Helen Hunt Jackson that goes like this: "Oh, if the world could only stop long enough for one generation of mothers to be made all right, what a Millennium could be begun in thirty years!"

I thought you might like to hear the story of the woman behind the quote, taken from a book called *Lives of Girls Who Became Famous* by Sarah Bolton,[87] written in 1886.

Thousands were saddened when, Aug. 12, 1885, it was flashed across the wires that Helen Hunt Jackson was dead. The Nation said, "The news will probably carry a pang of regret into more American homes than similar intelligence in regard to any other woman, with the possible exception of Mrs. Harriet Beecher Stowe."

How, with the simple initials, "H.H.," had she won this place in the hearts of the people? Was it because she was a poet? Oh no! many persons of genius have few friends. It was because an earnest life was back of her gifted writings. A great book needs a great man or woman behind it to make it a perfect work. Mrs. Jackson's literary work will be abiding, but her life, with its dark shadow and bright sunlight, its deep affections and sympathy with the oppressed, will furnish a rich setting for the gems of thought which she gave to the world.

Born in the cultured town of Amherst, Mass., Oct. 18, 1831, she inherited from her mother a sunny, buoyant nature, and from her father, Nathan W. Fiske, professor of languages and philosophy in the college, a strong and vigorous mind. Her own vivid description of the "naughtiest day in my life," in St. Nicholas, September and October, 1880, shows the ardent, wilful child who was one day to stand out fearlessly before the nation and tell its statesmen the wrong they had done to "her Indians."

She and her younger sister Annie were allowed one April day, by their mother, to go into the woods just before school hours, to gather checkerberries. Helen, finding the woods very pleasant, determined to spend the day in them, even though sure she would receive a whipping on her return home. The sister could not be coaxed to do wrong, but a neighbor's child, with the promise of seeing live snails with horns, was induced to accompany the truant. They wandered from one forest to another, till hunger compelled them to seek food at a stranger's home. The kind farmer and his wife were going to a funeral, and wished to lock their house; but they took pity on the little ones, and gave them some bread and milk. "There," said the woman, "now, you just make yourselves comfortable, and eat all you can; and when you're done, you push the bowls in among them lilac-bushes, and nobody'll get 'em."

Urged on by Helen, she and her companion wandered into the village, to ascertain where the funeral was to be held. It was in the meeting-house, and thither they went, and seated themselves on the bier outside the door. Becoming tired of this, they trudged on. One of them lost her shoe in the mud, and stopping at a house to dry their stockings, they were captured by two Amherst professors, who had come over to Hadley to attend the funeral. The children had walked four miles, and nearly the whole town, with the frightened mother, were in search of the runaways. Helen, greatly displeased at being caught, jumped out of the carriage, but was soon retaken. At ten o'clock at night they reached home, and the child walked in as rosy and smiling as possible, saying, "Oh, mother! I've had a perfectly splendid time!"

A few days passed, and then her father sent for her to come into his study, and told her because she had not said she was sorry for running away, she must go into the garret, and wait till he came to see her. Sullen at this punishment, she took a nail and began to bore holes in the plastering. This so angered the professor, that he gave her a severe whipping, and kept her in the garret for a week. It is questionable whether she was more penitent at the end of the week than she was at the beginning.

When Helen was twelve, both father and mother died, leaving her to the care of a grandfather. She was soon placed in the school of the author, Rev. J.S.C. Abbott, of New York, and here some of her happiest days were passed. She grew to womanhood, frank, merry, impulsive, brilliant in conversation, and fond of society.

At twenty-one she was married to a young army officer, Captain, afterward Major, Edward B. Hunt, whom his friends called "Cupid" Hunt from his beauty and his curling hair. He was a brother of Governor Hunt of New York, an engineer of high rank, and a man of fine scientific attainments. They lived much of their time at West Point and Newport, and the young wife moved in a fashionable social circle, and won hosts of admiring friends. Now and then, when he read a paper before some learned society, he was proud to take his vivacious and attractive wife with him.

Their first baby died when he was eleven months old, but another beautiful boy came to take his place, named after two friends, Warren Horsford, but familiarly called "Rennie." He was an uncommonly bright child, and Mrs. Hunt was passionately fond and proud of him. Life seemed full of pleasures. She dressed handsomely, and no wish of her heart seemed ungratified.

Suddenly, like a thunder-bolt from a clear sky, the happy life was shattered. Major Hunt was killed Oct. 2, 1863, while experimenting in Brooklyn, with a submarine gun of his own invention. The young widow still had her eight-year-old boy, and to him she clung more tenderly than ever, but in less than two years she stood by his dying bed. Seeing the agony of his mother, and forgetting his own even in that dread destroyer, diphtheria, he said, almost at the last moment, "Promise me, mamma, that you will not kill yourself."

She promised, and exacted from him also a pledge that if it were possible, he would come back from the other world to talk with his mother. He never came, and Mrs. Hunt could have no faith in spiritualism, because what Rennie could not do, she believed to be impossible.

For months she shut herself into her own room, refusing to see her nearest friends. "Any one who really loves me ought to pray that I may die, too, like Rennie," she said. Her physician thought she would die of grief; but when her strong, earnest nature had wrestled with itself and come off conqueror, she came out of her seclusion, cheerful as of old. The pictures of her husband and boy were ever beside her, and these doubtless spurred her on to the work she was to accomplish.

Three months after Rennie's death, her first poem, Lifted Over, appeared in the Nation:—

> As tender mothers, guiding baby steps,
> When places come at which the tiny feet
> Would trip, lift up the little ones in arms
> Of love, and set them down beyond the harm,
> So did our Father watch the precious boy,
> Led o'er the stones by me, who stumbled oft
> Myself, but strove to help my darling on:
> He saw the sweet limbs faltering, and saw
> Rough ways before us, where my arms would fail;
> So reached from heaven, and lifting the dear child,
> Who smiled in leaving me, He put him down
> Beyond all hurt, beyond my sight, and bade
> Him wait for me! Shall I not then be glad,
> And, thanking God, press on to overtake!"

The poem was widely copied, and many mothers were comforted by it. The kind letters she received in consequence were the first gleam of sunshine in the darkened life. If she were doing even a little good, she could live and be strong.

And then began, at thirty-four, absorbing, painstaking literary work. She studied the best models of composition. She said to a friend, years after, "Have you ever tested the advantages of an analytical reading of some writer of finished style? There is a little book called Out-Door Papers, by Wentworth Higginson, that is one of the most perfect specimens of literary composition in the English language. It has been my model for years. I go to it as a text-book, and have actually spent hours at a time, taking one sentence after another, and experimenting upon them, trying to see if I could take out a word or transpose a clause, and not destroy their perfection." And again, "I shall never write a sentence, so long as I live, without studying it over from the standpoint of whether you would think it could be bettered."

Her first prose sketch, a walk up Mt. Washington from the Glen House, appeared in the Independent, Sept. 13, 1866; and from this time she wrote for that able journal three hundred and seventy-one articles. She worked rapidly, writing usually with a lead-pencil, on large sheets of yellow paper, but she pruned carefully. Her first poem in the Atlantic Monthly, entitled Coronation, delicate and full of meaning, appeared in 1869, being taken to Mr. Fields, the editor, by a friend.

At this time she spent a year abroad, principally in Germany and Italy, writing home several sketches. In Rome she became so ill that her life was despaired of. When she was partially recovered and went away to regain her strength, her friends insisted that a professional nurse should go with her; but she took a hard-working young Italian girl of sixteen, to whom this vacation would be a blessing.

On her return, in 1870, a little book of Verses was published. Like most beginners, she was obliged to pay for the stereotyped plates. The book was well received. Emerson liked especially her sonnet, Thought. He ranked her poetry above that of all American women, and most American men. Some persons praised the "exquisite musical structure" of the Gondolieds, and others read and re-read her beautiful Down to Sleep. But the world's favorite was Spinning:—

> Like a blind spinner in the sun,
> I tread my days;
> I know that all the threads will run
> Appointed ways;
> I know each day will bring its task,
> And, being blind, no more I ask.
>
> *   *   *   *   *
>
> But listen, listen, day by day,
> To hear their tread
> Who bear the finished web away,
> And cut the thread,
> And bring God's message in the sun,
> 'Thou poor blind spinner, work is done.'

After this came two other small books, Bits of Travel and Bits of Talk about Home Matters. She paid for the plates of the former. Fame did not burst upon Helen Hunt; it came after years of work, after it had been fully earned. The road to authorship is a hard one, and only those should attempt it who have courage and perseverance.

Again her health failed, but not her cheerful spirits. She travelled to Colorado, and wrote a book in praise of it. Everywhere she made lasting friends. Her German landlady in Munich thought her the kindest person in the world. The newsboy, the little urchin on the street with a basket full of wares, the guides over the mountain passes, all remembered her cheery voice and helpful words. She used to say, "She is only half mother who does not see her own child in every child. Oh, if the world could only stop long enough for one generation of mothers to be made all right, what a Millennium could be begun in thirty years!" Some one, in her childhood, called her a "stupid child" before strangers, and she never forgot the sting of it.

In Colorado, in 1876, eleven years after the death of Major Hunt, she married Mr.

William Sharpless Jackson, a Quaker and a cultured banker. Her home, at Colorado Springs, became an ideal one, sheltered under the great Manitou, and looking toward the Garden of the Gods, full of books and magazines, of dainty rugs and dainty china gathered from many countries, and richly colored Colorado flowers. Once, when Eastern guests were invited to luncheon, twenty-three varieties of wildflowers, each massed in its own color, adorned the home. A friend of hers says: "There is not an artificial flower in the house, on embroidered table-cover or sofa cushion or tidy; indeed, Mrs. Jackson holds that the manufacture of silken poppies and crewel sun-flowers is a 'respectable industry,' intended only to keep idle hands out of mischief."

Mrs. Jackson loved flowers almost as though they were children. She writes: "I bore on this June day a sheaf of the white columbine—one single sheaf, one single root; but it was almost more than I could carry. In the open spaces, I carried it on my shoulder; in the thickets, I bore it carefully in my arms, like a baby…. There is a part of Cheyenne Mountain which I and one other have come to call 'our garden.' When we drive down from 'our garden,' there is seldom room for another flower in our carriage. The top thrown back is filled, the space in front of the driver is filled, and our laps and baskets are filled with the more delicate blossoms. We look as if we were on our way to the ceremonies of Decoration Day. So we are. All June days are decoration days in Colorado Springs, but it is the sacred joy of life that we decorate—not the sacred sadness of death." But Mrs. Jackson, with her pleasant home, could not rest from her work. Two novels came from her pen, Mercy Philbrick's Choice and Hetty's Strange History. It is probable also that she helped to write the beautiful and tender Saxe Holm Stories. It is said that Draxy Miller's Dowry and Esther Wynn's Love Letters were written by another, while Mrs. Jackson added the lovely poems; and when a request was made by the publishers for more stories from the same author, Mrs. Jackson was prevailed upon to write them.

The time had now come for her to do her last and perhaps her best work. She could not write without a definite purpose, and now the purpose that settled down upon her heart was to help the defrauded Indians. She believed they needed education and Christianization rather than extermination. She left her home and spent three months in the Astor Library of New York, writing her Century of Dishonor, showing how we have despoiled the Indians and broken our treaties with them. She wrote to a friend, "I cannot think of anything else from night to morning and from morning to night." So untiringly did she work that she made herself ill, and was obliged to go to Norway, leaving a literary ally to correct the proofs of her book.

At her own expense, she sent a copy to each member of Congress. Its plain facts were not relished in some quarters, and she began to taste the cup that all reformers have to drink; but the brave woman never flinched in her duty. So much was the Government impressed by her earnestness and good judgment, that she was appointed a Special Commissioner with her friend, Abbott Kinney, to examine and report on the condition of the Mission Indians in California.

Could an accomplished, tenderly reared woman go into their adobe villages and listen to their wrongs? What would the world say of its poet? Mrs. Jackson did not ask; she had a mission to perform, and the more culture, the more responsibility. She brought cheer and hope to the red men and their wives, and they called her "the Queen." She wrote able articles about them in the Century.

The report made by Mr. Kinney and herself, which she prepared largely, was clear and convincing. How different all this from her early life! Mrs. Jackson had become more than poet and novelist; even the leader of an oppressed people. At once, in the winter of 1883, she began to write her wonderfully graphic and tender Ramona, and into this, she said, "I put my heart and soul." The book was immediately reprinted in England, and has had great popularity. She meant to do for the Indian what Mrs. Stowe did for the slave, and she lived long enough to see the great work well in progress.

This true missionary work had greatly deepened the earnestness of the brilliant woman. Not always tender to other peoples' "hobbies," as she said, she now had one of her own, into which she was putting her life. Her horizon, with her great intellectual gifts, had now become as wide as the universe. Had she lived, how many more great questions she would have touched.

In June, 1884, falling on the staircase of her Colorado home, she severely fractured her leg, and was confined to the house for several months. Then she was taken to Los Angeles, Cal., for the winter. The broken limb mended rapidly, but malarial fever set in, and she was carried to San Francisco. Her first remark was, as she entered the house looking out upon the broad and lovely bay, "I did not imagine it was so pleasant! What a beautiful place to die in!"

To the last her letters to her friends were full of cheer. "You must not think because I speak of not getting well that I am sad over it," she wrote. "On the contrary, I am more and more relieved in my mind, as it seems to grow more and more sure that I shall die. You see that I am growing old" (she was but fifty-four), "and I do believe that my work is done. You have never realized how, for the past five years, my whole soul has been centered on the Indian question. Ramona was the outcome of those five years. The Indian cause is on its feet now; powerful friends are at work."

To another she wrote, "I am heartily, honestly, and cheerfully ready to go. In fact, I am glad to go. My Century of Dishonor and Ramona are the only things I have done of which I am glad now. The rest is of no moment. They will live, and they will bear fruit. They already have. The change in public feeling on the Indian question in the last three years is marvellous; an Indian Rights Association in every large city in the land."

She had no fear of death. She said, "It is only just passing from one country to another…. My only regret is that I have not accomplished more work; especially that it was so late in the day when I began to work in real earnest. But I do not doubt we shall keep on working…. There isn't so much difference, I fancy, between this life and the next as we think, nor so much barrier…. I shall look in upon you in the new rooms some day; but you will not see me. Good-bye. Yours affectionately forever, H.H." Four days before her death she wrote to President Cleveland:—

"From my death-bed I send you a message of heart-felt thanks for what you have already done for the Indians. I ask you to read my Century of Dishonor. I am dying happier for the belief I have that it is your hand that is destined to strike the first steady blow toward lifting this burden of infamy from our country, and righting the wrongs of the Indian race.

"With respect and gratitude,

"HELEN JACKSON."

That same day she wrote her last touching poem:—

> Father, I scarcely dare to pray,
> So clear I see, now it is done,
> That I have wasted half my day,
> And left my work but just begun;
>
> So clear I see that things I thought
> Were right or harmless were a sin;
> So clear I see that I have sought,
> Unconscious, selfish aim to win
>
> So clear I see that I have hurt
> The souls I might have helped to save,
> That I have slothful been, inert,
> Deaf to the calls Thy leaders gave.
>
> In outskirts of Thy kingdoms vast,
> Father, the humblest spot give me;
> Set me the lowliest task Thou hast,
> Let me repentant work for Thee!

That evening, Aug. 8, after saying farewell, she placed her hand in her husband's, and went to sleep. After four days, mostly unconscious ones, she wakened in eternity.

On her coffin were laid a few simple clover-blossoms, flowers she loved in life; and then, near the summit of Cheyenne Mountain, four miles from Colorado Springs, in a spot of her own choosing, she was buried.

> Do not adorn with costly shrub or tree
> Or flower the little grave which shelters me.
> Let the wild wind-sown seeds grow up unharmed,
> And back and forth all summer, unalarmed,
> Let all the tiny, busy creatures creep;
> Let the sweet grass its last year's tangles keep;
> And when, remembering me, you come some day

And stand there, speak no praise, but only say,
'How she loved us! It was for that she was so dear.'
These are the only words that I shall smile to hear.

Many will stand by that Colorado grave in the years to come. Says a California friend: "Above the chirp of the balm-cricket in the grass that hides her grave, I seem to hear sweet songs of welcome from the little ones. Among other thoughts of her come visions of a child and mother straying in fields of light. And so I cannot make her dead, who lived so earnestly, who wrought so unselfishly, and passed so trustfully into the mystery of the unseen."

All honor to a woman who, with a happy home, was willing to leave it to make other homes happy; who, having suffered, tried with a sympathetic heart to forget herself and keep others from suffering; who, being famous, gladly took time to help unknown authors to win fame; who, having means, preferred a life of labor to a life of ease.

Mrs. Jackson's work is still going forward. Five editions of her Century of Dishonor have been printed since her death. Ramona is in its thirtieth thousand. Zeph, a touching story of frontier life in Colorado, which she finished in her last illness, has been published. Her sketches of travel have been gathered into Glimpses of Three Coasts, and a new volume of poems, Sonnets and Lyrics, has appeared.

Month 8 Podcasts

Podcast #73 Lessons from the Songs of the Slaves

I noticed when we last visited Mount Vernon, a section of the museum that used to house personal items of Washington's family was closed and they were creating an exhibit to highlight slavery. I've heard they are doing the same thing at Thomas Jefferson's home, Monticello. In fact, it seems there is a movement everywhere to bring awareness of the slavery issue to us.

I deplore slavery. It was a black mark on our history. But I fear they—whoever they are—are using it to further divide us as a people and making it an issue of race. Slavery has never cared about the color of skin. Joseph was sold as a slave into Egypt, Daniel was carried as a slave into Babylon. The Lord's chosen people served as slaves to the Egyptians for 400 years. The Greeks were slaves to the Romans. Aesop was a slave. As was Saint Patrick for a time. Captain John Smith of Pocahontas fame was sold as a slave by the Turks. Cervantes who gave the world Don Quixote was a slave. There was a time when white Christians were captured from coastal cities in Europe and forced into slavery in the Ottomon Empire. In Africa, Africans captured and traded fellow Africans.

It is estimated that today, worldwide, there are 45.8 million people subject to some form of slavery, the most common is referred to as human trafficking. Even debt bondage is a form of slavery today.

So, yes, do teach your children about slavery. But it's not the single story of evil white people subjecting black people into slavery. Such a story makes us hate ourselves, when what we should really be focusing on is the fact that we actually abolished it!

Instead of focusing on the cruel stories of slavery, I'd like to spend some time focusing on the tremendous gifts the Africans brought to the soil of America. They played a vital role and provide us with some of the most inspirational stories ever of overcoming tremendous odds. Today I want to focus on their hearts as expressed through the beautiful Negro spirituals. And in the next podcast, I want to highlight the story of a hero of mine, Mary Macleod Bethune.

Most of what I am going to share with you came from a book written in 1915, *The Folk Song of the American Negro* by John Wesley Work.[88] This man spent ten years hunting in out-of-the-way places, following trails from state to state to learn the story from the songs themselves and from the makers of the songs. The history and description came to him first hand from those who have been a part of them.

> Folk song is the unguarded, spontaneous expression of a people's soul. It is their natural means of communication, which they understand among themselves. We know for a fact that it was never intended that the world should understand the slave music. It was a kind of secret pass-word into their lives. … [T]he only reliable source of truth in regard to the fundamentals of his character, is his songs.
>
> The African soul for some inexplicable reason expresses himself in its own peculiar

scale—1,2,3,5,6,—. Every shout of triumph, every note of endurance, every wail of sorrow, every cry of pain, every heart-throb of love, every prompting of religion, is expressed in that scale.

[I will add—what that means is that all his songs can be played on the black keys alone on the piano.]

When the Africans were snatched away to the new world to fell the forest and cultivate the fields, they left their all save their song. This they brought, because the All-wise knew the New World had great need of it.

Thirty centuries ago, amidst the dawning civilization of the Mediterranean shores, science taught that the earth was a circular disc surrounded by the ocean. Contemporaneous legends told of the swarthy Ethiopians living in two divisions; one in the extreme East, the land of the rising sun, and the other in the extreme West, the land of the setting sun. Consequently the Ethiopians dwelt in perpetual light. This light was symbolic of their own souls; pure, bright and happy. So worthy were they that the Gods from Olympus honored them with regular visits. Homer in narrating these events calls them the 'blameless Ethiopians' and Vergil speak of the black King of the Ethiopians, as the son of Aurora, the Goddess of the Morning and of Light.

Ruthless centuries have not overcast that brightness, nor have they destroyed the soul happiness of the Son of Light. His soul is a song. He expresses his every experience, his whole life, in terms of melody and he passes through the Valley of the Shadow of Death with a song upon his lips.

Mark Twain tells the story of an old negro servant of his, who seemed always to be happy. Her face was ever lighted with a smile and she shed a brightness where ever she went. "She was sixty years old, but her eye was undimmed and her strength unimpaired. It was no more trouble for her to laugh than for a bird to sing." "Aunt Rachel, how is it that you've lived sixty years and have no trouble?" She told the story of her life. Of course, she had been a slave. She once had as happy a family as a slave could have. She had seen her husband and six children sold from her in one day. She saw them carried away into different directions, some away down South; and only one of whom, a boy, she had ever seen or heard of since. And yet, as Mark Twain says, "It was no more trouble for her to laugh than for a bird to sing." Aunt Rachel is an epitome of her race. She lives at the mountain top.

The human heart cannot perceive righteousness in being torn from those it loves, from the memories and attachments that make up the happiness of life, to be forced to labor hard and long that another may eat, rest and be comfortable—yea, to suffer and die at the whim of a master. This is surely beyond a mortal's comprehension of justice. Still through all these crushing experiences, the Negro slave trusted God. What faith!

Great souls are souls of great faith. Great faith is a mighty weapon for fighting battles and winning victories. No faithless, doubting soul has been a positive blessing to mankind…. Judged by his own soul-thoughts, his supreme virtue is faith; for every one of his songs is a song of faith. Faith is the all-pervading power of all the Negro's music. Someone has stated that if the Bible should be lost, it could be recovered and reconstructed from the mind of the Negro.

Some masters who did not believe in the slave's God or in his religion had some extraordinary experiences. In Southern Kentucky, a slave, John by name, was known for his piety, religion and seasons of prayer and praise. Like Daniel in Babylon, nothing could prevent him from turning his face toward Jerusalem in prayer. The time came when John had to be sold. The master who was about to buy him said, "John, they tell me that you are one of these great praying negroes. Now, I want to tell you that when I buy you, all that stuff must stop." John answered, "Massa, if that's the case, you better not buy me, for I'se bound to pray, and I'se goin to pray." "All right, we'll see about that," said the master and John was bought. It was not long before this master missed John, and upon learning from the slave's own lips that he had been praying, his wrath blazed in angry flame, and with curses he tore John's flesh with the cruel lash. He did his best to kill him. That night, the master lay down in complacency, while John lay down in torture. But peace and complacency soon flew away on the dark wings of the night, and the master was troubled in mind. His soul was like a stormy sea. He left his bed and walked the floor. The love of a wife could not comfort him, and the physician he refused to see. The God of John and of John's religion had convicted the master of his sinfulness. When no help came to his tempestuous soul, in his extremity he said, "Send for John." With labored step, John struggled to the big house with a prayer on his lips, and when the master saw him, he cried, "John, pray for me." In bloody pain, John sank down upon his knees and prayed for his weeping master. God heard that prayer, and the light a new life broke in upon the master's vision. He expressed, "The best investment I ever made, the best money I ever spent, was when I bought John."

A most natural consequence of having faith is having joy, for the soul that believes that all things will eventuate according to the laws of right, and that "God's in his Heaven," has joy in his security. … The believer can smile through tears and shout Hallelujah! The Negro has the habit of being happy.

In all his song there is neither trace nor hint of hatred or revenge. It is most assuredly divine in human nature, that such a stupendous burden as human bondage, with all its inherent sorrows and heart breakings could fail to arouse in the heart of the slave sentiments of hatred and revenge against his master.

"No man can drag me so low as to make me hate him," the slave would say. The world needs to know that love is stronger than hatred.

Uncle Anthony was owned by an August County master, and lived happily with this faithful wife. Their cabin was a realm of melody. It was singing, singing, singing! One day, Heaven sent a child to them, and there was more singing, with a tenderer, more ecstatic note. The glad father worked at odd times upon a rude cradle for his babe, in which she could lie, rock and go to sleep in the comforting lullabies from the full-hearted mother. At last the cradle was finished, and with an overflowing soul he bore it home. His joy grew with every step; anticipations of opening the door of that cabin, seeing the baby in the cradle, and beholding the smile upon that mother's face made his heart swell and his breath come short and fast! The cabin was there; that was all! Mother and babe were gone with the trader, somewhere toward the South. The bud of his happiness was dead! He searched the whole creation for his wife and child. The forest, hills, and fields mocked his cries. Days and days he was a madman in his grief. No threats or lashings could quiet him or force him back to his work. His usefulness as a slave was destroyed, and when a man whose heart had been touched and softened by the poor slave's sorrow offered to buy him, his offer was at once accepted. Two thousand dollars was paid. The bargain closed, he immediately made out "free papers" for Anthony and told him to go find his wife and child, promising that if he found them, they, too, should be purchased and freed. The last account of him was that he was still pursuing his quest somewhere in North Carolina, with this song upon his lips:

> Nobody knows the trouble I see, Lord,
> Nobody knows the trouble I see;
> Nobody knows the trouble I see, Lord,
> Nobody knows like Jesus.

In the darkness of bondage, it was his light; ... The songs of the slave were his sweet consolation and his messages to Heaven, bearing sorrow, pain, joy, prayer and adoration. ... [H]e could always unburden his heart in these simple songs pregnant with faith, hope and love. The man, though a slave, produced the song, and the song, in turn, produced a better man.

These songs are to us a storehouse of comfort. How can we ever forget those by gone days when our mothers sang them to us as our lullabies? "This old-time religion, makes me love everybody." Think of the great blessing of being sung to sleep by such a lullaby—"Makes Me Love Everybody!" Think of the great favor of being reared in the atmosphere of "Lord, I Want to Be Like Jesus!" In times of sorrow, we have heard our mothers sing "Keep Me From Sinking Down," and often, oh! So often, "March on and You shall Gain the Victory," has run with such meaning through the humble home. Can you blame us for loving these songs which have so much inspired us to be and to do?

Thus we find faith, hope, patience, endurance, prayer, joy, courage and humility and the love of mankind, of home, and of God to be the salient qualities of the Negro's soul. Such is the testimony of the only true expression of his soul, his songs. ... And although the story brings tears to our eyes, our hearts swell with pride that we can claim such ancestors...with their sweet inspirations.

The picture is before you: Virtues powerfully blended upon an ample background of love, energized by the spirit of the eternal.

No, these songs cannot die. They are eternal.

Podcast #74 Lessons from the Life of Mary McLeod Bethune

Many years ago, when I was involved with a little school in Africa through a friend, she asked if I could put together a story of someone who inspires the hearts of some of these young girls. I loved the story of Mary Bethune because it shows what faith and determination can overcome. So I put together this story that I'm going to share with you in this podcast. One of Mary's greatest desires was to go to Africa and teach the children there, but it never happened in her life. When my friend carried the story over there, I thought perhaps through her story, her influence will be a small realization of her dream. I like to think that.

The Story of Mary McLeod Bethune

How does a little girl, born under the poorest of circumstances, grow up to be a friend and advisor of presidents, guest of royalty, founder of a college, and an inspiration to millions of people?

This is the story of Mary McLeod Bethune. All her life she worked with youth. She begged for them and fought for them. Hers was not an easy road. But she said very few of her generation found life easy or wanted it that way. She overcame staggering obstacles. In her own words, "I'm poor and I'm ugly and I'm not very smart. But the Lord has chosen me for an instrument." She shows us how all things are possible when one has faith in God and faith in one's self.

The day Mary McLeod came into the world, July 10, 1875, was a joyous occasion. Although she was the fifteenth of Sam and Patsy McLeod's seventeen children, this was the first child born to them in freedom. The Civil War had just ended and slavery was abolished. That meant there would be no worrying in the middle of the night if this baby, in a few years, would be sold and sent away to another master. This baby was theirs to raise.

Mary was born into a simple log cabin with few material goods. A treasured Bible, even though no one in the household knew how to read, was kept on the shelf next to a blue china pitcher, a sewing box and an oil lamp. But hers was a home full of love. Both of her parents had been born into slavery. One day, her father was visiting a neighboring plantation where he first saw Patsy and immediately knew he wanted to be with her. She had soft, keen features and spoke with a gentle voice. She carried herself like a queen, which was only natural for one who came from a long line of African royalty. The slave owners had tried to erase any memories of the slaves' former lives in Africa, but Patsy's mother made sure she kept the stories of her family's heritage alive.

Sam needed his master's permission to marry her. He got the permission, but first had to earn enough money to buy her from her current owner. Sam was willing to do anything to be with Patsy. So, for two years, he walked an extra six miles a day after his normal chores were done where he put in long, hard hours hauling lumber, putting aside every penny he could earn. Finally, the wedding day arrived and a wedding dress and a suit were provided to make their day special. They became a well-respected, hardworking couple who were devoted to each other for the rest of their lives.

When Mary was 9 or 10 years old, something happened that hurt her very much, but proved to be a driving force that changed her life. It was not unusual for slaves, after being freed, to continue working for former masters to earn money. Patsy often returned to the Wilsons to cook for them or to help with laundry. When Mary was old enough, she was allowed to go with her. This particular day, Mr. Wilson's golden-haired granddaughters invited Mary out to their playhouse. Mary looked around wide eyed at the dolls with beautiful silk dresses and delicate shoes. There were slates and pencils and magazines and books all around. She walked over to a table and opened a book that was sitting there. Immediately, one of the granddaughters snatched the book away and slammed it shut. "Don't you touch that book with your black hands! Don't you know reading is for white folks? You can't never read…you're black."

It was true that during the years of slavery, many states had put laws into effect forbidding anyone from teaching a black person to read. It wasn't laws that kept them from reading now, just no one willing to teach them. Nevertheless, the words, "You can't read" pierced Mary's heart. She made up her mind right then and there that somehow, someday, she was going to learn how to read. She had seen the comfortable homes the white boys and girls lived in and the opportunities they had that she didn't, and she sensed, even at her young age, that knowing how to read had something to do with the difference.

As she walked back home past the broken-down shanties of her people, she told her mother of her dream to learn how to read. She said later, "You know, my mother was one of those grand educated persons that did not have letters. She had a great vision, a great understanding of human nature. When I told her, she said to me—child, your time will come. You will learn some day. My mother had a great philosophy of life. She could not be discouraged. No matter what kind of plight we found ourselves in, she always believed there was, through prayer and work, a way out. And it was one of the greatest things she stimulated life with…that determination that there was a way out if we put forth effort ourselves."

And so Mary's prayers began in earnest, "Please, Lord, help me find a way to learn how to read."

You had to be strong and fast to work in the cotton fields, and Mary was both. One day, as she was working her way down the cotton rows, her mother and father not far away, she looked up to see a stranger walking towards them. It was Miss Emma Wilson, a teacher with light, brown skin who had just been given authorization by the Presbyterian church to open a school and she was looking for students. Sam and Patsy could only spare one of their children because there was so much work to be done, but there was no question which of their children it would be. Mary sank to her knees, raised her hands towards heaven and thanked God for hearing her prayers.

The five miles each way to the little school in Mayesville was more like an adventure than a hardship. The school wasn't much to look at—a small, one-room shack with hard wooden benches inside. But Mary remembered her teacher's beautiful smile she always had on her face. And she remembered her patience, and her tenderness and the kindly way she handled the students. They were not afraid of her. They could approach her at any time. Years later, Mary became that kind of teacher.

Mary was an eager learner and was reading in a very short time. Every Sunday afternoon, she would gather the farm children from miles around to teach them whatever she had learned during the week—poetry, reading, songs. In her words, "I would give to them as often as I got. As I got I gave. They gave me a broader capacity for taking in and I feel that up to today, I feel it in all things, and I feel that as I give, I get."

As soon as she could do counting, all the papers—of both the whites and the colored people— were put in her lap. They wanted to make sure they weren't being cheated when they took their cotton in to be weighed. Unfortunately, for the most part they had been cheated. Many of her neighbors started turning a profit for the first time and were able to pay off their mortgages with Mary's help.

She said, "I became useful…I won their respect and admiration. I made my learning, what little it was, just from the beginning, spell service and cooperation, rather than something that would put me above the people around me. When I went off to school and came back, I was accepted and they looked forward to my coming back. They knew that whatever I had, they knew I would adapt to use of the people there."

For the first time, the people of her community saw in Mary something to aspire to. They had never before seen what their possibilities were. She brought a desire to learn, and an understanding that they just did not have to continue in darkness—that there was a chance.

After four years at the little school in Mayesville, when Mary was just 15, Miss Wilson told Mary there was nothing else she could teach her. So Mary went back to the cotton fields, praying all the time for a way to open up to get more education. It would cost money though, something they didn't have. As if the way didn't already seem impossible, one day her dad came into the house and announced that Old Bush had collapsed and died in the fields. Old Bush was their mule, the single most important possession of their family. Without the mule, there could be no plowing. No plowing meant no crops. No crops, no money. No money, definitely no school. Whatever money they did earn would have to first go towards replacing the mule. Never ones to give into discouragement, Mary's older brother, without a word, went over to the plow and strapped the harness around his own waist. It would be hard and strenuous work, but each member of the family took a turn pulling the plow.

Meanwhile, many hundreds of miles away in Denver, Colorado, a schoolteacher, Mary Crissman had faithfully been setting aside a tenth of her meager earnings for many years. She had supplemented her teaching salary by sewing dresses when school wasn't in session, and was waiting for the right opportunity to use the money to help someone who needed it, when she became aware of the plight of the former slaves and their children who had little opportunity for education. She sent the money to the Presbyterian board to be used as a scholarship by someone who would make good with it. She could have scarcely imagined at the time the good that would come from her modest donation.

Can you imagine the excitement Miss Wilson had the day she once again found Mary in the cotton fields, and was able to deliver the good news. Mary was astonished. Why, this woman didn't even know who she was. "Oh, the joy of that glorious morning! I can never forget it," is the way she herself told the story. "To this day my heart thrills with gratitude at the memory of that day. I was but a little girl, groping for the light, dreaming dreams and seeing visions in the cotton and rice fields, and away off in Denver, Colorado, a poor dressmaker, sewing for her daily bread, heard my call and came to my assistance. Out of her scanty earnings, she invested in a life—my life!—and while God gives me strength, I shall strive to pass on to others the opportunities that this noble woman toiled and sacrificed to give me."

For a second time, she pulled off her cotton sack, got down on her knees, clasped her hands and turned her eyes upward to thank God for the chance that had come. The whole community was excited about Mary's selection to go to Scotia Seminary. Some neighbors knitted her a little linsey dress and socks and provided other clothes she would need. Her father bought her a trunk to pack her belongings. All the neighbors stopped work that October afternoon to see their Mary take her very first train ride.

Her arrival at the new school was full of so many firsts. It was the first brick building she had ever seen, she climbed her first stairs, slept in her very own bed with crisp linens for the very first time, ate with a fork, and saw people with black skin and people with white skin eating at the same table as equals.

Mary quickly made friends with everyone there. It would seem her greatest gift was the ability to love absolutely everyone. Homesick girls always found her. Girls came with their problems, difficulties, and disappointments for her advice.

The scholarship didn't cover all of Mary's expenses, so she worked any way she could find; doing laundry, cooking, scrubbing. She said, "Nothing was too menial or too hard for me to find joy in doing, for the appreciation of having a chance."

Mary was starved for learning and couldn't get enough. She never considered herself an exceptional student, but took advantage of everything offered during her seven years at Scotia. She learned public speaking and debate and discovered she had a beautiful contralto voice. She had so many questions and soon learned she could find answers in books at the library. It was in books she learned such principles as inalienable rights and the history of her people. Why had there been slavery? It must have hurt her heart as she read how her ancestors were kidnapped by traders, dragged away in chains from their homes and families in Africa and placed in stinking, rat-infested holds of ships, many dying along the way. Once in America, they were sold as property.

Reading such things reawakened in her heart desires that had been placed there years earlier as she listened to a Reverend Bowen tell the stories of the people in darkest Africa. She had decided long before that her life's work was to travel to Africa as a missionary and bring light to the people there.

She shared these ambitions with her principal, who helped her make application to Moody Bible Institute in Chicago where she could be trained as a missionary. Her two years at Moody included much time on the streets, learning how to reach out and help the less fortunate. One time her missionary group had traveled to the Dakotas where they spent the night at the home of a minister and his wife. They had a five-year-old daughter who had never seen someone with black skin before, but immediately fell in love with Mary. When it came time for dinner, the little girl, not understanding, said, "Mother, tell the lady to wash her face and hands. She's all dirty." The parents were embarrassed and started to apologize, but Mary simply smiled and said, "I am not at all ashamed of my color. I'm proud of my black skin." Then she lifted the girl up on her lap and let her touch her skin so she could see that the color would not rub off. "Look; my skin is just like your skin. It stays the way God made it." Then she took a vase of flowers from a nearby stand and held it in front of her. "Look at all the different colors of these flowers. God made men just the way he made flowers, some one color, some another, so that when they are gathered together they make a beautiful bouquet." A grateful mother thanked her for her graciousness and this most important lesson that had been taught to her daughter.

As soon as graduation day was over, Mary traveled to New York, anxious and excited to receive her missionary appointment to Africa. However, the members of the board explained there was simply no opening for her at that time. Her whole life Mary regretted that she was not able to go to Africa and described that that was the greatest disappointment of her life.

It was with a heavy heart she accepted, instead, an assignment to teach school at Haines Normal Institute in Augusta, Georgia. It was there she met Lucy Lainey who taught her that there was much work to be done right here in America for her people.

Other teaching assignments followed. One day a tall handsome young man appeared at choir practice—his name, Albertus Bethune. The two fell in love and were married a short time later. Their only son, Albert, (Sam and Patsy's 90th grandchild!) came quickly. She adored her new little baby, but a new dream had taken hold of Mary. She dreamed of opening a school for little girls so they could be given all the same advantages and opportunities that had been given to her. Even though Albertus was a teacher, he didn't share his wife's passion for education, and although they were friendly towards each other, most of their nineteen years of marriage were spent apart. He died long before seeing Mary achieve the great successes of her life.

Mary carefully considered where to open this new school. She wanted it to be in a place that was hard; she wanted it to be somewhere where no one else was reaching out to help the children. She found out that a railroad was being built down the eastern coast of Florida and that many of the workers had their families with them. So she took the 3 day trip down to Daytona, arriving with just $1.50 and her dreams.

As she walked down the dusty streets, she saw broken down shacks and dirty children running wild everywhere. This would be the perfect place. The first order of business: find a building to hold class. At the end of a peninsula with the ocean in view, she saw an old empty shack, nothing beyond it but an old dump heap. Most of the paint had peeled off and the windows were broken or cracked. She held onto a rickety stair rail as she climbed the wobbly stairs and looked inside. It was filled with cobwebs and had a leaky roof. But it would do just fine. She located the owner who wanted $11.00 a month rent. Problem was she didn't have anything, but there was something about Mary that made the owner trust that she would find the money somehow.

She quickly found her first five students—five little girls who helped scrub and clean the old shack to get it ready. The neighbors pitched in, too, clearing the weeds away and nailing boards back in place. Mary started scouring the junk piles for anything usable. Cracked dishes, old lamps, even clothes thrown out behind hotels, were brought back to be cleaned up and mended. Old crates and barrels were used for desks and chairs. She didn't have any pencils, so she used charcoal slivers from burned logs. Elderberry juice was used for ink. She made sure the few supplies she was able to buy from the store were wrapped individually in paper. The paper was brought back to the school and smoothed out and flattened so the girls would have something to write on.

October 3, 1904, was the big opening day of the Daytona Educational and Industrial Training School for Negro Girls. Over the door was written the words, "Enter to Learn Depart to Serve." Mary knew just what to teach. She said "This is a new kind of school. I am going to teach my girls crafts and homemaking. I am going to teach them to earn a living. They will be trained in head, hand, and heart: their heads to think, their hands to work, and their hearts to have faith."

The burden of having to raise money was to be Mary's constant companion. She was able to acquire an old used bicycle, and once a week she could be seen riding up and down the streets, knocking on doors, begging for money. Many were kind to her and even grew to look forward to her visits. But others were downright rude. "I had learned already that one of my most important jobs was to be a good beggar! I rang doorbells and tackled cold prospects without a lead. I wrote articles for whoever would print them, distributed leaflets, rode interminable miles of dusty roads on my old bicycle, invaded churches, clubs, lodges, chambers of commerce. If a prospect refused to make a contribution, I'd say, "Thank you for your time." No matter how deep my hurt, I always smiled. I refused to be discouraged, for neither God nor man can use a discouraged person."

One day she had an idea. Sweet potatoes down there in Florida were plentiful and dirt cheap, and she knew how to cook up the tastiest sweet potato pie. She had her girls get up early in the morning with her and they'd boil and peel the sweet potatoes. By the time the railroad workers got off work, she was right there with her delicious, fresh pieces of pie which they eagerly bought.

Daytona Beach had become the winter retreat for many of the wealthy white Northerners. She taught her girls how to sing the beautiful spiritual hymns of the south and would take them to perform at the fine hotels nearby. They caught the attention of many prominent people who looked forward to their performances and rewarded them handsomely with donations.

She believed, like Gandhi, that no good cause suffers from the want of money and added trustfully, "God will shake money out of the trees." One Saturday night she went to the grocer's and pled with him to carry just four more dollars on her account until the next week. There was no food at home for her girls and she couldn't bear for them to go hungry.

He firmly refused. As she approached her school, trusting that God would somehow provide, there were four scruffy looking men on her porch. At first she was alarmed, but then she recognized them as students who attended some of her classes as adults. They said they had just been paid and wanted to thank her for what she had taught them. Each held out $1.00, which Mary thankfully took and rushed back to the store for the groceries.

She had learned from Lucy Lainey that a school had to be properly organized with a Board of

Trustees who could advise and help her. She perused the society pages of the newspaper and decided on the name of James N. Gamble, of Proctor & Gamble. She sat down and wrote him a letter, to which a prompt reply came back, inviting her to his home at noon the next day. She pedaled her old bicycle, arriving at his house fifteen minutes early. Wanting to impress him with promptness, she had borrowed a watch and waited for the exact strike of noon before she strode up to the front door.

Mr. Gamble looked surprised at the woman who was ushered into his study. "Are you the woman trying to build the school here? Why, I thought you were a white woman!" The jet-black Mary Bethune burst out laughing. "Well, you see how white I am."

She didn't want to waste his time, so she quickly told him how desperately the school was needed and invited him to serve as one of its trustees. He appeared interested, but seemed to hesitate just a bit, so Mary quickly invited him to take a look at the school. He agreed to a visit the next day.

Mary hurried home and quickly enlisted the help of her girls to scrub and clean and straighten so that everything would be in order for their distinguished guest.

A tall, slim white-haired Mr. Gamble showed up the next day in his chauffeured car. He looked around in amazement, staring at the wooden crates used as desks and the students lined up in their altered, mended and patched dresses.

"Just where is this school that you want me to take a look at?"

Mary had always looked at her school through the eyes of her dreams, and having this visitor must have been a harsh reality check. But she straightened herself and with great confidence replied, "In my mind, and in my spirit. I'm asking you to be a trustee of a glorious dream, trustee of the hope I have in my heart for my people."

Mr. Gamble was a kindly and a gracious man and must have been quite taken in by this courageous woman who had done so much with so little. He instantly agreed and handed her a check for $150, the first of a lifetime of generous donations by this good man.

With Mr. Gamble on board, it wasn't as hard to attract others who willingly became friends and partners of Mary Bethune's dream.

The school was growing and new buildings needed to go up. True to her nature, she moved forward, not quite knowing how it was going to come about, but trusting a way would be provided. She doubled and redoubled her begging efforts. "I hung on to contractors' coattails, begging for loads of sand and secondhand bricks. I went to all the carpenters, mechanics, and plasterers in town, pleading with them to contribute a few hours' work in the evening in exchange for sandwiches and tuition for their children or themselves." As soon as the roof went up, she moved her students in, even though the building was far from finished. Often the construction would have to stop altogether until more funds were found.

It was at one of her choir's performances at the Palmetto Hotel that her path first crossed with a gentleman who would become a great benefactor of her school. He placed a twenty-dollar bill in the collection plate, such a generous donation! Not too many days later, Mary was on her usual cycling rounds when a huge automobile drove up to her side and stopped.

"Aren't you the one I saw with the children at the Palmetto Hotel?" Without another word, he had his chauffeur put Mary's bike in the back of the car and they drove back to her school. He looked around at the unfinished construction, at the unplastered walls, at the homemade mattresses made from boiled, dried Spanish moss from the trees that were then stuffed in corn sacks. He noticed a bag of meal standing in the corner and asked what else there was to eat. Mary replied that was all they had at the moment. He walked over to where a young girl struggled to sew on an old broken-down Singer sewing machine. He turned back to Mary and said, "I believe you are on the right track. This is the most promising thing I've seen in Florida," and handed her a check for $200.

The visitor was Mr. Thomas H. White, manufacturer of White sewing machines. "I wept, called the children in for a special meeting. We knelt and thanked God. He came back the next day with a new sewing machine and with an architect and carpenter, and they brought materials and plaster to put on the walls. And he said, 'I will have bathrooms put in.' He brought pillow slips, and sheets."

Often he would drop by with a few pairs of shoes or blankets or whatever he thought they might need. Tears of gratitude would fill Mary's eyes whenever he came by, but his simple reply to her was, "I've never invested a dollar that has brought greater returns than the dollars I've given you."

That building was named Faith Hall and officially opened in 1907, "prayed up, sung up and talked up" in two years. Mary now had 250 girls who looked up to her as a mother. The field across the street had been cleared and they were taught to plant and grow vegetables and strawberries. They were of such quality, that well-to-do people traveled from all around to buy their produce there.

There needed to be more buildings built which meant more land needed to be purchased. She found the owner of the old dump next door. He wanted an outrageous $1,000 for that piece of property. Mary had grown confident in her bargaining power and asserted herself. "I don't suppose you know this, Sir, but people around here call this land of yours, "Hell's Hole." It's full of mosquitos, weeds and snakes. The way it is, I'm not sure it's good for anything." The man lowered the price down to $200, $5.00 down and $5.00 a month until it was paid off. He didn't know it at the time, but Mary didn't even have the $5.00 down payment. But she knew she could get it.

Once again neighbors pitched in and drained the swamp, clearing out the weeds and debris along the way. Bushes and shrubs, flowers and trees were planted in place of it and it became a beautiful piece of property.

One Sunday Mary took her girls for a picnic out by the Piney Woods. She had heard about the turpentine camps. These were horrible places. The riff-raff around town had been hired to drain the sap out of the pine trees to make turpentine in exchange for all the rum they could drink on the weekends. Sadly, some of them had brought their families with them and the conditions they lived in would make anyone shudder. Drunks were sprawled out on the ground everywhere and she saw ragged, unkempt women hiding timidly in the trees. Sickness was all around. They looked more like animals than human beings.

At first her girls were reluctant to be there, but Mary encouraged them to have faith. She invited as many as would to gather together into a meeting. At first, they laughed, they jeered, even told vulgar jokes, rum bottles in hand. But Mary started to sing a hymn in her beautiful contralto voice and soon the girls joined in. Then they sang another hymn followed by another. The laughter started to die down, the rum bottles were lowered to the ground. She now had their attention and she spoke to them with simple, eloquent words, encouraging them to a better life. She said she would return each Sunday and that eventually she would start a school for their children where they could learn to read and write and sew. As she gained their confidence, she was invited to their homes, such as they were, and showed them how to clean and make them pretty. She had always taught her students that neatness, cleanliness and beauty in a home were like another kind of prayer to God. Week after week, Mary and her girls sang and read to them. They encouraged and admonished them. The girls were able to practice their nursing skills. And many of the people of the turpentine camps felt human again; like they were a part of the world again. Five mission schools were set up in the camps over the next five years.

Wherever Mary saw a need, she would say, "I prayed to God to let me do something about that." One of her young girls became deathly ill with acute appendicitis. Mary tried in vain to find a hospital that would treat her. All refused because she had the wrong color of skin.

Finally, she found a doctor who compassionately agreed to perform the surgery. Mary left her in his care, but was outraged when she returned the next day and found the little girl left to herself on a cot on a drafty back porch. This was just not acceptable. Mary stayed up all night writing letters, begging for money to raise the $5,000 she would need to open a small hospital that could treat her people. Within a month, she had the money. And within a short time, McLeod Hospital, named after her father, was dedicated.

The Ku Klux Klan was a dreaded, secret society of those who hated, among other things, people with colored skin. They used fear as a weapon to force people into compliance with what they wanted. They stopped at nothing to exert their power—burning buildings, torturing and even killing innocent victims. It was no secret that Mary had long been teaching her people to courageously stand up for their inalienable rights. The next day was to be another election day and rumor was the Klan was riding out to Mrs. Bethune's school that night to persuade her it would be in her best interest to keep her people away from the voting polls. This was not a time to show cowardice in any way. Mary ordered every light be turned on in the school. She encouraged the choir to continue its practice as usual and fearlessly placed herself in between the two white columns on the steps leading up to the school. What an imposing figure she must have been, her long cape fluttering in the wind. She waited. Maybe they weren't coming after all. But then, out in the darkness, she could see the flicker of flames coming closer; the muffled sound of horse's hoofs making their way toward her. Silently, eighty ghostly figures lined up in front of her, their eyes glaring from behind their hooded masks.

"We hear you're teaching colored folks around here to vote. We've just come to warn you about filling their heads with such ideas." They threatened her that if she didn't stop, they would come back and burn every building until there was nothing left. Mary was more angry than afraid now. She straightened herself and with deliberate words told them, "If you must burn my buildings, go ahead. But let me tell you. Once you've burned them, I'll build them back again. Then if you burn them a second time, I'll build them again, and again, and again." She must have been startled by her own boldness, but slowly, the masked men turned and walked back out into the dark of night. They left behind the can of kerosene, which the groundskeeper quickly retrieved. The school could use it.

The next morning, Mary led a procession of 100 voters, many of them exercising their rights for the first time. They were kept waiting all day, but they voted. The story of this obscure schoolteacher in Florida who had stood up to the Klan made newspaper headlines all over America.

Mrs. Bethune was becoming a speaker in high demand. She raised awareness of the needs of her people; of the need for equal rights and opportunities. She would be seated on the stands in her plain, shabby clothes next to prominent and fashionably dressed club members. But Henry Winslow observed, "There was a magnificent dignity about her person and carriage that awed her audiences."

People who heard her speak said she was electrifying.

Her natural ability to unite and organize combined with her warmth and dignity soon led to her appointment as the president of the National Association of Colored Women. Her school had grown and was now a fully accredited college, admitting men as well as women, after a merger with Cookman College. Friends convinced her to turn the college over to other capable hands as the level of her influence widened.

She never kept any of the money she raised for herself. But when friends offered to pitch in and pay for her to enjoy a trip to Europe, she excitedly accepted the opportunity. She had long had the desire to know just a little more about the setting of foreign people in their own homes and in their own surroundings.

She thrilled at visiting Westminster Abbey, the Louvre, Christopher Columbus' birthplace. Teas and parties were held in her honor by the Lord Mayor of London, by Lady Astor and Lady McLeod. What a different world Europe was, far from the Jim Crow laws back home that wouldn't allow her to eat in restaurants and forced her to go through certain doors. In Europe, she was treated like royalty. "We were wonderfully received there. My dark skin did not hamper them at all. They were very fond of me and I liked them." When her group got to Vatican City, they were received by the Pope, the spiritual leader of the Catholic Church. They were assembled in a large room and the pope gave his blessing to the body as he always did. Then everyone kissed his ring. But when the pope came to Mary, he stopped and held his hands over her head and said something in Latin. Mary never knew what he said. But when she looked up, the men in her group were weeping, and strangely, the attendant who was with the Pope put his arms about her shoulders and said, "Oh blessed art thou among women."

As she saw first hand much of poverty in the different countries she visited, she observed, "One gets very many different ideas—we are not the only sufferers and burden bearers in the world. I stiffened my back and got new courage to come back to America with greater appreciation for the blessings we did have."

Back home in America, Mary was invited to a special luncheon by the mother of soon-to-be president Franklin D. Roosevelt. There were about 35 guests, but Mary was the only guest with dark skin. Two of the guests were ladies from the South, and as the announcement was made that lunch was to be served, these ladies were waiting for Mrs. Bethune to be escorted out. It was unheard of to sit at the same table. Anyone who allowed it would be socially ostracized. Imagine the startled looks on their faces as Mrs. Roosevelt graciously held out her arm to personally escort Mary Bethune to the table where she was seated as the guest of honor. She remembered how the faces of the servants lit up with pride when they saw her seated at the center of that imposing gathering of women leaders from all over the United States. Mrs. Roosevelt introduced her to her daughter-in-law, Eleanor, wife of Franklin, and they became immediate friends.

Her circle of influence grew wider and wider, with appointments to various boards, committees and even advisory roles to the Presidents of the United States. She fought hard to open doors for her people. When asked what they wanted, she would reply without hesitation: "Protection that is guaranteed by the Constitution of the United States and which we have a right to expect; the opportunity for development equal to that of any other American; to be understood; and finally, to make an appreciable contribution to the growth of a better America and a better world."

As conditions in the country became desperate in the Great Depression, President Roosevelt personally selected Mary to be Director of Minority Affairs of the National Youth Administration, or the NYA. The appointment overwhelmed her and her first inclination was to decline. But then she was reminded this was the first post created at such a high level for a black woman in the United States. Think of what it would mean to her people. She was paving the way for others to follow. She had accomplished so much in her life, overcoming so many insurmountable barriers. With her faith, she surely could do this. And so she went to work.

"Let those who can read go out to teach the children who can't," Mary Bethune directed. Young men and women just out of school themselves, under her inspiration, gathered in the children of the sharecroppers who had no schools and others who had not had an education and set up schools without buildings. In the NYA schools over the next few years, more than a million children got the basics of education. Reading did make a difference. But she didn't stop there. She set up projects in agriculture, shop work and dressmaking. Mothers' clubs were organized, bringing modern standards of health and child care. More than 40,000 young people were able to complete their college work and obtain their degrees.

Her desk was flooded with touching letters: "I am a colored boy 19 years old and am in very bad need of work. Please help me get a place in the National Youth Administration. They say it helps poor boys and girls like me."

Or, "I've been out of school for five school terms. I have no father and my mother isn't able to work regular on account of a run-down condition. So you see I must have work, so please help me." She criss-crossed the country, looking for ways to help take care of their needs.

For ten years, she worked tirelessly for "her children." President Roosevelt trusted her and depended on her. Once he said to her, "I am always glad to see you, Mrs. Bethune, because you never ask for anything for yourself."

She ignored her doctor's advice to slow down. There were just too many young people who needed her. But she had been distressed with a severe asthmatic condition for years, and announced that she needed to undergo an operation. Now, this woman who was the personal friend of presidents; who held a high rank in the national government; who was beloved by the millions of young people she had given hope to still faced the cruel realities of Jim Crow. Upon entering Johns Hopkins Hospital, she was told there were no private rooms in the medical or surgical divisions, where she should be, for a black woman. A special gesture was made because she was so outstanding, to place her in a room in a completely different part of the hospital. She soon discovered every nurse and every doctor on the staff were white. She persisted in a request to allow two distinguished black physicians in the city to participate in her case. She won and from that time on, doctors of all races have been allowed on the staff at Johns Hopkins hospital.

Mrs. Bethune kept a careful diary of her six weeks there, and although she must have had times of severe pain, there were no records of complaints. Years before, John D. Rockefeller, Sr., had given her his personal copy of *The Optimists Good Morning*, a book of wise sayings and comforting thoughts she had read for years. Her own log always began with a cheery thought, "Thank God for light, or Thanks for life, thanks for morning." "Glorious Day." "All my trust in Thee."

When World War II started, she spent countless hours writing words of encouragement and hope in letters. This 200-pound grandmother in her 60s became the unlikely pin-up girl in lockers of servicemen all over the world. How they loved her. And how she loved them.

The last five years of her life were spent at what was called "The Retreat," a home that was built for her on a corner of the Cookman-Bethune campus. The school now covered 32 acres and had 14 beautiful buildings surrounded by manicured lawns, dazzling flower beds and tall, shady trees. She watched the students as they hurried from class to class. Did they know how dear a price had been paid for the opportunities they now enjoyed? She remembered how the school had been built on an old dump heap with just $1.50 in her pocket. Gone were the days of the white-dress inspection tour. When she appeared dressed in white, everyone scrambled to their rooms to make sure no clothes had been stuffed under the bed or their rooms left untidy. The walls of her retreat were covered with photos and memories of her life of service. So much progress had been made, but there was still so far to go.

She sat down to write her last will and testament.

> Sometimes I ask myself if I have any legacy to leave. My worldly possessions are few. Yet, my experiences have been rich. From them I have distilled principles and policies

in which I firmly believe. Perhaps in them there is something of value. So, as my life draws to a close, I will pass them on in the hope that this philosophy may give inspiration. Here, then is my legacy.

I leave you love. "Love thy neighbor" is a precept which could transform the world if it were universally practiced.

I leave you hope.

I leave you a thirst for education.

I leave you faith. Without faith, nothing is possible. With it, nothing is impossible. Faith in God is the greatest power, but great faith too is faith in oneself.

I leave you racial dignity. We must recognize that we are the custodians as well as the heirs of a great civilization. As a race we have given something to the world, and for this we are proud.

I leave you a desire to live harmoniously with your fellow men.

I leave you finally with a responsibility to our young people. They must not be discouraged from aspiring toward greatness, for they are to be the leaders of tomorrow.

One of Mary Bethune's biographers closes her story with these words:

On the afternoon of May 18, 1955, Mary McLeod Bethune was rocking gently on her front porch. She rose and entered the house, and her heart suddenly stilled. She did not need time to make her peace with God; that had been done long ago, and they were companions.

Beside her dearly beloved Retreat, a hill was built and what was left of earth was laid within it. In flowers above her was spelled out MOTHER. And anyone who listened with hope and belief might hear the strong echo of her voice, "Life is wonderful!"

Podcast #77 Lessons from Abraham Lincoln

On April 9, 1865, at about 1:00 in the afternoon, two war-weary generals met in the parlor of the McLean house at Appomattox Court House, just a few miles from where I live. General Lee came in full formal military attire while General Grant rushed to the unexpected meeting in his mud-splattered field uniform. After a few awkward social exchanges, General Lee surrendered his troops and the war was over. As Grant left the house, he quieted the band eager to play the songs of celebration. He told them, "The war is over. The Rebels are our countrymen again." The Union soldiers were ordered to feed the starving Confederate troops from their provisions. It was time for a nation to heal.

Just five days later, relieved from the crushing pressures of war, President Abraham Lincoln and his wife were enjoying a play at Ford's Theater. He was looking forward to returning to his Illinois home in the not-too-distant future and resuming the quiet life of a country lawyer. It was not to be. The next morning, both North and South were stunned at the news Lincoln was dead.

As one of his biographers wrote: "All the world loves a lover and Lincoln loved everybody. He was the great-heart of the White House. The secret of his true greatness was in his heart. So hearty was his kindness toward everybody that the most casual remark of his seems to be charged with deep human affection. He knew just how to sympathize with everyone. The people felt this; without knowing why, and recognized it in every deed or word or touch, so that those who felt the grasp of his great warm hand seemed to have been drawn into the strong circuit of 'Lincoln fellowship,' and were enabled…to speak of him ever after with a deep and tender feeling."[89]

No wonder that thousands of books have been written about this great soul. I knew I wanted to do a podcast on him, but how could I begin to narrow down the focus? I thought of doing one on Lincoln: the great storyteller, for that was one of his great gifts. People were endeared to him through his stories. When tempers and disagreements were running hot, one of his stories would bring clarity and diffuse the heat of the moment.

Or I could do one just on Honest Abe, for his example of honesty and personal integrity are legendary. Or how about the stories of his compassion and kindness? His attention to little birds that fell out of their nests or little girls that needed a tear wiped from their faces? Or desperate parents, pleading for the lives of their soldier sons facing disciplinary executions? I could do one on Lincoln: the poet, for he was a great lover of poetry and even wrote poetry himself. Or on the education of his childhood, in which you would recognize many Well-Educated Heart principles in action. A discussion of the kinds of books he read would be interesting in itself! Or I could highlight Lincoln the family man with the picture of him carrying his boys on his shoulders or romping with them in the White House; or the grief-stricken father at the death of his little boy whom he loved dearly in the midst of the terrible war. Or how about the wisdom of Lincoln of which I find a never-ending supply.

Narrowing down the choices reminded me of when I was choosing what I would include about Lincoln in the volume dedicated to him in the Forgotten Classics Family Library. You may have heard me talk about it elsewhere as I have frequently been asked how I chose the stories and books included in that library. And the answer is, it came down to feelings and impressions. Often I would sit down at the computer and a keyword or an idea would come to my mind and as I perused the books on Internet Archive, it was almost as if they 'lit up'—there we go again trying to find words to describe an experience of the heart. All I can say is there's a purpose for every story that was included and that purpose was that each of them teach a life lesson or principle for happy living.

At the time that I was searching for stories about Lincoln, we had subscribers to our Freedom Series and we were using a company who published hard-bound editions with dust covers. So we had deadlines to keep as they expected a new volume each month and we had to allow time for our printer to do his work. My husband and I were out of town and we were way past the deadline. My husband had spent over 40 hours formatting the book and getting it ready for the printer. I had planned on submitting it the next morning, but as I went to bed that night, I had this unsettling feeling come over me that something wasn't right or that something was missing. It wasn't the first time. But I knew I couldn't send it off until it was right. I hated to tell my husband after all his long hours of work, but he patiently does whatever I ask of him. I told him we needed to delete one of the sections all together and there was something else that should go in its place.

It was late at night, but I got on Internet Archive and started searching. The impression that came to me was that I was looking for a book that had short character sections about Lincoln. Internet Archive wasn't as user friendly as it is now; all that came up were long lists of titles of books. So for the next couple of hours I scrolled through those lists, opening and checking out the titles. But nothing 'felt' right. I got up early the next morning and started searching again and when I came to a little book written by a Samuel Scoville,[90] my heart said "This is the right one." It matched the impression of the book I was looking for. I started reading through it and when I came to a section on Lincoln: The Christian, I read a passage that brought tears to my eyes and this overwhelming feeling came to me that this is what I was looking for. This is what needed to be included in the book.

I'll tell you what the specific incident is in a minute, but let me preface it by saying that at the time I was doing this, I couldn't imagine that within a few years, statues of Lee and Washington and other American heroes would be toppled. And even Lincoln is under attack. Part of that attack is that he was not a Christian or a religious man; that he has done horrible things to our country; that he was a vulgar man and that every act he committed as president was purely strategic, including the Emancipation Proclamation.

This particular chapter I felt to include in the book contains his farewell speech to his friends in Springfield, Illinois, as he leaves for the White House: "I now leave, not knowing when or whether I may ever return, with a task before me greater than that which rested upon

Washington. Without the assistance of that Divine Being who ever attended him I cannot succeed. With that assistance I cannot fail."

After the Emancipation Proclamation had been signed, he said to some men who had called to congratulate him:

> On many a defeated field there was a voice louder than the thundering of cannon. It was the voice of God crying, Let my people go. We were all very slow in realizing that it was God's voice, but after many humiliating defeats the nation came to believe it as a great and solemn command. Great multitudes begged and prayed that I might answer God's voice by signing the Emancipation Proclamation, and I did it, believing that we should never be successful in the great struggle unless we obeyed the Lord's command. Since then the God of battles has been on our side.

And here is the part I read that struck my heart:

> Just before the Battle of Gettysburg all the members of the Cabinet were in a state of terrible anxiety. General Lee with a powerful army had swept up into Pennsylvania. On the eve of the battle General Meade, almost an untried general, had been placed in command. A defeat meant the loss of the Capital and perhaps the occupation of Philadelphia and even New York. Everywhere was panic. Only Lincoln remained unmoved and unafraid. After the battle he told General Sickles the reason of his confidence:

> "In the pitch of your campaign up there, when everybody seemed panic-stricken and nobody could tell what was going to happen, I went to my room one day and locked the door and got down on my knees before Almighty God, and prayed for victory at Gettysburg. I told him that this was his war, and our cause his cause, but that we could not stand another Fredericksburg or Chancellorsville. Then I made a vow to Almighty God that if he would stand by our boys at Gettysburg, I would stand by him, and he did stand by you boys and I will stand by him. And after that, I don't know how it was and I can't explain it, but soon a sweet comfort swept into my soul that God Almighty had taken the whole business into his own hands, and that is why I have no fears about you."

To Chittenden, the Register of the Treasury, Lincoln said:

> That the Almighty does make use of human agencies, and directly intervenes in human affairs, is one of the plainest statements in the Bible. I have had so many evidences of his direction, so many instances when I have been controlled by some other power than my own will, that I cannot doubt that this power comes from above. I frequently see my way clear to a decision when I am conscious that I have not sufficient facts upon which to found it. I am satisfied that when the Almighty wants me to do or not to do a particular thing, he finds a way of letting me know it.

It was this deep and achieved faith in God that made John Hay, who had been one of his private secretaries, say of him:

Abraham Lincoln, one of the mightiest masters of statecraft that history has known, was also one of the most devoted and faithful servants of Almighty God who have ever sat in the high places of the world.

On the day of the receipt of the news of Lee's surrender, the President held a meeting of the Cabinet. Neither Lincoln nor any member was able for a time to speak. Finally, at the suggestion of the President, all dropped on their knees and thanked God in silence and in tears for the victory that had been granted to the Union. It is doubtful whether there is any other recorded instance where the meeting of the Cabinet of a great country ended in prayer.

In his Second Inaugural Address, he said:

"The Almighty has his own purposes…. The judgments of the Lord are true and righteous altogether."

For whatever reason, these words needed to be part of this book on Lincoln, maybe not so much as a reflection on him, but as a reminder to us as we face the challenges of our nations today.

So I would like to focus on Lincoln's faith, but more importantly, what lessons we gain from his life that will teach us how to instill such a great faith in our children today, which is completely tied into his great heart of love.

As another biographer wrote, "There were smarter men than Lincoln…. True greatness is made of goodness rather than smartness…. The people loved him for his big heart because he loved them more than he loved himself and they knew it. In his second inaugural address, he used this phrase: 'With malice toward none and charity for all.' This was not a new thought, but it was full of meaning to the country because little Abe Lincoln had lived that idea all his life, with his own family, his friends, his acquaintances and his employers. He became the most beloved man in the whole world, in his own way or any other time, because he himself loved everybody."

Where did his well-educated heart come from? Lincoln himself said, "All that I am or ever hope to be I owe to my angel mother."

> His first mother, Nancy, was with him in those first open and impressionable nine years of his life before she was called home to heaven. But her work laid a foundation in his heart that saved a nation. Henry Rankin who worked with Lincoln in his law firm listened to his stories of his childhood and recorded:

> "We learn from his words how vividly he recognized, and recalled with generous tenderness, the deep and lasting impressions those nine years of mother-love had made on him. From more than one friend I have heard of Lincoln's remarking that he owed all that he was, or ever would be, to the inspiration so early instilled into his mind by his mother. The isolation of their home made their companionship in every way closer than is usual between mother and son. Her memory ever should be held in sacred reverence for the influence she had on the life she gave our country."

At one point, there was a debate over what age children should be admitted into the Sunday Schools, and Lincoln's opinion was asked for. He replied that he was not an authority in such matters; that there were no such schools in his childhood, and that he had never attended a Sunday-school except by request to make a short address. But the age limit, he thought, should find no place in any Sunday-school. He might illustrate this, he said, by mention of his own boyhood and the influence that biblical and moral instruction given in early years could, and did, have in his life. He said he was nine years old when his mother died; that his instruction by her in letters and morals, and especially the Bible stories, and the interest and love he acquired in reading the Bible through this teaching of his mother, had been the strongest and most influential experience of his life. He referred with evident sadness to the lonely months after his mother's death, and said that the Bible she had read, and had taught him to read, was the greatest comfort he and his sister had after their mother was gone. It was from this Bible of hers, that he had asked Dr. David Elkin to read when he came into their home to preach the funeral sermon of his mother several months after her death.

Lincoln continued speaking of the vividness of childhood's impressions and how potent they were to influence and control mature years. He recalled how his mother had interested him in Bible stories before he had learned to read. He said that for years afterwards, and even yet, when he read certain verses which he had in early boyhood committed to memory by hearing her repeat them as she went about her household tasks, the tones of his mother's voice would come to him and he would seem to hear her speak those verses again.

When his mother knew that she was going to die, she called the children to her bedside. She was very weak and 9-year-old Lincoln and his slightly older sister leaned over her while she gave them her dying message. "Be good to one another," she said to them both, while expressing her hope that they both might live, as she had taught them to live, in the love of their kindred and the service of God.

It's no wonder Lincoln…used and quoted more scripture than any man in the nation, and that he quoted the parables and language of Christ oftener than any public man living. Not only did Lincoln quote scripture, but he used it as being of Divine authority, and applicable to the affairs of earth.

Yet, Lincoln, even in his day, was accused of being an infidel, an unbeliever. The fact that he didn't regularly attend a church was used against him. There were some writings taken out of context and even fabricated. He never engaged in the rivalries of sects and doctrines. He didn't talk about religion directly. But, there, according to another biographer, were times, in the privacy of the home life or in an interview with a friend in the office, when Lincoln spoke freely of what religion meant to him. Such times, however, were not frequent. They were rare occasions. He did not wear his religion as a personal exhibit on his sleeve, as some have done. He lived his religion. It was a constant, pervasive part of the man, but he was averse to advertising it and never used it for purposes of display. It was in only quiet, private moments that he spoke of his beliefs."

I believe it's worth sharing one of those private moments that took place in 1846 when Lincoln was opposing a preacher, Peter Cartwright, for a seat in Congress. Cartwright's team had brought up the infidel charge. Lincoln was visiting in a home with friends, and the mother in that home brought up the question of his faith.

He rose from his chair where he had been sitting and walked slowly across the room and stood at one end of the hearth, at the side of the chimney breast before the old-fashioned fireplace. He rested an elbow on the wide mantel, leaning his head on his hand, with the long fingers thrust through his hair. Although so young at the time, I clearly recall [him] as he stood there, facing those in the room in silence for a few moments. Then he began to speak quite slowly…

"Mrs. Rankin, you have asked me a question opening up a subject that is being thrust into this Congressional campaign and which I have resolved to ignore. It is one having no proper place, or call for an answer by me, in the political present or future before us. I will not discuss the character and religion of Jesus Christ on the stump! That is no place for it, though my opponent, a minister of His gospel, thinks it is. But in the private circle of friends, with the inquiry coming from you, Mrs. Rankin, who have known me as long as any of my Salem friends, and in some respects more intimately than any of them, I will frankly answer your question…

"At the time you refer to I was having serious questionings about some portions of my former implicit faith in the Bible. The influence that drew me into such doubts were strong ones, men having the widest culture and strongest minds of any I had known up to that time. In the midst of these shadows and questionings, before I could see my way clear to decide on them, there came into my life sad events and a loss that you were close to and you knew a great deal about how hard they were for me, for you were, at the time, a mutual friend. Those days of trouble found me tossed amidst a sea of questionings. They piled big upon me, experiences that brought with them great strains upon my emotional and mental life. Through all I groped my way until I found a stronger and higher grasp of thought, one that reached beyond this life with a clearness and satisfaction I had never known before. The Scriptures unfolded before me with a deeper and more logical appeal, through these new experiences, than anything else I could find to turn to, or ever before had found in them.

"I do not claim that all my doubts were removed then, or since that time have been swept away. They are not. Probably it is to be my lot to go on in a twilight, feeling and reasoning my way through life, as questioning, doubting Thomas did. But in my poor maimed, withered way, I bear with me as I go on a seeking spirit of desire for a faith that was with him of the olden time, who, in his need, as I in mine, exclaimed: Help, thou my unbelief.

"I do not see [he went on to say, after leaving his position on the hearth and resuming his former seat], I do not see that I am more astray though perhaps in a different direction than many others whose points of view differ widely from each other in the sectarian denominations. They all claim to be Christian, and interpret their several creeds as infallible ones. Yet they differ and discuss these questionable subjects without settling them with any mutual satisfaction among themselves.

"I doubt the possibility, or propriety, of settling the religion of Jesus Christ in the models of man-made creeds and dogmas. It was a spirit in the life that He laid stress on and taught, if I read aright. I know I see it to be so with me.

"The fundamental truths reported in the four gospels as from the lips of Jesus Christ, and that I first heard from the lips of my mother, are settled and fixed moral precepts with me. I have concluded to dismiss from my mind the debatable wrangles that once perplexed me with distractions that stirred up, but never absolutely settled anything. I have tossed them aside with the doubtful differences which divide denominations sweeping them all out of my mind among the non-essentials. I have ceased to follow such discussions or be interested in them.

"I cannot without mental reservations assent to long and complicated creeds and catechisms. If the church would ask simply for assent to the Saviour's statement of the substance of the law: 'Thou shalt love the Lord thy God with all thy heart, and with all thy soul, and with all thy mind, and thy neighbor as thyself,' that church would I gladly unite with."

Oh, there is so much I love about Abraham Lincoln. There are good reasons I devoted a whole month to him in the rotation schedule. For today, I present to you Abraham Lincoln: a man of deep faith who loved his Father in Heaven and thereby, his fellow man.

I'll close with a few lines from one of his favorite poems, written by William Cullen Bryant, a poem he memorized while visiting with his wife's family and which he recited for them.

> So live, that when thy summons comes to join
> The innumerable caravan, that moves
> To that mysterious realm, where each shall take
> His chamber in the silent halls of death,
> Thou go not, like the quarry-slave at night,
> Scourged to his dungeon, but sustained and soothed
> By an unfaltering trust, approach thy grave,
> Like one who wraps the drapery of his couch
> About him, and lies down to pleasant dreams.

Podcast #165 Abraham Lincoln

Today is April 15, not a favorite day for many Americans scrambling to get their taxes filed. But today is also the 154th anniversary of the day Abraham Lincoln died. He had been shot the night before Good Friday while watching a play with his wife at Ford's theater and passed away without regaining consciousness about 7:00 the next morning on April 15th. Those who were there said his face relaxed into a smile when death came.

I just finished recording a favorite book about Lincoln written by Wilbur Gordy that you will find at mybelmonde.com under Month 8, Abraham Lincoln. This book will not only help you and your children begin to appreciate this giant of a man in every way, they will get a clear overview of key Civil War events without getting bogged down in details. I would guess it will appeal to upper elementary and older aged children. As I read it aloud, I was swept into the emotion of the story and could almost feel the heavy weight Lincoln bore on his shoulders. No one thought this backwoodsman was capable of doing the job and they didn't hesitate to let him know. Yet, with a firm faith in the guiding hand of Providence he navigated the stormy seas and brought the Ship of State safely to port. After the crushing pressure he had been under, I can well imagine his face relaxing into a smile. We owe so much to this man and each year as I return to him in the rotation schedule, I learn another facet of his character and personality that makes me love him even more.

One of his most endearing qualities was his sense of humor as well as his storytelling and I thought you might enjoy a letter he wrote. I'll let it speak for itself. But I smile just thinking about it. You might also keep in mind, it is dated April 1st.

Here is the letter.[91]

Dear Madam:

Without appologising[sic] for being egotistical, I shall make the history of so much of my own life, as has elapsed since I saw you, the subject of this letter. And by the way I now discover, that, in order to give you a full and inteligible [sic] account of the things I have done and suffered since I saw you, I shall necessarily have to relate some that happened before.

I was, then, in the autumn of 1836, that a married lady of my acquaintance, and who was a great friend of mine, being about to pay a visit to her father and other relatives residing in Kentucky, proposed to me, that on her return she would bring a sister of hers with her, upon condition that I would engage to become her brother-in-law with all convenient dispatch [sic] I, of course, accepted the proposal; for you know I could not have done otherwise, had I really been averse to it; but privately, between you and me, I was most confoundedly well pleased with the project. I had seen the said sister some three years before, thought her intelligent and agreeable, and saw no good objection to plodding life through hand in hand with her. Time passed on, the lady took her journey, and in due time returned, sister in company sure enough. This stomached me a little; for it appeared to me, that her coming so readily showed that she was a trifle too willing; but on reflection it occurred [*sic*] to me, that she might have been prevailed on by her married sister to come, without any thing concerning me ever? having been mentioned to her; and so I concluded that if no other objection presented itself, I would consent to waive this. All this occurred to me upon my hearing of her arrival in the neighbourhood; for, be it remembered, I had not yet seen her, except about three years previous, as before mentioned.

In a few days we had an interview, and although I had seen her before, she did not look as my immagination [*sic*] had pictured her. I knew she was over-size, but she now appeared a fair match for Falstaff; I knew she was called an "old maid," and I felt no doubt of the truth of at least half of the appellation [*sic*]; but now, when I beheld her, I could not for my life avoid thinking of my mother; and this, not from withered features, for her skin was too full of fat to permit its contracting in to wrinkles; but from her want of teeth, weather-beaten appearance in general, and from a kind of notion that ran in my head, that nothing could have commenced at the size of infancy, and reached her present bulk in less than thirty-five or forty years; and, in short, I was not all pleased with her. But what could I do? – I had told her sister that I would take her for better or for worse; and I made a point of honor and conscience in all things, to stick to my word, especially if others had been induced to act on it, which in this case, I doubted not they had, for I was now fairly convinced, that no other man on earth would have her, and hence the conclusion that they were bent on holding me to my bargain. Well, thought I, I have said it, and, be consequences what they may, it shall not be my fault if I fail to do it. At once I determined to consider her my wife; and this done, all my powers of discovery were put to the rack, in search of perfections in her, which might be fairly set-off against her defects. I tried to imagine [*sic*] she was handsome, which, but for her unfortunate corpulency, was actually true. Exclusive of this, no woman that I have seen, has a finer face. I also tried to convince myself, that the mind was much more to be valued than the person; and in this, she was not inferior, as I could discover, to any with whom I had been acquainted.

Shortly after this, without attempting to come to any positive understanding with her, I set out for Vandalia, where and when you first saw me. During my stay there, I had letters from her, which I did not change my opinion of either her intelect or intention; but on the contrary, confirmed it in both.

All this while, although I was fixed "firm as the surge repelling rock" in my resolution, I found I was continually repenting the rashness which had led me to make it. Through life I have been in no bondage, either real or imaginary, from the thraldom of which I so much desired to be free. After my return home, I saw nothing to change my opinion of her in any particular. She was the same and so was I. I now spent my time between planing [*sic*] how I might get along through life after my contemplated change of circumstances should have taken place; and how I might procrastinate the evil day for a time, which I really dreaded as much—perhaps more, than an irishman [*sic*] does the halter.

After all my suffering upon this deeply interesting subject, here I am, wholly unexpectedly, completely out of the "scrape"; and I now want to know, if you can guess how I got out of it. Out clear in every sense of the term; no violation of word, honor or conscience. I don't believe you can guess, and so I might as well tell you at once. As the lawyers say, it was done in the manner following, towit. After I had delayed the matter as long as I thought I could in honor do, which by the way had brought me round into the last fall, I concluded I might as well bring it to a consummation [sic] without further delay; and so I mustered my resolution, and made the proposal to her direct; but, shocking to relate, she answered, No. At first I supposed she did it through an affectation of modesty, which I thought but ill-become her, under the peculiar circumstances of her case; but on my renewal of the charge, I found she repeled [*sic*] it with greater firmness than before. I tried it again and again, but with the same success, or rather with the same want of success.

I finally was forced to give it up, at which I very unexpectedly found myself mortified almost beyond endurance. I was mortified, it seemed to me, in a hundred different ways. My vanity was deeply wounded by the reflections, that I had so long been too stupid to discover her intentions, and at the same time never doubting that I understood them perfectly; and also, that she whom I had taught myself to believe nobody else would have, had actually rejected me with all my fancied greatness; and to cap the whole, I then, for the first time, began to suspect that I was really a little in love with her. But let it all go. I'll try and out live it. Others have been made fools of by the girls; but this can never with truth be said of me I most emphatically, in this instance, made a fool of myself. I have now come to the conclusion never again to think of marrying; and for this reason; I can never be satisfied with any one who would be block-head enough to have me.

When you receive this, write me a long yarn about something to amuse me. Give my respects to Mr. Browning.

Your sincere friend.

A. Lincoln

Podcast #166 William Lloyd Garrison

We'll be moving into the Civil War next month and it's time for another reminder. Just as not all the colonists wanted to break away from England, not all of the Northeners were against slavery and not all the Southerners were for it. So while you'd think a group of abolitionists who wanted to get rid of slavery all together would get support from their Northern neighbors, it just wasn't the case. Many Northern businessmen benefited from slave labor. Even those who agreed that slavery was wrong couldn't see the way for the slaves to be assimilated into society if they were suddenly freed. So they, too, did not support the Abolitionist cause.

One Northerner who lived in Massachusetts took the unpopular stand as an abolitionist against slavery and demanded its immediate end. His name was William Lloyd Garrison. In 1830 he started an abolitionist newspaper—the Liberator—to promote his views. For 35 years he did not miss publishing a single issue—1,820 in all! Think about that. Many of you who are listening haven't even been alive 35 years—that is a long time to fight for a cause. Which is why I believe he is a great soul worth highlighting.

He never gave up until the task was done. Once the slaves were freed, he closed his newspaper and went home.

His life was in constant danger because of his views. He was a Northerner who believed the Union should be dissolved because he viewed the Constitution as pro-slavery. Yet, when Abraham Lincoln who was fighting to save the Union issued the Emancipation Proclamation, he praised the effort, even though he had been at odds with President Lincoln.

I want to share a scene from his life that illustrates his courage and calm, even in the face of death. I found it in one of Eva March Tappan's Children's Hour volumes—*Adventures and Achievements*.[92]

> The time appointed for the meeting was three o'clock in the afternoon, and a little before that time Garrison went to Congress Hall and joined the little band of devoted women, mostly white, but including some negroes and mulattoes, who were undaunted by the presence of a group of howling, swearing, outrageous enemies of human freedom. Garrison appealed to the chivalrous feelings of this disorderly crew, but the effect of his words speedily wore off. As Garrison was the only male Abolitionist in the meeting, it was thought that his withdrawal would prevent the gentlemanly mob of auditors from attempting any violence. Acting upon the advice and suggestion of Miss Parker, he retired into the adjoining anti-slavery office. It was impossible to leave the building, for the staircase was now filled by an angry crowd, and below the streets were also filled. Thousands of voices were demanding "Thompson, Thompson!" The mayor assured the yelling mob that George Thompson was not in Boston, and that Garrison had left the building. If the men had escaped, there were still thirty women to be annoyed by the mob of five thousand respectable gentlemen. Miss Parker opened the meeting with a

fervent and untremulous prayer, apparently not concerned by the attitude of the threatening mob around her. The mayor ordered them to go home, but they at first declined. Then a letter was read inviting them to meet at the house of Mr. Francis Jackson.

"Ladies," exclaimed the mayor, "do you wish to see a scene of bloodshed and confusion? If you do not, go home."

"Mr. Lyman," retorted Mrs. M. W. Chapman, "your personal friends are the instigators of this mob; have you ever used your personal influence with them?"

"I know no personal friends," he replied. "I am merely an official. Indeed, ladies, you must retire. It is dangerous to remain."

"If this is the last bulwark of freedom," Mrs. Chapman answered, "we may as well die here as anywhere." Finally, it was decided to adjourn. They filed out, two and two, each white lady, where necessary, having with her a colored friend. This heroic band walked through the howling mob, in solemn procession, to Mr. Jackson's house, and finding that he was ill, walked from there to Mrs. Chapman's home. When the ladies had left the hall, there were cries of "Garrison is there. We must have Garrison. Lynch him." The antislavery sign-board excited their indignation, and it was, with the mayor's connivance, if not by his orders, torn off its hooks and thrown into the street, where it was promptly broken to pieces, some of the bits being secured as precious relics by the friends of the slaveholders.

Garrison continued calmly writing in the anti-slavery office until the partition was broken down. There was no hope that the mob would disperse whilst he was in the building. It was impossible for him to leave by the front door, as all the avenues were in possession of the mob. The mayor begged that he would escape from the back of the building. One of the Abolitionists, righteously angry at the baseness with which the civil authorities truckled to the lawlessness of the mob, said:—"I must henceforth repudiate the principle of nonresistance. When the civil arm is powerless, my own rights are trodden in the dust, and the lives of my friends are put in imminent peril by ruffians, I will hereafter prepare to defend myself and them at all hazards."

Garrison, putting a hand affectionately on his shoulder, said: "Hold, my dear brother! you know not what spirit you are of. This is the trial of our faith, and, the test of our endurance. Of what value or utility are the principles of peace and forgiveness, if we may repudiate them in the hour of peril and suffering? Do you wish to become like one of these violent, bloodthirsty men, who are seeking my life? Shall we give blow for blow, and array sword against sword? God forbid! I will perish sooner than raise my hand against any man, even in self-defense, and let none of my friends resort to violence for my protection. If my life be taken, the cause of emancipation will not suffer. God reigns, His throne L is undisturbed by this storm; He will make the wrath of man to praise Him, of the remainder He will restrain; His omnipotence will at length be victorious."

Garrison's friends now joined their entreaties to those of the mayor. At length he consented, and made his way by a window on to a shed, and thence into a carpenter's shop, which opened into Wilson's Lane. He was accompanied by Mr. J. R. Campbell, but they found that their retreat was cut off by the mob. Garrison wanted to face them, but Campbell thought it was his duty to avoid capture as long as possible. He was put into a corner of the room, and loose timber put in front to hide him. In a moment the room was entered and Campbell was seized. "This is not Garrison," the captors shouted to the mob outside, "but Garrison's and Thompson's friend, and he says he knows where Garrison is, but won't tell." A moment later and then Garrison was discovered and dragged to the window.

"Don't let us kill him outright," one of them cried; then they tied a rope round his body, and he descended a ladder, placed for the purpose, into the street. He now extricated himself from the rope, and was seized by Daniel and Aaron Cooley, who, although opponents of the Abolitionists, were no friends of mob violence. They led him along, bareheaded, and cried aloud to the immense crowd, "He shan't be hurt; he is an American." The cry excited some sympathy, and the bearing of Garrison was one to increase it. As an eyewitness testifies, he walked erect, with a calm countenance and flashing, eyes, like a martyr going to the stake full of faith and manly hope. Mr. Josiah Quincy, Jr., the president of the common council, had from his window seen the action of the mob and at once hastened to his side. The news of the capture had also reached the mayor, and an appeal was made to him to save the life of Garrison.

There was a tremendous struggle between the lynchers and those who were attempting to rescue their victim. The human tide set towards the Old State House, and for a moment it was doubtful which side would be successful; the appeal of the mayor to the mob was little heeded, but the fierce rush to prevent Garrison from being taken into the hall was unsuccessful, and he was carried into the mayor's room. Here the authorities decided to commit him to jail as a rioter. He had been supplied with fresh clothing to take the place of the garments torn to pieces by the mob. Whilst a carriage, placed at the south door with a double line of guards, was attracting attention there, Garrison was hurried into a hackney coach at the north door. Notwithstanding what he had experienced he kept saying, "Oh, if they would only hear me for five minutes, I am sure I could bring them to reason." His perfect courage and self possession never deserted him throughout the trying ordeal. No sooner was he in the carriage than the mob recognized that he was being spirited away from their vengeance. They clung to the wheels, forced open the doors, and tried to overturn the vehicle. The driver used his whip freely to both horses and men, and drove at a furious pace and by a circuitous route to the city jail. All the way there was danger, and even at the prison door there was another ineffectual effort made to seize him. Finally, he found the "refuge of liberty" in a prison cell, where he was visited that same evening by Whittier, Bronson Alcott, and other friends.

Garrison had made no objection to his removal to the jail, and it was not until next morning that he learned that he had been committed as a rioter. Next morning he was brought before Judge Whitman and discharged. The examination was held in the jail, as the mayor and sheriff were afraid to have the trial in the court-house. The city authorities anticipated further trouble, and earnestly solicited Garrison to leave Boston for a few days, until a more tranquil spirit prevailed. This he consented to do, all the more readily that the condition of Mrs. Garrison was one that demanded his anxious attention.

The "rioter" Garrison placed on the walls of his cell this inscription: —

"Wm. Lloyd Garrison was put into this cell on Wednesday afternoon, Oct. 21, 1835, to save him from the violence of a 'respectable and influential' mob, who sought to destroy him for preaching the abominable and dangerous doctrine, ' that all men are created equal,' and that all oppression is odious in the sight of God. 'Hail, Columbia!' Cheers for the Autocrat of Russia and the Sultan of Turkey!

"Reader, let this inscription remain till the last slave in this despotic land be loosed from his fetters.

> When peace within the bosom reigns,
> And conscience gives th' approving voice;
> Though bound the human form in chains,
>   Yet can the soul aloud rejoice.

> 'Tis true, my footsteps are confined—
> I cannot range beyond this cell;—
> But what can circumscribe my mind?
>   To chain the winds attempt as well!

> Confine me as prisoner — but bind me not as a slave.
> Punish me as a criminal — but hold me not as a chattel.
> Torture me as a man — but drive me not like a beast.
>   Doubt my sanity— but acknowledge my immortality.

Podcast #167 David Livingstone, I Presume

The audio story of David Livingstone by Vautier Golding can be found in BelMonde, and if you don't yet know his story, this will be a great introduction, although I bet you'll want to learn more about this great soul. He was determined to open up the continent of Africa or perish trying. No sacrifice, no danger, no illness was too awful to deter him. His purpose was this: he could not bear to allow the slave trade to continue and he devoted his entire life trying to end it.

He had a plan. He felt that if he could find the right waterways into the interior of Africa and could promote trade and commerce, this new prosperity could replace the lucrative slave trade going on. He originally went to Africa as a Christian missionary. He only converted one native to Christianity, yet he did more to spread Christianity on the continent of Africa than anyone else

It wasn't by his preaching; he was a terrible preacher. It was by the conduct of his life. His heroic and relentless efforts caught the attention and the imagination of the entire European continent. When he went missing for six years, Henry M. Stanley was hired to find him no matter what the cost. He wrote: "No living man shall stop me. Only death can prevent me; but death not even then. I shall not die. I will not die; I cannot die. Something tells me that I shall find him. And I write it larger, find him. FIND HIM."

Stanley's courageous story is no less gripping. When the two men finally met, they became immediate friends. He wrote of Livingstone: "I challenge any man to find a fault in his character. The secret is that his religion is a constant, earnest and sincere effort."

Stanley could not persuade Livingstone to return to civilization, though. Livingstone would not give up his quest. Perhaps he felt he had failed in those last days of his life because his original plans to end the slave trade had not come to pass. The candle was still burning when his companions found him, not in bed, but kneeling at his bedside, with his head buried in his hands upon the pillow. The sad, yet not unexpected truth, soon became evident; he had passed away on the furthest of all his journeys he had traveled over 29,000 miles and covered a third of the African continent. He died alone. At least no earthly companion was by his side. He died in the act of prayer. In his diary, on his 59th birthday, he had written: "My birthday! My Jesus, my King, my Life, my All. I again dedicate my whole self to thee."

God magnified his efforts. As the news spread of his death, the story of his life in Africa quickened the hearts of countless individuals who now desired to travel to Africa and inspired the movement that changed the face of a continent, including the end of the slave trade at that time.

The study of Africa is incomplete without knowing the story of this remarkable man. It's amazing to see the influence one individual can have. Listen to his story in Month 8 under Africa at mybelmonde.com.

Podcast #187 Lessons from Harriet Beecher Stowe

President Abraham Lincoln was sitting by the fireplace in his office when Harriet Beecher Stowe entered the room with her twelve-year-old son and her grown-up daughter. The object of her visit was to deliver an "Affectionate and Christian Address" which had been signed by 500,000 women in Great Britain and Ireland, by duchesses, countesses, wives of generals and ambassadors, as well as by hands that evidently were unused to hold the pen. This "Address" had been sent to "their sisters, the women of the United States of America," through Harriet Beecher Stowe, in her efforts to remove slavery from the Christian world.

In part, it read: "We acknowledge with grief and shame our heavy share in this great sin. We acknowledge that our forefathers introduced, nay, even compelled the adoption of slavery in those mighty colonies. We humbly confess it before Almighty God; and it is because we so deeply feel and unfeignedly avow our own complicity that we now venture to implore your aid to wipe away our common crime and our common dishonor."

Upon seeing Harriet, Mr. Lincoln quickly rose from his chair. "So you're the little woman who wrote the book that made this great war."

She replied, "I did not write it, not I myself alone. It seemed to me that God himself made me write it, that I wrote it at his dictation."

The book was *Uncle Tom's Cabin*. Slavery had been a subject of debate for decades, but Harriet finally gave eyes to see and hearts to feel the horrors of the institution and stirred the hearts of the people to do something about it.

I'm taking excerpts from a biography of Harriet Beecher Stowe written by her son, Charles Edward Stowe.[93]

Harriet had established herself as a writer when her brother Edward's wife wrote her, "Hattie, if I could use a pen as you have, I would write something to make this whole nation feel what an accursed thing slavery is."

Harriet replied, "I will write something. I will if I live."

> Uncle Tom's Cabin came from the heart rather than the head. It was an out outburst of deep feeling, a cry in the darkness. The writer no more thought of style or literary excellence than the mother who rushes into the street and cries for help to save her children from a burning house thinks of the teachings of the rhetorician or the elocutionist.

It was in the month of February that Mrs. Stowe was seated at communion service in the college church at Brunswick.

> Suddenly, like the unrolling of a picture, the scene of the death of Uncle Tom passed before her mind. So strongly was she affected that it was with difficulty she could keep

from weeping aloud. Immediately on returning home she took pen and paper and wrote out the vision which had been as it were blown into her mind as by the rushing of a mighty wind. Gathering her family about her she read what she had written. Her two little ones of ten and twelve years of age broke into convulsions of weeping, one of them saying through his sobs, "Oh, mamma! Slavery is the most cruel thing in the world." Thus Uncle Tom was ushered into the world, and it was, a cry, an immediate, an involuntary expression of deep, impassioned feeling.

Twenty-five years afterwards Mrs. Stowe wrote a letter to one of her children, of this period of her life: "I well remember the winter you were a baby and I was writing 'Uncle Tom's Cabin.' My heart was bursting with the anguish excited by the cruelty and injustice our nation was showing to the slave, and praying God to let me do a little and to cause my cry for them to be heard. I remember many a night weeping over you as you lay sleeping beside me, and I thought of the slave mother whose babes were torn from them."

Uncle Tom's Cabin made the enforcement of the Fugitive Slave Law an impossibility. It aroused the public sentiment of the world by arousing in the concrete that which had been a mere series of abstract propositions. People are like children, and understand pictures better than words…. So Uncle Tom's Cabin made the crack of the slave-driver's whip, and the tortured Blacks ring in every household in the land, till human hearts could endure it no longer.

"I could not control the story; it wrote itself…. I, the author of Uncle Tom's Cabin? No, indeed. The Lord himself wrote it, and I was but the humblest instrument in his hand. To Him alone should be given all the praise."

There is so much in this biography of this wonderful woman I wish I could share. Do yourself a favor and find a copy in Internet Archive: *The Life of Harriet Beecher Stowe* by Charles Stowe. In the meantime, let's take a couple of snapshots of the childhood that produced the writer.

Although her mother died when just 5 years old, there was a bond between her that influenced all Harriet's life, and is revealed in nearly everything she wrote.

Her father believed thoroughly in playtime, and when long or hard tasks were well done, he often rewarded the small workers with a fishing trip or nut-gathering. The pleasure seekers tramped happily away at daybreak for a holiday that often lasted until after dark. He was better known as a playmate than a disciplinarian.

He possessed a stimulating personality that always brought forth the best efforts of his large brood in whatever tasks they undertook, and he tried to make those tasks so interesting that no one would want to shirk. If tasks were indoors, one of them would read Scott's novels or some other interesting work, while the rest busied themselves with their hands, and the long evenings slipped by so rapidly that no one could believe bedtime was at hand when the old clock struck the hour.

Even when sawing hickory logs, they strengthened their minds debating some topic suggested by their father. Often he would purposely take the wrong side of a question in order to create a lively argument. Thus he developed their reasoning powers to an unusual degree, making strong speakers of his children, and in this manner fitting them to become the powerful preachers which six of them afterward became.

He loved music and they had quite a respectable orchestra under their own roof.

The Beecher children lacked toys, but the lack was not greatly felt, for all of the little Beechers possessed vivid imaginations and could readily think up new games. They never lacked for rag dolls with real, painted faced and clothes to dress them in.

The children almost lived in the open air. There were gardens to tend to, especially flower gardens with hollyhocks and marigolds. "The wild beauty of the place held the child enthralled even before she could tell what it was that seemed so beautiful about her surroundings. She would sit on the stone parsonage steps and watch the glorious sunsets fade into purple twilights, too deeply moved for tears."

The day started with an early breakfast—simple but hearty. Family prayers followed breakfast, and every member of the household took part. So impressive were these brief morning services that they were never forgotten by any of them. Long evenings were given to family discussions, or household tasks, then family prayers were held again, and good-nights spoken.

Her little town was visited by many of the chief Revolutionary heroes of the time and the stories were repeated—she heard many stories of those stirring times which stirred her heart with patriotism.

There were also stories of her mother, and stories from her uncle who brought home wonderful treasures from around the world and told tales of adventure of his trips around the world as a sea-captain. All made impressions never to be forgotten by the sensitive child.

She loved her father's study and the books that lined the wall. She says, "High above all the noise of the house, this room had to me the air of a refuge and sanctuary. Its walls were set round from floor to ceiling with the friendly, quiet faces of books, and there stood my father's great writing-chair, on one arm of which lay open his Bible. Here I loved to retreat and niche myself down in a quiet corner with my favorite books around me. I had a kind of sheltered feeling as I thus sat and watched my father writing, turning to his books, and speaking from time to time to himself in a loud, earnest whisper. I vaguely felt that he was about some holy and mysterious work quite beyond my little comprehension, and I was careful never to disturb him by question or remark." She dug up "The Tempest" and Arabian Nights—her delight knew no bounds. She read Ivanhoe seven times in one summer. They weren't content to just read them— they must play them out, discuss them with their friends, and compare their merits and faults with those of other books which they had read. They acted out many of the scenes with simple costumes put together.

She wrote, "I was married when I was twenty-five years of age to a man rich in Greek and Hebrew, Latin and Arabic, and, also, rich in nothing else." The first year, twin daughters were born while her husband was away in England. Five more babies arrived quickly after that. She always declared that she would never exchange her children for all the ease, leisure and pleasure she could have without them. She said, "God invented mothers' hearts, and He certainly has the pattern in His own."

Her children received much of their early education under her. She said, "The most fearful thing about this education matter is that it is example more than word. Talk as you will, the child follows what he sees, not what he hears. The prevailing tone of the parent's character will make the temper of the household; the spirit of the parent will form the spirit of the child."

With this thought uppermost in her heart, she succeeded in making the atmosphere of her home sweet, harmonious and happy, and between the members of her family existed a bond of understanding that is rarely found.

Harriet became a musician and artist of considerable ability, and had a positive genius for homemaking. She was well-read and spoke French fluently and did beautiful needlework and lace. When problems of any sort arose about homemaking duties, she promptly went to the encyclopedia for advice and studied until she solved the problem. She built her own Russian stove according to the description seen in an encyclopedia and it heated six rooms more efficiently on less fuel it took for a single fire in an open fireplace.

One time she made a carpet out of a bale of cotton her husband brought home, which was unheard of at that time. The church deacons chided Mrs. Beecher for "trying to make the house so splendid that Heaven would lose its attractiveness!"

There was never enough money and her husband was often gone. Some of you might relate to this letter to her husband:

"My dear husband,

"It is a dark, sloppy, rainy, muddy, disagreeable day, and I have been working hard (for me) all day in the kitchen, washing dishes, looking into closets, and seeing a great deal of that dark side of domestic life…. I am sick of the smell of sour milk, and sour meat, and sour everything, and then the clothes will not dry, and no wet things does, and everything smells mouldy; and altogether I feel as if I never wanted to eat again….

"I feel no life, no energy, no appetite, or rather a growing distaste for food…. I suffer with sensible distress in the brain, … a distress which some days takes from me all power of planning, or executing anything; and you know that, except for this poor head, my unfortunate household has no mainspring, for nobody feels any kind of responsibility to do a thing in time, place, or manner, except as I oversee it."

Her husband was very dependent on her and pessimistic by nature, and she had to cheer him on when he became down-hearted. "If you were not already my dearly beloved husband, I should certainly fall in love with you."

But with her unswerving faith in her God, she bore her burden bravely.

Another time it fell on her to move to Brunswick, Maine. There was furniture to be bought, a house to be found and put in order, in the midst of a cold, northeastern storm that continued for days. She found many of her adventures funny, and laughed heartily over them with family and friends.

The kitchen had no sink. So she solved the problem and created one herself. She finished the house the first of July; gave birth to their seventh child on July 8th. Yet, she still managed to teach school an hour a day to her children and read to them for two hours every evening. While her husband was away.

In spite of the numberless tasks that absorbed her time night and day, she found time to keep at her writing through all these years; or perhaps it would be better to say that she made the time, for she certainly learned to do several things at once, and in this way managed her stories when a less determined or a less talented soul would have given up in despair.

An amusing and at the same time most interesting account of her struggles to accomplish literary work amid her distracting domestic duties is furnished by the letter of one of her intimate friends, who writes:—

It was my good fortune to number Mrs. Stowe among my friends, and during a visit to her I had an opportunity one day of witnessing the combined exercise of her literary and domestic genius in a style that to me was quite amusing.

"Come, Harriet," said I, as I found her tending one baby and watching two others just able to walk, "where is that piece for the 'Souvenir' which I promised the editor I would get from you and send on next week? You have only this one day to finish it, and have it I must."

"And how will you get it, friend of mine?" said Harriet. "You will at least have to wait till I get house-cleaning over and baby's teeth through."

"As to house-cleaning, you can defer it one day longer; and as to baby's teeth, there is to be no end to them, as I can see. No, no; today that story must be ended. There Frederick has been sitting by Ellen and saying all those pretty things for more than a month now, and she has been turning and blushing till I am sure it is time to go to her relief. Come, it would not take you three hours at the rate you can write to finish the courtship, marriage, catastrophe, and all; and this three hours' labor of your brains will earn enough to pay for all the sewing your fingers could do for a year to come. Two dollars a page, my dear, and you can write a page in fifteen minutes! Come, then, my lady housekeeper, economy is a cardinal virtue; consider the economy of the thing."

"But, my dear, here is a baby in my arms, and there is a great baking down in the kitchen, and there is a 'new girl' for 'help,' besides preparations to be made for house-cleaning next week. It is really out of the question, you see."

"I see no such thing. I do not know what genius is given for, if it is not to help a woman out of a scrape. Come, set your wits to work, let me have my way, and you shall have all the work done and finish the story, too."

"Well, but kitchen affairs?"

"We can manage them, too. You know you can write anywhere and anyhow. Just take your seat at the kitchen table with your writing weapons, and while you superintend Mina fill up the odd snatches of time with the labors of your pen."

I carried my point. In ten minutes she was seated; a table with flour, rolling-pin, ginger, and lard on one side, a dresser with eggs, pork, and beans and various cooking utensils on the other, near her an oven heating, and beside her, Mina, waiting orders.

"Here, Harriet," said I, "you can write on this atlas in your lap; no matter how the writing looks, I will copy it."

"Well, well," said she, with a resigned sort of amused look. "Mina, you may do what I told you, while I write a few minutes, till it is time to mould up the bread. Where is the inkstand?"

"Here is it, close by, on the top of the tea-kettle," said I.

At his Mina giggled, and we both laughed to see her merriment at our literary proceedings.

She fell into a muse, as she attempted to recover the thread of her story.

"Ma'am shall I put the pork on the top of the beans?" asked Mina.

"Come, come!" said Harriet, laughing. "You see how it is. Mina is a new hand and cannot do anything without me to direct her. We must give up writing for today."

"No, no; let us have another trial. You can dictate as easily as you can write. Come, I can set the baby in this clothes basket and give him some mischief or other to keep him quiet; you shall dictate and I will write. Now, this is the place where you left off: you were describing the scene between Ellen and her lover: the last sentence was, 'Borne down the tide of agony, she leaned her head on her hands, the tears streamed through her fingers, and her whole frame shook with convulsive sobs.' What shall I write next?"

"Mina, pour a little milk into this pearlash," said Harriet.

"Come," said I. "'The tears streamed through her fingers and her whole frame shook with convulsive sobs.' What next?"

Harriet paused and looked musingly out of the window, as she turned her mind to her story. "You may write now," said she, and she dictated as follows:

"'Her lover wept with her, nor dared he again to touch the point so sacredly guarded'—Mina, roll that crust a little thinner. 'He spoke in soothing tones'—Mina, poke the coals in the oven."

"Here," said I, "Let me direct Mina about these matters, and write a while yourself."

Harriet took the pen and patiently set herself to the work. For awhile my culinary knowledge and skill were proof to all Mina's investigating inquiries, and they did not fail till I saw two pages completed.

"You have done bravely," said I, as I read over the manuscript; "now you must direct Mina awhile. Meanwhile dictate and I will write."

Never was there a more docile literary lady than my friend. Without a word of objection she followed my request.

"I am ready to write," said I. "The last sentence was: 'What is this life to one who has suffered as I have?' What next?"

"Shall I put in the brown or white bread first?" said Mina.

"The brown first," said Harriet.

"'What is this life to one who has suffered as I have?'" said I.

Harriet brushed the flour off her apron and sat down a moment in a muse. Then she dictates as follows—

"Under the breaking of my heart I have borne up. I have borne up under all that tries a woman—but this thought—oh, Henry!"

"Ma'am, shall I put ginger into the pumpkin?" queried Mina.

"No, you may let that alone just now," replied Harriet. She then proceeded:—

"I know my duty to my children. I see the hour must come. You must take them, Henry; they are my last earthly comfort."

"Ma'am, what shall I do with these egg-shells and all this truck here?" interrupted Mina.

"Put them in the pail by you," answered Harriet. "They are my last earthly comfort," said I. What next?

She continued to dictate.

"You must take them away. It may be—perhaps it must be—that I shall soon follow, but the breaking heart of a wife still pleads, 'a little longer, a little longer.'"

"How much longer must the gingerbread stay in?" inquired Mina.

"Five minutes," said Harriet.

"A little longer, a little longer," I repeated in a dolorous tone, and we burst into a laugh.

Thus we went on, cooking, writing, nursing, and laughing, till I finally accomplished my object. The piece was finished, copied, and the next day sent to the editor.

Harriet wrote, "I thank God that there is one thing running through my life from the time I was thirteen years old. It is the intense unwavering sense of God's educative presence and care." Jesus was the friend and comforter whom she had always sought; she could love Him with all her heart and soul…. She had no further need of worry; Jesus would take care, He really would. He would take care of Hattie Beecher because He loved her; He would give her life beauty and meaning.

The day these truths unfolded to her soul, she walked home in a state of exaltation. Treading upon rarified air, she felt one with life's mysteries; Jesus had taught her. As she shared her experience with her father, he held Hattie close to him. "Then has a new flower blossomed in the Kingdom this day.

When Harriet finished *Uncle Tom's Cabin*, she wondered if anyone would ever read what she had written. She had looked for neither fame nor money, but overnight, she went from a modest, retiring little mother one day to the author of the world's best seller overnight. Three thousand copies were sold the first day the book appeared on the market, and over 300,000 copies in a year. By 1857, over 2 million copies had been sold worldwide.

And we know the rest of the story.

Month 9 Podcasts

Podcast #168 William Prescott

I thought I'd open Month 9's podcasts with a writer whose best-known works had to do with the Conquest of Mexico by Cortez and the Conquest of Peru by Pizarro, both Month 9 topics. But I also chose him because, as a great writer, he fits in nicely with this month's Mother's University topic as well.

Let me first introduce him by sharing a story from a book written by Mary Stimpson, *A Child's Book of American Biography*.[94] And then I have a few more things to add that I've gleaned from other places.

> George Washington was a daring soldier himself and of course noticed how other men behaved on a battlefield. He liked a man who had plenty of courage—a real hero. There was a certain Colonel Prescott who fought at the battle of Bunker Hill whom Washington admired. He always spoke of him as Prescott, the brave.
>
> Colonel Prescott had a grandson, William Hickling Prescott, who was never in a battle in his life and did not know the least thing about soldiering, but he deserved the same title his grandfather won—"Prescott, the brave"—as you will see.
>
> William was born in Salem, in 1796. His father, a lawyer who afterwards became a famous judge, was a rich man, so William and his younger brothers and sisters had a beautiful home; and as his mother was a laughing, joyous woman, the little Prescotts had a happy childhood.
>
> William was much petted by his parents. His mother taught him to read and write, but when he was very small he went to school to a lady who loved her pupils so well that she never allowed people to call her a school-teacher—she said she was a school-mother. Between his pleasant study hours with Miss Higginson, this school-mother, and his merry play hours at home, the days were never quite long enough for William.
>
> When he was seven, he was placed in a private school taught by Master Knapp. And there he was asked to study rather more than he liked. He had loved story books almost from his cradle, and what he read was very real to him. Sometimes, when he was only a tiny boy, he felt so sure the goblins, fairies, and giants of which he had been reading might suddenly appear, unless his mother were at hand to banish them, that he would follow her from room to room, holding on to her gown. Still these books were much nicer, he thought, than the ones Master Knapp told him to study. He was full of fun and frolic and took all Master Knapp's rebukes so cheerfully that the teacher could not get angry with him. His schoolmates adored him. Even if he did play a good many jokes on them, they were not mean, vicious jokes. He had altogether too kind a heart to hurt a person or to say unkind things. He did manage to get his history lessons, and he liked to read lives of great men. But he did not study any great amount until after his father moved to Boston, and William began to fit himself for Harvard College. He was proud

of his father and fancied that he would like to be a lawyer like him.

Young Prescott had been in college but a short time when, one night at dinner, a rough, rude student hurled a hard crust of bread across the table, not aiming at any one in particular. But it hit Prescott in his left eye and destroyed the sight in it. The poor fellow fell to the floor as if he were dead and was very ill for weeks. Then it was that he began to earn his title of Prescott, the brave. He did not complain, he did not say: "Well, of course, I shall never try to do anything now that I have only one eye to use." Instead, he kept up his spirits and finished his course at Harvard gayly. Everybody talked of his pluck. He was asked to be orator of his class, and he wrote for graduation day a Latin poem on Hope, which he recited with such a happy face and manner that the people clapped their hands and cheered. His parents were so pleased that William could finish his college work, in spite of his accident, and that he could keep right on being a rollicking, laughing boy, that they spread a great tent on the college grounds and feasted five hundred friends who had come to see William graduate.

Then William went on a wonderful visit to the Azores. His mother's brother, Thomas Hickling, was United States Consul at St. Michael. This uncle had married a Portuguese lady, and there was a large family of cousins to entertain the New England boy. Mr. Hickling had a big country house and a lot of spirited horses. As William drove over the lovely island, he used to laugh at the funny little burros the working people rode and the strange costumes they wore. Of course, he found St. Michael a different looking place from Boston, with its brick, or sober-colored houses. At the Azores, you know, everything is bright and gay. A salmon-pink castle stands next a square, box-like house, painted yellow; a blue villa and a buff villa probably adjoin dainty green and lavender cottages, and occasionally a fancy little dwelling, all towers and balconies, will be painted cherry red. Then the mountain peaks behind all these houses are vivid green. So William felt almost as if he were in fairyland.

When he had been looking at these beautiful things about six weeks, he found suddenly, one morning, that they had turned black. He could not see a bit with his well eye! A doctor was sent for and he said: "A perfectly dark room for you, William Prescott, for three months, and only enough food to keep you alive!" In all the ninety-five days the doctor kept him shut in, William was never heard to utter one word of complaint. His cousins sat with him a good deal (thankful that he could not see them cry), and he told them funny stories, sang songs, and paced back and forth for exercise, with his elbows held way out at his sides to avoid running into the furniture. He finally saw again but had to be very careful of that one useful eye all the rest of his life. The minute he used it too much, the blindness would come on again.

As studying law was out of the question for him, he thought he would write histories. He had already learned a good deal about the different countries but knew most about Spain. So he set about learning all he could of that country as far back as the days of Christopher Columbus. Of course, this brought in King Ferdinand and Queen Isabella (you remember she offered to sell her jewels to help Columbus) and stories of Peru and

Mexico, so that William Prescott spent most of his life gathering facts together about the Spanish people. And the histories of them he wrote (eight large books) sound almost like story books; when you read them you seem to see the banquet halls, the queens followed by their pages and ladies-in-waiting, the priests chanting hymns in their monasteries, and the Mexican generals in their showy uniforms.

Think how hard it was for William Prescott to make these histories. He dared use his eye but a few hours a week. So he hired people to read to him, to go to libraries to look at old papers and letters, and to copy the notes he made on a queer machine. You can see this instrument that he contrived at the Massachusetts Historical Society. Some pieces of wood held sheets of paper in place; other strips of wood kept the pencil going in fairly straight lines. But sometimes when he used this at night, or when his eye was bandaged, he would forget to put in a fresh sheet of paper and would scribble ahead for a long time, writing the same lines over and across until his secretaries would have a hard time to find out what he meant. He did not want to waste time by asking to have the same thing read twice to him, so he trained his memory until he could carry the exact words on a page in his mind, and after a while he could repeat whole chapters without a mistake. But it was slow work making books this way. He was ten years getting his first one, the history of Ferdinand and Isabella, ready for the publisher.

Prescott did not talk about this work. No one but his parents and the secretaries knew that he was busy at all, because in his resting hours he was often seen at balls and parties, laughing and chatting in his own lively way. And one day one of his relatives drew him aside (this was when he had been grinding away in his library for eight years) and said: "William, it seems to me you are wasting your time sadly. Why don't you stop being so idle and try some kind of work?"

This same relation and all Prescott's friends were astonished and proud enough when, two years later, three big volumes of Spanish history were for sale in the book-stores, with William Hickling Prescott's name given as the author. That season every one who could afford it gave their friends a Christmas present of the Prescott books. He had compliments enough to turn his head, but he was too sensible to be vain. He wrote several other books and soon became famous. When he was in London, he had many honors shown him.

Prescott was fond of children and always kept a stock of candy and sweets on hand for small people. His servants adored him and so did his secretaries. They used to tell how he would frolic, even at his work. Sometimes when he had got to a place in one of the books where he must describe a battle scene, he would dash about the room, singing at the top of his lungs some stirring ballad like: "Oh, give me but my Arab steed!" And then when he felt he really "had his steam up" he would begin to write. He was kind and generous and showed so much courtesy to rich and poor alike that he has been called the finest gentleman of his time. No doubt he was, but it is true, too, that he was Prescott, the Brave!

Some of you may have seen a post in the Facebook group where I shared I was facing some problems with my vision. The doctor told me I was at high risk for a retinal detachment. I knew that if it actually detached, if it wasn't treated immediately, it could result in blindness. My concern was that I knew we were going to be out of the country. About a week before our trip, I went in for one last check. I had been symptom free, so I was surprised when she told me it had torn on three sides and that she needed to perform laser surgery immediately.

I am so thankful I was in the right place at the right time. And that I can see.

But I can tell you William Prescott was my companion through all those weeks of uncertainty. He reminded me that there are ways to compensate for that which we lose. I read. A lot. So I imagined trying to do what I do with the vision of only one eye—and it made me appreciate Prescott's accomplishments and patience all the more.

Those who knew him said they never knew anyone who loved as much as he did and who was so genuinely happy. A friend wrote, "He could be happy in more ways, and more happy in any one of them, than any other person I have ever known." His mother said that, in some of his most difficult times, people would go to comfort him—and he would comfort them instead!

Speaking of his mother, Prescott wrote:

"My mother had a warm and sympathetic nature, a heart full of love, a hand open to charity…. She had, indeed, a generous nature, wishing ever to do good and to make those around her better."

Her influence as a mother is reflected in Prescott's life, not only in his nature and character, but in his love of books and reading. He said that he could recall no time in his childhood that he did not love books and he read primarily stories which powerfully quickened his imagination. His mother was his first teacher. Prescott continued:

> Though her reading in early life had been left much to her own direction, she had read a great deal more than was usual at her day; and the Shakespeare which she had when a girl…bears testimony on every page to her accurate perusal. It is the same with others of the old English writers, and through life, and to last day of it, the love of reading and writing has been a chief solace of her hours when alone. One book was her study by day and by night—the Scriptures. This was visible to those admitted to her privacy, for her piety was not of that ostentatious kind which commends itself to the notice of the world.

She lost 4 of her 7 children in infancy, William being the eldest of her 3 surviving children.

When Prescott decided to become a writer, he took the matter very seriously. The first year, he took upon himself an additional concentrated study of grammar and correct writing as well as a focused study on the great English authors. His objective was to discover the means by which the great writers produced their effects. The second year, he moved on to French Literature, the third year, Italian literature and then Spanish literature, and consequently, he decided upon Spain as the subject of his first book. To help familiarize himself with the Spanish language, he hired someone to read Spanish literature to him two hours a day, even though he didn't understand a word a of it. He made a list of several hundred volumes to be read or consulted. He had hoped to finish his first book in 5 to 6 years, but it took nearly twice as long. It took him three and a half years to research just the first chapter.

He would digest while sitting alone in his study the material of four hours reading which he had been listening to. He would then think over and compose and polish what would become 50 to 60 pages of written text, holding it for several days in his memory, running it over and over through his mind. Once, he went over a single chapter of one of his histories 16 times before actually writing it down.

All I can say to that is, "Wow!" I think I'm a pretty lazy writer. But he makes me want to be more diligent and careful in my writing. And more importantly, he makes me want to be a kinder and happier person.

Before he died, he expressed that he would like to have his body placed in the library where he had spent so many studious and happy hours, and there allowed to remain for a time. And it was done. There he lay in the silent presence of the great host whose thoughts had been such joy and strength and inspiration to him.

And surely, they welcomed him as one of their own.

Podcast #169 David Crockett

A couple of years ago, a friend of mine, Jeff Hymas, called me and told me he had been working on a book to help families teach basic Constitutional principles to their children. He had identified 12 of the most important principles of freedom and for each one offered a simplified explanation for children, an LDS scriptural reference, a quote from an LDS prophet, a constitutional reference, and a founding father quote. What he was missing was a story to illustrate each principle and he wondered if I might have any.

Well, I just happen to have some in my reservoir of stories and as I looked at each principle, immediately a story came to mind for all of them except one of them. And that just happened to be the one he had a story for. So the book was finished—it's called *Founders and Prophets*—and when someone at Deseret Book heard about it, he contacted Jeff and told him they were anxious to carry it in the stores. Which I believe they did and maybe still do. But I do know it's available on Amazon.

Since we are talking about Mexico this month, I thought I'd like to share the story about Davy Crockett that I provided for Founders and Prophets that went along with the chapter on the proper role of government. So what does Davy Crockett have to do with Mexico? I included the study of Texas and California in connection with the study of Mexico in Month 9 because originally they were a part of Mexico. And if you Remember the Alamo in Texas, that's where Davy sacrificed his life in defense of liberty and independence.

His life was full of adventure and he has long been a hero of young boys. Maybe some of you remember Fess Parker in Walt Disney's Davy Crockett series. I have found some on YouTube. He was loved for his backwoods simple ways and storytelling and was elected to serve in Congress from Tennessee. Which brings me to the story selection I sent to Jeff. I think we could use some Davy Crocketts in Congress today, don't you agree?

Here it is.

> [The following story about the famed American icon Davy Crockett was published in Harper's Magazine in 1867, as written by James J. Bethune, a pseudonym used by Edward S. Ellis. The events that are recounted here are true, including Crockett's opposition to the bill in question, though the precise rendering and some of the detail are fictional.]

> One day in the House of Representatives, a bill was taken up appropriating money for the benefit of a widow of a distinguished naval officer. Several beautiful speeches had been made in its support. The Speaker was just about to put the question when Davy Crockett arose:

> "Mr. Speaker–I have as much respect for the memory of the deceased, and as much sympathy for the sufferings of the living, if suffering there be, as any man in this House,

but we must not permit our respect for the dead or our sympathy for a part of the living to lead us into an act of injustice to the balance of the living. I will not go into an argument to prove that Congress has no power to appropriate this money as an act of charity. Every member upon this floor knows it. We have the right, as individuals, to give away as much of our own money as we please in charity; but as members of Congress we have no right so to appropriate a dollar of the public money. Some eloquent appeals have been made to us upon the ground that it is a debt due the deceased. Mr. Speaker, the deceased lived long after the close of the war; he was in office to the day of his death, and I have never heard that the government was in arrears to him.

"Every man in this House knows it is not a debt. We cannot, without the grossest corruption, appropriate this money as the payment of a debt. We have not the semblance of authority to appropriate it as a charity. Mr. Speaker, I have said we have the right to give as much money of our own as we please. I am the poorest man on this floor. I cannot vote for this bill, but I will give one week's pay to the object, and if every member of Congress will do the same, it will amount to more than the bill asks."

He took his seat. Nobody replied. The bill was put upon its passage, and, instead of passing unanimously, as was generally supposed, and as, no doubt, it would, but for that speech, it received but few votes, and, of course, was lost.

Later, when asked by a friend why he had opposed the appropriation, Crockett gave this explanation:

"Several years ago I was one evening standing on the steps of the Capitol with some other members of Congress, when our attention was attracted by a great light over in Georgetown. It was evidently a large fire. We jumped into a hack and drove over as fast as we could. In spite of all that could be done, many houses were burned and many families made homeless, and, besides, some of them had lost all but the clothes they had on. The weather was very cold, and when I saw so many women and children suffering, I felt that something ought to be done for them. The next morning a bill was introduced appropriating $20,000 for their relief. We put aside all other business and rushed it through as soon as it could be done.

"The next summer, when it began to be time to think about the election, I concluded I would take a scout around among the boys of my district. I had no opposition there, but, as the election was some time off, I did not know what might turn up. When riding one day in a part of my district in which I was more of a stranger than any other, I saw a man in a field plowing and coming toward the road. I gauged my gait so that we should meet as he came to the fence. As he came up, I spoke to the man. He replied politely, but, as I thought, rather coldly.

"I began: 'Well, friend, I am one of those unfortunate beings called candidates, and–'

"'Yes, I know you; you are Colonel Crockett, I have seen you once before, and voted for you the last time you were elected. I suppose you are out electioneering now, but you had better not waste your time or mine. I shall not vote for you again.'

"This was a sockdolager…I begged him to tell me what was the matter.

"'Well, Colonel, it is hardly worth-while to waste time or words upon it. I do not see how it can be mended, but you gave a vote last winter which shows that either you have not capacity to understand the Constitution, or that you are wanting in the honesty and firmness to be guided by it. In either case you are not the man to represent me. But I beg your pardon for expressing it in that way. I did not intend to avail myself of the privilege of the constituent to speak plainly to a candidate for the purpose of insulting or wounding you. I intend by it only to say that your understanding of the Constitution is very different from mine; and I will say to you what, but for my rudeness, I should not have said, that I believe you to be honest.… But an understanding of the Constitution different from mine I cannot overlook, because the Constitution, to be worth anything, must be held sacred, and rigidly observed in all its provisions. The man who wields power and misinterprets it is the more dangerous the more honest he is.'

"'I admit the truth of all you say, but there must be some mistake about it, for I do not remember that I gave any vote last winter upon any constitutional question.'

"'No, Colonel, there's no mistake. Though I live here in the backwoods and seldom go from home, I take the papers from Washington and read very carefully all the proceedings of Congress. My papers say that last winter you voted for a bill to appropriate $20,000 to some sufferers by a fire in Georgetown. Is that true?'

"'Well, my friend; I may as well own up. You have got me there. But certainly nobody will complain that a great and rich country like ours should give the insignificant sum of $20,000 to relieve its suffering women and children, particularly with a full and overflowing Treasury, and I am sure, if you had been there, you would have done just as I did.'

"'It is not the amount, Colonel, that I complain of; it is the principle. In the first place, the government ought to have in the Treasury no more than enough for its legitimate purposes. But that has nothing to do with the question. The power of collecting and disbursing money at pleasure is the most dangerous power that can be entrusted to man, particularly under our system of collecting revenue by a tariff, which reaches every man in the country, no matter how poor he may be, and the poorer he is the more he pays in proportion to his means. What is worse, it presses upon him without his knowledge where the weight centers, for there is not a man in the United States who can ever guess how much he pays to the government. So you see, that while you are contributing to relieve one, you are drawing it from thousands who are even worse off than he. If you had the right to give anything, the amount was simply a matter of discretion with you, and you had as much right to give $20,000,000 as $20,000. If you have the right to give to one, you have the right to give to all; and, as the Constitution neither defines charity nor stipulates the amount, you are at liberty to give to any and everything which you may believe, or profess to believe, is a charity, and to any amount you may think proper. You will very easily perceive what a wide door this would open for fraud and corruption and favoritism, on the one hand, and for robbing the people on the other. No, Colonel, Congress has no right to give charity. Individual members may give as much of their own money as they please, but they have no right to touch a dollar of the public money for that purpose. If twice as many houses had been burned in this county as in Georgetown, neither you nor any other member of Congress would have thought of appropriating a dollar for our relief. There are about two hundred and forty members of Congress. If they had shown their sympathy for the sufferers by contributing each one week's pay, it would have made over $13,000. There are plenty of wealthy men in and around Washington who could have given $20,000 without depriving themselves of even a luxury of life. The congressmen chose to keep their own money, which, if reports be true, some of them spend not very creditably; and the people about Washington , no doubt, applauded you for relieving them from the necessity of giving by giving what was not yours to give. The people have delegated to Congress, by the Constitution, the power to do certain things. To do these, it is authorized to collect and pay moneys, and for nothing else. Everything beyond this is usurpation, and a violation of the Constitution.

"'So you see, Colonel, you have violated the Constitution in what I consider a vital point. It is a precedent fraught with danger to the country, for when Congress once begins to stretch its power beyond the limits of the Constitution, there is no limit to it, and no security for the people. I have no doubt you acted honestly, but that does not make it any better, except as far as you are personally concerned, and you see that I cannot vote for you.'

"I tell you I felt streaked. I saw if I should have opposition, and this man should go to talking, he would set others to talking, and in that district I was a gone fawn-skin. I could not answer him, and the fact is, I was so fully convinced that he was right, I did not want to. But I must satisfy him, and I said to him:

"'Well, my friend, you hit the nail upon the head when you said I had not sense enough to understand the Constitution. I intended to be guided by it, and thought I had studied it fully. I have heard many speeches in Congress about the powers of Congress, but what you have said here at your plow has got more hard, sound sense in it than all the fine speeches I ever heard. If I had ever taken the view of it that you have, I would have put my head into the fire before I would have given that vote; and if you will forgive me and vote for me again, if I ever vote for another unconstitutional law I wish I may be shot.'

"He laughingly replied: 'Yes, Colonel, you have sworn to that once before, but I will trust you again upon one condition. You say that you are convinced that your vote was wrong. Your acknowledgment of it will do more good than beating you for it. If, as you go around the district, you will tell people about this vote, and that you are satisfied it was wrong, I will not only vote for you, but will do what I can to keep down opposition, and, perhaps, I may exert some little influence in that way.'

"'If I don't,' said I, 'I wish I may be shot; and to convince you that I am in earnest in what I say I will come back this way in a week or ten days, and if you will get up a gathering of the people, I will make a speech to them. Get up a barbecue, and I will pay for it.'

"'No, Colonel, we are not rich people in this section, but we have plenty of provisions to contribute for a barbecue, and some to spare for those who have none. The push of crops will be over in a few days, and we can then afford a day for a barbecue. This is Thursday; I will see to getting it up on Saturday week. Come to my house on Friday, and we will go together, and I promise you a very respectable crowd to see and hear you.'

"'Well, I will be here. But one thing more before I say good-by. I must know your name.'

"'My name is Bunce.'

"'Not Horatio Bunce?'

"'Yes.'

"'Well, Mr. Bunce, I never saw you before, though you say you have seen me, but I know you very well. I am glad I have met you, and very proud that I may hope to have you for my friend.'

"It was one of the luckiest hits of my life that I met him. He mingled but little with the public, but was widely known for his remarkable intelligence and incorruptible integrity, and for a heart brimful and running over with kindness and benevolence, which showed themselves not only in words but in acts. He was the oracle of the whole country around him, and his fame had extended far beyond the circle of his immediate acquaintance. Though I had never met him before, I had heard much of him, and but for this meeting it is very likely I should have had opposition, and had been beaten. One thing is very certain, no man could now stand up in that district under such a vote.

"At the appointed time I was at his house, having told our conversation to every crowd I had met, and to every man I stayed all night with, and I found that it gave the people an interest and a confidence in me stronger than I had every seen manifested before.

"Though I was considerably fatigued when I reached his house, and, under ordinary circumstances, should have gone early to bed, I kept him up until midnight, talking about the principles and affairs of government, and got more real, true knowledge of them than I had got all my life before.

"I have known and seen much of him since, for I respect him—no, that is not the word—I reverence and love him more than any living man, and I go to see him two or three times every year; and I will tell you, sir, if every one who professes to be a Christian lived and acted and enjoyed it as he does, the religion of Christ would take the world by storm.

"But to return to my story. The next morning we went to the barbecue, and, to my

476

surprise, found about a thousand men there. I met a good many whom I had not known before, and they and my friend introduced me around until I had got pretty well acquainted–at least, they all knew me.

"In due time notice was given that I would speak to them. They gathered up around a stand that had been erected. I opened my speech by saying:

"'Fellow-citizens–I present myself before you today feeling like a new man. My eyes have lately been opened to truths which ignorance or prejudice, or both, had heretofore hidden from my view. I feel that I can today offer you the ability to render you more valuable service than I have ever been able to render before. I am here today more for the purpose of acknowledging my error than to seek your votes. That I should make this acknowledgment is due to myself as well as to you. Whether you will vote for me is a matter for your consideration only.'

"I went on to tell them about the fire and my vote for the appropriation and then told them why I was satisfied it was wrong. I closed by saying:

"'And now, fellow-citizens, it remains only for me to tell you that the most of the speech you have listened to with so much interest was simply a repetition of the arguments by which your neighbor, Mr. Bunce, convinced me of my error.

"'It is the best speech I ever made in my life, but he is entitled to the credit for it. And now I hope he is satisfied with his convert and that he will get up here and tell you so.'

"He came upon the stand and said:

"'Fellow-citizens–It affords me great pleasure to comply with the request of Colonel Crockett. I have always considered him a thoroughly honest man, and I am satisfied that he will faithfully perform all that he has promised you today.'

"He went down, and there went up from that crowd such a shout for Davy Crockett as his name never called forth before.

"I am not much given to tears, but I was taken with a choking then and felt some big drops rolling down my cheeks. And I tell you now that the remembrance of those few words spoken by such a man, and the honest, hearty shout they produced, is worth more to me than all the honors I have received and all the reputation I have ever made, or ever shall make, as a member of Congress.

"Now, sir," concluded Crockett, "you know why I made that speech yesterday.

"There is one thing now to which I will call your attention. You remember that I proposed to give a week's pay. There are in that House many very wealthy men–men who think nothing of spending a week's pay, or a dozen of them, for a dinner or a wine party when they have something to accomplish by it. Some of those same men made beautiful speeches upon the great debt of gratitude which the country owed the deceased–a debt which could not be paid by money–and the insignificance and worthlessness of money, particularly so insignificant a sum as $10,000, when weighted against the honor of the nation. Yet not one of them responded to my proposition. Money with them is nothing but trash when it is to come out of the people. But it is the one great thing for which most of them are striving, and many of them sacrifice honor, integrity, and justice to obtain it."

Podcast #170 The Legends of El Dorado

I'm afraid I didn't learn much about our neighbors down south in school. I remember filling out a map of South America but that's about it. So I have really enjoyed filling in the gap and learning more about them. They, too, have their freedom stories and heroes. But what I'd like to focus on today are their myths and legends, particularly as they are related in a 1904 book I came across called *The Stories of El Dorado* by Frona Eunice Wait.[95]

In her preface, she writes: "As to where these myths originated, or how old they are, I have nothing to suggest, since in presenting these simple variants, it is no concern of mine. It is sufficient for my purpose to know that they exist. To me they lend a dignity to our country by investing it with a misty past, replete with a mythology as rich and sublime as that of any of the races of antiquity."

The central hero was a Great Heart who came from the East and taught the people the peaceable arts of civilization. So great was his influence on them, that all the tribes had essentially the same hero in their lore, though he was called by different names. The preface opens with a quote by Professor A.F. Bandelier who wrote: "It has only recently been recognized as a fact that on the whole America continent, the mode of life of the primitive inhabitants was formed on one sociological principle, and consequently the culture of these people has varied, locally, only in degree, and not in kind. The religious principles were fundamentally the same among the Sioux and the Brazilians...."

This hero was a bearded white man in white robes, and when he left the people, he promised he would one day return. Temples were built to remember him. Many generations passed, and still the people watched for his return. He had taught them of making sacrifices of the heart, and as they degenerated, they engaged in actual sacrifices of hearts in hopes of bringing him back.

When the bearded Europeans landed—Columbus, Cortez, Pizarro—these simple people were submissive because they believed the Great Heart had finally returned. What happened next is one of the saddest pages of all history—a history that has largely been erased because the Spanish priests burned and destroyed so many of their records. But I can't help but hope there will be records that will yet come forth to teach us more of these people.

In another old book, which I regretfully have been unable to locate again, but I'm still looking, I read that, at a time of great conflict and turmoil, a people had been led to a place of refuge where they were taught by—and this book used the term—'celestial beings' who taught them the peaceable arts of civilization. Their place of refuge was Machu Picchu and if you have ever been there, you know the wonder of the world that it is. When things settled down, they were instructed to take what they had learned and build a holy city-Cuzco. The story of the Incan Empire is incredible and I am only scratching the surface. I read how, at one time, millions of them lived in a cashless society. Each person had a spirit of self-reliance and each one looked after his neighbor's needs.

As I talk about these things, many of you who are of my faith, will recognize a connection. For those of you who are not of my faith, I hope you won't mind if I share some of my beliefs, not in a spirit of persuasion, but in a spirit of understanding.

I believe the Book of Mormon to be a record of these people. In 600 BC when the Babylonians laid siege to Jerusalem, there was a prophet named Lehi. He was warned in a dream to take his family away from Jerusalem and they were brought across the waters to a Promised Land—the Americas. The Book of Mormon is a record of their story as well as others on this continent. The culminating event to the story was the fulfillment of a promise— that a Savior would be born in a land from which they had come. And after his death and resurrection, He would visit them and teach them in the Americas. They were the other sheep of another fold.

One of the sweetest scenes I have ever read is of Jesus blessing their children.

What followed was 200 years of peace. There were no wars and no contentions in the land. And He promised that He would return.

Of course, I can't help but connect these legends of the Great Heart that are common among all Native tribes to this visit of Jesus in my Book of Mormon.

Returning to Stories of El Dorado, back in the preface again, Frona writes: "No words incorporated into the English language have been fraught with such stupendous consequences as El Dorado. When the padres attempted to tell the story of the Christ, the natives exclaimed, "El Dorado," or what the imperfect translations have made El Dorado—the golden. As the ignorant sailors and adventurers had been kept from mutiny by Columbus' promise of gold, it is no wonder that they seized upon the literal meaning instead of the spiritual one…. The great heart of humanity will ever ache with sympathy for the melancholy and pitiful end of the natives, who at the time of the conquest of Mexico were confidently expecting the return of the mild and gentle Quetzalcoatl…. None of the cruelties attributed to the Indian had its origin in resistance to the acceptance of a new faith. On the contrary, he fought solely in defense of his home, and from Patagonia to Alaska was always willing to listen to the Christian ideas of God and hereafter."

The natives prized the Golden Rule. The conquerors prized only the Gold.

Let me share the first chapter in Frona's retelling of the myth of the Great Heart and if you'd like to read more, the book is linked in the Middle School section of Latin America.

> A long time ago there was a beautiful island close by the place in the east where the sun rises. The sea was all around it, and at noonday the sun in the sky seemed to slant just above it. Being near the equator and in a tropic clime the winds were soft and warm and full of the odor of sweet flowers. Sometimes the sea was smooth and clear as glass and then the goldfish and sea mosses floated near the surface and glittered in the sunlight.
>
> At night the moon came out big and round like a silver ball and the stars shone very

clear because there was no smoke nor fog in the air. In the moonlight the queer little flying fish would jump up out of the water and dart forth and back in the funniest way as if they were playing some kind of game. Their tiny wet wings glistened like silver gauze, and, when everything else was still, made a peculiar whirring sound by all flapping at once.

The beach was strewn with quantities of conch and abalone shells, also other species of all shapes and sizes and they were as dainty in color as it is possible to imagine. The children of the Happy Island often held the larger ones to their ears to listen to the murmurs and complaints of the insects and other forms of life living inside them. This was only a fancy, but many sea shells do have a soft musical cadence if we care to hear it. Some poets believe that they were the first musical instruments, and that the inhabitants of the sea send messages ashore in this manner.

The ferns grew almost as tall as the trees and there were hundreds of birds skimming through the air, or flitting through the branches singing and chattering and having a very happy time. They were not afraid because no one threw stones at them or tried to frighten them. Everybody was glad to see them put up their little bills and ruffle up their throats in singing, or else spread out their wings and splash water all over their backs while they stood on a pebble or twig taking a morning bath. The people said that when the birds were twittering and chirping they were talking to each other. When they were singing they were telling God how thankful they were for the warm sunshine and plenty to eat.

There was a wonderful city in the center of the island named the City of the Golden Gates because it was surrounded by a high wall of very thick stones, with a great number of gates of gold through which the animals and people passed in and out. Here lived the Old Man of the Sea, as the king was called, and his son was a beautiful youth known as the Golden Hearted because he was so gentle and kind. He was a swift runner and could shoot well with a bow and arrow and was strong enough to wrestle with a big man, but he preferred to make gold ornaments and vessels for his father and was often permitted to go into the king's treasure house to watch the workmen polish the precious gems which they found in great abundance by digging into the mountains near the city.

The people knew all about white and black pearls and how to get them from the bed of the ocean. In full sight of the island was a large reef of pink and white coral and the young prince went there many times to see the curious little insects building their graceful, airy houses over some rock hidden by the water. He sometimes imagined that he heard the mermaids calling to him. What he really did hear was the wind dashing the waves in and out of the coral chambers as if it were determined to wash them away. The reef was an excellent place to fish, and the Golden Hearted and his companions had many a fine day's sport there while the divers were searching for the pearl oysters. He fished with a drag-net made by himself, and he could let it out and haul it in again like a regular sailor. He never killed any of the fish, and the divers would not give him the pearls they found because they were compelled to kill the oysters to get them, and this they said made the pearls unlucky and was the reason why they are round and shining like tear drops. The miners brought him all the emeralds they could find, because this was the happiness-bringing stone. Its color is like the soft grass in the springtime, and they wanted him to be always young and have everything his heart desired.

The royal gardens were his special care and in them he was allowed to cultivate any kind of tree or plant or grain. Then from them he must learn the names and habits of the trees producing the best wood for building houses, what plants were good to heal the sick, and all about the grains useful for food either for man or animals. Every flower that had a perfume grew in a separate part of the garden, and those shedding their fragrance at night only were in a bed by themselves. He was required to know the difference between single and double species and why there is such a difference in the same family of plants.

Honey bees, big-winged butterflies, crickets and beetles hid in the flowers or flew above them, and these all taught a lesson to the young prince who had no other books. The honey bee was an industrious little fellow continually building a piece of comb or else filling it with honey. The butterfly, on the other hand, did not work at all but changed from an ugly grub into a caterpillar and finally into a gorgeous butterfly with spotted wings and bright eyes. The king told his son that the butterfly was like a soul—the immortal part of ourselves—and he wished him to be as busy as the bee, and to do no more harm to other creatures than does the pretty butterfly.

The cricket was a cheerful, merry chap, usually singing at the top of his voice, and the beetle tried to push all of the dirt out of the garden. If he found anything he did not like he would roll and tumble with it, even if it were much bigger than himself. This amused the Golden Hearted very much, and when he grew tired of his own occupations he would run out into the garden and watch the beetles.

One day he went into the splendid throne-room where his father was giving audience to some wise old men who were foretelling what was going to happen to the king and the people of the Happy Island. They urged the king to send some member of his household to the strange land over the sea, toward the setting sun, where the people were in barbarism.

The Golden Hearted was much interested and thought here was an opportunity to do some good for the weak and helpless. Springing forward he said:

"Dear father, let me go. I am able to sail the seas and am willing to devote my life to teaching these poor people how to live like brothers."

The king felt proud of the young prince, but he loved him so dearly that it was hard to let him go, and also hard to refuse such a noble, manly request.

"Do you know, my son, this will entail a great deal of hardship and self-denial?" he asked.

"Yes, father, but God intends us to earn all the good things in life; He will not give them to us for nothing. That is His good law, which makes us healthy, happy and wise—three of the most precious possessions in the world."

"Go, my Golden Heart, and may God bless and keep you always," said the king. "Take a green-throated humming-bird for your guide, and when you find the land, journey on until you come to a place where a cactus grows at the base of a rock and there is a golden eagle soaring in the air above it. Halt there and found a city, and name it in honor of the sun."

Then all the wise men begged to go with him, and for days after there were great preparations made for the departure of the king's son. At daybreak one morning he set sail in a snake-skin boat, and all the inhabitants came with the king to throw flowers and emeralds into the sea because they wished to show respect to the Golden Hearted. It was their method of blessing him and wishing him good luck. The whole shore line, as far as he could see, was lighted up by bonfires where the people burned resin and perfume to commemorate his going.

At the water's edge stood the old sea king with his long white hair and beard blowing in the wind. By his side was a cream-white horse with three plumes in the top of its bridle reins and a square, red blanket edged with deep fringe on its back. Crowns and moons and stars of gold and silver were scattered over the blanket to show that the horse belonged to the royal prince. Back of the king was a long line of young warrior priests mounted on white horses, with red blankets, and carrying reversed spears in their hands. They bowed their heads when the poor old father leaned over on the horse's neck and cried as if his heart would break as the boat with his only son in it pushed off from the shore. Snatching a torch from the hand of an attendant, the Golden Hearted waved it on high. Fire with them was a symbol of wisdom, and when the king saw it, he answered the signal by waving a torch, and the warrior priests flashed their spears in the bright sunlight, and the people sent up a deafening shout.

This meant that they were willing to sacrifice their future king for the good of a strange race of men who needed a teacher to show them how to cultivate the land and how to build cities and live civilized. The people of the Happy Island would not send a common man for a teacher. No, indeed; they gave the best they had—their dearly loved prince with the golden heart—to help their less fortunate neighbors. And he gave up all luxury and comfort because he would rather be useful, than live in ease as a king. The name of the island was Atlantis, and the new country was our own—America.

Month 10 Podcasts

Podcast #76 Lessons on Happiness from Helen Keller

I am in the middle of treasure hunting for additional books for the new website and I found a rare jewel I just have to share with you. It's an article from an old 1930 *Better Homes and Gardens* magazine contributed by Hazel Gertrude Kinscella[96] following an interview with Helen Keller. I'll get to the article in a minute, but the ads on the pages were also interesting—for example: "If good taste says 'white or light-tinted walls and woodwork,' And more and more greasy dust sifts indoors from increasing traffic and high-priced domestic help balks at endless scrubbing of walls and woodwork which you haven't time to do yourself, how can you have lasting cleanliness and beauty? Thousands have found the answer in Barreled Sunlight, the paint enamel whose flawless surface can't hold dirt embedded!"

Or to the wives of desk-bound men… "Sanitarium records show an amazing number of people who live sedentary lives suffer from faulty elimination. It causes most human ills. Ridding the body of waste must be done regularly and thoroughly, else poisons are formed that tend to get into the blood stream. These poisons prematurely age and cause many serious diseases. From Battle Creek comes a new drugless way to regular habits…."

Some things never change!

Which leads me back to the article. The principles of tending to the heart are universal and true. There is a part of us that cannot be expressed and cannot be seen. But it is very real. There are so many faculties within us that can add to our joy and happiness, but they lie dormant because they are unused. Helen was blind and deaf, yet she could see flowers and hear music which gave her abundant joy. She said, "Flowers have personalities, too, and Music is more than sound." We who have sight and hearing often see and hear very little.

Let me share parts of this beautiful article with you.

> My most startling lesson in seeing and hearing, in learning of the unseen personality of flowers and of the enchanting inner beauties of the world of sound, came to me today as I visited for an hour with Helen Keller, who can neither see nor hear, and yet finds joy in a flower garden and in the music of the spheres. I asked her how she is able to enjoy these things.
>
> "In replying to your question," Miss Keller said to me, during the course of our conversation, "my ways of seeing and hearing the outer world are difficult to analyze. Indeed, I am almost convinced that my impressions cannot be expressed except in mystical symbolism. When I try to tell people my idea of natural phenomena beyond the reach of my hands, I am profoundly troubled by the remoteness of my inner life, and yet the intensity of it is as fresh and throbbing as a physical reality. Things perceived by the spirit are imperfectly articulate. Only the greatest poets can put into words shades of soul experience.

"I put my hand on the violin or the sensitive diaphragm of the radio, and my body is flooded with rhythmical vibrations. My mind transmutes the silvery nerve thrills into bird songs and wind songs, the tripping of tiny streams, the chattering of moth and bee, the tremulous whispering of leaves. Thus my conception of music is built up of association and analogy.

"I am extremely sensitive, not only to musical vibrations, but also to the exhalation of flowers. Beside their delicate texture and fragrance, I feel a soul in them. By this I mean the personalities of flowers. Subtly they suggest human attributes. Some flowers are friendly, adapting themselves to our moods. The sense lends itself to all our human experiences, like a versatile companion. Some flowers have shy spirits that seem embarrassed when I touch them. The mimosa actually shrinks from the human hand. Other flowers caress my palm with tenderest speech of curling petal and nestling leaf. Everyone feels the modesty of the violet and the thought that looks out of the upturned face of the pansy. Who does not welcome the hearty laugh of the peony, the childlike gaiety of daffodils, the mystical quality of lilacs, the pungent good sense of chrysanthemums and marigolds? Anyone can see that geraniums are cheerful, good-natured, workaday friends of man, and that the sunflower is an optimist, keeping its face ever towards the sun...."

Unexpected is Miss Keller's constant use of the words "see" and "hear," in view of her personal handicap. "Miss Keller will see you at 1 o'clock Saturday afternoon" had come the telegram signed by Polly Thomson, Miss Keller's loyal friend and secretary for many years.

When I arrived at the Forest Hills Station a little after 3, my first impression was that of a Tudor village, the ivy-covered red brick building, the great tower, and the big speaking clock, all reminding a visitor of an old English scene.

My first impression of [Miss Keller's] house, standing behind the iron fence and rather high-clipped hedge, was of a three-story pink brick and stone dwelling, partly overhung with glistening ivy, the windows to the south being all shielded with striped awnings....

No portrait can, or does, do justice to the great personal beauty of Miss Keller. I thought instantly, as with high-held head, and erect, high-spirited person, she came towards me across the hall and the parlor to greet me graciously and hospitably.

"I am glad to meet you," she said quietly but distinctly, as she took my hand....

The impression of Miss Keller's great charm deepened, as sitting there so quietly in her modish gray dress—her only decoration a string of pearls—she asked and answered questions as naturally as any hostess might.

That my questions and conversation were conveyed to her hand by Miss Thomson seemed, after the first instant, not at all an unusual way to converse. Miss Keller's diction and her command of the English language are such as to call for comment in this day of careless speech.

"You wish to know what home and garden mean to me," she said, at once. "My garden is my greatest joy. I feel that I am in the seventh heaven when among my plants. I feel the little heads pop up to look at me—my poppies, pansies, and pinks. We had a fine time in our garden last night with the hose. We have just set out a little Siberian elm tree, and not knowing that it was going to rain in the night, we watered it well. It took two of us to drag the hose around, and I got so dirty. You should have seen me then!"

"There in my garden I have my 'green circle' where I walk for at least an hour every day or evening. It is very narrow, but it reaches to the stars! On one side of this narrow walk is a privet hedge; on the other, small evergreen trees to guide me in my walk.'

"We have as many things as we can. Our clematis is just planted. It is always a miracle to see young trees grow. I take unusual joy in the dogwood and the wisteria, of which there has been a profusion. And here is syringa earlier than usual," she concluded, indicating with her right hand an exquisite cluster of syringa and white peonies which stood in a quaint blue bow on a low table in the hallway.

"Are all these flowers from your garden?" I asked, for the room was fragrant with the odor of the blossoms which were everywhere so tastefully arranged.

"Yes, indeed," was the reply, "but you must not think we have a big garden because we seem to have so many flowers. We shall show you what we have before you go. At best, it is not much," she concluded modestly.

"Miss Kinscella is looking at our flowers," Miss Thomson told Miss Keller and as I looked at each of the lovely bouquets, the two hostesses united in telling me of their history.

At one end of the divan upon which we sat was a low table and on this was another bowl full of white peonies.

"I adore the peonies," said Miss Keller. "Since my childhood I have adored them and have been glad each spring when the miracle of their bloom has been wrought again."

Beside me, at the other end of the divan was a higher table, and on it was a tall bouquet of violet and cream iris. On the library table near the fireplace was another bouquet, this one of fragrant red roses and white peonies. I mentioned their fragrance.

"I really like no flowers without fragrance, as fragrance is their soul, to me," said Miss Keller. "As color is to the eye, so is fragrance to me my way of recognizing them. Also I feel them—their form, shape, stem, even their pistils. Such a joke was played on me," she added with a characteristic little gesture. "What I took, one day, for a petunia, bless you, was a tobacco flower. So I had to 'look' very closely again to see whether the stem was round, or square: Yes, I like those red roses. We have some nice red buds on another bush out by the front walk, a bush we thought dead from insects. The bugs like my flowers, too!"

There was still another wonderful spray of flowers in the room—a gorgeous spray of salmon-colored gladiolus which set at the opposite end of the fireplace under a life-size oil portrait of Miss Keller at the age of 14.

Hans—the beautiful big Dane was sent Miss Keller just a year ago by her German publisher—was meanwhile interestedly watching every movement in the room, and when his mistress rose and started to take me thru the house before going out into the garden, he rose and followed closely behind her.

We went thru the dining-room. Cheery sunshine flooded it, streaming across the blue rug and onto the table. Here Miss Keller must stop to "see" with her fingers a dainty centerpiece of old-fashioned flowers. There on to the "radio" room, so called because in it is installed the device which is one of Miss Keller's greatest pleasures.

"Here is my radio. It enables me to feel the beautiful music every night. I like the Goldman band concerts, the quaint old melodies some entertainers sing, comic opera, Gilbert and Sullivan, and Wagner. It is so tantalizing when one feels the announcer's voice. I can distinguish the various instruments, the human voices, and the applause. This age of invention is so astonishing! What is my favorite music? One of my favorites is the Wagner 'Fire Music.' Then one time Heifetz, the famous violinist, played for me especially, while we both chanced to be in Denver. I like best of all that he played the 'Hunting Song,' but—I could feel the song of the deer at its end."

With a skillful twist of the hand, Miss Keller turned the radio going, touched it lightly, adjusted it again, then with one hand barely touching the frame, and head slightly tipped, she "listened," while instantly her free hand indicated the rhythmic pulsations she was feeling.

A thrill went thru me as I recognized the music which the radio pianist was playing, for the coincidence was so startling! In a moment Miss Keller turned her face slightly toward me. "It is the Moonlight Sonata, which Beethoven, the deaf pianist, played for the blind girl."

Then we went upstairs. On the third floor are Miss Keller's bedroom, personal library—all four walls full of books—and her sleeping porch and study. Here was another light and airy spot, all windows. An easy daybed stood near the window at one end of the room. On her table were typewriter and books....

"What are your favorite books?" I asked.

"They are many," was the answer. "Just now I have been reading 'Out of the East,' by Lafeadio Hearn; a book of Conrad's; Hudson's 'Green Mansions'; The River and here is a book given me by a friend in Philadelphia not long ago—put into Braille for me. It is Abraham Lincoln and the Hooker Letter. Louis Kolb, who gave it to me, has several Lincoln keepsakes, among them a pen with which the great president signed many momentous documents. When they put that pen into my hand I couldn't help kissing it!" and she suggested the act with a simple gesture.

The Bible lay on a table near the bed. "My Bible is always within reach of my hand. It is my ever-increasing fountain of sun and courage. I read it so much."

It has been commented upon that Miss Keller has possibly acquired much of her lovely command of the English language thru reading the Bible. When this was mentioned, she assented. "It is more than possible. If we read the Bible we get all the English we need—a combination of simplicity and greatness. We may well read it for style as well as for our heavenly inspiration."

Then we went downstairs to go out into the garden, Miss Keller leading the way down the stair ahead of us as quickly and lightly as a little child at night.

"You will be surprised what a tiny thing our garden really is," she warned me, as we stepped outside. "Most people expect an extensive garden or a banked-up one. It is just a pile of sun, songs, blossoms, and butterflies, for what else matters? One lady wrote me in a letter, 'You must have a gorgeous estate.' I answered her, 'We have just a wee bird's nest!'"

Here she stopped, felt for a moment, then located her rose geranium plants and broke off some leaves, of which she smelled the spicy odor, then handed them to me.

Next to the house was a spot where the tulips and daffodils had just finished their blooming. Now the later flowers were coming into blossom, and all along the house, inside the front hedge and along the wall hedge at the side of the lawn, were representatives of almost every lovely flower that grows. Here were Canterbury-bells, high delphinium, rosy columbine, multi-colored phlox, modest violas, daylilies, spotless fragrant Madonna Lilies; and for the fall, chrysanthemum, dahlia, and late gladiolus plants. Near the fence was a showy bunch of gaudily colored oriental poppies. When Miss Keller slipped her fingers under the cup of one of those flowers to show it to me, the petals, already full-blown, fell off into her hand.

"A pool of crimson beauty in my hand," she said, then tossed the petals aside.

"My impressions of color are emotional, symbolical. I am interested in the theory that there is a correspondence between all the colors in the visible world and the soul within."

"Here is my bird-bath—I really do have a garden full of songs!"

Right before the bird-bath, near which Miss Keller often sits, is a long cement seat, and not far away is the real heart of the garden—an exquisite marble statue of 'Rebecca at the Well,' a gift to Miss Keller from her teacher, Miss Mary.

"We thought it so appropriate a gift," said Miss Thomson, "as 'water' was the first word that Helen learned and realized as the name of something."

At the foot of the statue is another bird bath, and green ivy covers the ground. Next to it, reached thru a trellis, is Miss Keller's green circle, a narrow gravel path lined by her evergreens—'to guide me.'

"They are my favorite trees," said my hostess. "They are, to me, all that is lovely and unfading in our natures. They symbolize words that breathe and speak after life is done, and that go on thru the air sweetening and ennobling it."

And as I said good-by and took my departure—after being given a fragrant little rose by Miss Keller to complete my bouquet—I carried with me a mental picture which will not fade, of a homemaking heart, of a joyous and valiant traveler on the Path of Happiness.

I'll leave you to savor her words and her beautifully well-educated heart. There are many layers of truth here. Her garden reminds me of what I read in Corrie Ten Boom's *The Hiding Place*: People can learn to love from flowers.

So I'll close with a poem by Maurice Thompson.

> In the oldest wood I know a brooklet,
> That bubbles over stones and roots,
> And ripples out of hollow places,
> Like music out of flutes.
>
> There creeps the pungent breath of cedars,
> Rich coolness wraps the air about
> While through clear pools electric flashes
> Betray the watchful trout.
>
> I know where wild things lurk and linger
> In groves as gray and grand as time;
> I know where God has written poems
> Too strong for words or rhyme.

Podcast #171 The Nuremberg Stove

I want to share a story with you today that was known by just about all school children in the early 1900s because it was included in many of their readers. It's the story of an old stove and the setting is Austria and Germany which goes along with this month's rotation topics. But I am more importantly sharing it because of the message. I know everyone takes away his or her own message, but for me, when I heard this story, it reminded me of the vital role beauty and inspired art plays in our lives.

The story was written by a woman named Marie Louise de la Rame. But when she was little, she had a hard time pronouncing Louise. It came out as Ouida—and Ouida spelled O-U-I-D-A became her preferred pen name. She was a famous novelist in her day, writing what was viewed as racy novels in strict Victorian days. And the facts in her historical romances were pretty sketchy. So it's not that I'm recommending her as a great writer you should study in depth, but still her life has left behind lessons worth paying attention to. And she did leave us this gem of a story.

Ouida had a good heart. She hated

> "All wrongdoing that is done
> Anywhere always underneath the sun."

It was less common in her day for women to voice their opinions in the public arena, but she was quick to speak up for any form of suffering, whether human or animals.

Her mother was her lifelong companion, but it was her father who was credited as her chief educator. He talked to her about many subjects and inspired her with a love of history and mathematics. —At least when he was home, which was rare. Ouida's book called *Friendship* is said to be her autobiographical work and in it, she wrote, "Her father had come and gone, come and gone, as comets do…. He would kiss her carelessly, bid her do a problem or write a poem, stay a few days, and go…until one day he ceased to come…. His death was mysterious, like his life."

She read very much and very widely, "studied in big books, and strayed about in the chestnut woods and orchards, and lived in her own fancies more than in anything around there…." An entry in her diary read, "I must study, or I shall know nothing when I am a woman." She wrote, "The treasures of scholarship are sweet to all who open them. But they are perhaps sweetest of all to a girl that has been led both by habit and nature to seek them…the mightiness and beauty of past ages become wonderful…the…element of faith and of imagination…becomes the strength of the girl-scholar…." and she wrote of "the all-absorbing happiness in the meditations of great minds, in the myths of heroic ages, in the delicate intricacies of language, and in the immeasurable majesties of thought."

Like other great souls, she had a love of nature and took daily walks in a beautiful park near her home. Her father would join her when he was around. "She knew the whereabouts of every rare wild flower; she knew every bird that haunted the woods or the streams; she loved the wind and the wild weather as she loved the heat and the still moonshine when the nightingale sang in the orchards; she was not dismayed if evening fell as she ran alone down a lone hillside, or if she bore down through the swift wild rain like a little white boat through a surging sea."

Near the end of her life, she wrote a letter to a friend in her hometown: "Tell the trees, the flowers, the birds—I do not forget the beauty of their home."

She deplored the loss of beauty in the crowded cities around her and it was this loss of beauty to which she attributed the evils of modern life.

I think you will see this idea reflected in the story I will now share with you. There are many adaptations out there—the one I chose appeared in the original My Book House series.[97]

> August lived in a little town called Hall. Hall is a favorite name for several towns in Austria and Germany; but this one especial little Hall, in the Upper Innthal, is one of the most charming Old-World places that I know, and August for his part did not know any other. It has the green meadows and the great mountains all about it, and the gray-green glacier-fed water rushes by it. It has paved streets and enchanting little shops that have all latticed panes and iron gratings to them; it has a very grand old Gothic church, that has the noblest blendings of light and shadow, and a look of infinite strength and repose as a church should have. Then there is the Muntze Tower, black and white, rising out of greenery and looking down on a long wooden bridge and the broad rapid river; and there is an old schloss which has been made into a guard-house, with battlements and frescoes and heraldic devices in gold' and colors, and a man-at-arms carved in stone standing life-size in his niche and bearing his date 1530.
>
> In this little town a few years ago August Strehla lived with his people in the stone-paved irregular square where the grand church stands. He was a small boy of nine years at that time—a chubby-faced little man with rosy cheeks, big hazel eyes, and clusters of curls the brown of ripe nuts. His mother was dead, his father was poor, and there were many mouths at home to feed.
>
> In this country the winters are long and very cold, and this night was terribly cold and dreary. The good burghers of Hall had shut their double shutters, and the few lamps there were, flickered dully behind their quaint, old-fashioned Iron casings. The mountains indeed were beautiful, all snow-white under the stars. Hardly any one was astir; a few good souls wending home from vespers, a tired post-boy who blew a shrill blast from his tasselled horn as he pulled up his sledge before a hostelry, and little August, were all who were abroad, for the snow fell heavily and the good folks of Hall go early to their beds. He was half frozen and a little frightened, but he kept up his courage by saying over and over again to himself, "I shall soon be at home with dear Hirschvogel."
>
> He went on through the streets into the place where the great church was, and where

near it stood his father's house with the Pilgrimage of the Three Kings painted on its wall.

The snow outlined with white every gable and cornice of the beautiful old wooden houses; the moonlight shone on the gilded signs, the lambs, the grapes, the eagles, and all the quaint devices that hung before the doors. Here and there, where a shutter had not been closed, a ruddy fire-light lit up a homely interior, with the noisy band of children clustering round the house-mother and a big brown loaf, while the oilwicks glimmered, and the hearth-logs blazed, and the chestnuts sputtered in {heir iron roasting-pot. At August's knock the solid oak door of his father's home, four centuries old if one, flew open, and the boy darted in.

It was a large barren room into which he rushed with so much pleasure, and the bricks were bare and uneven. It had a walnutwood press, handsome and very old, a broad deal table, and several wooden stools for all its furniture; but at the top of the chamber, sending out warmth and color together as the lamp shed its rays upon it, was a tower of porcelain, burnished with all the hues of a king's peacock and a queen's jewels, and surmounted with armed figures, and shields, and flowers of heraldry, and a great golden crown upon the highest summit of all.

It was a stove of 1532, and on it were the letters H. R. H., for it was the handwork of the great potter of Nuremberg, Augustin Hirschvogel, who put his mark thus, as all the world knows.

The stove no doubt had stood in palaces and been made for princes, had warmed the crimson stockings of cardinals and the gold-broidered shoes of archduchesses; no one knew what it had seen or done or been fashioned for; but it was a right royal thing. Yet perhaps it had never been more useful than it was now in this poor desolate room, sending down heat and comfort into the troop of children tumbled together on a wolf-skin at its feet, who received frozen August among them with loud shouts of joy.

"Oh, dear Hirschvogel, I am so cold, so cold!" said August, kissing its gilded lion's claws. "Is father not in, Dorothea?" "No, dear. He is late."

Dorothea was a girl of seventeen, dark-haired and serious. She was the eldest of the Strehla family; and there were ten of them in all. Next to her there came Jan and Karl and Otho, big lads, gaining a little for their own living; and then came August, who went up in the summer to the high alps with the farmers' cattle, but in winter could do nothing; and then all the little ones, who could only open their mouths to be fed like young birds—Albrecht and Hilda, and Waldo and Christof, and last of all little three-year old Ermengilda, with eyes like forget-me-nots.

They were of that mixed race, half Austrian, half Italian, so common in the Tyrol; some of the children were white and golden as lilies, others were brown and brilliant as fresh-fallen chestnuts. The father was a good man, but weak and weary so many to find food for and so little to do it with. He worked at the salt-furnaces, and by that gained a few florins. Dorothea was one of those maidens who almost work miracles, so far can their industry and care and intelligence make a home sweet and wholesome and a single loaf seem to swell into twenty. The children were always clean and happy, and the table was seldom without its big pot of soup once a day. Still, very poor they were, and Dorothea's heart ached with shame, for she knew that their father's debts were many for flour and meat and clothing. Of fuel to feed the big stove they had always enough without cost, for their mother's father was alive, and sold wood and fir cones and coke, and never grudged them to his grandchildren.

"Father says we are never to wait for him; we will have supper, now you have come home, dear," said Dorothea.

Supper was a huge bowl of soup, with big slices of brown bread swimming in it and some onions bobbing up and down; the bowl was soon emptied by ten wooden spoons, and then the three eldest boys slipped off to bed, being tired with their rough bodily labor in the snow all day. Dorothea drew her spinning-wheel by the stove and set it whirring, and the little ones got August down upon the old worn wolf skin and clamored to him for a picture or a story. For August was the artist of the family.

He had a piece of planed deal that his father had given him, and some sticks of charcoal, and he would draw a hundred things he had seen in the day, sweeping each out with his elbow when the children had seen enough of it and sketching another in its stead—faces and dogs' heads, and men in sledges, and old women in their furs, and pine-trees, and cocks and hens, and all sorts of animals, and now and then—very reverently—a Madonna and Child. It was all very rough, for there was no one to teach him anything. But it was all life-like, and kept the whole troop of children shrieking with laughter, or watching breathless, with wide open, wondering, awed eyes.

They were all so happy; what did they care for the snow outside? Their little bodies were warm, and their hearts merry; even Dorothea, troubled about the bread for the morrow, laughed as she spun; and August, with all his soul in his work, cried out loud, smiling, as he looked up at the stove that was shedding its heat down on them all:

"Oh, dear Hirschvogel! you are almost as great and good as the sun! No; you are greater and better, I think, because he goes away nobody knows where all these long, dark, cold hours; but you—you are always ready; just a little bit of wood to feed you, and you will make a summer for us all the winter through

The grand old stove seemed to smile through all its iridescent surface at the praises of the child. No doubt, though it had known three centuries and more, it had known but very little gratitude.

It was one of those magnificent stoves in enamel, of great height and breadth, with all the majolica lustre which Hirschvogel learned to give to his enamels. There was the statue of a king at each corner. The body of the stove itself was divided into panels, which had the Ages of Man painted on them; the borders of the panels had roses and holly and laurel and other foliage, and Gennan mottoes in black letters. The whole was burnished with gilding in many parts, and was radiant everywhere with that brilliant coloring of which the Hirschvogel family were all masters.

Nothing was known of the stove at this latter day in Hall. The grandfather Strehla, who had been a master-mason, had dug it up out of some ruins where he was building, and, finding it without a flaw, had taken it home, and only thought it worth finding because it was such a good one to burn. That was now sixty years past, and ever since then the stove had stood in the big, desolate, empty room, warming three generations of the Strehla family, and having seen nothing prettier perhaps in all its many years than the children tumbled now in a cluster, like gathered flowers, at its feet.

To the children the stove was a household god. In summer they laid a mat of fresh moss all round it, and dressed it up with green boughs and the numberless beautiful wild flowers of the Tyrol country. In winter all their joys centered in it, and scampering home from school over the ice and snow, they were happy, knowing that they would soon be cracking nuts or roasting chestnuts in the broad ardent glow of its noble tower, which rose eight feet high above them with all its spires and pinnacles and crowns.

Once a traveling peddler had told them that the letters on it meant Augustin Hirschvogel, and that Hirschvogel had been a great German potter and painter, in the city of Nuremberg, and had made many such stoves, that were all miracles of beauty and of workmanship, putting all his heart and soul and faith into his labors, as the men of those earlier ages did, and thinking but little of gold or praise.

So the stove had got to be called Hirschvogel in the family, as if it were a living creature, and little August was very proud because he had been named after that famous old German who had had the genius to make so glorious a thing. All the children loved the stove, but with August the love of it was a passion; and in his secret heart he used to say to himself, "When I am a man, I will make just such things too, and then I will set Hirschvogel in a beautiful room in a house that I will build myself. That is what I will do."

For August, a salt-baker's son and a little cow-keeper when he was anything, was a dreamer of dreams, and when he was upon the high alps with his cattle, with the stillness and the sky around him, was quite certain that he would live for greater things than driving the herds up when the spring-tide came among the blue sea of gentians, or toiling down in the town with wood and with timber as his father and grandfather did every day of their lives. He was a strong and healthy little fellow, fed on the free mountain air and he was very happy, and loved his family devotedly, and was as active as a squirrel and as playful as a hare. But he was always thinking, thinking, thinking, for all that.

August lay now in the warmth of the stove and told the children stories, his own little brown face growing red with excitement as his imagination glowed to fever-heat. That human being on the panels, had always had the most intense interest for August, and he had made, not one history for him, but a thousand; he seldom told them the same tale twice.

In the midst of their chatter and laughter a blast of frozen air and a spray of driven snow struck like ice through the room, and reached them even in the warmth of the old wolf-skins and the great stove. It was the door which had opened and let in the cold; it was their father who had come home. The younger children ran joyous to meet him, Dorothea pushed the one wooden arm-chair of the room to the stove, and August flew to set the jug of beer on a little round table, and fill a long clay pipe; for their father was good to them all, and they had been trained by the mother they had loved to dutifulness and obedience and a watchful affection.

Tonight Karl Strehla responded very wearily to the young ones' welcome, and came to the wooden chair with a tired step and sat down heavily, not noticing either pipe or beer. He was a fair, tall man, gray before his time, and bowed with labor.

"Take the children to bed," he said, suddenly, and Dorothea obeyed. August stayed behind, curled before the stove.

When Dorothea came down again, the cuckoo-clock in the corner struck eight; she looked to her father and the untouched pipe, then sat down to her spinning, saying nothing.

There was a long silence; the cuckoo called the quarter twice; August dropped asleep; Dorothea's wheel hummed like a cat.

Suddenly Karl Strehla struck his hand on the table, sending the pipe on the ground.

"I have sold Hirschvogel," he said; and his voice was husky and ashamed in his throat. The spinning-wheel stopped. August sprang erect out of his sleep.

"Sold Hirschvogel!"

"I have sold Hirschvogel!" said Karl Strehla, in the same husky, dogged voice. "I have sold it to a- traveling trader for two hundred florins. What would you owe double that. He saw it this morning when you were all out. He will pack it and take it to Munich tomorrow."

Dorothea gave a low shrill cry: "Oh, father!—the children—in mid-winter!" She turned white as the snow without.

August stood, half blind with sleep, staring with dazed eyes. "It is not true?" he muttered. "You are jesting, father?" Strehla broke into a dreary laugh.

"It is true. Would you like to know what is true too?—that the bread you eat, and the meat you put in this pot, and the roof you have over your heads, are none of them paid for, have been none of them paid for, for months and months. If it had not been for your grandfather, I should have been in prison all summer and autumn, and he is out of patience and will do no more now. Boy, you stare at me as if I were a mad dog! You have made a god of yon china thing. Well—it goes: goes tomorrow. Two hundred florins, that is something. It will keep me out of prison for a little, and with the spring things may turn—"

August stood like a creature paralyzed. His eyes were wide open, fastened on his father's with terror and incredulous horror; his face had grown as white as his sister's; his chest heaved with tearless sobs.

"It is not true!" he echoed, stupidly. It seemed to him that the very skies must fall, if they could take away Hirschvogel. They might as soon talk of tearing God's sun out of the heavens.

"You will find it true," said his father, doggedly, and angered because he was in his own soul bitterly ashamed to have bartered away the heirloom and treasure of his race and the comfort of his young children. "The dealer has paid me half the money tonight, and will pay me the other half tomorrow. No doubt it is worth a great deal more—but beggars cannot be choosers. The little black stove in the kitchen will warm you all just as well. Who would keep a gilded, painted thing in a poor house like this, when one can make two hundred florins by it? What is it, when all is said?—a bit of hardware much too grand-looking for such a room as this."

August gave a shrill shriek, and threw himself at his father's feet. "Oh, father!" he cried, his hands closing on Strehla's knees. "Oh, father, dear father, you cannot mean what you say? Send it away—our life, our sun, our joy, our comfort? Sell me rather. But Hirschvogel! You must be in jest. You could not do such a thing. It is not a piece of hardware, as you say; it is a living thing, for a great man's thoughts and fancies have put life into it, and it loves us though we are only poor little children, and we love it with all our hearts and souls! Oh, listen; I will go and try and get work tomorrow! I will ask them to let me cut ice or make the paths through the snow. There must be something I could do, and I will beg the people we owe money to to wait; they are all neighbors, they will be patient. But sell Hirschvogel never! never! never! Give the florins back to the man. Oh, father, dear father! do hear me, for pity's sake!"

Strehla was moved by the boy's anguish. He loved his children, and their pain was pain to him. But stronger than emotion, was the anger that August roused in him: he hated and despised himself for the barter of the heirloom of his race, and every word of the child stung him with a stinging sense of shame.

And he spoke in his wrath rather than in his sorrow.

"You are a little fool," he said, harshly, as they had never heard him speak. "Get up and go to bed. There is no more to be said. Children like you have nothing to do with such matters. The stove is sold, and goes to Munich tomorrow. What is it to you? Be thankful I can get bread for you. Get on your legs, I say, and go to bed."

Then Strehla took the oil-lamp that stood at his elbow and stumbled off to his own chamber.

August laughed aloud; then all at once his laughter broke down into bitterest weeping. He threw himself forward on the stove, covering it with kisses, and sobbing as though his heart would burst from his bosom. What could he do? Nothing, nothing, nothing!

"August, dear August," whispered Dorothea, piteously, and trembling all over—for she was a very gentle girl, and fierce feeling terrified her—" August, do not lie there. Come to bed. In the morning you will be calmer. It is horrible indeed, but if it be father's will—"

"Let me alone," said August through his teeth, striving to still the storm of sobs that shook him from head to foot. "Let me alone. In the morning!—how can you speak of the morning?" "Come to bed, dear," sighed his sister. "Oh, August, do not lie and look like that! you frighten me. Do come to bed."

"I shall stay here."

"Here! all night!"

"They might take it in the night. Besides, to leave it now!"

"But it is cold! the fire is out."

"It will never be warm any more, nor shall we."

All his childhood had gone out of him, all his gleeful, careless, sunny temper had gone with it; he spoke sullenly and wearily, choking down the great sobs in his chest. To him it was as if the end of the world had come.

His sister lingered by him while striving to persuade him to go to his place in the little crowded bed chamber with Albrecht and Waldo and Christof. But it was in vain. "I shall stay here," was all he answered her. And he stayed—all the night long.

The lamps went out; the rats came and ran across the floor; as the hours crept on through midnight and past, the cold intensified and the air of the room grew like ice. August did not move; he lay with his face downward on the golden and rainbow-hued pedestal of the household treasure, which henceforth was to be cold for evermore, an exiled thing in a far off land.

Whilst yet it was dark his three elder brothers came down the stairs and let themselves out, each bearing his lantern and going to his work in stone-yard and timber-yard and at the saltworks. They did not notice him; they did not know what had happened.

A little later his sister came down with a light in her hand to make ready the house ere morning should break.

She stole up to him and laid her hand on his shoulder timidly. "Dear August, you must be frozen. August, do look up! do speak! It is morning, only so dark!"

August shuddered all over. "The morning!" he echoed. He slowly rose up to his feet. "I will go to grandfather," he said, very low. "He is always good: perhaps he could save it."

Loud blows with the heavy iron knocker of the house-door drowned his words. A strange voice called aloud through the keyhole: "Let me in! Quick!—there is no time to lose! More snow like this, and the roads will all be blocked. Let me in! Do you hear? I am come to take the great stove."

August sprang erect, his fists doubled, his eyes blazing.

"You shall never touch it!" he screamed; "you shall never touch it!"

"Who shall prevent us?" laughed a big man, who was a Bavarian, amused at the fierce little figure fronting him.

"I!" said August. "You shall never have it!"

"Strehla," said the big man, as August's father entered the room, "you have got a little mad dog here: muzzle him."

One way and another they did muzzle him. He fought like a little demon, and hit out right and left. But he was soon mastered by four grown men, and his father flung him with no light hand out from the door of the back entrance, and the buyers of the stately and beautiful stove set to work to pack it heedfully and carry it away.

When Dorothea stole out to look for August, he was nowhere in sight. She went back to little 'Gilda, and sobbed, whilst the others stood looking on, dimly understanding that with Hirschvogel was going all the warmth of their bodies, all the light of their hearth. In another moment Hirschvogel was gone—gone forever and aye.

August had stood still for a time, leaning against the back wall of the house. The wall looked on a court where a well was. Into the court an old neighbor hobbled for water, and, seeing the boy, said; "Child, is it true your father is selling the big stove?" August nodded his head, then burst into a passion of tears. "Well, for sure he is a fool," said the neighbor. "Heaven forgive me for calling him so before his own child! but the stove was worth a mint of money. If sell it he must, he should have taken it to good Herr Steiner over at Spruz, who would have given him honest value. But if I were you I would do better than cry. I would go after it."

Then the old man hobbled away.

August remained leaning against the wall; his head was buzzing and his heart fluttered with the new idea which had presented itself to his mind. "Go after it," had said the old man. He thought, "Why not go with it?"

He was by this time in that state of exaltation in which the impossible looks quite natural and commonplace. He ran out of the court-yard, and across to the huge Gothic porch of the church. From there he could watch unseen his father's door.

Presently his heart gave a great leap, for he saw the straw-enwrapped stove brought out and laid with infinite care on the bullock dray. Two of the Bavarian men mounted beside it, and the sleigh-wagon slowly crept over the snow of the place. The noble old minster looked its grandest and most solemn, with its dark-gray stone and its vast archways, and its strange gargoyles and lamp-irons black against the snow; but for once August had no eyes for it: he only watched for his old friend. Then he, a little unnoticeable figure enough, like a score of other boys in Hall, crept, unseen by any of his brothers or sisters, out of the porch and followed in the wake of the dray.

Its course lay towards the station of the railway. August heard the Bavarians arguing a great deal, and learned that they meant to go too and wanted to go with the great stove itself. But this they could not do, for neither could the stove go by a passenger-train nor they themselves go in a goods-train. So at length they insured their precious burden for a large sum, and consented to send it by a luggage-train which was to pass through Hall in half an hour.

August heard, and a desperate resolve made itself up in his little mind. Where Hirschvogel went, would he go. He gave one terrible thought to Dorothea—poor, gentle Dorothea!—sitting in the cold at home, then set to work to execute his project. How he managed it he never knew very clearly himself, but certain it is that when the goods-train from the north moved out of Hall, August was hidden behind the stove in the great covered truck, and wedged, unseen and undreamt of by any human creature, amidst the cases of wood-carving, of clocks, of Vienna toys, of Turkish carpets, of Russian skins, which shared the same abode as did his swathed and bound Hirschvogel.

It was very dark in the closed truck, which had only a little window above the door. But August was not frightened; he was close to Hirschvogel, and presently he meant to be closer still; for he meant to do nothing less than get inside Hirschvogel itself. Being a shrewd little boy, and having had by great luck two silver groschen in his breeches-pocket, which he had earned the day before by chopping wood, he had bought some bread and sausage at the station of a woman there who knew him, and who thought he was going out to his uncle Joachim's chalet above Jenbach. This he ate in the darkness.

When he had eaten, he set to work like a little mouse to make a hole in the withes of straw and hay which enveloped the stove. He gnawed, and nibbled, and pulled, and pushed, making his hole where he guessed that the opening of the stove was—the opening through which he had so often thrust the big oak logs to feed it. No one disturbed him; the heavy train went lumbering on and on, and he saw nothing at all of the beautiful mountains, and shining waters, and great forests through which he was being carried. He was hard at work getting through the straw and hay and twisted ropes; and at last he found the door of the stove, which he knew so well, and which was quite large enough for a child of his age to slip through. Slip through he did, as he had often done at home for fun, and curled himself up there to see if he could anyhow remain during many hours. He found that he could; air came in through the brass fret-work of the stove; and with admirable caution in such a little fellow, he leaned out, drew the hay and straw together, and rearranged the ropes, so that no one could ever have dreamed a little mouse had been at them. Then he curled himself up again, this time more like a dormouse than anything else; and, being safe inside his dear Hirschvogel and intensely cold, he went fast asleep as if he were in his own bed at home with Albrecht and Christof on either side of him. The train lumbered on, and the child slept soundly for a long while. When he did awake, it was quite dark; he could not see, and for a while he was sorely frightened, and sobbed in a quiet heart-broken fashion, thinking of them all at home. But August was brave, and he had a firm belief that God and Hirschvogel would take care of him. So he got over his terror and his sobbing both.

The goods-trains are usually very slow, and are many days doing what a quick train does in a few hours. This one was quicker than most, because it was bearing goods to the King of Bavaria; still, it took all the short winter's day and the long winter's night and half another day to go over ground that the mail-trains cover in a forenoon. It passed pretty Rosenheim, that marks the border of Bavaria. And here the Nuremberg stove, with August inside it, was lifted out heedfully and set under a covered way. When it was lifted out, the boy had hard work to keep in his screams; he was tossed to and fro as the men lifted the huge thing, and the earthenware walls of his beloved fire-king were not cushions of down. However, though they swore and grumbled at the weight of it, they never suspected that a living child was inside it, and they carried it out on to the platform and set it down under the roof of the goods-shed. There it passed the rest of the night and all the next morning, and August was all the while within it.

He had still some of his loaf, and a little—a very little—of his sausage. What he did begin to suffer was thirst. It was many hours since he had last taken a drink from the wooden spout of their old pump, which brought them the sparkling, ice-cold water of the hills. But, fortunately for him, the stove, having been marked and registered as "fragile and valuable," was not treated quite like a mere bale of goods, and the Rosenheim station-master resolved to send it on by a passenger-train that would leave there at daybreak.

Munich was reached, and August, hot and cold by turns, and shaking like a little aspen-leaf, felt himself once more carried out on the shoulders of men, rolled along on a truck, and finally set down, where he knew not, only he knew he was thirsty—so thirsty! If only he could have reached his hand out and scooped up a little snow! He thought he had been moved on this truck many miles, but in truth the stove had been only taken from the railway-station to a shop in the Marienplatz. Fortunately, the stove was always set upright on its four gilded feet, an injunction to that effect having been affixed to its written label, and on its gilded feet it stood now in the small dark curiosity shop of one, Hans Rhilfer.

"I shall not unpack it till Anton comes," he heard a man's voice say; and then he heard a key grate in a lock, and by the unbroken stillness that ensued he concluded he was alone, and ventured to peep through the straw and hay. What he saw was a small square room filled with pots and pans, pictures, carvings, old blue jugs, old steel armor, shields, daggers, Chinese idols, Vienna china, Turkish rugs and all the rubbish of a brica-brac dealer's. It seemed a wonderful place to him; but, oh! was there one drop of water in it all? That was his single thought. There was not a drop of water, but there was a lattice window grated, and beyond the window was a wide stone ledge covered with snow. August cast one look at the locked door, darted out of his hiding-place, ran and opened the window, crammed the snow into his mouth again and again, and then flew back into the stove, drew the hay and straw over the place he entered by, and shut the brass door down on himself.

Presently the key turned in the lock, he heard heavy footsteps and the voice of the man who had said to his father, "You have a little mad dog; muzzle him!" The voice said, "Ay, ay, you have called me a fool many times. Now you shall see what I have gotten for two hundred dirty florins. Potztausend! never did you do such a stroke of work!"

Then the other voice grumbled and swore, and the steps of the two men approached more closely, and the heart of the child went pit-a-pat, pit-a-pat. They began to strip the stove of its wrappings; that he could tell by the noise they made with the hay and the straw. Soon they had stripped it wholly; that, too, he knew by the oaths and exclamations of wonder and surprise and rapture which broke from the man who had not seen it before.

"A right royal thing! A wonderful and never-to-be-rivalled thing! Grander than the great stove of Hohen-Salzburg! Sublime! magnificent! matchless!"

After standing by the Nuremberg master's work for nigh an hour, praising and marvelling, the men moved to a little distance and began talking of sums of money and divided profits, of which discourse he could make out no meaning. All he could make out was that the name of the king—the king—the king came very often in their arguments. He fancied at times they quarrelled, for they swore lustily and their voices rose hoarse and high; but after a while they seemed to agree to something, and were in great glee. He made out that they were going to show Hirschvogel to some great person. He kept quite still and dared not move.

Presently the door opened again sharply. He could hear the two dealers' voices murmuring unctuous words, in which "honor," "gratitude," and many fine long noble titles played the chief parts. The voice of another person, more clear and refined than theirs, answered them curtly, and then, close by the stove and the boy's ear, ejaculated a single "Wunderschon!"

The poor little boy, meanwhile, within, was hugged up into nothing, dreading that every moment the stranger would open the stove. And open it truly he did, and examined the brass-work of the door; but inside it was so dark that crouching August passed unnoticed, screwed up into a ball like a hedgehog as he was. The gentleman shut to the door at length, without having seen anything strange inside it; and then talked long and low with the tradesmen. The child could distinguish little that he said, except the name of the king and the word "gulden" again and again. After a while he went away, one of the dealers accompanying him, one of them lingering behind to bar up the shutters. Then this one also withdrew, double-locking the door.

He would have to pass the night here, that was certain. He and Hirschvogel were locked in, but at least they were together. If only he could have had something to eat! He thought with a pang of how at this hour at home they ate the sweet soup, sometimes with apples in it from Aunt Maila's farm orchard, and sang together, and listened to Dorothea's reading of tales, and basked in the glow that beamed on them from the great Nuremberg fire-king. After a time he dropped asleep.

Midnight was chiming from all the brazen tongues of the city when he awoke, and, all being still, ventured to put his head out the door of the stove to see why such a strange bright light was round him. What he saw was nothing less than all the bric-a-brac in motion.

A big jug was solemnly dancing a minuet with a plump Faenza jar; a tall dutch clock was going through a gavotte with a spindle-legged ancient chair; an old violin of Cremona was playing itself; a queer shrill plaintive music that thought itself merry came from a painted spinnet covered with faded roses, and a Japanese bronze was riding along on a griffin. A great number of little Dresden cups and saucers were all skipping and waltzing; the teapots, with their broad round faces, were spinning their own lids like teetotums; and a little Saxe poodle, with a red ribbon at its throat, was running from one to another. August looked on at these mad freaks and felt no sensation of wonder. He only, as he heard the violin and the spinnet playing, felt an irresistible desire to dance too. No doubt his face said what he wished; for a lovely little lady, all in pink and gold and white, with powdered hair, and high-heeled shoes, and all made of the very finest and fairest Meissen china, tripped up to him, and smiled, and gave him her hand, and led him out to a minuet.

"I am the Princess of Saxe-Royale," she said with a smile.

Then he ventured to say to her: "Madame, my princess, could you tell me kindly why some of the figures dance and speak, and some lie up in a corner like lumber? Is it rude to ask?"

"My dear child," said the powdered lady, "is it possible that you do not know the reason? Why, those silent, dull things are imitation; lies, falsehoods, fabrications! They only Pretend to be what we are! They never wake up; how can they? No imitation ever had any soul in it yet."

Then from where the great stove stood there came a solemn voice. All eyes turned upon Hirschvogel, and the heart of its little human comrade gave a great jump of joy. At last he would hear Hirschvogel speak.

"My friends," said that clear voice from the turret of Nuremberg faience. "We were made in days when men were true creatures, and so we, the work of their hands, were true too. We derive all the value in us from the fact that our makers wrought at us with zeal, with integrity, with faith—not to win fortunes, but to do nobly an honest thing and create for the honor of the Arts and God. I see amidst you a little human thing who loves me and in his childish way loves Art. Now I want him forever to remember that we are what we are, and precious in the eyes of the world, because centuries ago those who were of single mind and of pure hand so created us, scorning sham and haste and counterfeit. Well do I recollect my master, Augustin Hirschvogel. He led a wise and blameless life, and wrought in loyalty and love, and made his time beautiful thereby. For many, many years I, once honored of emperors, dwelt in a humble house and warmed in successive winters three generations of little, cold, hungry children. I warmed them they forgot that they were hungry; they laughed and told tales, and slept at last about my feet. Then I knew that, humble as had become my lot, it was one that my master would have wished for me, and I was content. That was better than to stand in a great hall of a great city, cold and empty, even though wise men came to gaze and throngs of fools gaped, passing with flattering words. Where I go now I know not; but since I go from that humble house where they loved me, I shall be sad and alone."

Then the voice sank away in silence, and a strange golden light that had shone on the great stove faded away. A soft pathetic melody stole gently through the room. It came from the old, old spinet that was covered with the faded roses.

Then that sad, sighing music of a bygone day died too; the clocks of the city struck six of the morning; day was rising over the Bayerischerwald. August awoke with a great start, and found himself lying on the bare bricks of the floor of the chamber, and all the bric-a-brac was lying quite still all around.

He rose slowly to his feet. Tramp, tramp, came a heavy step up the stair. He had but a moment in which to scramble back into the great stove, when the door opened and the two dealers entered, bringing candles with them to see their way.

August was scarcely conscious of danger more than he was of cold or hunger, now that he had heard Hirschvogel speak. A marvelous sense of courage, of security, of happiness, was about him, like strong and gentle arms enfolding him and lifting him upwards—upwards—upwards! Hirschvogel would defend him.

The dealers undid the shutters, and then began to wrap up the stove once more in all its straw and hay and cordage. Presently they called up their porters, and the stove, heedfully swathed and tended as though it were some prince going on a journey, was borne on the shoulders of six stout Bavarians down the stairs and out of the door. Even behind all those wrappings August felt the icy bite of the intense cold at dawn of a winter's day in Munich. The men moved the stove with exceeding gentleness and care, so that he had often been far more roughly shaken in his big brothers' arms than he was in his journey now.

The stout carriers tramped right across Munich to the railway station. Whether for a long or a short journey, whether for weal or woe, the stove with August still within it, was once more hoisted up into a great van; but this time it was not all alone, and the two dealers as well as the six porters were all with it.

Though the men grumbled about the state of the roads and the season, they were hilarious and well content, for they laughed often, and August, like a shrewd little boy as he was, thought to himself, with a terrible pang: "They have sold Hirschvogel for some great sum! They have sold him already!"

It is but an hour and a quarter that the train usually takes to pass from Munich to the Wurm-See or Lake of Starnberg; but this morning the journey Was much slower, because the way was encumbered by snow. When it did reach Possenhofen and stop, and the stove was lifted out once more, August could see through the fretwork of the brass door that this Wurm-See was a calm and noble piece of water, with low wooded banks and distant mountains, a peaceful, serene place, full of rest. Before he had time to get more than a glimpse of the green gliding surface, the stove was again lifted up and placed on a large boat that was in waiting. The boat then moved across the lake to Leonie Presently they touched the pier at Leoni.

"Now, men, for a stout mile and half!" said one of the dealers to his porters, who, stout, strong men as they were, showed a disposition to grumble at their task. Encouraged by large promises, they shouldered sullenly the Nuremberg stove, grumbling again at its preposterous weight, but little dreaming that they carried within it a small, panting, trembling boy.

The way the men took was a mile and a half in length, but the road was heavy with snow, and the burden they bore was heavier still. The dealers cheered them on, swore at them and praised them in one breath. The road seemed terribly long to the anxious tradesmen, to the plodding porters, to the poor little man inside the stove, as he kept sinking and rising, sinking and rising, with each of their steps.

Where they were going he had no idea, only after a very long time he lost the sense of the fresh icy wind blowing on his face through the brass-work above, and felt by their movements beneath him that they were mounting steps or stairs. Then he heard a great many different voices, but he could not understand what was being said. He felt that his bearers paused some time, then moved on and on again. Their feet went so softly he thought they must be moving on carpet, and as he felt a warm air come to him, he concluded that he was in some heated chambers. What he fancied was that he was in some museum, like that which he had seen in the city of Innsbruck.

The voices he heard were very hushed, and the steps seemed to go away, far away, leaving him alone with Hirschvogel. He dared not look out, but he peeped through the brass-work, and all he could see was a big carved lion's head in ivory, with a gold crown atop. It belonged to a velvet fauteuil, but he could not see the chair, only the ivory lion. There was a delicious fragrance in the air—a fragrance as of flowers. "Only how can it be flowers?" thought August. "It is November!" From afar off, as it seemed, there came dreamy, exquisite music.

He did not know it, but he was in the royal castle of Berg, and the music he heard was the music of Wagner, who was playing in a distant room.

Presently he heard a fresh step near him, and he heard a low voice say, close behind him, "So!" An exclamation no doubt, of admiration and wonder at the beauty of Hirschvogel. Then the same voice said, after a long pause, during which, as August thought, this new-comer was examining all the details of the wondrous fire-tower, "It was well bought; it is exceedingly beautiful! It is undoubtedly the work of Augustin Hirschvogel."

Then the hand of the speaker turned the round handle of the brass door, and the fainting soul of the poor little prisoner within grew sick with fear. The door was slowly drawn open, some one bent down and looked in, and the same voice called aloud, in surprise, "What is this in it? A live child!"

Then August, terrified beyond all self-control, and dominated by one master-passion, sprang out of the body of the stove and fell at the feet of the speaker.

"Oh, let me stay! Pray, meinherr, let me stay!" he sobbed. "I have come all the way with Hirschvogel!"

Some gentlemen's hands seized him, not gently by any means, and their lips angrily muttered in his ear, "Little knave, peace! be quiet! hold your tongue! It is the king!"

They were about to drag him out of the august atmosphere as if he had been some dangerous beast come there to slay, but the voice he had heard said in kind accents, "Poor child! he is very young. Let him go. Let him speak to me."

The word of a king is law to his courtiers; so, sorely against their wish, the angry and astonished chamberlains let August slide out of their grasp, and he stood there in his little rough sheepskin coat and his thick, mud-covered boots, with his curling hair all in a tangle, in the midst of the most beautiful chamber he had ever dreamed of, and in the presence of a young man with a beautiful dark face, and eyes full of dreams and fire; and the young man said to him,—

"My child, how came you here, hidden in this stove? Be not afraid, tell me the truth. I am the king."

August in an instinct of homage cast his great battered black hat with the tarnished gold tassels down on the floor of the room, and folded his little brown hands in supplication. He was too intensely in earnest to be in any way abashed; he was too lifted out of himself by his love for Hirschvogel to be conscious of any awe before any earthly majesty. He was only so glad—so glad it was the king.

"Oh, dear king!" he said, with trembling entreaty in his voice, "Hirschvogel was ours. We have loved it all our lives; and father sold it. When I saw that it did really go from us, then I said to myself I would go with it; and I have come all the way inside it. And last night it spoke and said beautiful things. And I pray you to let me live with it. I will go out every morning and cut wood for it and you, if only you will let me stay beside it. No one ever has fed it with fuel but me since I grew big enough, and it loves me;—it does indeed; it said so last night; and it said that it had been happier with us than if it were in any palace—"

And then his breath failed him, and, as he lifted his eager, pale face to the king's, great tears were falling down his cheeks.

Now, the king liked all poetic and uncommon things, and there was that in the child's face which pleased and touched him. He motioned to his gentlemen to leave the little boy alone.

"What is your name?" he asked him.

"I am August Strehla. My father is Karl Strehla. We live in Hall; and Hirschvogel has been ours so long—so long!" His lips quivered with a broken sob.

"And have you truly traveled in this stove all the way from Tyrol?"

"Yes," said August, "no one thought to look inside till you did."

The king laughed; then another view of the matter occurred to him. "Who bought the stove of your father?" he inquired.

"Traders of Munich," said August.

"What sum did they pay, do you know?"

"Two hundred florins," said August, with a great sigh of shame. "It was so much money, and he is so poor, and there are so many of us."

The king turned to his gentlemen-in-waiting. "Did these dealers of Munich come with the stove?"

He was answered in the affirmative. He desired them to be sought for and brought before him. As one of his chamberlains hastened on the errand, the monarch looked at August with compassion.

"You are very pale, little fellow: when did you eat last?"

"I had some bread and sausage with me; yesterday afternoon I finished it."

"You would like to eat now?"

"If I might have a little water I would be glad; my throat is very dry."

The king had water and wine brought for him, and cake also; but August, though he drank eagerly, could not swallow anything. His mind was in too great a tumult.

"May I stay with Hirschvogel he said, with feverish agitation.

"Wait a little," said the king, and asked, abruptly, "What do you wish to be when you are a man?"

"A painter. I wish to be what Hirschvogel was—I mean the master that made my Hirschvogel." "I understand," said the king.

Then the two dealers were brought into their sovereign's presence. They were so terribly alarmed, not being either so innocent or so ignorant as August was, that they were trembling as though they were being led to the slaughter, and they were so utterly astonished too at a child having come all the way from Tyrol in the stove, as a gentleman of the court had just told them this child had done, that they could not tell what to say or where to look, and presented a very foolish aspect indeed.

"Did you buy this stove of this boy's father for two hundred florins?" the king asked; and his voice was no longer soft and kind as it had been when addressing the child, but very stern. "Yes, your majesty," murmured the trembling traders.

"And how much did the gentleman who purchased it for me give to you?"

"Two thousand ducats, your majesty," muttered the dealers, frightened out of their wits, and telling the truth in their fright.

"You will give at once to this boy's father the two thousand gold ducats that you received, less the two hundred Austrian florins that you paid him," said the king. "You are great rogues. Be thankful you are not more greatly punished."

He dismissed them by a sign to his courtiers.

August heard, and felt dazzled yet miserable. Two thousand gold Bavarian ducats for his father! Why, his father would never need to go any more to the salt-baking! And yet, whether for ducats or for florins, Hirschvogel was sold just the same, and would the king let him stay with it?—would he?

"Oh, do! please do!" he murmured, joining his little brown weather-stained hands, and kneeling before the young monarch. He looked down on the child and smiled once more.

"Rise up, my little man," he said, in a kind voice; "kneel only to your God. Will I let you stay with your Hirschvogel? Yes, I will; you shall stay at my court, and you shall be taught to be a painter. You must grow up worthily, and win all the laurels at our Schools of Art, and if when you are twenty-one years old you have done well and bravely, then I will give you your Nuremberg stove. And now go away with this gentleman, and be not afraid, and you shall light a fire every morning in Hirschvogel, but you will not need to go out and cut the wood."

Then he smiled and stretched out his hand; the courtiers tried to make August understand that he ought to bow and touch it with his lips, but August could not understand that anyhow; he was too happy. He threw his two arms about the king's knees, and kissed his feet passionately.

Podcast #175 Leo Tolstoy—Where Love Is, There God Is Also

When I was a little girl, I loved it when my mom or dad would lie down on the bed next to me while I fell asleep. It was in the dark, away from my brothers teasing, that I felt safe to ask any questions and I remember vividly as a little girl of 5 or 6 asking my mother what Communism was. Where I came up with that question, I'm not exactly sure. But it was the early 60s and it was the days of Kruschev and the Cuban Missile Crisis, so I must have picked it up in conversations.

I remember my mother told me that children who lived under Communism didn't have any freedom to choose what they wanted to do or what they wanted to learn or where they could live and they weren't even allowed to believe in God. That little discussion made a lasting impression on me and I have to admit, whenever I heard of Russia, those childish impressions came back to me. And it still jolts me when I hear someone in our country today embracing Communism. So I have to admit, because of these initial negative impressions, I grew up with a negative and fearful view of Russia, but I am enjoying now unfolding layers and discovering all the beautiful contributions Russia has made to the world.

And one of those wonderful contributors is Count Leo Tolstoy, who I'm sure you recognize as the author of *War and Peace*. In trying to highlight what might be of most interest to you in light of our discussions here, I had a hard time deciding where to land.

Should I tell you of his wife, Sonia, 16 years his junior? Together they had 13 children, 8 of whom survived infancy. During four of those pregnancies, in a seven-year span, she completely copied by hand the entire *War and Peace* manuscript for her husband eight times. Some sections, she copied thirty times as her husband revised and perfected his work. She often had to use a magnifying glass to decipher the scribbling that crammed every bit of space on the page. And by the way, she did this while managing their estate and business affairs as well.

Or maybe I should mention Leo's mother who died when he was only two years old, yet, he wrote: "Such was the figure of my mother in my imagination. She appeared to me a creature so elevated, pure and spiritual that often in the middle period of my life, during my struggle with overwhelming temptations, I prayed to her soul, begging her to aid me, and this prayer always helped me much."

Ahh. The influence of a mother.

Or maybe we could talk about his deep interest in education. If you ever have a chance to study his writings, you'll recognize some Well-Educated Heart principles there. He set up thirteen free schools for children of peasants who had recently been emancipated from serfdom. He hated what he saw in the traditional schools. He wrote, "It is terrible! Everything by rote; terrified, beaten children." He said all education should be free and voluntary—that no authority or government should have the right to force it. The sign over the door to his school room read: "Enter and leave freely." Pupils carried nothing in their hands—no homework books or exercises. They had not been obliged to remember any lesson. They brought only themselves, their receptive natures, and the certainty it would be as happy in school that day as it had been the day before. He understood that Art could be used to get kinder ideas into the minds of others. Teaching was not a method—it was an art. Finality and perfection were never achieved; development and perfecting continued endlessly. In his schools, he told people it was impossible to send the children away—they always begged for more.

He believed, "If education is good, then the need for it will manifest itself like hunger."

As I studied him, I found a connection back to Pestalozzi—Froebel, who was a follower of Pestalozzi's philosophy had a nephew who had conversations with Tolstoy. I see Pestalozzi's fingerprints all over Tolstoy's educational views.

Tolstoy used his writing skills to write books and stories for children to learn from that included folk tales, moral parables and the lives of the Saints; that which had 'the spark of life.' I'll share one of his stories for children in a minute.

Maybe some day I'll devote a whole podcast to his views on education.

But what I'd like to land on is the turning point of his life—his spiritual awakening. He was born in an aristocratic family and attended the orthodox church, but by the time he was eighteen, he had grown tired of all the rituals and couldn't see the point. He joined the Russian army and later wrote: "I put men to death in war. Lying, robbery, adultery, drunkenness, violence and murder all were committed by me. This was my life of years."

For years he tried to get those decadent years out of his mind. He was so ashamed of them. He turned to the sciences, religion and philosophy to discover the meaning of life—and find a purpose for living. Following the death of three babies in a row, he was nearly driven to suicide.

And then he taught himself Greek and translated the Four Gospels for himself and finally found the answers for which he was seeking. He was deeply moved by the teachings of Jesus Christ and especially the Sermon on the Mount. He wrote, "Seize the moments of happiness, love and be loved! That is the only reality in the world, all else is folly. It is the one thing we are interested in here!"

That's in *War and Peace*, by the way.

Do good to those who despitefully use you. Turn the other cheek. His non-violent ways influenced a young Gandhi and later Dr. Martin Luther King. Jane Addams, a personal hero of mine, was also influenced by his peaceful writings.

"The Kingdom of Heaven is Within You," he taught, which eventually caused him to be excommunicated from his church. He turned to selfless living and despised his wealth, which brought increasing contention between he and his wife. He wanted to give his money away to help others. He even sought to sign away the copyrights on his books, which did not set well with Sonya who did not embrace his new lifestyle and eventually, when he was 82 years old, in 1910, he left his home in the middle of winter in the dead of night to start a new, simpler life without her. He didn't even make it to the next train station—he caught pneumonia and in a couple of days, he was dead. They brought him home and buried him in the garden under a tree where he loved to play as a child.

Thousands of people all over the world mourned his death and his influence continues to reach into our hearts as we read his works.

Like I said, he turned to writing children's school books and one of my favorite stories there is called *Where Love Is, There God Is* and you can see his own spiritual transformation in the life of Martin Avdyeich. A good lesson for well-educated hearts and our search for joy.

And by the way, one of the secrets of Tolstoy's success as a writer was he kept a daily journal of experiences, observations and personal insights. I read that everything we read in his books can be traced to his journal. Louisa May Alcott did the same. So if you want to raise a good writer, encourage your children to keep a personal journal!

Now the story.[98]

> In a certain town there lived a cobbler, Martin Avdeitch by name. He had a tiny room in a basement, the one window of which looked out on to the street. Through it one could only see the feet of those who passed by, but Martin recognized the people by their boots. He had lived long in the place and had many acquaintances. There was hardly a pair of boots in the neighbourhood that had not been once or twice through his hands, so he often saw his own handiwork through the window. Some he had re-soled, some patched, some stitched up, and to some he had even put fresh uppers. He had plenty to do, for he worked well, used good material, did not charge too much, and could be relied on. If he could do a job by the day required, he undertook it; if not, he told the truth and gave no false promises; so he was well known and never short of work.
>
> Martin had always been a good man; but in his old age he began to think more about his soul and to draw nearer to God. While he still worked for a master, before he set up on his own account, his wife had died, leaving him with a three-year old son. None of his elder children had lived, they had all died in infancy. At first Martin thought of sending his little son to his sister's in the country, but then he felt sorry to part with the boy, thinking: "It would be hard for my little Kapitan to have to grow up in a strange family; I will keep him with me."
>
> Martin left his master and went into lodgings with his little son. But he had no luck with his children. No sooner had the boy reached an age when he could help his father and be a support as well as a joy to him, than he fell ill and, after being laid up for a week with a burning fever, died. Martin buried his son, and gave way to despair so great and overwhelming that he murmured against God. In his sorrow he prayed again and again that he too might die, reproaching God for having taken the son he loved, his only son while he, old as he was, remained alive. After that Martin left off going to church.
>
> One day an old man from Martin's native village who had been a pilgrim for the last

eight years, called in on his way from Troitsa Monastery. Martin opened his heart to him, and told him of his sorrow.

"I no longer even wish to live, holy man," he said. "All I ask of God is that I soon may die. I am now quite without hope in the world."

The old man replied: "You have no right to say such things, Martin. We cannot judge God's ways. Not our reasoning, but God's will, decides. If God willed that your son should die and you should live, it must be best so. As to your despair – that comes because you wish to live for your own happiness."

"What else should one live for?" asked Martin.

"For God, Martin," said the old man. "He gives you life, and you must live for Him. When you have learnt to live for Him, you will grieve no more, and all will seem easy to you."

Martin was silent awhile, and then asked: "But how is one to live for God?"

The old man answered: "How one may live for God has been shown us by Christ. Can you read? Then buy the Gospels, and read them: there you will see how God would have you live. You have it all there."

These words sank deep into Martin's heart, and that same day he went and bought himself a Testament in large print, and began to read.

At first he meant only to read on holidays, but having once begun he found it made his heart so light that he read every day. Sometimes he was so absorbed in his reading that the oil in his lamp burnt out before he could tear himself away from the book. He continued to read every night, and the more he read the more clearly he understood what God required of him, and how he might live for God. And his heart grew lighter and lighter. Before, when he went to bed he used to lie with a heavy heart, moaning as he thought of his little Kapitan; but now he only repeated again and again: "Glory to Thee, glory to Thee, O Lord! Thy will be done!"

From that time Martin's whole life changed. Formerly, on holidays he used to go and have tea at the public house, and did not even refuse a glass or two of vodka. Sometimes, after having had a drop with a friend, he left the public house not drunk, but rather merry, and would say foolish things: shout at a man, or abuse him. Now, all that sort of thing passed away from him. His life became peaceful and joyful. He sat down to his work in the morning, and when he had finished his day's work he took the lamp down from the wall, stood it on the table, fetched his book from the shelf, opened it, and sat down to read. The more he read the better he understood, and the clearer and happier he felt in his mind.

It happened once that Martin sat up late, absorbed in his book. He was reading Luke's Gospel; and in the sixth chapter he came upon the verses:

"To him that smiteth thee on the one cheek offer also the other; and from him that taketh away thy cloke withhold not thy coat also. Give to every man that asketh thee; and of him that taketh away thy goods ask them not again. And as ye would that men should do to you, do ye also to them likewise."

He also read the verses where our Lord says:

"And why call ye me, Lord, Lord, and do not the things which I say? Whosoever cometh to me, and heareth my sayings, and doeth them, I will shew you to whom he is like: He is like a man which built an house, and digged deep, and laid the foundation on a rock: and when the flood arose, the stream beat vehemently upon that house, and could not shake it: for it was founded upon a rock. But he that heareth and doeth not, is like a man that without a foundation built an house upon the earth, against which the stream did beat vehemently, and immediately it fell; and the ruin of that house was great."

When Martin read these words his soul was glad within him. He took off his spectacles and laid them on the book, and leaning his elbows on the table pondered over what he had read. He tried his own life by the standard of those words, asking himself:

"Is my house built on the rock, or on sand? If it stands on the rock, it is well. It seems easy enough while one sits here alone, and one thinks one has done all that God commands; but as soon as I cease to be on my guard, I sin again. Still I will persevere. It brings such joy. Help me, O Lord!"

He thought all this, and was about to go to bed, but was loth to leave his book. So he went on reading the seventh chapter – about the centurion, the widow's son, and the answer to John's disciples – and he came to the part where a rich Pharisee invited the Lord to his house; and he read how the woman who was a sinner, anointed his feet and washed them with her tears, and how he justified her. Coming to the forty-fourth verse, he read:

"And turning to the woman, he said unto Simon, Seest thou this woman? I entered into thine house thou gavest me no water for my feet: but she hath wetted my feet with her tears, and wiped them with her hair. Thou gavest me no kiss; but she, since the time I came in, hath not ceased to kiss my feet. My head with oil thou didst not anoint: but she hath anointed my feet with ointment."

He read these verses and thought: "He gave no water for his feet, gave no kiss, his head with oil he did not anoint…." And Martin took off his spectacles once more, laid them on his book, and pondered.

"He must have been like me, that Pharisee. He too thought only of himself – how to get a cup of tea, how to keep warm and comfortable; never a thought of his guest. He took care of himself, but for his guest he cared nothing at all. Yet who was the guest? The Lord himself! If he came to me, should I behave like that?"

Then Martin laid his head upon both his arms and, before he was aware of it, he fell asleep.

"Martin!" he suddenly heard a voice, as if some one had breathed the word above his ear.

He started from his sleep. "Who's there?" he asked.

He turned round and looked at the door; no one was there. He called again. Then he heard quite distinctly: "Martin, Martin! Look out into the street to-morrow, for I shall come."

Martin roused himself, rose from his chair and rubbed his eyes, but did not know whether he had heard these words in a dream or awake. He put out the lamp and lay down to sleep.

Next morning he rose before daylight, and after saying his prayers he lit the fire and prepared his cabbage soup and buckwheat porridge. Then he lit the samovar, put on his apron, and sat down by the window to his work. As he sat working Martin thought over what had happened the night before. At times it seemed to him like a dream, and at times he thought that he had really heard the voice. "Such things have happened before now," thought he.

So he sat by the window, looking out into the street more than he worked, and whenever any one passed in unfamiliar boots he would stoop and look up, so as to see not the feet only but the face of the passer-by as well. A house-porter passed in new felt boots; then a water-carrier. Presently an old soldier of Nicholas' reign came near the window spade in hand. Martin knew him by his boots, which were shabby old felt ones, goloshed with leather. The old man was called Stepanitch: a neighbouring tradesman kept him in his house for charity, and his duty was to help the house-porter. He began to clear away the snow before Martin's window. Martin glanced at him and then went on with his work.

"I must be growing crazy with age," said Martin, laughing at his fancy. "Stepanitch comes to clear away the snow, and I must needs imagine it's Christ coming to visit me. Old dotard that I am!"

Yet after he had made a dozen stitches he felt drawn to look out of the window again. He saw that Stepanitch had leaned his spade against the wall, and was either resting himself or trying to get warm. The man was old and broken down, and had evidently not enough strength even to clear away the snow.

"What if I called him in and gave him some tea?" thought Martin. "The samovar is just on the boil."

He stuck his awl in its place, and rose; and putting the samovar on the table, made tea. Then he tapped the window with his fingers. Stepanitch turned and came to the window. Martin beckoned to him to come in, and went himself to open the door.

"Come in," he said, "and warm yourself a bit. I'm sure you must be cold."

"May God bless you!" Stepanitch answered. "My bones do ache to be sure." He came in, first shaking off the snow, and lest he should leave marks on the floor he began wiping his feet; but as he did so he tottered and nearly fell.

"Don't trouble to wipe your feet," said Martin "I'll wipe up the floor – it's all in the day's work. Come, friend, sit down and have some tea."

Filling two tumblers, he passed one to his visitor, and pouring his own out into the saucer, began to blow on it.

Stepanitch emptied his glass, and, turning it upside down, put the remains of his piece of sugar on the top. He began to express his thanks, but it was plain that he would be glad of some more.

"Have another glass," said Martin, refilling the visitor's tumbler and his own. But while he drank his tea Martin kept looking out into the street.

"Are you expecting any one?" asked the visitor.

"Am I expecting any one? Well, now, I'm ashamed to tell you. It isn't that I really expect any one; but I heard something last night which I can't get out of my mind Whether it was a vision, or only a fancy, I can't tell. You see, friend, last night I was reading the Gospel, about Christ the Lord, how he suffered, and how he walked on earth. You have heard tell of it, I dare say."

"I have heard tell of it," answered Stepanitch; "but I'm an ignorant man and not able to read."

"Well, you see, I was reading of how he walked on earth. I came to that part, you know, where he went to a Pharisee who did not receive him well. Well, friend, as I read about it, I thought now that man did not receive Christ the Lord with proper honour. Suppose such a thing could happen to such a man as myself, I thought, what would I not do to receive him! But that man gave him no reception at all. Well, friend, as I was thinking of this, I began to doze, and as I dozed I heard some one call me by name. I got up, and thought I heard some one whispering, 'Expect me; I will come to-morrow.' This happened twice over. And to tell you the truth, it sank so into my mind that, though I am ashamed of it myself, I keep on expecting him, the dear Lord!"

Stepanitch shook his head in silence, finished his tumbler and laid it on its side; but Martin stood it up again and refilled it for him.

"Here drink another glass, bless you! And I was thinking too, how he walked on earth and despised no one, but went mostly among common folk. He went with plain people, and chose his disciples from among the likes of us, from workmen like us, sinners that we are. 'He who raises himself,' he said, 'shall be humbled and he who humbles himself shall be raised.' 'You call me Lord,' he said, 'and I will wash your feet.' 'He who would be first,' he said, 'let him be the servant of all; because,' he said, 'blessed are the poor, the humble, the meek, and the merciful.'"

Stepanitch forgot his tea. He was an old man easily moved to tears, and as he sat and listened the tears ran down his cheeks.

"Come, drink some more," said Martin. But Stepanitch crossed himself, thanked him, moved away his tumbler, and rose.

"Thank you, Martin Avdeitch," he said, "you have given me food and comfort both for soul and body."

"You're very welcome. Come again another time. I am glad to have a guest," said Martin.

Stepanitch went away; and Martin poured out the last of the tea and drank it up. Then he put away the tea things and sat down to his work, stitching the back seam of a boot. And as he stitched he kept looking out of the window, waiting for Christ, and thinking about him and his doings. And his head was full of Christ's sayings.

Two soldiers went by: one in Government boots the other in boots of his own; then the master of a neighbouring house, in shining goloshes; then a baker carrying a basket. All these passed on. Then a woman came up in worsted stockings and peasant-made shoes. She passed the window, but stopped by the wall. Martin glanced up at her through the window, and saw that she was a stranger, poorly dressed, and with a baby in her arms. She stopped by the wall with her back to the wind, trying to wrap the baby up though she had hardly anything to wrap it in. The woman had only summer clothes on, and even they were shabby and worn. Through the window Martin heard the baby crying, and the woman trying to soothe it, but unable to do so. Martin rose and going out of the door and up the steps he called to her.

"My dear, I say, my dear!"

The woman heard, and turned round.

"Why do you stand out there with the baby in the cold? Come inside. You can wrap him up better in a warm place. Come this way!"

The woman was surprised to see an old man in an apron, with spectacles on his nose, calling to her, but she followed him in.

They went down the steps, entered the little room, and the old man led her to the bed.

"There, sit down, my dear, near the stove. Warm yourself, and feed the baby."

"Haven't any milk. I have eaten nothing myself since early morning," said the woman, but still she took the baby to her breast.

Martin shook his head. He brought out a basin and some bread. Then he opened the oven door and poured some cabbage soup into the basin. He took out the porridge pot also but the porridge was not yet ready, so he spread a cloth on the table and served only the soup and bread.

"Sit down and eat, my dear, and I'll mind the baby. Why, bless me, I've had children of my own; I know how to manage them."

The woman crossed herself, and sitting down at the table began to eat, while Martin put the baby on the bed and sat down by it. He chucked and chucked, but having no teeth he could not do it well and the baby continued to cry. Then Martin tried poking at him with his finger; he drove his finger straight at the baby's mouth and then quickly drew it back, and did this again and again. He did not let the baby take his finger in its mouth, because it was all black with cobbler's wax. But the baby first grew quiet watching the finger, and then began to laugh. And Martin felt quite pleased.

The woman sat eating and talking, and told him who she was, and where she had been.

"I'm a soldier's wife," said she. "They sent my husband somewhere, far away, eight months ago, and I have heard nothing of him since. I had a place as cook till my baby was born, but then they would not keep me with a child. For three months now I have been struggling, unable to find a place, and I've had to sell all I had for food. I tried to go as a wet-nurse, but no one would have me; they said I was too starved-looking and thin. Now I have just been to see a tradesman's wife (a woman from our village is in service with her) and she has promised to take me. I thought it was all settled at last, but she tells me not to come till next week. It is far to her place, and I am fagged out, and baby is quite starved, poor mite. Fortunately our landlady has pity on us, and lets us lodge free, else I don't know what we should do."

Martin sighed. "Haven't you any warmer clothing?" he asked.

"How could I get warm clothing?" said she. "Why I pawned my last shawl for sixpence yesterday."

Then the woman came and took the child, and Martin got up. He went and looked among some things that were hanging on the wall, and brought back an old cloak.

"Here," he said, "though it's a worn-out old thing, it will do to wrap him up in."

The woman looked at the cloak, then at the old man, and taking it, burst into tears. Martin turned away, and groping under the bed brought out a small trunk. He fumbled about in it, and again sat down opposite the woman. And the woman said:

"The Lord bless you, friend. Surely Christ must have sent me to your window, else the child would have frozen. It was mild when I started, but now see how cold it has turned. Surely it must have been Christ who made you look out of your window and take pity on me, poor wretch!"

Martin smiled and said; "It is quite true; it was he made me do it. It was no mere chance made me look out."

And he told the woman his dream, and how he had heard the Lord's voice promising to visit him that day.

"Who knows? All things are possible," said the woman. And she got up and threw the cloak over her shoulders, wrapping it round herself and round the baby. Then she bowed, and thanked Martin once more.

"Take this for Christ's sake," said Martin, and gave her sixpence to get her shawl out of pawn. The woman crossed herself, and Martin did the same, and then he saw her out.

After the woman had gone, Martin ate some cabbage soup, cleared the things away, and sat down to work again. He sat and worked, but did not forget the window, and every time a shadow fell on it he looked up at once to see who was passing. People he knew and strangers passed by, but no one remarkable.

After a while Martin saw an apple-woman stop just in front of his window. She had a large basket, but there did not seem to be many apples left in it; she had evidently sold most of her stock. On her back she had a sack full of chips, which she was taking home. No doubt she had gathered them at some place where building was going on. The sack evidently hurt her, and she wanted to shift it from one shoulder to the other, so she put it down on the footpath and, placing her basket on a post, began to shake down the chips in the sack. While she was doing this a boy in a tattered cap ran up, snatched an apple out of the basket, and tried to slip away; but the old woman noticed it, and turning, caught the boy by his sleeve. He began to struggle, trying to free himself, but the old woman held on with both hands, knocked his cap off his head, and seized hold of his hair. The boy screamed and the old woman scolded. Martin dropped his awl, not waiting to stick it in its place, and rushed out of the door. Stumbling up the steps, and dropping his spectacles in his hurry, he ran out into the street. The old woman was pulling the boy's hair and scolding him, and threatening to take him to the police. The lad was struggling and protesting, saying, "I did not take it. What are you beating me for? Let me go!"

Martin separated them. He took the boy by the hand and said, "Let him go, Granny. Forgive him for Christ's sake."

"I'll pay him out, so that he won't forget it for a year! I'll take the rascal to the police!"

Martin began entreating the old woman.

"Let him go, Granny. He won't do it again. Let him go for Christ's sake!"

The old woman let go, and the boy wished to run away, but Martin stopped him

"Ask the Granny's forgiveness!" said he. "And don't do it another time. I saw you take the apple."

The boy began to cry and to beg pardon.

"That's right. And now here's an apple for you," and Martin took an apple from the basket and gave it to the boy, saying, "I will pay you, Granny."

"You will spoil them that way, the young rascals," said the old woman. "He ought to be whipped so that he should remember it for a week."

"Oh, Granny, Granny," said Martin, "that's our way – but it's not God's way. If he should be whipped for stealing an apple, what should be done to us for our sins?"

The old woman was silent.

And Martin told her the parable of the lord who forgave his servant a large debt, and how the servant went out and seized his debtor by the throat. The old woman listened to it all, and the boy, too, stood by and listened.

"God bids us forgive," said Martin, "or else we shall not be forgiven. Forgive every one; and a thoughtless youngster most of all."

The old woman wagged her head and sighed.

"It's true enough," said she, "but they are getting terribly spoilt."

"Then we old ones must show them better ways," Martin replied.

"That's just what I say," said the old woman. "I have had seven of them myself, and only one daughter is left." And the old woman began to tell how and where she was living with her daughter, and how many grandchildren she had. "There now," she said, "I have but little strength left, yet I work hard for the sake of my grandchildren; and nice children they are, too. No one comes out to meet me but the children. Little Annie, now, won't leave me for any one. 'It's grandmother, dear grandmother, darling grandmother.'" And the old woman completely softened at the thought.

"Of course, it was only his childishness, God help him," said she, referring to the boy.

As the old woman was about to hoist her sack on her back, the lad sprang forward to her, saying, "Let me carry it for you, Granny. I'm going that way."

The old woman nodded her head, and put the sack on the boy's back, and they went down the street together, the old woman quite forgetting to ask Martin to pay for the apple. Martin stood and watched them as they went along talking to each other.

When they were out of sight Martin went back to the house. Having found his spectacles unbroken on the steps, he picked up his awl and sat down again to work. He worked a little, but could soon not see to pass the bristle through the holes in the leather; and presently he noticed the lamplighter passing on his way to light the street lamps.

"Seems it's time to light up," thought he. So he trimmed his lamp, hung it up, and sat down again to work. He finished off one boot and, turning it about, examined it. It was all right. Then he gathered his tools together, swept up the cuttings, put away the bristles and the thread and the awls, and, taking down the lamp, placed it on the table. Then he took the Gospels from the shelf. He meant to open them at the place he had marked the day before with a bit of morocco, but the book opened at another place. As Martin opened it, his yesterday's dream came back to his mind, and no sooner had he thought of it than he seemed to hear footsteps, as though some one were moving behind him. Martin turned round, and it seemed to him as if people were standing in the dark corner, but he could not make out who they were. And a voice whispered in his ear: "Martin, Martin, don't you know me?"

"Who is it?" muttered Martin.

"It is I," said the voice. And out of the dark corner stepped Stepanitch, who smiled and vanishing like a cloud was seen no more.

"It is I," said the voice again. And out of the darkness stepped the woman with the baby in her arms and the woman smiled and the baby laughed, and they too vanished.

"It is I," said the voice once more. And the old woman and the boy with the apple stepped out and both smiled, and then they too vanished.

And Martin's soul grew glad. He crossed himself put on his spectacles, and began reading the Gospel just where it had opened; and at the top of the page he read

"I was an hungred, and ye gave me meat: I was thirsty, and ye gave me drink: I was a stranger, and ye took me in."

And at the bottom of the page he read

"Inasmuch as ye did it unto one of these my brethren even these least, ye did it unto me." (Matt. xxv)

And Martin understood that his dream had come true; and that the Saviour had really come to him that day, and he had welcomed him.

References

[1] *Book of Prophecies*, by Christopher Columbus (c. 1501-1502).

[2] *The Voyages of Christopher Columbus*, by United States Catholic Historical Society (New York: 1892).

[3] *The Story of Christopher Columbus*, by Charles W. Moores (New York: 1912).

[4] *The Adventures of Marco Polo, the Great Traveler*, by Marco Polo, edited by Edward Atherton (New York: 1912).

[5] *Wild Swans: Three Daughters of China*, by Jung Chang (New York: 1991).

[6] *The Story of John G. Paton or Thirty Years Among South Sea Cannibals*, by John Gibson Paton (New York: 1892).

[7] *Light in My Darkness*, by Helen Keller (New York: 1927).

[8] *Stories of American History*, by N.S. Dodge (Boston: 1879).

[9] *The Discovery of New Worlds*, by M.B. Synge (Edinburgh: 1903).

[10] *Restoring the Art of Storytelling in the Home*, by Marlene Peterson (Appomattox: 2012).

[11] *Explorers and Settlers*, by Charles L. Barstow (New York: 1912).

[12] *Stories from Hans Andersen*, by H.C. Andersen (Denmark: 1911).

[13] *Mrs. Leonowens*, by John Macnaughton (Montreal: 1915).

[14] *The English Governess at the Siamese Court: Being Recollections of Six Years in the Royal Palace at Bangkok*, by Anna Harriette Crawford Leonowens (Philadelphia: 1870).

[15] *Famous Authors for Young People*, by Ramon P. Coffman and Nathan G. Goodman (New York: 1943).

[16] *Kipling: Storyteller of East and West*, by Gloria Kamen (New York: 1985).

[17] *Gladys Aylward: The Little Woman*, by Gladys Aylward (Chicago: 1970).

[18] *Christ and the Fine Arts*, by Cynthia Pearl Maus (New York: 1938).

[19] *Five Brothers: The Story of Mahabharata*, by Elizabeth Seeger (New York: 1948).

[20] *Of Plimoth Planation*, by William Bradford (Boston: 1898).

[21] *Brave Little Holland, and What She Taught Us*, by William Elliot Griffis (Boston: 1922).

[22] *Stories of American History*, by N.S. Dodge (Boston: 1879).

[23] *True Stories of the American Fathers, for the Girls and Boys All Over the Land*, by Rebecca M'Conkey (New York: 1874).

[24] *Id.*

[25] *Georgia History Stories*, by Joseph Harris Chappell (New York: 1905).

[26] Heritage History website, found at https://www.heritage-history.com/

[27] *Historical Tales: The Romance of Reality*, by Charles Morris (Philadelphia: 1908).

[28] *Id.*

[29] *Tales from the Alhambra*, by Washington Irving (Boston: 1910).

[30] *The Story of the Cid for Young People*, by Calvin D. Wilson (Boston: 1901).

[31] *Stories of Great Artists*, by Olive Brown Horne (New York: 1903).

[32] *High Adventurers*, by Mary Rosetta Parkman (New York: 1931).

[33] St. Nicholas: An Illustrated Magazine for Young Folks, Volume 32, Part II (New York: 1905).

[34] *Robert Louis Stevenson*, by Amy Cruse (New York: 1915).

[35] *Stories of Great Writers*, by Selected Authors, Compiled by Libraries of Hope (Appomattox: 2016).

[36] *Stories of Great Americans*, by Selected Authors, Compiled by Libraries of Hope (Appomattox: 2012).

[37] *Historic Americans: Sketches of the Lives and Characters of Certain Famous Americans Held Most in Reverence by the Boys and Girls of America*, by Elbridge Streeter Brooks (New York: 1899).

[38] *Pioneers and Patriots in Early American History*, by Marguerite Dickson (New York: 1915).

[39] *A Treasury of Heroes and Heroines: A Record of High Endeavor and Strange Adventure, from 550 B.C. to 1920 A.D.*, by Clayton Edwards (New York: 1920).

[40] *Children's Stories in English Literature: From Taliesin to Shakespeare*, by Henrietta Wright (New York: 1899).

[41] *King Arthur and His Knights*, by Maude Radford Warren (Chicago: 1905).

[42] *Stories of King Arthur and His Knights: Retold from Malory's "Morte D'Arthur"*, by U. Waldo Cutler (London: 1905).

[43] *King Arthur and His Knights*, by Maude Radford Warren (Chicago: 1905).

[44] *Heroes of the Middle Ages*, by Eva March Tappan (London: 1912).

[45] *Fifty Famous Stories Retold*, by James Baldwin (New York: 1896).

[46] *Roman People*, by Olivia Coolidge (Boston: 1959).

[47] *Lew Wallace: An Autobiography*, by Lew Wallace (New York: 1906).

[48] *The Story-Life of Washington: A Life-History in Five Hundred True Stories, Selected from Original Sources and Fitted Together in Order*, by Wayne Whipple (Philadelphia: 1911).

[49] *The Real George Washington*, by Jay A. Parry, Andrew M. Allison, and W. Cleon Skousen (Malta: 1991). Used with permission.

[50] *The Mothers of Great Men and Women, and Some Wives of Great Men*, by Laura C. Holloway (Baltimore: 1892).

[51] *Stories of Great Wives and Mothers*, by Selected Authors, compiled by Libraries of Hope (Appomattox: 2015).

[52] *Id.*

[53] *Id.*

[54] *Fifty Famous People, a Book of Short Stories*, by James Baldwin (New York: 1912).

[55] *Aunt Charlotte's Stories of Greek history for the Little Ones*, by Charlotte Mary Yonge (London: 1885).

[56] *Tales of Wonder Every Child Should Know*, by Kate Douglas Wiggin and Nora Archibald Smith (New York: 1909).

[57] *The Heroes*, by Charles Kingsley (London: 1869).

[58] *Old Greek Stories*, by James Baldwin (New York: 1895).

[59] *Legends and Stories of Italy for Children*, by Amy Steedman (New York: 1909).

[60] *Knights of Art: Stories of the Italian Painters*, by Amy Steedman (Philadelphia: 1907).

[61] *The Old Bell of Independence, or Philadelphia in 1766*, by Henry C. Watson (Philadelphia: 1851).

[62] *True Stories of the American Fathers, for the Girls and Boys All Over the Land*, by Rebecca M'Conkey (New York: 1874).

[63] *Pioneers and Patriots in Early American History*, by Marguerite Dickson (New York: 1915).

[64] *Stories of the American Revolution*, by Everett T. Tomlinson (Boston: 1898).

[65] *Pioneers and Patriots in Early American History*, by Marguerite Dickson (New York: 1915).

[66] *Heroines of Service*, by Mary R. Parkman (New York: 1923).

[67] *Stories of Great Writers*, by Selected Authors, Compiled by Libraries of Hope (Appomattox: 2016).

[68] *The Boys' Life of Mark Twain*, by Albert Bigelow Paine (New York: 1916).

[69] *Boys and Girls Who Became Famous*, by Amy Cruse (New York: 1929).

[70] *The Mothers of Great Men and Women, and Some Wives of Great Men*, by Laura C. Holloway (Baltimore: 1892).

[71] *The Children's Longfellow*, by Henry Wadsworth Longfellow (Boston: 1908).

[72] *The Americanization of Edward Bok*, by Edward William Bok (New York: 1922).

[73] *Acadian Reminiscences: The True Story of Evangeline*, by Felix Vorrhies (New Orleans: 1907).

[74] *The Madonna in Art*, by Estelle M. Hurll (Boston: 1898).

[75] *The Story of Our Constitution*, by Eva March Tappan (Boston: 1922).

[76] *Stories of American History*, by N.S. Dodge (Boston: 1879).

[77] *Young Folks' Bible Library, Vol: 5 Lessons from the Great Teachers*, by William Barton (Chicago: 1911).

[78] *The Soul of the Indian*, by Charles Alexander Eastman (Boston: 1911).

[79] *The Discovery of Freedom*, by Rose Wilder Lane (New York: 1943).

[80] *Had You Been Born in Another Faith*, by Marcus Bach (Englewood Cliffs: 1961).

[81] *The Fairyland Around Us*, by Opal Stanley Whiteley (Los Angeles: 1918).

[82] *The Story of Opal: The Journal of an Understanding Heart*, by Opal Stanley Whiteley (Boston: 1920).

[83] *In My Youth*, by Robert Dudley (Indianapolis: 1914).

[84] "Why I Think My Father and Mother Were Great", *American Magazine*, October 1926 issue.

[85] *The Life of Dr. J.R. Miller: "Jesus and I Are Friends"*, by John T. Faris (Philadelphia: 1912).

[86] *Week-Day Religion*, by J.R. Miller (Philadelphia: 1880).

[87] *Lives of Girls Who Became Famous*, by Sarah Bolton (New York: 1923).

[88] *Folk Song of the American Negro*, by John Wesley Work (Nashville: 1915).

[89] *The Story of Young Abraham Lincoln*, by Wayne Whipple (Philadelphia: 1915).

[90] *Abraham Lincoln: His Story*, by Samuel Scoville (Philadelphia: 1918).

[91] "Letter to Mrs. Orville Browning, Abraham Lincoln, April 1, 1838." Taken from https://teachingamericanhistory.org/library/document/letter-to-mrs-orville-browning/ on August 3, 2020.

[92] *Adventures & Achievements*, by Eva March Tappan (Boston: 1907).

[93] *Life of Harriet Beecher Stowe, Compiled from Her Letters and Journals*, by Charles Edward Stowe (Boston: 1890).

[94] *The Child's Book of American Biography*, by Mary Stoyell Stimpson (Boston: 1915).

[95] *The Stories of El Dorado*, by Frona Eunice Wait (San Francisco: 1904).

[96] "Helen Keller Sees Flowers and Hears Music", *Better Homes & Gardens*, May 1930 issue.

[97] *My Book House*, by Olive Beaupre Miller (Chicago: 1920).

[98] *Walk in the Light & Twenty-Three Tales*, by Leo Tolstoy. Copyright 2011 by The Plough Publishing House. Used with permission.